The Western Dream of Civilization: The Journey Begins

Volume I

Fifth Edition

The Western Dream of Civilization: The Journey Begins

Volume I

FIFTH EDITION

Doug Cantrell
Mary A. Rigney
Elizabethtown Community and Technical College
Elizabethtown, Kentucky

Donald L. Barlow
Thomas D. Matijasic
Big Sandy Community & Technical College
Prestonsburg, Kentucky

Barbara D. Ripel
Suffolk County Community College
Selden, New York

John Moretta
Houston Community College System
Houston, Texas

Abigail Press **Wheaton, IL 60189**

casey

Design and Production: Abigail Press
Typesetting: Abigail Press
Typeface: AGaramond
Cover Art and Maps: Sam Tolia

The Western Dream of Civilization: The Journey Begins

Volume I

Fifth Edition, 2011
Printed in the United States of America
Translation rights reserved by the publisher
10 digit ISBN 1-890919-65-9
13 digit ISBN 978-1-890919-65-8

ABOUT THE AUTHORS

Doug Cantrell is an Associate Professor of History and head of the history program at Elizabethtown Community College in Elizabethtown, Kentucky where he has taught for 15 years. He holds a B.A. from Berea College, an M.A. from the University of Kentucky, and has completed 30 hours toward the Ph.D. He is co-author of *American Dreams & Reality: A Retelling of the American Story* and *Historical Perspectives: A Reader and Study Guide* published by Abigail Press. He also has written numerous journal and encyclopedia articles and contributed book reviews to academic journals. Professor Cantrell also teaches various history courses on the web, and serves as the social science discipline leader for the Kentucky Virtual University, He is listed in *Who's Who in America, Who's Who in the World,* and *Who's Who in the South and Southwest.* In addition, he is former editor of the Kentucky History Journal and past president of the Kentucky Association of Teachers of History.

Mary Rigney is an Associate Professor of History at Elizabethtown Community and Technical College in Kentucky where she teaches European History survey courses. She earned a B.A. degree from Lindsey Wilson College and a M.A. in History from Western Kentucky University. She has taught full time for Elizabethtown Community and Technical College since 2001, serving as an adjunct faculty member since 1999. She also served as an adjunct professor at McKendree College in Louisville, KY where she taught American History. Ms. Rigney is a member of the Kentucky Association of Teachers of History.

Donald L. Barlow earned a B.S. from Indiana Wesleyan University, and a M.A. and Ph.D in History from Ball State University. He is currently an Associate Professor of History at Prestonsburg Community College in Prestonsburg, Kentucky where he teaches European and American History. Dr. Barlow previously taught at Bartlesville Wesleyan College and Oral Roberts University. He has served on the Board of the Historical Confederation of Kentucky since 1999, and as a District Coordinator of National History Day in two different states since 1985. He was chosen to attend an NEH summer seminar at Yale in 1989, and he participated in a humanties seminar for the University of Kentucky Community College System for the purpose of developing a comprehensive, interdisciplinary approach to the study of history and the humanities for the university and its community college system.

Barbara D. Ripel is Professor of History at Suffolk County Community College, Selden, New York. Her B.A. and Ph.D are from SUNY Stony Brook, and her M.A. is from Rutgers University in New Jersey. The *West Georgia Quarterly* published her article on Harbottle Dorr, and *The William and Mary Quarterly* published her research on Early ProSlavery Petitions from the 1780s. Professor Ripel has taught American History, Western Civilization, Political Science, Anthropology, and Sociology. She recently directed the Honors Program on the Suffolk Campus. In 1998, she received the New York State Chancellor's Award for Excellence in Teaching. In 2002 she received a NEH (National Endowment for the Humanities) Summer Fellowship at Harvard University for an integrated Study of Eurasia and has spoken at the National Social Science Asso. Annual Conference. Dr. Ripel serves as the campus advisor to Phi Theta Kappa, the International Honor Society for Two Year Colleges.

John A. Moretta earned a B.A. in History and Spanish Foreign Language and Literature from Santa Clara University in CA, an M.A. in History from Portland State University in Oregon, and a Ph.D. in History from Rice University in Houston, TX. He is currently Professor of History and Chair of the Social Sciences Dept. of Central College of the Houston Community College System in Houston, Texas. He is also Visiting Professor of History at the University of Houston, Main Campus. He also teaches in the Honors College at UH. Dr. Moretta has published several articles and books during his twenty-two year career in higher education. His biography of Texas lawyer William Pitt Ballinger won the best book award in Texas history (2002) given by the San Antonio Conservation Society and it was runner-up for the best book in Texas history awarded by the Texas State Historical Asso. Dr. Moretta's book did win the best research award given by that same organization for 2001. Dr. Moretta also wrote a biography of William Penn for Pearson Longman Publishers' Library of American Biography series.

Thomas D. Matijasic earned a B.A. from Youngstown State University, a M.A. from Kent State and a Ph.D. in History from Miami University. He is currently a Professor of History at Big Sandy Community & Technical College in eastern Kentucky. Dr. Matijasic has received four Great Teacher Awards and five NISOD Awards for teaching excellence. He has served as President of the Kentucky Association of Teachers of History and is a member of the National Council for History Education. In 1994, governor Brereton Jones appointed him to a seat on the Kentucky Heritage Council. He was re-appointed to the Council in 1998 by Governor Paul Patton when his first term expired. Dr. Matijasic has published more than twenty articles and thirty book reviews. He has also contributed entries to the Kentucky Encyclopedia and to reference works published by Salem Press.

PREFACE

Before we tackle the chronological advance of "Western Civilization," it is important to discuss just what we will be studying. Each word is chosen for specific reasons and the definitions will set the tone, as well as the development of this course.

As we look around the world today in the twenty-first century, the word "western" has acquired many meanings. To some, it is the height of human political, social, and economic progress, and some even add to that the supreme religious interpretation of people's drive to understand their world. The definition certainly represents the settled, urban, materialistic societies of western Europe (possibly minus Spain and Portugal) and the United States. "Western Europe" is in itself a problem to define as the evolution of the nation state has been marked with a sliding group of participants.

Many historians equate western civilization with the rise of the nation state and that political unity certainly directs a definition that can explain participation in the idea of Western Civilization. In the West, nationhood is the product of devotion to a political, economic and social system, such as monarchy or democracy or some combination. It could be described as the "advance" from personal loyalty to institutional loyalty. In "non-Western" formats of society, personal loyalty, loyalty to family, ancestry, and/or tribe are the basis of political organization. This of course breeds a different kind of societal organization, which is on a much smaller and local scale than that of a "nation state." Blood and tradition rule over formal legal systems.

"Civilized" areas kept written records, composed written laws, and produced written histories. They termed their nomadic neighbors "barbarians" (from the Latin term "*barbarus,*" which means strange or foreign) and led future generations to determine those who did not join the ways of the settled populations to be inferior to themselves. The term "civilization" comes from the Latin term "*civitas,*" which means an urban community and also gave us the terms city and citizen. Cities cause the dissolution of family ties and kinship groups because masses of unrelated peoples are gathered together so a different format other than the patriarch or tribal chieftain for their organization is necessary. Individuals in a Western society are not related by blood but by the format of their government, which terms them a "nation," or a "people" rather than a tribe.

We have titled our text as the "Western Dream of Civilization" because the blend of possibilities that form its societies contain many dissident elements in which the notion of "people" and "tribe" create competitions between neighbors, as well as those beyond the borders of Western Civilization. In the United States, we have seen the development of the Civil Rights movements, which include those of African Americans, Amerindians (Native Americans) and other minority groups. In Europe, the struggles between England and France, the Western nations and Central Europe, and the arrival of "barbarians" during various periods, all point to a confrontation between the "civilized peoples" and the nomadic "barbarian tribes."

If, however, we look beyond the political barriers and see the movement of ideas to improve the conditions of humans on earth, we gain a broader picture of the real sense of "civilization." Settled citizen and nomadic trader both contributed to the rise of the Modern World. We see social, economic, and religious trends, which gave and still give meaning to the lives of those touched by both elements. Although this is a text about Western Civilization, the rise of the nation state and the arena in which it still exists and affects our world today, we hope we have presented a balanced picture of the many peoples who have given both meaning and questions to our own place in history. The process of history is really a goal or dream to benefit humanity.

Barbara D. Ripel
Suffolk County Community College
Selden, New York

Contents in Brief

Contents

CHAPTER TWO
THE GREEKS

CHAPTER THREE
ALEXANDER AND THE HELLENISTIC AGE

CHAPTER FOUR
THE ROMANS

CHAPTER FIVE
THE POST-ROMAN EAST: BYZANTIUM, ISLAM & EASTERN EUROPE

CHAPTER SIX
GERMANIC EUROPE & THE EARLY MIDDLE AGES A. D. 378 - 1000 A.D.

CHAPTER SEVEN
FEUDAL EUROPE, 1000-1215

CHAPTER EIGHT
THE CHURCH IN THE HIGH MIDDLE AGES c. 900 to 1216

CHAPTER NINE
CIVILIZATION OF THE LATE MIDDLE AGES 1100-1300

CHAPTER TEN
FROM FEAR TO HOPE, THE 1300s

CHAPTER ELEVEN
THE RENAISSANCE 1350 TO 1650

PHOTO CREDITS

Special thanks to the following authors for sending their personal photos to be included in this text.

Barbara D. Ripel: 25 (both), 26, 101, 102, 103, 126, 127 (both), 128, 163, 256, 269, 329.

Tom Matijasic: 234, 237, 240, 241 (both), 242, 243, 244, 246, 247, 253.

Chapter 1

THE FOUNDATIONS OF WESTERN CIVILIZATION

Western civilization traces its roots to the Near Eastern cultures of the Mediterranean region. The Near East is a name given to identify the area from the Mediterranean Sea to modern day Iran where the Mesopotamian peoples built the first known cities and began using written language. Meanwhile, in North Africa the Egyptians took a similar, yet distinctive path. These initial civilizations established the foundation for subsequent cultures, and their achievements continue to fascinate modern scholars.

While the first known written language developed around 3500 B.C.E., people had existed in some evolutionary form for much longer. The prehistoric period, the time before writing, provided a foundation of what would later become civilization. The very word ***civilization*** *implies progress and development of a culture. This was not possible until prehistoric early man made significant agricultural advances that resulted in the end of the nomadic hunter-gatherer era. It was at this point that the first cities were established in the Sumerian region of Mesopotamia and in Egypt.*

Much of what happened in the prehistoric era by definition remains unknown. Exploration of these peoples is securely within the realm of archaeology. To attempt any understanding of the peoples in this vast prehistoric era, one must examine the artifacts and relics that were left behind. Cultural anthropologists work closely with archaeologists and spend their careers aspiring to an overwhelming task: making sense of the residue of long dead cultures.

The advances that helped propel the primitive peoples from itinerant hunter gatherers into civilized inhabitants of urban areas are abundant. This transformation is what will be explored in this chapter in beginning the quest of discovering the roots of Western civilization.

Chronology

(all dates are approximate and B.C.)

2 million	Beginnings of Paleolithic culture
200,000	*Homo sapiens* appears
by 30,000	Cro Magnon man had emerged
10,000-8000	End of Paleolithic Age
8000-7000	Neolithic Revolution begins Agriculture and pottery developed
4500	Farming villages appear in Holland
3500	Civilization arises in Mesopotamia
3300	The "Ice Man" dies in the Alps
3100	Egypt unified by King Narmer (Menes) Early construction at Stonehenge
2600	The Great Pyramid built at Giza
by 2300s	Indo-European migrations have begun
2371-2316	King Sargon I forms Akkadian Empire
2000-1400	Minoan civilization flourishes
1792-1750	Amorite King Hammurabi rules
1600-1200	Mycenaean civilization flourishes
1490-1468	Hatshepsut rules Egypt
1400-1200	Hittite Empire flourishes
1300-700	Urnfield culture flourishes in Europe
1270	Israelite exodus from Egypt
1200	Invasion of "Sea Peoples" and others Egyptian & Hittite Empires collapse
1000-971	King David rules Israel
814	Phoenicians establish Carthage
700-51	Celtic culture flourishes in Europe
600s	Zoroaster teaches his religion
612	Chaldeans & Medeans crush Assyria
586-538	Babylonian Captivity of the Jews
550	Cyrus the Great begins Persian Empire

PREHISTORY: THE TIME BEFORE WRITING

The prehistoric era is divided into two broad stages: the Paleolithic Period (Old Stone Age) and the Neolithic Period (New Stone Age). In some history books one can find a third designation, the Mesolithic Period (Middle Stone Age), credited as an intermediate phase. These prehistoric periods are generally categorized as **Stone Age** because the contemporary human-like ancestors relied greatly on stone to make their functional tools. In this era humans evolved and dispersed to the Near Eastern region, Europe, and eventually throughout the world. The term prehistory is usually used to refer to the time before writing, but this chapter will categorize it more specifically as stretching from the earliest pre-humans until the origins of written language.

The hominoid family (humans and relatives of humans classified taxonomically as the great apes) itself is very old, with the first tool-making hominoids probably evolving about two million years ago. It is believed that the first humanlike organisms appeared in Africa as long as four million years ago. The earliest anatomically modern humans, *Homo sapiens* from the genus *Homo*, species *sapiens*, subspecies *sapiens* appeared somewhere from 100,000 to 200,000 years ago.

The Paleolithic Period

The Paleolithic Period covers the time from around 2.5 million years ago and the introduction of stone tools to the time when the rudiments of agriculture developed approximately 20,000 to 10,000 years ago. Obviously the numbers are approximations with wide variations among scholars.

Roughly 200,000-50,000 years ago there emerged a close forerunner of modern humans: the Neanderthal peoples. These peoples, categorized as a*rchaic homo sapiens*, lived in Europe and the western regions of Asia until around 30,000 years ago when they became extinct. Although Neanderthals share some similarities with today's humans, they differed in various ways. Their build was somewhat shorter and stouter than modern humans, and they are said to have had a brain that was larger than modern humans, some scholars say by as much as 5 to 10 percent. They were probably much stronger than humans today, likely due to their active, physically challenging lifestyle.

Early modern humans (formerly designated Cro-Magnons), also called anatomically modern humans, evolved from the *archaic homo sapiens* in Africa around 100,000 years ago. In some regions Neanderthals and early modern humans co-existed for several thousand years. Early modern humans migrated throughout Europe about 35,000 years ago. These groups lived a parallel nomadic hunter-gatherer lifestyle until about 30,000-35,000 years ago when the Neanderthals disappeared. Early modern humans were physically similar to modern humans with some differences. Like the Neanderthals, the early moderns were likely more stocky and solid with brains that were about 2 to 4 percent larger than modern humans.

By the time the Neanderthals vanished, they, alongside early modern humans, had made many advances. For one thing, the Neanderthals exhibited a belief in an afterlife as shown by their elaborate burial rituals. These ceremonies also indicate that Neanderthals were emotional and grieved for their dead. The peoples of this period also created cave paintings and improved on the basic stone tools that their ancestors used. The Paleolithic era also marks the time when spoken languages began to develop. This advance was monumental because with the advent of spoken language, communication transcended gestures and amorphous sounds. Communicating basic facts became much simpler and this undoubtedly accelerated progress as elders transmitted their own discoveries to the young.

The Neolithic Revolution

Paleolithic family units and tribes had traveled behind migrating animal herds and gathered plants, fruits, nuts and berries to survive. At some point around 10,000 years ago the Neolithic Period or the New Stone Age dawned and ended the nomadic way of life. Although scholars debate the exact causes of this enormous change, many argue that climate change was at the root of the vast transformation that occurred. Europe and the Near East had been exposed regularly to vast glaciers that periodically ebbed and flowed. When not covered with these icebergs, many areas were grassy and fertile, teeming with vegetation. When this frost-bound latter ice age ended sometime prior to 20,000 years ago, the climate began to warm. These climatic changes caused the grassy, productive areas to become less common. At the same time many varieties of wild animals the peoples depended on for food could not adapt to the conditions and became extinct. Peoples of the time also had to modify their lifestyles or perish. Human beings were on the threshold of discovering agriculture and, with it, a future with unlimited progress.

The Neolithic Period was a time of such extensive ***change***s that it is synonymously referred to as the Neolithic Revolution. Neolithic achievements are vital to the existence of modern cultures and taken together comprise an unquestionable revolution. There were three major interrelated breakthroughs of the time: agriculture, domestication of animals, and pottery. Each of these innovations pushed people closer to establishing societies.

Agriculture and the domestication of animals allowed people to modify their environments in accordance with their own needs and desires. The earliest domesticated animals were likely sheep, goats and dogs. Wheat and forms of barley were likely the first crops that humans learned to manage. While it is likely that some peoples had learned how to farm previously, it was not until 13,000-7,000 B.C.E. (Before Common Era–equivalent to B.C.) that agriculture deeply impacted humanity. For a time the wandering lifestyle evidently existed alongside newly settled agricultural regions, but over several generations growing numbers of people came to rely on the crops they grew and the animals they raised instead of on hunting and gathering. This made it possible for permanent settlements to emerge.

Agriculture and settlements led to surplus food supplies as people no longer just gathered what they needed for the immediate future. With a stable food supply people became healthier overall and populations expanded. The reliable food source also freed many people to explore skills other than finding and securing food. Some people were able to hone their tool-making ability while others perfected pottery making, and so on. This diversity led to further innovations, propelling the Neolithic Revolution forward.

Neolithic peoples made great advances in what modern people would refer to as technology. Their creation of pottery is arguably as significant as their discovery of farming and the taming of animals. They learned that by shaping and baking clay, they could make containers to store and carry food and liquids. They also used metals, starting with copper as the first to be utilized in tools by c. 6400 B.C.E. Over time Neolithic man discovered how to make bronze (by combining copper and tin). Since it is stronger than copper, bronze began to replace copper in many practical ways. Bronze became an essential material for everyday tasks, as people learned how convenient, durable, and efficient it was to use. Historians commonly designate the period from c. 3000-1200 B.C.E. as the Bronze Age.

Once people began to stay in one spot for long times, communities formed, and people began to settle down into villages. Archaeologists have uncovered Neolithic villages that allow a quick glance into the lives of these ancestors. Jericho is considered one of the oldest, if not the oldest, continuously inhabited cities of the world. Located near the Dead Sea in the modern day West Bank region about twenty miles from Jerusalem, Jericho was originally settled between 9,000 and 7,000 B.C.E. Starting in 1900 with Ernst Sellin, the first person to excavate the ancient territory, archaeologists have uncovered many important items about Jericho. There is a religious shrine in the region that may have been built before 9,000 B.C.E. It also appears that there are several layers to this city, with one atop the other. Jericho did indeed have walls like the Biblical story, with tall and impressive stone fortifications as early as 7,500 B.C.E.

Another Neolithic settlement existed at Çatal Hüyük, in modern day Turkey. This town was likely founded around 7500 B.C.E. and lasted until about 5500 B.C.E. Çatal Hüyük is the largest known settlement from the period. With upwards of eight to ten thousand inhabitants by 6000 B.C.E., it displays the early development of a complex and advanced culture. Their homes had cooking areas with ovens, and evidence shows that these homes were decorated with artwork and figurines. It is at Çatal Hüyük that there is also some very early evidence of domesticated cattle.

Neolithic advances resulted in peoples' lives becoming more orderly and systematic, which encouraged further progress. The prehistoric period ended with the arrival of written language and the emergence of cities that were much more complex than Neolithic villages. The first two locations to leave Neolithic ideals behind and develop a new, more complex way of life were Mesopotamia and Egypt. Both areas' foundations were based on organization and structure; clearly the presence of these principles denotes the first true Western civilizations.

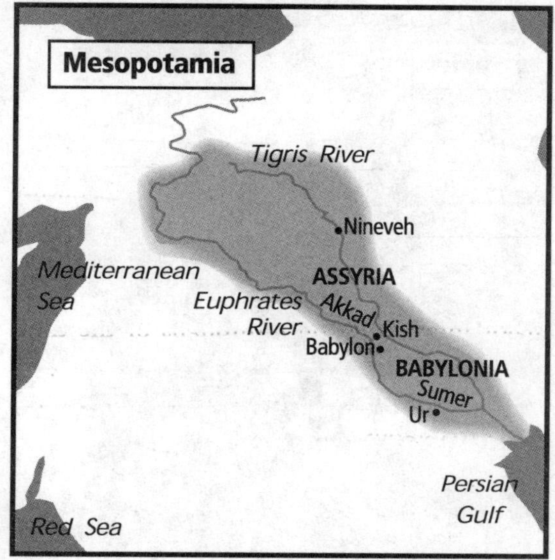

MESOPOTAMIA: THE LAND BETWEEN THE RIVERS

The first known urban civilization began in Mesopotamia or modern day Iraq. This region is part of "the fertile crescent," an expanse in the shape of an arc that reaches from the northern part of Syria to the Nile to the Tigris and Euphrates Rivers and finally to the Persian Gulf. Sometime before 5,000 B.C.E. the first genuine cities (which functioned as independent city-states) were constructed by residents of southern Mesopotamia in the region called Sumer. People in this area created the earliest known written language, formalized religious rituals and temples, as well as one of the oldest pieces of literature in the Western world. Unfortunately, along with these positive advances, these people also originated systematic organized warfare, which was more destructive than the intermittent random violence of the Neolithic peoples. As a result, Mesopotamian peoples endured many wars and frequent changes in leadership and governments. Civilization got off to a shaky start, and the story of how these people adjusted to the difficulties is, in essence, the story of humanity, for good or bad.

The name Mesopotamia comes from the Greek for "land between the rivers." The area is located between the Tigris and Euphrates Rivers in an easily accessible basin. The climate of Mesopotamia is diverse, and one's quality of life in the ancient Mesopotamian world varied from the north to the south. The northern region, later controlled by the Assyrians, had a more moderate climate. It was easier to grow crops because the region received more dependable rainfall. However, in looking at southern Mesopotamia, where the Sumerians founded early cities and developed writing, there is a harsh and bleak climate. In the desert environment, where temperatures reach up to 120 degrees Fahrenheit

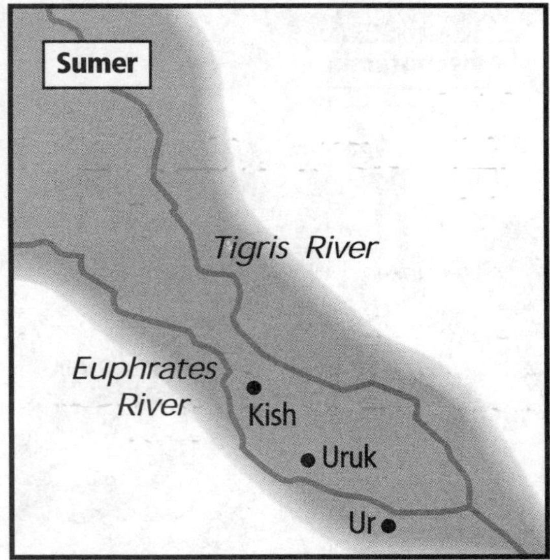

in the summer, weather heavily influenced the early settlements. There was simply not enough annual rainfall to sustain agriculture. Out of necessity, inhabitants learned to irrigate the land, but much of the land remained unavoidably infertile. Irrigation also played a part in taming the wild Tigris and Euphrates, which were prone to erratic flooding. People had to find ways to not only protect their crops and homes from the flooding but also to store the water for later use to irrigate plants during dry spells. Since the Tigris and Euphrates depend on the rainfall and melting of any snowfall from the mountains to the north and east, the water level of the rivers is inconsistent. Scientists have shown that in the spring, due to sudden heavy rainstorms, the Tigris River can rise by 20 feet over the course of a day. This must have been terrifying for these pre-scientific people who were unaware of the laws of nature and could not comprehend the reasons for such volatile events.

Mesopotamia is located in a place that was prone to invasions in ancient times. The area has no natural barriers and is the crossroads to three continents, (Africa, Asia and Europe) so it must have presented an attractive target for invaders. The story of Mesopotamia became a narrative of constant change in government after the Sumerians were conquered by the Akkadians sometime before 2300 B.C.E.. But first it is important to examine the lifestyle of those innovators of cities and writing, the Sumerians, in some detail.

The Sumerian people of southern Mesopotamia developed a system of writing called *cuneiform* from the Latin *cuneus*, which literally means "wedge or wedge-shaped." While some scholars believe the Sumerians got the idea from earlier peoples' record-keeping methods, they made it their own. Sumerians widely used cuneiform in the marketplace to keep accurate records of business and trade. It began as a pictographic system that used symbols, but it eventually advanced toward phonetic representation of language. By 3500 B.C.E. the Sumerians had developed their own script that was read from left to right and was written in horizontal lines. The early cuneiform was later adapted by different Mesopotamian inhabitants such as the Akkadians and the Assyrians. The last traces of cuneiform are dated to the period between 100 and 200 C.E.

Writing in cuneiform was cumbersome and awkward because the process was complicated. It involved taking a reed stylus and making wedge-shaped impressions on a wet clay tablet. Once the impressions were set in the clay, the tablet could be baked in the sun or in a kiln-like oven. The writer could simply reuse the clay tablets without baking them if a permanent record was not necessary. Once the tablets were baked, they became incredibly durable and long lasting. Modern archaeologists have discovered tens of thousands of these well-preserved clay tablets at ancient sites.

Sumerian cuneiform used several thousand characters, and it was difficult to master. Some of

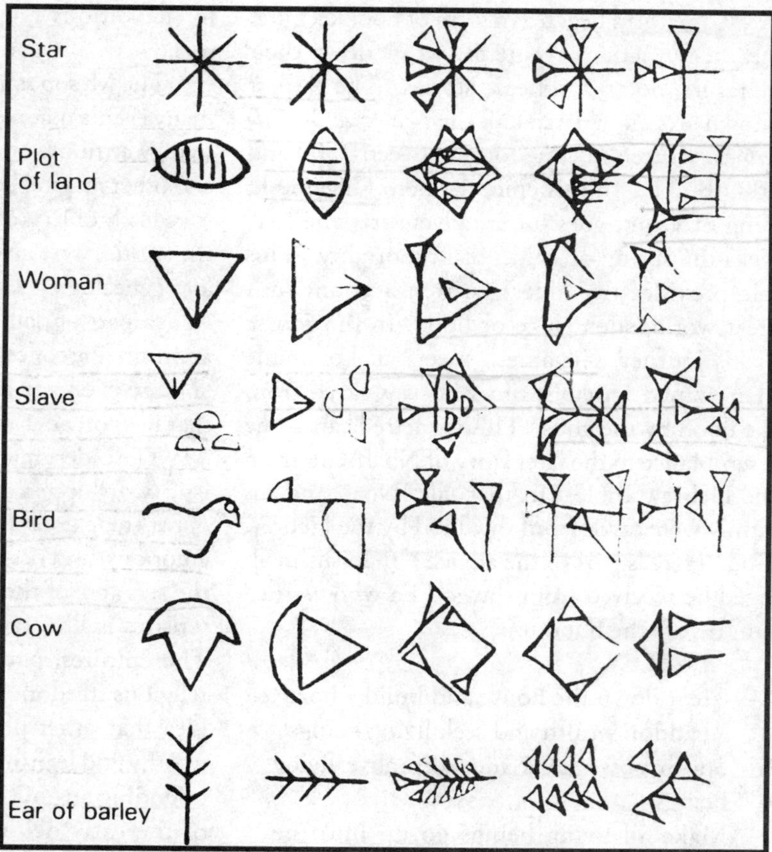

Writing developed from pictogram to cuneiform. Scribes began writing in horizontal lines instead of columns.

the characters stood for specific words, and others represented sounds from their spoken language. Some sounds could be written several different ways, and some characters that signified words were combined to make compound words. This complicated writing system meant that only a few talented and intelligent people learned to read and write.

By 2500 B.C.E. schools called *edubbas*, or tablet houses, had been established in the Sumerian region. Those who graduated from the arduous schools had acquired a valuable skill and would be guaranteed a prestigious job as a scribe. These educated scribes played an important part in management of the temples, in commerce, and in the government. But schooling was reserved for boys only. Since it was expensive, the sons of the wealthy were the only ones who could afford to attend. As a result commoners never got accustomed to reading and writing; therefore, most remained illiterate for many generations. This created an elite class of literate people, an early example of social stratification and an archaic class hierarchy.

*B*ecause the Sumerians were active in commerce and regularly encountered people from other areas, cuneiform spread beyond Sumer. Various peoples who encountered cuneiform through trade began to modify it to fit their own spoken languages. The many adaptations over time resulted in several different versions of cuneiform in diverse regions.

Cuneiform began as a form of bookkeeping, but the Sumerians eventually wrote down their literature, poetry, and epic stories. The earliest known extant written tale is *The Epic of Gilgamesh* written in cuneiform between 2500 and 2000 B.C.E. In this epic, the hero Gilgamesh, King of Uruk, goes on an adventure where he seeks the spring of youth or immortality. This tale provides the oldest written account of a great worldwide deluge or flood. In the course of his journey, Gilgamesh meets an honorable man named Utnapishtim who was saved from the flood by the gods. This vignette bears some resemblance to the later story of Noah's ark from the Hebrew Bible. In that tale, Noah and his family were saved from the flood by the Hebrew God. Here is part of the advice Utnapishtim alleged he received from the god Ea who warned him before the flood to:

> "Tear down the house and build a boat!
> Abandon wealth and seek living beings!
> Spurn possessions and keep alive living beings!
> Make all living beings go up into the boat.
> The boat which you are to build,
> Its dimensions must measure equal to each other:
> Its length must correspond to its width."
> (Tablet XI, *Epic of Gilgamesh*)

The Epic of Gilgamesh is written on twelve clay tablets, which were discovered in Nippúr by Hormuzd Rassam in the 1850s. The first modern translation of the work was published in the 1870s allowing today's readers a glimpse into the worldview and the religion of the Sumerians as the anonymous author deals with the gods, life, death, and the prospect of immortality. The poem also illustrates some commonalities found in the various religions of ancient Mesopotamia.

The Mesopotamians believed that there were many events that mankind could not understand, so they attributed the unknown realm to the gods and other magical beings. The superhuman beings were likely objects of musings and ponderings, and the entities were given names, emotions, passions, and genealogies. The mysterious and miraculous were a part of daily life. The people believed in animism, the concept that everything in nature has an unseen energy represented by a spiritual force that lives on after the body has died.

The oldest religions of the area were polytheistic (worshipped many gods), anthropomorphic (gave their gods human characteristics such as emotions) and pessimistic (believed humans were the servants of the gods). Each of these characteristics is illustrated in *The Epic of Gilgamesh*. The cultures, particularly in Sumer, practiced religious freedom because they were open to the idea that other peoples' gods might be equally worthy and legitimate. They did not want to risk offending any of these powerful creatures. Most of the early deities were rooted in observable natural elements such as the earth, sky, fire and water. The gods (and goddesses) were considered to be more powerful than mere humans and to possess eternal life. The Sumerians created an entire pantheon of gods and goddesses, and their mythology influenced Mesopotamian religious practices throughout the region. Some of the chief deities were given prominent roles and were worshipped by all Sumerians. One primary Sumerian god was called *An*, which meant sky. As the sky god, he was believed to transcend all cultures and as a truism the Sumerians felt he should be worshipped by everyone. Other major deities were Enlil, the god of air (sometimes known as the king of heaven and earth) and Enki, the god of wisdom.

People devised mythologies and complex stories about their gods. In one variant, Enki was credited with pouring the water that became the Tigris and Euphrates Rivers. The people imagined the gods gathering in an assembly to discuss the future of mere humans. Eventually the Sumerian gods spread, and many of the basic gods were also worshipped, sometimes under different names, by various Mesopotamian peoples. For instance, Enki was referred to as Ea by the Akkadian people. There were also several hundred minor deities revered by various cities such as Nanna, the god of the moon, and the patron god of the city of Ur, and Inanna, a fertility goddess who was the major deity of the city of Uruk.

Due to the strong emphasis on religion, a powerful priest class arose that acted as mediators between the people and the gods. The priests helped organize society around religious principles, and in return they received a portion of the crops at every harvest. While the priests exercised power as advisors to community leaders, scholars now believe that priests did not actually enjoy such powerful leadership roles in the government itself. Administrative control in Sumer was wielded by the *lugal* or king of each city-state. Provincial governors were also important in deciding local matters. The lugals and governors were responsible for supervising temple administration, construction of city walls, and other practical concerns as the early inhabitants labored to establish civilization.

The importance of religion is evident in the construction of temples called *ziggurats*. The word ziggurat can be translated roughly as "hills of heaven," and these structures were vital to the culture of the Sumerians. The design of a ziggurat, tiers with steps leading up toward the heavens, was meant as an invitation or a respectful appeal for the gods to descend those steps and interact with the people. Most Sumerian cities would have had a *ziggurat*, usually constructed of mud and clay bricks, positioned in a central location. Priests would dedicate the ziggurat to the city's own patron deity, and people were encouraged to offer sacrifices to this god or goddess. There were sections of the ziggurats that were considered holy, and only priests were allowed access to these inner chambers. The typical ziggurat was built as part of a larger worship complex that might take up many acres of land in the center of a city. In addition to the religious functions, public areas of the ziggurats also served as a social hub in most urban areas. People conducted business, met to discuss the news of the day, and merchants even sold goods in these large compounds.

Religion also provided the Mesopotamians with a way to retain control over the growing urban population. With patron deities who could punish or reward humans on a divine whim, the people were encouraged to openly venerate the gods in a show of meekness and submission. It was important for the people in a city to participate in religious ceremonies in order for the gods (especially the city's patron god/goddess) to realize their loyalty. They thought that unless a good number of the populace participated in the religious services, the gods might feel insulted and would perhaps remove their protection from the city.

The Mesopotamians by and large believed that placating and worshipping the gods was beneficial, but it still did not ensure that the gods would treat humans well. Even providing regular sacrifices and paying homage to the gods did not mean the gods would view those supplicants kindly. The prevalent belief was that natural phenomena like earthquakes and destructive storms were the result of annoyed or angered gods. Essentially the conventional Mesopotamian view of religion was that the gods would favor who they wanted, harm who they wanted, and all humans could do was attempt to appease and mollify these much more powerful beings.

The people of Mesopotamia conceived of an afterlife that was unpleasant at best. They believed that everyone, from the most evil to the most pious, would go to a dark and gloomy hereafter. This leads historians to wonder if these people's lives were so harsh that they did not anticipate any improvement in the next world or even a reward system for the devout. This pessimism is unusual since most religions envision a pleasurable afterlife. However, as mentioned previously, Mesopotamia was prone to intermittent flooding by the two major rivers, which left the inhabitants at the mercy of the environment. Also, the area withstood scores of outside invaders, and the consistent lack of rainfall made agriculture uncertain. These fears likely carried over into their religion as they tried to account for the inexplicable events that surrounded and controlled their lives. The Sumerian and most other Mesopotamian religions reserved their main focus for the present, with practitioners striving to lead a good life and to alleviate the sufferings of others. Sacrifices and ceremonies for the dead were means to slightly ease some of the most unpleasant aspects of the afterlife such as being hungry or thirsty. This is a rather melancholic and fatalistic religious view, but when considered in relation to the exacting and capricious lifestyle endured by the average person of the time, it makes sense.

The Rise and Fall of the Akkadians

The Sumerian people established the foundations of civilization in Mesopotamia, but the widespread dissemination of this early culture came from the Semitic peoples. The term *Semitic* describes many different groups who share a common linguistic background. Some Semitic peoples from the region this chapter will examine include the Akkadians, Amorites, and Hebrews. Historians who specialize in ancient history believe that the Semitic peoples migrated to the region, perhaps from modern day Saudi Arabia and proceeded to adapt Sumerian notions of religion, writing and commerce. By the year 3000 B.C.E. there is evidence of mutual cultural communication as well as a growing fusion of the Akkadian and Sumerian languages.

The Akkadians were the first to succeed the Sumerians as rulers of Mesopotamia led by their powerful King Sargon I, also known as Sargon of Akkad (Agade) (c. 2300 B.C.E.). While the Sumerian government had been based on the concept of independent, sovereign city-states, Sargon is credited with introducing the west to a new governing body: the empire. After overthrowing the king of Kish, a city-state in Sumer, Sargon centered his government at the city of Akkad, and guided his people in the conquest of all of Sumer.

Like many great historical figures, legends surround Sargon. One legend will sound familiar to people with a Judeo-Christian background. According to an old Semitic tale written down in cuneiform text, Sargon, whose name literally means "the king is legitimate," was put adrift on a river by his mother, found and raised by a kindly man, and grew up to be a great leader. This ancient tale, passed down for a long time through oral culture, may have provided a basis for the story of Moses found in the Hebrew Scriptures. From *The Legend of the Birth of Sargon*:

> My humble mother conceived me; she brought me forth in secret. She laid me in a basket of reeds, she smeared the door with bitumen (a sticky substance), and

> she committed me to the river which did not submerge me. The river carried me to Akki . . . . (who) lifted me out of the basket . . . . (and) made me his own son . . . Ishtar fell in love with me . . . and I ruled the kingdom.

After conquering major Sumerian cities like Ur and Uruk, Sargon marched his well trained, highly prepared military into Upper Mesopotamia and conquered the territory west of the Euphrates and east of the Tigris. Historians have evidence that his army conquered Syria, crossed the Mediterranean, and then took possession of Cyprus as well. Merriam-Webster.com defines an empire as "a major political unit having a territory of great extent or a number of territories or peoples under a single sovereign authority." In other words, Sargon was the first to extend his authority over people who were not originally part of his sphere of influence.

Starting with Sargon, the Akkadian emperors managed their conquests in a *laissez-faire* (hands off) fashion, choosing not to micromanage the subjugated regions of their vast empire. They let the indigenous people keep local autonomy, essentially requiring military service and taxation from the residents while providing protection to their subjects. For the most part, the emperors allowed retention of existing traditions and customs, and it can even be said they promoted a form of multiculturalism. The Akkadians clearly practiced synthesis in many ways with the subjugated peoples. For one thing they adopted vital tenets of the Sumerian religion, learned to write their spoken Akkadian language in cuneiform, and used Sumerian models for trade with other countries.

Sargon I was succeeded by his son Rimush, whose short reign of less than ten years was marked by upheaval. Almost as soon as he took the throne, he had to put down rebellions in numerous Sumerian cities. Several cities including the larger municipalities of Umma, Ur and Lagash attempted to remove Akkadian control from their territories. Rimush was able to quash the insurgencies, and in the aftermath he treated the rebels harshly. According to some sources, he enslaved as many as one-third of the adult male population in those cities and put them to work tearing down the city walls of the rebel states. Rimush was murdered as a result of a conspiracy, perhaps spearheaded by his power-hungry brother, Manishtusu, who followed him and ruled for nearly twenty years. Monarchs from the lineage of Sargon retained control of the empire until about 2200 B.C.E. By this point the Akkadian Empire fragmented into a series of smaller states. It was around this time, because of the diminishing power of the Akkadians, that the Sumerians were able to make a temporary return to power.

The Neo-Sumerian Empire, also called the Third Dynasty of Ur, likewise shows a tendency toward assimilation and amalgamation of cultures. Instead of removing all Akkadian influences and reverting back to traditional Sumerian culture, the Neo-Sumerians merged the best of both societies. The Sumerian language supplanted Akkadian as the official state language for commerce and government, but Akkadian influence was clearly present. For one thing, all the new cities that were founded in this period were given Akkadian names.

The Neo-Sumerian Empire left behind two significant items at the city of Ur that have helped modern scholars piece together more details about their culture. King Ur-Nammu likely commissioned the Great Ziggurat of Ur, which was uncovered by archaeologists in the nineteenth century. King Ur-Nammu also is credited with ordering a law code (c. 2100 B.C.E.). This law code was probably not the first, but it is the earliest one that is still extant, at least in fragments. This code was written using cuneiform and has been at least partially translated. It seems to focus on various aspects of legal codes such as taxes, trial procedures, and punishments for breaking the laws.

The Neo-Sumerian reign ended less than 400 years after it had begun. As the Amorites, a Semitic people from Arabia, conducted progressively more violent raids and attacks on the Sumerians, the Neo-Sumerian Empire was shattered. By the mid 1800s B.C.E. the Amorites had conquered not only the Sumerians, but they had also re-unified Mesopotamia and set up their own empire. Even though the government of the Sumerians again disappeared, their culture continued to influence the region as later peoples adapted Sumerian discoveries and knowledge to their own civilizations.

The Amorites

The Amorites, under their powerful king, Hammurabi (r.c.1790-1750 B.C.E.) controlled all of Mesopotamia. Their government was centered at so some historians refer to them as the Babylonians. This city proved to be a perfect choice for a capital due to its convenient position near the Tigris and Euphrates Rivers. The Amorites established Babylon as a great trade city due to its location, and Babylon grew wealthy. It became a great metropolis with an intricate bureaucracy and capable governors, businessmen, scribes, and builders.

Hammurabi proclaimed that the patron god of Babylon, Marduk, had become first in authority and reigned supreme over other gods. Marduk had thus become the chief deity, presumably in an assembly of the gods, and was therefore free to exercise control over the lesser gods. The implication is, of course, that Babylon was the legitimate, divinely sanctioned ruling city of Mesopotamia, or the leader of the gods wouldn't be the patron of Babylon. In another wise move, Hammurabi allowed people to continue to worship the lesser gods if they wished, but everyone in his empire would be required to worship Marduk as the principal deity. This shows a parallel to the physical re-unification of Mesopotamia; Hammurabi deemed Babylon superior to the other cities, but also allowed the peoples to retain their own traditions and customs.

While Hammurabi made several contributions to commerce and religion, he is best known for the Code of Hammurabi, the most complete ancient law code that is still in existence. An ancient slab of stone was uncovered in 1901-1902 on an archaeology expedition led by Jacques de Morgan in modern day Iran. The code was carved on this eight foot high block of black diorite stone that would have been displayed prominently for all to see. The code begins by mentioning many gods and by establishing Hammurabi as a favorite of the gods who was meant to "destroy the wicked and evil-doers so that the strong shall not harm the weak" because Hammurabi was an "exalted prince who feared god." The code is broken into three parts. Part I tells of the greatness of the king and what he has done for the people. Part II contains the 282 laws, and Part III returns to the gods with a blessing for those who observe the laws and a curse for those who disregard them.

Hammurabi's decrees tried to prohibit the arbitrary judgments where judges would mete out punishments according to their whims. Once the laws were written down, it symbolically elevated their magnitude. Hammurabi's code gave rise to the expression "written in stone" because the laws literally were. But emblematically, once a law is written in stone, it is unchangeable. That means even a monarch cannot issue impulsive and erratic punishments if the offense is covered in the legal code.

The code was exceedingly strict and severe, and its punishments varied according to class. In Hammurabi's society, social stratification played a vital role. Everyone was either a noble (upper class), a commoner, or a slave. Punishments in the law code were tailored to the specific classes. The nobility received lighter sentences if they committed a crime against someone of a lower status, and the commoners and slaves faced much harsher sentences if they committed a crime against their social superiors. So although the laws did favor higher ranking citizens, all people in any social class could count on receiving the same penalty for the same crime.

The sometimes callous and unforgiving punishments were meant to act as a deterrent. Many of the punishments were designed to suit the offense, or to use a later Italian word, *contrapasso*, which can be translated simply as "counter-suffering." For example: "If a man is caught stealing during a fire, he shall be thrown into the fire" and "a house-breaker (burglar) shall be buried in the hole he dug" (to get into the house). The meaning of other laws is obvious: "If anyone brings an accusation of any crime before the elders, and does not prove what he has charged, he shall, if it be a capital offense charged, be put to death." This was plainly meant to deter frivolous cases from being brought before the judges. If someone put out the eye of his equal, his eye would be put out also as punishment. However, in the class conscious society, if one put out the eye of a person from a lower status, he had the option of paying a fine. Hammurabi's code was studied and parts of it even appropriated by later generations. Today it is considered an important step on the road toward formalized legal systems.

By c.1700 B.C.E. there were various Amorite-controlled kingdoms all over Mesopotamia, with Amorite leaders controlling at least part of Syria. But in the politically unstable region, the Amorites would soon be unseated by fierce interlopers.

INDO-EUROPEAN INVASIONS

The Amorite kingdom had disappeared by c.1600B.C.E., and in the period that followed, (c1600-1100B.C.E.) many changes came to Mesopotamia. Occasionally this period is referred to as a "dark age" because of the instability of the time. Diverse peoples of Indo-European descent began to infiltrate the region. Indo-European, like Semitic, refers to a collection of related languages sharing a common source. This adjective can be applied to groups such as the Hittites, who are considered an Indo-European people. The Hittites came from Anatolia, or modern day Turkey. The aggressive Hittites attacked both Mesopotamia and Egypt, attempting to transform their militaristic society into an empire. Hittite soldiers brutally attacked and pillaged the city of Babylon in the 1590s B.C.E., officially ending Amorite rule in Babylon. The Hittites perfected chariot warfare, which made them formidable opponents for any enemy in the ancient world. They battled the Egyptians ferociously from c. 1300-1200 B.C.E. before finally forming an alliance with them.

The Hittite Empire grew large and prosperous. They controlled most of Anatolia, Syria, and Northern Mesopotamia. In the period from c. 1475-1200 B.C.E. their empire reached its height. Since they were heavily involved in trade, the Hittites became vital to the continued spread of Mesopotamian culture to areas as far away as Egypt and even Greece. Instead of destroying the indigenous cultures, the Hittites chose to merge their lifestyles, keeping the best from both. The Hittites adopted many Mesopotamian ideas including their deities, religious rituals, and ideas of commerce. Hittites spoke an Anatolian branch of the Indo-European languages, and their extant writing provides the earliest known instance of a written Indo-European language; Historians are fortunate that over 20,000 tablets of Hittite writing, both cuneiform and hieroglyphics, have been discovered. The Hittites also adapted the Mesopotamian monarchial system, with provincial governors being assigned jurisdiction over subjugated cities.

While the Hittites were in power, another group took control of Southern Mesopotamia: the Kassites. The Kassites were likely Indo-European, but some sources speculate that they were Asian peoples who were displaced by the vast Indo-European migration. The Kassites ruled Southern Mesopotamia including Babylon from c. 1500-1200 B.C.E. They were actually the longest ruling dynasty in Babylonian history.

The Age of Small Kingdoms

By the 1200s B.C.E. the region suffered a return to a period of violence and uncertainty. A series of invasions wracked the Near East, with various Indo-European groups settling in and inhabiting the area. The "Sea Peoples" who moved into the eastern Mediterranean are at once the most well-known and least understood of these invaders. The name "Sea Peoples" is given to a loosely defined group of peoples with ambiguous origins. Some of the groups believed to have made up this diverse collection of peoples were the Libyans, Philistines, and some groups from Anatolia. The "Sea Peoples" are infamous for their violent attacks on Egypt and the Hittite Empire. Historians disagree about their exact role in halting Egyptian expansion and toppling the Hittite Empire, but they agree that the widespread upheaval led to drastic changes that altered the governments in both areas.

In retrospect, one can see that the ensuing time of small kingdoms was actually an interval between periods of great kingdoms and empires. This provisional era of small kingdoms is identified by its confusion and unrest. During the subsequent disorder, as the old governments fell apart, new societies began to take shape. Many different peoples built societies during this time. The Phoenicians, Arameans, Syrians, Palestinians (Philistines), Hebrews, and others prospered after the decline of the large, overshadowing kingdoms. Perhaps the two most significant to European history were the Phoenicians and the Hebrews.

The Phoenicians

The Phoenicians were a Semitic people who migrated from the area that includes modern day Israel, Lebanon, and Jordan. After the destabilization of Egyptian power in the period following c. 1200 B.C.E., the Phoenicians employed their talent for commerce to create a wealthy society. They established a civilization based on trade, and as they spread their culture, they also launched numerous moneymaking provinces in far-reaching sites such as present day Sicily and Spain. Their colonies provided access to new types of raw materials and supplied additional trade markets for the original Phoenician coastal cities. One of the most profitable colonies was located in the city of Carthage in North Africa, which they founded around 812 B.C.E.

The Phoenicians are recognized for the development of a phonetic (derived from the word Phoenician) alphabet. This system of writing was much simpler than most others in the ancient world. Writing systems such as early cuneiform and Egyptian hieroglyphics were generally pictographic and cumbersome to learn and to use. With the introduction of the Phoenician alphabet and as a result of its dissemination throughout their extensive trade markets, writing became more common. Other cultures borrowed the idea of a phonetic alphabet, with each letter representing one sound, and modified it to their own spoken languages. The Greek alphabet is the most prominent example of this adaptation; the Greeks added vowels, which the Phoenician alphabet did not have. The Greek alphabet was transmitted to various regions through trade and eventually influenced the Roman Latin script. In turn, the Roman symbols were passed down and helped develop the alphabets of many modern European based languages.

Egyptian writing was based on pictograms. Ancient pictographs were colorfully painted using red, yellow and blue.

The Hebrews

During the ascension of these new smaller states, the one that arguably had the most dramatic and long lasting influence on Western civilization was the Hebrew culture. The Hebrews, also known as Israelites (and later as the Jews), were a Semitic people with obscure origins who ended up in the Levant (the modern-day eastern Mediterranean regions of Israel, Palestine, Jordan, Lebanon and Syria). They settled mainly in what they called the land of Canaan (Israel, Lebanon and Syria) and built a culture based on a monotheistic religion.

The principal existing source for the history of the Hebrew people is the Bible (Hebrew Scriptures) which, as a religious work, cannot be considered strictly objective. The Bible is a multifaceted collection of literature, and as such it gives much insight into the culture and beliefs of the people who wrote it. But along with the purported historical records, the Bible also contains works of poetry, allegories, and moral stipulations that quite likely held very different connotations for contemporary Bronze Age nomads than for modern-day people.

The Hebrews were the first group in the ancient world to have specifically written down such a chronicle with historical references, but it was composed as a religious narrative. Their morality and didactic tales are carefully told alongside and as part of a larger account of the Israelites and their relationship with their God. The Hebrew Bible is called the Old Testament by Christians, who practice a religion that evolved from Judaism. These scriptures were composed by many people over a lengthy period of time from c. 1200 B.C.E. up to c. 100 B.C.E., and their composition relied heavily on earlier oral tradition. The Hebrew Bible includes several stories that appear to have been shared and circulated amongst peoples of Mesopotamia and the surrounding areas. Some examples are the story of a great deluge or flood also found in the Sumerian *Epic of Gilgamesh*; the creation story in Genesis (the first book of the Bible), which has a Sumerian parallel; and the account of Moses and the story of Sargon I of Akkad are variants of the same legend. Historians are always judicious when using Biblical stories to glean historical perspective. Above all, the Bible imparts the underlying belief that there is one true God who is actively involved in guiding the progress of humankind, particularly his "chosen people," the Hebrews or the Jewish people. As such, it is naturally subjective. However, the influence of the Hebrew Scriptures, combined with the later Christian "New Testament," is so far-reaching that it is worthwhile to examine the claims of this enduring work.

According to the Bible, the story of the Jewish people begins with the patriarch, Abraham. If he can be considered a historical personage, he likely was a nomadic herdsman who migrated to the land of Canaan, probably from Mesopotamia, sometime around c. 2000 B.C.E. The Biblical account says God made a covenant with Abraham:

> And I will bless them that bless thee, and curse him that curseth thee: and in thee shall all families of the earth be blessed. (Genesis 12:2-4)

Abraham left his homeland and headed for the land of Canaan, which the Bible says God promised him, as part of the covenant, in return for his faithfulness. God also assured Abraham that his descendants would be numerous and powerful:

> And I will make thee exceeding fruitful, and I will make nations of thee, and kings shall come out of thee. And I will establish my covenant between me and thee and thy seed after thee in their generations for an everlasting covenant, to be a God unto thee, and to thy seed after thee. And I will give unto thee, and to thy seed after thee, the land wherein thou art a stranger, all the land of Canaan, for an everlasting possession; and I will be their God.
> (Genesis 17: 6- 8).

Abraham, his son Isaac, and his grandson Jacob form the trio of Jewish forefathers. The term Israelite is derived from the patriarch Jacob, who was renamed Israel by the Hebrew God. Jacob was said to have had twelve sons who became the heads of the twelve tribes of Israel.

The Bible goes on to describe a great famine in the land of Canaan sometime prior to the 1400s B.C.E. This food shortage led some of Abraham's descendants to leave the region in order to survive. Many of these émigrés settled in Egypt, which boasted an expanding, successful economy. According to Hebrew tradition, the Hebrews in Egypt were enslaved and subjected to horrible treatment by their Egyptian overlords. The Bible describes how they were led out of slavery by a man named Moses, whose historical identity is uncertain. Many aspects of Moses' story can be found in earlier legends, but, regardless, the Israelite people believed in his existence. Jewish sources have attempted to place him and the so-called "exodus" of the Israelites from Egypt in the thirteenth century B.C.E. This is the time when the Bible says that Yahweh renewed his covenant with Abraham's descendants, and they were led back to the land of Canaan.

Around 1000 B.C.E. the Hebrews were attacked by another group who had arrived in the Levant at nearly the same time: the Philistines. The homeland of the Philistines is not certain, but there is speculation that they were part of the "Sea Peoples" that invaded the territory in the 1200s B.C.E. Some scholars look to their language and cultural remnants and believe they originated in Mycenae on mainland Greece. Regardless of their origins, the Philistines came to occupy the southern part of ancient Canaan, and they were far more organized and advanced militarily than their neighbors. They used iron weapons, and as a result, they were able to defeat many nearby societies that still relied on bronze tools and weapons. Because the Philistines had conquered so much of the region, it became known as Palestine, which literally means Philistine country. The loosely allied Israelite tribes were led by tribal chieftains called judges until the Philistines began to present an aggressive military threat. For their protection the Israelites were forced to unify under a strong monarchy.

The first king of this unified nation was Saul, who was appointed king around 1025 B.C.E. He is portrayed in the Bible as a troubled leader who stopped the Philistines from completely defeating the Kingdom of Israel. His legacy was incomplete because he was unable to remove them from the surrounding areas, which meant the threat was not extinguished. By this point Saul had lost God's favor, and he was soon replaced by a brave young man named David, who became the second King of Israel.

David (r. c.1000-965 B.C.E.) is considered Israel's most remarkable king. He led the Israelites to victory over the Philistines, and solidified the Kingdom of Israel. By the time of David's death his kingdom was large, encompassing sections of Jordan, Lebanon, and Syria with its capital in the former Canaanite city of Jerusalem. Under David, the Israelites captured considerable Canaanite territories, and after his reign the Hebrews and the native Canaanites successfully blended their cultures.

Solomon (r. c. 965-930 B.C.E.) was David's son, and even though it was hard to follow the powerful reign of his father, Solomon is remembered as a great king in his own right. He is known for building a grand and stunning temple to honor the Israelite God, Yahweh (sometimes called Jehovah). Solomon's temple had a certain inner room that was prepared to contain and protect the "Ark of the Covenant," which was believed to contain the original Ten Commandments on stone tablets. But Solomon was a despotic leader who forced many of his subjects, 30,000 according to the Bible, to work on his building projects against their will and with no compensation. In the northern part of the kingdom, there was widespread anger and resentment at this conscription. Soon after Solomon's death, the Kingdom of Israel split into two kingdoms. The southern kingdom retained Jerusalem as its capital and became known as Judah. In the north, ten Israelite tribes united calling their nation the Kingdom of Israel. The two kingdoms co-existed for centuries, but much like the time before Saul, the fragmented Israelites were no longer the powerful force they had been under a centralized monarchy. The Kingdom of Israel fell in c.722 B.C.E., but the Kingdom of Judah, whose people eventually became known as Jews, held on until c.586 B.C.E. Individually they had become significantly more vulnerable to attack. Both kingdoms of the original Hebrew people had fallen, but they were not alone in this fate. Most of the other small nations of the region also collapsed due to the efforts of a formidable foe: the Assyrians.

The Assyrians

By c. 1200 B.C.E. the Indo-European invaders and the resulting small kingdoms were beginning to be displaced by the Assyrians, a Semitic people who reclaimed control of the region. The Assyrians were descendants of the earlier Akkadian peoples, and after the Akkadian Empire fragmented, the Assyrians remained in Northern Mesopotamia. They were farmers who settled in the region of Assur, a small city-state. The region was perilous and unstable, with invaders constantly battling them for control of their fields and homes. As a result, the Assyrians built a vast, remarkable military out of necessity. They constructed iron weapons, using iron in many objects from spears to shields. This gave them a distinct advantage over most of their enemies who still used bronze weaponry. They also expanded and improved on an earlier concept of chariot warfare. The Assyrian armies had superior tactics and weapons, but they were also highly organized and well-trained. What began as a way to survive became a way of life, and the Assyrians transformed into a military society.

As the Hittite government weakened, the Babylonians and the Assyrians fought for control of Syria. The Assyrian king Ashur-resh-ishi I (r. 1133-1115 B.C.E.) defeated the Babylonian king Nebuchadnezzar I of Babylon (c.1125-1103 B.C.E.). However, it was not until the time of their celebrated king, Tiglath-Pileser I (c. 1115 -1077 B.C.E.) that the Assyrians were able to assert their power over the Kassite controlled regions in Southern Mesopotamia and claim the entire area, including Syria, as their kingdom. Tiglath-Pileser I is sometimes referred to as the first genuine Assyrian emperor because under his guidance, the Assyrians revived and then expanded the model of empire. Instead of simply reducing the subject peoples to a life of servitude under their conquerors, the Assyrians began a process of a genuine amalgamation of diverse cultures under one leader. Although their methods of conquest were brutal, they did allow the varied customs and traditions to co-exist with Assyrian society. But in order to produce a unified empire, they strongly advised loyalty to the government.

Sometimes after a particularly strong leader dies, the society goes into crisis mode; this happened after Tiglath-Pileser I's death. The Assyrian government deteriorated for a time as the Arameans, another Semitic people, took control of the area. It was generations later under Assyrian leaders such as Tiglath-Pileser III (c.774-727 B.C.E.) and Sargon II (r. c. 722-705 B.C.E.) that the Assyrian Empire triumphed again. These two powerful kings led the expansion of the Assyrian domain to such an extent that their territory stretched from Egypt to Persia. This revived Assyrian empire is referred to as the Neo-Assyrian Empire.

When Tiglath-Pileser III took the throne of Assyria, he brought with him his own management style for the empire. He is sometimes credited with originating centralized government in the western world. He controlled his conquered territories through a formal hierarchical system. The emperor was the leader and commander of his realm, and the subjugated regions would be required to pay taxes to the empire and provide soldiers for the military. As the Neo-Assyrian Empire became vast, one emperor could no longer manage it effectively. They set up a complicated system of administration that included provincial governors to supervise the various areas and enforce the laws.

Tiglath-Pileser III put together one of the first and best standing armies of the ancient world, which the emperors used to secure imperial expansion. This military exercised what would be referred to in modern times as a draft, whereby all able-bodied men had to serve for a time. The military was broken into smaller, manageable units, with foot soldiers playing an important role. Assyrian military commanders

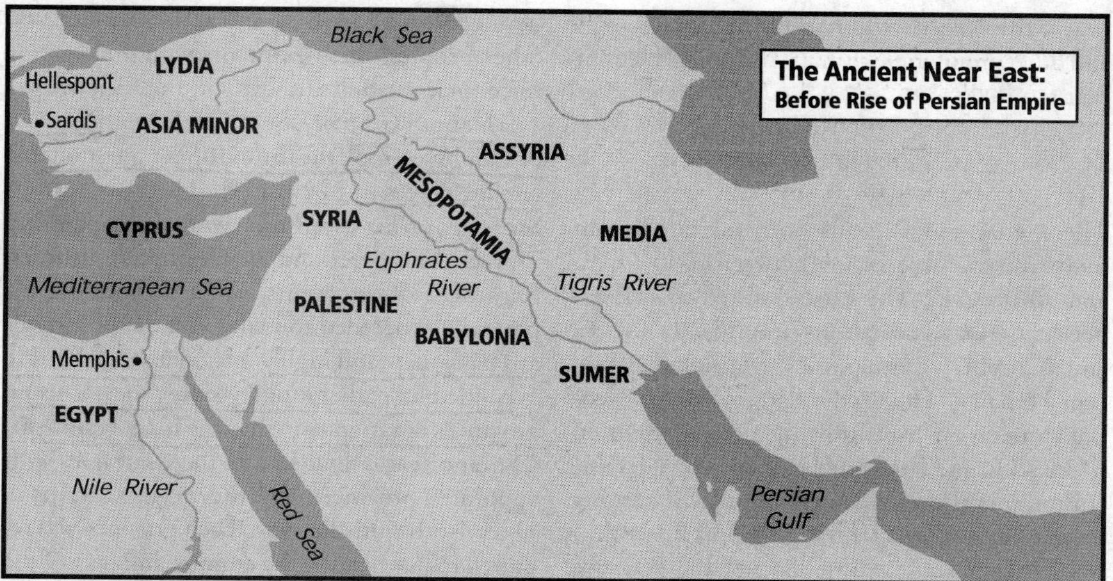

were exceptional innovators in their preparation and performance on the battlefield. They were among the first to utilize scientific expertise to increase their effectiveness in combat. Their design of elaborate mounted (on wheels) battering rams that were used to knock down fortifications provides one of the best examples. While the Assyrian tactics were brutal and vicious, they were also undeniably effective. Assyrian soldiers were encouraged to terminate rebellions by any means necessary. There are accounts of dissenters being burned alive, skinned alive, and impaled on a variety of objects. The emperors also liberally used the practice of deportation, or forcible removal. The message was unambiguous: submit or this is your fate! This was virtually a pledge that any resistance would be short-lived.

But all the ingenious strategies and methods used by the Assyrians were unable to keep them in power indefinitely. There were so many rebellions against the hated and feared Assyrians that the empire became progressively destabilized. After a long period of wars, revolts and attempts to regain control, finally the Neo-Assyrian Empire came to an end. In 612 B.C.E. a coalition of Medes and Chaldeans (also known as Neo-Babylonians) pillaged and plundered the Assyrian capital of Nineveh. This ended the government of the militaristic Assyrians, and these brutal conquerors were finally dominated.

The end of Assyrian domination led to a renewed interest in Babylonian culture. The Neo-Babylonians joined with the Medes to take control of the defunct Assyrian empire, and they retained military control in the region until the coming of the Persians. The Neo-Babylonian king Nebuchadnezzar II (c. 605-562 B.C.E.) was responsible for rebuilding Babylon into a great cultural center. His people studied astronomy, providing a foundation for later analyses focusing on the movement of stars, and they developed systems to calculate the timing of lunar eclipses. Nebuchadnezzar II is vilified in the Bible for capturing the cities of Jerusalem and Judah and for relocating many Hebrews out of their homeland during an event referred to as the Babylonian Captivity or the "Exile of the Sons of Judah," (c. 600– 538 B.C.E.). After Nebuchadnezzar II's death, the Neo-Babylonian Empire lost power, and other groups quickly filled the power vacuum that resulted.

The Persian Empire

The Medes and Persians both migrated from modern-day Iran sometime between 1600 B.C.E. and 900 B.C.E. The Medes united their independent tribal associations around 700 B.C.E. and as a cohesive group, they overtook the adjacent Persians. The Medes had joined the Neo-Babylonians in overthrowing the Assyrians in 612 B.C.E. and continued to enjoy considerable authority in the region until the reign of a strong Persian king: Cyrus II (r. c. 559-530 B.C.E.).

When Cyrus became king of the Persians, he went to work planning his conquest of the governing Medes. By 550 B.C.E. he had made this suppression a reality, and the Medes became part of what eventually evolved into the Persian Empire. Cyrus conquered the Lydian kingdom and the Greek cities in Anatolia, Babylon, and he continued to the borders of northwestern India. The Persian Empire represented the last and most impressive empire to emerge from the ancient Near Eastern cultures.

Cyrus believed in treating his subjugated peoples with tolerance and lenience, allowing them to keep their customs, as long as they also paid respect to the Persian Empire. Beginning with Cyrus, Persian kings were benevolent rulers over their subjects to encourage loyalty to the empire. He allowed the Hebrews, who had been exiled by Nebuchadnezzar II, to return to their land, ending the Babylonian Captivity in 586 B.C.E. Cyrus' son Cambyses II (c.529-522 B.C.E.) continued his father's policies, and he was able to add the conquest of Egypt to his list of accomplishments. Under Cambyses' successors the Persian Empire increased its clout through new territorial conquest, and as they vanquished other peoples, these emperors would also reinforce their existing authority in the region.

Darius I (r.c.550-486 B.C.E.), brother in law of Cambyses, took the throne under questionable circumstances in 522 B.C.E. There are various accounts of his ascension, with some painting him as a murderer and an illegitimate usurper. Regardless of the events, when he became emperor, he proceeded to make a name for himself as a passionate and highly imaginative leader. He expanded on earlier kings' visions, such as using provinces or satrapies to manage his government. The empire was divided into these satrapies with appointed provincial governors called satraps to supervise the jurisdictions. Each province was required to pay taxes to the empire, and part of the satraps' job was to collect these taxes. Darius, also known as Darius the Great, employed a group of spies called the "eyes and ears of the king" who were dispersed throughout the domain to make sure the satraps were respecting imperial policies and adhering to the king's will.

Earlier ancient peoples, notably the Assyrians, had believed in building a unified population. In keeping with this tradition, Darius made Aramaic the official imperial language for conducting business. While the people could use their own traditional languages in their private affairs, when performing administrative and governmental matters, Aramaic was used exclusively. Since he showed respect to the diverse groups in his domain, (at one time he had 26 different subject peoples) he was highly regarded as a leader by the various groups.

Darius the Great's Persian Empire stretched from Egypt to India. As emperor he was admired by his subject peoples, but this did not mean everything was peaceful. In 499 B.C.E. the Ionian Greeks in Anatolia began a large scale insurrection against their Persian overlords. The Ionian

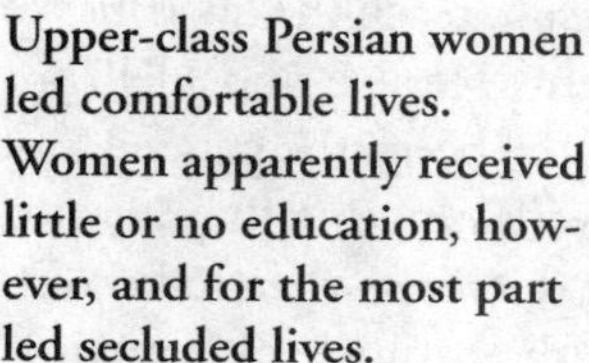

Upper-class Persian women led comfortable lives. Women apparently received little or no education, however, and for the most part led secluded lives.

Greeks were displaced Greeks, who had migrated to Anatolia centuries earlier to flee from a period of invasions in their homeland. They had long chafed at their status under Persian hegemony, and they were frustrated with the amount of tribute they were required to pay the Persians, so the rebellion was no real surprise. The revolt went well at first for the Ionians, and they received military support from Athens and Eretria, two mainland Greek poleis. In 498 B.C.E. the combined Greek forces took Sardis, a prominent Persian city and attempted to burn it to the ground. But the joint Greek forces were no match for the formidable Persian army, and by 494 B.C.E. the Ionian uprising had been quashed. At this point Darius believed that it was necessary to punish Athens and Eretria and make them an example for their insolence in challenging his rule. He also wanted to prevent any further rebellions, so he decided to reduce Greece to a Persian province.

In 492 B.C.E. Darius ordered the Persian army to Greece. Within a year he brought Macedonia under Persian dominance. Instead of using further military resources, he then tried diplomatic means in his efforts to subdue the Greeks. He sent ambassadors to various poleis in Greece to obtain an official surrender and capitulation to Persia. Many Greek cities acquiesced out of a valid fear of the Persian army, but Athens and Sparta both refused to give in. Eretria was destroyed by the Persians, and the citizens almost certainly sold into slavery. After defeating Eretria, the Persian forces headed for Athens, where the Athenian forces were able to gain a decisive victory in the Battle of Marathon (490 B.C.E.). This victory was imperative; if the Persians had won, they likely would have followed through with the plan to make Greece part of the Persian Empire. After Darius' death, his son Xerxes invaded Greece a second time in 480 B.C.E., but again the Persians were unsuccessful. After this second defeat, the Persians no longer attempted expansion into Europe.

In addition to their military conquests and administrative structure, the Persians also gave the Western world one of the oldest monotheistic religions: Zoroastrianism. Emperor Darius I embraced the religion, and with his endorsement, Zoroastrianism spread throughout Persian controlled territories. Before Zoroastrianism, the Indo-Iranian religion was polytheistic, having a large pantheon of gods and goddesses. Devotees of Zoroastrianism believed that the truth was revealed to a prophet, a man named Zoroaster (Zarathustra in Greek) who set out to align the Indo-Iranian beliefs with his revealed knowledge.

Zoroaster is difficult to place definitively in history; some scholars believe he lived around the 6th century B.C.E. while others position him as early as the 15th century B.C.E. There are many legends about his life, but few verifiable facts. According to Zoroastrian sacred writings, Zoroaster was preparing for a religious ritual when he had a striking vision. He said he was escorted to the god Ahura-Mazda, who provided him with the fundamentals of the one true religion. Zoroaster believed it was his mission to spread this vision, and at age 30 he began to preach a monotheistic religion to the polytheists. The former deity of wisdom from the Indo-Iranian pantheon, Ahura-Mazda, was elevated to the status of the "wise lord" or "uncreated creator god." Ahura-Mazda became the supreme deity in Zoroaster's revealed religion, but Ahura-Mazda continually had to subdue an evil and destructive spirit called Ahriman or Angra Mainyu.

Zoroastrianism stresses the importance of personal responsibility in one's eternal destination. Humans have free will, and one's choices determine whether the afterlife is a reward or punishment. If a person makes good choices, following the dictates of Ahura-Mazda, the afterlife will be a bright, happy place. On the other hand, if one is wicked, pursuing the temptations of Ahriman, the afterlife will be a place of eternal despair. The Avesta, the main Zoroastrian holy book, explains how to combat the malevolent spirit: "Ahriman is best fought by joy; misery is a symptom of his victory." And the basics of the religion can be summed up in the pithy phrase: "Good thoughts, good words, good deeds."

The parallels between Zoroastrianism and the later religion of Christianity are obvious and numerous. According to scholar Mary Boyce, who has written extensively on the religion, ""Zoroaster was thus the first to teach the doctrines of an individual judgment, Heaven and Hell, the future resurrection of the body, the general Last Judgment, and life everlasting for the reunited soul and body. These doctrines were to become familiar articles of faith to much of mankind, through borrowings by Judaism, Christianity and Islam." Zoroastrianism is one of the oldest religions still in existence in the twenty-first century. As of 2010, it has been estimated that there are between 100,000 and 200,000 devotees of this ancient religion living in Iran and India. The culture of the Near East would simultaneously influence and be shaped by the Persians for centuries. With a stable economy, steady expansion, and a growing population, the Persians carved out the largest empire in the world. This empire would endure until it was conquered by Alexander the Great in the 300's BCE.

THE EGYPTIANS

The Egyptian civilization seems to have developed at virtually the same time as the Mesopotamian civilization, but in many ways the cultures were very different. In Mesopotamia, the Tigris and Euphrates Rivers provided life-giving water to the people, but the rivers were also viewed with apprehension since they could be volatile and dangerous. The Egyptians had the security of the Nile River, which flooded reliably every year with such predictability that the inhabitants of the river valley learned to measure the years according to the annual flood. While Mesopotamia had no real natural barriers to prevent invasion, Egypt was bordered by the Mediterranean Sea in the north and the Red Sea in the east. In

Paintings in the Egyptian tombs depicted the lifestyle to which the nobility were accustomed. In this painting servants carry items to fill their pharaoh's tomb.

the southern regions Egypt had rough, unstable rocky protrusions called cataracts, a word which loosely translated means "rushing downward." These cataracts were impossible to navigate by boat. Much of Egypt outside of the river valley consisted of bleak, uninviting deserts, including the vast Sahara and the Libyan Deserts. The deserts and the seas acted as sentinels, keeping the people secluded and making successful invasion much less likely. These geographic guardians, together with the perpetually reliable Nile, offered the Egyptians a sense of security that was unique in the ancient world. Because of this unique situation, the Egyptians had a more optimistic view of the afterlife, which they considered to be an extension of the known worldly pleasures and gratifications.

The country of Egypt is located in a long, narrow valley with a flat delta region where the Nile meets the Mediterranean Sea. The earliest inhabitants had to settle close to the Nile so they could farm the small amount of arable land in the region. The Nile allowed agriculture in Egypt, and as the fertile soil gave the Egyptians reliable crops, their culture thrived. Archeologists believe that around 4700 B.C.E. villages were forming in the Nile Valley and that by 3100 B.C.E. the growing population had begun settling into small communities such as Nekhen and Abydos. This era corresponds to prehistory, or the time before writing, and is usually designated Predynastic Egypt (c. 5000–3100 B.C.E.).

Egyptians divided their land into two clearly delineated regions: Upper and Lower Egypt. Lower Egypt, (located in the north) was in the delta, a triangle shaped section of land where the Nile divides into smaller offshoots that join the Mediterranean Sea. Upper Egypt (located in the south) included the southern edge of the delta region all the way to the first cataract. The designations of Upper to the southern region and Lower to the northern region may seem counterintuitive until one realizes that the Nile flows from the south to the north.

Upper and Lower Egypt were unified around 3150 B.C.E. under a semi-legendary ruler called Menes or Narmer. Whether he was a real person, a legend, or a combination of reality and myth-making, King Menes is given credit for founding the first of thirty-one royal dynasties or families of Egypt. The Archaic Period, also known as the Early Dynastic Period, (c. 3150-2700 B.C.E.) began with King Menes and included the First and Second Egyptian Dynasties. During the Archaic Period the kings continually found themselves engaged in battles for control of Egypt, so true political unification would not arrive until the next chapter of Egyptian development: the Old Kingdom.

The Old Kingdom (c. 2700- 2200 BCE)

The Old Kingdom was a prosperous, peaceful, and creative time for Egypt. The Egyptians perfected their system of trade, particularly with Nubia, which had plentiful mineral deposits, ivory and gold. As a result, the Egyptian economy flourished, and the country became wealthy. During this period artists produced some of the earliest known life-sized three-dimensional sculptures using a wide range of mediums such as stone and wood. They decorated their temples and public buildings with beautiful scenes from their environment. Art during the Old Kingdom

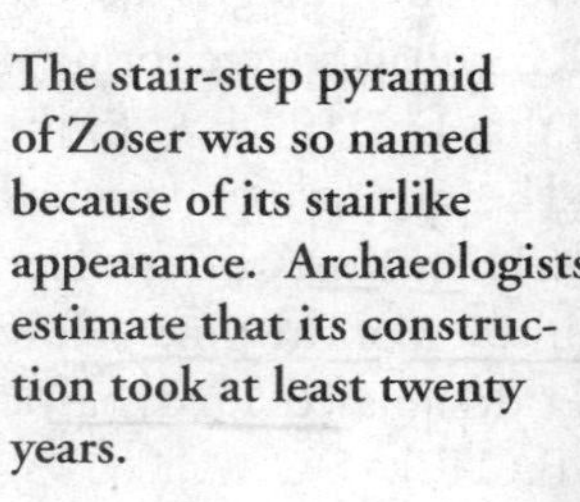

The stair-step pyramid of Zoser was so named because of its stairlike appearance. Archaeologists estimate that its construction took at least twenty years.

was created mainly for religious purposes as the Egyptians honored their deities with imaginative accomplishments.

Ancient Egyptians believed their continued success rested on the king, who would be called a pharaoh starting in the New Kingdom. They believed this leader was an actual god personified. The people thought that each king was the god Horus incarnate while he was living, and at his bodily death he became the god Osiris, judge of the dead in the spirit world. The political and religious worlds of the Egyptians were therefore inextricably linked. During the Old Kingdom the artistic, political and religious worlds converged under the reign of King Zoser (also spelled Djoser) through a new building style that would eventually lead to some of the most long lasting and prominent structures in the world.

King Zoser (c. 2600s), who was an early ruler of the Third Dynasty, wanted to leave a monument to his twenty year reign that would instill wonder and admiration in future generations. He instituted a building program in his capital of Memphis, which culminated in the creation of the first pyramid structure in Egypt around 2630 B.C.E. His architect, Imhotep, designed the step pyramid, which is one of the earliest sizable structures built out of dressed stone. It was 204 feet high with a base of 389 by 462 feet, and built in six layers, or as they would appear, steps. Later kings built step pyramids, but it took some time for the architectural style to evolve into the traditional "true" pyramid shape that is well-known today.

Since the ancient Egyptian pharaohs were considered to be gods, their ornate burial rituals and tombs served as memorials of their glory on earth. Additionally, the pharaoh's tomb had to store all the physical luxuries his ka (spirit) would need for a smooth transition to the afterlife. The people believed that his status in the next life would have an effect on the living, and by giving him an elegant farewell, they hoped he would continue to bring them success and enrichment from the hereafter. This is a major reason the kings were given such elaborate burials, complete with remarkable treasures to access in the next world. For example, in King Zoser's pyramid complex, there were underground storerooms and galleries filled with all sorts of riches. The compound was encircled by a stone wall that was at least 30 feet high with numerous false entrances to discourage thieves.

While several pharaohs after King Zoser tried to surpass his burial monument, they had little success. It was during the Fourth Dynasty that the renowned pyramids at Giza were constructed. The ruler Khufu (r. c. 2589-2532; also known as Cheops) went south of Memphis to the flat desert

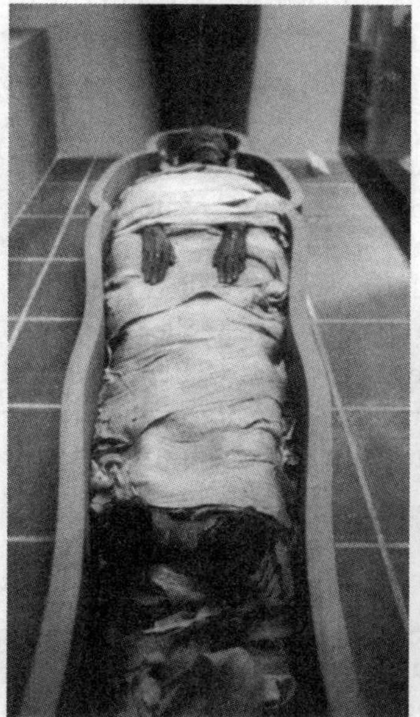

Mummification was an important step in the process of preparing the body for the afterlife. This process was practiced for over three thousand years. This Egyptian mummy and organ jars are displayed in an Egyptian museum in Turin, Italy.

lands of Giza near Cairo to build the largest of the great pyramids. His pyramid originally towered above the plateau at 481 feet with a base of 756 feet square. The pyramid was constructed using over two million limestone blocks. The visible outer portion was covered with polished glossy white limestone, and there is speculation that there was once a gilded capstone.

The splendor and complexity of this structure has led to debates regarding its actual construction. Scholars have mused for centuries about building techniques and engineering methods. Historians also wonder who the laborers were and how many there were. Though many theories have been proposed over the years, there has been no scholarly agreement on these questions. The Greek historian Herodotus visited Giza roughly two thousand years after the pyramids were built. He speculated that it took twenty years using thousands of slaves. Today archaeologists are constantly uncovering pieces of this ancient puzzle. One of the latest theories is that slaves were not used exclusively in the construction; rather the laborers were compensated manual workers.

While Khufu's pyramid is called the Great Pyramid, next to it stand two smaller pyramids built by his successors Khafre (Chephren) and Menkaure (Mycerinus). If one looks at a picture of the three structures, it may seem that Khafre's pyramid is larger, but it is actually a bit smaller (471 feet tall and 707 feet square). The impression is misleading because Khafre's pyramid was built on higher ground. The third pyramid in the trio at Giza is the pyramid of Menkaure, which had an original height of about 218 feet with a base of approximately 339 feet square.

Khafre is given credit for also commissioning the so-called Great Sphinx, a massive reclining lion with the head of a human, which is the largest and most ancient extant statue. The Great Sphinx was carved out of a strong limestone outcropping east of the pyramid of Khafre. Many scholars believe that in ancient times the Sphinx was decorated elaborately with colorful adornment. The sculpture also originally had a nose and a beard, which have not lasted to modern times. For thousands of years, the Great Pyramids and the Sphinx have remained a symbol of the wealth and power of Egyptian culture. Like the reliable Nile, these structures have timelessly endured, heralding the might and mystery of ancient Egypt to later peoples.

The First Intermediate Period, the Middle Kingdom, and the Second Intermediate Period (c. 2200-1600 BCE)

By the end of the Old Kingdom the pharaohs lost most of their power, and by around 2200 B.C.E.

The pharaoh's coffin was taken by priests into the pyramid and placed inside a sarcophagus. This is an Egyptian sarcophagus.

The Great Sphinx features the head of a man and the body of a lion. The Great Sphinx was built at the same time as the Giza Pyramids. The Sphinx measures 240 feet in length and stands 66 feet tall. At its widest point it measures 13 feet 8 inches.

the orderly absolutism they had cultivated had all but disappeared. A devastating drought in neighboring Nubia caused flooding and as a result, famine struck Egypt. A time of uncertainty and disunity descended upon Egypt. Political and economic pressures led to a fragmented government, and a series of insignificant rulers attempted to revive Egypt. This bleak time is usually called the First Intermediate Period, a reference to a temporary breakdown in authority. This chaotic interlude lasted until Amenamhat I of the Twelfth Dynasty (c.2052) was finally able to establish firm control over both Upper and Lower Egypt and usher in another prosperous era called the Middle Kingdom.

While the pharaohs of the Middle Kingdom (c. 2052-1640 B.C.E.) were still considered gods, in practice these "gods" were concerned with pleasing their subjects to retain the hard won stability of the kingdom. Regardless, the pharaohs of the Middle Kingdom are remembered as humane rulers who showed benevolent concern for their people. The Middle Kingdom is also known for the conquest of wealthy Nubia as well as exploration of new trade markets in places like Mesopotamia. Unfortunately for the Egyptians, the Nubian people rebelled and regained their autonomy. This had a disastrous effect on the economy of Egypt and also served to undermine the king's supremacy. With both a weakened economy and king, it didn't take long for invaders to overrun and inhabit the region.

Extensive immigration into Egypt during the late Middle Kingdom caused the region again to descend into a tumultuous episode filled with conflict. As more and more of these peoples entered Egypt, they chose not to assimilate into the culture. Instead they insisted on keeping their foreign practices and beliefs while ignoring the traditions and customs of the Egyptians. These groups from distant lands brought the Middle Kingdom to an end and what followed is referred to as the Second Intermediate Period (c. 1640-1550 B.C.E.).

For close to one hundred years foreign-born kings grappled almost constantly for control of Egypt. The state decentralized once again, and many small kingdoms were set up all across the Nile Valley under the leadership of various immigrant kings. The Egyptians referred to these kings as "foreign rulers," commonly referred today by the Greek name: *Hyksos*. These people ruled Egypt for about a century until the Egyptians defeated them in a series of wars. Then, with the establishment of the Eighteenth Dynasty around 1550 B.C.E., Egypt was back in the hands of the Egyptians. The New Kingdom had begun.

The New Kingdom (c. 1550-1075 B.C.E.) brought with it foreign expansion and stanch military expeditions. With conquests in the Levant region, Palestine, Syria, and the Sudan, Egypt was experiencing a golden age of development and growth. Prosperity and growth are the main characteristics of the New Kingdom, with some historians believing this to be the first genuine Egyptian empire.

Having such success on the battlefield brought much glory and prestige, but it is also when slavery became commonplace in the empire. Men, women and children from many areas lost their freedom and were required to serve under their Egyptian captors. It was also a practice for some poor families to sell a child they could not support into slavery. Slaves performed many different jobs in Egypt, ranging from working on building projects to domestic labor.

The New Kingdom's Eighteenth Dynasty had its share of well-known and exceptional pharaohs. Amenhotep IV (c. r. 1350s-1330s B.C.E.) attempted to spark a religious revolution in polytheistic Egypt. While it is likely that he was raised practicing the typical Egyptian religious rituals and ceremonies, at some point he turned from polytheism and called for a type of monotheism in his kingdom. The god Amon-Re (also called Amon or Amun) had previously been elevated to the top of the Egyptian pantheon, but Amenhotep IV insisted that the creator and universal god was Aten, the sun disk. Amenhotep IV also insisted that he was in contact with Aten, and that he was to act as an intercessor between Aten and the people. Amenhotep IV changed his name to Akhenaten, which loosely translated means "all is well with the Aten" or "the spirit of the Aten" and began reforming the religion of Egypt around a solar cult. During his reign he built his capital city of Amarna, where he tried to remove all traces of the earlier powerful god Amon-Re, and he outlawed worship of all gods except Aten. His religious innovation was short-lived because after Akhenaten's death, within a short time the former priests of Amon were restored to their powerful positions, and Aten was relegated to a low position in the pantheon. Historians have many unanswered questions about Akhenaten's reign. Is it possible that the Hebrews who came in contact with Egyptians got their idea for monotheism from this religious anomaly? Some wonder if it could have been the other way around, with the Hebrews influencing Akhenaten. Regardless, his insistence on a single god caused confusion among the people, and it was not well received.

The pharaoh Amenhotep IV's reign is rarely mentioned without referencing the fact that he was married to Nefertiti. We do not know a great deal about her life, but Nefertiti was immortalized in a limestone sculpture of her head and shoulders (a bust). This work was discovered in 1912, and it is still on display in the modern world. The well preserved figure has been studied by Egyptologists during the last century, and it provides historians with a unique glimpse of one of the queens from the powerful Eighteenth Dynasty.

Akhenaten was succeeded by his son Tutankhamen, who reigned for a short time in the 1330s B.C.E. Tutankhamen was born Tutankhamen, which was another reference to the power of Aten, but he renounced monotheism and changed his name. He began the process to restore the god Amon-Re to his former elite status, undoubtedly at the behest of the priests and the people. His reign was short. He took the throne at nine and died at eighteen or nineteen of unknown causes. The boy king's reign was largely insignificant and would have likely been lost to history except for the discovery in the 1920s of his tomb, complete with many preserved treasures including a gold funeral mask and his mummified body. The discovery caused an extensive sensation that became even more frenetic when news of a "curse" began to spread. The deaths of a number of people who were involved in some way with the expedition fueled the rumors of a deadly curse on all who dared to disturb the tomb. Eventually King Tutankhamen's tomb was emptied of more than 5000 relics, most of which are housed in the Cairo museum today and occasionally are exhibited briefly in other countries. King Tut, as he is sometimes called, was succeeded by a general, Harmhab (r.c. 1320-1290 B.C.E.), who completed the restoration of polytheism to Egypt.

The New Kingdom essentially ended during the reign of a Twentieth Dynasty pharaoh called Ramses III (r.c.1185- 1155 BCE). While he held the throne, the "Sea Peoples" invaded and forced the Egyptians to fight for control of Egypt. The fierce assaults and frequent battles served to weaken Egypt's economy. When combined with periods of drought and famine, this effectively marked the end of a powerful era. Ramses III is considered the last truly sovereign, noteworthy pharaoh. However, the New Kingdom managed to hold on ostensibly through the reign of Ramses XI (r.c. 110 -1078 B.C.E.), when Egypt fragmented and finally split politically into the Upper and Lower regions once again.

The Third Intermediate Period (c. 1070-530 B.C.E.)

After Ramses XI, Egypt fell into another time of uncertainty and discord that is known as the Third Intermediate Period. Remember, the designation of intermediate period in Egyptian history refers to the collapse of government and the subsequent societal and political chaos that follows. While the dynasties continued to yield pharaohs, they essentially became figureheads during this time.

The latter part of the Third Intermediate Period was a time of war between Egypt and the Assyrian Empire. Many of Egypt's powerful allies had been conquered by the Assyrian forces, and Egypt was forced to either submit or fight to retain her independence. The Assyrians became more aggressive toward Egypt, and by c. 675 the Assyrian military occupied Egypt. The Assyrians were still building their vast empire, so they chose to leave the everyday operations of the country to the Egyptians. However, Assyrian domination was brief; they were expelled from Egypt after only twenty years. Egypt's subsequent return to autonomy was also fleeting. The Persian Empire had noticed the riches of Egypt, and it was only a matter of time until the Persians came to seize this wealth.

In c. 525 B.C.E. Cambyses II captured Egypt as a province of the Persian Empire. From this point on, Egypt never regained her sovereignty, but the governing bodies changed periodically. In the 300s B.C.E. Alexander the Great seized Egypt for the Greek/Macedonian Empire, and in 30 B.C.E. Rome annexed Egypt. Even though the Egyptians were permanently overpowered by these magnificent empires, Egypt's cultural advances and innovations have continued to impact various aspects of Western civilization.

Egyptian Culture: Writing

By approximately 3000 B.C.E. the Egyptians had devised a means of written language. It is unclear (but likely) if they were influenced by the Sumerians, or if they devised their writing technique on their own. However the system originated, the Egyptian form of writing called *hieroglyphics*, (sacred engravings) provides a wealth of information about the ancient Egyptian culture. The hieroglyphic writing, which used several hundred symbols, did not change greatly over several millennia. The surviving texts include religious documents, medical writings, poetry, and stories. Although most of these works are incomplete, their existence has been instrumental in furthering modern day knowledge and appreciation of Egyptian culture.

The process of deciphering hieroglyphics started around 1799 when French troops found a portion of black granite stone in the small Egyptian village of Rosetta. This rock, now called the Rosetta Stone, boasted an inscription written in three different languages. Egyptologists believe it was engraved in the 190s B.C.E. First, at the top of the stele is hieroglyphic text, which was often used for religious pronouncements. But because a large portion of the top is missing, a great deal of the original hieroglyphic engraving is lost. The second section is written in another Egyptian script (demotic), which was used for more commonplace messages. The bottom section has a complete text written in Greek, the formal language of the government. The three sections repeat a rather banal decree, but the Rosetta Stone's importance is not found in the content. The routine announcement was repeated in the three common scripts used in Egypt at the time of the inscription. Utilizing the Greek text, which many scholars in the early nineteenth century were familiar with, the hieroglyphic writing was eventually decoded and provided more clues about the seemingly exotic and remote culture of the ancient Egyptians.

Everyday Life

While archaeologists have uncovered many relics and valuables that reveal useful information about the ancient Egyptians, most of these items fall into two main categories. By far the largest category is the vast array of objects found in the temples and in the tombs of kings and the nobility. Obviously much has been learned about the Egyptian culture from these things, but their scope is rather narrow, covering predominantly religious/funerary rituals and then only those of the wealthy. The other category is made up of artifacts and articles that are found mainly at commoners' burial places and at laborers' village sites. It is this second grouping that will be discussed, since the grandeur of the pyramids and temples is more familiar to most readers and has been alluded to earlier in this chapter.

Unlike the pyramids, homes along the Nile were simply not constructed to last for millennia. Due to the dry climate, most homes were built using baked mud bricks; therefore, they were impermanent. By studying the villages, archaeologists have pieced together some information about the surroundings of the common people. According to Ian McMahan in *Secrets of the Pharaohs*, "The walls of a typical house (of four rooms) were as much as twenty inches thick, which helped protect the interior from the terrible heat of summer as well as the chilly nights of winter . . . The few small windows were placed high up . . . . the inside walls were usually plastered and whitewashed, sometimes with painted decorations as well." Of course, the nobility would have had grander homes and features with more expensive flooring, more luxurious decorations, and more rooms.

As for fashion, most Egyptians went barefoot, regardless of their social class or gender, and men of all classes generally went shirtless. Men of all groups were found in kilts generally, with the distinction being in length: nobles wore longer kilts as a rule than commoners. Women's clothing was also lightweight and comfortable for the climate. Typical female attire was an unadorned, plain tunic made from a buoyant type of linen. Over time, the tunics gained more decorative aspects, but by today's standards, they remained rather mundane—except for the fact that most tunics were made of virtually translucent linen—and most women wore nothing underneath.

CONCLUSION

For an indefinite period of time, prehistoric peoples and their ancestors lived a nomadic lifestyle, as they drifted from place to place seeking food. Once the Neolithic Revolution introduced agriculture, pottery, and domestication of animals, early people were able to put down roots and build permanent settlements. The earliest villages appeared, and over several generations, towns and cities emerged, first in Mesopotamia then shortly thereafter in Egypt.

The Mesopotamian and Egyptian societies were affluent and advanced, and, as such, they must have fascinated outsiders. These cultures were so innovative and exceptional that their traditions, values, and technologies spread readily throughout the regions. These initial Western civilizations not only developed cities but also the first known written language, religious codes and principles, and large scale architectural endeavors. Regrettably, not all the concepts they originated were positive. In addition to the beneficial constructs, the earliest communities also spawned social inequity, wars and subjugation, crime, and the necessitation of preventative and punitive legal codes.

Ultimately the Mesopotamian and Egyptian societies were incorporated and assimilated into larger, more powerful emergent empires, but they had established such a strong cultural base that their influence persisted. Even as they defeated these early cultures, many of the conquerors were attracted to their way of life. Often the conquerors kept elements of the subjugated cultures, and in this way kept their legacies alive.

Suggestions for Further Reading

Mary Boyce, *Zoroastrians: Their Religious Beliefs and Practices* (1984).

John Bright, *A History of Israel* (1972).

A. Rosalie David, *The Ancient Egyptians: Religious Beliefs and Practices* (1982).

Margaret Ehrenberg, *Women in Prehistory* (1989).

Richard N. Frye, *The History of Ancient Iran* (1983).

Thorkild Jacobsen, *The Treasures of Darkness: A History of Mesopotamian Religion* (1976).

T.G.H. James, *An Introduction to Ancient Egypt* (1990).

Arthur Bernard Knapp, *The History and Culture of Ancient Western Asia and Egypt* (1988).

Samuel N. Kramer, *History Begins at Sumer* (1981).

Richard E. Leakey, *The Making of Mankind* (1981).

J.P. Mallory, *In Search of the IndoEuropeans: Language, Archaeology and Myth* (1989).

J. Maxwell Miller and John H. Hayes, *A History of Ancient Israel and Judah* (1986).

Sabatino Moscati, *The Face of the Ancient Orient*(1962).

Leonard R. Palmer, *Mycenaeans and Minoans* (1980).

Georges Roux, *Ancient Iraq* (1980).

W.W. Hallo and W.K. Simpson, *The Ancient Near East* (1971).

Barbara Watterson, *Women in Ancient Egypt* (1991).

Raymond Weill, *Phoencia and Western Asia to the Macedonian Conquest* (1980).

Robert J. Wenke, *Patterns in Prehistory: Humankind's First Three Million Years* (1990).

Chapter 2

THE GREEKS

It was the year of the great invasion, 480 B.C. The greatest power in the world, Persia, was sending an army of at least 150,000 men plus a huge navy of over 100 ships to take revenge on the Athenians because they had humiliated the Persian army ten years earlier at Marathon. Many of the Greeks decided to give in and try to get the best deal possible from the great emperor, Xerxes. Who could blame them for wanting to save their own lives, or perhaps avoid slavery in a distant land, which was worse than death for these free people?

Only thirty-one out of hundreds of Greek city-states (poleis) joined in an alliance to stop this seemingly unstoppable force. Many must have called them fools and argued that they would bring the wrath of the great king down on all as a punishment for their vain opposition. Sparta, which had the most formidable army in all Greece, was chosen to lead this alliance, known as the Greek Alliance. As the Persian army crossed the Hellespont (Turkish Straits) and marched around the northwest end of the Aegean Sea, every city-state in its path surrendered without a fight. But when they turned south along the coast, they came to a narrow pass about 50 feet wide, Thermopylae. This was the place that the Greeks had been chosen to halt the Persian invasion. King Leonidas, one of two kings in Sparta, was the chosen leader of the Greek armed forces. He had 300 Spartan soldiers with him but a total of about 9,000 men to hold the pass. Since the Greek soldiers were equal to the Persian troops man to man in courage and skill, the larger Persian army could gain no advantage from their greater number. According to Herodotus, the "Father of History," who wrote the ***History of the Greek and Persian War*** *and is our main source for this event, Xerxes waited for four days, as he expected them to capitulate. When they didn't, the attack began and went on for two days, The Persian army could not break through despite sending in the king's special bodyguard called the "Immortals" by Xerxes.*

Then a Greek from a polis that was not allied against Persia offered to show the Persians a mountain path that would bring the Persian troops out on the far side of the pass and dislodge the Greeks from their defensible position. This was done during the second night. By morning of the third day, it was clear that the Greeks must abandon their position or die. Leonidas commanded most of the allies to retreat but he determined that he and his 300 men, along with 400 Thebans which he forced to stay as hostages (to insure that their polis did not go over to the Persians), would stay and fight to the death. Another 700 Thespians, who would not abandon him, also remained by his side. Strange as this action might seem to modern civilians, Leonidas refused to retreat to gain glory for Sparta and because Spartans were never supposed to retreat. His polis had sent him to defend that place, and he would not break that command. Furthermore, he had a religious reason in that the oracle (source of divine revelation to the Greeks) at Delphi had foretold "that either Sparta must be overthrown by the barbarians or one of her kings must perish." He and his men fought to the death that morning, and Herodotus tells us that they fought with such fury that the enemy "fell in heaps." At last Leonidas fell in the battle. There was a great struggle for his body, which was won by the Greeks after four counterattacks were made to drive the Persians back so they could carry his body back with them. The remaining Greeks retreated to a small hill in the narrowest part of the pass. They formed a circle to protect their backs and fought to the last man, except for the Thebans who surrendered after Leonidas' death. Herodotus described it thus: "Here they defended themselves to the last, such as still had swords using them, and the others resisting with their hands and teeth; till the barbarians . . . overwhelmed and buried the remnant which was left beneath showers of missile weapons."

The defiant courage of these men was perhaps best expressed by a Spartan named Dieneces who heard a fellow Greek from Trachinia complain before the battle began that the monstrous army they faced would produce so many arrows that they would darken the sun. Dieneces answered "Our Trachinian friend brings us excellent tidings. If the Medes darken the sun, we shall have our fight in the shade." Their heroic stand won not only the admiration of all Greeks at that time, but it has echoed down the centuries to inspire and touch human beings even today.

Chronology
(all dates B.C.)

2,900	Minoan Period
2,000	First Palace at Knossos
1,900	First appearance of Greek-speaking people on the mainland
1600-1150	Mycenaean Period
1,400	Linear B tablets first appear on Crete
1,200-1,150	Mycenaean palace culture is destroyed
1,150 -750	The Greek Dark Age
776	First Olympic Games are held
750	Homer writes *Iliad* and *Odyssey*
750-500	The Archaic/Lyric: Poleis develop and expand through colonization
725-710	First Messenian War
657	Cypselus takes over Corinth as Tyrant
650	Second Messenian War followed by Lycurgan Reforms
621	Draco publishes first law code in Athens
594	Solon reforms the law code of Athens
546-527	Pisistratus is Tyrant of Athens
510	Hippias, son of Pisistratus, is deposed and Athens is free of tyranny
508-501	Cleisthenes brings democratic changes to Athenian constitution & politics
500-323	Classical Age
499	Ionian poleis revolt against Persian rule and Athens sends military assistance
490	Persian War begins; Athenians defeat Persians at Marathon
480	Second Persian invasion of Greece:
479	Battles of Plataea and Mycale
478	Delian League formed
474-462	Cimon is the leader of Athens
467	Cimon defeats Persians at the Battle of the Eurymedon River
465-463	The revolt of Thasos
462	Pericles becomes the leader of Athens
460-445	First Peloponnesian War
449	Persian War ends
431-404	Second Peloponnesian War
405	Spartans destroy Athenian fleet at Aegospotami
404	Second Peloponnesian War ends Thirty Tyrants rule Athens under Sparta
403	Democracy restored in Athens – Tyrants driven out
399	Socrates' trial and execution
400-387	Spartan war against Persia
395-387	Corinthian War
387	Plato founds the Academy
378	Second Athenian Confederation formed
371	Thebes defeats Sparta at Leuctra – end of Sparta's hegemony of Greece
362	Battle of Mantinea – death of Epaminondas and of Theban hegemony of Greece
350	Appearance of Corinthian columns in architecture

HELLENIC CULTURE AND CIVILIZATION

Greece is a land of mountains with little arable soil that can be used for farming. These mountains were barriers to political unity, causing communities to form that were unique and fiercely independent. While the communities of the interior region of this rugged extension of the Balkan Peninsula were isolated by geography, a brief look at a map of Greece will immediately impress the observer with the fact that it is surrounded by water.

Jutting out into the Mediterranean Sea, this peninsula is cut off from Anatolia (modern Turkey) by the Aegean Sea to the east, from Italy by the Ionian Sea to the west, and from Africa and the Middle East by the Mediterranean Sea itself. Because of this extensive coastline, many Greeks were seafaring people, particularly those who had direct access to the sea. Eventually the Greeks expanded north into the Black Sea and around the Anatolian coast of the Aegean to the east, over the Ionian Sea west to southern Italy, and on across the Mediterranean to North Africa and what is today southern France and Spain. These people naturally turned to the sea for their livelihood, developing skills in fishing, boat building, seamanship, and trade.

Their position astride a peninsula, which forms a spearhead into the heart of the sea, led the Greeks quite naturally to share not only the economic goods of the region through trade but also cultural and religious developments as well. Greek sailors and merchants frequently traveled to Egypt and the ports of the Near East where they learned new ideas about religion, technology, and other aspects of culture. Some historians of ancient Greece stress this process of transferal of knowledge from other parts of the world when they describe the cultural development of the Greeks. Others emphasize the self-development

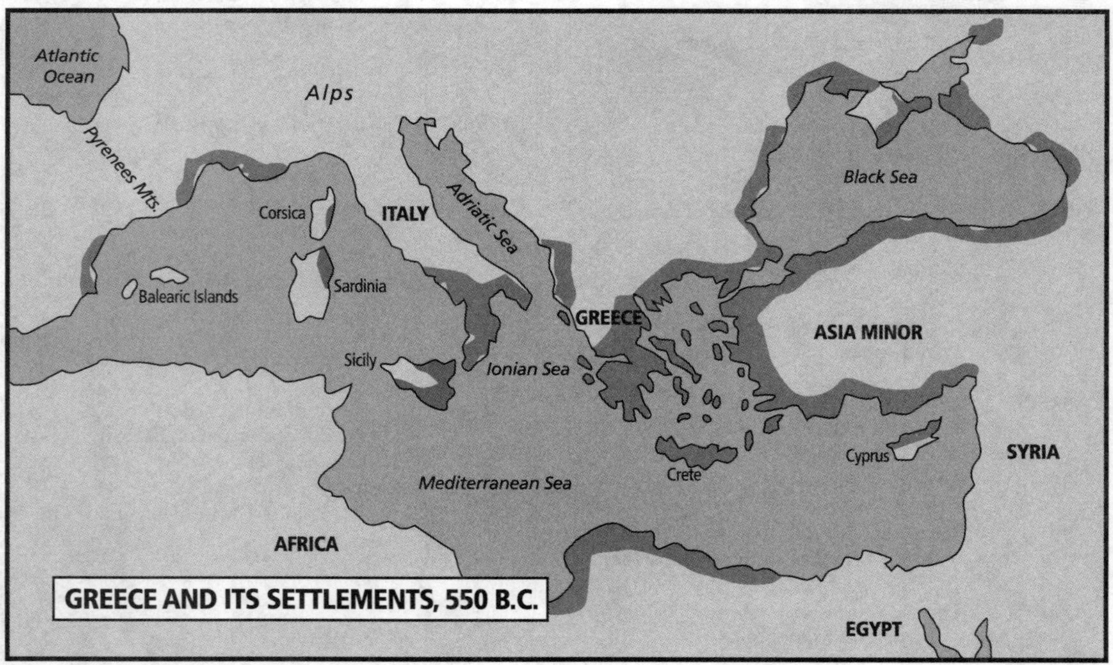

GREECE AND ITS SETTLEMENTS, 550 B.C.

of these people instead of seeing them as being dependent on outside influences. We cannot say with certainty, which of these was predominant, but most historians would agree that there was a mixture of the two, which produced Hellenic (Greek) culture and civilization.

The Minoans (1900-1150 B.C.)

Whether the development of Hellenic civilization is interpreted as spontaneous self-development, the spreading of civilization from Mesopotamia, the Near East and Egypt, or a blending of the two, it is on the island of Crete that we find the first advanced civilization in this region. Sir Arthur Evans, an early archeologist who discovered the site of a palace at Knossos, named the Minoans after the legendary ruler of Crete, King Minos. The Minoans developed Bronze Age technology shortly after 3000 B.C. These people traded with the Egyptians, Hittites, and other peoples of the Mediterranean Sea. The Minoans extended their influence into the Aegean Sea islands by establishing colonies and thus trade. Much about Minoan society and culture is unknown today. However, continual archaeological work provides new information, which slowly fills in missing pieces of the puzzle of what they believed and practiced religiously, and how they lived in society and with their neighbors of that time and place. The evidence is clear that the Minoans loved creature comforts, as we do today, and that they were able to build complex buildings up to five stories tall with many rooms, running water, and beautiful fresco paintings on the walls. The palace at Knossos is known as a labyrinth, or maze, because it had so many rooms in it that strangers could easily get lost. This was reinforced by a Greek myth, which claimed that King Minos exacted a tribute of Athens each year, seven young men and seven maidens, who disappeared in the maze to be eaten by the Minotaur who was part man and part bull. The bull was very important in the Minoan religious belief and ritual system. Rodney Castleden, author of *Minoans: Life in Bronze Age Crete,* describes the bull-leaping rituals of the Minoans as a rite of passage for males and females that symbolized human struggle with, and obedience to, their deity.

The first palace at Knossos was built around 2000 B.C. Castleden argues that the palaces were actually temples and that these temples were the center of religious, social, and economic activity, led by the priests and priestesses, much as the Mesopotamians did at that same time. About 1700 B.C., an earthquake destroyed the building. It was rebuilt on an even grander scale and survived until a catastrophe occurred in 1470 B.C. with the eruption of a volcano on the island of Thera, 50 miles to the north. The resulting earthquake, tidal wave, or a combination of the two caused major destruction on Crete and damaged the temple/palace at Knossos extensively, as well as many other buildings on the island. Within 100 years, the Knossos building was abandoned. This period marks the end of a dominant Minoan culture, which was then replaced by the mainland center of Mycenae.

Before moving on to the Mycenaens, let us note several other significant Minoan developments. First, they developed or adopted several forms of writing, which are preserved on tablets today. So far, the written records that are readable only reveal business transactions of the palace/temples. No literature revealing the way they lived and thought has been discovered, but there is hope something will be unearthed in future excavations that will unlock the mysteries of these important people. The Minoans used hieroglyphics apparently adopted from the Egyptians and a non-Greek language, which has not been deciphered, called Linear A. Around 1400 B.C.

another written language named Linear B appeared, which Briton Michael Ventris deciphered in 1952. This language was Greek and as far as we know now was used for record keeping. The appearance of this language indicates the increasing importance of the Greek Mycenaens to the Minoans. In fact, most historians believe that the Mycenaens took over Crete, either peacefully or by force, around 1400 B.C.

The Minoans have been interpreted by many scholars, beginning with Evans, as a peace-loving people due to the lack of walled cities. An alternative view is that, like England, the Minoan walls of defense consisted of her ships. Seemingly there was no need to defend themselves against each other, so as in any stable, strong country, forts and walled cities were not necessary. Again, Castledon takes a contrarian view of the peace-loving inhabitants of Crete. He finds that recent archaeological evidence shows a darker side to Minoan society. Castledon cites new frescoes that reveal naval battles, armor in graves, and evidence of the sacrifice of teenage boys. He theorizes that Minoans produced art that portrayed themselves and nature idealistically, not as they really were, just as Victorian Britons preferred flowers and bric-a-brac while conquering and exploiting other people in their empire.

Perhaps the last word on the Minoans should be about women in their society. Women are noticeable in Minoan culture as goddesses and priestesses. The Great Mother Goddess, a bare-breasted fertility symbol, was accepted as the chief deity. It is not known whether this female dominance in the religious world transferred to the secular world, but it is reasonable to conclude that women in Minoan society held a higher status and were closer to equality with men there than anywhere else in ancient society. This widely-held view is supported by the existence of a chief god that is female and by the prominent portrayal of women in art who are shown as engaging in a wide range of activities.

The Mycenaeans (1600-1200 B.C.)

The Minoans had a great impact on mainland Greece through trade and cultural exchange. The mainland people spoke a language that was Indo-European in origin, an early Greek form of language, which corresponds to the Linear B tablets. Once again, there is no written history or literature of these people. They appear to have invaded Greece shortly after the beginning of the second millennium B.C. While the name of Mycenae is used to represent the mainland Bronze Age civilization, these early Greeks spread across the Peloponnesus and the Attic Plain, establishing the cities of Pylos, Thebes, Athens, and Tiryns. Mycenae was known as the home of King Agamemnon in Homer's *Iliad.* Thus, it was the first mainland site to be identified and excavated by Heinrich Schliemann, the German businessman/archeologist who set out to prove that Homer's tale was not just a myth.

Mycenaean civilization was centered in the city, and political control was in the hands of powerful kings. Even at this early stage of Greek development, there was no political unification. Individual city-states, which included the surrounding territory, were the norm then as well as later during the classical period. Existing art and artifacts make it very clear that this was a warrior society. Shaft graves, which were used for burial from about 1600 to 1500 B.C., contained hundreds of bronze swords, daggers, arrowheads, shields, and other weapons of war. These graves also contained beautiful jewelry and items made of gold and silver. In fact, the Mycenaean kings lived in fine palaces and developed a high standard of living with complex methods of economic production and trade.

MYCENAEAN & MINOAN CIVILIZATIONS

A new type of grave marks the second general period of Mycenaean development around 1500 B.C., known as the beehive, or Tholos tombs. These tombs were built with large blocks of stone, which were cut to fit perfectly. One of the large lintel stones is estimated to weigh over one hundred tons. The best known of the tombs is the Treasury of Atreus. The vault of this tomb is over 40 feet high and was only surpassed in size by the building of the Pantheon in Rome 1500 years later. This vault, which has stood for over 3,000 years, attests to the wealth and power of the kings of that era and to the architectural skill of this civilization.

The Mycenaeans flourished from about 1600 B.C. to 1200 B.C. As we have already noted, they came to dominate the Minoans by 1400 B.C., perhaps as a result of the volcanic devastation to Crete from the explosion of Thera. Egyptian records show that the Mycenaeans sometimes raided their shores and at other times traded with them. In fact, the people of mainland Greece replaced the Minoans as traders who ranged across the Mediterranean Sea. Homer's *Iliad* tells the story of their siege and eventual ransacking of the city of Troy. This event is estimated to have taken place at around 1250 B.C., if, indeed, the Greeks are the cause of the destruction of Troy at that time.

Then Mycenaean civilization fell apart and disappeared into a Dark Age where writing and higher forms of political organization and cultural achievement ceased to exist. The cause of the fall of the Mycenaeans is uncertain. The

The epic poems, the *Iliad* and the *Odyssey*, attributed to Homer, were important examples of European literature. According to Homer, the kidnapping of Sparta's Queen Helen by a Trojan prince supposedly provoked the war. Whether this part of the legend is factual remains unknown.

Greeks themselves told of an invasion by the Dorians, a less civilized people from the north that spoke a different dialect of the Greek language. These Dorians, according to the legend, teamed up with the Heraclidae and eventually overran the Peloponnesus, except for Athens and the Attic Plain. Greeks from the west and south fled to the east through Athens to the islands of the Aegean Sea and to the coast of Asia Minor, now known as Turkey. There they were known as Ionian Greeks, and the west coast of Asia Minor became Ionia.

Some scholars theorize that the Mycenaeans fell apart from within. They believe that bands of Mycenaean marauders began to attack the Greek kingdoms, perhaps as part of a rebellion against the over-centralized system of economic and political control exercised by the kings. It is important to note that this came at a time when groups known as the "sea peoples" overran the Hittite kingdom to the east in Asia Minor about 1200 B.C. and attacked Egypt and the coastal cities of the Mediterranean. Thomas Martin, author of *Ancient Greece* and an important American scholar of this period today, argues that the internal conflict explanation is the most plausible. He finds that there is evidence that the "sea peoples" were composed of different groups, which could very well have included Greeks from the mainland, as well as from the islands. All historians agree that, whatever the cause, the period after 1200 B.C. witnessed the destruction of Mycenaean palaces and the widespread movement of people.

The Dark Age (1150-750 B.C.)

For the next 200 years, there was chaos and economic insecurity as the centralized systems of the kings in their palaces were destroyed, and the population of Greece shrank. The only record of this period is archaeological evidence, since the Greeks lost their knowledge of writing. According to that record, this was a period where less land came under cultivation, and people relied more on the herding of animals to make a living. This naturally led to constant movement by small bands of people with their animals as they

In this woodcut from Guido delle Colonne's *Trojan History*, the Trojans prepare to drag the famous wooden horse into their city unaware that Greek warriors are hiding inside.

searched for new pastures. They lived in small huts that were built for temporary use. The days of great architecture and cultural advancements in the arts were over.

By 1000-900 B.C. the chaos and destruction had ended, and life for the Greeks became more stable. The increase of wealth is apparent from the valuable objects uncovered in burial sites. Iron weapons and tools began to replace those made of bronze. The first Geometric style art appeared by 850 B.C., so-called because of the use of geometric forms, such as circles and rectangles, used to form parallel bands around the vase or other decorated objects. Agricultural production began to increase as did the population, and Greece began to emerge into a new age.

The Archaic Age (750-500 B.C.)

The Greeks adapted the Phoenician alphabet to the sounds of their language by the end of the Dark Age, and the resulting literature informs us about Greek life and culture. Homer is considered the father of Greek literature. His epic poems, the *Iliad* and the *Odyssey*, were gathered from tales of heroes passed down orally for generations. The subject of the *Iliad* is the Trojan War, which was set in the Mycenaean period about 1250 B.C. Homer, whether he was one person as the Greeks believed or several people, wrote these stories about 400 years after the events took place. We can tell that some of his facts about the Mycenaeans are correct, but the lifestyle and values portrayed in these tales are taken from the Dark Age Period. It is believed that Homer lived at the end of that period in about 800-750 B.C., and that he and the poets who passed these tales on to him placed Mycenaean events and people within the context of their own time.

The *Iliad* and the *Odyssey* describe a tribal, rural society led by chieftains who governed them with the assent of their warriors. The Greeks had assemblies, and certain constitutional limits of power were applied to their governments in many cases, although this was never a uniform development since each group evolved their own local laws and customs as a result of their political

Winners at the Panathenaic games received awards and honor. This nineteenth-century reconstruction of the north section of the Parthenon's Ionic frieze inaccurately depicts a judge crowning a chariot driver. More recent scholarship suggests that the man is a marshal in the Panathenaic Procession who is signaling for the driver to stop so as to avoid running into the marchers ahead.

independence. Their society was organized along class lines and was dominated by the nobles. Below the nobility were the freemen who owned small farms. The lowest class consisted of slaves. The noble code of values placed excellence (arete) at the top of the list of virtues. One was to excel in courage and the physical attributes, whether in battle, sports contests, or public speaking. This code of excellence emphasized the individual warrior but also bound him to the honor of his fathers and his family.

The Olympic Games

This code of excellence led to competition not only in battle but also in sports. The Olympic games began in 776 B.C. and lasted for over a 1000 years. They were held at Olympia to honor Zeus, father of the gods, so there was a strong religious connection to the games. Held every four years, the games provided a common cultural heritage for all Greeks, as did the gods and their religious observances. Although in the beginning competitors were individuals who sought excellence for themselves in the panhellenic games that were open to all Greeks, over time this changed and became an effort to gain honor for the community.

The Polis

During the next 250 years, the Greeks developed their characteristic political organization called the polis. The polis was a community usually considered to be a group of people who were descendants of a common ancestor. Although translated as the word city-state, many of these poleis (plural form of the word) were actually just small towns of less than 2,000 people, but they included the surrounding countryside and perhaps several villages. The original center of a polis was an elevated citadel where the people of the area could gather to defend themselves. In Athens, this area was called the Acropolis. Later, the Athenians built their temples on this hill. Eventually some of these villages grew to become cities of some size. Athens was the largest city in Greece, and it grew to about 155,000 people by the fourth century B.C., while Sparta only had a population of 40,000.

Overtime a marketplace developed, the agora, where the members of the polis traded goods and discussed politics. Each male citizen was expected to participate in these discussions and the decision-making process of the polis. Women were members of the polis socially, legally, and religiously, but they were excluded from direct participation in politics. In fact, the modern word "politics" derives from the word polis, as do other words we use today, such as metropolis and police.

Each polis was independent from the others and developed its own particular laws and policies in war and peace. This independence was preserved by fierce loyalty to the polis, preventing the development of a unified Greece and leading to eventual subjugation by more powerful forces. While they worshipped all the gods, each Greek polis had one that presided over and protected it. The members of the polis, in return for that protection, were obligated to honor the god in special religious observances. The uniqueness of each polis provided its citizens with an identity, which they seldom willingly gave up. In fact, exile was one of the worst punishments possible for a member of a polis. Socrates, the famous philosopher, chose death when he could have slipped away from prison and fled from Athens because he thought exile from his beloved polis was worse than death.

The Hoplite Phalanx

The polis included the ideal of equality before the law for all of its members, whether they were rich or poor. Through this ideal of equality, which was unusual in the ancient world, the political inclusion of all male members of society must have been effected. However, citizenship and equal rights did not exist for slaves and metics, which were foreigners who had been granted limited rights to live and work in the polis. Many historians believe that the emergence of a citizen-army toward the end of the eighth century played a critical role in this political development. This new style army was composed of common citizens who were wealthy enough to buy their own weapons and armor. These heavily armed soldiers were called hoplites. They stood shoulder to shoulder and used their shields to form a rectangular wall called a phalanx, which was usually eight ranks in depth. The hoplite's

Zeus, leader of the Greek gods, is depicted in this bronze statue dated to c. 450 B. C. His right hand once held a thunderbolt, one of his chief symbols.

main weapon was the spear, but each man also carried a sword for hand-to-hand combat. As long as the men of the phalanx maintained discipline, they were almost unbeatable except by a stronger hoplite phalanx. This method of battle gave the Greeks a military superiority that they would not surrender until the Romans improved it centuries later.

The hoplites became necessary to the defense of the polis, replacing the older style aristocrats who fought as "heroic" individuals with great skill. This development gave them an importance that could not be denied by the nobility. This evolution in military tactics and the type of people who performed them may not have been the only cause of political rights being extended to all male citizens because the poor could not afford to buy armor, yet, they were included in many of the poleis, and it must have been one of the major causes.

Most of the poleis of Greece, and it is estimated that there were 1,500 of them, followed a similar pattern of development during the archaic age from 750 to 500 B.C. In the beginning, most poleis were under the control of the nobles. Some had kings who might be elected or were hereditary, but they were part of the aristocratic system of government. From 700 B.C. until 500 B.C. most of the poleis were taken over by tyrants. These tyrants were often members of a leading noble family who aspired to gain power for personal reasons, such as revenge against their enemies. They were assisted by economic and social changes, which destabilized society and caused a crisis that these men used to gain control in an unconstitutional manner. A rising population, the growth of wealth from new sources such as trade, the flow of new ideas and knowledge from the outside world, and the development of hoplite warfare combined to pave the way for tyranny.

Greek tyrants often played a positive role in the development of democracy and in providing a higher standard of living for the people of their poleis. Since they had to appeal to a broad political base to gain and keep control, the tyrants often extended economic development and trade. They built temples and other public buildings in their cities to provide jobs and income for the poor while undoubtedly lining their own pockets and those of their friends. Most important of all was the role they played in the destruction of aristocratic power. When the aristocrats were driven out, as they were all over Greece by 500 B.C., democracy replaced them. Not all poleis turned to democracy, as we shall see, for there were those who followed the Spartans in an oligarchical form of government. Before turning to the divergence between Athens and Sparta in their form of government, an element of this period needs to be considered that was very important to the spread of Greek culture: the colonization movement that began around 750 B.C. and continued for about 200 years. Due in some cases to population pressure and in others to the revival of trade, Greeks aggressively colonized around the shores of the Mediterranean Sea along the coast of North Africa, Spain, southern France, and the Black Sea. Before establishing a colony, the leaders of a polis always consulted their gods. Those who went to the colony were expected to retain ties to their mother polis (metropolis) even though they were to become an independent polis. The colony was never supposed to join in a war against the mother polis. Instead, they were to trade with them and honor the same religious festivals.

The tyrants played an active role in the colonization process, providing new opportunities to members of their poleis while relieving growing pressures at home. Colonization provided several long-term benefits. It increased trade, stimulated the production of new goods, reduced the population pressures in the Greek homeland, and helped to avoid civil wars while providing new opportunities for people who otherwise would have been trapped in the old socio-economic system. Even more important to the development of Western civilization was the spreading of Greek culture around the Mediterranean world.

Sparta

Sparta was one of the leading poleis of Greece. Its development was different from Athens, a rival to Sparta in many ways. Sparta was similar to most of the other poleis in the beginning. Their government was aristocratic and as descendants of the Dorian invaders, they held the original inhabitants as slaves. In 725 B.C. during the first Messenian War they turned to conquer neighboring Messenia, which was located in the southwestern corner of the Peloponnesus. They took the land of Messenia and reduced the people to slavery. These slaves, called Helots, were owned by the state. They were bound to the land where they lived, and their role in life was to till the soil and produce goods for the Spartans. The total number of slaves was far greater than that of the Spartans by a ratio of about 10 to 1.

The great change in Spartan development came in 650 B.C. when the Helots rose in rebellion and almost destroyed Sparta with the help of some neighboring poleis, such as Argos in the Second Messenian War. Once this threat was defeated, the Spartans realized that they were going to have to give up Messenia or completely change their social structure to maintain control. They chose the latter, and the result was a disciplined, militaristic society. In that new society, all adult males constantly trained for war from the age of seven, when they were taken from their mothers, until they reached the age of sixty. As a result, the Spartan army was a professional force, which was ready to march at a moment's notice to put down rebellion or destroy an invading army. The internal threat of a Helot rebellion forced them to be very conservative in their foreign policy because the army had to remain close to home.

The Spartans became very conservative in politics and social development in some ways, while in others they were liberal for the times. For example, while the Spartans never accepted democracy nor the cultural advancements in philosophy, literature, and the arts, they allowed women a certain amount of freedom to learn, compete in sports, or oversee property that was forbidden to other Greek women. The conservative form of government they produced was unique. The Spartans had a "mixed constitution" that included three forms of government. The first part was a monarchy with two equal kings that were hereditary in that they came from two royal families but were elected by the assembly. The second part of the government operated on the principle of an oligarchy (rule of the few), and representative government existed in an assembly composed of all male warriors who were over 30 years of age. This strange combination was guided by a council of 28 elders who were over the age of 60 plus the two kings. It was this body that seemed to lead the government of Sparta based on oligarchical principles. This council, known as the gerousia, presented all proposals to the assembly, which could then vote for or against them. The assembly probably accepted the proposals of the gerousia most of the time, but on occasion it voted against these proposals. It now is considered to have been more powerful than earlier historians concluded. If the gerousia saw that a proposal was generating opposition in the assembly, they could withdraw it. The assembly also had limited power to amend these proposals.

In addition to the legislative powers of the assembly, it also annually elected five overseers (ephors). These men were chosen from the members of the assembly and were originally supposed to provide a balance to the power of the kings and council. They could bring charges against the kings, and they convened and presided over meetings of the assembly and the gerousia. The ephors were given the responsibility of seeing that the law was followed in all things, which was a very important emphasis of the Spartans. Eventually the ephors were given control of foreign policy, oversight of the kings in war, and the prevention of uprisings by the Helots. This system of government was very stable. The Spartans attributed their form of government and the changes in their society to a man named Lycurgus, the lawgiver. There is doubt today that this was the work of one man. Instead, it appears to have developed over time as a reaction to the Second Messenian War.

Despite the control of the state over the individual, which forced conformity to the ideals of the polis, many Greeks admired the Spartan constitution and way of life. The Athenians, who seemed the opposite of the Spartans in so many ways, admired them too. The philosopher, Plato, used Sparta as the model for his ideal polis in the *Republic*.

The Spartans continued to expand their control of the Peloponnesus by defeating their neighbors in war. In these cases they required an alliance with the defeated polis, which made the polis promise to follow Sparta's foreign policy and provide a given number of warriors in case of war. This Peloponnesian League, as it is known by historians today, included all of the poleis of the Peloponnesus except Argos. Through this league Sparta gained protection from invasion while it became the most powerful polis in all Hellas.

Plato joined Socrates' circle and saw his mentor condemned to death. From then on Plato sought to vindicate Socrates by constructing a philosophical system based on Socratic precepts.

Athens

Athens is the other polis that we use as a model for the Greeks. In fact, Athens is synonymous with Greece for most people because Western civilization inherited the political ideal of democracy that the Athenians developed. Athens went through these stages of political development in the Archaic Age. The monarchy was replaced by aristocratic rule early in the seventh century. The people of the Attic Plain (Attica) slowly combined into one polis with four tribes and several clans and brotherhoods called phratries. The nobility owned most of the land and ran the government through a council known as the Areopagus and elected magistrates (archons).

Late in the seventh century the Athenians began to experience internal dissension due to a growing crisis in agriculture. Evidently the soil became depleted, resulting in small farmers going into debt due to lower yields of crops such as wheat and barley. As they failed to make payments to the aristocrats, they lost their land and their freedom, since many became slaves to pay for their debt. In 632 B.C. an attempt was made to overthrow this government and establish a tyrant. The attempt failed, but the basic cause of unrest continued until in 621 B.C. the legendary lawgiver, Draco, established harsh laws, which were written and made public for the first time. Draco's laws were so harsh that it is said they were written in blood. Even today we use the term "draconian" to signify harsh treatment.

Still the pressures of poor agricultural production, a growing population, and enslavement of their own people led to the development of a society ripe for revolution. In 594 B.C. Solon was elected as the sole archon for one year and given special powers to deal effectively with the growing crisis. He reformed the constitution to restrain the excessive power of the aristocrats. He canceled debts of the poor and stopped the practice of using people as collateral for loans, which had resulted in growing numbers of Athenians becoming slaves. Solon encouraged trade abroad and industry at home, in part, by offering citizenship to foreign craftsmen. He altered the constitution, dividing Athens into four groups based on wealth. While archons could only be elected from the two wealthiest groups, the third class of hoplites could sit on a new council of 400, made up of 100 men from each tribe. This council was supposed to represent the people and limit the power of the aristocratic Areopagus. The Thetes were the poorest class. They could vote in assembly for the archons and members of the Areopagus, as well as all matters brought to the assembly. They could also sit on a new court of appeals. Solon retired voluntarily from what was practically a dictatorship, warning the nobility to voluntarily restrain their abuses of the common people. Then, he left to live abroad to escape the stress of appeals that were made to him for help. Solon's name, today, is a synonym for wisdom or a wise man.

The basic problems persisted, however, until Pisistratus became tyrant in 560 B.C., and again in 556 B.C., then permanently in 546 B.C. until he died in 527 B.C. Pisistratus fit the norm for tyrants in Greece. He won control and kept it by force, but he also had to improve the economy and social conditions to avoid rebellion. Therefore, he used public works to keep people employed, built temples to the gods to gain religious support, and supported the arts and artists. Pisistratus strengthened his government at the expense of the power of the aristocrats, thus opening the way for truly democratic rule later. His son succeeded him but became harsh as a ruler, and in 510 B.C. the Spartans intervened and deposed him.

In the power struggle that followed, Cleisthenes emerged the winner. Cleisthenes was a noble by birth but a democrat at heart. He was the founder of democracy in Athens, an ironic outcome of the Spartan intervention and a development of which they disapproved. In 508 B.C. Cleisthenes reorganized the basis of representation by making the deme the basic unit of government. He increased the number of tribes to 10 and increased loyalty to the polis while reducing old regional and aristocratic rivalries. A new council of 500 replaced the old council of 400 with each tribe electing 50 members. This council proposed legislation to the assembly and supervised public finances and foreign policy. The assembly was composed of all free males, and it had final authority in all things. Democracy

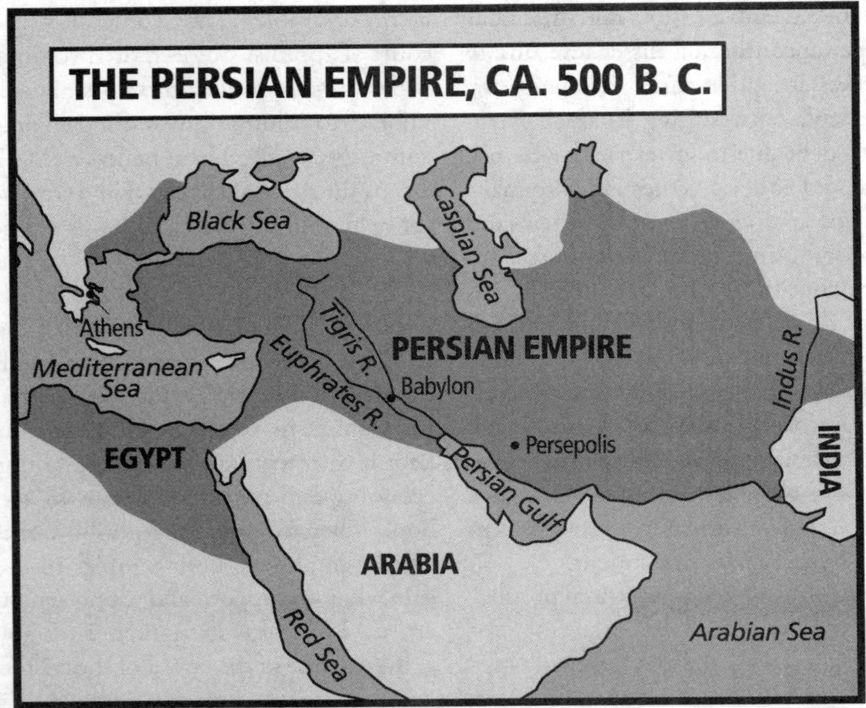

had arrived in Athens and would spread to other poleis throughout Greece.

The Persian War

The Greeks were blessed with relative isolation and thus were free to develop their way of life in each independent polis until the fifth century B.C. As noted earlier, the Greeks had expanded across the Aegean Sea to the coast of Asia Minor (Turkey) during the early Dark Age as people fled the chaos and invasions. During the sixth century, the Greek poleis of Ionia were over-run by an expanding Persian Empire. By 540. B.C., all of Ionia had been added to that empire. In 499 B.C. the Ionians rebelled with the support of ships and warriors from Athens and Eretria. The Persians had the rebellion under control by 495 B.C., but Darius, the Persian Emperor, decided to punish the mainland Greeks who had interfered in what he considered to be an internal affair.

The first Persian War began in Ionia, but in 490 B.C. the Persian navy transported an army to strike directly at Athens and Eretria. The Athenians met and defeated the Persian forces on the plains of Marathon under the brilliant generalship of Miltiades. The defeat of the Persian army gave the Athenians self-confidence for they had beaten the forces of the most powerful empire in the world, and they had done it without the Spartans! (Eretria did not fare so well; it was defeated, and its people were sent far away to Persia, probably as slaves.) This confidence directly contributed to the achievements of Athens in the "Golden Age" of the Classical period.

The Persians waited ten years before they made a second attempt to invade Greece and take revenge on Athens. By that time their goal was revenge and control of the whole Greek peninsula. Sensing this, some of the Greeks banded together in a rare display of unity to fight the invader. Darius was dead by that time, and his successor, Xerxes, gathered a mighty army of perhaps 150,000 or more men, and a navy of 600 ships. Ironically, much of this navy consisted of ships and men from the Greek Ionian poleis, since they were part of the Persian Empire. In 480 B.C. the invasion began. One of the leaders of Athens, Themistocles, had foreseen this danger and built additional ships, so that the Athenian navy had 200 ships. Yet with its allies included, there was only a total of about 333 Greek ships to face that massive armada. Xerxes' strategy was to march his army from Asia Minor across the Hellespont and along the coast until it reached

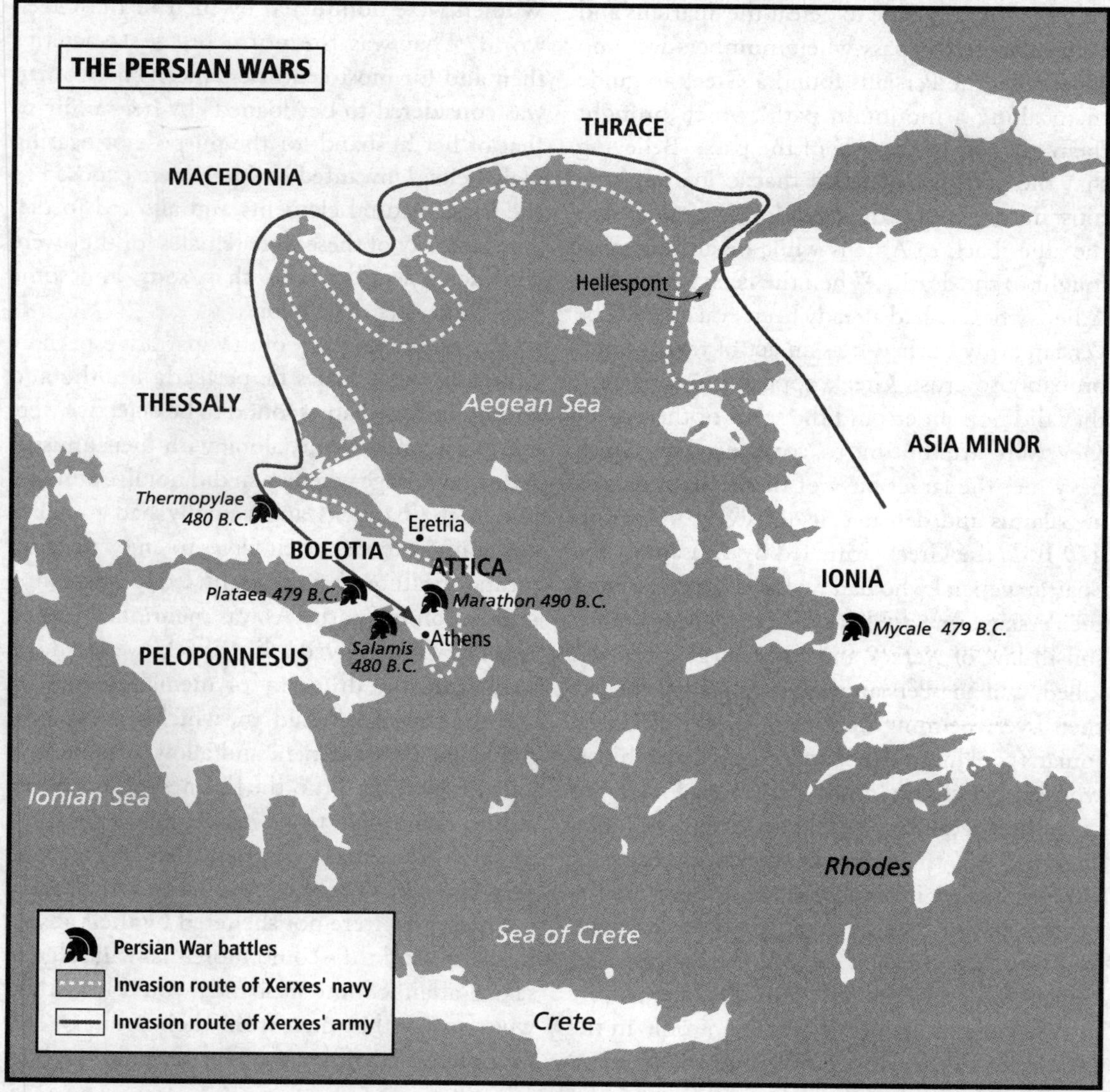

Athens. The navy would be used to supply the army and destroy the Greek navy.

The Greek League, consisting of only 31 out of about 1,500 total poleis , chose Sparta as their leader in this war. As the Persian army approached the narrow pass of Thermopylae to the north of Athens, a legendary battle took place between the Greek warriors that included 300 Spartans led by their king, Leonidas, and the Persian army. Unable to defeat the Spartans and their allies at the pass where numbers were no advantage, the Persians found a Greek to guide them along a mountain path, which brought them out on the far side of the pass. Believing that the gods had decreed that a Spartan king must die to preserve their freedom, Leonidas sent the allies back to Athens while he and his men fought to the death. When the Persians reached Athens, the city had already been evacuated. The Persian army burned it as an act of revenge and probably to crush Greek opposition. However, they did not understand the spirit of the people they were attempting to conquer. The Greek navy met the larger navy of the Persians nearby at Salamis and defeated it decisively. Then, in 479 B.C. the Greek army led by Pausanius, the Spartan general who had replaced Leonidas, met the Persian army at Plataea. General Mardonius, son-in-law of Xerxes and his best general, was killed, and the Persian army was routed despite their overwhelming numbers. In 478 B.C. the Ionians convinced the Spartan king, Leotychidas, who was in command of the Greek forces, to cross the Aegean and attack the Persians in Ionia. In 478 B. C., the Greek navy won the battle of Mycale, which finished the destruction of the Persian navy. The Persians abandoned Ionia, and Greece seemed to be safe once more. The Persian Wars and the retreat of the great empire of Asia were momentous events not only in the history of Greece but of Western civilization. The defeat of the greatest power in their world gave the Greeks unprecedented self-confidence and led them to achievements in politics and the arts that still influence Western culture today.

THE CLASSICAL AGE (500-323 BC)

Women, Children and Slaves

Women were dominated by men in the Greek world. That was the norm in most societies then and for most centuries since. The woman was considered to be "loaned" by her family to that of her husband for the purpose of bearing male heirs. Unwanted children were exposed to the harsh natural elements and allowed to die. The majority of these were females for they were considered less desirable than sons, and some were imperfect male babies.

The military society of the Spartans especially demanded that males be perfectly healthy and strong, and any babies found to be defective were left to die. Infanticide, along with their unusual style of marriage where men did not live at home but in the barracks and actually had to sneak out at night to visit their wives to enjoy physical intimacy without being caught, led to a declining population in Sparta. As was mentioned earlier, Spartan women lived a life of relative freedom, both from the drudgery of menial housework and the rearing of children, which was done by the Helot slave women, and allowed to participate in sports and run the business affairs of the family. (Boys went to military camp at age seven to stay.) The Athenians were shocked at what they claimed were the loose morals of Spartan women, who were not sheltered by their absent husbands and thus could more easily indulge in sexual affairs Some husbands would lend their wives to another man from their military unit for procreation if that man's wife could not bear children. Spartan girls kept in good physical condition like their male counterparts and were supposed to be among the most beautiful women in Greece. Condemned by Greeks from other areas for their loose morals, nude sports and loose clothes that revealed far more of the body than other Greek women were allowed to show, the Spartan women were noted for winning at sports and running the economy while their husbands spent their entire lives in the army until they were 60 years old.

Most Greek women were expected to live very differently. They were to stay quietly in their homes supervising slaves if they had any, bearing and raising their children, and caring for their husbands. In his *Funeral Oration*, Pericles described the best woman as the type that was "least talked about by men, whether for good or bad." Women could not vote or participate in public political debates or sit on juries, even at the height of Athenian democracy. If they were not prostitutes (these were usually slave women) or courtesans, who were considered high class female "companions," then the Greek woman's chastity was prized and protected by the males of her family.

This was the accepted view in that society, although the poor working class woman enjoyed greater freedom because she had no slaves to do her house work, go to the market and raise the children for her. As a result, women of that class had to have more social contact just to live. But the traditional view set forth in their laws, customs and literature has come to be challenged by women historians as a result of the women's revolution today. While one radical view of young Athenian wives probably went too far when a historian claimed in 1971 that they were undisciplined nymphs, there is the growing recognition that women from Athens were less secluded and had a wider range of social contacts and experiences than has been considered the norm. Certain religious festivals that women took part in, like the *Haloa* festival, featured ribald jokes and replicas of private male parts. Still, most Greek women followed the mores of their polis, but perhaps not as completely as was once thought to be the case.

Children in Sparta have been mentioned above. The military training of the boys was harsh (A young man had to catch and kill a helot before he was accepted as a full soldier in the Spartan army.) and included the idea that mothers expected their sons to come home with their shields (which means they had not thrown them away to run and escape) or on them as a corpse. The rigors of their training and the general lack of any type of luxury in the lives of all people there, not just soldier boys, provides the basis for the term "Spartan" to this day. However the younger boys from 7 until they reached the age of 17, experienced the lighter duty of learning to dance and sing, and of course do gymnastics and compete in sports.

All children were a part of their polis and took part in the religious festivals, learning the proper way to behave and how to fulfill the roles expected of them. Boys began to train for military duty early in life, for each polis had to defend itself against its neighbors as well as enemies from further away. Naturally boys helped their fathers and girls helped their mothers and learned skills from them that were necessary for them to live. All children in working families before the present time, had to help with household chores or work at something to help the family survive. While the children of the rich and famous aristocrats would be expected to avoid menial labor and gain an education along with learning the martial arts, working class children had to work hard from early in their lives, and they could not expect to receive a formal education nor would poor boys be able to learn military skills or become citizens in some of the poleis if their family was too poor to afford the cost of the helmet, sword and shield necessary to join the hoplite army, for usually each man had to provide his own equipment. Slave children would have worked their entire lives unless they could earn their freedom. Slave boys and girls would have experienced what we would consider to be abuse as they became sex objects to their masters.

Slaves were a major component of the Greek economy and indeed of their entire society. The Spartans held an entire group of their neighbors as state slaves. These people basically lived without protection and could be killed at the whim of a Spartan citizen, who of course was male. Undoubtedly the Spartan women were tough on these people too, for toughness was a trait of the Spartans. The helots rose in rebellion several times, partly with the assistance of the Athenians in those times that they were at war with Sparta. Those rebellions were the worst nightmare of the Spartans and the reason that their men were members of a professional army most of their adult lives.

Female slaves have already been mentioned in relation to prostitution, housework, and child rearing. The male slaves worked in the fields as did female slaves, and they also worked in the mines, did heavy construction, ran shops, were rowers on the triremes (the basic naval vessel during the classical age, that had three levels of seating for the rowers who were the main means of propulsion during battle) and in general were indispensable to the Greek economy and cultural achievement. Slaves made up a large portion of the population even in Athens. In fact without them to do the dirty work of their society, the Greeks would not have had the leisure time to make their great contributions in literature, philosophy, politics, or art and architecture to Western Civilization! People who fell into debt at times were sold as slaves to pay for that debt, but normally they came from foreign countries as a result of purchase due to the age-old practice of selling the people of conquered countries as slaves. Slaves were quite often teachers and other educated people, or skilled workers who plied their trade for their master, sometimes making enough on the side to earn their freedom. Zeno, the originator of the Stoic philosophy, was a slave who earned his freedom.

The Delian League

With the defeat of the Persians, the Greeks of Ionia and the Aegean Sea islands formed a defensive alliance with Athens known as the Delian League, knowing that the Persian threat was not over. The league was named after the sacred island of Delos, where they met in 478 B.C. Athens was chosen as the leader of the Delian League because the Spartans refused to accept a commitment that would place their armies far from the Helots at home and because Athens was the largest polis and the greatest naval power among the allies. By 467 B.C., the remaining Greek cities under Persian control were liberated by the league, and Persian forces were driven back into the interior of Asia Minor.

Over time the Delian League became the Athenian Empire. The smaller city-states in the league increasingly converted their obligation to provide men and ships for the common defense into cash payments. The Athenians provided not only their own contribution of ships and men for the league's naval forces, but they also used the cash payments to supply substitute ships with trained crews. Athens had the largest population of any member of the Delian League with a large pool of laborers who sought work as rowers, and she had the skilled shipbuilders who were capable of building the necessary warships in large numbers. More and more, the men of Athens came to rely on the military activities of the Delian League as a source of income. Since they dominated the Athenian assembly, which in turn dominated the Delian League assembly, the league and its activities reflected the Athenians' desire for an active policy. Furthermore, no polis was allowed to withdraw from the league since contributions provided an income for Athens and the original oath bound them to remain members of the league forever. The Athenians had the means and motive to compel rebellious members to remain in the league.

In 465 B.C. the polis of an island in the Aegean Sea, Thasos, decided to withdraw from the Delian League. Cimon, the son of Miltiades, victor at Marathon, was the leading Athenian statesman and general of the day. He laid siege to Thasos for two years before the "revolt" was put down. Thasos was forced to remain in the league and pay a huge tribute and fines while losing her own navy. Cities had already begun to level the charge against the Athenians that they desired to take over all of Greece. Athenian actions seemed to confirm that suspicion to a growing number of Greeks. This suspicion, coupled with Spartan distrust of Athens' democratic form of government and jealousy on both sides, led to a series of wars among the Greeks that would eventually destroy the Greek way of life.

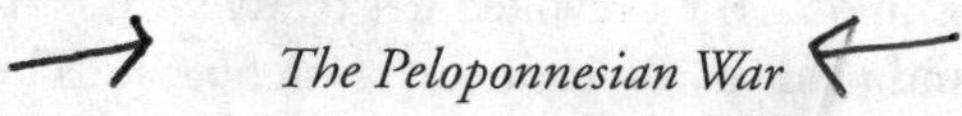

The Peloponnesian War

Under the leadership of Cimon, the Athenians sought to maintain good relations with Sparta and her Peloponnesian League. The Spartans, however, did not like the democratic tendencies of the Athenians, whose constitution continued to change whereas the Spartans remained stable and unchanging. Democracy, of course, could undermine their control of the Helots, which threatened the entire Spartan way of life. In 462 B.C., following a gigantic earthquake two years earlier that killed many Spartans and allowed the Helots to rebel, Sparta called on the Athenians for help to end the siege of Mt. Ithome where the Helots were holding out. Cimon won the reluctant permission of the Athenian Assembly to take an army of hoplites to assist the Spartan army. The Spartans sent them home soon after they arrived, according to Thucydides, the great chronicler of the wars, in his *Peloponnesian Wars,* because they feared the "revolutionary spirit" of the Athenian soldiers might only make matters worse with their slaves. The Athenian assembly was enraged at this affront.

While Cimon was in the field for the Spartan campaign, his political adversary, Ephialtes, stripped the Areopagus of much of its political power, leaving it to function only as a court with limited jurisdiction over certain crimes. A whole new system of courts using juries consisting of the male citizens of Athens was put in place by the Ephialtic reforms. Ephialtes was assassinated by reactionaries, and the following year, 461 B.C., Cimon was ostracized due to the disfavor he had gained over the insult Sparta had given to the Athenians. With his pro-Spartan influence removed, the Athenian-Spartan relationship deteriorated further. Athens formed an alliance with Argos, the enemy of Sparta, and then accepted Megara as an ally. Megara had been a member of the Peloponnesian League but due to a boundary dispute with Corinth, another member of that league, the Megarians left to become an ally of Athens with the hope that they might win the territorial dispute.

With Cimon gone, the anti-Spartan, democratic party was clearly in power. Its leader was the young Pericles, a descendant of Cleisthenes, founder of Athenian democracy. Pericles was an

A bust of Pericles

aristocrat who wanted to broaden the democratic base of the Athenian constitution. Under his leadership the assembly passed legislation that allowed the hoplites to become archons, the highest office in the polis. They began the practice of paying jurors so poor men could afford public service. The assembly of Athens made the final decision for all things, including war or peace. Public officials were openly criticized and could be removed from office as Pericles was when people lost faith in him.

While pursuing democracy at home, Pericles and his supporters were unwilling to back down when the Spartans demanded that they end their alliance with Megara. This led to the First Peloponnesian War (460-445 B.C.) when the Athenians seemed to gain the upper hand. They took advantage of their alliance with Megara to fortify the northern end of the isthmus that connects the Peloponnesus to the Attic Plain, occupied an island in the Saronic Gulf, and gained control of the area known as Boeotia. Then, as the Athenians seemed to have the upper hand in the war, they over-reached themselves by joining with the Egyptians who rebelled against Persia in 460 B.C. Victorious at first, they were defeated in 455 B.C. and lost an entire fleet of ships and men. As a result of this defeat, some of Athens' allies in the Delian League took advantage of this moment of weakness to rebel. Athens moved the treasury from Delos to Athens for safety, but they also began to keep one-sixtieth of the annual contributions for the building or repair of temples that had been destroyed in the fighting. This money was used to help pay for the building on the Acropolis, such as the Parthenon. Cimon was recalled from exile, and a 5-year truce was agreed on with Sparta. This gave the Athenians time to rebuild their fleet, and in 450 B.C. Cimon led a 200-ship fleet to attack the Persians in Cyprus. He defeated the Persians but died the following year. In 449 B.C. the Persians and the Delian League ended the war. Persia accepted the Greek states as independent of their control except for Cyprus.

The five-year truce with Sparta did not hold. Argos in 451 B.C. revoked her treaty with Athens and made a 30-year treaty with Sparta. The Boeotia and Megara rebelled, Sparta invaded, and Pericles accepted a 30-year peace. For about 15 years, the peace lasted while Pericles (elected Archon a total of 30 times) reorganized what was now the Athenian Empire. This was the Golden Age of Athens. Democracy reached its fullest development, though it excluded women, slaves, and metics, or foreigners. The Acropolis reached the form that we see the remains of today, with buildings and sculptures that still inspire us with its beauty and technical perfection.

War broke out again in 431 B.C. after a series of conflicts between the two alliances, which resulted in an invasion by Sparta and her allies. The Athenian strategy under Pericles' leadership was to attack with her navy along the coast of the Peloponnesus against the Spartan forces. Athens relied on her empire for food and income through trade while defending herself with walls that held off the Spartans. The Spartans invaded each year, burned, and destroyed the crops, then went home when the Athenians refused to battle. From 431 to 404 B.C., with intermittent periods of truce, war continued until Athens was forced to surrender.

Pericles planned the defensive strategy and expected that Sparta would be forced to ask for peace in one to three years, due to the empire's attacks on Sparta's allies. This might have worked, but a great plague struck Athens in 429 B.C., and one-third of Athens' population died, including Pericles. The Athenian generals followed Pericles' plan and placed strategic bases to surround, blockade, and attack such poleis as Megara, Pylos, and Messenia. At Pylos in 425 B.C., the Athenians won a major victory and trapped a group of over 400 of Sparta's warriors on an island. Sparta was facing yet another Helot revolt, and those men were a significant part of their forces, so they sued for peace. Two Athenian political parties had emerged by that time. Nicias favored continuing Pericles' more conservative policy while Cleon and his followers wanted a more aggressive approach. Cleon won, and Athens refused the Spartan peace offer, opting instead for total victory since the peace plan offered no real guarantee of security for Athens. Some historians conclude that this policy resulted from Athenian pride and aggressiveness, causing them to over-reach the limits of their power and resources. The Greeks, of course, would have appreciated that interpretation and called it hubris, which offends the gods and leads to defeat.

Whatever the cause, the more aggressive policy of Cleon failed as Athens attempted to invade and conquer neighboring Megara and Boeotia. A truce was agreed upon in 432 B.C. Then, a Spartan general, Brasidias, attacked in the areas of Thrace and Macedonia on the northern coast of the Aegean. He took the important ally and colony of Athens, Amphipolis. General Thucydides commanded the naval forces of the area, so he was blamed for the defeat and sent into exile as punishment by the assembly. Thucydides wrote the *Peloponnesian Wars* in exile, which provide us with the most important source of information about this epic war. Thucydides, unlike the earlier historian, Herodotus, does not explain the war in terms of the gods and religious forces; rather, he gathered evidence in a scientific manner and attempted to explain causality in terms of human behavior.

The Athenians tried to retake Amphipolis in 422 B.C. Both generals, Cleon of Athens and Brasidias of Sparta, were killed in the failed attempt. Nicias now asked for peace, and the Spartans agreed in 421 B.C., but some of their allies, such as Megara, refused and so remained at war with Athens. The peace terms demanded that both sides give up captured territory. Brasidias had followed a policy of urging rebellious members of the Athenian empire to revolt. Now some of those poleis did not want to return to the empire, and the Spartans would not force those poleis to rejoin. Thus, the terms of the peace were not fully carried out by both sides.

This war was fought in terms of ideology, meaning a fight between those who wanted democracy and those who wished to return to oligarchy, as well as for power. At Corcyra, the

The remains of the Dionysus Theatre are frequently remodeled and expanded. By the mid-fourth century B.C., the facility held an estimated 14,000 spectators.

civil war continued after the Peace of Nicias and brought a bloody massacre to the inhabitants of that island. Both sides continued to lure the allies of their opponent to join them, and the young Alcibiades, who was related to Pericles, involved Athens in several ventures during this period of tense peace.

In 415 B.C. Alcibiades persuaded the Athenian Assembly to begin the war again by attacking and conquering Sicily. The expeditionary force at Syracuse was totally lost by 413 B.C., including about 200 ships and 50, 000 men. This time Persia joined the war, as well as Sparta, which was an ally of Syracuse. Alcibiades, who had been recalled to answer charges that he had acted in an irreligious manner, escaped to Sparta, advising them as to ways to defeat Athens. He then moved on to advise the Persians, who were providing money to the Spartans. Under Lysander, the victorious general of Sparta, the Peloponnesian League began to build a navy and cut off Athenian trade and their supply of grain from colonies in the Black Sea coastal area. The Spartan fleet destroyed the Athenian fleet at Aegospotami in 405 B.C. Athens surrendered unconditionally in 404 B.C. An oligarchy was put in power whose members came to be known as the Thirty Tyrants, and the walls of Athens were torn down. Her fleet was gone, as well as her empire.

Spartan and Theban Hegemony

Following the end of the Peloponnesian War, the struggle for power among the Greek city-states continued. At first, Sparta was dominant, but other city-states, such as Corinth, Thebes, and Athens, resented her insolent treatment and banded together to end Spartan rule. This resulted in the Corinthian War of 395-387 B.C. Athens took advantage of these events to rebuild her walls and fleet. Spartan hegemony was destroyed by the Thebans defeat at the Battle of Leuctra in 371 B.C. The Peloponnesian League was broken up, and the Helots freed, as Thebes replaced Sparta as the dominant power.

Meanwhile, Athens had put together the Second Athenian Confederation. This confederation, and what remained of the Peloponnesian League, met Thebes at the Battle of Mantinea in 362 B.C. The Thebans won the battle but lost their great commander, Epaminondas. Without him they returned to their former position. Athens briefly regained power but without a threat from Sparta or Thebes, the other city-states began to secede from Athens's second empire. The Greek poleis continued arguing and fighting, while to the north a new power began to emerge, which eventually united them by force. The Macedonians changed the Greek world forever.

CLASSICAL CULTURE

Despite the wars and instability of the Classical Age, which has been defined as 500 B.C. to 323 B.C., it was the Athenians greatest period of cultural creativity. With the defeat of the Persian army on the plains of Marathon, the greatest power of their world, the Athenians gained confidence in themselves, believing they could do anything. "Man is the measure of all things," said the Sophist Protagoras, and the Athenians believed it. As a result, along with the wealth extracted by the state slaves from the silver mines at Laurium and from their "allies" in the Delian League, the Athenians achieved new heights of perfection in the arts, literature, and philosophy.

Literature

The epic poems of Homer and the mythological stories of the gods are the basis of Greek literature. Concern about ethical values and the forming of good citizens to build the good community underlay much of the Greek effort in the arts. That was especially true of poetry, which then became drama acted out on the outdoor theater, which was synonymous with Greek culture. Many of the Greek city-states promoted competition in drama, with the winner's play enacted in the public theater, usually as a part of the yearly religious festivals. The tragedy, the oldest form of drama, was probably first developed at Athens. This poetic drama dealt with serious issues in the context of religious mythology. At Athens these plays were performed as a part of the yearly festival honoring the god Dionysius. They included interaction between human beings and the gods often resulting in violence and irreconcilable conflicts. The audience was forced to consider their own flaws as humans and the possibility of self-destruction through hubris, or pride and overconfidence. Especially talented dramatists were Aeschylus (525-456 B.C.), Sophocles (496-406 B.C.), and Euripides (485-406-B.C.). With Euripides, the tragedy began to evolve toward the concerns of the person and his/her own psychological make up.

Comedy was introduced at the festival of Dionysius in the early fifth century. The best known to us, because we have some of his complete plays, is Aristophanes, who lived from 450 to 385 B.C. Known as Old Comedy, Aristophanes and his contemporaries wrote plays of political satire aimed at well-known leaders like Pericles. Comedy developed similar to tragedy

Socrates not only pursued knowledge and the meaning of life but also shared both with his fellow citizens, spending hours asking and answering questions.

and eventually turned to the personal love story in the Hellenistic Age.

History is the earliest form of prose literature. Herodotus is known as the "Father of History" and he was discussed earlier in relation to the Persian War. His account of that epic struggle is the first written history. Thucydides, too, has been discussed earlier as we considered the Peloponnesian War. His method of objective analysis and critical use of sources set the standard for writing history from that day until now.

Philosophy

The word "philosophy" means the pursuit of wisdom, not simply knowledge, and the philosopher is one who seeks or pursues wisdom. The Greeks were not the first people to produce wisdom literature, and surely they were not the first people to pursue the truth, but they were the originators of philosophy as a rational, systematic field of study. Beginning in the sixth century B.C., and sometimes referred to as Pre-Socratic philosophy, Greek philosophy before the Classical Age dealt with the origins and physical nature of the universe. Thales of Miletus is the earliest known philosopher. He undoubtedly encountered several ideas in Egypt, which he brought back and taught in Greece, such as astronomy, geometry, and that water was the basic substance of the universe. Empedocles of Acragas in the fifth century B.C. believed that there were four basic elements in the universe: air, water, fire, and earth. Another theory put forward by Leucippus of Miletus and his pupil, Democritus, was that all things are composed of tiny building blocks called atoms. Anaximander developed the idea of evolution and thought that the universe was a limitless, constantly expanding system. Hippocrates, the father of medicine, began using the empirical method in science, basing conclusions on rational evidence after careful experimentation and observation. Finally, Pythagoras believed that the basis of the universe was mathematical. He also believed that the earth orbited the sun.

During the fifth century, Sophists traveled and taught certain skills, such as rhetoric, for pay. Their use of rational analysis of human behavior and beliefs was disturbing to many people. They questioned everything and some went so far as to question the basis of law and religion. These were fundamental values of the polis, and this school of philosophy with its questioning of all things helped to undercut the basis of the polis and bring on the crisis of that institution, which was central to the Greek way of life. The Sophists argued that truth was relative, not absolute, and that the end justified the means. The Sophists, who gave us the term "sophistry" (subtly deceptive reasoning or argumentation), also gave us the term that has been used to symbolize the achievements of both the Classical Age and the Renaissance. Protagoras, the leader and probably the originator of the Sophists, placed human beings at the center of the cosmos, suggesting that they determined their own truth and could do anything they chose to do.

A number of Greeks agreed with this new emphasis on man rather than on the universe but were troubled by the Sophists' rejection of eternal or absolute truth. That was akin to a rejection of the gods, and while the Greeks of the fifth century had become more cynical of the religious myths, the worship of the gods was still a deeply ingrained value of the citizens of the polis. Charges of impiety could be used to bring down an opponent, resulting in punishments ranging from public dishonor to exile or death.

Socrates, an Athenian who lived from 470-399 B.C., is considered to be the father of philosophy. He was a humanist, for he centered his philosophy in the quest for truth to improve the soul and lead a just life in the polis. He believed that knowledge led to a life of virtue because the person who knows what is right will choose to do the right or virtuous thing. Socrates held no view similar to the later Christian doctrine of the sinful nature, but he did believe that ignorance was evil and caused people to lead unjust lives.

Socrates conducted his search for truth by questioning the citizens of Athens and causing them to examine their own assumptions, beliefs, and actions. If he found contradictions among these beliefs and actions, he was quick to point it out, but he did it in such a way that the person being questioned realized their own ignorance of the truth. This method of teaching by asking questions is called the Socratic method. Socrates' reliance on reason to discover the virtuous life did not preclude his belief in absolute truth, which he was searching for, but it did cause him to question the Greek understanding of the gods who acted in unethical, immoral ways according to religious mythology. Socrates rejected that kind of religion but affirmed a higher deity that was just and ethical.

His questioning of people and the gods, along with his rejection of democracy at the very time that Sparta forced oligarchy on Athens with the rule of the Thirty Tyrants at the end of the Peloponnesian War, led to trouble for Socrates. Since the traitor, Alcibiades, had been one of his students, as well as two of the thirty tyrants, his opponents claimed that he had corrupted the youth of the city and introduced strange gods. Socrates was convicted by a jury of 501 men and condemned to die. Socrates refused to leave the polis where he had lived for 70 years. He argued that he had taught obedience to the law all of his life, and he would not throw away the work of a lifetime just to exist as a foreigner in another country for a few more years. One of the most poignant scenes of classical age literature is that of Socrates drinking the poison hemlock while he speaks with some of his disciples about truth and the virtuous life to the very end.

Plato, who lived from about 428 to 347 B.C., was a devoted student of Socrates. He recorded Socrates' death scene in the *Crito*. It is largely through the writings of Plato that we learn the philosophy of Socrates. Plato accepted the political philosophy of Socrates that rejected democracy and called for a system in his *Republic* that was led by a few wise men or women, the guardians. His ideal estate granted equality to men and women and was based on ability and achievement of knowledge through systematic education. Plato abandoned the practice of politics after the death of his teacher, convinced that the mobocracy of Athens would do the same thing to any honorable man.

Plato's basic philosophical position on truth is that it is absolute. He is known as a philosophical idealist because he believed that the things we see in material form are only imperfect reflections of the ideal or perfect form, which exists beyond this world. Later, Christianity would equate that place of perfection with Heaven and the Power who established the ideal forms with God. In 386 B.C. Plato began his academy where he taught philosophy, mathematics, and astronomy. Considered the first college in the history of Western civilization, the academy lasted for 900 years and laid the foundation for education.

Aristotle, who lived from 384 to 322 B.C., was a student of Plato and studied with him at the academy. Later he opened his own school in Athens, the Lyceum. Aristotle was born in Macedonia where his father was a doctor to the king. Eventually, Aristotle became a tutor to the son of the king of Macedonia. That young son was Alexander, known down through history as "The Great."

Aristotle is important for his scientific approach to gathering knowledge about the natural world and placing it in a systematic form for study and practical use. He and his students applied this in many fields of knowledge, such as politics, where they gathered 158 copies of constitutions. Today, only one out of the original 158 remains in existence, which is the Athenian constitution. This brilliant yet practical scientist-philosopher believed the goal of life was to find happiness. Finding balance between extremes in life, or the golden mean, is the way to achieve that happiness. Aristotle was more comfortable with democracy and tended to see men as good and capable of self-government in the polis. His written works that still exist include the *Politics* and *Metaphysics*.

One other branch of philosophy that deserves mentioning is that of the Cynics. This school of philosophy taught that one should reject wealth and physical comfort and live the simple life close to Nature to find the good life and wisdom for the individual. Diogenes (400-325 B.C.) is the best known of the Cynics, and he was famous for his rudeness and filthy, unkempt personal attire. He wore rags, lived in a barrel, and rejected formal study for the simple lifestyle.

Classical Art

In the field of aesthetics, the Greek artists established the highest standard of excellence. While they produced beautiful things for everyday use, such as jewelry, the greatest art was produced in architecture and sculpture. Painting was also im-

The Doric style is sturdy, and its top (the capital) is plain. This style was used in mainland Greece and the colonies in southern Italy and Sicily. The Ionic style is thinner and more elegant. Its capital is decorated with a scroll-like design. This style was used in eastern Greece and the islands. The Corinthian style was seldom used in the Greek world, but often appeared in Roman temples. Its capital is elaborate and decorated with acanthus leaves.

portant for their public buildings and sculptures, however, the paint has been completely erased by time, and we cannot determine its quality.

Architecture

Greek achievement in architecture in the Classical Age affects us still. The symmetry, balance, and order that are characteristics of the religious temples built on the Acropolis of Athens, cause one to gaze in awe at the beauty created by those architects of long ago. The basic construction of a temple like the Parthenon was post-and lintel with many columns in front and along the sides to hold up the roof. These temples were decorated with carvings of their patron god or goddess, as well as scenes from mythology about the gods and heroes. The Parthenon had seventeen columns along each side and eight on each end. It was different from many of the other temples because the Athenians, full of confidence after defeating the Persians, decorated this temple to Athena with freestanding sculptures of recognizable, contemporary Athenians. Three styles, or orders, of columns developed over time. The oldest, the Doric column, was used in building the Parthenon. This was the largest of the columns and stood directly on the stone floor. Larger at the bottom than at the top, the gradually tapered shape made the columns appear to be straight. The Doric column was simple in style with no intricate carving. The Ionic column came next in development and was a thinner, more graceful column with a scrolled capital. The Corinthian column was basically the Ionic column with a capital that had intricately carved leaves on

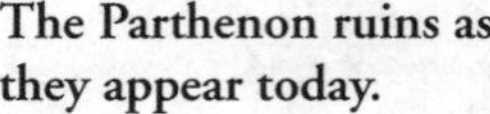

The Parthenon ruins as they appear today.

the capital. Both the Ionic and Corinthian columns were set on a base that in turn sat on the stone floor. The Greeks put their best work into the public temples instead of fine homes and palaces.

Sculpture

Beginning with the more formal, one might even say bland and impersonal, sculpture of the Archaic Age, the Greeks began to experiment with little, individual changes, like a smile or changing the stance of the legs. By the Classical period, this innovativeness brought a new freedom to Greek sculpture. The search for ideal beauty brought them to portray the nude human body, male and female, in lifelike detail where muscles rippled across the chest, legs and arms of the ideal athlete. Myron's *Discobolus* in 450 B.C. portrays a discus thrower in motion, represented by two intersecting arcs that give the impression of a bow that is drawn the moment before the arrow is released. Phidias, the famous fifth-century artist who decorated the Parthenon, and Praxiteles of the fourth century achieved perfection in rendering the human form both real and sensually idealistic at the same time. Not until the Renaissance were great artists again able to approach their skill and vision in portraying the human form.

CONCLUSION

This chapter covers a long period of history, beginning with 3,000 B.C. and ending in 30 B.C. Bronze Age technology had begun to develop on the island of Crete at the beginning of this period. It was not until 2,000 B.C., however, that the history of the Minoans emerged. This period has no known written record, and the interpretation of their history is based completely on archeological evidence. The Minoans were influenced by the contemporary Mesopotamian and Egyptian civilizations and, in turn, spread their culture to the Greek mainland where it blended with the native culture to produce what is known today as Mycenaean culture. This ancient Aegean civilization reached a high level of development including writing, urban centers, centralized government, advanced engineering skills demonstrated by the building of extensive palace-temples, international trade, and the appreciation of aesthetics as seen in the beautiful frescoes on palace walls.

A Dark Age followed the fall of that civilization where knowledge of earlier accomplishments faded, and the culture sank to a more primitive level of existence. Legends of that great period lived on, however, and by 750 B.C. Homer had written the great literary epics of the *Iliad* and the *Odyssey*. These epics provided a unified set of religious beliefs about the gods and basic values such as arete, or excellence, that were basic for Hellenic culture.

Believing they must strive to excel in all things led the Greeks to great heights of human accomplishment. One of the greatest of those accomplishments, which certainly affects our world today, was the development of majority rule or democracy. Within their independent poleis the Greeks realized a new concept of citizens, not as subjects but as responsible partners in the defense and governance of their social order. Despite the successful evolution of that concept, it also had a dark side. There was continual warfare and independence among the poleis, which prevented Hellenic unity and led to the demise of the polis and democracy.

The Greeks achieved great things in the arts, literature and drama, philosophy, and science, particularly at Athens, during the Golden Age of the fifth century. Perhaps their greatest achievement was in the emphasis they placed on human beings and their ability to inquire after the truth and find it. This philosophy, known as humanism, placed humankind at the center of all things, believing that human beings could discover truth through rational inquiry.

Suggestions for Further Reading

John Boardman, *Greek Art* (1985).

J. Boardman, J. Griffin & O. Murray eds., *Greece and the Hellenistic World* (1986).

W. Burkert, *Greek Religion* (1977).

A.R. Burn, *The Lyric Age of Greece* (1960).

Paul Cartledge, *Agesilaus and the Crisis of Sparta* (1987); *The Spartans* (2002); (ed) *The Cambridge Illustrated History of Ancient Greece* (1998).

Rodney Castleden, *Minoans: Life in Bronze Age Crete* (1990); *Mycenaeans* (2005).

John Chadwick, *The Mycenaean World* (1976).

James Davidson, *Courtesans and Fishcakes* (1997).

M.I. Finley, *The Ancient Economy*, 2nd Ed. (1985); *Ancient Slavery and Modern Ideology* (1980); *Politics in the Ancient World* (1983).

Y. Garlan, *Slavery in Ancient Greece* (1988).

Michael Grant, *The Classical Greeks* (1989).

P. Green, *The Greco-Persian Wars* (1998).

Victor Hansen, *The Western Way of War* (1989); *A War Like No Other* (2005).

Herodotus, *The Histories.*

B. Hughes, *Helen of Troy* (2005).

Donald Kagan, *The Outbreak of The Peloponnesian War* (1969); *Pericles of Athens and the Birth of Democracy* (1991).

G.B. Kerferd, *The Sophistic Movement* (1981).

Thomas R. Martin, *Ancient Greece: From Prehistoric to Hellenistic Times* (1996)

J.D. Mikalson, *Athenian Popular Religion*(1983).

D. Brendan Nagle, *The Ancient World: A Social and Cultural History* (1979).

S. Pomeroy, *Goddesses, Whores, Wives, and Slaves* (1975).

Barry Strauss, *The Battle of Salamis* (2004); *The Trojan War* (2006).

Thucydides, *History Of The Peloponnesian War.*

Chapter 3

ALEXANDER AND THE HELLENISTIC AGE

Alexander the Great

Archimedes (287-212 B.C.) is one of the major scientist/mathematicians of the Hellenistic Age, which is also the Golden Age of science in the ancient world. He was born in Syracuse, a Greek colony in Sicily. His father was an astronomer and he sent his son to study in Alexandria, Egypt, the center of scientific study in the world at that time, due to the great library and museum built there by Ptolemy I. Everyone has heard the story of his discovery of the 1st law of hydrostatics, which deals with the idea that a solid displaces an equal amount of liquid, which can be used to determine the weight of the solid item. He realized this as he climbed into a bath and saw the water rise. Ecstatic that he had solved the problem he had been wrestling with, Archimedes is supposed to have run naked through the streets of the city shouting "Eureka," which means "I have found it" in Greek. This man evidently possessed the power of concentration to such a degree that he didn't even realize he had forgotten to put on his clothes!

That same power of concentration when applied to solving scientific problems and allied with his genius produced so many things that we still use today. He calculated the value of pi, the approximate area of circles without calculus, and according to a webpage dedicated to him:

> *He found the area and tangents to the curve traced by a point moving with uniform speed along a straight line which is revolving with uniform angular speed about a fixed point. This curve, described by r = aq in polar coordinates, is now called the "spiral of Archimedes." With calculus it is an easy problem; without calculus it is very difficult.*

Archimedes applied his knowledge to machines, such as the screw of Archimedes, which could be used to raise water as a modern pump does from mines, wells, or the hold of a ship. He built compound pulleys and catapults, as well as other weapons of war. Polybius, a Greek historian who wrote about the rise of Rome, described the use of his catapults to bombard their ships during the Second Punic War with lead weights and rocks, and another machine that picked up the Roman warships with grappling hooks and using the compound pulley, dumped the contents of the ships including the sailors and soldiers on board into the sea when they attempted to bridge the walls of the city from their ships. This broke up the Roman attack from the sea on his city, and when his catapults of varying sizes were used against troops attacking by land, the Romans had to give up the attack. Eventually the Romans took Syracuse by a surprise attack and according to Plutarch:

> *Archimedes, who was then, as fate would have it, intent upon working out some problem by a diagram, and having fixed his mind alike and his eyes upon the subject of his speculation, he never noticed the incursion of the Romans, nor that the city was taken. In this transport of study and contemplation, a soldier, unexpectedly coming upon him, commanded him to follow to Marcellus, which he declined to do before he had worked out his problem to a demonstration; the soldier, enraged, drew his sword and ran him through.*

In this case, his powers of concentration led to his death!

Chronology
(all dates B.C.)

359-336	Philip II of Macedon's reign as king
338	Battle of Chaeronea, Philip II gains hegemony of Greece
336	Philip II assassinated and his son, Alexander III (the Great), becomes king; Aristotle establishes the Lyceum
334-326	Alexander the Great invades Persia, Battle of the Granicus River
333	Alexander and his army of Greeks win the Battle of Issus
331	Alexander wins the Battle of Gaugamela-final defeat of the Persian Emperor
326	Alexander's forces reach the Indus River but mutiny and refuse to go on
323	Death of Alexander the Great
322	Death of Aristotle
320-301	Establishment of the Antigonid kingdom
310	Alexander's son murdered, Zeno founds school of Stoicism at Athens
307	Epicurus founds his school of philosophy at Athens
306-304	Seleucid and Ptolemaic kingdoms established
342-290	Menander lives and writes New Comedy style drama
310-230	Aristarchus of Samos – astronomer who develops helio-centric theory
300	Euclid's *Elements of Geometry*, Museum of Alexandria with great library
287-212	Archimedes of Syracuse develops the basis of physics
276-194	Eratosthenes, founder of mathematical Geography
272	Library of Alexandria destroyed by fire
238-227	Attalus I, king of Antigonid kingdom of Pergamum defeats the Gauls
225	*Dying Gaul* sculpted for the monument of Attalus, example of Hellenistic emotion and portrayal of the individual in art
214-205	King Philip V of Macedonia fights first war with the Romans
200-118	Polybius, Greek historian who writes a history of Rome during the Punic and Greek wars
190	*Winged Victory of Samothrace*
168	Rome conquers the Antigonid dynasty to rule Macedon
150	*Venus de Milo*
146	Roman conquest of Corinth
133	Attalid kingdom of Pergamum bequeathed to Rome on the death of the last king
100	*Laocoon and His Sons* by Polydoros, Hagesandros, and Athenodoros of Rhodes
64	Rome conquers remains of the Seleucid kingdom
30	Death of Cleopatra VII; Rome adds Egypt to its empire; End of the Ptolemaic line of monarchs and the Hellenistic Age

THE HELLENISTIC WORLD AND CIVILIZATION

The Hellenic period was a time of intense development of Greek culture and a period of conflict between the poleis. The world of the individualized polis as the basic political unit of Greece gave way in the fourth century to the period of the cosmopolitan world empire of the Macedonian, Alexander the Great. The term Hellenistic refers to the three century period from the death of Alexander in 323 B.C. to the death of Cleopatra, the last Macedonian ruler of Egypt in 30 B.C. During this period, Greek culture was diffused throughout the eastern Mediterranean region, including Egypt and the Near East, in the wake of Alexander's army as he invaded and conquered the Persian Empire. Earlier historians dating from the 19th century interpreted this to mean a fusion of the local cultures in the East took place with the Greek culture, forming a new synthesis dominated by the superior culture of the Hellenes. It has long been noted that this blending was not perfect and often seemed to be superficial at best, with the Greeks forming a separate ruling class.

Others have recently come to question this view and instead see the Hellenic conquerors as acting like normal imperial conquerors who imposed their culture on their subjects, but the spreading of their *superior* culture took place incidentally rather than deliberately, and it was only accepted by those who hoped to gain personally from their compliance. Peter Green, a well-known Greek historian, is among those who have adopted this view. He found that almost no Greek literature was translated into the Persian, Egyptian, or other eastern languages and the same was true in the other arts and to a lesser degree in the sciences, and thus little integration of ideas took place. The one great exception was the Romans who came from the West and conquered the Hellenistic kingdoms, but in turn were conquered by the Hellenes intellectually. The Romans admired and accepted Hellenic culture despite some resistance to it by the older Romans, who saw it as being degenerate due to the nudity and debauchery of the Greeks at that time.

During this period, Sparta, which had retained a certain amount of autonomy, slowly decreased in power as her pool of available warriors dropped to 700 or less, and she had to look for allies and at times hired mercenaries to defend the Peloponnesus. The city states she had dominated broke free of Spartan control, and 1st the Macedonian kingdom and then the Romans defeated and gained control of Sparta as well as the rest of Greece. This was the period of Roman expansion in Italy culminating in the wars with Carthage and the great struggle with Hannibal during the 2nd Punic War. Some Greek kings allied with Carthage while others such as Sparta allied with the Romans. Regardless, all would become part of the Roman Empire by the end of the Hellenistic Age, and democracy was nowhere to be found in Greece.

Philip II of Macedonia and Alexander the Great

In northeastern Greece, there arose a king with the skill, knowledge, political ambition, and boldness necessary to build his kingdom into a powerful force. Philip II (359-336 B.C.) of Macedonia overthrew his infant nephew to become king. Philip had lived in Thebes during his youth when that polis was at the height of its power under Epaminondas. He learned not only Greek culture (the nobility of Macedonia considered themselves to be Greek, and the royal family claimed to be descendants of Heracles) but also the military skills of the Greeks. The Macedonians spoke a dialect of the Greek language and admired Greek culture. With Philip's ambition and military-organizational skill, he began to build a superb fighting force. Unlike the citizen-soldier of the polis, the Macedonian army was a professional army because Philip, as king, was able to fund it with money from the gold mines of Macedonia and Thrace. Philip employed the phalanx of the Greeks in his army, but he used a more open formation with longer pikes. He relied on the cavalry, which was placed on the flanks of the phalanx, to protect them and to over-run the flanks of the opposing army. This proved to be a superior form of organization of the army and led to victory after victory. The cavalry were Macedonian nobility, called *Companions,* who fought on horseback. They lived with the king and fought beside him, developing an extreme loyalty to him.

Philip began to involve Macedonia in the internal politics and wars of the poleis when he convinced the leaders of Thessaly in the 350s B.C. to elect him as the leader of their confederacy. This was a cunning move, giving him legitimacy as a Greek leader. In the 340s B.C., he led the armies of the Thessalonian confederacy in battle against the Phocians, who had a long-running dispute with Thessaly, called the Holy War over the oracle of Apollo at Delphi. Defeating the Phocians, along with their allies which included Athens, Philip then took over not only Phocis but Thessaly as well. He gained control of Thrace along the northern coast of the Aegean Sea adjacent to the Hellespont. By the late 340s B.C., Philip had bribed, cajoled, or forced the northern and central poleis of Greece to submit to his leadership. Philip began to call for a united Greek and Macedonian army to invade the Persian Empire as revenge for the Persian War over a century before. His main detractor was Demosthenes, the great orator of Athens. Athens was no longer the powerful polis she had been a century earlier, for her empire was gone and her population was declining. Philip needed the resources of southern Greece, in addition to those he already controlled, to carry out his plan of building a great empire. Demosthenes rallied Athenian opinion with his warning that Greece would lose her freedom to this "barbarian" king, and he won Thebes over to this point of view. However, in 338 B.C., Philip's coalition defeated the Athenian alliance at the battle of Chaeronea, ending the independence of the poleis of Greece. Chaeronea was an important turning point in Greek history. Philip granted generous terms to the city-states he had just defeated, giving them autonomy over local affairs but requiring them to follow his foreign policy and join a league that was formed in 338 B.C.

The following year, the Greek representatives met at Corinth and declared war on Persia. Philip claimed this was to be a crusade to free the Greek city states of Ionia in Asia Minor from Persian control and to gain revenge for the Persian invasion and desecration of their temples more than a century earlier. However, the undoubted purpose was to gain wealth, power and glory for Philip and his kingdom. To do this, he needed the resources and support of a unified Greece. Before he could carry out his plan, Philip was assassinated and replaced by his oldest son, Alexander. There has been a great deal of speculation about Alexander's role in the death of his father. Peter Green in his biography of Alexander details the unhappy background of the tragedy: a competitive father-son relationship, which was promoted by Olympias, Alexander's mother; Philip's decision to take his fifth wife in order to produce a new heir to the throne as he repudiated Olympias as an adulteress, and by implication questioned the

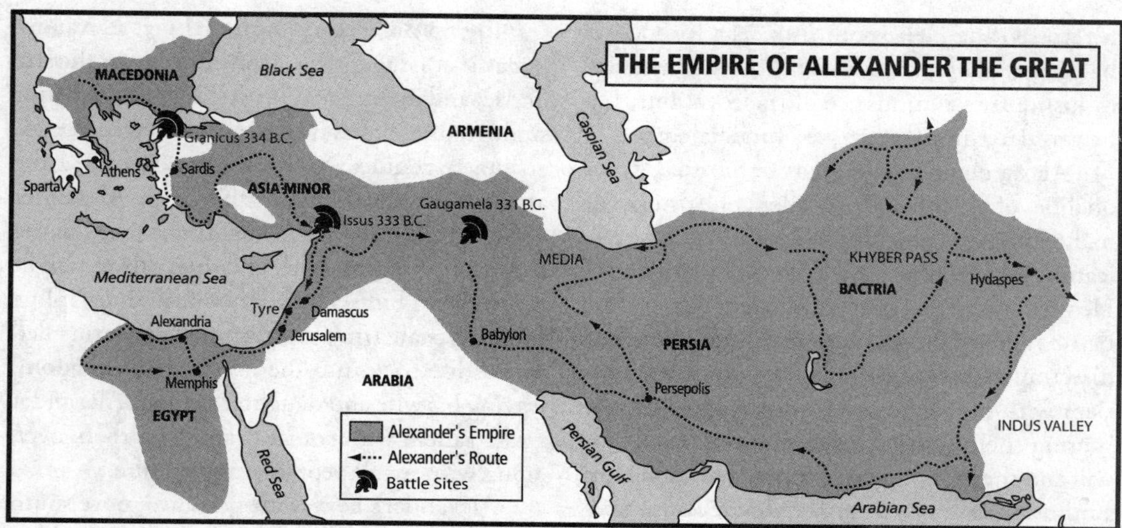

legitimacy of Alexander's birth; palace plotting and intrigue. Then in a drunken brawl at the wedding feast, Philip threatened Alexander with his drawn sword but fell down and was taunted by his son as being unable to stand on his feet, let alone lead the invasion of the Persian Empire. Alexander and his mother then fled to her home kingdom of Epirus. Alexander was eventually recalled when the new baby was a girl, and a male heir was needed after all. In the midst of preparations for the great invasion in 336 B.C., a second child was born, and this time it was a boy. Then in the midst of a wedding procession for his daughter, Philip was stabbed by one of his own bodyguards named Pausanias, who had also been one of his lovers. He had suffered a serious indignity at the hands of some other men of the court, for which Philip failed to grant justice, and Pausanias bore a grudge. Green believes, along with ancient historians like Plutarch, that his grievance may have been inflamed by Olympias and that Alexander was a party to the assassination plot. All evidence that Alexander was involved is circumstantial; however, Alexander was immediately proclaimed king, and he was the chief beneficiary of what amounted to a coup. Many believe that Olympias was involved to protect her son and out of spite for her treatment by her husband, she openly rejoiced that Philip was dead and is supposed to have placed a gold crown on the head of the assassin as his body was hung up on the gibbet for public disgrace.

Alexander had already shown his military ability and courage by participating in the Battle of Chaeronea in 338 B.C., which he helped to win by leading the cavalry charge that broke the Athenian-Theban line. With the death of his father, Alexander took the Macedonian crown and quickly put down revolts in Greece and in the tribal areas of northern Macedonia. He ruthlessly destroyed the city of Thebes in 335 B.C. in a fit of rage and sold the inhabitants into slavery when it rebelled a second time (upon the word of Demosthenes and others who spread stories that he was dead) in order to intimidate the other city-states of Greece and establish his control. Although he was only 20 years old, Alexander gathered his forces, which included men from all of Greece as well as Macedonia, and in 334 B.C.

he crossed the Hellespont into Asia Minor. He had been advised to wait until he was married to insure the continuance of the royal line, but he was determined to strike immediately.

Alexander inherited many of the exceptional qualities of his father. As a student of Aristotle, he had demonstrated his intelligence and desire to learn. Like his father, he was ambitious and bold. He was a masterful general who led his men into battle rather than sending them into battle and directing them from behind the lines. He ate and slept with his soldiers and won their loyalty by sharing their hardships. Alexander had an iron will and the discipline and courage to back it up. Enthusiastically accepting certain Hellenic ideals, Alexander, who slept with a copy of the *Iliad* (and a dagger for protection), saw himself as living up to the heroic image of Achilles as portrayed in that great work of literature by Homer. He believed that he was chosen for greatness by the gods and that he must achieve arête (excellence) to be worthy of that fate. Upon crossing the Hellespont, Alexander drove his spear into the earth, claiming it like a Homeric hero as "won by the spear."

Leading an army of 30,000 foot soldiers and a cavalry of about 5,000, Alexander invaded an empire far greater in size than all of Greece to fight an army that was several times the size of the combined Greek and Macedonian army. The first serious battle was fought at the Granicus River in 334 B.C. Alexander hazarded his life by leading the cavalry charge across the river and straight into the Persian army line, causing it to break and giving him the victory. In doing so, he almost lost his life, but by such courage he led his men to victory. After defeating and scattering the Persians, young Alexander led his army south along the coast of Asia Minor, liberating the Greek city-states and depriving the Persian navy of ports.

In 333 B.C., King Darius III met Alexander in battle at Issus with an army three times the size of Alexander's army. With good luck, a superior strategy, disciplined troops, and courageous leadership, Alexander's smaller army destroyed the army of the great king. In this battle Alexander again led a cavalry charge that broke through the left flank of Darius' army and then drove straight for the king himself. The morale and discipline of the Persian army disintegrated as Darius fled for his life back into the heart of his kingdom, leaving his wife and daughter behind. Alexander treated them with courtesy and won them over, along with many people of the empire.

Alexander's next strategy was to move south along the coast of the Mediterranean Sea, taking Egypt rather than immediately pursuing King Darius. He captured Egypt with relative ease and was deified as the son of Ammon (their equivalent of Zeus) after laying siege to the ancient city of Tyre and destroying its walls, a feat that no one else had been able to do in 700 years. Darius put another army together and met Alexander's forces at Gaugemela in 331 B.C. near the site of what had been Ninevah in northern Mesopotamia. Once again, Alexander's army smashed a much larger Persian army, and the great king fled. That was the last flight of Darius. He fled to the east pursued by Alexander and a select group of soldiers. After a long chase they learned he had been deposed and taken prisoner by two of his top officials in order to bargain with Alexander. One of them, a general named Bessus, claimed the title of Great King and planned to carry on a fight of national resistance against the invaders. Then as they found Alexander was in hot pursuit, these two men speared Darius with javelins and left him to die. A Macedonian soldier found him chained in a wagon with only a dog for company, and gave him water before he died. Alexander covered the body with his own cloak and sent it back for a proper royal burial in Persepolis.

Alexander found all of the wealth needed to fund his empire at Persepolis, the Persian capital. After confiscating the gold, jewels, and other rich goods, he burned the royal city to symbolize the revenge of Greece and to destroy the loyalties to the center of the old empire. One source estimates that the value of the gold and silver confiscated there was equal to 300 years of the income of the former Athenian empire, and 3,000 camels were required to transport it to Ecbatana.

Alexander pushed on across the Persian Empire into the northeast where in Bactria (now a part of Afghanistan and Uzbekistan) he married the princess Roxane to confirm an alliance with the Bactrians. He also established one of the many cities bearing his name, as he usually did (estimates differ from 30 to 70 or more cities named after him), but this one was named Alexandria Eschate, which means "farthest Alexandria." He tried to conquer the area of modern India, crossing the Indus River and in 327 B.C. led his army through the Khyber Pass. They had now been gone from home for about eight years, and his troops refused to go any further. Although Alexander evidently had heard of China from Aristotle, and must have planned to go all the way to the sea, he listened to his mutinous troops and turned back. As he traveled down the Indus River, Alexander was injured. He had thrown himself into the front of a battle and to motivate his troops, climbed over the wall of the city being attacked and fought alone when his troops would not act with the aggressiveness that he demanded. His warriors were forced to come to his rescue or let him die due to their dishonorable cowardice. They rescued Alexander but not before he received a spear wound that must have punctured his lung during the fight. As a result, Alexander lay near death for several days. Eventually he was able to travel, and they moved south to where the Indus River flows into the sea. He sent part of his party around the coast while the remainder crossed the desert to return to the center of Persia.

Once back in Persia, Alexander the Great began to make his plans to consolidate and expand his empire. First he was determined to invade and possess the Arabian Peninsula. Then he would move west along the coast of North Africa taking control of Carthage and going on to the Atlantic Ocean. He would have undoubtedly attempted to take control of the Italian Peninsula and thus united the entire Mediterranean world within his empire too. But the following year, in 323 B.C. he died at the early age of almost 33 years. He died of a fever, probably from a combination of malaria and his terrible wound received on the Indus River, which weakened his body that had seemed indestructible throughout his years of continual fighting. One of his recent biographers, Peter Green, has noted that all of the ancient historical sources record the belief at that time that Alexander was poisoned. Green says it cannot be ruled out, and he draws on the evidence that powerful men around Alexander feared him for he had put several of his closest associates to death with only a mock trial if he believed they were disloyal and killed others in fits of rage, usually accompanied by excessive drinking. Both he and his boyhood friend and lover, Hephaestion, died within a short time of each other and with similar symptoms, which could have been induced by the use of strychnine. Whatever the cause, Alexander had not prepared for his succession. When asked who he left his kingdom to, Alexander is supposed to have whispered "To the strongest." His son by Roxane was born a few months after his death. The boy and his mother were put to death 13 years later by Cassander, one of Alexander's own generals.

What is the significance of this man and how shall we interpret his actions? He has been seen as the great conqueror who never lost a battle, overcame tremendous odds and performed seemingly impossible physical feats so that he is the personification of the Greek ideal of the hero. He certainly was all of that and one of the greatest battlefield generals of all time combined with leadership and organizational skills that enabled him to hold an army together from many different countries, defeat a huge empire and organize that empire as he invaded it. Alexander was also a man who could be magnanimous in victory, granting mercy and bestowing certain favors on the defeated, so that he has been interpreted as the enlightened leader who brings peace and order on a universal scale to his subjects and to the entire world he conquered, leading to the later Pax Romana of the Roman Empire, and even to the modern organizational attempts to prevent war such as the United Nations. This last extrapolation seems to reach beyond the believable for this man who was soaked in the blood of so many and made war his continual profession, looking always for new lands to conquer that in no way threatened him or his people. His empire fell apart as soon as he died, yet his name is known to this day and his exploits still capture the imagination of almost all who study his life, and that was certainly one of the things he wanted to achieve. Whether Alexander truly wanted to Hellenize the world as he claimed, it is incontestable that Greek culture spread throughout the area of his empire. He also must be credited, along with his father, Philip II, for bringing an end to the independent, democratic governments of the poleis of Greece and replacing that ideal with the new one of world empire ruled by an absolute emperor in the West.

Hellenistic Cities and Kingdoms

With the death of Alexander, his generals began a struggle for power that ended in the formation of three major kingdoms. All of the royal family were murdered or executed, including Roxane and her son. One of Alexander's generals, Ptolemy, took control of Egypt and established the 31st dynasty of pharaohs. There the great city of Alexandria, first established by Alexander, became a center of cosmopolitan living and education with one of the great libraries and academic centers of the ancient world. Ptolemy's last and best known descendant in modern times was Cleopatra.

The second general, Antigonus, ruled Macedonia and some of the Greek city-states of northern Greece where he established the Antigonid dynasty. The remainder of Greece was divided between two leagues of city-states that survived until the Romans conquered them in the second century B.C.

The third kingdom was the heartland of the old Persian Empire that stretched from Asia Minor on the Aegean/Mediterranean Sea through Mesopotamia to India. Seleucus founded the Seleucid Dynasty that lasted until the Romans conquered it, though it had lost considerable territory in the east by that time. This kingdom experienced an influx of thousands upon thousands of Greek immigrants who brought their culture with them.

Alexander was the first to induce people to leave their homes in Greece and resettle in his new empire as a part of the governing class necessary to run it reliably and harmoniously. He also seemed to see this as an opportunity to Hellenize that part of the world, since he believed in those values so strongly, at least in the beginning. Realizing the importance of establishing a permanent basis for his empire,

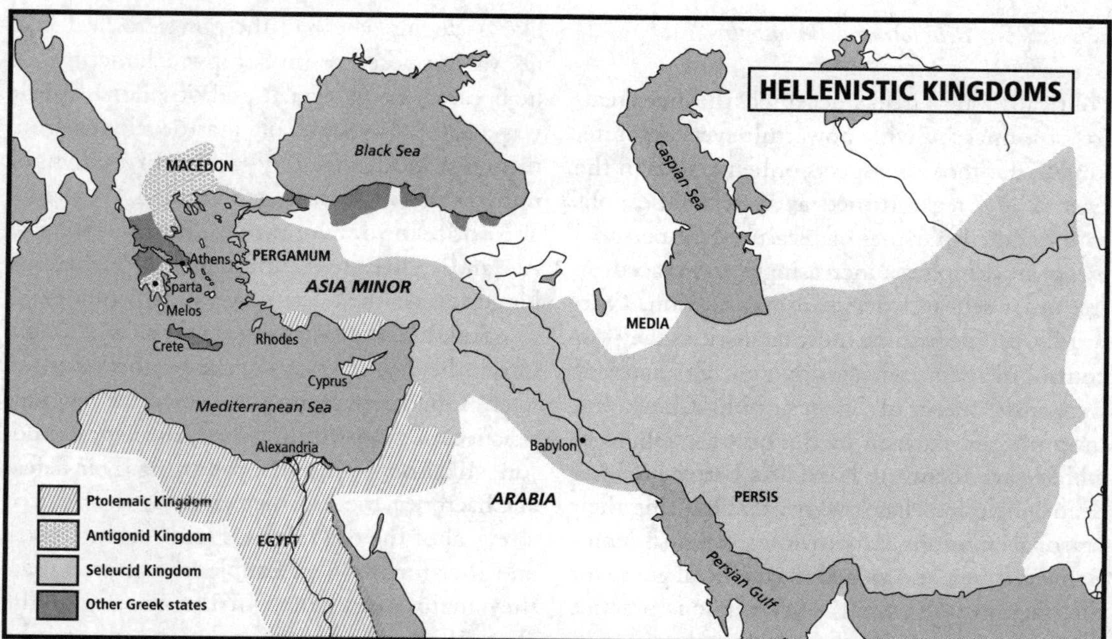

Alexander decreed that all were to be citizens of the empire and equal members of the state. This gave rise to the belief in the "Brotherhood of all mankind" and some have interpreted Alexander as a visionary who wanted to establish a world where all men were brothers, under his rule, of course. He urged his soldiers to follow his example and take wives of the region they were in, evidently hoping to blend not only culture but races, despite the fact that some of them had wives back in Greece. After his death, this movement of people from Greece and Macedonia continued, blending the Greek and Eastern culture to form the culture we know as Hellenistic. The Greek language was used among the educated ruling class, but Eastern ways of living and religion were established in most other ways. A truly urban society developed due to emphasis being placed on the cities and the events held there, despite the fact that most people lived in rural areas. This was a cosmopolitan world where people and goods moved about with considerable ease. Their loyalty was no longer to the polis or local region but to the person of the king and the kingdom in which they lived.

The economy tended to thrive at first. The Greeks implemented crop rotation and irrigation, leading to more efficient and productive use of the land. But the main advances came in industry and trade, as goods were made in one place and shipped over wide areas with fewer obstacles to the flow of trade. For example, many thousands of shipping pots (amphoras) made in Rhodes have been found in Egypt. The island of Delos handled the transshipment of many goods, including ten thousand slaves per day. As time passed, there was a tendency to rely more and more on slaves, making it difficult for the poor to compete and make a living. Gradually poverty increased and the separation between the upper class and the lower classes widened.

Religion and Philosophy

Politically, the Greeks accepted the new reality of monarchy with powerful, even absolute, kings, who took on aspects of being gods in the East. The Greeks turned away from the polis to individual pursuits of pleasure and personal escapism. Emphasis increasingly was placed on the inner-self and personal gratification. Outwardly, people became more fatalistic as they lost control of their own destiny and felt that they were at the mercy of Chance or blind Luck, but inwardly they turned to the mystery religions, which gave them the hope of a better life after death, included elaborate rituals involving their personal emotions and providing catharsis (emotional release), and as well as an ethical guide for their actions. Classical Greek religious practice was based on the gods of the polis and as a result, was essentially meaningless to other people. In the East, Greek religious practices never took root among the common people and soon died out. Even in Greece, people were looking for inner fulfillment in their lives. They often found it in one of the major mystery cults, such as that of Isis, the goddess of the Nile who renewed life and in addition gave immortality to her followers and helped them to avoid the bad results of Chance. This cult spread rapidly throughout the Hellenistic world including Greece. Mithra originated as the Persian sun god and became the god of life-eternal but only spread through the Hellenistic world late in that era. It became popular with the Roman soldiers in the empire era because it viewed life as a battle and involved the slaughter of a bull and the washing of the cult initiate in the blood of the slain bull to gain salvation. Serapis was a new cult god established in Egypt by Ptolemy I as a blend of the Egyptian god of the underworld, Osiris, who was consort to Isis, and included characteristics of Greek gods like Asclepius who had the power to heal, and he was supposed to save shipwreck victims, so he became the particular god of sailors. Cybele was another mystery cult that developed from the Great Mother fertility goddess of Asia Minor into a mystery cult during this period. We should also notice the development of the ruler cults, as Alexander's heirs to the thrones of the Hellenistic kingdoms claimed that they were divine too.

Still, the religion changed very slowly, for the Greeks held to the ways of their fathers instinctively. One scholar who has studied the religious practices of Athens during the Hellenistic period, Jon Mikalson, found that following their defeat at Chaeronea, the Athenians actually experienced a revival of the old religious faith in their gods, and that for the next couple of hundred years they maintained much of the essence of the classical era religion. Thus, he and others who challenge the idea that Greek religion declined or changed in ways that prepared them for the coming of Christianity, find considerable continuity in Greek religion in some of the poleis they have studied carefully. Yet Mikalson admits that eventually the foreign cults did become popular, but they were accepted within, or adapted to, the framework of religion that already existed.

Philosophy followed a similar pattern of appealing to the individual's need for fulfillment and happiness during the Hellenistic Age. Metaphysics, which is concerned with establishing the nature of being and those things which exist beyond the human senses such as the supernatural, became less important in philosophical inquiry while ethics (the study of moral principles that lead to happiness and fulfillment) became more important. Philosophy was increasingly separated from the factual knowledge of science, as fields of knowledge became more specialized. Philosophy itself was divided into three areas: ethics, physics (the scientific study of physical processes in nature to determine how they exist) and logic (the system and theory of reasoning to determine the truth). Of course, philosophy was largely the domain of the educated upper class, yet it reached more people than ever before (Theophrastus, a student of Aristotle and a popular lecturer, is supposed to have attracted crowds of 2,000 people in Athens), because there were more people who were affluent and thus they had more leisure time to spend in the pursuit of learning. Also, as Greeks migrated to the new cities of the Hellenistic world, they brought their culture with them and that included philosophy. For example, in small towns in rural Afghanistan, archeologists have discovered a philosophical text and other evidence of interest in Aristotle's philosophy. Women had not been permitted to attend philosophy lectures during the Classical period, but now women of the upper classes attended lectures and joined the group of followers of the philosopher of their choosing. Kings of the new Hellenistic kingdoms promoted philosophy and learning at their courts and went so far as to compete with each other for the attendance of the greatest minds of the day at their courts.

Epicurus lived in Athens (342-271 B.C.) and taught that pleasure was the goal of life. Pleasure, however, was the absence of pain, not uncontrolled indulgence of the appetites, for that often leads to pain. The Epicureans believed that one should ideally escape the busy life and avoid things like politics. Epicurus taught that there is no life after death, for the soul, as well as the body, is made up of atoms, which disintegrate back into the universe upon death. This philosophy of avoidance fit the age. Politics as the purpose of life was gone, as was the city-state. The earlier polis had become simply a local unit of an empire.

Stoicism is the other major philosophy that came out of the Hellenistic Age. A freed slave, Zeno (333-262 B.C.), taught the brotherhood of all men and the existence of reason and universal law because there is a divine providence that rules over all and determines the destiny of each person. The duty of each person is to live the virtuous life, bear your fate without flinching and take action to make the world around you a better place. The Stoics believed that God is in Nature and in each person, and the result was to treat human beings with greater respect. Through self-control, one could find happiness, or at least tranquility. This philosophy was the opposite of Epicureanism except for the finding of tranquility for the inner soul. It was accepted by the ruling classes and fit in with the idea of the cosmopolitan kingdom or empire, whose subjects were to serve the state for the good of all.

Two other philosophies, the Cynics and Diogenes, developed that were less popular than Stoicism and Epicureanism. Cynicism was discussed earlier in chapter 2. Antisthenes started this philosophy. He was a student of Socrates who lived from 450 B.C. to 350 B.C. His student, Diogenes (400-325 B.C.), is the best known leader of this school of thought. A good example of his crude behavior that rejects social norms of behavior and relates to both Alexander the Great and this Cynicism is when Alexander went to visit him prior to the invasion of the Persian Empire. Diogenes was meditating and sunning himself when Alexander approached with a crowd of people. Diogenes continued to lay on the ground as the young man approached him but simply stared and did not speak. Embarrassed, Alexander asked if there was anything he could do for Diogenes, whereupon the old philosopher is supposed to have answered "Yes, stand aside, you're keeping the sun off of me." Despite this humiliating treatment, Alexander defended the old man as his followers attempted to make light of Diogenes, saying "If I were not Alexander, I would be Diogenes." This reveals

This large black-figured amphora jar, made in Attica during the Classic Age, shows artisans working in a bootmaker's shop.

both the way Cynics acted in an anti-social way and the independence of Diogenes, as well as the complex nature of Alexander. Cynicism opposed conformity and the pursuit of pleasure of any kind. Instead, they taught that the simple life was best. Whatever came naturally should be followed, whether it was defecating in public or refusing to show respect. Crudeness was completely acceptable for the Cynics.

Skepticism claimed that one couldn't know the truth for certain, so one should not worry about what happens in life. Acceptance of things as they were was the result. Their goal was to achieve individual freedom and to be unaffected by the tragedies and trials of life, and in that respect were similar to the Epicureans. This school of philosophy followed the thinking of Pyrrho of Elis (360-270 B.C.) who argued that almost nothing can be known for certain, for even the physical senses provide us with information that is unreliable and contradictory. To reach a state where nothing disturbs our inner tranquility is the goal of this philosophy, and to reach that goal, the individual must stop making judgments and accept life as it comes. This philosophy replaced Platonism at the Academy, the school begun by Plato, during the Hellenistic Age.

Science

The Hellenistic Age was one of the most productive ages in the history of western civilization in the development of scientific knowledge. That is one reason why the Hellenistic Age is similar to the modern world in which we live. Why did it occur? First, it was based on the rational inquiry of the Greek philosophers, particularly Aristotle. Second, it received the support of Alexander the Great who brought a number of scientists along on his triumphal invasion of Persia to collect flora and fauna, among other kinds of scientific data, and later the support of the Ptolemies in Egypt. Finally, the cross-fertilization of knowledge from the East with that of the Greeks led to the sharing of knowledge and greater development. Alexandria in Egypt became the most advanced center for the study of science where the greatest library in the ancient world developed with over 500,000 volumes before it was destroyed in 272 A.D. Scientists found employment, a scholarly atmosphere, and resources for research at the first Museum (which means "place of the Muses") there. However, science was studied throughout the Hellenistic kingdoms and received the support of kings.

In astronomy, Aristarchus (310-230 B.C.) set forth the theory that the earth revolves around the sun, although later the competing theory by

Hipparchus won out and the geocentric model was believed to be correct, until Copernicus disproved it 1,700 years later. In geography Eratosthenes (276-194 B.C.) estimated the circumference of the earth close to the actual distance, which meant that he anticipated the earth being a globe, rather than flat.

In mathematics, Euclid (383-325 B.C.) compiled a textbook on geometry, *Elements of Geometry*, one of the most important texts on math ever produced. Archimedes (287-212 B.C.) of Syracuse was educated at Alexandria but then returned to his native city to work and live, and he died as you read earlier in the opening story of this chapter. He was an important researcher who calculated the value of pi, a concept learned by every student of advanced mathematics today. He also worked on catapults and developed the screw of Archimedes, which is the application of the inclined plane and was used to pump water from below the decks of ships. He wrote *On Plane Equilibriums*, a description of levers and their principles and discovered the displacement of a liquid by a solid could be used to determine the weight of the solid. In other words, Archimedes invented hydrostatics. Scientists and mathematicians produced a clocklike mechanism referred to as the Antikythera, named for the island where this mechanical device was found. X-rays have revealed that the device had metal gears and pointers, which could predict the motion of the planets and probably served as an aid to navigation. It was a forerunner of the modern computer.

In medicine and anatomy, Herophilus learned the functions of arteries and veins and described various organs like the cerebrum, cerebellum, optic nerve, uterus, ovaries, and the prostate. Erasistratus, the founder of physiology, explained how the valves of the heart function and described the difference between the sensory and motor nerves. These men dissected bodies of the dead to understand the body and its individual parts, and according to the ancient source *On Medicine* by Celsus, even performed vivisection on living criminals! Human rights had not progressed to the point they have in modern times.

Science began as a part of philosophical inquiry conducted by the philosophers but during the Hellenistic Age it became increasingly separated from that discipline. Science became a specialized area for scientists who spent their entire lives developing scientific theories and researching them to prove or disprove those theories. Despite this growth of scientific knowledge, it is important to note here that most of it was not applied in a practical manner to improve the standard of living for the common people.

Literature and Art

The library at Alexandria became the center of literary effort during the Hellenistic Age, but all of the courts of the major kingdoms competed for the presence of the popular authors. This competition became so intense that the Ptolemies who ruled Egypt supposedly refused to allow the export of papyrus to Pergamum in order to prevent the Attalid kings from producing written literature there. As a result, the court of Pergamum began using parchment, which is made of animal skins. Much of the work was dry, scholarly writing, and over 1,100 writers have been identified. The development of cataloguing and the use of literary criticism were necessary for intellectual development, academic pursuits similar to those that are so important today in colleges and universities throughout the world.

Poetry is the form of literature at which the Hellenistic writers excelled, according to Robin Lane Fox in his essay on "Literature and Patronage." However, Fox points out that much of the literature of this period has vanished and so that judgement is based only on what is available to us today. Apollonius in the third century B.C., wrote *Argonautica,* which tells the story of Jason and the Golden Fleece. Apollonius, librarian at Alexandria from 260 to 247 B.C., used the romantic love of Medea for Jason as the main theme of an epic for the first time. Theocritus (310-250 B.C.), a Greek poet like Apollonius, wrote thirty-two poems and developed the idyll, a poetic form that pictures an idealized version of rural life.

This was the age of the New Comedy in drama that avoided the theme of politics, which had been predominant in the older comedies, and played on timeless themes with plots that revolved around the private lives and problems of lovers, much like the "soap operas" of today. Menander (342-290 B.C.) wrote one hundred comedies that dealt with love intrigues and sentimental themes, using a witty, polished style. Philemon (360-263 B.C.) is another of the New Comedy dramatists. Finally, Polybius (203-120 B.C.) wrote a forty volume *Universal History* of Rome, covering the period 221-146 B.C. Only five volumes remain today. Polybius is considered to be very accurate. He wrote a great deal about the two Punic Wars in that series. Eratosthenes wrote a chronology of important events from the Trojan War to the second century B.C.

Architecture was affected by the development of the Hellenistic monarchies, for they had plenty of money. The simple Greek temple of the Classical Age was replaced by public structures built on a magnificent scale. Size and excessive ornamentation were characteristics of the period, as was the use of the Corinthian column with its foliage ornamented capital (see examples of column styles in chapter 2). The Temple of Zeus, which was built at Athens, was 363 feet long and 182 feet wide and was considered by many to be a wonder of the ancient world. The giant-sized lighthouse, or Pharos, at Alexandria, and the massive library are examples of buildings built on a grand scale not only to perform an important service but also to project the power and glory of the king who built it. Of the *Seven Wonders of the World,* two were built during the Hellenistic Age. The first was the Pharos and the second was the Colossus of Rhodes, the huge bronze sculpture that stood astride the entrance to the harbor.

Sculpture became increasingly emotional and dramatic. For example, the *Dying Gaul* arouses the emotions of the person looking at it, in part because the death is a tragic scene and in part because each viewer must eventually face death. The sculpture on the *Altar of Zeus* at Pergamum, built by the Attalid King Eumenes II about 170 B.C., is considered to have been the largest work of Greek sculpture and "was meant to outdo the Parthenon frieze" according to the great classical historian Michael Grant. In fact that massive piece of sculpture included 1200 gods and giants that were partially human and partly-animal and was over 400 feet long and seven feet high. It portrayed a chaotic struggle full of pain and terror out of which the victorious gods brought order and civilization. In *Laocoon and His Sons,* the realism of the priest and his sons being strangled by the serpents is interwoven with the emotional impact of the death struggle that the artist displayed by exaggerating the muscles and portraying agony on the faces of the victims. Particularly good examples of realism are the *Boxer, Drunken Old Woman*, and *Old Market Woman*. The latter is a bent and bowed older woman with a mole on her face. Praxiteles in the Classical Age would never have portrayed such a person. This realism would point the way to the art of the Roman world. Other trends in Hellenistic art included the use of the naked female figure and the use of sculpture as symbols of abstract ideas like peace or liberty, similar to our own *Statue of Liberty* in the harbor of New York. Busts of famous people also became prominent during this period, led by those made of Alexander the Great by Lysippus, the outstanding sculptor who worked at Alexander's court and is supposed to have amazed his contemporaries by his realistic portrayal. The natural bust, though often romanticized (idealized) for Alexander and perhaps other great patrons of the arts, is another example of the realism that developed in Hellenistic art, which became a characteristic of Roman art.

CONCLUSION

The Hellenistic period saw a major change take place in the dominant political concept of the times. With the conquest of Greece by the Macedonian kings, Philip and Alexander the Great, the independent poleis were incorporated into an empire and the ideal of democracy was replaced by that of individuals as subjects of a vast empire, or kingdoms that were cut out of the cloth of Alexander's empire. This led quite naturally into the later "world" empire of Rome. The loss of the polis caused people to turn inward for individual satisfaction in religion, philosophy and the arts.

The Hellenistic Age provided a higher standard of living for many in the beginning, but it also saw a growing disparity between the rich and the poor. This period saw an even greater development and application of scientific knowledge. The emphasis on individual fulfillment was demonstrated in the growth of the mystery cults, the individuality, realism and emotion in the arts, and the philosophies of Epicurus and Zeno. Beyond the achievements in the arts and sciences of that age, probably the greatest is the dissemination and preservation of Hellenic culture for the Roman Age and beyond that time to all of later Western civilization.

Suggestions for Further Reading

John Boardman, *Greek Art* (1985)

J. Boardman, J. Griffin & O. Murray eds., *Greece and the Hellenistic World* (1986)

Paul Cartledge, *Alexander the Great: The Hunt for a New Past* (2004); *Ancient Greece* (1998)

M.I. Finley, *The Ancient Economy*, 2nd Ed. (1985)

Robin Lane Fox, *The Classical World* (2006)

E.H.Gombrich, *The Story Of Art* (1995)

Michael Grant, *The Founders of the Western World* (1991)

Peter Green, *Alexander the Great* (1972); *From Alexander to Actium* (1990)

Peter Green ed., *Hellenistic History and Culture* (1993)

A.A. Long, *Hellenistic Philosophy: Stoics, Epicureans, Skeptics* (1974)

Thomas R. Martin, *Ancient Greece : From Prehistoric to Hellenistic Times* (1996)

J.D. Mikalson, *Athenian Popular Religion* (1983);

Religion in Hellenistic Athens (1998)

D. Brendan Nagle, *The Ancient World: A Social and Cultural History* (1979)

J. Onians, *Art and Thought in the Hellenistic Age* (1979)

F.W. Wallbank, *The Hellenistic World* (1981)

Chapter 4

THE ROMANS

According to legend, Rome, the ancient world's greatest city, was founded by twin brothers—Romulus and Remus. Descendents of the Trojan prince Aeneas, the twins were fathered by the war god Mars when he impregnated their mother the virgin-priestess Silvia in a temple where she served the goddess Vesta. Shortly after birth, the twin's uncle, Amulius, throws them into the Tiber River to die. Fortunately, Romulus and Remus did not die. They washed ashore where both were found by a female wolf that, aided by a woodpecker, cared for the infants until Faustulus, the king's herdsman, finds and brings them to his wife. The good shepherd and Acca Larentia, his wife, raise the twins as their own. After reaching adulthood Romulus and Remus leave home, kill Uncle Amulius, restore the throne to Numitor, their grandfather, and return to the shores of the Tiber River to build a new town.

The twins disagree about where to build the town and decide to seek signs from the Gods regarding its location. Romulus and Remus both claim that the signs favor their town site. Romulus begins his town on the Palatine Hill while Remus starts construction on the Aventine Hill. Remus mocks Romulus by jumping over the low town walls. Humiliated, Romulus kills Remus and continues to build his city, which he calls Rome after himself.

Rome needed people so Romulus allows criminals and outcasts from other cities to live there. Despite the acceptance of outlaws, Rome's population does not grow rapidly enough to suit Romulus, who decided to abduct women from Sabine, a neighboring tribe, so that Rome's population could increase through natural reproduction. The Sabine warriors, furious at the abduction and rape of their women, attack Rome under the leadership of Titus Tatius, their king. After several years of war between the Romans and Sabines, the Sabine women, who had come to accept their Latin husbands, brokered a peace between the two sides. The Sabines and Romans joined together as one people, and Romulus and Titus Tatius shared the throne until Titus Tatius was killed in battle. Afterwards, Romulus governed Rome alone for the rest of his earthly life, proving himself in war and peace. He created both the Roman Legion and the Roman Senate. Romulus did not die a mortal death. According to Rome's foundation myth, Mars, his godly father, took him into the sky in a fiery chariot during a violent storm. Thereafter, the Romans worshipped him as the god Quirinus. Rome, the town founded by Romulus the wolf child and murderer of his brother, eventually becomes the greatest empire in the Ancient World, conquering nation after nation and imposing Roman culture, influence, and government throughout the Mediterranean regions of Europe, West Asia, and Northern Africa.

Chronology

c. 507 Tarquin expelled the beginning of the Republic.

c. 494 First Secession of Plebeians. Establishment of tribunes.

471 Tribal Assembly established

451-450 The Twelve Tables

264-241 First Punic War

218-201 Second Punic War – Hannibal

149-146 Third Punic War

146 Destruction of Carthage

73-71 Revolt of Spartacus

60 First Triumvirate – Pompey, Crassus, Caesar

59 Full Consulship of Caesar

49-45 Civil War

44 Dictatorship and assassination of Caesar

43 Second Triumvirate: Octavian, Antony, Lepidus

36 Octavian is victorious over Lepidus

31 Defeat of Antony and Cleopatra by Octavius at Actium. Egypt annexed.

27 BC-14 AD Octavian Augustus

6 BC – 4 BC Birth of Jesus

66-70 First Jewish revolt

79-81 Titus

115-118 Jewish revolts

132-135 Second Jewish Revolt

161-180 Marcus Aurelius

249-251 Persecution of Christians

257 Renewed persecution of Christians

303-311 Great persecution of Christians

312 Constantine I the Great defeats Maxentius at the Milvian Bridge

312-337 Constantine I the Great and Licenius (d. 324)

313 Toleration to Christianity – Edicts of Milan

324-330 Eastern Capitol at Constantinople

325 Council of Nicaea – Establish Nicene Creed

363-364 Julian the Apostate – Restoration of Paganism
Jews told they could rebuild Temple of Solomon

373-397 Ambrose, bishop of Milan

395-430 Augustine bishop of Hippo in North Africa writes *Confessions*, *City of God*, hundreds of letters

404 Ravenna on Adriatic becomes new capitol of Western Empire

EARLY HISTORY AND DEVELOPMENT

While the story of Romulus and Remus is merely a myth, the city whose founding it depicts developed into the Ancient World's greatest empire. Modern archaeology indicates that the area near Rome on the Italian Peninsula had been inhabited by humans as early as 1000 B.C. By the middle of the eighth century B.C. two mud hut villages existed on the Palatine Hill near where legend says Romulus established Rome on April 21, 753 B.C. Defensive structures, a cemetery, and other artifacts have been discovered at that site. By 700 B.C. Sabine people had settled on the Esquiline Hill and other tribal people had likely settled on other of the seven hills on which Rome was eventually built. Early people likely were attracted to the seven hill region because of its fertile soil and its easily defensible location.

The Italian Peninsula is an extremely fertile agricultural region that extends more than 700 miles from the Alps in the north to the Mediterranean in the south. Only about 125 miles wide from east to west, the area stretches from the Adriatic Sea on the east to the Tyrrhenian Sea to the west. Separated from the peninsula by a narrow strait in the south lies the island of Sicily, which is about 90 miles from the North African coast. Soil throughout the Italian Peninsula was deposited by rivers and enriched by volcanic ash from eruptions of Stromboli, Etna, Vesuvius, and other volcanoes. Early human inhabitants of this region lived on a land whose agricultural, economic, social, and political potential was virtually limitless. Tribal people, including Greek colonists in the south, Etruscans in the north, Sabines and Samnites in the mountains, and the Lucanians and Latinums in central Italy, spoke various dialects of Indo-European languages, including Latin, and fought with neighboring peoples until all were eventually conquered by Rome.

Rome's geographical location gave its people the opportunity for expansion. The seven hills on which the city developed were high enough to protect its inhabitants from the flooding of the Tiber River and provide security against invasion. Because the Tiber flowed to the sea, Rome realized trade opportunities with other peoples throughout the Mediterranean region.

Several human groups were important to Rome's early development. Perhaps the most important was the Latinums. These people, from whom the word Latin is derived, lived on the Tiber River in central Italy near where present-day Rome is located. The small Latin villages began to grow during the eighth century B.C., developing into a large city over the next two centuries as a result of contact with two other peoples—Greeks who had established colonies in southern parts of the Italian Peninsula and Etruscans in the north. Contact between Rome and Magna Graecia, as the Greek colonies established in the south during the seventh and eighth centuries B.C. were called, brought Latin people into contact with the most advanced civilization in the Mediterranean at that time. Latin people began to adopt many aspects of Greek culture.

Latin contact with Etruscan people in the northern part of the Italian Peninsula also furthered the development of Rome. Although historians disagree about the degree of influence Etruscan civilization had on Roman culture, the fact that Rome was influenced by the Etruscans is undeniable. For two centuries—from the eighth to the sixth century B.C.—the twelve city-states of people who inhabited the province of Etruria dominated northern regions on the Italian Peninsula. The Etruscans were organized into a loose confederation located between the Arno River to the north, the Tiber River in the south and east, and the Mediterranean Sea on the west. Etruscans engaged in mining metals such as silver, copper, and iron, were excellent mariners who traded throughout the Mediterranean, engaged in piracy, and contacted most peoples living in the Mediterranean region. Etruscan artifacts have been unearthed by archeologists in most lands bordering the Mediterranean.

Etruscans likely influenced Rome's art, architecture, alphabet, calendar, government, and religious development. Numerous buildings in Rome, such as the Temple of Jupitor on the Capitoline Hill, appear to be Etruscan in origin. The Roman alphabet was likely borrowed from the Etruscans who by 700 B.C. had adopted it from the Greeks. The Etruscans eliminated some of the Greek vowels not needed in their language and changed some of the consonants. The Romans then adopted this alphabet that originally consisted of 21 letters. Rome also appears to have adopted the Etruscan system of two names for each individual—a personal name and a family or clan moniker—and the Etruscan calendar that consisted of twelve months. Politically, the Etruscans introduced the city-state form of government to Italy and other Mediterranean cultures and forced inhabitants of the Italian Peninsula to develop tightly organized political systems to maintain their independence. Etruscans also served as Roman kings in Rome's early years and evidence suggests that the Etruscans dominated Rome during much of the sixth century B.C. The great triad—fate, fortune, and unpredictability—important in Roman religion also appears to be partly adopted from Etruscan religious beliefs. Roman art, like that of the Etruscans, depicts realism. Examples include images of deceased people placed on or near burial coffins and urns.

The Romans, like the Etruscans and other Mediterranean peoples, were heavily influenced by the Greeks. Archeological evidence suggests that Latin people adopted their religion from Greece. Prior to contact with Greek civilizations, inhabitants of the Italian Peninsula worshipped various gods as protective spirits in the open air. Economic and social intercourse with the Etruscans and Greeks led the Romans to adopt the Greek family of Gods and the custom of depicting gods and goddesses in the form of statues and erecting temples in which to worship them. Ancient Romans believed that spirits were present everywhere—in the house, on the farm, and in the woods. Spirits also determined all things, including the weather and the fate of individuals. The Lares, or ghosts of dead ancestors, for example, watched over the home and its occupants while the Penates guarded grain stored for human and livestock food. Vesta guarded the hearth and Janus the door. The father of all gods was Jupiter (this was Zeus in Greek civilizations). He watched over the heavens and ruled all other deities. Mars, known as Ares to the Greeks, oversaw livestock, and Genius was responsible for male reproduction. Within the temples and shrines, Roman priests performed ceremonies and rituals to appease the gods and goddesses so they would leave humans alone and allow them to prosper. Romans often tried to strike bargains with various deities through prayers and offerings. Initially, Roman religious beliefs were aniministic (the Gods were believed to take the form of animals) but due to Greek influence gradually became anthropomorphistic (took the form of humans).

Once Roman government developed, household deities were modified into state deities. Vesta, the hearth goddess, for example, became the guardian of the state. Mars became the protector of soldiers and armies while Janus, the door god, became protector of Rome's entry ways. Priests employed by the state attempted to appease all Rome's gods and goddesses so that the city state would prosper. The Roman government operated schools to train priests in state religious rituals. At first, these institutions were open only to individuals from noble families but over time evolved to accept commoners. While a few priests were employed full time, most were part time positions in which the priest followed another occupation to earn a livelihood. The head priest was the Pontifex Maximus. Elected to the position, he oversaw all state clergy and until the fourth century B.C., he administered Roman law with the aid of lesser pontiffs. Priests were allowed to interpret and administer law because Romans believed that a violation of the law offended the gods. The pontifex maximus also was responsible for selecting the six Vestal Virgins whose job was to ensure that the fire at the civic hearth was never extinguished. The Vestal Virgins were chosen between the ages of six and ten and required to remain virgins for thirty years. A Vestal Virgin who engaged in sexual intercourse before the 30-year period elapsed faced execution.

Astrology was also an important component of Roman religious life. Many Romans could not accept that life was controlled merely by fate and fortune or by Gods far removed from humans. For them, life's direction was found in the sun and planets and their position in relation to the earth and each other. Planetary alignment determined good or bad luck, life or death, sickness or health, success or failure. The problem was creating a system that enabled humans to know what affect cosmic forces had on life. Emperors, nobles, and commoners all consulted astrologers in an attempt to divine the future. Few Romans would make an important decision without consulting an astrologer. Military leaders, for example, would not take troops into battle, legislatures would not enact laws, the emperor would not begin construction of a building, and farmers would not plant a field until an astrologer said the time was right for these activities. Roman coins usually displayed signs of the zodiac, which is an indication of the importance Romans attached to astrology.

Magic, like astrology, was an important component of religion among Ancient Romans. Although magic was not as important as the cosmic forces in directing life, it was believed to be instrumental over lesser matters. Witches, for example, had the ability to cast spells on people and animals but could not control the gods and goddesses or movement of the planets or their relationship to the earth and each other. Even though some Romans were skeptical, in general Roman culture embraced any idea that might give humans control over all unseen and little understood forces in life. After Rome became an empire and dominated the Mediterranean world, it generally adopted the religious beliefs of conquered people, incorporating them into Roman society. Romans thus exhibited a religious toleration and developed numerous religious cults centered around a particular deity. An individual could belong to as many cults as he desired.

THE EARLY KINGDOM

Pre-Expansion 800-509 B.C.

Although Rome's foundation myth involving Romulus and Remus is probably not true, reliable evidence indicates that Latin peoples living in the vicinity of Rome began to create a city-state around 800 B.C. The earliest inhabitants of Rome were likely a mixture of tribes including Latins, Sabines, Etruscans, and others that lived in central Italy. By about 700 B.C. the population of Rome had expanded to the point that ancient religious festivals such as the fertility rite of the Luperci in which individuals ran naked through the village every February 15 and the Palilia ceremony to protect livestock being sent out to pasture on April 21 were being held. Archeological evidence also suggests that some sort of religious union of tribal people living in the vicinity of Rome had occurred by 700 B.C. as the festivals of the Septimontium and the Argei were held at Rome. Contact with Greek and other Mediterranean peoples had also occurred by 700 B.C. as archaeologists have unearthed foreign vases dating to this period. It was also around this time that Romans began to construct temples for worship, likely an adaption from the Ancient Greeks.

Recent archaeological evidence also suggests that significant change occurred in Rome about 600 B.C. Historians generally conclude that this was around the time that Rome became an official city state. Burials where the Forum would be located were halted, swampy areas in the city were drained, streets were paved, the area around the Forum was also paved, and construction on a number of buildings was completed by 500 B.C. These activities apparently mark the beginning of Roman political history and signify a growing economy and development of a cultural consciousness among tribal peoples of west central Italy.

From 700-509 B.C. the Roman city-state was ruled by numerous kings. Roman mythology says seven different kings ruled during this period, but historians have generally discounted the accuracy of that figure. The exact number of kings that ruled Rome is unknown. Most likely, Rome was ruled by Etruscan kings during this period. The last one, Tarquin, was certainly Etruscan. Evidence indicates that under Etruscan control, Rome developed a tradition of military expansion that would later define the empire. Etruscan/Latin armies apparently destroyed the religious site of Alba Longa, marched up the Tiber River, conquering villages such as Gabii, and captured the coastal salt mining town of Ostia.

The Roman king, who was chiefly a military and religious leader, was elected by the army. As the primary military commander, the king led an army organized into legions. This army, comprised of soldiers armed with spears, swords, and shields, was grouped in the phalanx formation. Before leading his legions into battle, the Roman king prayed to the gods and sought to know the outcome of the battle through the auspices. During periods of war, the king had absolute authority over Roman citizens. He could tax the population, enforce laws, force individuals to serve in the army, and order executions of state enemies.

Assisting and advising the king was the Senate. The Senate was made up of prominent men whom the king called into session. When in session, the Senate was divided into thirty groups, and a resolution had to receive a majority of votes from each group before it was accepted. Only issues raised by the king could be considered, and no Senator could speak without permission from the king.

The ancient Roman city-state was divided into three tribes, each of which were generally required to pay taxes, provide soldiers for the army, and contribute two Vestal Virgins for the Vesta cult. Within each tribe, individuals were divided into family clans called gentes. Each family carried the name of the clan along with an individual personal name. The clans were politically powerful in Ancient Rome. Lower classes, called plebians, were often dependent on the clan head for support. In return for this support, the plebian pledged political and military allegiance to the clan head, called the patrician. There was a vast chasm economically, politically, and culturally between plebians and patricians.

Only patricians could serve in the Senate or become priests. All peoples, including clans, and their heads, were expected to obey the state.

Roman families were organized patriarchially. Fathers were head of the family for as long as they lived. All children, even adult sons, were legally under the control of the father. Only at the father's death was the son an independent adult. Mothers and daughters held honored places in Roman families but were legally under the control of fathers and husbands.

ROMAN EXPANSION 509-133 B.C.

The Early and Middle Republic

Like most governments, Rome desired to expand its territory. Rome's early expansion was largely confined to conquest of the Italian Peninsula. From 509 to 264 B.C. Roman legions marched north and south, conquering all peoples living on the Italian Peninsula. At the beginning of the Republic Period (about 509 B.C.) Rome's total territory comprised no more than 500 square miles. Over the next 175 years the land Rome controlled quadrupled. By 338 B.C. Roman legions had conquered all 2,000 miles of Latium and were marching into both Etrurian and Samnite lands. By 265 B.C. Rome controlled nearly 50,000 square miles on the Italian Peninsula from modern Pisa, which was then called Pisae, to modern Rimini, then called Ariminum. By 146 B.C. Rome had added Sicily, Cisalpine Gaul, Sardinia, Corsica, Spain, Tunisia (formerly Carthage), Macadeonia, and Greece. Rome's empire was the most powerful the ancient world had known.

Rome's conquest of the Mediterranean World was largely unplanned and was not carried out according to a set time table. Roman expansion was mostly built on threats to its interests as the city-state's territory grew. Over time, Rome was drawn into foreign conflicts and eventually acquired an empire. A desire for economic and territorial expansion likely played a role in Rome's aggression against its neighbors as did fear of and prejudice against outsiders. Rome also engaged in conquest for political reasons, to placate its citizens by providing them with plunder, and because of personal ambitions of military leaders such as Julius Caesar. Leaders and soldiers who were victorious in battle could often claim honor, riches, and political advancement. Victorious generals, for example, were viewed as heroes within Roman society and allowed to celebrate victories by leading their troops in a parade through Rome to Jupiter's Temple.

Conquest begat more conquest. After gaining control of territory surrounding the city in the fourth century B.C., Rome felt threatened by the Samnites in central and southern Italy. Once the Samnites were conquered, Rome felt threatened by Carthage across the Mediterranean in North Africa. After Carthage was defeated in the third century B.C., Rome felt threatened by the Macedonian Empire. After the Macedonians were defeated, Rome turned toward the Seleucid kingdom in Syria. Thus, conquest of one territory created new threats that Rome had to meet.

Roman military success was largely the result of organization, flexibility, discipline, and tactics used by its armies. The Roman army was organizationally flexible enough to borrow tactics from foreign foes that suited the situation the army faced at the time. For example, Roman armies borrowed from the Greeks the Hoplite Phalanx that was particularly effective when fighting on level plains. When the Hoplite Phalanx proved inadequate in mountainous terrain, Rome, after a defeat at the hands of the Samnite in 321 B.C.,

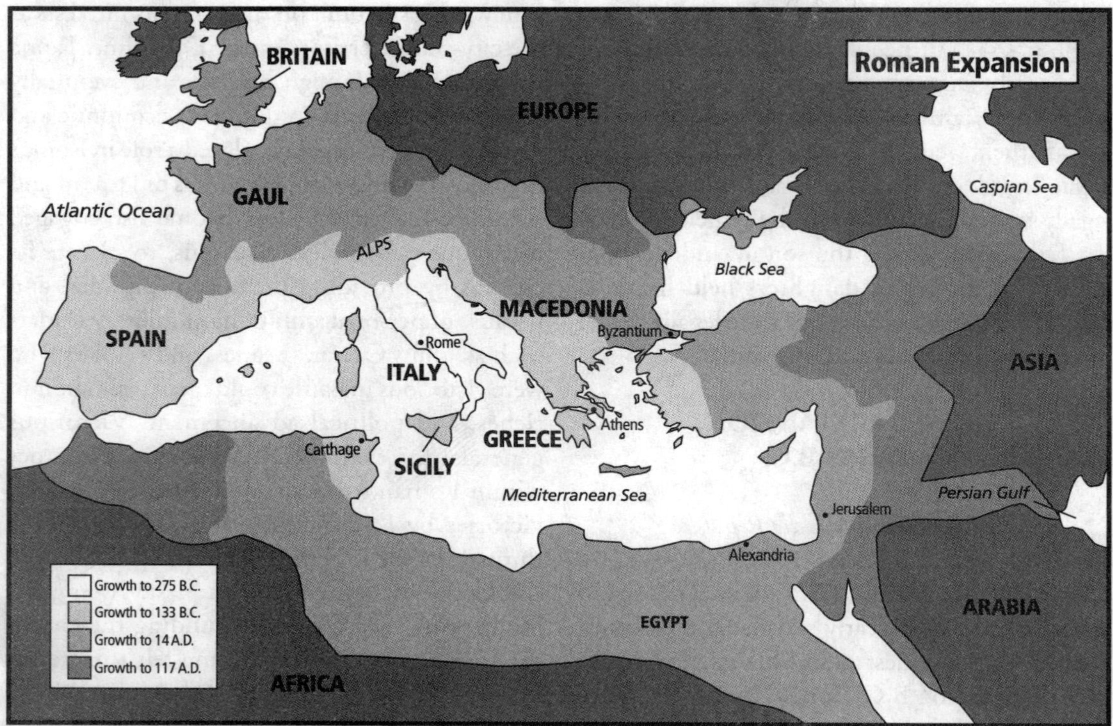

adopted the Samnite method of fighting by organizing their soldiers into legions. Unlike the phalanx, which basically was a large group of troops massed together into one unit, the legion was comprised of three lines divided into thirty maniples and sixty centuries. Each century, whose number varied, was led by an officer called a centurion. Each legion was organized into squares with space left between groups of soldiers. During battle, each legion closed the gaps between the groups of soldiers. During the initial phases of battle, each legion threw its spears at long range, which was a tactic designed to create disorder within the enemy's ranks. After having discharged their spears, the Roman legions then engaged the enemy with sword and shield. The Roman army was the most maneuverable in the Ancient World, which accounted for its success against Rome's foes.

Rome's military success was also aided by the treatment of soldiers. Rome, unlike most governments, paid soldiers on a regular basis and rewarded them with land taken from defeated foes. This system meant that morale among Roman soldiers was generally high and the promise of conquered land gave Roman soldiers an incentive to fight that enemy soldiers lacked.

Roman diplomacy was another factor that sometimes led to war and conquest. Rome sometimes joined into military and economic alliances with other peoples. In most of these alliances Rome provided protection to other states in return for economic concessions. When outsiders threatened Rome's allies, Roman armies were often sent to defend the client state, and Rome usually added territory to its domain as a result. After becoming the dominant city-state on the Italian Peninsula, Rome created an alliance of city-states called the Latin League. While Rome was the dominant city-state in the Latin League, other cities generally had rights under law equal to Rome's. For example, citizens of any League member could marry a member from any other state within the Latin League and could also claim citizenship in any Latin polis they chose to live in. All Latin League members could trade freely with Rome and were afforded military protection by their association with Rome.

The Latin League was dissolved after Rome successfully defeated a revolt from League members from 340 to 338 B.C. After dissolution of the Latin League, Rome annexed outright several former members, allowed others to retain military and political alliances with Rome. Others, however, aligned, for a time, with non-Latin states against Rome. Eventually, Rome defeated all its Latin enemies and controlled the entire Italian Peninsula. Rome also annexed many non-Latin territories its armies conquered, giving their people the status of near citizen, meaning that they had all rights of Roman citizens except voting. Non-Latin peoples were also given the right of local self-determination. Rome was thus the first nation to make outsiders citizens. Before, in the Ancient World, defeated peoples were usually killed, adopted, enslaved, or banished from their homeland. Rome's leniency with defeated peoples won support and loyalty from these people for the government. Conquered provinces often provided many soldiers Roman armies used to conquer other peoples. In fact, non-Latin soldiers enabled Rome to defeat the Gauls, Etruscans, Samnites, and Greeks.

Vital to Roman conquest of its Mediterranean Empire were roads. Rome constructed a series of stone paved roads throughout the Mediterranean World. These roads were used by the army to quickly dispatch troops to deal with any riot, rebellion, invasion, or disturbance within its lands. These roads also linked various colonies and provinces to Rome economically. As the saying went, "all roads led to Rome." Manufacturers, farmers, and merchants could quickly and easily transport crops, products, and merchandise to markets throughout the Roman Empire.

THE PUNIC WARS AND THE ROMAN EXPANSION FROM 264-133 B.C.

Carthage, an empire across the Mediterranean in North Africa, challenged Rome's expansion, and the two empires fought three major conflicts between 264 and 146 B.C. The city of Carthage, founded by Phoenician sailors around 750 B.C. in North Africa, had by 264 B.C. become the dominant empire on the southern side of the Mediterranean. Carthaginian lands included the northern areas of Africa, along with southern Spain, Sardinia, Corsica, and part of Sicily. After Rome began to expand, a clash between the two empires became inevitable.

War first broke out between Carthage and Rome in 264 B.C. over Sicily. Rome felt threatened by the Carthaginian conquest of Messana, a Sicilian city-state. Roman leaders decided that intervention was necessary to protect Roman interests. Carthage was a naval power while Rome was a land power at the beginning of the First Punic War. Rome had to construct a navy to deal with the Carthaginian fleet. Rome's army, however, proved decisive. Although Carthage had perhaps the most brilliant and capable generals the Ancient World produced in the Barca family (the most famous would be Hannibal), Roman military policies were superior to those of Carthage. Roman soldiers were simply more loyal to the empire because they had Roman citizenship, were paid a regular salary, and given lands from Rome's conquests while Carthaginian soldiers were mostly mercenaries who were treated badly by their commanders and held in contempt by political leaders. Consequently, Roman soldiers fought harder and were loyal to the empire while some Carthaginian soldiers exhibited a great deal of disloyalty and often rebelled against their commanders.

Rome, despite losing numerous ships and thousands of soldiers, defeated Carthage after more than two decades of war in 241 B.C. Polybius, a Roman historian, called the First Punic War the deadliest war even fought. Under the settlement with Carthage, Rome took Sicily. In 238 B.C. Rome forced Carthage to surrender Corsica and Sardinia and pay tribute to Rome.

A second conflict, called the Second Punic War, broke out in 218 B.C. This war, which lasted until 201 B.C., occurred after Carthage decided to challenge Rome's dominance of the Mediterranean and seek revenge for its defeat in the First Punic War. To effectively challenge Rome, Carthage, under leadership of the Barca kings, decided to expand their territory in the Iberian Peninsula (modern day Spain) in 237 B.C. Hamilcar Barca, father of the soon to be famous Hannibal, hoped to use metal deposits, especially silver and copper, to make Carthage the dominant power in the Mediterranean. Rome became concerned about Carthaginian expansion in Spain, and in the mid 220s B.C. tensions between the two empires began to increase. Hannibal Barca, the new Carthaginian general, decided that he would attack Rome on the Italian Peninsula. Since Carthage did not have a naval fleet (the Carthaginian fleet had been destroyed in the First Punic War) Hannibal decided to launch a surprise attack on Rome by marching his army across the Alps from Spain. In 218 B.C. Hannibal left Spain with a veteran army, making a dangerous crossing of the snow covered Alps. Included in Hannibal's army were war elephants. Overall, about 25,000 soldiers survived the trek across the Alps. Once across, Hannibal recruited another 15,000 soldiers from tribal people in the Po River Valley. Hannibal, perhaps the most brilliant general the Ancient World produced, defeated Roman forces at the Battle of Cannae in 216 B.C. Here, Hannibal's smaller army of about 40,000 defeated 60,000 Roman soldiers, which at the time was the largest army Rome had ever amassed, killing approximately 30,000 Roman soldiers. This represented the worst defeat in Roman History.

After the defeat at Cannae, Roman generals refused to fight another major battle, a strategy which bought them time to regroup and strengthen their forces. Instead of rushing into another decisive battle, Roman commanders fought skirmishes against Hannibal in a campaign designed to harass the Carthaginian army. Hannibal, try as he might, could not force Rome into a decisive battle that would enable Carthage to completely defeat Rome, and Hannibal lacked the forces necessary to attack Rome itself. During the time that Rome regrouped, a new general—Publius Cornelius Scipio—took command of Roman forces. Scipio, unlike previous Roman generals, understood Hannibal's strategy and countered it. Scipio invaded Spain, capturing Carthaginian colonies there before crossing the Mediterranean to attack Carthage proper. This Roman strategy forced Hannibal to retreat back into North Africa to defend his homeland. Scipio then met Hannibal in a decisive battle at Zama in modern day Tunisia. Scipio defeated Hannibal, and Rome's domination of the Mediterranean World was complete.

Rome and Carthage fought a third war from 149 to 146 B.C. Most historians have concluded that the Third Punic War was unnecessary. The treaty that ended the Second Punic War gave Rome practically all colonies Carthage owned, stripped the city of its wealth, and generally made it vastly inferior in military power to Rome. Roman leaders, particularly Scipio Aemilianus, wanted to claim glory in battle and revived old fears about Carthage to achieve his objective. Aemilianus laid siege to Carthage for three years, forcing the city to surrender in 146 B.C. Roman troops then completely destroyed the city, enslaved its population, and added Carthaginian land to Rome's empire as the province of Africa.

Victory in the Punic Wars whetted Rome's appetite for more conquest, which led to conflict against Philip V of Macedonia. Roman forces won the First Macedonian War in 205 B.C. The Roman government decided to attack Philip after winning the Second Punic War because he had made an alliance with Hannibal after Rome's defeat at Cannae. The Roman legions easily defeated Philip's forces at Cynoscephalae, Greece in 197 B.C. during the Second Macedonian War and began the process of making Greece into a Roman Province. The Greeks did not easily submit to Roman authority, however, and Rome had to fight a third war with Macedonia before completely subduing the city in 148 B.C. and adding the Province of Macedonia to the Roman Empire.

The Macedonia Wars caused Rome to fight wars in the Middle East against Greek colonies in Egypt, Seleucia, and Pergamum. King Antiochus III, the Seleucid leader, was perhaps Rome's most formidable Hellenistic foe in the Middle East. Aided by Hannibal, Antiochus challenged Roman control of Greece. The Seleucid challenge did not succeed. Roman forces easily defeated the Seleucids, driving them out of both Greece and Anatolia in 188 B.C. This victory, coupled with the annihilation of Carthage, meant that Rome would be the supreme empire in the Ancient World. The Greeks and other people were forced to submit to Roman domination. Any challenge to Roman authority and power was met by force. In 146 B.C., for example, Rome completely destroyed the Greek city-state of Corinth to crush a rebellion against Roman authority. The destruction of Corinth served to warn other peoples about the futility of resistance to Rome.

Roman victory provided an impetus to add land to the empire. After Rome annexed Greece, Macedonia, and Carthaginian lands, Rome did not hesitate to add other territory when the opportunity arose. Eventually, Rome annexed parts of Gaul, took territory in Asia (modern Turkey and the Middle East), and Northern Africa. Rome got the Kingdom of Pergamum in 133 B.C. after Attalus III died without a male heir. Attalus, who was a Roman ally, simply decreed that Rome should annex his lands. Rome made Pergamum the Province of Asia. Rome also annexed the Seleucid kingdom (modern Syria) and Ptolemaic Egypt during the first century B.C.

THE LATTER REPUBLIC 133 B.C.- 14 A.D.

Modern historians generally view the year 133 B.C. as a watershed year, one that marks a turning point in Roman History. Rome was at its height of power, having conquered much of the Mediterranean world and adopted large parts of Greek civilization. The century and a half from 133 B.C. to 14 A.D. was one of tremendous change for Rome, which had grown from a small republic to a far-flung empire. Decades of warfare gripped the Mediterranean world as conquered people struggled to overthrow their Roman masters and the republic became a monarchy.

Rome's trouble was rooted in economic and social change acquisition of an empire brought.

By 133 B.C. Roman traders dominated the Mediterranean economy, importing slaves, gems, spices, and various manufactured goods into Italy and sending various Italian products, including olive oil, wine, metal products, textiles, and other goods to both its eastern and western provinces. Facilitation of this vast trade required the replacement of Rome's traditional barter economy with a monetary one. As the use of coinage increased, poverty increased among the masses. Many free land holders lost their land and were forced to work on farms of large landowners or move to cities in search of work. As land increasingly became consolidated into the hands of the wealthy, slavery was used more and more to work the land. The economic position of ordinary Romans became more precarious. Food, in particular, became difficult for agricultural workers, household servants, and workers in shops and factories to acquire at times. Much of Rome's countryside was inhabited by agricultural slaves who were literally worked to death by landowners. This situation produced numerous revolts throughout the empire. In 133 B.C., for example, a revolt occurred in Sicily. Other slave insurrections later broke out across Italy, terrifying the Roman population.

Rome's military system was also altered due to the economic and social changes wrought by empire. In the middle and early republic periods Rome had relied upon the land owning peasant for the bulk of its soldiers. As the ranks of peasant land owners decreased, Rome increasingly turned toward forced military conscription to meet its military needs. All Roman males between the age of 17 and 46 were required to serve in the army for a period of time that ranged from five to twenty-two years. The required military service made it difficult for Roman families to survive economically.

Corruption within the Roman government and economy added to problems the empire faced during the period of the latter republic. Wealthy Romans became even wealthier. Army generals, diplomats, tax collectors, judges, businessmen, and others amassed great wealth in land, slaves, and money through graft. Roman officials commonly skimmed from the public treasury. Gaius Verres, the governor of Sicily from 73 B.C. to 71 B.C. skimmed thousands of pounds of silver from Sicily. Cicero, the famous orator, also stole much silver from Cilicia, the Roman province he governed from 51 to 50 B.C.

Wealthy Romans also took more than their fair share of public land (land Rome conquered). Under Roman law, an individual could legally claim 320 acres of land. Many wealthy Romans, however, claimed much more land than the law permitted. A common practice wealthy Romans often used to acquire even more land was to drive families of conscripted soldiers off the land through use of the court system or by physical force. Roman law made it difficult for citizens of modest means to sue wealthy people who illegally took their land because the displaced farmer was required to physically bring the wealthy crook into court himself, a task that most poor people could not accomplish.

In general, after 133 B.C. Rome's ordinary citizens were in a bad state. Wealthy citizens displayed their wealth in ostentatious ways and got laws passed that segregated rich from poor, insulating them from the worst elements of Roman society. The poor, however, faced a dire situation. The most that a poor person could expect was a life that was brutal, nasty, and short. Given this situation, it is not surprising that most of Rome's population increasingly became embittered and turned toward religious emotionalism for solace, which the Roman government eventually banned in a Senatorial decree.

Two brothers, Tiberius and Gaius Gracchus attempted to solve the problems besetting Rome. Tiberius became the Roman Tribune in 133 B.C. and shortly thereafter began a program of land reform. In particular, Tiberius proposed to limit acreage held by the wealthy and allow renters or tenant farmers to claim up to 600 acres of land they worked. Tiberius' reform also provided state funds to help the poor peasants make improvements on the land they owned and allowed the government to confiscate all surplus land, which would be subdivided into small parcels and given to the poor. Tiberius' objective was to create within Rome a flourishing peasant middle class that could be used to provide soldiers for the army.

Wealthy Romans, as might be expected, strongly opposed the land reform law and persuaded Octavius, another Tribune, to veto the bill. Tiberius reacted by using the veto to force an election to vote Octavius out of office. This election was illegal under Roman law, but with the ouster of Octavius the land reform bill became law. Tiberius then appointed himself, brother Gaius, and Appius Claudius to a commission to reclaim and redistribute surplus lands. Wealthy conservative landowners who controlled the Senate, however, voted not to appropriate funds for the commission to carry out its purpose. Tiberius again violated Roman law, which allowed the Senate to control public money, by asking the people to vote on a declaration allowing the Pergamum treasure given to Rome in the last king's will to be used to fund land reform. When Tiberius announced that he was going to seek another term as Tribune, a revolt broke out. An ex-Tribune led a group of conservative landowners into the Senate chamber who clubbed Tiberius and about 300 of his supporters to death.

Tiberius' death did not stop the land reform. In 123, Gaius Gracchus was elected Tribune after promising to continue his brother's reforms. Gaius not only revived the land commission but enacted even more liberal social programs. Perhaps the most important was enactment of a law that stabilized the price of grain and prevented it from rising so high that Rome's poor could not afford to eat. Gaius also gave the equestrian class (best defined as upper middle class businessmen a step below aristocrats) authority to collect taxes in Asia and serve on juries that tried aristocrats. Many political analysts believe that Gaius enacted these laws to secure support of the poor and businesses classes against aristocratic landowners.

While these and other programs, such as building roads, throughout the empire were popular and generally successful, Gaius ran into trouble when he tried to establish a Roman colony on the site of Carthage for the poor and give Roman citizenship to non-Romans. Sensing that Gaius had lost popular support as a result of these proposals, wealthy conservatives succeeded in electing Livius Drusus Tribune. After Gaius' defeat, a civil war broke out between conservatives and liberals. Gaius was eventually killed along with several thousand supporters. Their wealth was confiscated and used to build a temple to Concord.

Rome's troubles had become more acute by 100 B.C. The economic crisis had evolved into a political and military crisis. The crisis worsened when conflict over succession in the Numidia kingdom, a state controlled by Rome, broke out. Roman armies commanded by Senators made little progress quelling rebellion in Numidia (modern Algeria) and in repelling Germanic invaders in Gaul. A newcomer to Roman politics, Gaius Marius was elected consul in 107 B.C. and saved the day. Marius, who was popular among the common people, initiated a series of reforms that improved the Roman army, including barring camp followers, making soldiers carry their weapons rather than having slaves carry them, expanding the army's size by allowing non-property holders to serve (this created a professional military as afterward landless peasants with no hope for the future could make the army a career), and combining smaller legions into larger units called cohorts. These reforms greatly strengthened the Roman army, enabling Marius to defeat Jugurtha (nephew of the deceased king Masinissa who had usurped the Numidian throne from Adherbal and Hiempsal, the sons of Masinissa) and defeat the Cimbri, Teutone, and other Germanic tribes in Gaul.

Marius became the most powerful politician in the Roman Empire because of his military success. He won six straight elections for Consul even though his elections were unconstitutional. Marius' popularity rested on concern for ordinary soldiers. In 100 B.C. he introduced legislation asking the Senate to provide land to soldiers. When the Senate refused to pass this law, common people rioted. The Senate ordered Marius to arrest the rioters but Marius refused and instead had several Senators murdered, which caused ordinary Romans to back strong leaders like Marius who promised to look after their interests.

Marius' downfall occurred as a result of the Social War, which gave rise to a new leader, Lucius Cornelius Sulla. The Social War began in 91 B.C. when Italian people revolted, demanding Roman citizenship. When their request was denied, the Italians broke away from Rome and created a country they called Italia (its capital was at Corfinium). Rome, in an effort to avoid war, quickly granted citizenship to the rebels, who would pledge allegiance to Rome. Some rebels, however, refused the offer of citizenship in return for loyalty and continued the effort to secede. Rome had to dispatch troops to crush the rebellion. Sulla, who commanded the Roman troops, easily defeated the Italian rebels and as a result, was elected Consul in 88 B.C. The most important result of this conflict was that all people on the Italian peninsula were now Roman citizens. Within the next 50 years Italian and Roman people would develop into a unified people, and Rome was no longer a city state.

The second conflict broke out with Mithridates ,a king in northern Anatolia, in 89 B.C. Mithridates invaded Roman territory in northern Anatolia and slaughtered in one day 80,000 people in Asia Minor. Mithridates also formed alliances with Athens and other Greek city states. Sulla led an army against Mithridates. Marius, jealous of Sulla, raised an army of his own and fought with Sulla over command of Roman forces. Rather than obey a Senate order giving command of Roman forces to Marius, Sulla turned his army around and marched it to Rome, forcing Marius and most Senators to flee in fear of their lives. Sulla, after securing Rome, marched east to meet Mithridates. During Sulla's absence Marius returned, took control of Rome and executed many of Sulla's supporters. After being elected Consul for the seventh time, Marius died of natural causes, and Cornelius Cinna replaced him as Consul.

Sulla fought against Mithridates from 87 to 85 B.C. After Mithridates was defeated, Sulla returned to Rome where he fought in a civil war for control of the empire. Sulla's forces had won the Italian Civil War by 82 B.C. This conflict ravaged much of the Italian countryside before the fighting ended with Sulla's victory at Colline Gate. Sulla than had himself appointed dictator in a guise to reform the Roman constitution. Rome was a republic no longer.

Sulla's first order as dictator was to settle things with his enemies from the rebellion. He declared all his political opponents as outlaws and offered rewards for their death. Their land was confiscated, their family's right to vote was taken away, and those captured were executed. Thousands of people perished under Sulla's dictatorship, and Sulla gave land to soldiers who supported him. Entire communities were sometimes displaced to make room for Sulla's soldiers. Sulla also tried to reestablish the Senate and added 300 new members who supported him. Sulla's most important reform was of the courts. He created seven permanent courts to hear trials. Juries in these courts were comprised of senators. Trials before popularity elected assemblies were abolished and wealthy Romans generally were the only people with access to the courts. Much of the Roman legal system was based on the system Sulla established. Sulla retired due to poor health in 79 B.C. and died the next year.

END OF THE ROMAN REPUBLIC

Many historians date the beginning of the end of the Roman Republic to difficulties Rome faced during the last century prior to the birth of Christ. In this century Rome's military problems multiplied as Germanic tribes from northern Europe migrated into southern Gaul in search of a warmer climate. Rome was thus forced to dispatch its legions to repel the invaders. The Germanic wars weakened the Senatorial government and gave ambitious generals opportunity for political advancement. Military reforms undertaken by Marius that transformed the Roman army from one of volunteers to a reliance on professional soldiers created an army whose soldiers expected their generals to economically provide for them. Economic pressures generated by Rome's soldiers caused generals to grab more power.

Adding to Rome's problems during the latter years of the Republic was an inept Senate. Senators were generally conservatives who were more interested in looking after their personal interests than doing what was best for Rome. The Senate itself was split into various factions. Each faction incited mobs to intimidate its opposition. This situation produced a government that had lost the ability to govern. The Roman political climate was ripe for an ambitious General flush with success from fighting in the Germanic wars to take control of the Republic.

Three ambitious generals, Pompey the Great, Julius Caesar, Marcus Licinius Crassus, began to jockey for political power. All three agreed that they, not the inept Senate, should control Rome. In 60 B.C., they entered into an agreement forming a coalition government. Known as the First Triumvirate, this government brought an end to republican government in Rome. Distrust of each other brought an end to the First Triumvirate. Crassus was killed in battle when his army was defeated at Carrhae in Syria in 53 B.C. Pompey, frightened by Caesar's military success against the Germanic invaders in Gaul, renounced the Triumvirate agreement and again joined the Senate led by Cato the Younger. In 49 B.C. the Senate ordered Caesar to relinquish his military command. Rather than obey the Senate's order, Caesar moved his army out of Gaul, crossed the Rubicorn River, the northern boundary of Rome, and initiated a conflict with Pompey and Cato for control of Rome. Caesar defeated Pompey at Pharsalus, Greece in 48 B.C. By 45 B.C. Caesar had defeated Cato's forces and won complete control of Rome. The Roman Republic existed no longer.

Once in power, Caesar instituted numerous reforms. He broke the power of old Roman families and gave Roman citizenship to many peoples throughout Italy and the Roman provinces. Caesar also stacked the Senate with his supporters by increasing its number by a third

Julius Caesar's head is graced by a laurel wreath, an ancient symbol of victory, honor, and glory.

(going from 600 Senators to 900) and made it possible for provincial supporters in Gaul to hold Senate membership. Caesar also began a public building program in Rome, lowered the nation's debt, established colonies in different parts of the Mediterranean for military veterans, and introduced the Julian calendar that had a year consisting of 365 ¼ days. Borrowed from Egypt, the Julian calendar became operational on January 1, 45 B.C.

Caesar also forced the Senate to name him dictator for life. Caesar's contempt for republican government, however, infuriated members of the Senate. They feared Caesar's power and wanted to restore republican government to Rome. Thus, a group of aristocrats plotted to kill Caesar. On March 15, 44 B.C. a group of conservative Senators led by Junius Brutus and Cassius Longinus stabbed Caesar to death in front of a statue of Pompey at the Pompey Theater, the place the Senate was meeting at that time. Brutus, Longinus and other conservatives erroneously believed that Caesar's assassination would restore republican government to Rome. Rather than being greeted as liberators by the Roman people, a mob forced the conspirators to take refuge on Capitoline Hill, as Rome was plunged into civil war yet again.

Mark Anthony, one of Caesar's lieutenants, briefly seized control of Rome's government. Anthony's dominance did not last long. Octavius, Caesar's grandnephew and adopted son returned to Rome. There, he raised a private army drawn partly from Caesar's veterans, marched on Rome, where he was elected consul. He then joined forces with Anthony and Aemilius Lepidus to defeat the forces of Brutus and Cassius. Octavius, Anthony, and Lepidus had previously entered into an agreement known as the Second Triumvirate in which they shared control of Rome's government. This arrangement did not last long, however. Lepidus was sent into exile, and Anthony and Octavius fought each other for control of Rome. In 31 B.C. Octavius defeated the forces of Anthony and his wife, the Egyptian Queen Cleopatra, at the battle of Actuim in western Greece. Both Anthony and Cleopatra committed suicide. Octavius was in complete charge of the Roman Empire at the age of 32. Four years later he became the first Roman Emperor even though he pretended to rule alongside the Senate.

Octavius, who as a result of his adoption by Julius Caesar took the name Octavian, made Caesar a god, and attempted to assimilate his military dictatorship with Republican principles. On January 13, 27 B.C. Octavius offered to relinquish his dictatorial powers, but the Senate refused his offer and instead voted to increase his powers. Three days later the Senate bestowed upon Octavius honors for virtue, valor, piety, and justice. On that date the Senate also conferred upon Octavius the title Augustus, a religious term that implied he was godlike. In return, Octavius reestablished many previous Roman political traditions. Magistrates, for example, were again elected, political assemblies still met, and the Sen-

Antony and Cleopatra are depicted during the Battle of Actium. Actually they commanded separate ships and did not rejoin each other until well after fleeing the conflict.

ate was allowed to retain its treasury, administer outlying provinces, and advise the emperor.

AUGUSTAN RULE AND THE PAX ROMANA

Even though the trappings of the Roman Republic remained, Octavius' reign effectively meant that the republic was, for all practical purposes, dead. Afterward, Rome would be ruled by one person. Octavius used his dictatorial power to impose order, stability, and peace throughout the empire. He forced all of Italy to take an oath of allegiance to the emperor, instituted reforms in the army to thwart the political ambitions of generals, provided land and money for soldiers discharged from the army, constructed aqueducts to provide water to Roman homes, organized a fire department, and created a police force to protect citizens against criminals. Octavius also built roads throughout Italy, had numerous public buildings constructed, passed reform laws to curb abuses by tax collectors, appointed competent governmental officials throughout Rome's provinces, and allowed Roman citizens to bring charges against corrupt officials.

Octavius' rule also marked the beginning of the Pax Romana, a 200-year period of peace and prosperity throughout the Mediterranean World. From Octavius' defeat of Anthony and Cleopatra at the Battle of Actium until the death of Marcus Aurelius in 150 A.D. the Mediterranean world enjoyed the most peaceful and prosperous period it had ever seen. The Pax Romana, or Roman Peace as this period is known, largely resulted from the wise leadership of Octavius. The emperor possessed extraordinary political skills and understood well the subtle art of diplomacy. Even though most of his enemies were dead after the Battle of Actium, he realized that the Roman aristocracy could make trouble for the emperor unless they were handled with tact. Rather than flaunting his power, Octavius chose to be called by the title Princeps (First Citizen) rather than emperor, which was a title that denoted respect for Roman customs and traditions. Octavius understood that using this title would not upset conservative senators and cause them to engage in assassination plots against him as they had against Julius Caesar. Octavius also pleased conservative aristocrats when he announced in 27 B.C. that the republic had been restored even though the republic was not actually restored.

Octavius also placated the Roman aristocracy by opening more public offices. Ambitious Romans could hold public office and make binding

This fanciful rendering of Cleopatra shows her pressing a poisonous asp to her breast. After her death, Octavian fulfilled her request to be buried with Antony.

decisions in those offices so long as they accepted Octavius' ultimate authority. Likewise, Octavius generally left the military alone when its commanders accepted Octavius' power. In order to prevent a new emperor from rising to challenge his power, Octavius divided Rome's provinces between himself and the Senate. The outlying provinces were mainly given to Octavius while provinces closer to Rome were mostly given to Senators. Military commanders in the outlying provinces generally owed their position to Octavius and thus remained loyal to the emperor.

Octavius also frequently sought advice from the Senate but did not tolerate unruly mobs. He divided the Senate into various groups or departments and used them as advisors when the need arose. Mobs that gathered from time to time were usually dispensed by the Praetorian Guard, or police force, which Octavius created to safeguard himself.

Improvements in governmental administration were instituted during Octavius' reign. The emperor established Rome's first professional bureaucracy. Different officials would be in charge of offices that oversaw various functions. One department, for example, oversaw Rome's water supply, another was in charge of the city's food, another collected taxes, and yet another constructed and maintained roads.

Overall, Rome thrived under Octavius' rule. Governmental control, especially in Rome's outlying provinces, was largely decentralized. Equestrians and freedmen both held civil service positions and usually supported the government's policies. Even though bribery was common place because government officials were not paid salaries, the Roman bureaucracy generally operated efficiently and effectively. Despite the presence of bribery, most bureaucrats were reasonably honest and interested in the welfare of the Roman population during the Pax Romana.

The Roman Empire enjoyed prosperity under Octavius' rule. Agricultural and industrial production blossomed. Roman industries produced goods that were sold throughout the Mediterranean World. Italian products made from iron, silver, bronze, and wax had no equal in the world and were highly sought commodities in the ancient world. The employment rate was high under Octavius. Elaborate public works programs created jobs for the urban poor. Rome's freedmen greatly benefited from the Octavian policy of "bread and circuses," a policy of free grain distribution and free admission to sporting and entertainment events designed to placate the general population.

Octavius decreased the size of Rome's military to reduce the chances of rogue generals deposing the emperor. Under Octavius, Rome maintained an army of about 300,000 men assigned to 28 legions. The decrease in defense expenditures lessened the empire's budgetary obligations but made it difficult for Octavius to conquer new lands and in some cases hold on to lands Rome already controlled. In 9 A.D. for example, a revolt of Germanic tribes destroyed three legions, forcing Rome to withdraw from the Elbe River and establish the Rhine River as Rome's boundary.

Military veterans who lost their position when Octavius downsized the army were compensated with land in Rome's outlying provinces. This policy, which Octavius funded by increasing taxes on the rich, kept the ex-soldiers relatively happy and likely prevented many from aligning themselves with ambitious generals who might have threatened Octavius' rule.

Socially, Octavius attempted to renew and revitalize Rome's ancient culture. He passed legislation that promoted marriage, encouraged childbearing, and forbad adultery and sexual promiscuity. To show that he was serious about enforcing laws against adultery and sexual promiscuity, Octavius banished his daughter Julia, whose sexual misdeeds were the subject of gossip throughout the empire, to a deserted Mediterranean island. Octavius also revitalized Roman religion. He remodeled ancient temples and encouraged worship of old gods and cults. After his death, Octavius was deified. Cults dedicated to his worship developed in both the eastern and western empire.

CULTURE, SOCIETY AND LAW

The Augustan Age, as the reign of Octavius is called, was generally perceived as a time of remarkable cultural flowering in the Roman world. Roman artists incorporated classic principles of heroism and traditional values in their work. Writers and poets likewise included similar themes in their works. Octavius and other prominent Romans patronized literacy figures, including Virgil, Horace, and Livy. Virgil's epic the *Aeneid* about the founding of Rome is perhaps the greatest literary work that survives from the ancient world. Horace's poetry, like that of Virgil, celebrates old Roman values and today influences modern western poets. Livy wrote a 142-volume history of Rome. Unfortunately, only about a fourth of his works survive today. Still, modern historians consult Livy's works, particularly when researching the Roman monarchy and Early Republic, even though his account is based more on myth than fact.

Octavius and wealthy Romans living during his reign were also patrons of the arts. Numerous building projects were completed, especially in Rome, including temples, the Forum of Augustus, the Theater of Marcellus, the Baths of Agrippa, the Pantheon, and the Mausoleum of Augustus. Roman architects included in these structures, the arch, the building feature most commonly identified with Rome. The Roman arch, which was incorporated into aqueducts, bridges, and buildings, gave structures great strength and stability. Making Roman buildings even stronger was a unique mortar made from a mixture of volcanic earth called pozzolana and stone. The bond created from this mixture was strong and flexible and, along with the arch, created buildings that survived the ravages of time into the modern world. Aqueducts were particularly important in the Roman Empire. Architects built these structures that transported by use of gravity millions of gallons of water to Roman cities.

This famous statue of Augustus Caesar shows him wearing a general's breastplate with embossed decorations. This statue is found at Prima Porta, near Rome.

Latin, the official language of the Roman Empire, which is no longer spoken, was an excellent communication vehicle because it enabled its users to communicate both simple and complex ideas to each other. Roman schools emphasized Latin and encouraged its use in public oratory and debate.

Philosophically, most Romans were adherents to Stoicism. Practitioners of Stoicism held that the world was rational and could be understood by the human mind. Philosophers, including Seneca, Epictetus, the slave, and the Emperor Marcus Aurelius strove for a higher plane of good in life that could be achieved through reason that every human was endowed with. Roman Stoics also believed that every person was self-sufficient and should control their lives by exercising rational faculties. The primary goal of Stoic philosophers was to search for good using reason and once found, do good. All people, according to Stoicism, held membership in the human race because of the innate ability to reason, which separated humans from animals.

Science was also an important component of Roman culture. Ptolemy, a mathematician, astronomer, and geographer, and Galen, a physician, were the most famous Roman scientists.

Etruscan Aqueduct

Ptolemy's the *Almagest* was the multivolume work that summarized the ancient world's astronomical knowledge. According to Ptolemy, the earth was the center of the universe. The sun, moon, and planets orbited the earth. Ptolemy's ideas were not disproven until Galileo's work with the telescope in the middle of the sixteenth century showed conclusively that the earth actually orbited around the sun. Just as Ptolemy's ideas dominated astronomy, Galen's ideas dominated medicine until relatively recent times. Galen used dissection of both deceased and living organisms to understand how the physical body works. His work, even though filled with errors, enabled doctors to better understand how the human body functions and treat diseases to some degree.

Law was, perhaps, the greatest Roman achievement in relation to the modern world. Roman emperors developed a legal system that protected all citizens under a common law. The same laws applied to all Romans regardless of where an individual lived. Roman law was founded upon reason and common sense and is the basis for most legal systems in the western world today. The Roman legal system can generally be divided into two main components—civil law and international law. Roman civil law (*jus civile*) developed during a two century struggle between classes. Conflict between patricians and plebians produced the Twelve Tablets, a document that contained written rules of law that applied to all citizens regardless of class. Over time, Roman written law expanded as the Senate, governmental assemblies, emperors, and judges added to it. Roman international law, or *jus gentium* as it was known in Latin, developed as a result of Rome's expansion outside Italy. Contact with Greeks and other peoples resulted in modification of Roman civil and criminal law.

The baths built by the Romans were large communal centers.

Roman legal experts took the best principles from foreign peoples they came into contact with, added them to Roman law, and then applied them to provinces throughout the empire. According to law, all free people anywhere in the empire were Roman and subject to the Empire's laws. Principles of Roman law are readily recognized today within the American legal system. For example, Roman law decreed that nobody could be punished for what he believed, required that consideration should be given as to whether a crime was accidentally or deliberately committed, and when punishing criminals the age of the criminal should be taken into account.

Roman entertainment would likely be considered barbaric by modern standards. Major entertainment events included battles to the death between armed gladiators, the torturing of dangerous animals, chariot races, and circuses. These events were extremely popular and drew large crowds who cheered on the participants. Often, the gladiatorial spectacles pitted slaves or condemned criminals against each other in bloody combat. If the slave won he was set free; if the criminal won, he also received freedom. Professional gladiators learned their trade as schools operated by professional fighters. Gladiators usually fought with a sword or a net and trident. During the combat, spectators exhibited a seemingly unquenchable blood lust. The bloodier the fight the more Romans liked it. If a losing gladiator displeased the crowd they flashed the thumbs down signal, which was a call for his immediate execution. The winning gladiator usually obliged, quickly dispatching his opponent. Women also battled in the gladiatorial ring as did animals and children. Roman entertainment was indeed brutal and bloody.

Roman law allowed and Roman culture tolerated slavery. As the centuries passed, Roman society became more stratified. A few people enjoyed privileges accorded to the upper class

The underground chambers of the Colosseum, once covered by the arena floor, are visible in this photo. Slaves and animals were led through underground tunnels and out onto the main area.

but the bulk of the population were rural peasants, the urban poor, and slaves. Over time, the Empire relied more and more on slavery and the status of free men changed as an increasing number were enslaved. Many slaves were added to Rome's domain as a result of territorial expansion when defeated people were enslaved as a result of conquest in war. By the time of the empire period, slavery had became one of the most important cornerstones of Rome's economy. Without slavery, the Empire likely would have collapsed. Millions of slaves were added to the empire as a result of the Punic and other wars. Hundreds of thousands more people were enslaved after being convicted of crime, falling into debt, or as a result of being sold by parents. Historians estimate that as many as one-fourth to one-third of Rome's population was enslaved at the Empire's height.

Slaves worked at a variety of occupations. Some were field hands, working on the Empire's farms and plantations. Others worked as house or personal servants, keeping house, cooking, and attending to the everyday needs of the master. A few slaves even entered the professions, becoming healers, teachers, lawyers, and philosophers. Many gladiators were also enslaved. They entertained the populace by fighting to the death in Roman arenas.

Masters commonly treated slaves inhumanly. Because of the abuse they endured, the average slave rarely lived beyond the early twenties.

Owners often worked slaves to death. Confinement in chains was common and generally accepted as a method of controlling slaves. Slaves who wanted to engage in sexual activity, other than with the slave master or mistress, had to get permission from the owner and then pay a tax.

Faced with such horrible conditions, slaves often escaped or rebelled. Insurrections were generally suppressed with absolute brutality and much loss of life. One of Rome's most famous slave rebellions was led by Spartacus. This rebellion from 73 to 71 B.C. terrified Rome. Spartacus and a group of gladiators escaped from their quarters in 73 B.C. and recruited thousands of runaway slaves in an attempt to escape into Gaul and Thrace, lands that many slaves originated from. Spartacus organized the slaves into an army that defeated several Roman armies and struck terror throughout the Italian Peninsula before being defeated by the Roman general Crassus in 71 B.C. Crassus decided to make an example of Spartacus and the rebellious slaves as a warning to others who might want to rebel. Six thousand were tortured and executed by cruxification on the road connecting Capua to Rome.

As time passed, Rome attempted to moderate just a bit the institution of slavery. Stoic ideas that stressed a common humanity caused some Romans to consider slaves human beings rather than animals. After all, Stoics taught that people, unlike animals, had souls. Octavius enacted legislation requiring a degree of humane treatment for slaves and gave them the legal status as slaves. Under Octavian law, for example, a master could no longer dispose of slaves when they became ill. Despite being given the legal status of slaves, a slave's status throughout the Roman Empire remained that of a slave. They were not free to do as they pleased and remained chattel property their entire life. As chattel, slaves remained under the absolute control of their master until death broke the bonds of slavery.

ROMAN LEADERS AFTER OCTAVIUS

Emperors who followed Octavius after his death in 14 A.D. were a mixed lot. Many had psychological or other problems that, coupled with the pressures of governing, made effective leadership difficult. Octavius died without a natural male heir. Despite repeated attempts, Octavius and his second wife Livia did not produce a male child. Octavius then adopted two grandsons born to his daughter Julie and intended to name one of them as his successor but both died before Octavius. Ultimately, Octavius had to adopt and name as his successor Tiberius, a stepson he disliked.

Tiberius, Livia's eldest son from a previous marriage, largely owed his power to his mother. Livia became perhaps the most powerful woman in Roman history due to her influence over Octavius. She was so determined to ensure that Tiberius became emperor that she likely murdered several people, including Julia's sons, and others who threatened Tiberius. Some evidence indicates that Livia poisoned Octavius in 14 A.D. Once Tiberius became emperor he tried many Romans for treason, cut governmental expenditures, refused to engage in harmful border wars, cut taxes, and demanded honesty from government officials.

Emperors who followed Tiberius were largely inept. Gaius, who succeeded Tiberius in 37 and ruled until 41 A.D., nicknamed Caligula or Baby Boots, was a poor ruler. He increased taxes, created a cult to worship himself, and made his favorite horse the high priest in the cult. He also appointed the horse to the Senate, confiscated private property, and attempted to have himself deified. He was assassinated and succeeded by his uncle Claudius.

Claudius, who was physically handicapped, was one of the best Julio-Claudian emperors, the dynastic name given to Roman Emperors from Octavius' family. During his reign Rome conquered England, constructed an artificial harbor at Ostia, and opened more governmental jobs to freemen. Claudius died in 54 A.D., likely poisoned by Agrippina, his wife, and niece so that Nero, her son by an earlier marriage, could become emperor.

Nero is generally considered a poor emperor. During his reign a fire destroyed much of Rome in 64 A.D. Nero accused a small religious sect, the Christians, of starting the fire and persecuted them relentlessly. Nero launched a massive program to rebuild Rome. Contemporary critics maintained that Nero actually set Rome afire so he would have an opportunity to create a legacy for himself as a builder. Nero was more popular with the public than with the military and Senate. Ordinary Romans liked the Emperor because his construction program gave them jobs; the military generally disliked him because he did not regularly pay soldiers. When the army revolted against him in 68 A.D., Nero took his own life.

After Nero's death, crisis gripped the Empire as Rome faced civil war for the first time in a hundred years. Eventually, Titus Flavius Vespasianus, a general, claimed the throne and founded a new ruling dynasty known as the Flavians who ruled until 96 A.D. The Flavians were followed by the Nero-Trajanic and Antonine dynasties.

The Flavian Emperors—Vespasianus and his sons Titus and Domitian, were generally good rulers who kept peace and maintained order within the Empire. Unlike the Julio-Claudian emperors, the Flavians were not members of the ancient Roman nobility. They instead were members of an Italian landowning family. Domitian, the last emperor in the line, was assassinated in 96 A.D. His death began the reign of Rome's five "Good Emperors"—Nerva, Trajan, Hadrian, Antonius Pinus, and Marcus Aurelius. These emperors generally tried to do what they believed was best for the Empire. Each, for example, named the person they thought most fit to rule as their successor rather than making an incompetent family member emperor. The five Good Emperors are also remembered for their generosity. All five listened to their constituents and tried to solve the Empire's problem.

Border security was a particularly acute problem of the Good Emperors. Rather than making defensive alliances with powerful tribes on the Empire's frontier as previous emperors had done, the Good Emperors decided to build walls, forts, and other defensive fortifications to secure the Empire's frontier. Soldiers were used

A fanciful depiction of Nero persecuting the early Christians for supposedly starting the great fire of A. D. 64.

to man these defensive structures. Hadrian's Wall is perhaps the best surviving example of these defensive fortifications. Constructed by Emperor Hadrian, this wall was approximately 80 miles long and separated the region that Rome controlled in England from hostile tribes in the north. About two thousand soldiers generally patrolled Hadrian's Wall to keep tribal invaders out of the Empire's territory.

Rome reached its largest geographical size under Trajan's rule. He sent Roman troops across the Danube River, establishing the new province of Dacia (modern Romania), and also conquered lands around the Persian Gulf. Trajan, however, had overreached. The Roman military was spread so thin that it could not hold on to all the conquered territory. After Trajan's death, Hadrian was forced to withdraw from the Persian Gulf and Mesopotamian regions.

THE RISE OF CHRISTIANITY

Roman expansion throughout the Mediterranean region brought numerous religions into the Empire. The most important such religion was one that began in the Roman province of Palestine during the reign of Tiberius. Called Christianity because its adherents were followers of a Jewish rabbi named Jesus Christ, this religion eventually changed Rome and the entire world.

Although little historically is known about Joshua ben Joseph or Jesus of Nazareth, who most likely was born between 6 and 3 B.C., in 6 A.D., his birthplace was annexed by Rome as the province of Palestine. In 28 or 29 A.D. John the Baptist began preaching to Palestine Jews that God's kingdom as prophesied in the Old Testament was at hand, and he urged the Palestinian people to repent of their sins and be baptized anew. Jesus was one of the people baptized by John in the Jordan River. After the baptism, Jesus also began preaching, but his message differed somewhat from that of John the Baptist. Whereas John had preached that the kingdom of God was near, Jesus preached that it was already underway and would be further established through his ministry. Jesus's teaching produced conflict with the Pharisees who rejected his claim of divinity as idolatry. Between 30 and 33 A.D. Jesus travelled to Jerusalem and visited Solomon's Temple. There, he initiated conflict with the Sadducees, a powerful Jewish group, when he said he was the Messiah whose arrival was prophesied by the Torah. While in Jerusalem, Jesus was betrayed by one of his followers, arrested, tried for and convicted of sedition, and executed by cruxification. After his death, Jesus's followers maintained that he had actually been resurrected and began to preach his message throughout the Mediterranean World.

At first, Rome paid little attention to Christianity, which was viewed as just another religious sect among hundreds of others. Over time, however, Christianity threatened the other pagan religions of Rome. In particular, the view that the Christian lived in the world but was not of it was viewed as subversive. After Nero blamed Christians for causing the fire that destroyed Rome, the sect became a favorite object of governmental persecution.

Other than Jesus himself, the second most important figure in the spread of Christianity was Paul of Tarsus. Initially, Paul, who was a Jew, engaged in the persecution of Christians whom he considered blasphemous. In 36 A.D. he claimed to have experienced a vision of Jesus while travelling to Damascus, Syria that changed him from a persecutor of Christians into a believer in Christ. Paul then devoted his life to spreading Christianity throughout the Roman Empire and was instrumental in separating the sect from Judaism. Jews could generally not accept Paul's view that following the law in the Torah would not lead to salvation. Paul instead taught that only faith in Jesus as Messiah could give one salvation and established numerous churches in the Roman Empire based upon his views. These churches grew and prospered, in part because of the Roman persecution. Christians who were executed were viewed as martyrs, and their deaths likely attracted others to the religion. In the second century Christian views changed somewhat as Christian writers attempted to make their faith less of a threat to the empire. Much of this literature supported the Roman government, and numerous Christians also began to argue against their pagan detractors and, as a result, persecutions decreased. Rome's emperors came to see Christianity as more of a nuisance than a threat to the government. Generally, Roman officials were willing to tolerate Christianity so long as its practitioners kept their faith private, did not criticize Roman officials, and obeyed Roman law. By the third century the number of Christians in the Empire was significant.

In the fourth century, Christianity became an officially acceptable religion within the Roman Empire. Emperors Constantine and Licinius issued the Edicts of Milan, granting official toleration and a return of church property previously seized by the government. These measures were undertaken largely because Rome was again engaged in Civil War. This conflict occurred in 305 A. D. after Emperor Diocletian abdicated. The war pitted Constantine and Licinius against Maxentius. Constantine and Licinius defeated Maxentius at the Battle of Milvian Bridge in 313. There, Maxentius drowned, and Constantine attributed his victory to Jesus Christ. The Emperor supposedly saw in the sky the Greek letters *chi* and *rho*, the first two letters for *Christos*, and the words *in hoc signo vicenes* (in this sign conquer). Constantine then ordered *chi* and *rho* to be inscribed on the shields of his soldiers.

The victory of Milvian Bridge persuaded Constantine to legalize Christianity within the Empire and undo the harm done to Christians under the Diocletian persecution. These persecutions from 303 to 305, which were the last official persecutions of Christians within the Empire, were brutal and harsh. Diocletian ordered all Christian churches closed, required all Roman citizens to make a public sacrifice in a pagan temple, seized all church buildings and land, and had all clergy arrested. His motivation for these actions probably was due to his belief that Christianity offended Rome's ancient gods, and the presence of Christian troops in the army so angered the traditional gods that they caused Rome's military to suffer defeat at the hands of barbarians on the Empire's frontier.

Constantine not only reversed what Diocletian had done but granted the Christian Church immunity from taxation, made clergy exempt from military service, and used government funds to rebuild churches and replace other church property destroyed during the persecution. Constantine's motivation for legalizing Christianity likely was due to the influence of Helena, his Mother, who was a devout Christian. She persuaded him to construct both St. Peter's Church in Rome and the Church of the Holy Sepulcher in Jerusalem at the site of Jesus' tomb.

At the time Constantine and his co-emperor Licinius issued the Edicts of Milan, only about 15 to 20 percent of the Roman population was Christian. Most Christians resided in the eastern part of the Empire in the general region where the religion had begun as a sect of Judaism and where most of the Empire's cities were located. Christianity had originated in an urban part of the Empire and was particularly attractive to lower class people in cities and towns. The number of Christians in the western half of the Empire, which was largely rural, was far less than in the more urban east.

Even though Constantine legalized Christianity, contrary to popular opinion, he did not make Christianity the official religion of the Roman Empire. This would not occur until near the end of the fourth century under the rule of Emperor Theodosius, who was granted the title "Great" by the church. Constantine may not have even been Christian. Throughout his reign, as Emperor, he headed Rome's pagan sect and did not change Roman coinage to reflect Christian themes. Until 324 Roman coins displayed an image of the Sun God. Regardless of whether Constantine was Christian, he apparently was convinced that the religion could be used to unify the Empire into one universal or Catholic entity. Had Constantine not have patronized Christianity it is doubtful that it would have become very influential within the Roman Empire.

After Constantine legalized Christianity, the issue of orthodoxy became an issue within the religion. Early Christians were concerned whether converts held the correct beliefs about Jesus, his death, and resurrection. Immediately after Jesus' death, the small number of Christians were eschatological in outlook, that is, they expected Christ's return at any moment, and found it unnecessary for the church to develop a formal theology. With each passing year without the occurrence of the "Second Coming," Christianity was increasingly diluted by false beliefs that took hold within the religion as the number of converts increased. Differences between different congregations on basic beliefs caused problems within the church. These problems became more acute after the Edicts of Milan allowed Christians to openly worship their God. In the first quarter of the fourth century a tremendous controversy erupted within the church over the idea of the Trinity. One faction, led by a priest named Arius, maintained that Jesus was not equal to God. This group believed that Jesus was more than divine. Arius and the faction he led thus questioned Jesus' divinity and the need for his death and resurrection. Opposing Arius was Athanasius, the bishop of Alexandria, who held that God was actually three different but equal entities: the Father, the Son, and the Holy Ghost. After Arius developed a large following, church leaders persuaded Constantine to call a meeting at Nicaea to settle the dispute. Between two and three hundred Catholic bishops met at the Council of Nicaea in 325 A.D. Constantine presided over the meeting, which rejected the views of Arius and adopted the Nicene Creed, a statement of faith that many Christians adhere to today. The Nicene Creed, in rejecting Arianism, confirmed that God, Christ, and the Holy Spirit were one and the same equal to each other throughout eternity.

Although the Council of Nicaea rejected Arianism, the controversy within the church did not immediately end. Constantius II, the son of Constantine, was openly Arian. Later emperors would likewise follow Arianism, even though the doctrine had been declared heretical by church officials. Arian beliefs were widely accepted by tribal peoples who lived along frontier regions after Ulfilas, a Visigoth priest, was converted to Arian Christianity and spread the doctrine among his people.

Constantine's legalization of Christianity did not bring an end to paganism within the Roman Empire. Julian the Apostate (so named by Christian historians because of his opposition to the religion), Constantine's nephew, tried to return Rome to paganism during his reign from 361 to 363. While he did not resort to persecution, Julian forbade Christians from holding official positions in the military, in government, and in the schools. Julian's effort to restore paganism failed because by 360 A.D. Christianity was so entrenched within the Empire that any attempt to root it out was doomed to failure.

Eventually Arianism was defeated, but other controversies arose within Christianity. One of the bitterest fights occurred in the fifth century over Monophysitism. Christian theologians at Alexandria and Antioch disagreed over how to discuss God's nature. Some theologians stressed the divinity of Christ while others emphasized the deity's humanity. In 451 A.D. the Council of Chalcedon met to deal with Monophysitism. Theologians at Chalcedon decided that Christ was equally divine and human and that Christian theologians had to recognize both natures without stressing one over the other. Anybody who believed differently was deemed a heretic.

By the end of the fifth century Christianity was the dominant religion within the Roman World. The Christian church itself was dominated by leaders who followed edicts issue by the Council of Nicaea and the Council of Chalcedon. Constantine's desire to unite the Empire through religion had been realized. The Catholic Church had become universal throughout the Roman World. Those who deviated from universal Catholic doctrine were themselves subject to persecution, just as Christians had been persecuted by the government and other religions earlier in Rome's history.

DECLINE OF THE EMPIRE

In the third century A.D. the Roman Empire began a permanent decline. The peace and prosperity enjoyed throughout the Empire during its glory years gave way to anarchy and warfare. Several factors were responsible for the Empire's disintegration, including problems within the military, invasion by Germanic tribes, and economic upheaval.

Military issues were perhaps the primary reason for the beginning of Rome's decline. Unlike in prior centuries when the Roman legionnaire was likely the best soldier in the world, the third century saw a decline in the quality of soldiers. Loyalty to the Empire, which was a quality Roman soldiers were noted for, declined as soldiers transferred loyalty to military commanders, who used them to further personal agendas. Soldiers also became greedy for war spoils and often attacked civilians when the spoils of war were not available. Emperors had to guard against assassination by lower ranking officers. The chaos in Rome's military destabilized the government and produced civil war. The army found it difficult to effectively guard the Empire's borders, and tribal peoples on the Empire's border launched raid after raid into Roman lands. These raids destabilized Rome economically, militarily, and politically, disrupting life for most residents in border regions. The Pax Romana had ended.

Germanic tribesmen took advantage of problems within the Roman military, crossing the Rhine and Danube River boundaries to loot and destroy Roman cities. These barbarians, as the Romans and Greeks called them, overran Roman territory in the west and ushered into western Europe the period historians call the Dark Ages. In reality, there was not one coordinated barbarian invasion of the western Roman Empire but a series of smaller invasions between 370 and 530 A.D.

The Germanic invasion actually began about 375 A.D. when the Ostrogoths and Visigoths—two Germanic tribes living near the Black Sea—were attacked by the Huns, a warrior people from the steppes of central Asia. Both the Ostrogoths and Visigoths seeking safety from the Huns, requested permission from Emperor Valens to settle in Roman territory in the Balkan Mountains.

When Valens did not respond to the request for shelter, the Visigoths crossed the Danube anyway, forcing the Emperor to reluctantly agree to their request to settle in the Balkans. Trouble between the Visigoths and Romans erupted when local merchants and governmental officials mistreated the new arrivals, charging extremely high prices for food and enslaving Visigoth children. The harsh treatment by the local populace caused the Visigoths to revolt. Valens decided to put down the revolt but did not commit enough troops to do the job. In 378 A.D. the Visigoths defeated Valens at the Battle of Adrianople. The Roman defeat convinced the Visigoths that the Empire could not protect its borders, and more groups from the Black Sea region migrated across the Danube to escape the Huns. In 382 A.D. Emperor Theodosius reached a settlement with Visigoth tribal leaders, granting them Balkan land and giving their king an officer's rank in the Roman army. Theodosius gave in to Visigoth demands to avoid war and settle the Balkan lands with farmers and warriors who could help protect Roman land from the Huns.

Theodosius' settlement with the Visigoths did not permanently end hostilities between the groups. Alaric, the Visigoth king, invaded Italy in 395 because Roman officials had not kept promises made to Visigoth leaders. Pressure from Germanic tribes increased as increasing numbers migrated into Roman territory. In 406 A.D. the Empire's border was completely breached as Vandals, Alans, Suebi, and other Germanic groups began a migration into Roman lands. Alaric attacked and sacked Rome itself in 410 A.D., which some historians consider to be the official date of the fall of the western Empire. After the attack on Rome, Visigoths marched into Gaul, taking the southern part of the province from Rome and forcing the Roman government to reach an accord allowing the Visigoths to settle in Gaul and receive a portion of taxes collected there in return for protecting southern Gaul from other invaders. This treaty made the Visigoths the first people to take Roman land since the Empire's establishment.

Rome, like Germanic tribes along the Danube frontier, faced trouble with the Huns. Hun raiding parties frequently attacked Balkan settlements, robbed traders traveling on long established trade routes in Roman lands, and threatened Constantinople, the capital of the eastern Roman Empire. These attacks became more acute after 434 A.D. when Attila murdered his brother and became sole rule of the Huns. To stop the Balkan raids, Roman officials were forced to pay an annual tribute to Attila. For a brief time Attila and the Huns formed an alliance with Rome against the Burgundians, a tribal people from the Rhineland whose migration into Roman lands threaten both the Huns and Romans. The alliance was successful as a combined Roman and Hun force defeated the Burgundians. Attila, sensing Roman weakness, broke the alliance in 451 A.D. when he attacked Gaul. After the Gaul attack was thwarted by an army of Romans, Visigoths, Burgundians, and Franks, Attila turned toward Rome. There Pope Leo I bribed Attila in 452 and the feared Hun force withdrew from the imperial city. The Hun threat to Rome ended with Attila's death in 454, after the Hunnic kingdom he had established disintegrated.

Rome's difficulties did not end with Attila's death. In 455 the Vandals sacked Rome, and more territory in the western Empire came under control of various Germanic tribes. Germanic soldiers employed by Rome gained enough power that they seized control of the government to a degree sufficient enough to grant them authority to control the choice of emperor. In 476 the German controlled army deposed Emperor Romulus and placed a German, Odovacer, on the Roman throne. This event generally signifies the end of Roman control in western Europe, and most historians cite it as the traditional date of the Empire's official fall. By about 530 the western Empire had virtually vanished. Roman forces had been pulled out of Britain in the fourth century, and the Anglos and Saxons seized control of southern and eastern Britain by 600. Clovis, a Frankish king, subjected most of Gaul to his rule after defeating, with Rome's cooperation, the Visigoths, who were driven into Spain. The Ostrogoth king Theodoric conquered most of Italy and established his capital at Ravanna, where he ruled until his death in 526.

The Germanic invasions produced economic upheaval throughout western regions of the Empire that contributed to its demise. One important economic factor that contributed to Rome's decline was a decrease in population. The various wars, couple with outbreaks of disease, shrank the western Empire's population. This meant that Rome lacked a tax base sufficient to adequately administer the government and fund the military, especially when faced with the Germanic invasions. The population decrease also meant that an insufficient agricultural workforce was available to produce the amount of food needed for the Empire's inhabitants. The population decline also meant that the military could not recruit enough soldiers to defend Rome's borders. Emperors were thus forced to allow Germanic people.

The lack of commerce and industry, along with the population decline, played a role in the western Empire's collapse. Rather than developing industry and commerce, towns and cities in Western Europe generally relied upon surrounding agricultural areas for economic prosperity and when agricultural production declined, urban prosperity declined also. Most towns in the Western Empire were controlled by non-resident agrarians who owned vast estates outside the village and who received income from farming rather than manufacturing. The little industry that existed was primitive in comparison with the Eastern Empire. The textiles, glassware, pottery, and furniture produced were generally inferior to similar products made elsewhere in the Empire, and, consequently, their market was limited, transportation costs were high, and labor was difficult to secure. These problems generally created an economic situation that made it impossible for the Roman Empire to survive in the west.

Despite the Empire's collapse in Western Europe, Rome created a rich heritage that benefits modern Europeans. The western cultural tradition was advanced by the spread of Roman civilization. The Latin that Romans spoke gave rise to the Romance languages that developed throughout Western Europe. The Catholic Church created by Roman Christians still survives and legal systems of most European nations are derived from Roman law. Had the Roman Empire not have existed, the world as modern people know it would have been vastly different.

Suggestions for Further Reading

A.E.R.Boak, *History of Rome to 565 A.D.* (1969)

John Boardman, Jaspar Griffin, and Oswyn Murray, *The Oxford History of The Roman World* (1991)

Julius Caesar, *The Gallic Wars*, (1951)

J.Ferguson, *The Religions of the Roman Empire* (1970)

Robin Lane Fox, *Pagans and Christians* (1987)

W.H.C.Friend, *The Rise of Christianity* (1984)

Edward Gibbon, *The Decline and Fall of the Roman Empire* (1909-1914)

Michael Grant, *The World of Rome*, (1987)

R.M.Grant, *Historical Introduction to the New Testament* (1972)

M.I.Rostovtzeff, *Social and Economic History of the Roman Empire* (1957)

THE POST-ROMAN EAST: BYZANTIUM, ISLAM & EASTERN EUROPE

CONSTANTINOPLE

Oleg, the Seer, a Viking Prince who succeeded Rurik as ruler of Kiev and who some credit with founding Russia, ruled Kiev until his death amid strange circumstances in 913. According to the Primary Chronicles of Russian History, during his life Oleg, who was by nature a superstitious person, consulted fortune tellers wanting to know in advance the cause of his death. One fortune teller told Prince Oleg that "it is from the steed which you love and on which you ride that you shall meet your death." Oleg thought about the prophesy and found a way to avoid death from his favorite horse, or so he thought. He ordered aids to remove the horse from his presence, keep it in an isolated location, and feed it well until the animal died. Oleg was determined to never mount, ride, or even see the horse again. Several years passed during which Oleg made war upon the Greeks, Byzantines, and nomadic tribes. Kiev prospered under his rule. One day, while reflecting upon his many successes and accomplishments, Oleg wondered what had become of the horse the magician had predicted would cause his death. Curious, Oleg summoned his aid and asked about the whereabouts of the horse. The aid informed Oleg that the horse had been dead for some time. Oleg felt that a black cloud that had hung over him since the magician had predicted his death had dissipated. He was so happy that he laughed and began dancing around, mocking the fortune teller that had predicted his death, saying: "Soothsayers tell untruths, and their words are nothing but falsehoods. The horse is dead, but I yet live." Oleg then had his squire saddle his horse so that he could ride out and see the bones of the dead horse. When he arrived at the field where the horse's bones lay, he dismounted and again mocked the magicians, exclaiming, "Am I to receive my death from this skull?" Oleg then kicked the skull, which aroused the wrath of a serpent sleeping inside. The angry serpent crawled out of the skull and bit Prince Oleg, killing him with its poisonous fangs. The Kievan people mourned Oleg and buried him in a tomb upon a hill called Shchekovitza.

Chronology

313	Constantine's Edict of Milan tolerating Christianity
325	First Ecumenical Council held at Nicaea Arianism was condemned as heresy
395	During the reign of the Emperor Theodosius the Great Christianity triumphs and becomes empire's official religion
527-565	Reign of Justinian Reconquest of portions of West Corpus Juris Civilis Constantinople rebuilt Great church of Hagia Sophia Golden Age of Byzantine culture
570-632	Life of Muhammad
622	Hejira – Muhammad's flight to Yathrib (renamed Medina)
610-641	Emperor Heraclius Great war with Persians – Byzantine victory Ongoing problems with Monophysites
632-661	First Four Muslim Caliphs: Abu Bakr 632-634 Omar 634-644 Uthman 644-658 Ali 658-661
661	Umayyad Dynasty established Capital at Damascus
717	Leo III, The Isaurian
726	Leo III issues decree banning icons
639-732	Islam conquerors Egypt, Syria, Palestine, Persia, North Africa, and Spain
750	Overthrow of Umayyads replaced by Abassids—new capital in Baghdad
827	Muslims conquer Sicily and Crete
843	Icons finally and officially restored
860	Constantinople attacked by Rus
862	Kiev becomes capital of Rus
956	Seljuk Turks become Muslims
957	Princess Olga of Russia receives Baptism in Constantinople
976-1025	Apogee of Byzantine power under Macedonian Emperors
989	Vladimir and Russia converted to Byzantium form of Christianity
1054	Schism between Rome and Byzantine churches
1071	Catastrophic military defeat of Byzantines at Manzikert (Asia Minor) by Seljuk Turks and at Bari in southern Italy against the Normans

Long after the Western Roman Empire fell to invading Germanic tribes, the Eastern Empire survived as the Byzantine Empire for several centuries more because the eastern provinces contained a larger population that lived in cities that were better fortified and were thus better able to resist invasion. From 324 until 1453 the Byzantine Empire included Greece, Asia Minor, Italy, southern Spain, parts of the Middle East, North Africa, and the Balkan Mountains.

Actually, usage of the term Byzantium or Byzantine to describe the Eastern Roman Empire is somewhat inaccurate because people living in Eastern Europe and parts of the Near East did not perceive themselves as separate from the Roman Empire as it existed in Western Europe at that time. Easterners recognized no separation between eastern and western parts of the empire and referred to themselves as Roman even after Rome was no longer the most powerful entity in the world. Most individuals living in eastern provinces of the empire continued to think of themselves as Romans even after Greek had replaced Latin as the official language of the Eastern Empire. The Roman Empire, in fact, did not collapse in the east until 1453, long after its demise in the west. However, western historians usually separate the Roman Empire into two parts after 324 A.D.—the Byzantine Empire in the east and the Roman Empire in the west. If one accepts this classification, then the age of the Byzantine Empire can generally be divided into three main periods: the Early Byzantine from 324 to 632; the Middle Byzantine from 633 to 1071; and the Late Byzantine from 1072-1453.

THE EARLY BYZANTINE PERIOD, 324 TO 632

Historians generally date the beginning of the Byzantine Empire at 324 when Emperor Constantine moved the capital from Rome to Constantinople. Constantine moved the capital to the eastern part of the empire because it enabled him to more easily protect that part of his territory from enemies, including Germanic tribes and Persians who were attacking Rome's eastern provinces, which were the most prosperous and profitable in the entire empire at that time. The new capital, which officially was called New Rome, was at the site where the ancient Greek colony of Byzantium (hence the name Byzantine Empire) was located when it was founded in 660 B.C. The name New Rome was soon discarded in favor of Constantinople or the City of Constantine in honor of the emperor.

The location Constantine chose for his new capital was excellent. Constantinople was situated on a peninsula that juts into the Sea of Marmara, a spot easily defended from attackers. There, also, two of the most important trade routes of the Roman World intersected—a land route between the Balkan Mountains and the Middle East and a sea route connecting the Black Sea to the Mediterranean Sea. This location meant that Constantinople became the economic and cultural center of the eastern Roman Empire. Because Constantinople was an entirely new city built to house the capital of the Roman Empire, it soon became an important center of Christianity. Unlike Rome, there was no tradition of pagan worship in Constantinople and no altars or statues of idols were present to remind residents of the empire's history of paganism. The Bishop of Constantinople became an important leader in the Catholic or universal church, ranking only behind the Pope in Rome in importance.

The secular goal of Constantine and his successors was to continue Rome's military, political, economic, and cultural domination of the world in both Europe and Asia. Moving the empire's capital from Rome to Constantinople did not

Constantinople's access to the Black Sea and the Mediterranean Sea made it the heart of trade in both Europe and Asia. Merchant ships conducted business and the vibrant economy supported the empire's great expenses.

signify abandonment of Rome's importance in the world. From the time Constantinople was founded in 324 until its fall to the Ottoman Turks in 1453, the city was home to a Christian government that dominated much of the world.

Byzantine power was at its apex during the reign of Emperor Justinian from 527 to 565 A.D. During this time Justinian's lands stretched from the Mediterranean to North Africa and included Greece, Asia Minor, Italy, southern Spain, and territory in the Middle East and Balkan Mountains. This territory contained over 1500 cities that had populations greater than 50,000. Constantinople, whose population numbered about 350,000, became the world's commercial center during Justinian's reign. The Empress Theodora, who once was a prostitute according to the historian Procopius, served not only as Justinian's wife but also as his most important advisor and was the most powerful woman in the world at this time. She provided her husband with much good counsel that helped him overcome several adverse crises that threatened the Byzantine government. Important among these was religious squabble between the Monophysites and the Dyophysites. Traditionally, Dyophysite Christians believed that Christ had two natures, human and divine. In other words, Christ was human while on earth, but at the time of the resurrection he became divine. However, Monophysites believed that Christ had only one nature, that he was partly human and partly divine while on earth and after the resurrection. Justinian, who was an orthodox

Constantinople was strongly walled and surrounded by water, which turned back many invaders.

Christian, accepted Theodora's offer of patronage for the Monophysites, which kept them loyal politically to the emperor even though they created a separate church in the eastern parts of the empire. Later, after Theodora's death, when the government attempted to outlaw the Monophysite heresy, this group provided little support for the government and offered little resistance when Persian and Arab forces attacked the empire.

Theodora's influence was also important in 532 when a rebellion broke out in Constantinople. Justinian and several governmental officials were so frightened by the rebellion that they planned to flee the city and abdicate the government until Theodora, in a passionate plea, begged Justinian to confront the rebels rather than flee into exile. The Emperor heeded his wife's advice and defeated the rebels. Justinian's victory strengthened his government so much that he could pursue three important objectives: restoration of western provinces to the empire, legal and institutional reform, and public works projects.

To achieve his first objective, Justinian launched attacks against the Vandals, Ostrogoths, and Visigoths. By 554 Byzantine armies had defeated the Vandals in North Africa, the Ostrogoths in Italy, and taken territory from the Visigoths in Spain. At least for a time, Justinian retook the empire's control over its territory in Western Europe.

Reform of the Roman legal system was perhaps Justinian's greatest accomplishment. By the time of Justinian's reign the Roman legal system was in chaos. This disorganization stemmed in large part because Roman law had developed

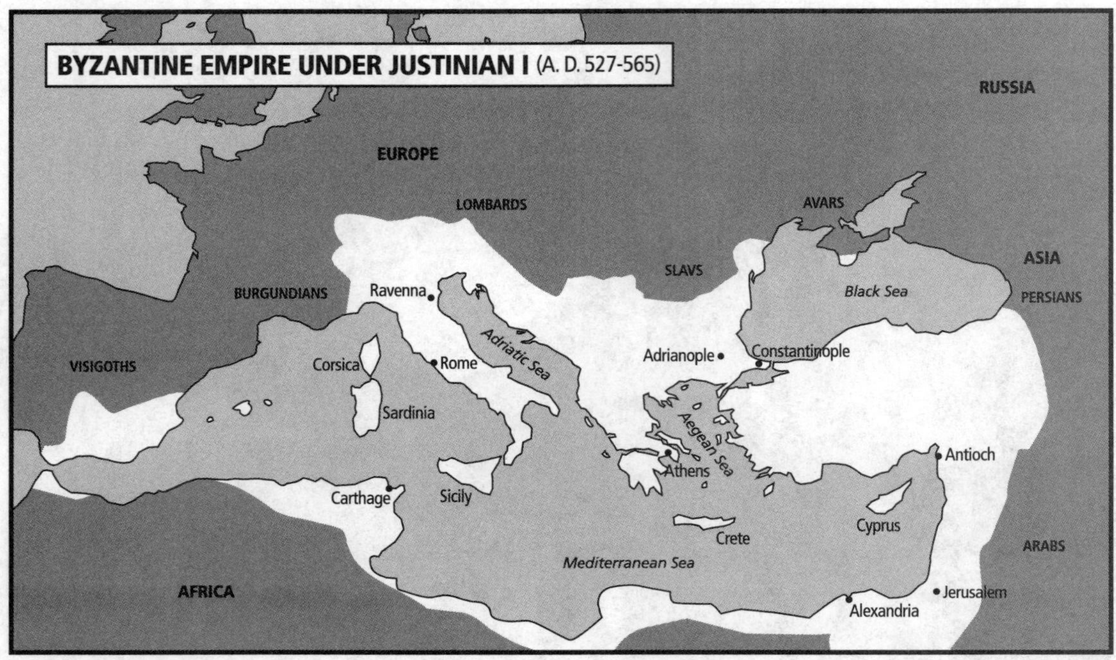

from many sources—judicial decisions, edicts from various emperors, legislation passed by the Roman Senate, and opinions issued by learned people recognized as expert legal scholars. Roman law was so vast and disorganized that lawyers often could not figure out which laws applied to a particular case and often laws contradicted each other. The great morass of Roman law had not been codified over the centuries, and the entire legal system bordered on collapse. It needed serious reform. In 528 Justinian established a commission of legal scholars led by the lawyer Tribonian to begin a systemic review of Roman law in order to clarify and simplify it. The work of this commission was remarkably successful. Their *Corpus Juris Civilis* (Body of Civil Law) was published in 533 and 534. The *Corpus Juris Civilis* was divided into four principle parts: the *Digest* or Pandects (a summary of previously issued opinions by legal scholars and other experts), the *Codex Justinianus* or Code of Justinian (all edicts issued by all Roman Emperors arranged according to subject), the *Novellae* or New Laws (all imperial edicts and laws issued after 534), and the *Institutes* (a law book explaining the new legal system). Justinian's work in this matter preserved Roman law for the medieval and modern worlds. These legal works have provided the best source of information on the Roman Byzantine Empire the world has. Moreover, the *Corpus Juris Civilis* exerted a tremendous influence on the development of modern legal systems in the western world. Most countries in Europe and in North and South America today live under legal systems of common law derived at least in part from the *Corpus Juris Civilis*. American and English common law are both largely derived from the *Corpus Juris Civilis*.

Justinian is also remembered for his extensive public works projects. The earlier rebellion in Constantinople destroyed much of the capital, giving Justinian an excuse to launch a project to extensively rebuild the Byzantine capital. Consequently, many new churches, palaces, and other public buildings were erected, including the spectacular Church of Holy Wisdom.

Overall, Justinian's reign was successful until near the end of his life. During the last two years of his rule, things began to disintegrate. The Emperor had to fight a war against the Persians in the Middle East and deal also with

Belisarius brings a captured Vandal to Emperor Justinian. The defeat of the Vandals brought North Africa, which had been overrun by the German Vandals a century before, once more under Byzantine rule.

Justinian was not an aristocrat. He was born to peasant parents near Sardica, deep in the Balkan Peninsula, several hundred miles northwest of Constantinople.

an Ostrogoth uprising in the western provinces. Justinian simply lacked the manpower and economic resources to wage war on two fronts simultaneously. Byzantine forces were losing on both fronts when Justinian died in 565.

THE MIDDLE BYZANTINE PERIOD, 633-1071

The emperors who came after Justinian generally lost interest in controlling the western part of Rome's empire, concentrating instead on maintaining power in the eastern provinces. Heraclius, who ruled from 610 to 641, especially

Heraclius

focused governmental attention toward the east. Unlike his predecessors, Heraclius spoke Greek rather than Latin and faced military problems in the empire's eastern provinces throughout his reign. Persian and Islamic invaders continually tried to take Byzantine territory. The Emperor strengthened his army by using funds donated from Christian churches to combat these invaders. He launched a successful campaign against the Persians in 622, recapturing Antioch, Jerusalem, and Alexandria, three Byzantine cities Persian armies had previously taken. In 628 Heraclius captured Ctesiphon, the Persian capital, and forced Persian leaders to accept a humiliating peace that restored lands previously controlled by the Byzantine Empire.

The peace Heraclius won against the Persians was fleeting, however, as new enemies began attacking the empire after 632. After the prophet Muhammad died in 632, Islamic armies began to attack vast areas in the eastern empire. By 642 Islamic forces had gained control of most Byzantine land. Constantinople was attacked by Islamic troops in 677. Eventually Leo III, who ruled from 717 to 740, would drive the Islamic forces out of Asia Minor and recover most Byzantine lands lost during Heraclius rule.

Not all things Heraclius did turned out badly. He enlarged upon a reform began by prior emperors that created military units and provinces settled by soldiers called "themes." Under this system, soldiers and sailors were awarded land in return for military service. Military personnel would settle in these themes and join with other soldiers on the land into a military unit to defend the territory. Because these soldiers were defending land they actually worked and lived on, they generally fought harder than the slaves, draftees, and foreign mercenaries Byzantine armies had previously relied upon.

The Islamic forces that had ravaged Byzantine lands during the reign of Heraclius remained in control of much of Asia Minor until Emperor Leo III began a campaign to reconquer Byzantine lands. The reconquest began after Leo repelled a Muslim siege of Constantinople in 717 and 718.

Leo III (left) forbade the worship and display of icons. This imperial act enraged the monasteries, whose monks were firmly attached to the practice of venerating icons.

Largely because of Leo's fight against Islam, he became embroiled in a controversy called "iconoclasm." In 726, Leo issued an edict against the use of images within Christian churches within Byzantine lands. Some historians think the Emperor's policy was initiated to give the state an excuse to take monastic lands which could be used to pay troops in his army. Others believe Leo's iconoclastic policy was devised to make it easier to convert Muslims in conquered lands to Christianity. Still others have concluded that iconoclasm arose because Leo himself was influenced by the Islamic condemnation of idol worship. Whatever the reason for issuance of the policy, it produced a crisis in relations between the eastern and western parts of the empire, hardening the chasm between the Roman Catholic and Eastern Orthodox churches.

The controversy over whether images of Christ, the Virgin Mary, and the saints were permitted in churches split the Byzantine Empire into two zealous factions. In the early period of organized Christianity, the Judaic belief that any graven images represented idolatry and that it is impossible to physically look upon God, generally kept icons out of Christian worship houses. Over time, the influence of Judaism waned and by the fifth century icons depicting Jesus, Mary, and various saints had become increasingly prevalent in churches. Moreover, such relics were venerated in many churches, giving the impression that some Christian worshippers were breaking the Second Commandment by engaging in idolatry (worshipping graven images). In this context, iconoclasts clashed with iconodules (people who favored allowing images in churches). Iconodules justified having images in churches due to their belief that in Jesus the word of God had become flesh and thus did not prohibit artists from creating images depicting Christ, Mary, and the saints. Iconoclasts, however, saw things differently. They believed that a reverence of images not only resulted in idolatry but took focus within worship services away from God.

The controversy over iconoclasm raged within the Byzantine Empire for half a century. Western parts of the empire and the Roman pope generally fell into the iconodules camp while eastern provinces wanted to completely eliminate images from churches. Riots, persecutions, and deaths resulted from the extreme zeal on both sides.

In 787 the Empress Irene attempted to end the controversy by calling into session the Seventh Ecumenical Council. Since Irene had been born and grew up in the western part of the empire, she favored the use of images in churches. Consequently, the Seventh Ecumenical Council voted to allow eastern churches to have icons because their use could possibly provide a means for nonbelievers to find God. The council's decision, however, did not permanently end the controversy.

Iconoclasm began to end in Byzantine lands as images were gradually permitted back into eastern churches between 784 and 813. However, in 813 Emperor Leo V again ordered all images removed from eastern churches, but the ban was not rigidly enforced. In 843 the Byzantine government officially ended the policy of iconoclasm but its repudiation did little to heal the rift between the eastern and western churches—a rift that remains to this day.

The Eastern Church

Leo's policy of iconoclasm, which was an attempt by the emperor to control the church, was an example of "Caesaro-papism" that the western church consistently opposed. Caesaro-papism was the belief that the emperor was head of both the church and state. Even though the Byzantine emperor was not considered a divine personage, as head of the state he served a sacred function within the church. The emperor's life was surrounded by pompous ceremony, and laypeople considered him to be a sacred figure. Byzantine emperors exerted tremendous influence over the Eastern Orthodox Church. Still, the emperor's power within the church was limited. The emperor, for example, could not modify or abolish the Nicene Creed. Byzantine emperors were also expected to live morally upright lives and because he was not ordained as a priest, the emperor could not preside over religious services or administer the sacraments. However, emperors exercised discipline in regards to church officials, chose bishops and determined bishopric territory, made rules for ordination of priests and other church officials, and had the power to investigate wrongdoing within the church and order reformation when necessary. Emperors could also call church councils into session, set the agenda for council meetings, settle theological disputes through royal decrees, and enforce decisions made by the church hierarchy.

Priests within the Eastern Orthodox Church had limited power. They were mostly allowed to settle disputes between parishioners, say mass, and perform the sacraments. Other duties were generally relegated to higher officials

Like its western counterpart, the Eastern Church considered itself the universal church that maintained the one true faith. Little difference in theological principles between the western and eastern churches exists. Beliefs in both the Roman Catholic and Eastern Orthodox churches are similar. A few differences are present, however. Perhaps the major theological difference is over where the Holy Spirit originates. The Eastern Church maintains that the Holy Spirit comes only from God, while the Roman Catholic Church believes that both God and Jesus are sources of the Holy Ghost. This difference between the Greek Orthodox and Roman Catholic churches is called the "filioque dispute." Another difference is that the Eastern Church does not accept the western idea of purgatory (a place between heaven and hell where some souls go to atone for sins before admission to heaven). Unlike its western sister, the Eastern Church allowed divorce, especially if one spouse had committed adultery, accepted married men into the priesthood, and allowed mass to be said in vernacular languages. Churches in Russia, for example, conducted services in Russian, Greek churches used Greek, and churches in other regions of the Byzantine Empire said mass in whatever language was spoken by common people in that region. The use of vernacular languages had a positive and negative effect on the Byzantine Empire. On the positive side, use of vernacular languages meant that literature written in native languages developed much more rapidly in eastern lands than in lands formerly part of the Western Roman Empire where Latin was the official language of the church. A negative associated with the use of various languages in Eastern Churches is that religious communication was hampered. Priests from churches in one region could not communicate with priests from other areas because of the language barriers. Western priests, in contrast, could communicate with all priests in all Western Churches because they knew Latin. Eastern Churches, consequently, became fragmented and isolated from each other while the Western Church was more unified. The ability to read Latin also meant that western priests could read Latin literary works, which their eastern counterparts could not read.

The Greek Orthodox Church was, as stated previously, more decentralized than was its Roman Catholic sister. Over time the Roman Pope became the dominant figure in the Western Church. He was the court of last resort in the Roman Church, which he controlled with an iron hand through canon law and the help of a large church bureaucracy. The Eastern Church, in contrast, became more decentralized over time. It existed as a loose assortment of more or less independent churches dependent upon the government to look after church interests. The relationship between church and state in the Byzantine Empire meant that the Eastern Church was not excessively involved in politics as was it western sibling. Instead, the Orthodox Church focused mainly on religious and spiritual matters.

In 380, Christianity became the official religion of the Byzantine Empire and the Patriarch of Constantinople was authorized to head the ceremony in which emperors were crowned. The Byzantine view afterward regarding religion was that the church was an institution used to promote centralization of governmental power. Individuals and groups who held different religions ideas were persecuted by both the government and religious leaders. As a result, many pagan practices within eastern lands were either stamped out or absorbed into mainstream Christianity. Neither persecution nor absorption was able to root out all nonChristian religious groups and practices. The Byzantine Empire had always contained a large Jewish population, which traditionally under Roman Law was protected so long as Jews did not try to convert Christians and construct new synagogues. Jews were, however, legally discriminated against as Byzantine law forbade members of this religious group from holding public office or entering professions such as law or medicine. Justinian and other emperors developed programs to convert Jews to Christianity and in some cases Jews who agreed to undergo Christian baptism were given tax breaks.

Byzantine Civilization

Byzantine civilization, economically and culturally, was more advanced than that of Western Europe during the Medieval Period. While commerce and cities declined in the west, the east experienced an increase in urbanization and trade. Whereas most Westerners were mired in the dark ages, eastern scholars studied Hellenistic philosophy, science, mathematics, and law. Byzantine cities contained schools, libraries, shops, and overflowing markets—things found but rarely in Western Europe.

Byzantine scholars generally adopted ideas from the ancient Greeks and Romans. One important idea was that all people were alike in the natural world and therefore controlled by natural law. Byzantine thinkers expanded upon this idea, which was first enunciated by Epicurean and Stoic philosophers in Greece and Rome. They maintained that since all were one in nature and that since there was but one God, one church, one true set of religious principles, all Christians should be ruled by one government, which would maintain order, enforce laws, and spread Christianity among heathen peoples. Because the empire's duty was to spread Christianity worldwide, Byzantine people generally believed that God would keep the government intact forever. This idea, perhaps more than any other thing, united the diverse people who lived in the Byzantine world, enabling the empire to survive in some form for over a thousand years. After all, Byzantine people reasoned, God had chosen them to preach the "good news" of Christianity worldwide and offer salvation and eternal life to those who were not Christian.

Byzantine people highly valued education. Language and literature within the empire was primarily written in Greek. Most Byzantine scholars read Greek fluently, and the most highly educated individuals spoke Latin as well. In fact, the *Codex Justinianus* was originally published in Latin.

A large percentage of the common population was literate, especially when compared to Western Europe and other civilizations at that time. Three institutions of learning existed in Byzantine lands: a palace school that trained civil servants and diplomats in language, law, and literature; a patriarchal school that taught theology and trained individuals for the priesthood; and a monastic school that instructed monks in ancient literature. Vocational education and training was generally provided for craftsmen through various guilds that existed within the empire.

Much attention was devoted to historical works. Herodotius, Thucydides, and other Greek historians were read widely. Byzantine scholars often expanded upon Greek histories or wrote new histories of their own. Procopius is perhaps the best known Byzantine historian. His work was multifaceted as on one hand he wrote a book praising Justinian's military campaigns in the Mediterranean world but in the *Anekdota* or Secret History, he criticized and poked fun at Justinian and the Empress Theoroda whom he accused of prostitution. In general, Byzantine historians wrote about wars and the conquest of territory by various rulers. Of interest to modern historians are Byzantine accounts of the Crusades from the eastern perspective. The western Christian crusaders were often depicted as semi-barbarians led by kings ignorant of the world around them.

Byzantine historical scholarship was better than their mathematical and scientific achievements. Most scientific achievements came in the context of military use. Perhaps the most important scientific-military discovery Byzantine scientists made was Greek Fire. Eastern scientists learned how to mix oil, sulfur, and other compounds that could be shot through a metal tube and ignited, shooting a flame some distance from the tube. Byzantine armies used these flame throwers to strike fear in their opponents. This weapon was used against Islamic forces to repeal assaults on Constantinople and other Byzantine cities.

The most important scientific advances within the Byzantine Empire came in medicine. Eastern doctors had a much greater medical knowledge than did physicians in Medieval Western Europe. Byzantine medical knowledge was based mainly on the work of ancient Greek doctors, especially Hippocrates' idea that the human body contained four fluids called humors—yellow bile, black bile, blood, and phlegm. So long as these substances were balanced in the body an individual was healthy. However, if an imbalance occurred, the body became disease ridden. To cure disease, doctors would have to restore balance between the four humors. In accordance with this theory, Byzantine doctors sought to cure illnesses through relaxation, a healthy diet, physical exercise, herbal medicines, and expulsion of body fluids through bleeding, burning, the use of leeches, and other methods. While the rest, exercise, and herbal medicines likely helped some patients, the bleeding and burning probably killed many patients already weakened by disease. Medical knowledge was certainly not what it is today. Despite what modern people would consider crude medical treatments, most cities within the Byzantine Empire had hospitals where ailing people were cared for. These institutions contained wards where specific illnesses were treated and beds to house ill patients. Specialists also operated in Byzantine hospitals. Gynecologists in female wards were often women. Other specialists treated intestinal and eye diseases, and most hospitals also contained general practitioners and

This is a modern view of the Santa Sophia. It stands today having survived fifteen hundred years of earthquakes, wars, riots, and fires.

provided outpatient services. Medical practices within the Byzantine Empire were socialized, that is, the government provided funds to operate the hospitals and patients were not charged for treatment.

Despite their medical knowledge, when an outbreak of Bubonic Plague, sometimes called the Justinian Plague, hit Byzantine lands, doctors were not able to cope with the illness any better than their western counterparts because medical knowledge was incapable of understanding its cause or treatment. This illness, which was at its height within the Empire from about 541 to 700, likely originated in Asia and was transported to Mediterranean lands on ships trading with India and China. Thousands of Byzantine people succumbed to this illness. Not only did the plague kill thousands, it also hampered Byzantine efforts to reconquer lost lands in the western empire and to repel Arab and Persian invaders from the east.

The Byzantine Empire was noted for its art and architecture. Excellent examples of eastern art and architecture are found in the Hagia Sophia (Church of the Holy Wisdom) constructed during Emperor Justinian's reign. The Hagia Sophia, considered one of the world's greatest churches, was designed by Anthemius of Tralles and Isidore of Miletus. This great cathedral, built according to Romanesque architectural style, is shaped like a cross. The church's interior contains a variety of art, including mosaic pictures made from rocks and silica glued into frames. Atop the church sits a large dome nearly 200 feet high. Around the dome are windows to let in outside light. The dome itself symbolizes the portal entrance into heaven from the earth that souls pass through after death.

Byzantine civilization is particularly noted for its large degree of urbanization during the Middle Ages, a time in which urban life declined in Western Europe. Numerous cities, including Constantinople, Tyre, Trebizond, Alexandria, Antioch, and Beirut, flourished within the eastern Empire. Constantinople and other cities offered residents streets that were paved with cobblestones and lighted by lamps at night. Byzantine cities also contained large and marvelous buildings as well as horrible slums. Wealthy Byzantines lived in large houses while most people who were poor lived in squalor inside small huts. Like modern cities, Byzantine cities faced problems with homeless people, economic distress, and crime.

Mosaic of Justinian and Theodora in Ravenna, Italy.

Not all Byzantines lived in cities. Many also lived in rural areas. Rural dwellers were generally classified as peasants. They usually lived in small villages and farmed lands surrounding the town, venturing forth from the villages at dawn and returning home at dusk. Villages were governed by councils of all property owners. These councils assembled when needed to decide by vote issues important to villagers and chose people to run the town's government.

Ordinary people within Byzantine lands were generally farmers or workers. Farmers produced all kinds of crops and livestock. Most manufacturing was done by skilled craftsmen who belonged to one of the numerous guilds operating in the empire. Guild members made all kinds of products, including silk cloth, gold jewelry, iron tools, and ivory trinkets. Both farmers and craftsmen were heavily regulated by the government, which profited handsomely from commercial activities. Prices, quality, and quantity of production were closely regulated by the government. Laws forbade the best products from being exported, and sometimes gave certain people or companies monopolies in an area.

Trade and commerce were important components of Byzantium civilization. In fact, Byzantium people were generally wealthier than people living in other places at the same time because of the vast amount of trade that passed through the empire's towns and cities. Trade flourished in various commodities throughout the east. Important products included wheat, fur, honey, wax, metals, livestock, spices, and wood. Byzantine merchants also traded in slaves, as did most medieval people. Underpinning this commerce

The Golden Mosaic of Justinian (top) in Ravenna, Italy and the Saintly Disciples (right).

was the gold coin of the realm called a "bezant." The central government ensured that its weight and purity were maintained so that trade could flourish. The bezant was used from the reign of Constantine until the early twelfth century. The international trade made Constantinople and other Byzantine cities virtual melting pots in which various ethnic groups and different religions existed in relative harmony alongside each other.

Byzantine government was centralized. Heading the government was the emperor who had legislative, executive, and judicial functions. Byzantine emperors had absolute authority in all things. They could make new laws, modify existing laws, abolish laws, punish or pardon lawbreakers, and appoint government officials. However,

Justinian's throne in Ravenna, Italy.

the empire was too large for a single individual to control by himself. Emperors had to rely upon a large bureaucracy to effectively govern. They chose individuals they could trust to run various governmental departments, including the treasury and the courts. Most department heads reported to the emperor's second in command, called the Master of Offices, with the exception of the military commander who reported directly to the emperor. While civil and military affairs were separated at the national level, they were generally combined at local governmental levels. Generals who headed the themes also controlled civil authorities within them. Although trials were held by courts throughout the land, individuals could appeal an unfavorable verdict directly to the emperor or one of his department heads who might then overturn the verdict. The Byzantine government also operated a system of mail delivery and had a secret police, called the agents in rebus, to keep tabs on enemies of the emperor. The government also engaged in diplomacy with other governments. Diplomats and civil service workers were generally literate people capable of doing the job they were hired for.

THE LATE BYZANTINE PERIOD: DECLINE OF THE EMPIRE, 1072-1453

As previously stated, Byzantine military might was based, to a large degree, on creation of themes. This system established a powerful army and navy populated by free peasant landowners willing to defend their farms and villages from outside threats. However, beginning in the tenth century, the theme system began to crumble as the peasant-farmer-soldier saw their land taken by more powerful neighbors, which crated a society dominated by large landowners who became a rural aristocracy. Many of the former landowners became serfs bound to the aristocratic manors, which lessened the number of people available for military service. Likewise, serfs that did serve in Byzantine armies had little incentive to fight hard because they now were defending the land of the aristocrat, not land owned and farmed by the soldier. Decline of the theme system was one factor contributing to decline of the Byzantine Empire.

Another factor contributing to the empire's decline was the increasing power of the landed aristocracy, which weakened control of the central government over its outlying provinces. This decline was hastened in the eleventh and twelfth centuries when weak Byzantine emperors, rather than squashing aristocratic power militarily, tried to assure the loyalty of aristocrats by giving them even more land from royal holdings. Instead of buying loyalty from landed aristocrats, this ill conceived policy only strengthened the power of large landowners, making it more difficult for the central government to control them.

A third factor that strengthened aristocratic power and contributed to the empire's decline was that large landowners were also given control over church lands. Church leaders began in the eleventh century to grant vast monastic holdings to wealthy aristocrats. These grants, called *charistikaria*, or donations to charity, were given aristocrats to run for the church. In reality, aristocrats rarely managed monastic lands in ways that benefitted the church but instead, used the lands to increase the manager's wealth and power.

The above factors meant that the Byzantine Empire was undergoing a social transformation from a land of independent land owners controlled by a strong central government into a feudal land controlled locally by wealthy aristocratic landowners with a weak central government. From a military perspective, this transformation was disastrous. Emperors had to hire foreign mercenaries to fight their wars and defend Byzantine lands from outside invaders. Control of the Mediterranean Sea was vital for the defense of Constantinople. Because of the decline of the naval themes, emperors found it increasingly harder to secure sailors and had to seek naval support from foreign nations, particularly Venice, an Italian city-state whose naval power had grown over time. In 998 and again in 1082 the Byzantine Empire signed treaties giving Venice most favored nation trade status. These trade concessions contributed greatly to the commercial and military growth of Venice, enabling this Italian city-state to dominate trade in the Mediterranean for a lengthy time.

Control of the Mediterranean was not the most serious military problem facing the Byzantine Empire. Defense of the eastern provinces from the Seljuks, or Turks as the Byzantine people called them, was an even greater problem. The Seljuks were a nomadic tribal people who originated in the steppes east and north of the Caspian Sea in what is today Turkestan. Warfare had occurred off and on between the Turks and Byzantines. In the eleventh century warfare between the two became more fierce as the Seljuks moved deep into the empire's land. Emperor Romanus Diogenes unsuccessfully attempted to expel the invaders but was defeated at the Battle of Manzikert in 1071. The Seljuks captured the Byzantine Emperor and routed the empire's forces, which were comprised of a mixture of foreign mercenaries and Byzantine citizens.

The defeat at Manzikert opened much of the empire's land to the Turkish invaders. Suleiman, a Turkish trial leader, captured land near Constantinople, making himself into the most powerful Seljuk leader and created the Sultante of Rum at Nicaea, his capital city. The Seljuk invasion forced Byzantine leaders to seek assistance from nations that had formerly been part of the Western Roman Empire. The appeal for

Muhammad was the prophet of Islam.

western assistance prompted the First Crusade and marked the permanent decline of Byzantine dominance in Eastern Europe and the Middle East.

ARABA AND ISLAM

By the seventh century Byzantine power was being challenged by Arabic people in the Middle East. In 610 Muhammad, the son of a merchant in Mecca (currently located in Saudi Arabia), began to experience religious visions. As a result of these visions, Muhammad began preaching to people on the Arabian Peninsula. He called upon them to cast aside their old polytheistic beliefs and accept the one true God, whom he called "Allah." Muhammad's preaching was successful. At the time of his death in 632, practically all peoples in the Arabian Peninsula had accepted his teachings, which formed the basis of the religion today called Islam. Within a century after Muhammad's death, Islam had spread far beyond Arabia. Islamic forces controlled lands that today include Syria, Palestine, Egypt, North Africa, Spain, and part of France. Territories controlled by Muhammad's followers would eventually be larger than the old Roman Empire. Today, Islam is considered one of the world's great religions.

Little is actually known about Muhammad's life. The Prophet himself, except for a few sentences in the Qur'an or holy book of Islam, said little about his early life. For over a century after Muhammad's death, stories about his life circulated among Arabic peoples throughout the Middle East. Eventually, these stories were recorded. According to the tales, Muhammad was orphaned when he was a young child and raised by his grandfather, who, like his father, was a merchant. During his teenage years, Muhammad found employment as a merchant in a trade caravan. He later married a wealthy widow, Khadijah, who previously had employed him as a personal servant. Marriage to the wealthy widow made Muhammad financially independent, giving him time to preach the message of Allah. As depicted in the Qur'an, Muhammad was a man devoted to Allah who was literate but not highly educated. He had been afflicted with seizures from the time of his childhood. During the seizures he generally lost consciousness and experienced visions. In one of these seizures in 610, the Angel Gabriel told Muhammad to preach Allah's message to the entire world.

The message Gabriel told Muhammad to preach was fairly simple, having five primary tenants. Allah, or the Islamic God, is supreme, and Muhammad was his prophet. This is called Shanda. All Muslims are required to submit themselves completely to Allah because all eventually will face a Judgment Day. All thoughts and actions of each person must be directed to the coming Day of Judgment at which devout Muslims will be awarded heavenly bliss—live in a lush garden dressed in fine clothes surrounded by beautiful people. According to Muhammad, whom Muslims believe to be the last heavenly prophet and a successor of Abraham and Christ, in order for an individual to enter heaven his or her earthly life must be lived according to God's will. Thus, Muslims are required to live according to a strict code of moral behavior. During the month of Ramadan, Muslims must not drink, eat, or engage in sexual intercourse from dawn to dusk and must fast and pray extensively. In months other than Ramadan, Muslims are required to pray five times each day facing Mecca. Called the Salat, these prayer ceremonies show love for and obedience to Allah. Within his or her life each Muslim, if possible, must undertake the Haij or pilgrimage to Mecca. There, he or she must visit the Ka'bah and pray to Allah along with the thousands of other pilgrims visiting Mecca. Islam also requires its adherents to give alms to the poor; this is called Zakat. This charity is given to the poor because the devout Muslim wants to express love for Allah. Muslims are not allowed to consume alcoholic beverages, gamble, practice usury (charging interest on money), or charge excessive prices for merchandise. Sexual activity is also strictly regulated by Islamic teachings and may occur only in the context of marriage but men are allowed to have as many as four wives, so long as each wife is treated equitably. Polygamy was a common practice in Arabic societies, especially among the wealthy, and likely developed because of the shortage of marriageable males in the warrior cultures that existed in the Middle East. In some respects, Islam protected women more than did Christianity. For example, at the time of marriage, Muslim women retained control over one-third of property owned before marriage. Women in Christian parts of Europe, in contrast, lost control over property to their husband when married.

Even though Muslims were required to live a devout life, this alone did not mean they would enter heaven, as Muhammad taught that God predestined each individual for heaven or hell before birth. Although a person's fate was sealed prior to birth, Muhammad stated that predestination gave each individual hope for eternal salvation. Martyrs, those who died in battle while fighting for Islam, automatically gained admission into heaven. Muslims, like Jews, generally gathered to worship and pray in groups on Fridays, the day before the Sabbath. Both Christians and Jews were viewed as protected people under Islam because, like Muslims, these religions emanated from the ancient Hebrew scriptures.

The Qur'an originated from the visions Muhammad had while experiencing one of his frequent seizures. While in the trance, Muhammad's personal secretary wrote down the words the Prophet uttered, which were often recited in an almost poetic manner. After Muhammad died, Islamic scholars organized the revelations according to topics into chapters. In 651 an official holy book—the Qur'an or Prayer Recitation—was published at the behest of Islamic religious cleric Othman.

The Schism of Islam

After Muhammad's death a schism developed within Islam. Muhammad, like the Hebrew prophets in the Old Testament, presented himself as a religious reformer. He considered himself to be the last in a line of prophets extending from Abraham and Jesus Christ. However, Muhammad died without having a son to inherit his position. His daughter, Fatima, was his only survivor, and she was married to the Prophet's cousin, Ali. Muhammad's successor was to be named at a meeting of a council of elders in 632, but they did not choose Ali. In fact, between 632 and 656 four other leaders were chosen to succeed Muhammad as Caliph. Finally, in 656 Ali became Caliph but was murdered in 661. His assassin was a member of the Kharijites, a group of radical Muslims who believed that only Arabs could be Muslims. In 661 the Kharijites broke from Ali when he sought compromise on a religious principle to give him political advantage. After his assassination, Ali's followers maintained that Allah had ordained Ali as the Prophet's successor on earth. Ali's supporters became known as Shiites, meaning supporters of Ali, and maintained that Ali and other blood descendants of the Prophet Muhammad, whom they called imans, had divine knowledge passed from Allah to Muhammad and then to the imans. Most Muslims rejected the Shiite belief in hereditary divinity. They believed instead that divine knowledge from Allah was revealed in the *Sunna*, a book that contained Muhammad's words and advice on how to cope with various issues. This group of Muslims became known as Sunni. Rather than consulting an iman or direct descendant of Muhammad when the Qur'an offered no answer to a problem, Sunni Muslims read the *Sunna*. Over the centuries since the 661 schism, Sunni Muslims have become known as orthodox believers, and Shiites are viewed as heretical by the majority of the Islamic population. The split between Sunni and Shiite still causes conflict in modern Middle Eastern countries such as Iraq and Iran. Ali's death marked the beginning of the Syrian Ommayad (sometimes spelled Umayyad) family rule, a hundred year period that saw Islam's greatest period of military conquest and expansion.

The Expansion of Islam

Mecca, the city of Muhammad's birth, was traditionally a holy city on the Arabian Peninsular because it was the location of the Ka'ba, a stone building that housed a black rock, most likely a meteorite that was an object of worship by pagan Arabs. After Muhammad began teaching in Mecca, he suffered rejection because his preaching threatened the established pagan religions. Mecca's leaders in particular felt threatened when Muhammad called the faithful to face toward Jerusalem—the Jewish capital—when praying rather than the pagan Ka'ba shrine. The order to face Jerusalem when praying did not remain in effect long. After the Jews refused to accept Muhammad as their promised Messiah, he then instructed Muslims to face toward Mecca when reciting prayers.

In 622 Muhammad undertook the Hejira to Yathrib, a city north of Mecca after leaders of Mecca forced him and about 40 followers to flee. Muhammad fled to Yathrib because leaders of that city extended him an invitation to preach there. Muhammad's preaching in Yathrib was so successful that the city was renamed Medina (the City of the Prophet) in his honor. Muhammad's flight from Mecca to Medina became year one in the Islamic calendar. Until his death in 632 Muhammad resided in Medina, becoming the city's spiritual and political leader. At Medina, the Prophet wrote a constitution used to govern the city, consolidated his military power, and converted numerous followers to his faith. Islamic converts were told that Allah wanted them to spread his word through peaceful conversion but if that did not work, then by military conquest.

After consolidating power in Medina, Muhammad began to make war against Mecca, beginning with successful raids on Meccan merchant caravans. In 624 Muhammad and his followers, against great odds, defeated a Meccan army. By 630 the Medinans had captured Mecca itself, and Muhammad returned briefly to his birth city, outlawed the worship of pagan gods, and made Mecca the central city in Islamic worship.

The greatest period of Islamic expansion occurred after Muhammad's death. The Prophet had united all the Arabic Bedouin tribes by 632, and Islamic expansion toward Byzantine lands began. Between 632 and 732 the four Caliphs and the succeeding Umayyad rulers (the first group of hereditary Caliphs) expanded Islamic territory further than in any other period. Several Byzantine provinces, including Syria, Palestine, Egypt, and North Africa, came under Islamic rule. Muslim forces also expanded across northern Africa and into Spain and attempted to invade Frankish lands before Charles Martel stopped them at Tours in 732. This defeat stopped Islamic advances into Western Europe. Islamic boundaries remained relatively unchanged for several centuries afterward. Muslim expansion was not confined to lands surrounding the Mediterranean Sea. Islamic warriors fought battles deep within the African continent and into the Indian subcontinent of Asia. Umayyad rulers also moved the Islamic capital from Mecca to Damascus, Syria and from that location ruled an enormous empire.

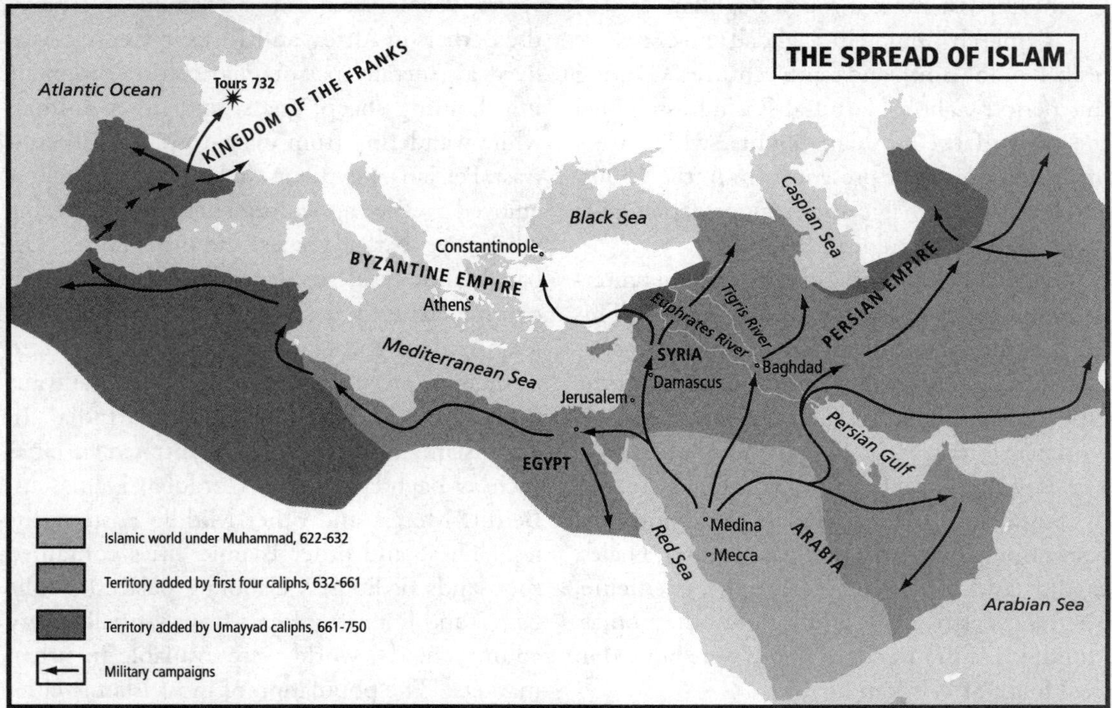

Islamic Civilization

Baghdad, a city on the Tigris River in modern day Iraq, was the leading center of Islamic culture and civilization. In a fertile agricultural area between the Tigris and Euphrates rivers, Baghdad became an important commercial center early in Middle Eastern history, controlling profitable trade routes between Mediterranean countries and Asian lands to the east. The city was expanded on orders from Caliph Mansur of the Abbasid dynasty in 762. Thousands of craftsmen and artisans were employed to build the city whose central feature was a splendid palace capped by a green dome. Entry into the palace was through a golden gate. Here, the Abbasid caliphs ruled during Islam's golden age. Trade goods from China and other Asian lands were carried through Baghdad on their way to Mediterranean countries, and goods from the west bound for the Orient likewise came through Baghdad.

Islamic civilization in Baghdad and elsewhere peaked in the ninth and tenth centuries. During this period Caliph Harun al-Rashid assembled the tales of the Arabian Nights, which were organized into their present form in the 1500s. These stories of magic and intrigue depict a life of luxury and splendor in Baghdad.

Baghdad also housed the first Islamic international "college," the House of Wisdom. This Muslim institution of higher education was established by Caliph Al-Mamun. Scholars at the House of Wisdom translated ancient documents written in Greek, Hebrew, Latin, Hindu and Chinese into Arabic and established a library for use by researchers. Islamic scholars could now read works from Plato, Aristotle, Hippocrates, Thales, Euclid, and others on philosophy, medicine, geography, astronomy, and various other topics. Hundreds of thousands of books were housed in the House of Wisdom library.

In Western Europe, Islamic civilization was centered in Spain. Muslim forces came across the Mediterranean Sea at the Strait of Gibraltar in 711 and defeated Visigoth forces at Guadalete, controlling Spain for the next five centuries. The Umayyad ruler, Abd al-Rahman, established a kingdom in Spain, making his capital at Cordoba where he constructed a magnificent mosque. Muslims built also the Alhambra palace in Granada and the Alcazar at Seville. Spain was the site of greatest contact between Islam and western Christianity. In fact, Islamic rulers in Spain allowed Christian, Jewish, and Muslim scholars to live and work together, and Spain enjoyed a flourishing artistic, literary, architectural, and philosophical society. Aristotle was translated into Latin by Jewish scholars, and Moses Majmonides, a Jewish philosopher, used Aristotelian logic to question God's existence.

Economically, the Islamic empire was diverse. People, such as the Bedouins in Arabia, the Berbers in Africa, and Turks in Central Asia, lived a generally pastoral/agricultural/nomadic life, herding sheep, goats, and other animals while wandering from place to place. In contrast, Persians, Egyptians, Italians, and Spaniards enjoyed a settled agricultural lifestyle, cultivating wheat, rye, barley, grapes, and other crops. Urban Islamic residents generally prospered from commercial activities in Baghdad and other cities. Artisans and craftsmen in cities produced numerous products carried on trade caravans for sale in places such as China and India. In fact, Islamic society was concentrated in cities such as Baghdad, Cairo, Cordoba, Damascus, Beirut, Mecca, and other Middle Eastern cities. These and other Islamic cities contained thousands of houses, elaborate palaces, public baths, and libraries. Items from virtually every country in the world were available in urban markets. The population of most Islamic cities was cosmopolitan. Merchants, artisans, traders, and businessmen from throughout the world set up shop in Middle Eastern cities.

Islamic religious beliefs and laws aided economic expansion in Muslim lands. Commercial communication was made easier when Arabic was legally declared to be the official language of the empire. Merchants, craftsmen, and traders from Spain to India now understood and could easily communicate with each other. Businessmen were also highly respected in Islamic lands. After all, the Prophet Muhammad had been a merchant, and Mecca and Medina, the two cities where Islam was born, had been important centers of trade. Muslim laws encouraged commercial activity. Much Islamic trade was carried on by ships on the Mediterranean Sea, the Red Sea, and the Indian Ocean. In fact, Muslim ships transported the bulk of products exchanged between Western Europe and Asia until the 1700s.

Trade between the Middle East, Africa, Asia, and Europe also stimulated agricultural development. Plants and livestock cultivated in one area were introduced into other areas. Rice, carrots, sugar cane, oranges, lemons, grapefruit, figs, eggplant, cotton, wheat, rye, and other crops were introduced into various areas controlled by Muslim people. New farming methods, such as irrigation of dry fields, were likewise introduced throughout Islamic countries and greatly improved lands' yields.

Academic thought also advanced in territories controlled by Islamic forces. Muslim mathematical and scientific knowledge, much of which was derived from the Greeks, Romans, and Hindus, was extensive. Al-Khwarizmi, a Muslim mathematician, wrote the first book on the discipline of Algebra and used it to solve problems in science, particularly in physics and astronomy. He also borrowed the use of the Hindu numerical system and introduced it into lands conquered by Islamic people. Arab mathematicians also discovered the number zero, making mathematical calculations easier. Al-Razi, an Islamic physician, wrote about 140 essays and books on medicine. Muslim medical knowledge was far superior to that of Western Europe. Al-Razi's writings were soon translated into Latin and read widely in the West. Al-Zahrawi, a Muslim surgeon at Cordoba, discovered how to prevent infection in open wounds by cauterizing them with a hot piece of metal and how to break up calcified stones in the human urinary system. Ibn-Sina wrote al-Qunun, a text that included all the medical knowledge known to the Greco-Roman, Hindu, and Muslim worlds in the eleventh century. This work described symptoms associated with most diseases, discussed how various contagious diseases spread, and included information on over 760 drugs known to treat illness and alleviate symptoms of illnesses.

Philosophy and religion were additional topics Muslim scholars addressed. Spaniard ibn-Rushd was perhaps the most gifted Muslim philosopher. He wrote extensively on Aristotle. Since the Islamic Empire was united by a common religion, Muslim scholars generally wrote books and essays praising Allah and exploring the relationship between faith and rational thought, between Allah and human beings, and Allah's all encompassing power as opposed to free will within humans.

As stated earlier, Islam theoretically sanctioned polygamy, the practice in which males could have as many as four wives. In reality, most males had only a single mate because the majority could not afford multiple wives given the economic realities of the time. Only wealthy Muslims could actually afford to support more than one wife and the household each presided over. Some Muslim scholars maintain that Islamic law provided greater protection to Islamic women because it required that males with multiple wives treat them equally. Divorce laws were fairly lax in Muslim countries. Husbands could generally initiate divorce proceedings against wives for almost any reason, but Muslim women retained more control over property in marriages than did women living in western societies. Muslim women, however, were required to cover their faces with a veil when in public. No man but the husband was allowed to view a woman's face, and women were generally not allowed to have male friends outside family members; Muslim women spent their time in the company of other women only.

Government within the lands conquered by Islamic forces was usually theocratic. After Muhammad's death, the first caliph, Abu Bakr, consolidated both secular and religious authority in his person. Afterwards, the caliph was the supreme religious and political leader in the Islamic Empire. No separation between church and stated existed in Muslim lands. Even though all political and religious authority was vested in the caliph, he could not arbitrarily dictate changes in Islamic law because all rules and regulations for Muslims theoretically came from Allah and were recorded in the Qur'an and other holy documents. Because Muslim laws already existed, the caliph and lesser governmental officials primarily served as administrators, judges, and interpreters of the law. Muslim rulers generally allowed conquered peoples to keep governmental institutions already operational in those lands unless they conflicted with the teachings of Islam. Local judges, called Kadi, resided in practically all Muslim communities. They chiefly adjudicated disputes among local people and kept order throughout the Muslim Empire.

Islamic expansion initiated change in Muslim civilization through the absorption of ideas and institutions created by other civilizations, especially the ancient Greek, Hebrew, and Hindus. Of these, Greek was perhaps the most important. Arabic scholars translated works of most Greek authors, including Plato and Aristotle into Arabic. These and other Greek writers, along with the teachings from the Qur'an and other Islamic holy books, were the base upon which education in Muslim schools rested.

Muslims generally divided the world into two spheres: Dar-al-Islam (the world or house of Islam) and Dar-al-Harb (the world of Infidels or House of War). Within Dar-al-Islam regions most of the people were Muslim and within Dar-al-Harb areas people were mainly Christian or some other non-Islamic religion. All Muslims were required to live according to the principle of jihad, which means struggle or exertion within and outside the self. Jihad required that every devout Muslim struggle to overcome sin within the individual by leading a morally upstanding lifestyle and to overcome worldly sin by spreading Allah's word among nonbelievers. War, in the name of Allah, was part of jihad and permitted to bring Allah's message to lands populated by infidels. In fact, some Muslim scholars teach that jihad, or holy war, in the name of Allah is one of the primary tenants of Islam. Other scholars, however, disagree with this idea, maintaining instead that jihad is primarily meant to apply to the struggle against evil that constantly occurs within each individual Muslim.

The Decline of Islam

Islamic civilization reached its zenith in the ninth and tenth centuries and also began to decline at the same time. Scholars generally date the beginning of the decline to the ninth century when Seljuk Turks mercenaries were employed by various caliphs to guard the royal family. Within a short period the Seljuks controlled the caliphs and could appoint or remove Islamic leaders. Because of their inability to control their Turkish guards a series of weak caliphs ruled the Islamic Empire, and over time the government lost control of conquered lands.

Islamic decline further escalated in the tenth and eleventh centuries when invaders from both Europe and Asia threatened the empire. Christian forces from Western Europe attacked Muslim strongholds in Spain and began to retake the Iberian Peninsula. Christian naval forces also defeated the Islamic fleet in the western Mediterranean, breaking Muslim domination within that area. The First Crusades also successfully captured Jerusalem from Muslim forces in 1099.

From the east, Turkish forces attacked Islamic lands. After infiltrating the Abbasid caliphate in large numbers, the Turks wrested control of Baghdad from the Arabs in 1055. In 1071, the Seljuks, led by Sultan Alp Arslan, defeated a Byzantine force at Manzikert, which opened all Middle Eastern lands to their armies. Weak caliphs within Islamic lands were unable to withstand the Turkish invasion, and over the next two centuries lost control of much Muslim land previously conquered by Islamic forces.

Economic changes also hastened the decline of the Islamic Empire. After the Muslim navy lost control of the Mediterranean, Italy and other Western European countries dominated international commerce by the thirteenth century. The decline in use of Islamic coins in international commerce, for example, was a sign that Muslim countries were no longer commercially influential.

A third factor that played a role in Islam's decline was that caliphs stopped the practice of paying soldiers salaries. Instead, soldiers received compensation through land grants. Some soldiers received vast amounts of land and through acquisition of neighboring land grants, became aristocrats, much like the situation that developed in feudal Europe. There large landowners maintained private armies to protect their personal holdings, which weakened the central control of the caliphs.

After the eleventh century Islamic civilization appeared to lose its vigor. Qualities such as openness, flexibility, a stimulating intellectual society, and toleration of minorities and of other religions began to wane within Muslim societies. In general, society became more closed, and intolerant, and exhibited less ability to question previous assumptions. The glory days of Islam were over.

Legacy of Islam for the Western World

Islamic civilization greatly influenced life in Western Europe during the Medieval Period. As previously noted, western agriculture benefitted as new farming techniques such as irrigation were introduced into western lands and new crops, including rice, fruits, and other plant foods were successfully cultivated by western farmers. Western societies also made use of the numerical system Arabic people got from the Hindus and brought to western lands they conquered. Western philosophical thought was also indebted to Islam.

In general, however, Muslim and Europeans distrusted each other even though both had a common religious and cultural heritage from the ancient Hebrews. As a result of this distrust, contact between the two cultures was limited mainly to commerce and war. Europeans, because of Islam's expansion into parts of Europe during the eighth and ninth centuries, viewed Muslims with fear and hatred. Religious differences between Islam and Christianity also fueled the hostility between the neighboring cultures. Christians were unwilling to tolerate a religion that viewed

Allah or God as creator of the universe but that rejected the Trinity and that denied the divinity of Christ but accepted him as a major prophet. Christian popes, theologians, and church councils condemned Islam. Most Europeans viewed Islam as an heretical religion and the Prophet Muhammad as an evil being. The Italian poet Dante, for example, placed Muhammad in the ninth circle of hell, next to Satan himself, where his body was constantly ripped to shreds as punishment in the classic *Inferno*.

Muslims, likewise, regarded Europeans and Christians with suspicion. Christians were assigned to the Dar-al-Harb and viewed as infidels. Little actual contact occurred between Muslims and Christians other than in the context of trade. Few Muslims would travel in Europe because few Mosques or Islamic communities, containing the things Muslims needed to maintain their faith, were available there. Muslims also were reluctant to travel in lands where Christians viewed them as heathens. When Muslims needed to make contact with Europeans in regards to government or business needs, they usually sent a dhimmis, a Jewish or Christian intermediary. Muslims generally perceived Europeans as culturally inferior people and viewed Christianity as an early religion that was flawed and that had been surpassed by Islam. Consequently, Muslims manifested little interest in or concern with European culture and people.

THE PRINCIPALITY OF KIEV

Russian society and civilization owes much to Byzantine civilization. Within what today is Russia, eastern Slavic people adopted Byzantine Christianity and established the Principality of Kiev. Modern Russians are direct descendants of Byzantine civilization. Between 700 and 1000 A. D. Slavic tribal people expanded in Europe as far east as the Volga River and north to the Baltic Sea. In these lands, the Slavs settled into a lifestyle dependent on agriculture and commerce and built numerous settlements, including Kiev on the Dnieper River. Early in the ninth century Norsemen or Vikings invaded Slavic settlements. The Viking invaders then opened trade routes between Russia and Constantinople. According to the *Primary Chronicles of Russian History*, which were written down in 1118 after being circulated as oral history for over 200 years, the Vikings ruled Russia until the Slavs drove them from their lands in the ninth century. After the Norsemen were expelled, Slavs fought among themselves so much that no effective government could be established to control the warring factions. In 862 Slavs asked a Viking prince named Rurik to govern them. Rurik and his family arrived in the land of the Slavs and briefly ruled before turning the lands over to Oleg, Rurik's associate. The name Russia supposedly was taken from Rurik and his followers who were known as Rus. Thus Russia means land of the Rus.

Under Oleg's rule, Slavic settlements, including Kiev and Novgorod, were united sometime after 873, which makes Oleg the actual person who founded Russia. Russians also attacked Byzantine lands near the middle of the ninth century. Oleg attacked Constantinople with a naval fleet supposedly having over 2000 ships early in the tenth century. His victory forced the Byzantine Empire to buy peace through trade and tribute. After Oleg's death in 913, his heirs consolidated power, bringing all Slavic tribes under their control. As a result, Russia stretched from the Baltic to the Black Seas and from the Danube to the Volga Rivers. In 957 the Russian princess Olga was converted to Byzantine Christianity while in Constantinople. In 989 Vladimir, the supreme Russian ruler, was baptized in the Eastern Church and ordered all Slavs to become Christian even though Russian nobles feared that Byzantine Emperors and the Orthodox church would exert too much power in their lands. Vladimir's conversion occurred, according to the *Primary Chronicles of Russian History,* after he sent an emissary to visit different religions—Muslims, Jews, Khazars, and Byzantines. Apparently, Vladimir's ambassador was impressed by Byzantine worship practices, especially the high level of pomp and pageantry in Eastern Church services, and recommended that the Russian ruler become Christian. Vladimir's conversion, which likely resulted from close economic connections between the Slavic kingdom and the Byzantine Empire, brought Russia deeper into Byzantine culture and religion. Kiev's strategic location made the city important in the trade between Northern and Western Europe and the Byzantine Empire.

The Russian Orthodox Church, despite maintaining close ties to the Byzantine Church, was generally independent from its beginning. Although the Metropolitan or Primary Bishop of the Russian Church was Greek and appointed by the Constantinople Church, practically all Russian clergy were Slavic. Conversion to Byzantine Christianity did, however, cause Russian society to experience drastic change. For example, under Slavic law, victims of crime were vindicated when family members extracted punishment on the criminal. After Russians adopted Christianity, punishment for crimes was now a state rather than family matter. Within Russia, pagan altars and statues were destroyed. Christian crosses and artwork were erected in their place. Orthodox priests became important people in most communities.

Kievan civilization reached its height under Yaroslav or Yaroslav l the Wise, as he is sometimes called, during the first half of the eleventh century. Yaroslav, the son of Vladimir, was successful in most of his undertakings. In terms of military conquest, he defeated the Pechenegs, a nomadic tribe who lived near the Black Sea south of Kiev, and the Fins, who inhabited lands north of Kiev (now Finland) and extended Russian territory at the expense of both groups. Yaroslav erected numerous churches and public buildings in territory he controlled, including the magnificent cathedral at Kiev, and also codified Russian law. He imported scholars from Byzantine lands and established schools for them to teach in. These scholars also translated many important Greek books, including the Bible, into the Slavic language.

Economically, Kiev prospered through trade with both the East and West. Various products, including slaves, fur, honey, beeswax, amber, wheat, silk, spices, and incense, were traded with Scandinavian lands to the north, Muslims and Byzantines to the east, and peoples living in England and France to the west. Agriculture was the foundation of Kievan civilization. The largest portion of the population was comprised of free peasants who farmed small plots but some Kievans were enslaved while others held the status of serfs. Most Kievan agriculturalists were concerned with daily survival, barely eking out a subsistence living on the land.

Not all Kievans were farmers. Some people lived in cities and towns. Kiev itself was a prosperous city that rivaled Constantinople and other cities in population and splendor, containing by several accounts hundreds of churches, thousands of people, numerous stores, ships, and open markets. Within the city aristocratic princes, merchants, soldiers, shopkeepers, craftsmen, day laborers, and homeless street people intermingled.

The Principality of Kiev was governed by a monarch who selected important nobles, called boyars, to advise him on most issues. Cities and towns were controlled by veches (assemblies of citizens) who also offered advice to the monarch when necessary. Courts of law, from which there was no appeal, administered justice.

After Russia's conversion to Christianity, Byzantine monks established schools to educate priests and children of noble descent. Scholars educated a these schools generally left a literary body comprised mainly of translations of the Bible and other religious works. The most important Kievan literary accomplishment was publication of the *Primary Chronicles of Russian History* detailing the coming of Christianity to Russia. Historians generally hold that this book created a national identity with the Slavic peoples of Russia. Although much of the information contained within the *Primary Chronicles* is not historically accurate, it is the best source of information available on medieval Russian life.

Architecturally, the Kievan Principality borrowed greatly from the Byzantine Empire. Church buildings, for example, usually were topped with domes similar to those found on Byzantine churches. Also, Kievan churches were decorated with paintings and icons similar to those found in Byzantine churches.

The Decline of Kiev

After Yaroslav's death in 1054, the Principality of Kiev began a decline. Several factors played a role in the decline. First, the capitol was moved from Kiev to Muscovy, which weakened the central government. Second, the rota system Yaroslav created to choose his successor did not function well. Under the system, all towns and cities were ranked according to their value and awarded to different members of the royal family based upon their degree of kinship to Yaroslav. The death of the monarch within this system often provoked wars between various princes wanting to be king. Third, the almost constant civil wars over who would be king weakened the kingdom so much that it could not fend off outside invasions. In 1061, the Cumans, a nomadic people from the Asian steppes, attacked Kiev and denied the principality access to the Black Sea, causing an economic decline as the primary trade route to Baghdad, Constantinople, and Western Europe was severed. In 1169 a northern prince, Andrew Bogoliubsky, attacked Kiev. Over the next several centuries Russia was generally isolated from both the East and the West. The invasion of Genghis Khan and the Mongols in 1240 marked the end of Kiev as a viable kingdom. For centuries afterward, Russia was under Mongol control. Moscow eventually replaced Kiev as the center of Russian culture.

CONCLUSION

Centuries after the Western Roman Empire ceased to exist, the Byzantine part of the empire survived until its collapse in 1453. From its beginning in 324, when Emperor Constantine moved the Roman capital to Constantinople, Byzantine civilization ebbed and flowed. The empire reached its zenith under the reign of Emperor Justinian from 527 to 565. Today, Byzantine influence is felt throughout the world, especially since most countries in Europe and in the Western Hemisphere base their legal systems on the *Corpus Juris Civilis* devised during Justinian's rule. After Justinian's death in 565, Byzantine power declined during the middle period of the empire's existence because a series of weak emperors lost control of its western provinces. As Byzantine interest shifted more toward the east, Greek replaced Latin as the empire's official language. Further splintering of the Byzantine civilization were conflicts over religion, especially iconoclasm. Despite the controversy over iconoclasm, Byzantine civilization was economically and culturally more advanced than western civilization during the Middle Ages. Scholars and physicians in the Byzantine world, for example, were much more knowledgeable than their counterparts in Western Europe and eastern cities flourished while western urban life declined. During the eleventh and twelfth centuries, the theme system practically ended as landed aristocrats acquired vast tracts of land, which weakened governmental power, making it harder to defend Byzantine territory from Islamic and other invaders. After the defeat at Manzikert, Byzantine lands were opened to Turkish invaders, and the empire eventually collapsed. Modern Russians, however, are today's direct descendents in the western world of the Byzantine civilization. Byzantine influence on Russia stretches back to establishment of the Principality of Kiev.

Throughout its history, Byzantine power was challenged by various outsiders. One of the greatest challengers came from Islamic peoples in the Middle East. Founded by Muhammad in 610, Islam spread throughout the Middle East and into Africa, Asia, and Europe. Muhammad's followers eventually conquered a territory larger than the original Roman Empire. Like other great civilizations, Islam faced problems, especially the schism between Sunni and Shiite. Despite the separation between Sunni and Shiite, Islamic civilization flourished in cities such as Baghdad, Damascus, and Beirut, reaching its peak during the ninth and tenth centuries. Afterwards, Islam began a decline when Turks gained influence over both the Islamic government and military. Hastening the decline was the invasion of Islamic lands by Europeans and Asians. Even after its decline, Islam remains one of the world's great religions.

Even though both the Byzantine and Islamic civilizations both declined, their influence is felt world wide today. Had these great civilizations not have existed, the world might not today be able to read works of the ancient Greek philosophers, use Arabic numerals to keep track of commerce and trade, and have legal systems based on the Code of Justinian.

Suggestions for Further Reading

Peter Arnott, *The Byzantines and Their World* (1973).

J. W. Barker, *Justinian and the Later Roman Empire* (1966).

Carl Brockelmann, *History of the Islamic Peoples* (1949).

Robert Browning, *Justinian and Theodora* (1971).

Charles Diehl, *Byzantine Portraits* (1925).

S. Franklin and J. Shepard, *The Emergence of Rus 750-1200* (1996).

Francesco Gabrieli, *Muhammad and the Conquests of Islam* (1968).

Hammilton A. R. Gibb, *Islamic Society and the West* (1949, 2nd ed. 1953).

Gustave von Grunebaum, *Medieval Islam: A Study in Cultural Orientation* (1961).

J. M. Hussey, *Church and Learning in the Byzantine Empire 867-1185* (1937).

Romily Jenkins, *Byzantium, The Imperial Centuries A.D. 610-1071.* (1969).

D. A. Miller, *Imperial Constantinople* (1969).

Gregor Ostrogorsky, *History of the Byzantine State* (1957).

Procopius, *The Secret History* (1966);
Qur'an, The (1949).

N. V. Riasonovsky, *A History of Russia* (1963).

A. A. Vasiliev, *History of the Byzantine Empire* (1952).

G. Vernadsky, *A History of Russia* (2000).

Montgomery Walt, *A History of Islamic Spain* (1965).

Chapter 6

GERMANIC EUROPE & THE EARLY MIDDLE AGES 378 -1000 A. D.

ALARIC THE VISIGOTH

By the latter years of the fourth century the Western Roman Empire was in shambles. After Odovacer overthrew the Roman Emperor Romulus in 476 A.D., peoples living within the western part of the Empire began to assert their independence. However, it looked as if Christianity, which had spread throughout Western Europe, might also be in decline along with the Roman Empire. Many inhabitants of Gaul and other territories worshipped pagan gods. One of the most important tribal groups living in western Europe were the Franks, who worshipped ancient Norse gods.

At the age of 16 in 486, a boy named Clovis became ruler of the Franks. According to legend, Clovis was a descendent of the Norse god Wotan. After defeating the remaining Roman forces in Gaul, Clovis and the Franks faced threats from the Allemanni, an alliance of various tribal people from modern Germany who invaded Gaul in 496. Clovis gathered his army to repel the invasion. Unfortunately, things did not go well for the Franks. The Allemanni were defeating them in battle until Clothilde, Clovis' Christian wife, persuaded him to abandon paganism and embrace Christianity. In the middle of a battle the Franks were losing, Clovis prayed to Christ, vowing that he would devote his life to Christ if God gave the Franks victory over their enemy. According to legend, God immediately instilled the Alemanni soldiers with a deadly fear, allowing Clovis' forces to defeat them. Clovis, impressed by God's power, fell on his knees, renounced paganism, and accepted Christ. After the battle was over, Clovis was baptized, destroyed pagan images throughout Gaul, encouraged his subjects to do likewise, made Paris his capital, and built the Church of Genevieve there. Clovis expanded his kingdom and established the Merovingian Dynasty. When he died in 511, Clovis had become one of the greatest Frankish kings ever. Over time his name would be altered to Louis, the most important name adopted by later French kings. Clovis was also the first important Frankish leader to become Christian. Some historians think he converted in part because he realized that Christians in neighboring lands would welcome his attacks on the kingdoms that were ruled by pagan leaders.

Chronology

306-337	Constantine I
311	Beginning of toleration of Christians in the Roman Empire
354-430	St. Augustine
392	Christianity made Roman religion
410	Visigoths sack Rome
476	Deposition of last Western Roman emperor
c. 480-524	Boethius
c. 481-515	Clovis
498-526	Theodoric the Ostrogoth King of Italy
c. 500-700	Decline of towns and trade in the West
c. 520	Benedictine monastic rule
527-565	Reign of Justinian
532-537	Byzantine church of Santa Sophia
c. 550	*Corpus* of Roman law
610-641	Byzantine emperor Heraclius
630	Muhammad enters Mecca in triumph
715-754	Missionary work of St. Boniface in Germany
726-843	Iconoclasm in Byzantine Empire

Historians traditionally view the Middle Ages as beginning after the collapse of Rome in the fourth century and the deposition of the last Roman Empire in the fifth century. Several decades ago, the prevailing view was that almost immediately after the last emperor was overthrown, western Europe fell into the Dark Ages. Actually, recent scholarship has shown this view to be inaccurate. After Rome collapsed, Germanic princes tried to maintain the political, economic, and social structure of the Empire. They vied with each other for control of territory and sought official recognition as princes from the Byzantine emperor in Constantinople. Even though a decline in learning, education, science, and culture occurred, Western Europe did not become overnight a land of barbarity and savagery. Trade still flourished in European lands bordering the Mediterranean and along navigable rivers. Still, things changed throughout Western Europe after the Roman Empire collapsed due to military and economic problems that allowed successful conquest of Roman territory by Germanic tribes.

By the arrival of the fifth century, Roman control of Western Europe was over. Various Germanic tribes now ruled lands previously controlled by Roman Emperors. Groups, including the Ostrogoths, Visigoths, Franks, Burgundians, Lombards, Vandals, and others fought each other for dominance in the region. The period from about 378 to 530 was critical in the development of Medieval Europe. At the beginning of this period, the Roman Valentinian dynasty controlled Western Europe. At the period's close, the region was divided into several independent kingdoms, most of which were recognized as sovereign nations by the Eastern or Byzantine Roman Empire.

THE GERMANIC MIGRATIONS INTO ROMAN TERRITORY

Contrary to popular imagination, the Dark Ages did not begin when barbarians, acting in concert, invaded the Western Roman Empire. In reality, the movement of Germanic people into Roman lands was more of a migration than an invasion. There simply was no single, coordinated invasion of the Roman Empire by outside barbarians. While different barbarian (the word barbarian generally meant a foreigner who spoke a different language) tribes did invade the Empire at various times, they were generally pushed into Roman territory by external forces. Romans and barbarians usually did not confront each other as enemies. In fact peaceful encounters between the two far outnumbered violent conflict. Both groups had maintained diplomatic and economic ties for decades before the Roman Empire collapsed. Thousands of barbarian soldiers had served in Roman armies, and emperors often concluded treaties with Germanic leaders in which the barbarians were given authority to defend the Empire's borders. At times, barbarians were given permission to legally settle in Roman lands.

Who, then, were the barbarians. Linguistically speaking, they are classified as part of the Germanic peoples within the Indo-European family of languages. While they differed from the Slavs and Celts that also inhabited central and eastern Europe, historians, archaeologists, and linguists have generally concluded that other than a few minor differences, the Lombards, Saxons, Franks, Vandals, Ostrogoths, and Burgundians were politically, economically, and socially very similar people who sometimes lived in confederations with other groups. The Germanic confederations were generally put together by strong leaders who forced neighboring groups to join them or by various villages who formed alliances to protect themselves from stronger groups. Within these confederations people from different villages often wed and established permanent kinship ties between different groups. Over time, as more and more alliances were formed, groups became larger, and eventually the group came to dominate a larger region.

As noted in the previous chapter on the Roman Empire, Hun raids into central and Eastern Europe was the catalyst that pushed the first Germanic peoples into the western provinces of the Roman Empire. Several factors, in addition to the Hun invasion, played a role in the Germanic migrations. Political upheaval in Germanic lands, shortages of food, the migration of other European tribes into Germanic lands, poor agricultural practices that stripped nutrients from the soil, the cold climate of central and eastern Europe, and a desire for fertile farmland in southern Europe all likely factored into the Germanic move into Roman territory. Regardless of why these people moved from their traditional homelands, by the fourth and fifth centuries, the Roman boundaries at the Rhine and Danube Rivers could no longer hold back the different groups wanting to move into the rich lands of the Roman Empire. Initially, many Germanic peoples were allowed into the Empire as *feodorati* or troops hired by the Roman army. Over time, they comprised a significant portion of the military and many of their leaders became powerful men within the Empire's western provinces. Certainly, the Empire influenced the Germans, and they in turn influenced the Romans.

During the early part of the migration, the Germans resembled the Romans in Western Europe. They had lived near the Roman border, interacted with Romans, and absorbed much of Roman culture. As the migrations proceeded and after the Roman Empire collapsed, the

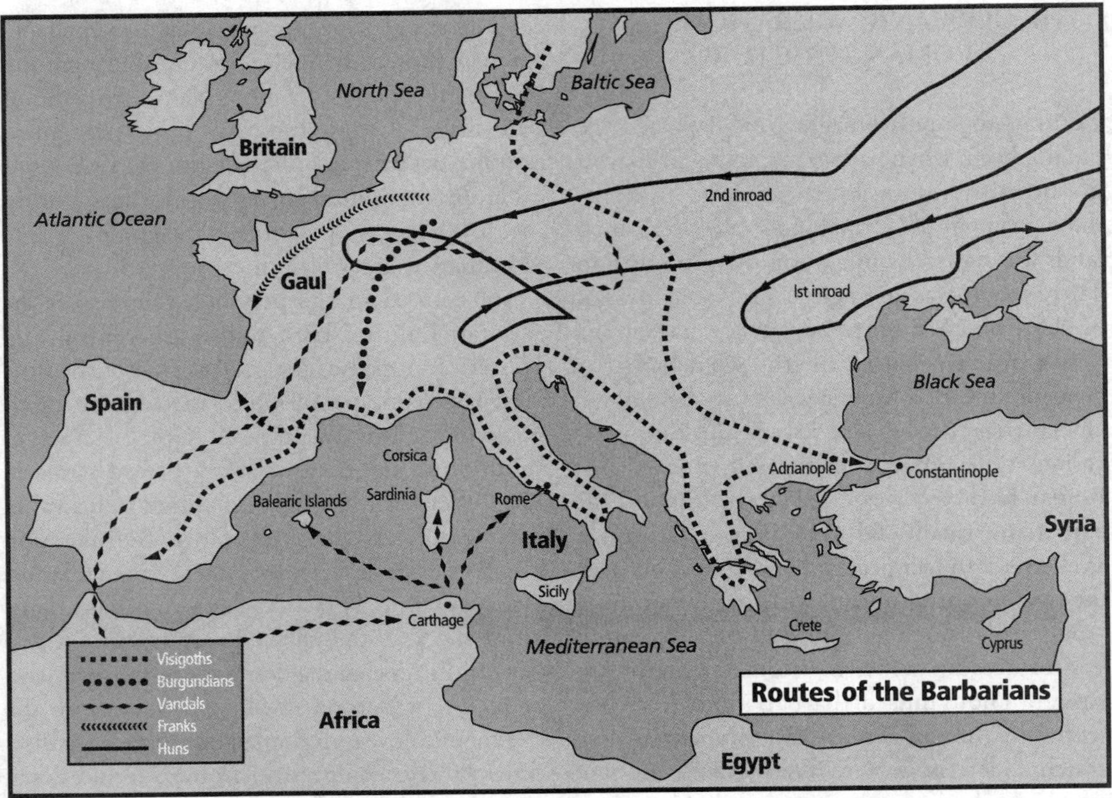

German kingdoms were often allies of the Byzantine Emperor, who saw them as protectors of Roman lands. In fact, the Germanic kingdoms were governmentally structured like the Roman government they replaced. Each nation was ruled by a monarch that generally served two primary purposes—military leader and magistrate. The king generally came from a wealthy family and presided over a dynasty that would produce an heir to the throne. As leader of the military, the monarch was expected to keep the nation safe from outside invaders and provide soldiers of the realm with land and booty. As magistrate, the monarch was expected to appoint officials throughout the realm that would disperse justice in a legal and fair manner. When a miscarriage of justice occurred, citizens could appeal directly to the king for a redress of their grievances.

Residents in most Germanic states dealt with a count. This position, which first appeared in Western Europe in the fifth century, was a method German monarchs used to control their kingdoms. Counts were initially appointed to the position by the king and had magisterial, economic, and military responsibilities. The king made sure that individuals appointed to the position of count came from the local population.

Cities and towns throughout Western Europe were centers of local government. There, local people paid taxes, part of which were then sent to the monarch who used the money for defense and other national purposes. Latin was the language governmental administration was conducted in across Western Europe during the Dark Ages. Legal codes in all Germanic kingdoms were based on Roman law. All legal transactions and documents were prepared and conducted according to this law. In short, the lives of ordinary people living in Western Europe changed little after Germanic kingdoms replaced the Roman government. They obeyed the same laws, paid taxes, worshipped, and generally lived as people lived during the period Rome controlled Western Europe. Likely, the average person in any of the German states was not aware that the Roman Empire had collapsed.

RELIGION AND THE MEDIEVAL CHURCH

The Roman Catholic Church was perhaps the most important institution in Medieval Europe. Christianity largely shaped civilization in Western Europe during the Middle Ages. After the Roman Empire disintegrated, the church took power and prestige, saw its membership increase, its wealth grow, and its influence on society and government increase. In fact, the church is largely credited with preserving civilized life during the Dark Ages. By the end of the Middle Ages, Christianity, not Germanic tribal customs, was the cornerstone of western civilization.

After the Empire's demise, the church maintained the Roman administrative system and, in doing so, preserved an important component of Hellenistic-Latin civilization. The Roman Catholic Church was the only unifying institution in Western Europe during the Middle Ages. It provided Europeans with a cultural tradition that dated to ancient Greek civilizations and also gave people a purpose in life—to serve God through work so that the individual would be rewarded with eternal life in heaven. Medieval Europeans were taught that the individual was a participant in a larger drama pitting God against Satan—good against evil that was cosmic in purpose. The Church was God's instrument on earth to fight the cosmic Satan, and individuals were pawns in the ongoing battle between good and evil. The only way a person could obtain heaven, or so Medieval Europeans were taught, was acceptance of God's salvation as a result of Christ's death. Membership in the Church became the avenue generally accepted for salvation.

Because the Roman Catholic Church was universal throughout Western Europe, membership in the Church replaced Roman citizenship as the unifying agent of society. Everywhere in Europe, a new society was being built around Christianity and the Church. In fact, the Church helped build the foundations of European society that developed in the centuries after the Roman Empire collapsed. After the seventh century, intellectual life throughout Western Europe was in serious decline. Had the Church not have preserved knowledge from the ancient world, this knowledge likely would have been permanently lost.

While learning was in decline across the European continent, Catholic monks copied and preserved numerous texts from the Ancient World and, in doing so, developed a new tradition of learning. Medieval monasteries became depositories for ancient texts. Their libraries contained works from Socrates, Plato, Marcus Aurelieus, and other ancient intellectuals. Monasteries also became cultural centers throughout Western Europe as cities and towns declined in importance, a position they held until cities and towns began to recover during the High Middle Ages. Monasteries also provided lodging for travelers, medical care for the infirmed, and religious education for those seeking a more complete understanding of Christianity. Monks and nuns became the primary agents by which Christianity spread to nonbelievers.

Several individuals were important to the preservation of ancient knowledge during the Medieval period. An early preservationist was Boethius. Descended from an Italian noble family, Boethius successfully translated numerous works by Aristotle into Latin during the first quarter of the sixth century. Cassiodorus, like Boethius, translated several Greek manuscripts into Latin and was one of the first monks to begin copying ancient texts. His work saved numerous classical works from disappearing during the middle decades of the sixth century. Isidore of Seville, working in a Spanish monastery, also preserved much ancient knowledge in *Etymologiae*, a vast work that included information on numerous topics. Although this work contained a number of errors, it nevertheless preserved much ancient knowledge from a large number of ancient texts Isidore consulted when compiling this important encyclopedic like reference work. The work that these and other scholars did was extensive and extremely important because most Europeans lost the opportunity to read, write, and speak both Latin and Greek. As more and more Roman schools closed, illiteracy spread across the continent. Individuals lost interest in learning and thousands of works by ancient authors disappeared. Of the hundreds of plays written by Sophocles, for example, only seven survive today. Had monks not have preserved these works, they likely would have vanished as well, especially after Vikings, Magyars, Mongols, and others raided libraries and destroyed books while searching for loot.

The Papacy and Early Medieval Church Leaders

Most organizations that exist for any length of time develop a leadership hierarchy that enables it to function efficiently. The Roman Catholic Church was no exception, developing a rigid hierarchy as the centuries passed. Initially, the church had five patriarchs located at Rome, Alexandria, Antioch, Jerusalem, and Constantinople. Early in the history of Christianity these patriarchs acknowledged the supremacy of the Roman patriarch because Christ told Peter, according to ancient texts that "Thou art Peter and upon this Rock I will build my church." Peter, whose ministry concluded with his execution and martyrdom in Rome, was later hailed as the first Pope and superior to other church leaders. His successors were generally considered to be head of the Christian Church in the Roman world. Over time, the political, economic, and religious power of the papacy increased. At the Council of Chalcedon in 451, Pope Leo I bestowed upon the papacy the authority to settle doctrine issues. Later popes would extend papal authority. Pope Hormisades in the early part of the fifth century ruled that papal statements were infallible and that salvation outside the church was not possible. Papal power became even greater when the Roman church separated from the eastern church in the eighth century after the Lombards invaded Italy and captured Ravenna, freeing the Roman Pope from control of the Byzantine governor. By the thirteenth century, the Pope was the most powerful and important person in Western Europe. Monarchs feared his power and generally feared to disobey a papal edict. Beginning with Gregory the Great, who served as Pope from 590 to 604, until 1517 when Martin Luther nailed his 95 Theses to the door of the Wittenburg, few dared question the authority of the Pope. Between the sixth and ninth centuries, Roman Popes defended orthodox Christianity from heresy, established bishophorics controlled by the Pope throughout Catholic Europe, and created a uniform literacy for true believers.

Initially, the five church patriarchs competed with each other for authority within the church. Each patriarch was jealous of the other's power and spent much time arguing among themselves for supremacy within the Empire. The patriarch in Constantinople generally was subservient to the Emperor while the bishops overseeing the church at Rome, Antioch, Alexandria, and Jerusalem had more autonomy because of the distance from the Empire's capital. Islamic invasions within the eastern Roman Empire eventually removed the church patriarchs at Jerusalem, Alexandria, and Antioch, leaving only the Bishop of Rome and the Bishop of Constantinople vying for power. This struggle continued until the Roman Pope formed an alliance with Pepin III, the King of the Franks in the eighth century. Afterwards, the Pope or Bishop of Rome was acknowledged as supreme head of the Catholic Church in Western Europe. He adopted the official title Pontifex Maximus, Latin for Little Father.

Jerome translated the Bible from the original Hebrew into Latin.

Several individuals in the early history of Christendom became important in regards to church development. St. Jerome translated ancient religious texts into Latin, producing the first medieval Bible in the common language of the day. This translation became the commonly accepted Bible used in the Catholic Church during Medieval Europe. St. Jerome, a devout Christian who gave up all his earthly wealth for life as a monk, was remarkable scholar who, when he received the order from Pope Damasus to translate the Greek version of the Old and New Testaments into everyday Latin, produced a work that survived for centuries. In 375 St. Jerome decided to reject earthly life and, in doing so, developed ideas still important in some Christian denominations. Jerome believed that all sexual activity was evil because it focused upon physical pleasure. The true Christian, according to St. Jerome, should instead focus on God and heaven. Any activity that did not glorify God and focus on heaven was, in St. Jerome's mind, evil.

St. Ambrose was another important leader in the early Christian Church. He was elected Bishop of Milan in 374, a position he held for the next quarter century. St. Ambrose was important in the development of early Christian theology. Educated in the classics and a gifted speaker, St. Ambrose defended Christian orthodoxy against various heresies. As a theologian, St. Ambrose incorporated principles advocated by Greek masters, including Plato, Aristotle, and Cicero, into Christian doctrine. In a work entitled *On Duties*, St. Ambrose urged Christians to follow the moral guidelines Cicero and other Hellenistic philosophers had outlined in classical works. St. Ambrose maintained that Christians had a duty to each other to live a morally just life and obey

Ambrose of Milan was among the most brilliant and talented, as well as militant and uncompromising.

civil law. Leaders, said St. Ambrose, should hold themselves to an even higher ethical code and be above reproach at all times, especially in their personal lives. St. Ambrose taught that Christians owed each other a high moral standard because they were united in a common community due to their acceptance of God's salvation through Christ.

St. Ambrose felt so strongly about the moral obligations of Christians that he did not hesitate to chastise political leaders. The Emperor Theodosius, on two occasions, ran afoul of St. Ambrose and was forced to do penance. The first event occurred when the Emperor punished Christian rioters who attacked a Jewish synagogue. St. Ambrose chastised Theodosius for his actions and forced the Emperor to repent. The second event also involved rioting. After General Butheric, a friend of Theodosius, was killed by rioters demanding the release of a favorite chariot-racer from prison, the Emperor lured the mob to an arena under false pretenses. Rather than being entertained as they had been promised, the crowd was executed when legionnaires stormed the theater. More than seven thousand people perished in this attack ordered by Theodosius to avenge the death of his general. St. Ambrose forcefully condemned the Emperor's actions, threatening to excommunicate him unless he did penance for the wanton massacre of so many citizens. Rather than face excommunication, Theodosius repented of his sin.

St. Augustine was the most important of all early church leaders. Born at Thagaste in north Africa into a mixed Christian/pagan family (his father was pagan and his mother Christian) Augustine became the most influential Christian theologian after St. Paul. *The City of God*, Augustine's seminal work, is second only to the Bible in importance to Roman Christians. Although Augustine's family was poor, both parents sacrificed so that their son could receive a good education. After completing school, Augustine became a professor of rhetoric. Later, he moved from his northern African homeland to Rome and then Milan. In Italy, Augustine met St. Ambrose and became Christian. In 395 Augustine became Bishop of Hippo, a position he held until his death in 430. Before his conversion to Christianity in 388, Augustine enjoyed the pleasures of the flesh and the material world in which he resided. After becoming Christian, Augustine felt a profound sense of guilt and engaged in a sort of intellectual penance when he wrote his first important book the *Confessions*. This work details Augustine's life and focuses in particular on his journey from paganism to Christianity. In the *Confessions*, Augustine describes how he grew spiritually, believing in Manichaeanism—a world in which good and evil are simultaneously present—to Neo-Platonism, an acceptance of Hellenistic moral truth, to Christianity.

In the 113 books, 218 letters, and more than 500 sermons he produced, Augustine never consciously attempted to develop a systematic Christian theology. Most of his writings were attempts to address particular problems encountered in daily life. Augustine's work is especially enlightening on the nature of the church, God's plan for humans, and the general relationship between God and humans. His most important book, *The City of God*, deals with all these issues. This book was written largely as a response to the claim that the Visigoth sack of Rome in 410 occurred because Christianity weakened the Empire. The Visigoths and other pagan Germanic tribes had maintained that Rome fell because God had abandoned the Empire. Augustine rejected this argument, maintaining instead that there were in fact two cities—the temporal city of man and the eternal city of God. The earthly city was a place filled with sin whose inhabitants were damned because they enjoyed pleasures of the flesh and the benefits of materialism. Rome fell, Augustine said, because it was a temporal city filled with sin. Paganism and the moral decadence it produced, rather than Christianity, caused Rome to fall. The eternal city of God in which all Christians resided in would stand forever. Visigoths, nor any other pagan tribe, could ever sack the eternal Rome, Augustine argued, so long as Christians believed in the death and resurrection.

Augustine's work also addressed the issue of salvation. During Augustine's life some Christian thinkers taught that an individual could attain salvation through the exercise of free will independently of God. Augustine rejected this idea. He maintained that although each person was given free will, humans usually exercised their abuse of free will by rebelling against God. A perfect example of the human abuse of free will occurred in the Garden of Eden when Adam and Eve partook of the forbidden fruit. Their rebellion, Augustine stated, damaged the entire human race. Afterwards, all people were predisposed to sin. Salvation, Augustine maintained, could be attained as a free gift from God. Humans, because of the original act of rebellion by Adam and Eve, could not affect their own salvation. As the Apostle Paul made clear in various letters to Christian communities throughout the Ancient World, God determined who was saved and who was damned before birth.

Another issue that arose in early Christendom that Augustine dealt with was the validity of church sacraments. This issue arose when some theologians in North Africa began to question the validity of sacraments administered by unworthy priests. Augustine, as Bishop of Hippo, settled this controversy by asserting that religious sacraments were vehicles by which God's grace was communicated to humans, and since they came from God, they were not dependent on human morality. Augustine thus ruled that priests acted as God's agent when administering Christian sacraments, and even though the priest might be a sinner, the sacrament was still valid because it came directly from God. Only God, Augustine said, is perfect. The church was a Christian community comprised of a sinful congregation led by an equally sinful clergy hoping for eternal salvation. In other words, the church, like all human institutions, was part of the temporal world, and like all humans and the institutions they had created, the church was imperfect.

Augustine likely was influenced by Jewish ideas that God was present in all things at all times. From the first moment of creation, Augustine wrote that God was present and God would be present until the last moment. God's presence was found in all things. This idea influenced later western ideas on God and humanity. Theologians after Augustine added to this idea.

Augustine also dealt with education in his writing. He was aware of the educational crisis Europe faced following the collapse of the Roman Empire. By the Middle Ages, public schools that primarily taught rhetoric, grammar, and logic during the days of the Roman Empire were closing as the need for education declined due to a lack of interest in learning. Despite the declining number of public schools, the church still needed an educated clergy. In a publication entitled *On Christian Doctrine,* Augustine set forth his ideas on education. He maintained that classical education was necessary so the individual could read and understand the Bible. After all, Augustine said, the Bible contained everything that a person needed to know but was difficult to understand because it was filled with illusions, metaphors, and parables. Education in the classics, Augustine argued, would enable individuals to gain the insight necessary to master the Bible, the greatest book of knowledge of all times. In short, Augustine valued education only because it gave people the ability to read the Bible and seek salvation as a result. Augustine's ideas on education were largely adopted throughout the western world for a thousand years after his death. Most educational institutions across western Europe existed to provide the church with an educated clergy.

One of Augustine's most important contributions to Medieval scholarship was a synthesis of classical thought with Christianity. Augustine's education, especially the emphasis Plato and Socrates place on universal truth, was easily joined with Christian theology and its emphasis on God and heaven. Augustine maintained that the Christian God was the universal truth that Socrates, Plato, and other classical philosophers were searching for. This idea appealed both to Christians and those educated in the classics. Christians could thus fully participate in the affairs of the world while also being committed to God and the church. Those who understood the classics could emulate examples set by Socrates, Plato, Aristotle, and others by searching through daily contemplation for the universal truth and goodness found only through the Christian deity.

Although Augustine is not generally regarded as a systematic thinker in that he did not attempt to devise a new or unique philosophy, he exerted more influence on Medieval Christianity and life than any other medieval person. In fact, Augustine's influence even reaches into the modern world and Christian theology as it exists today.

Monasticism became an important component of religion and society in Medieval Europe. St. Benedict established an early monastery at Monte Casino in 520. Benedict of Nursia originally wanted to study law and pursue a career with the government but gave up this plan after receiving salvation. He believed God had instructed him to seek truth through solitude and prayer. He then abandoned all worldly possessions and sought solitude in a cave near Rome. Benedict's lifestyle and his abandonment of worldly possessions attracted others who also sought God through solitude and prayer. Benedict established the Monte Casino Monastery near Rome so that his followers could reside within a community of believers with prescribed prayer rituals. Residents of Monte Casino supported the community through manual labor. Benedict used his legal and organizational skills to draft a rigorous set of rules for his monastery. These rules required monks to strictly obey the abbot, love each other unselfishly, and dress, eat, and live modestly. The abbot was given great authority over monks but was cautioned to use

Benedict helped to lay the foundations of medieval monasticism.

his powers wisely. Monks could be physically and mentally punished for transgressions, but Benedict's code generally recommended light correction rather than harsh punishment. Over time most monasteries adopted Benedict's rules. Hundreds of men across Western Europe left homes and families, gave up their wealth, and abandoned worldly pleasures for a life of poverty, chastity, and obedience in a monastery. Practically all monasteries organized the day around prayers, meals, work, and sleep. Monks generally lived a difficult life, rising early to work and pray throughout the day, wore rough clothing, ate simple meals, slept on thin straw pallets, unquestionably obeyed the abbot's orders, and had no personal possessions. The monastic lifestyle was not intended as punishment but as an avenue whereby the faithful could find God. Benedict's method that required each monk to pray every three hours enabled the individual to achieve spiritual freedom away from the world's material and physical distractions.

Benedict's monastic rules also required monks to spend part of each day studying. This requirement provided monks with an opportunity to copy and preserve numerous classical works that likely would have disappeared in an age of declining literacy. Thus, monasteries were largely responsible for keeping learning alive during Medieval Europe. As previously noted, many became learning centers where ancient knowledge was preserved.

GERMANIC KINGDOMS

Various kingdoms arose across Western Europe as the Roman Empire disintegrated. The most powerful and important was that of the Franks, a tribal group that originated in the Rhine Valley. The Frankish migration into Roman territory occurred mainly in the fourth and fifth centuries. By the end of the fourth century Frankish groups had moved into modern Holland and Belgium and were set to expand farther into Western Europe. The most important Frankish leader was Clovis, a tribal chieftain who united all the Frankish tribes into one people and became their king in 481. He then led armies into Western Europe that conquered all of Gaul. His greatest military success was achieved in 507 when his army defeated the Visigoths, driving them out of Gaul and into Spain. After his conversion to Roman Catholicism in 496, Clovis formed an alliance with the Italian Pope by which the Franks would protect the Church from Germanic tribes outside Gaul and pirates raiding coastal villages in return for formal recognition of the Merov-

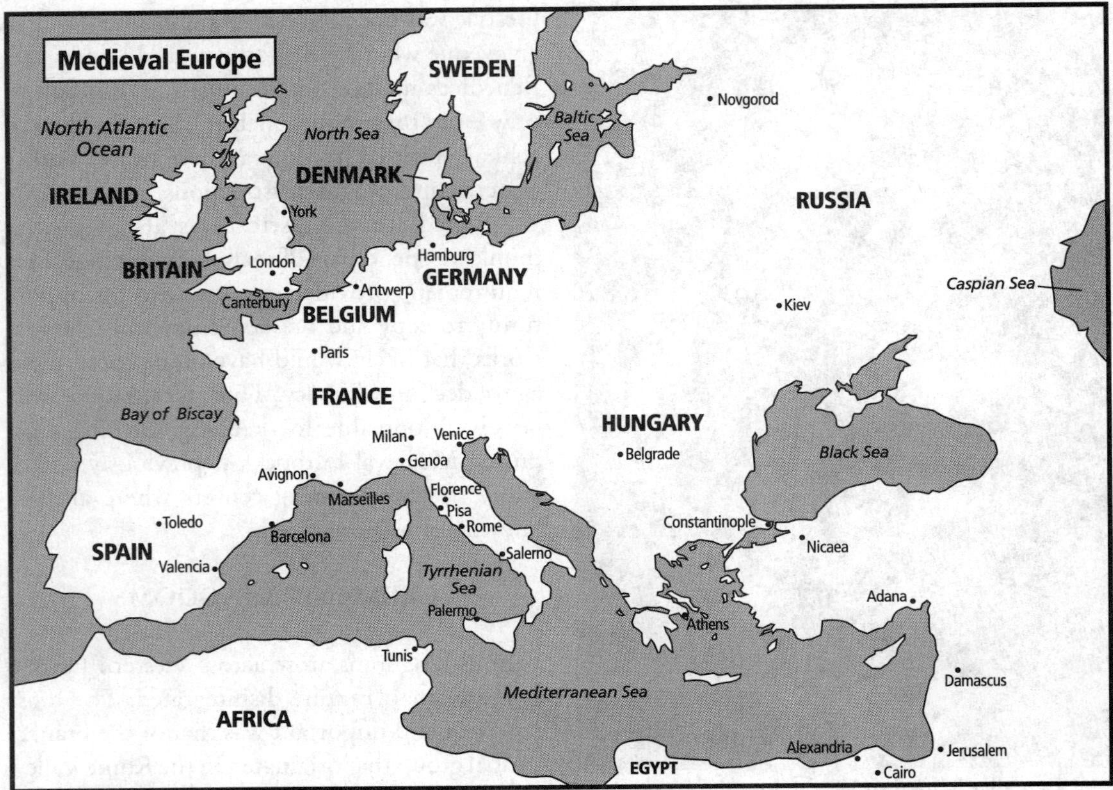

ingian dynasty that Clovis had founded. As a result of the alliance with Rome, the Frankish Merovingian kingdom was the most important of all the ancient Germanic states. When Clovis died in 511, the kingdom he had created largely disappeared after being divided among his sons. For a time, several Merovingian states existed side by side in western Europe—Neustria, Burgundy, and Austrasia.

Many Germanic states in Western Europe were not successful and disappeared after a short period of existence. The Vandals, Ostrogoths, and Burgundians are examples of unsuccessful Germanic nations. The Vandals, who moved from Germany into Spain and North Africa, were defeated by Roman forces in 534 after refusing to make peace with the Italians and continued to follow their Arian Christian beliefs, persecuting Roman Christians. The Franks defeated the Burgundians in the 530s and incorporated the state into the Frankish kingdom. Theodoric, the leader of the Ostrogoths, ruled Italy during the first quarter of the sixth century. After his death in 526, his daughter, Amalasuntha, ruled as regent for Theodoric's son until 534. Because she pursued a policy that would have united Italy with the Ostrogoth kingdom, enemies murdered her, which prompted the Gothic War from 534 to 554 with the eastern Roman Empire. This conflict, which the Eastern Emperor Justinian won in 554, completely destroyed the Ostrogoth kingdom.

A new Frankish dynasty arose to replace the Merovingian dynasty Clovis established. After it became clear that Clovis' successors could not keep the kingdoms they inherited, Frankish power was given to Charles Martel in 717. He conquered all Frankish states and halted the Muslim advance into Western Europe from North Africa at the Battle of Tours in 732. The Moors, as the Islamic North Africans were called, were relegated to the Iberian Peninsula. Martel was succeeded by his son, Pepin the Short, who deposed his father in 751. Pepin renewed the Frankish alliance with the Roman Church when Pope Stephen II named him King of the Franks in return for military help against the Lombards, the last Germanic tribe to migrate into western Europe. Pepin defeated the Lombards and gave lands they occupied in Italy between Rome and Ravenna to the Pope. This event, called the Donation of Pepin, allowed the Catholic Church to create the Papal States, a territory the Pope ruled.

Pepin's successor was his son who became Charles the Great, better known as Charlemagne. He ruled the Franks from 768 to 814. Under his reign the Franks continued their expansion. Charlemagne defeated the Lombards and incorporated their kingdom into that of the Franks. He also invaded Bavaria and added it to his holdings. The Saxons were defeated and forced to convert to Christianity. In fact, thousands were beheaded for refusing to convert. Charlemagne attacked the Moors, conquering part of northern Spain in the Spanish March and establishing a buffer between Christianity and Islam. In 800, Pope Leo III named Charlemagne emperor in an attempt to reestablish the Western Roman Empire. In reality, although Charlemagne was anointed emperor, the kingdom he ruled was far smaller and less influential than the Roman Empire. Charlemagne's governmental structure was primitive when compared to the Roman, Byzantine, and Islamic administrative structure. The Frankish kingdom consisted of about 250 counties headed by a count loyal to Charlemagne.

Charlemagne, King and Emperor

Economically, socially, and culturally, the Franks were not equal to the Romans. Frankish lands had no cities that served as cultural and economic centers, lacked professional governmental administrators, and were largely controlled by tribal chiefs loyal to Charlemagne.

The Carolingian dynasty that Charlemagne headed first became prominent in the early 600s when it gained control of the office of mayor of the palace. This office, which today would be similar to that of prime minister, enabled the Carolingians to steadily increase their power over the next two centuries until they dominated the western European world by the time Charlemagne established his empire.

Carolingian leaders used whatever opportunity that presented itself to increase their power. When possible, they formed alliances through treaties or marriage with other prominent families that might threaten their power. If an alliance was not possible the Carolingians engaged in warfare to achieve their objectives. Charles Martel, for example, defeated a Muslim army at Poitiers in 733 that stopped Islamic raiding in Gaul, consolidating Frankish power in the region. Spoils gained from conquest were distributed to other Frankish peoples in return for loyalty. The Carolingians also gained power by aligning themselves with the church when necessary and opposed the church if the situation dictated. When Pepin the Short usurped the Frankish throne in 751 against the Pope's will, he sought papal approval, which came only after he turned back the Lombard threat to the papacy. A few years later, the Pope visited Frankland and anointed Pepin and his sons with sacred oil, similar to the way ancient Israelite rulers were anointed in Biblical days.

Charlemagne was the most successful of all the Frank rulers. Although enemies fell before his armies, Charlemagne seldom led them in battle or accompanied them in the field. His success as a leader was not predicated on his military genius or leadership but on force of personality and governmental organization. One of his greatest accomplishments was installation of a new governmental order in Western Europe. In 789 Charlemagne ordered all males in his kingdom to take an oath of allegiance to him and granted equality to all regardless of their ethnic origin. Thus, Charlemagne made no distinction between Franks, Saxons, Angles, Banarians, or any other person in his kingdom.

Charlemagne did not separate church and state in the government he established. In his mind, they were one and the same. He believed the Franks were God's chosen people and that he was God's chosen leader on earth. Charlemagne, according to biographer Einhard, saw the world divided into two opposing sides—God and Satan—an idea he got from Augustine's *The City of God.* The earthly realm was inhabited by sinners, pagans, criminals, and heretics while the heavenly realm contained those who accepted Roman or Catholic Christianity. For Charlemagne, government existed to promote salvation, not military success or a national agenda. Thus, church and state could not be separated as both existed for the same purpose. Even though Charlemagne saw no need to separate church and state, the government he established functioned efficiently. In fact, many governmental institutions he created lasted several centuries after his death.

Heading the governmental system Charlemagne established was the monarch, who ruled because God deemed that he rule. Because the king was divinely chosen to rule, he was a law unto himself and in theory did not have to answer to anybody. In practice, however, the monarch sought counsel from leading nobles residing within his realm. The king had absolute authority to appoint all governmental officials and often rewarded loyal supporters with titles, land, office, and wealth. Likewise, the king's opponents were often stripped of land, wealth, titles, and office.

Charlemagne and later Carolingian rulers maintained a cadre of employees tied to the king through kinship and friendship. Officially known as the royal court, these officials looked after the monarch's every need. The constable, for example, oversaw the king's transportation needs and supervised a large staff specially trained for the job. The treasurer oversaw a staff that maintained the king's sleeping quarters because that was where the nation's treasure chest was stored. The royal minister kept official records for the court, counseled the king on religious matters, conducted religious services, administered Christian rites, and generally met the religious needs for the king and his court. Charlemagne and monarchs that followed him kept a

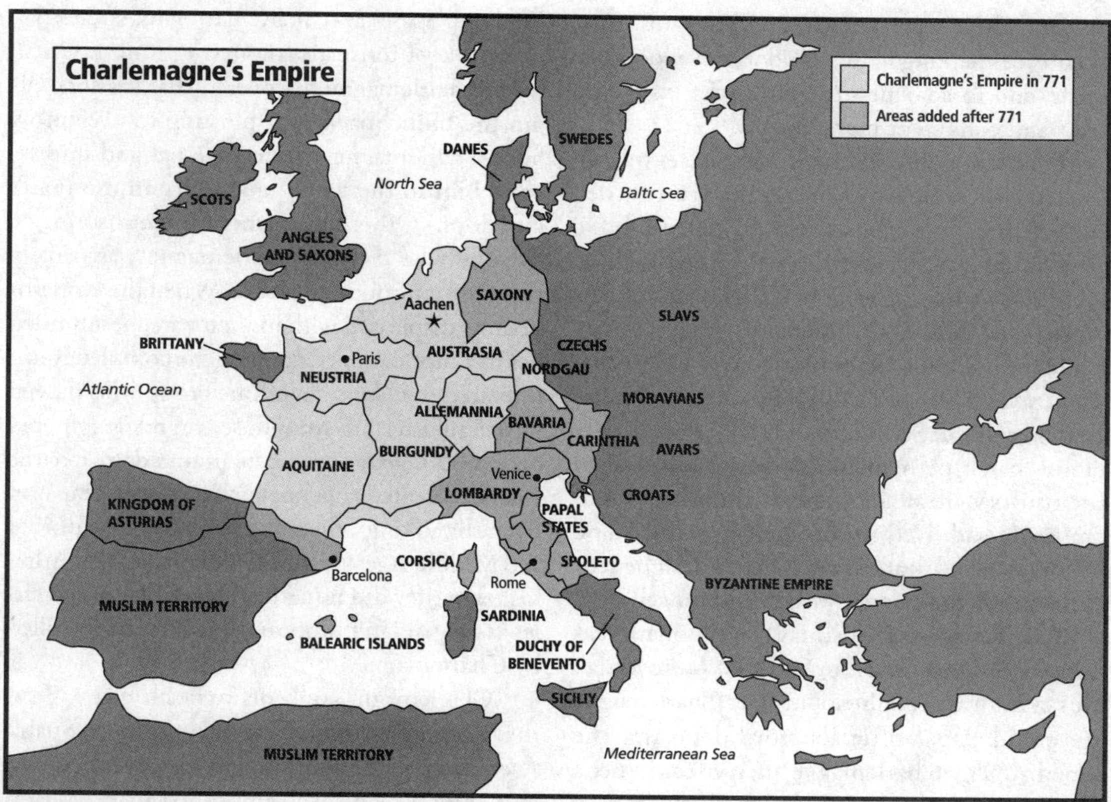

large domestic staff—maids, butlers, gardeners, etc.—supervised by the queen.

Charlemagne's realm was divided into smaller administrative and judicial districts known as counties. Each district was headed by a count. As in Roman times, the count served an administrative, judicial, and military function, commanding local troops, presiding over local courts, and enforcing royal laws. Most counts came from aristocratic families and enriched themselves through fines imposed on lawbreakers. Counts had to pledge complete loyalty to the king, were beholden to the king for their position, and were socially above most inhabitants of Carolingian lands. Counts and other prominent residents generally met together in a type of congress once or twice a year to advise the king. Within these assemblies laws and reforms were suggested and usually adopted by the king. These assemblies let the king know what nobles throughout his realm were concerned about and also served to diffuse threats to the monarchs power.

Carolingian kings usually travelled widely throughout their lands. Most monarchs owned great estates scattered across the realm and visited each one regularly. While travelling, the king and his companions usually stayed at Catholic monasteries. The extensive travel around the kingdom enabled the monarch to check on conditions locally, rectify wrongs, remove corrupt officials, and engender goodwill from the kingdom's populace. When the king could not travel to an area personally, he often dispatched envoys. These representatives had the authority to enforce the king's law, could remove local officials, and force courts to administer justice in a fair and consistent manner.

Charlemagne's primary residence was at Aachen, where he lived during the last two decades of his reign. His palace at Aachen was built in 788 and was elaborate for the time period. Monarchs who succeeded Charlemagne also constructed palaces considered their permanent residence. There, elaborate courts existed in grand style. The officials comprising the court lived an existence commoners could only dream about. Such permanent residences and elaborate courts were an adoption of the way Roman Emperors had lived in the ancient world. The elaborate palaces and courts were designed to showcase the monarch's wealth and power.

Charlemagne's Christmas Day coronation as emperor by Pope Leo III in 800 was controversial. This event was brought about after Charlemagne prevented papal officials from deposing the pope in 799. Charlemagne then became Leo's protector and punished those who had attacked the pope. Leo apparently decided to reward his protector. After Charlemagne arose from prayer at St. Peter's Basilica, Leo crowned him and proclaimed to all assembled that the Frankish king was now the new emperor of Rome. This event was controversial because previously popes did not have authority to name the Roman Emperor, and many people refused to accept the Frankish ruler as emperor. Regardless of whether one accepts Charlemagne's coronation as valid, the issue was largely moot because the western Roman Empire no longer existed. Charlemagne was the Roman Emperor in name only.

Charlemagne was brutal when the situation required brutality. His military exploits were legendary. He conquered much of Western Europe with the exception of southern Italy, England, Spain, and Sicily. Part of his success lay in his use of terror to frighten enemies. Once, when Charlemagne discovered that his son, Pepin the Hunchback, was plotting to overthrow him, Charlemagne arrested the lad and imprisoned him in the worst monastery in the Frank kingdom. Other opponents were not so lucky. Anyone who crossed Charlemagne was usually executed without hesitation. When the emperor became displeased with his first wife, he confined her to a monastery. Charlemagne completely annihilated the Avars, an ethnic group who moved into Frankish lands from the east, and slaughtered over 4,000 Saxon prisoners in one day after the Franks defeated the Saxons in a thirty-year war. Even the Vikings, the most vicious raiders during the Middle Ages, feared Charlemagne. During his reign they did not attack Frankish coastal cities as they did in European regions not controlled by Charlemagne.

Charlemagne's only defeat occurred in 778 at the hands of an Islamic force in northern Spain. A contingent of Frankish troops commanded by Count Roland was ambushed by a Muslim army. Roland's forces were completely destroyed. Frankish poets memorialized this defeat in an epic poem "The Song of Roland." Even though many details in the poem are inaccurate, it cemented Charlemagne's legendary status among the Franks and recorded for posterity the feudal ideas of chivalry, honor, death, and courage. According to the poem, the Frankish soldiers are slaughtered mercilessly after fighting bravely. Only one soldier lived to tell the tale, and he was branded a coward and killed in a duel.

Brutality was not the only thing Charlemagne used to control his vast empire. He understood, perhaps from the Roman past, that controlling a far flung empire required good organizational skills. To keep invaders out of his lands, Charlemagne created military buffer zones called marks. Each mark was ruled by a count and staffed with Frankish soldiers. The count and the army he commanded was expected to keep the peace, administer justice, maintain loyalty to Charlemagne, and keep invaders from taking Frankish lands.

A particularly difficult situation Charlemagne had to confront was the large number of different ethnic groups that inhabited his kingdom. Each group had its own laws, languages, customs, and traditions. Age old ethnic rivalries and jealousies often produced conflict between different groups. Charlemagne and his counts often had to spend much time and effort to keep order within his kingdom. Counts made use of the traditional Germanic court system to settle disputes among individuals and ethnic groups. Under this system, each party to a dispute swore an oath that their testimony was truthful. When the count could not reach a clear decision based on evidence presented in the case, both parties were often ordered to settle the dispute through combat. Guilty parties and individuals were usually required to pay damages, called wergild, to victims. The amount of wergild paid varied according to the severity of the crime as well as the age, gender, and social class of the victim. Murder required the greatest wergild while lesser amounts were awarded for less severe damage to the victim.

Charlemagne, to encourage commerce, created a stable monetary system that was used throughout Frankish lands. This system divided a pound of silver into twenty equal parts. Each part was shaped into a disk or coin called a shilling, which was equal in weight to one-twentieth of a pound of silver. The primary English unit of currency is still called the pound, and it is divided into shillings. English consumers still use this monetary system to pay for goods they purchase.

Charlemagne's greatest legacy was the Carolingian Renaissance that began during his reign. Unlike his father and grandfather, Charlemagne was interested in learning. This interest probably developed due to the influence of his mother, Bertrada, who was also interested in learning. In fact, some historians believe the popular Mother Goose stories originated with her as she was sometimes called Queen Goosefoot because of her large feet. Whether these stories came from Bertrada or not, Charlemagne had a close relationship with his mother who remained part of the royal household throughout her life. When Charlemagne built his primary palace at Aachen, he invited scholars, writers, artists, and musicians to live and work in the town that developed around the palace. Many structures within the town, including the palace, church, library, and school were built in the style of the ancient Romans and Greeks. Eventually, the new interest in scholarship and learning at Aachen spread throughout the Carolingian realm, initiating a revival of learning historians call the Carolingian Renaissance. Charlemagne required schools to be established by each church and monastery in his kingdom, and for the first time since the collapse of the Roman Empire, literacy increased among the European population. Many of the church schools Charlemagne created would evolve into universities that contributed greatly to the enlightenment of later centuries.

Charlemagne also reformed both religious practices and the legal code during his reign. Local law codes were updated and made uniform, and from the pope Charlemagne got a copy of the Roman Church's canon law, the *Sacramenty*, a book of worship for use in religious services, and made the Rule of St. Benedict a requirement for all monasteries. The centralization of law and worship was the first attempt by a western

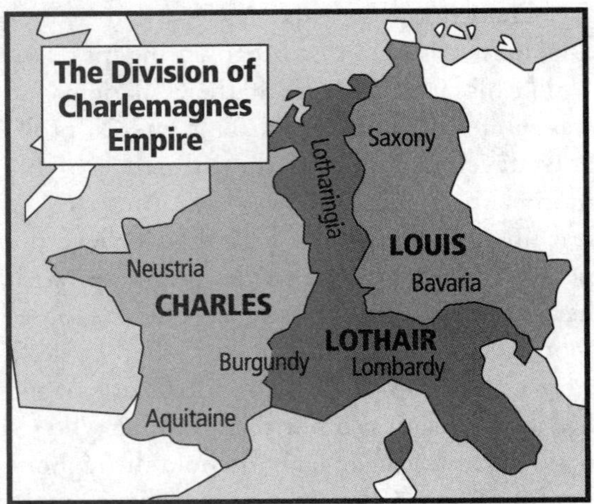

government to deal with these issues since before the collapse of the Roman Empire.

Like all empires, Charlemagne's could not last forever. By the end of the ninth century the Frankish kingdom had began to fragment. The unified kingdom Charlemagne had established was broken into several smaller states. The size and ethnic makeup of the Carolingian Empire contributed to its demise. The Frank kingdom was comprised of numerous small regions, including Lombardy, Saxony, Bavaria, and Brittany that contained various ethnic groups, each with its own culture and tradition that had existed long before the Carolingians and Merovingians conquered them. The common law, government, and culture Charlemagne and the Franks imposed on their subjects simply could not overcome the ethnic and cultural differences throughout the empire.

After Charlemagne died, political and dynastic issues plagued the kingdom. The Carolingians attempted to give each of their sons a kingdom within a larger kingdom. One son, the eldest, was made Emperor over all the land, but the younger sons were not willing to submit to the authority of their older brother and the empire eventually broke into separate kingdoms. The fighting among Charlemagne's heirs also caused difficulty for local counts and other government officials whose position depended on remaining loyal to the monarch.

Before he died, Charlemagne crowned Louis the Pious, his only surviving son co-emperor. When Charlemagne died in 814, Louis was not capable of leading the kingdom he had inherited. In 817 he made Lothair, his eldest son, co-emperor but also gave sub-kingdoms to Louis the German and Charles the Bald, two younger sons. This arrangement did not satisfy either son. Each plotted against their father and siblings until Louis died in 840. After his death the three brothers fought each other for control of the empire until 843 when the kingdom was permanently divided into separate realms by the Treaty of Verdun. Lothair emerged with the title of emperor and ruled the Middle Kingdom that comprised northern Italy. Louis the German was given control over East Frankish, which includes most of modern Germany. Charles the Bald got West Frankish, which today is modern France. Later the Middle Kingdom was swallowed by the East and West Kingdoms. Over time, several smaller kingdoms were also created from Charlemagne's empire, and the modern map of Europe began to take shape. The Treaty of Verdun, to some degree, was symbolic of the changes in Europe since the collapse of the Roman Empire. It was the first treaty drafted in three languages—Latin, French, and German. Although Charlemagne's successors ruled Germany until 911 and France until 987, the family never again produced a leader as capable as Charlemagne.

EUROPE UNDER ATTACK

Fragmentation of the Frank kingdoms opened the door for invasion and raids from external groups.

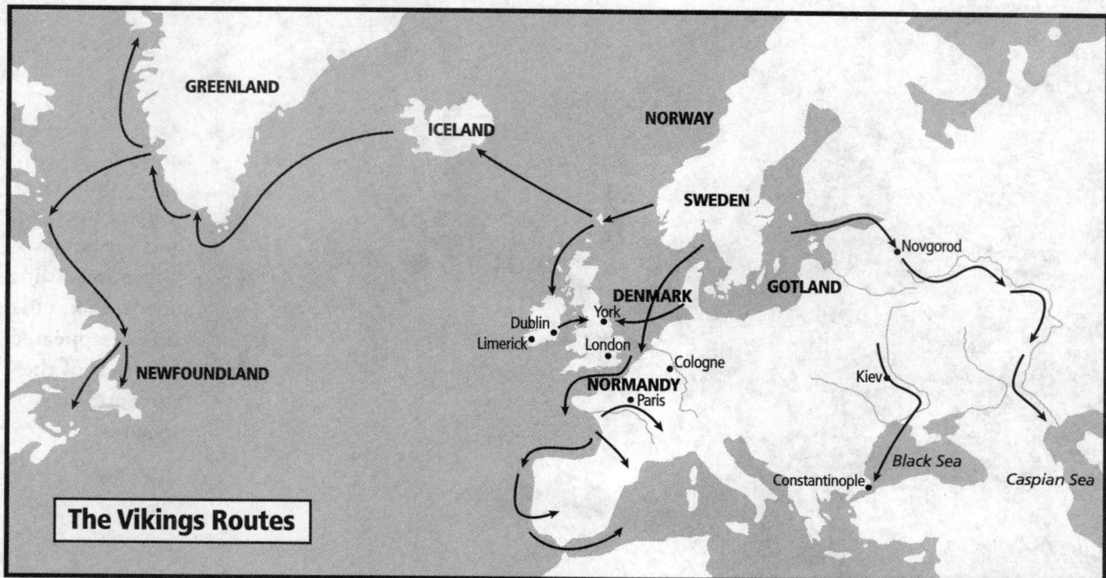

The most feared of these people were Vikings who hailed from the European northlands—now the countries of Norway, Sweden, and Denmark. The Viking invasions, which began about 780 and lasted until 1070, largely resulted from the harsh, frozen climate residents of Scandinavia had to endure. Viking people were simply trying to find a more hospitable land to live in where the summer growing season was longer and the winters were not as harsh. Vikings were a tough people who endured extreme hardship in the northern European lands they inhabited. They cast envious eyes on warmer lands to the south that by Viking standards were populated by wealthy people. As the Scandinavian population increased, farmers needed more land to produce food. Unfortunately, sufficient land was not available, and Vikings became seafaring people who depended on the ocean for survival. The ships they built to sail the cold, rough waters of the North Sea were the most sturdy and seaworthy of the day.

As Viking ships ventured farther from Scandinavia to fish, they encountered lands and people wealthier than any who lived in Norseland, and they began to raid coastal villages. The first documented contact between Vikings and western Europeans occurred in 5 A.D. when Scandinavian people began to trade with the Roman Empire. Evidence indicates that the trade and raids both increased until the Roman Empire disintegrated. In fact, Viking raids may have played some role in destabilizing the Roman Empire before its collapse. Regardless of whether Viking raids accelerated the collapse of Rome, the raids on Germanic tribal settlements and trade between Germanic people and Vikings continued during the Dark and Middle Ages.

Three major periods of Viking raids occurred. The first began in 793 when a Scandinavian party attacked a Catholic monastery at Lindisfarne, England, killing all monastery residents and destroying their settlement. Afterwards, the raids continued and increased in number until they ended about 840. Raids during this period served mainly to enrich members of the raiding party and struck fear into European inhabitants who lived outside Charlemagne's domain. Scan-

The Vikings were raiders and explorers. Often in settling down, their culture disappeared into that of the surrounding society.

dinavian raiders generally avoided the Frankish kingdom because they believed Charlemagne was so powerful that he could not easily be defeated. After Charlemagne died, the Frank kingdoms were not exempt from Viking raids. Numerous French coastal towns and villages were hit by Viking raiders.

About 840, Viking raids entered a second phase when raiders began to establish permanent settlements in England, Ireland, and elsewhere in Western Europe. Several European towns and cities likely grew up around Viking settlements. Dublin, Ireland is an example. Prior to the establishment of a Viking settlement there in the 840s, the site of Dublin was largely uninhabited. Viking raiders, operating from Dublin and other sites, ranged far inland, attacking towns and villages far from the coast. In 854, for example, Scandinavian raiders attacked Hamburg, Germany, setting the city ablaze. Numerous Viking settlements were established throughout Western Europe and played an important role in attacks by Viking raiders across the continent. Vikings were so successful after 840 that they attacked towns in North Africa, Spain, southern France, and throughout the Mediterranean region.

England and the British Isles probably suffered more from Viking attacks than did any other western European nation. Danish raiders were particularly hard on England. In 789, according to the *Anglo-Saxon Chronicles*, three Danish ships docked at Wessex slaughtered a party of local residents sent out to trade and then attacked neighboring villages and monasteries over the next several years. A large army of Vikings arrived in East Anglia in 865. This group, led by Halfdan and Ivar the Boneless, invaded England intent on conquering the island and remaining permanently and began the third and final period of Viking invasions. Halfdan and Ivar the Boneless captured East Anglia, moved into Northumbria, took York, the region's primary town, imprisoned and murdered King Edward the Martyr and caused general havoc wherever they raided. By 870, Anglo-Saxon lands in northern England had fallen under Viking control. Anglo-Saxon kingdoms disappeared, their governments collapsed and their leaders were killed after the Vikings imposed Dane Law on the region. The only Anglo-Saxon kingdom in England that survived the Viking onslaught was Wessex, ruled by Alfred, the only English king to earn the title Great.

Alfred was likely born to King Ethelwulf around 849 and became king at the age of 23 when his brother died after the Vikings invaded Wessex. Initially, Alfred defeated the Danes but later lost an important battle and was forced to pay tribute to prevent Danish forces from ravishing Wessex. After receiving payment from Alfred, the Vikings focused on northern England. Halfdan marched his army north and conquered Northumbria, which he divided among his soldiers. The Danes then moved their families from Denmark to England, where they became farmers. In southern England, King Guthrum, successor to Ivar the Boneless, was determined to finally conquer Wessex. In 878 Gutrum's forces attacked Alfred's kingdom, routed his army, and generally controlled the region. Alfred's army scattered across the land and Alfred fled, hiding in the Somerset Swamp to avoid capture and execution by the Danes. According to legend, an encounter with an illiterate, impoverished Anglo-Saxon woman in the swamp convinced Alfred that he must rally English forces and drive the Danes from Britain.

Whether the encounter with the swamp woman occurred, Alfred's forces established a fort at Athelney and began to attack Viking settlements. By Easter of 878, Alfred and the Anglo-Saxons he commanded were strong enough to take Edington, a Viking stronghold. There, Alfred's forces completely defeated the Danes, forcing King Guthrum to sue for peace. Alfred, rather than slaughtering the Vikings, treated them with kindness. During the course of negotiations, Guthrum and his tribal chiefs were showered with food and gifts. Alfred supposedly convinced Guthrum to accept Christianity, making the Dane leader the first Viking king to be baptized. Guthrum and Alfred then signed the Treaty of Wedmore that ended the conflict.

Alfred, despite making peace with the Vikings, did not trust the Norsemen. To protect his kingdom, Alfred constructed forts 20 miles apart at strategic sites and staffed then with Anglo-Saxon soldiers capable of fending off future Viking attacks. Alfred also ordered construction of a naval fleet to protect England's coastal villages from Norse raids and created a military system in which half the English army was on duty every six months while the other half was sent home.

Alfred the Great
Winchester, England

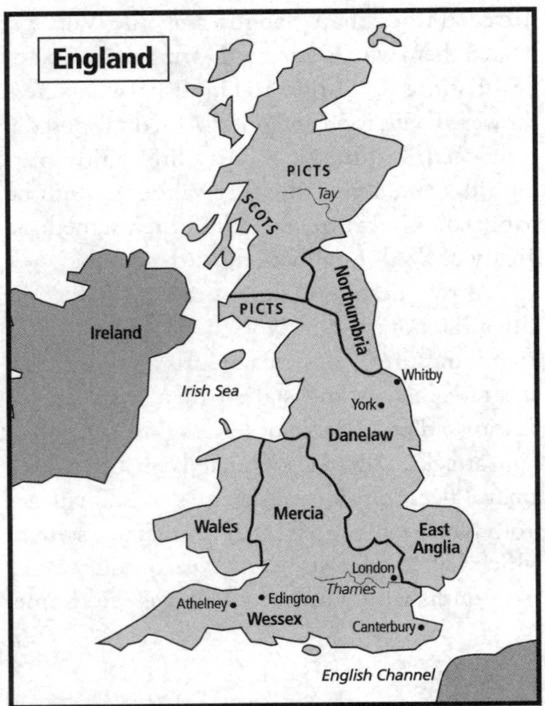

Alfred was determined to protect England at all costs and never to be caught flat footed again.

Viking raids throughout England continued until 866. In that year, Alfred and the Anglo-Saxons captured London and forced the Danes to withdraw from part of the territory they controlled. Alfred and Guthrum agreed to divide England in half. Alfred got control of southern England while the Danes retained power in northern England. Alfred and his army had rolled Dane law back in the area surrounding London and in parts of Mercia. After the English victory, Alfred did everything possible to liberate England from the Vikings. One tactic he used to check Viking power was marriage. Alfred himself married a woman from Mercia, a Viking province in England, married one daughter to a Viking leader, and married other daughters to English leaders to secure alliances against the Vikings. These measures enabled Alfred to gain power peacefully. Alfred, in order to maintain control over English nobles, established an English court and required each noble to reside at court for a portion of each year. Alfred also required each noble to maintain an army that could be deployed quickly when needed.

Alfred is generally considered the most important of the Anglo-Saxon kings because he laid the foundation for the creation of modern England and is the father of both the English army and navy. Like Charlemagne, Alfred was interested in learning and scholarship. He rebuilt monasteries destroyed in Viking raids and established schools across England. Alfred was something of a scholar himself. Fluent in both Latin and English, Alfred read the classics and wrote books on English history. The king also promoted literacy among English nobles. He ordered several classic works translated into English so that Englishmen could more easily read them. During Alfred's reign from 871 to 899 the *Anglo-Saxon Chronicles* were begun. This important reference work is perhaps the most important source of information on the Anglo-Saxon peoples that populated England. The Anglo-Saxon Chronicles was an encyclopedic work that begins with the year 1 A.D. and continues until 1154. Alfred was fascinated with this book and ordered copies made and enshrined in practically every school, monastery, and church library within his realm. Even today, historians conducting research about ancient Anglo-Saxons consult the *Anglo-Saxon Chronicles* out of necessity.

Although England suffered the brunt of Viking attacks, these fearsome warriors raided other European nations as well. After Charlemagne's death, France was no longer immune to Viking attacks. During the ninth century Vikings twice raided Paris and were paid tribute to leave the city on both occasions. Most regions within France contained Viking settlements. At the beginning of the tenth century the French government made peace with the Vikings. In 911 Charles the Simple, king of the West Franks, ceded the province of Normandy to the Viking chief Rollo in return for help defending French land from other Vikings groups. Rollo and his descendents became Christian and later produced the Norman king William the Conqueror who successfully invaded England in 1066.

Viking raiders also attacked Spain, which originally left the Roman Empire due to the Visigoth invasion in the fifth century. In 814 Vikings attacked Spanish settlements along the Iberian Peninsula. While these attacks allowed Vikings to plunder Spanish wealth, they generally did not result in establishment of Scandinavian settlements on the Iberian Peninsula.

Russia and regions in central England experienced raids by Vikings. Scandinavians from Sweden raided throughout the region and likely founded Russia and intermarried with Slavic people living in the area.

Vikings were not the only group that invaded Europe during the ninth and tenth centuries. Magyars invaded from the east, and Muslims came from the south. Magyars, relatives of the Huns and Avars, who had invaded the Roman Empire, were accomplished horsemen who, like Vikings, struck fear into the hearts of Europeans they threatened. In 889 Magyar cavalry attacked Italy, Germany, and France. Magyar raids disrupted commerce, education, and government. Nobody anywhere, it seemed, was safe from the fierce Magyar horsemen.

Muslim raiders from North Africa crossed the Mediterranean Sea in 711 and attacked Visigoth Spain. Within a short period Muslim forces, called Moors, controlled about half of modern Spain. There, these Islamic peoples constructed elaborate cities, improved the Spanish economy, encourage the study of law, science, and literature, and ushered in a golden age in Spain that dwarfed anything that existed elsewhere in Western Europe. Cordoba and Granada were centers of Islamic culture in Spain. The Moors used Spain as a base from which they launched attacks on territory throughout the Mediterranean region. Southern France was a particularly inviting target. At one time nearly a third of modern France was controlled by Muslims. In 827 Moors invaded Sicily and then attacked southern Italy, reaching Rome in the middle of the ninth century. There, they ravaged churches and took large amounts of gold and silver from Catholic institutions. Duke Sergius of Naples stopped Muslim attacks on Rome when he defeated the Moor navy in 847. To protect the city from future attacks, Romans built the Leonine Wall in 847 and 848.

ESTABLISHMENT OF THE HOLY ROMAN EMPIRE

Raiders, especially the Magyars in central Europe, played a role in creation of a new political entity in central Europe, the Holy Roman Empire. This political entity developed because Magyar raids created a need to establish centralized control over middle regions of the European continent. The groundwork for creation of the Holy Roman Empire was laid when Otto I became leader of Saxony in 936. Otto defeated relatives, including his brothers and sons, who claimed parts of Saxony, by forming an alliance with the Roman Catholic Church and marrying the daughter of the English king, in the Ducal Rebellions. By 941 Otto had defeated his rivals and consolidated his power. In 962 Pope John XII made Otto the Holy Roman Emperor, following the tradition began when Charlemagne was initially crowned. Conflict soon erupted with the Church when Pope John XII realized that Otto was interfering too much in Church business. Otto eventually drove the Pope from power and gave the Holy Roman Emperor power to appoint future popes when he drafted the *Privilegium Ottonianum.* According to this document, no pope could hold the office without the Emperor's consent. Otto then appointed Leo VII, one of his strong supporters, pope. Afterward, papal appointments were controlled by the German kingdoms.

Central Europe's greatest threat was the Magyars. Originally from central Asia, this group had reached Otto's kingdom by 954. The Roman Catholic Pope and the people of central Europe were dependent on Otto to save them from the Magyars who were believed to be as bloodthirsty as the Vikings were in Western Europe. Like other tribes from the Asian plains, the Magyars were fierce warriors who struck fear into people living in areas they invaded. In 955, Otto and his German army defeated Magyar forces near present-day Augsburg at the Battle of Lechfeld. This battle, which was one of the bloodiest during the Middle Ages, halted the Magyar advance into central Europe but did not drive them from territory they had already conquered. After their defeat at Lechfeld, however, Magyar leaders began to cooperate with surrounding leaders and became less hostile toward other people. As time passed, Magyar leaders consolidated their power and became firmly established in Hungary and other regions of central Europe. Duke Geza was the first person to unite the various Magyar tribes in Hungary. He served as the Hungarian king until his death in 997. Thereafter, Vajak, his son, ruled Hungary and ushered in a period of economic prosperity and economic stability. Vajak eventually married into the German royal family of Otto the Great, became Christian in 1000, and changed his name to Stephen in honor of the Christian martyr. Over time, Hungarian Magyars assimilated into central European society where they created a stable agricultural community.

ECONOMY AND SOCIETY

Agriculture dominated the European economy during the Middle Ages. Most Europeans, like their counterparts in the Ancient World, lived in rural areas and existed as part of a larger economic system called feudalism, which was itself based on control of large land areas by a wealthy individual. Sometimes known as manorialism, feudalism bound most Europeans to the land and provided the economic underpinning for Europe's economy during the Middle Ages. Although not every agricultural worker was bound to the land (a few individuals remained free) most peasant farmers lived in a village dominated by the surrounding manor.

Because Medieval Europe was primarily agrarian, few towns or cities existed. Most urban centers in Western Europe were not large. Rome, for example, contained less than fifty thousand inhabitants in 800 and was the largest city in Western Europe at the time. Paris, the second largest city in 800 had a population of about twenty thousand. London, Madrid, and other western cities contained fewer residents. Whereas governmental functions were based in urban areas during the Roman Empire, during the Middle Ages, these functions were increasingly moved to rural manors. Manorial lords, for example, held courts and administered justice outside cities. Although towns and cities lost their position as governmental centers during the Middle Ages, they retained their importance as centers of church administration. Large Catholic churches and cathedrals required a large cadre of administrators who generally lived in the town surrounding the cathedral. Merchants also often settled on the outskirts of towns, creating what Medieval people called "burghs."

Society in Western Europe during the Middle Ages was generally divided into three primary classes. At the top of society were the lords. They were generally large landowners who controlled serfs and exerted influence on government. Merchants, church officials, including parish priests, estate stewards, free land holders, and governmental administrators comprised the middle class while serfs and others dependent on manorial lords—the bulk of Western Europe's population—were part of the lower class.

Women faced discrimination in medieval society. In general, males dominated society. They were the soldiers, statesmen, judges, rulers, and clergymen. Women generally were expected to obey men in most instances. About the best most women could hope for was a good marriage to a man who could provide his mate with economic security. Because Medieval society was family orientated, marriage was the glue that held the family together. Marriage usually occurred from economic necessity. Among the elite, marriages were arranged to unite powerful families. The idea of romantic love did not exist. Even within the lower class, marriage occurred for materialistic security. Women generally had little choice in marriage partners. As noted earlier, nobles generally chose the marriage partner for serfs. Mates for middle -class women were usually selected by a father, grandfather, uncle, older brother, or other male relatives. As part of the matrimonial arrangements, the groom paid a bride fee to the woman's family, which gave him ownership of his future wife.

Because family lineage was important and because bearing children was a woman's most important marital function, brides were expected to be virgins at the time of marriage. Having a virgin bride was the only way husbands and families could ensure that children born to the couple were legitimately those of the husband and thus entitled to inherit the family estate. Marriage, according to Medieval custom, was not considered legal until the union was consummated sexually. Thus, it was customary for the couple to be placed in bed together as part of the marriage ceremony and forced to have sex so that wedding guests would know the marriage was legal.

After marriage, most medieval women were expected to bear a large number of children. Some women bore more than a dozen children, and many died of complications caused by pregnancy. In addition to bearing children, medieval women were expected to serve as the primary caregiver to children and husbands. Women were responsible for food preparation and storage, raised a vegetable garden, spun thread from wool and other fibers, and sewed clothing for husbands and children. Women from upper class families did not have life as rough as did peasant women. Noble women generally had servants to prepare food and make the family clothing. Noble women, however, supervised servants and managed the household budget. Women from all classes were generally controlled by husbands. Widows generally did not remain single for a long period. Social and economic pressures dictated that women should remarry as soon as possible after a spouse's death. As soon as the marriage was consummated, the new husband became the woman's master.

Sexual relations outside marriage were generally forbidden for women. Any woman who was caught in an adulterous relationship was punished by death. Males, however, were usually not punished for adultery. In fact, some noblemen kept women as concubines and engaged in sex with as many women as possible. A man who was unhappy with his wife for any reason could return her along with her dowry to her family. Divorce was not part of medieval society. Women could not seek divorce for brutal treatment or adultery. Many women were subject to both physical and mental abuse. About the best a Medieval European woman could wish for was marriage to a husband who did not beat her too often or too severely.

While most women were restricted by law and custom to servile positions, a few broke through the sexual boundaries and became important leaders. Ethelflaed, the daughter of Alfred the Great, was such a woman. After her father arranged a marriage with the Lord of Mercia to secure an alliance against Danish invaders, Ethelflaed ruled Mercia alongside her husband until he died in 911. Afterwards, she ruled Mercia alone until she died. Ethelflaed personally led soldiers into battle against Viking forces and helped England and Edward, her brother, who was King of Wessex, defeat the Danish invaders. After Ethelflaed's death in 918, the kingdom of Mercia became part of Wessex and later part of the larger English nation. Another prominent woman in Medieval Europe was the Viking Freydis, daughter of Eric the Red. She crossed the ocean with brother Leif Ericson and helped establish Viking colonies in present-day Canada. After Eric the Red died, Freydis was left in charge of the Viking colonies in North America when Leif returned to govern the Greenland colony Eric the Red had established. Freydis and another brother, Thorvald, remained in charge of the Viking colony in Canada as long as it survived.

Ethelflaed and Freydis were exceptions, however. The European legal, cultural, and social systems generally did not permit women to hold prominent military, political, economic, or religious leadership positions. While husbands were away from home, women might control the household, but as soon as the husband returned, the wife relinquished control to him. Marriage was the cornerstone of European society, and women held the family together, having few legal and political rights. Even in lands such as England where women gained limited legal status, they generally remained subordinate to males despite, in many cases, having to work harder than men and dying younger after having too many children too closely together.

Medieval Christianity presented a problem for women. On one hand, Christians honored Mary, the mother of Jesus, because she bore the Christ child. On the other hand, Christians blamed women for the condemnation of humanity because Eve succumbed to the serpent's temptation in the Garden of Eden and in turn tempted Adam to also consume fruit from the tree of knowledge of good and evil. Male church leaders tended to equate women with evil and maintained that a man's sexual desire for a woman was the origin of all bad things. Because women were blamed for original sin, early Christian leaders such as St. Augustine demanded that females place themselves under control of males in their life. Women were only permitted to engage in sexual relations with husbands for purposes of procreation. Any woman caught having sex for pleasure or profit was subject to harsh punishment. Assertive women were generally condemned by church officials as witches and burned alive at the stake or executed by another horrible method. Single women or widows who chose not to remarry were also viewed with suspicion. Medieval people simply believed single women threatened the underpinning of society because they created sexual desire within men reminiscent of Eve's original sin.

Women who did not marry were left with little alternative other than to join a convent or live in a monastery where they prepared meals, made clothing, and cleaned for monks. Women who were sent to convents or who joined female religious orders generally lived under the authority of an abbess, the equivalent of a male abbot. Nuns living in convents were believed to be married to God and tried to live a holy life apart from worldly temptations. England even had "double" monasteries where orders of nuns and monks lived side by side. The most famous English double monastery was Whitby Abbey, founded by St. Hilda, a Northumbrian princess. This institution attracted a large following and grew large and wealthy over time as women who chose to reside within its confines donated all possessions, including land that they might have inherited from fathers or husbands who died without leaving a male heir to the abbey. The Council of Whitby was held as Whitby Abbey to settle doctrinal disputes between English and Roman Christians in 663. Nuns were sometimes able to acquire an education in convents. Like monks, they copied ancient manuscripts. Hroswitha of Gandersheim, a nun in Saxony, Germany, wrote several volumes of poetry, history, and drama during her life from 935 to 1001.

Although the western church viewed women as the cause of human damnation, Christianity also provided some protection for woman against domineering males. Christian doctrine, for example, forbade divorce, polygamy, incest, prostitution, and the sacrifice of virgins, practices generally allowed by pagan religions.

Noblewomen had life better than did peasant women. Still, life was not a bed of roses for most noblewomen. Like all women, they were viewed as evil temptresses who were inferior to men in all spheres and whose primary goal was to cause men to sin. Therefore, noblewomen also had to belong to a man. Fathers generally arranged marriage for aristocratic daughters. Most noblewomen were married by the time they were sixteen. Husbands were generally much older than wives. Noblewomen, like peasant women, were subject to much physical abuse from husbands, often for the most minor offense. Noblewomen were responsible for education in the castles. They taught young girls important domestic skills they needed to live in Medieval society, such as sewing, spinning, weaving, food preservation, and doctoring.

Males were treated much better during the Middle Ages. Noblemen believed that manual labor was beneath their social rank. The only profession that appealed to them was making war. Warrior noblemen lived for combat, which was a way they could prove their self-worth and increase their wealth. Over time, a code of warrior behavior called chivalry developed. Under this code a feudal warrior could not show cowardice, must remain loyal to his lord, rescue damsels in distress, treat other knights in a courteous manner, and aid the church in spreading Christianity to nonbelievers. Feudal warriors, or knights, as they were commonly called under the code of chivalry, pledged loyalty in an elaborate ceremony to a particular lord. The knight was then required to fight for the lord whenever called upon, and the lord in turn awarded the warrior a grant of land called a fief. ,The fief usually contained serfs who worked the land and provided the knight with food and other material needs. Providing military service to the lord was not the only duty knights were required to perform for their fief. They also judged cases in the lord's court involving feudal obligations, provided lodging whenever the lord travelled through their fief, attended knighting and wedding ceremonies, and made every effort to secure the lord's release if he was captured and imprisoned by a rival lord.

Both lord and knight were generally honor bound to abide by the terms of the oath of allegiance they had pledged to each other. Upon occasion, however, knights renounced their loyalty to a lord. Renouncement was a rare event and occurred under the most extraordinary circumstances, such as when a lord became too weak to protect his vassels, required the knight to do more than normal feudal obligations, or if the lord did not provide the promised fief. Lords also could break the feudal contract if knights did not honor their obligations. A knight who refused to serve in the lord's court would be tried for treason and if found guilty lost his fief and often his life.

Knights sometimes took oaths of allegiance to several different lords and were in turn awarded several fiefs. These knights could then award fiefs to knights willing to pledge loyalty to them. Knights who owed allegiance to more than one lord sometimes had to choose which lord he owed primary loyalty to. This was particularly true for knights who had pledged loyalty to two different lords who went to war with each other. Knights sometimes found themselves in the awkward situation of fighting for a lord they had previously fought with.

Under the Medieval feudal system, the king was considered the lord of all lords. In theory, he was more powerful than all other lords and granted fiefs to the main or great lords who in turn granted lesser fiefs to lesser lords who then gave fiefs to knights. In reality, the king was not always the most powerful noble in the realm. Sometimes one of the great lords exercised more authority than the king.

Feudalism remained as the primary economic and social system in Western Europe throughout the Middle Ages, declining only when kings broke the power of great lords. This decline was gradual and occurred at different times in different countries. Eventually, the modern nation state with its centralized government replaced feudalism. The transformation from feudalism to nationalism did not occur easily or quickly as later chapters will make clear. Conflict between great lords and kings persisted for several generations before the transformation was complete.

CONCLUSION

Although Medieval Europe is often called the Dark Ages, this term is a misnomer for the period was not dark at all. Scholarship and learning did decline after the fall of the Roman Empire, but monks and nuns copied and preserved many ancient manuscripts. Europe did, however, undergo a great transformation from 378 until 1000 A.D. During this period the centralized government that existed under the Roman Empire was replaced by regional governments as geographically Europe fragmented into several independent states as rulers such as Charlemagne consolidated power and expanded their kingdoms. Within these larger realms, however, fragmentation was the rule as under the feudal system great lords controlled vast land areas inhabited by serfs who were legally bound to the land. These manorial lords raised great armies by awarding fiefs to warrior knights who pledged loyalty to the lord.

Life for most Europeans was cruel and unforgiving. Peasants generally lived on land owned by manorial lords who controlled their lives through work, taxes, various fees, and the legal system. Women also had life hard. They were at best accorded second-class citizenship and were strictly controlled by males. Although a few Medieval European women achieved status outside marriage, most were confined to a life of drudgery within matrimony. Women could not even choose husbands. Marriages were usually arranged by families to secure economic benefits for the family. Outspoken or assertive women were generally viewed as a threat to society and were not tolerated and social pressures to marry, or remarry, were exerted on them. About the only avenue open to women who did not wish to marry was service to the church as nuns living in convents.

Militarily, the Middle Age was a period in which Europeans face invasion from various groups. The most feared group in Western Europe was Vikings from Scandinavian lands to the north. These fierce raiders attacked England, Ireland, France and other lands in search of plunder at first and colonial possessions later. Within England, Alfred the Great arose and united English people against the Viking threat. From the south, Muslim raiders attacked Europe. Spain, France, Italy, and other lands along the Mediterranean Sea were most vulnerable to Muslim raiders. Part of Spain, France, and other lands bordering the Mediterranean were controlled by Muslims for a lengthy period. Magyars from central Asia attacked Central and Eastern European nations, disrupting commerce and government. Like Vikings from the north, Magyar raiders who were fearless horsemen, created fear and produced panic among inhabitants of lands they attacked. These raids led to establishment of the Holy Roman Empire in Central Europe as the Catholic Church made an alliance with Otto I to protect itself against Magyar attacks.

Suggestions for Further Reading

Frederick B. Artz, *The Mind of the Middle Ages* (1965).

Augustine, *The City of God*

T. Baker, *The Normans* (1966).

Boethius, *Consolation of Philosophy*

Norman Cantor, *The Civilization of the Middle Ages* (1993).

W. H. C. Frend, *The Rise of Christianity* (1984).

R. L. Fox, *Pagans and Christians* (1987).

Gregory of Tours, *History of the Franks*

Pope Gregory the Great, *Pastoral Care*

E. James, *The Franks* (1988).

Jordannes, *History of the Goths*

Rosamund McKitterick, *The Early Middle Ages* (2001).

F. Stenton, *Anglo-Saxon England* (1947).

Chapter 7

FEUDAL EUROPE, 1000-1215

Norman mounted knights charge Harold's troops in the Battle of Hastings.

Pierre Clergue, The Priest of Montaillou

Records abound of the activities of popes, cardinals, and bishops during the Middle Ages, but there is a dearth of information about the most important cleric of the period: the local parish priest. Occasionally, documentation emerges about such individuals. Such is the case for Pierre Clergue, parish priest of the remote mountainside village of Montaillou in southern France, not far from the Spanish border. In the early fourteenth century, Montaillou had a population of about 200-250 souls, ministered by a single priest. It was not a typical village nor was Pierre a typical priest. Montaillou was poor, backward, and a hotbed of support for the Albigensians. Indeed, it was one of the last bastions in France to cling to the ascribed heresy—not because its inhabitants were zealous followers of the movement but because their community was so isolated and unimportant that it was easily ignored.

Not until the early fourteenth century did Montaillou get the Inquisition's attention. Between 1318 and 1325 Jacques Fournier, bishop of Pamiers, (later the Avignonese pope Benedict XII), conducted a thorough and meticulously recorded inquest to identify and punish Albigensians in his diocese, and his documentation included many detailed interviews with the peasant inhabitants of Montaillou. From these interviews, the modern French historian, Emmanuel Le Roy Ladurie created a pioneering work of social history, ***Montaillou: The Promised Land of Error,*** *which has been widely praised and widely criticized—the appropriate makings of an interesting book. Ladurie provides, among other things, a vivid portrait of the priest Pierre Clergue.*

Father Pierre was of peasant heritage, but his family was the most powerful and prosperous household in Montaillou. His brother, Bernarrd, was the bayle, or the village's chief secular official. Pierre was literate, articulate, assertive, and, above all, most charming and persuasive. He seems to have performed his priestly duties most conscientiously, saying Mass on Sundays and holy days, hearing confessions regularly, attending diocesan meetings, and collecting tithes. Like the majority of his flock, Clergue was neither a rabid Albigensian nor a fanatical Catholic—he like his parishioners was somewhere in the middle. He was rather fluid in his religious convictions, moving without much strain of conscience between orthodoxy and heresy. Sometimes, he would behave as an Albigensian missionary, reading heretical doctrines to his people. On other occasions he would intimidate his enemies by threatening to accuse them of heresy before the Inquisition. Clergue's most passionate interest, however, was not religious doctrine or any real abiding concern for the physical or spiritual well-being of his charges; it was sex. Fournier's records provide the names of no less than a dozen mistresses, and the list is clearly incomplete. "He scattered his desires among his flock," Ladurie writes, "as impartially as he gave his benediction." And his flock was astonishingly tolerant of his behavior. At least one woman, however, disapproved of Clergue's fornicating habits and told him "You are committing an enormous sin by sleeping with a married woman."

"Not at all," he replied. "One woman is just like another. The sin is the same, whether she is married or not. Which is as much to say that there is no sin about it at all."

One of those who was interviewed by Fournier had this to say about Clergue's activities: "One summer about seven years ago," testified a young woman, named Grazide, "the priest Pierre Clergue came to my mother's house while she was out harvesting, and he was very persistent, 'allow me to have sex with you,' and I said 'all right.' I was very young at the time and a virgin. I think I was about fourteen or fifteen years old. After that, in January, the priest gave me in marriage to my late husband, Pierre Lizier, and after he had given me to this man, the priest continued to have sex with me, frequently during the remaining four years of my husband's life."

Grazide loved Clergue dearly and defended her own innocence with an argument straight out of the southern French troubadours: "A lady who sleeps with a true lover is purified of all sins." And she added, "With Pierre Clergue, I liked it. And so it could not displease God. It was not sinful."

Father Clergue, in turn, declared, "I love you more than any woman in the world"—not only to Grazide but to his other sexual partners as well. Clergue's most serious love affair was with a widow of the lesser nobility named Beatrice de Planisoles. When Beatrice went to the parish church to confess her sins to Clergue, he cut her off with the words, "I prefer you to any other woman in the world" and embraced her passionately. Beatrice managed to elude his blatant sexual harassment and slip away but after a courtship of several months, she finally succumbed. Their relationship lasted some two years, and Beatrice, in her Inquisition transcript, tells of tender moments with Pierre. Sitting beside him by the fire, or sometimes in bed, she would carefully remove all the lice from his body, a ritual known as "delousing" that was both hygienic and an expression of deep affection. She also reported that they committed the deliberate sacrilege of having intercourse in the parish church. In time, however, Beatrice remarried and moved from Montaillou.

Clergue's amorous behavior is a reflection not of medieval society as a whole but of life in an isolated, impoverished mountain village in which the church's dictums on monogamy and celibacy were irrelevant to the inhabitant's daily lives, regardless of occupation or status. "At an altitude of 1,300 meters," Ladurie wryly comments, "rules of priestly celibacy ceased to apply." Nor did religion speak with one voice in Montaillou. Albigensians had an even stricter sexual code than Catholics, but the Aligensian teaching that all sex was wicked deprived many of its followers of a set of sexual standards to which they could realistically aspire.

Father Pierre served for some time as the official representative of the Inquisition in Montaillou. In this capacity he prosecuted some Albigensians but protected others. Eventually, he himself was convicted by the Inquisition—not for licentiousness but for Albigensian leanings. Despite his family's efforts to obtain his release with lavish bribes, Clergue died in prison.

Chronology

955	Otto I defeats Hungarians at Lechfield, securing Europe's eastern border.
1066	Normans win the Battle of Hastings and assume English rule.
1152	Frederick I Barbarossa becomes first Hohenstaufen emperor; reestablishes imperial authority.
1154	Henry II assumes English throne.
1164	Henry II forces the Constitutions of Clarendon on the English clergy.
1170	Thomas a Becket is assassinated.
1176	Papal and other Italian armies defeat Frederick I at Legnano.
1194	Birth of future Hohenstaufen ruler Frederick II, who becomes a ward of the Pope.
1198	Welf interregnum in the empire begins under Otto IV.
1212	Frederick II crowned emperor in Mainz with papal, French and German support.
1214	French armies under Philip II Augustus defeat combined English and German forces at Bouvines in the first major European battle.
1215	English barons revolt against King John and force the king's recognition of Magna Carta.
1227	Frederick II excommunicated for the first of four times by the Pope; conflict between Hohenstaufen dynasty and papacy begins.
1250	Frederick II dies, having been defeated by the German princes with papal support.
1257	German princes establish their own electoral system to elect future emperors.
1270	French King Louis IX, having unified and reformed France, dies a Crusader in the Holy Land.

By the late eighth century, the contours of a new European civilization were beginning to emerge in Western Europe. Increasingly, Europe would become the focus and center of Western civilization. Such dynamism was built upon a fusion of Germanic, Christian, and classical elements. The first, visible beginning of medieval Europe emerged in Charlemagne's Carolingian empire. The agrarian foundations of the eighth and ninth centuries, however, were inadequate for sustaining a monarchial political system. Consequently, a new political and military system based on the decentralization of political power evolved to become an integral part of the political world of the Middle Ages. This new order was called feudalism, and its concomitant social and economic counterpart was called manorialism.

The new European civilization that emerged in the ninth and tenth centuries began to come into its own in the eleventh and twelfth centuries, as Europeans established new economic, social, and political institutions that provided better security and stability for increasing numbers of individuals. The High Middle Ages (1000-1300) was a period of recovery and growth for Western civilization. Both the Catholic Church and the feudal states recovered from the invasions and internal dissension of the Early Middle Ages. New agricultural practices that increased the food supply helped give rise to a commercial and urban revival that, accompanied by a rising population, created new dynamic elements in a formerly static society.

By the fifth century A.D., the town and cities that had been such an essential part of the Roman world declined, and the world of the Early Middle Ages continued to be predominantly agricultural. The late tenth and early eleventh centuries, however, witnessed a renewal of commercialism, leading to the revival of cities. Old Roman sites came back to life while new towns arose at major trading crossroads. Some of these new commercial entrepots were inland cities while others gained preeminence as natural harbors or ports. By the twelfth and thirteenth centuries, both the urban centers and their populations were experiencing a dramatic expansion. Although European society in the Middle Ages remained overwhelmingly agricultural, the growth of trade and cities along with the development of a money economy and new commercial practices and institutions constituted a veritable commercial revolution that affected most of Europe, including many country's political systems. Commerce, cities, and a money economy helped to undermine feudal institutions while strengthening monarchial authority as some medieval kings exerted centralizing authority and inaugurated the process of developing new kinds of monarchial states. By the thirteenth century, European monarchs were consolidating their governmental institutions in pursuit of greater power.

ORIGINS OF FEUDAL EUROPE

The Middle Ages were characterized by a chronic absence of effective central government and the constant threat of famine, disease, and foreign invasions. In this state of affairs the weaker sought the protection of the stronger, and the true rulers became those who could provide immediate protection from rapine and starvation. The term *feudal society* refers to the social, political, and economic system that emerged from these conditions. Feudal society of the Middle Ages was dominated by war lords. What people needed most was the assurance that others could be depended upon in time of dire need. Lesser men pledged themselves to powerful individuals—war lords or princes—recognizing them as superiors and promising them *fealty,* faithful service when called upon. Large warrior groups of *vassals* emerged and developed into a professional military class with its own code of knightly conduct. The result was a network of complex relationships based on mutual loyalty that allowed warlords to acquire armies and to rule over territory whether they owned land or had a legitimate royal title. The emergence of these military organizations, warlords and their retinue of professional military vassals or knights was a necessary adaptation to the absence of strong central government and the predominance of a noncommercial, rural, and agrarian economy.

Vassalage

Feudalism contained two important components: a personal element called *vassalage* and a property element called the *benefice*. These two essential features combined both Germanic and Roman practices. Vassalage originated from Germanic society and was based upon a lord gathering followers to himself on certain conditions, primarily military. In Germanic custom, this relationship between chief and followers was a perfectly honorable one, a relationship between social equals.

Feudalism also contained a property element that was ultimately fused with the personal element of vassalage. In the late Roman Empire, it became customary for great landowners to hire retainers. To provide for the latter's maintenance, the lord gave land known as a benefice, or fief. This granting of land emerged out of a king's or lord's need for fighting men, especially in the newly developing cavalry. Vassals were expected to live on these fiefs, or benefices, and maintain horses and other accouterments of war in good order. Originally, vassals were little more than gangs-in-waiting.

Since vassalage involved the swearing of "fealty," or allegiances, to the lord, a vassal promised to refrain from any action that might threaten his lord's welfare. Most important among the services required of a vassal was military duty as a mounted knight. The Frankish armies of Charlemagne originally consisted of foot soldiers dressed in coats of mail and armed with swords. By the eleventh century a military change had occurred when larger horses were introduced. Earlier, horsemen had been mobile archers and throwers of spears. Eventually, they were armored in coats of mail and wielded long lances that enabled them to act as battering rams. For almost five hundred years, heavily armored cavalry or knights would dominate European warfare. These particular warriors came to have the greatest social prestige and form the essence of Europe's aristocracy.

A knight's service involved a variety of activities: a short or long military expedition, escort duty, standing castle guard, or the placement of one's own castle or fortress at the lord's disposal, if the vassal was of such stature to have one. Frequently bargaining and bickering occurred between lord and vassal over the terms of service. As the relationship between lords and vassals became more formal, limitations were placed on the number of days a lord could require of his vassal's services. By the eleventh century in France about forty days of service a year were considered sufficient. It was also possible for vassals to buy their way out of military obligations by a monetary payment, known as scutage. The lord, in turn, applied this payment to the hiring of mercenaries, who often proved more efficient than contract-conscious vassals.

Beyond his military duty, a vassal was also expected to give his lord advice when requested and to sit as a member of the lord's court when it was in session. Many vassals were also obliged to provide hospitality for their lord when he stayed at a vassal's estate or castle. This obligation was especially important to medieval kings since they tended to be highly itinerant. In addition, a vassal could be called upon for financial assistance when his lord was in obvious need or distress. For example, such would be the case when a lord had been captured by his enemies and needed to be ransomed or when he was outfitting himself for a crusade or a military campaign. Gifts of money might also be expected when the lord's daughters married and his sons became knights.

The lord's obligations to his vassals were also very specific. Foremost was his obligation to protect the vassal from physical harm and to stand as his advocate in public court. After fealty was sworn and homage paid, the lord provided for the vassal's physical maintenance by the granting of the benefice or fief. The fief was simply the material wherewithal to meet the vassal's military and other obligations. It could take the form of liquid wealth, as well as the more common grant of real property. There were also money fiefs, which empowered a vassal to receive regular payments from the lord's treasury. Such fiefs, however, created potential conflicts because they made it possible for a nobleman in one land to acquire vassals among the nobility in another. More often than not, the fief was a landed estate of anywhere from a few to several thousand acres. It could also take the form of a castle, which also varied in size and construction from a simple, crude stone or even wooden tower to an elaborate edifice of the finest stone masonry.

As this system of mutual obligations between lord and vassal evolved, certain practices became common. If a lord acted improperly toward his vassal, the bond between them could be dissolved. Likewise, if a vassal failed to fulfill the requirements of his fealty, he was subject to forfeiture of his fief. Upon a vassal's death, his fief theoretically reverted back to the lord since it had been granted to him to use, not to own as a possession. In practice, however, by the eleventh century fiefs tended to become hereditary. Following the principle of primogeniture, the eldest son inherited the father's fief. If a man died without heirs, the lord could once again reclaim the fief.

By the eleventh century the fief acquired a new dimension involving the exercise of political power. While the fief remained, in essence, a landed estate held from the lord by a vassal in return for military service, increasingly, vassals came to have complete political and legal authority within their fiefdoms. Fief-holding also became increasingly complicated as subinfeudation occurred. The vassals of a king, who were themselves great lords, might also have vassals who owed them military service in return for a grant of land from their estates. Those vassals, in turn, might have their own vassals, who at such a level would be simple knights with barely enough land to provide their own equipment. The lord-vassal relationship bound together both greater and lesser landowners. Historians used to present feudalism as a hierarchy with the king at the top, greater lords on the next level, lesser lords on the next, and simple knights at the bottom, followed by the rest of medieval society, i.e., peasants and serfs. This was only, however, a model and rarely reflected reality. Such a hierarchy implied a powerful king at the top, exercising a substantial degree of authority and control over his kingdom. The reality of eleventh century France, for example, negates this image. The "kings" of France actually controlled no more land than the Ile-de-France, the region around Paris. By contrast, their supposed "vassals," the dukes of Normandy and Burgundy, controlled far more extensive territory and exercised greater political power and authority than did the kings. Indeed, as will be seen later in the chapter, it will be William, Duke of Normandy, who will conquer England in 1066.

As the centuries passed, personal loyalty and service became secondary to the acquisition of property, especially among the various levels of vassals. In developments that signaled the waning of feudal society beginning in the eleventh century, the fief came to overshadow fealty; the benefice became more important than vassalage, and freemen proved themselves prepared to swear allegiance to the highest bidder. Feudalism, nonetheless, provided stability throughout the Early Middle Ages and aided the difficult process of political centralization during the High Middle Ages. The advantage of feudal government lay in its adaptability. Agreements of different kinds could be made with almost anyone, as circumstances required. The process embraced a broad spectrum of people, from the king to the lowliest vassal in the remotest part of the kingdom. The foundations of the modern nation-state would emerge in France and England from the fine tuning of essentially feudal arrangements, as kings sought to adapt their goal of centralized government and authority to the reality of local power and control. In many countries, it took several centuries for monarchs to consolidate their power and centralize authority in their personage. Constantly obstructing this process were the forces of an entrenched nobility, who believed that the king was usurping power and legitimate authority because he was violating feudal arrangements between himself and his vassals that extended back to the Middle Ages.

THE MANORIAL SYSTEM

Peasants and Serfs

Feudalism rested upon an economic system known as manorialism. The agrarian economy of the Middle Ages was organized and controlled through village farms known as manors. Frequently, a manor and village were synonymous; one agricultural village constituted the lord's estate. Or, a manor might consist of two or more villages. There was no single formula. Manorialism grew out of earlier practices and was especially encouraged by the unsettled conditions of the Early Middle Ages when many peasants gave up their freedom in return for protection.

On manors, peasants labored as tenants for a lord, who allotted them land and tenements in exchange for their services and a portion of their crops. The part of the estate worked for the lord was called the demesne, on average about one-quarter to one-third of the cultivated lands scattered throughout the manor. All crops grown on the demesne were harvested for the lord. The manor also included common meadows for grazing animals and forests reserved exclusively for the lord to hunt in.

Peasants were treated according to their personal status and the size of their tenements. A freeman, a peasant possessing his own land, or hereditary property (property free from claims of an overlord), became a serf by surrendering his property to a greater landowner—a lord—in exchange for protection and assistance. Although the land was no longer his property, he had full possession and use of it, and the number of services and amount of goods he was to supply to the lord were carefully spelled out.

Peasants who entered a lord's service with little real property (perhaps only a few farm implements and animals) ended up as unfree serfs. Such individuals were more vulnerable to the lord's demands for their labor and service, often spending up to three days a week working the lord's fields. Truly impoverished peasants, those who had nothing to offer a lord except their hands, had the lowest status on the manor and were the least protected from exploitation.

The supervision of manors varied considerably. If the lord of a manor was a simple knight, he probably lived on the estate and supervised it personally. Great lords possessed many manors and relied on a steward or bailiff to run each estate. Lords controlled the lives of their serfs in a number of ways. Serfs were not only required to cultivate the lord's lands but also build barns, dig ditches, drain swamps, clear forests, and any other type of work deemed necessary by the lord for his manor's general sustenance and maintenance. Serfs of all classes were subject to various dues, including a share of every product raised by the serfs. Serfs, moreover, paid the lord for the use of the manor's common pasturelands, streams, ponds, and surrounding woodlands. For example, if a tenant fished in the manor's pond or stream, he turned over part of the catch to his lord. If his cow grazed in the common pasture, he paid a rent in cheese produced from the cow's milk. Serfs were also obliged to pay a tithe (one-tenth of their produce) to their local village church. Thus, the lord, who furnished shacks and small plots of land from his vast domain, had at his disposal an army of servants of varying status who provided him with everything from eggs to boots.

Legal Rights

In addition to complete control of their labor, lords also possessed legal rights over their serfs as a result of their unfree status. Serfs were legally bound to the lord's land; they could not leave without his permission. Although free to marry, serfs could not marry anyone outside their manor without the lord's approval. Due to the decentralization of public power that was part of feudalism, lords sometimes exercised public rights or political authority on their lands. This gave the lord the right to try serfs in his own court, although only for lesser crimes (called "low justice"). In fact, the lord's manorial court provided the only law most serfs knew. Finally, the lord's political authority allowed him to establish monopolies on certain services that provided additional income. Serfs could be required to bring their grain to the lord's mill and pay a fee to have it ground into flour. Thus, the rights a lord possessed on his manor gave him virtual control over both the lives and property of his serfs. Weak serfs often fled to monasteries rather than continue to be exploited in such a fashion. That many serfs were discontented is reflected in the high number of recorded escapes. Escaped serfs wandered the land as beggars and vagabonds until they found, if ever, new and more benevolent masters.

AGRICULTURAL REFORMS AND INNOVATIONS IN THE MIDDLE AGES

Medieval Europe was an overwhelmingly agrarian society and remained so for several more centuries, even though by the beginning of the thirteenth century commerce and a revival of town and city life had occurred. The revitalization of trade and urban life was, in large part, the result of important agricultural and technological changes that took place in the eleventh and twelfth centuries that dramatically increased the food supply that preceded and accompanied population explosion. Although some historians have questioned whether the medieval developments deserve the appellation "revolution," significant changes did take place in the way Europeans farmed.

Although the improvement in climate played an important role in producing longer and better growing seasons, another important factor in increasing food production was the expansion in the amount of land cultivated. This was accomplished primarily by intense clearing of forests. Millions of acres of trees were felled and the land cleared for farming. Cleared forests not only provided more arable land for agriculture but also timber for fuel, houses, mills, bridges, fortresses, ships, and charcoal for the nascent iron industry. Eager for land, peasants cut down trees and drained swamps. In the area of the Netherlands, peasants began to reclaim the land from the sea. Religious orders, such as the Cistercian monks, (a new religious order founded in 1098), proved particularly ambitious in clearing forests, draining marshes, and plowing fields. By the beginning of the thirteenth century, Europeans had available a total acreage for farming greater than any used before or since.

Technological Advancements

Technological advancements also furthered agricultural development. The Middle Ages witnessed an explosion of labor-saving devices, many of which depended upon the use of iron, which was mined in various areas of Europe and traded to places where it was not found. Iron was in demand to make swords and armor, as well as scythes, axeheads, and new types of farming tools, such as hoes, saws, hammers, and nails for building purposes. It was crucial to the development of the heavy-wheeled plow, the *carruca*, which was a great boon to farmers north of the Alps, who unlike their counterparts to the south (Mediterranean and Near Eastern farmers) could not use the *aratum*, a light, nonwheeled wooden scratch plow suitable only for the light soils of those regions. Interestingly, the aratum helped to preserve the family farm as the basic social unit rather than the village in the Mediterranean world. Farmers could afford to have one since it could be pulled by a donkey or a single animal.

Farming north of the Alps, however, required the "carruca" with its iron ploughshare to till the heavy clay soils of northern Europe. The carruca could turn over heavy soils and allow for their drainage. Because of its weight, several oxen were required to pull it. Oxen were slow, however, and two new inventions for the horse made greater productivity possible. A new horse collar appeared in the tenth century. Although horses were faster than oxen, the amount they could pull with the traditional harness was limited because it tended to choke the horse if it pulled too much weight. The new collar distributed the weight around the horse's shoulders and chest rather than the throat and could be used to hitch up a series of horses, allowing them to pull the new heavy plow faster and cultivate more land. The use of the horseshoe, an iron shoe nailed to the horse's hooves, spread in the eleventh and twelfth centuries and allowed for greater traction and better protection for the animal against the rocky and heavy clay soils of northern Europe.

Besides using horsepower, the Middle Ages saw the harnessing of water and wind power to do jobs previously done by human or animal power. The watermill, although invented as early as the second century B.C., was not used much in the Roman Empire, since it was considered disruptive to slave labor and free wage earners. Not until the Middle Ages, with the spread of metallurgical technology, making it easier to build, did its use become widespread. In 1086, the survey of English land, known as the Domesday Book, listed 6,000 of them in England. Located along streams, they were used to grind grains for flour. Even dams were constructed to increase waterpower. The development of the dam enabled millwrights to mechanize entire industries; waterpower was used in certain phases of cloth production and to power triphammers for the working of metals.

Where rivers were unavailable or not easily dammed, Europeans developed windmills to harness wind power. Historian are unsure if windmills were imported into Europe or designed independently by Europeans. (They were invented in Persia.) In either case, by the end of the twelfth century, windmills dotted the northern European landscape. The windmill and watermill were the most important devices for the utilization of natural power before the invention of the steam engine in the eighteenth century. Their use had a profound impact on the ability of Europeans to produce more food.

Finally, the transition from a two-field to three-field system contributed to the increase in agricultural production. In the early Middle Ages, it was common to plant one field, allowing another of equal size to lie fallow to regain its fertility. Now estates were divided into three parts: one field was planted in the fall with winter grains, such as rye and wheat, while spring grains, such as oats, barley, and vegetables, were planted in the second field. The third remained fallow. By rotating their use, only one-third rather than one-half of the land lay fallow at any time. Crop rotation also prevented soil exhaustion. Grain yields increased to levels that would not be surpassed until the next agricultural revolution that occurred in the eighteenth century. The three-field system was not adopted everywhere. It was not used in the Mediterranean lands, and even in some parts of northern Europe, the two-field and three-field systems existed side by side for centuries.

Medieval Europe was an overwhelmingly rural society with most people living in small villages. In the eleventh and twelfth centuries, however, new dynamics were introduced that began to transform Europe's economic foundation: a revival of trade, expansion in the circulation of money, the emergence of a new class of crafts-

Woodcut image of Venice, a leading city in the revival of trade.

men and artisans, and the concomitant growth of towns. Helping to stimulate these changes were the new agricultural practices and new uses of energy, which freed part of the European population from the need to produce their own food and allowed diversification in economic functions. Merchants and craftsmen could now buy their necessities.

THE REVIVAL OF TRADE

The revival of commercial activity was a gradual process. Although trade had never completely died out in Western Europe, the political chaos and related economic decline of the Early Middle Ages caused large-scale trade to all but disappear. The only amount of substantial trade taking place during those centuries was between Italy and the Byzantine Empire and the Jewish traders who moved back and forth between the Muslim and Christian worlds. By the end of the tenth century, however, individuals were appearing in Europe with both the skills and products essential for a revitalization of trade. Although most villages produced what they needed locally, other items were made that were unique to the region and could be sold elsewhere. These included a variety of goods, such as flax and wool for clothes, wine for drinking and for use in Catholic mass, salt for preserving food, furs for clothing, hemp for rope, and metals for weapons or tools. Some regions and countries became particularly well known for their specialized products: England for raw wool, Scandinavia and Germany for iron, and Germany for silver.

Cities in Italy, most notably Venice in the eighth century, assumed a leading role in the revival of trade. By that time Venice had assumed strong and profitable commercial connections with Byzantium. The city developed a merchant fleet and by the end of the tenth century had become Europe's main entrepot for Byzantine and Islamic commerce. Venetians traded grain, wine, and timber to Constantinople in exchange for silk cloth, which was then sold or traded to other northern Italian communities, which turned the silk into clothing. The Italians furthered their trading enterprises with the advent of the Crusades at the end of the eleventh century. (See Chapter 8) Italian merchants were able to establish new mercantile settlements in eastern ports, obtaining silks, sugar, and spices that they carried back to Italy and the west. Although these items were not entirely new to Western Europe, they were now traded in increasingly large quantities.

While northern Italian cities were enlarging the scope of Mediterranean trade, the towns of Flanders, the area along the coast of present day Belgium and northern France, became the centers for the production of woolen cloth. Flanders' location made it a logical entrepot for northern European traders. Merchants from England, Scandinavia, France, and Germany congregated there to trade their wares for the much desired woolen cloth; England, in particular, became the chief supplier of raw wool for the Flemish woolen industry. Flanders became one of the most prosperous regions in all of Western Europe by the end of the twelfth century, and its towns, particularly Bruges and Ghent, became centers for the trade and manufacture of woolen cloth.

By the twelfth century, both Italy and Flanders had become the leading centers of the trade revival, and it only seemed natural that these two areas witnessed a regular exchange of goods. The dangers and difficulties of sea travel around Western Europe, however, and the expense of overland journeys made such a connection unlikely. Powerful feudal lords and princes, moreover, charged tolls to merchants going through their lands and did not hesitate to plunder caravans carrying goods when they needed money or supplies.

As trade contacts increased, even lords began to see the advantage of promoting trade. The best example of such a change in attitude comes from the counts of the Champagne region in northern France. Beginning in the twelfth century, the feudal counts instituted an annual event of six fairs held in the chief towns of their territory. The counts guaranteed the safety of visiting merchants, supervised the trading activities, and, for their services, collected a sales tax on all goods sold or exchanged at the fairs. The Champagne fairs became the largest commercial marketplace in Western Europe for the exchange of goods between northern and southern Europe and the Byzantine and Muslim East. At the fairs, northern merchants brought furs, woolen cloth, tin, hemp, and honey of northern Europe and exchanged them for the cloth and swords of northern Italy and the silks, sugar, and spices of the East.

Money and Banking

As trade increased throughout Europe in the twelfth century, the demand for coins or the use of money instead of barter increased as well. Without gold mines of its own, Western Europe had few gold coins in circulation before the thirteenth century. Silver and copper coins were most frequently used as money. For several decades Germany had a monopoly on the production of silver coins because it had the richest silver deposit in Western Europe in the Harz Mountains of central Germany. England also produced coins, the silver penny, called sterling for its stability, and so did France, the pennies of Paris, Tours, and Anjou, together with the English penny became the most widely circulated coins in France and England in the twelfth century.

As trade expanded throughout Europe and competition increased, as more Western European regions emerged as manufacturing/

trade centers, the Italian merchants discovered that their trade (if they hoped to maintain their preeminence) required new ways of raising capital and new commercial practices. They created partnerships to raise capital for ships and goods in overseas journeys. The *commenda* was the most common form of partnership, a temporary association amongst a group of related enterprises where one partner contributed money while the other(s) supplied labor and time. If the venture was successful, the partners simple shared in the profits. The Italians also developed insurance to protect their investments, although rates were exorbitant. New methods of credit, such as bills of exchange or notes on credit, were established to circumvent the problem of insufficient reserves of money or the inconvenience of exchanging coins for larger transactions. By the beginning of the thirteenth century the Italians, because of their trade connections with the East, began minting gold coins that became standard in Western Europe over the next few decades. The gold florin of Florence was first struck in 1252 and the Venetian gold ducat in 1284.

A moneylender works with clients in the center of a medieval fair. Such men were the earliest bankers, issuing loans and credit.

Financial matters were complicated by the practice of usury. The Church regarded economic activity as an ethical affair and disapproved of usury, defined as pure interest on a loan. The Church condemned usury in 1139 and damned usurers, as malevolent and unworthy of Christian burial. The Church's attitude was troublesome because the lending of money for productive purposes was essential to the further expansion and development of trade, manufacturing, and banking. Consequently, Church officials discovered rationalizations and merchants found ways to circumvent the Church's ban. Most economic historians question whether the usury laws actually handicapped Europe's economic growth, although the laws undoubtedly caused many merchants grief and financial hardships.

It should also be noted that banking grew out of mercantile necessity. The existence of many different coinages required professional moneychangers who knew coins' respective values and could exchange them. Soon moneychangers became involved in lending money as well. As merchants accumulated wealth, they were able to hold large deposits of money and function as bankers. Because of their dominance of trade, the richest and most prominent early banking houses were Italian. Italians took the lead in developing the institutions and methods of the new capitalist system. Northern Europeans looked to the Italians as their role models.

In Spain and Portugal, Muslims and Jews dominated banking and financing. Together they dominated the mercantile and banking enterprises of both countries. Since they were non-Christian, the Church could only frown on their activities and not completely shut down their money-lending operations. Muslims and Jews, moreover, had coexisted harmoniously and profitably in both countries for centuries and had become invaluable fixtures in medieval Iberian society. They remained so until the Reconquista finally unified all of Spain under the Catholic rulers Ferdinand and Isabella at the end of the fifteenth century. When that was accomplished, the monarchy along with the Church unwisely decided to drive all non-Christians out of Spain if they did not convert. Most Muslims and Jews refused to convert and were driven out of both countries. Going with them was incredible financial acumen, something Spain and Portugal would sorely need in the centuries to come.

RISE OF MEDIEVAL CITIES

Without question, the most important dynamic resulting from the revitalization of trade in medieval Europe was the emergence of cities and urban life and society. Merchants could not function in a world that emphasized the exaction of labor services and attachment to the land. They needed places where they could build warehouses to store their goods for shipment elsewhere and personal residences that could serve as permanent bases. In short, their livelihood demanded a complete reorientation of their physical environment and existence. Cities did not develop just anywhere. To meet merchants' needs, they were located near sources of protection and alongside rivers or major arteries that provided favorable transportation routes.

Towns in the economic sense, as centers of population where merchants and artisans gathered and exchanged goods, services, and ideas and purchased their food from surrounding areas, had greatly declined in the Early Middle Ages, especially in Europe north of the Alps. Old Roman cities continued to exist but declined dramatically relative to size and population. Many were transformed into administrative centers for dukes and counts or sees or seats for bishops and archbishops. With the revival of trade, merchants began to gather in these old cities, followed by craftsmen or artisans, skilled individuals who saw in these places the opportunity to further develop their trade and produce objects that could be sold by the merchants. In the course of the eleventh and twelfth centuries, old Roman cities came alive with new populations and growth. By 1100 the old areas of these cities had been repopulated; after 1100, the population outgrew the old walls, requiring the construction of new city walls outside the old.

In the Mediterranean world, cities had survived the Western empire's decline and remained viable entities of habitation and commercial centers. After the Moors conquest of southern Spain in the eighth century, Islamic cities had a flourishing urban life, centered in such locales as Grenada and Seville. Urban life in southern Italy also thrived in such places as Bari, Salerno, Naples, and Amalfi. Although greatly reduced in size, Rome, the old capital of the Roman world, had survived as the center of papal administration. In northern Italy, Venice already had emerged by the end of the eighth century as a town because of its commercial connections with Byzantium.

Beginning in the late tenth century, many new towns and cities were established, particularly in northern Europe. The usual pattern for development would be a group of merchants establishing a settlement near some fortified stronghold, such as a castle or monastery. Castles were especially favored since they were usually located along major transportation routes or at the intersection of two such trade routes; castle lords also offered protection (for a fee, of course). If the settlement prospered and expanded, new walls were built to protect it. Most of these new towns were closely tied to their immediate surroundings since they were dependent on the countryside for their sustenance. In addition, they were often part of the territory belonging to a lord and were subject to his jurisdiction. Although lords wanted to treat towns and its folk as they would their vassals and serfs, cities had totally different needs and a different perspective toward life than their rural counterparts.

Townspeople and Self-government

The new class of townspeople did not fit into the structure and pattern of rural life in the Middle Ages. Since they were not lords, they were not subject to the customs that applied to lords. They were not serfs or peasants either and were reluctant to subject themselves to manorial services and mandates, even though many originally came from such ranks. Merchants and artisans needed mobility to trade. Consequently, townspeople were a sort of "revolutionary" group who needed their own identity and laws to meet the different requirements of their lives. Since townspeople were profiting from the growth of trade and the sale of their products, they were willing to pay to make their own laws and govern themselves. In many instances, lords and kings (especially the latter as they tried to weaken their feudal ties with powerful lords because of their desire to consolidate and centralize power in their own hands) saw the potential for vast new sources of revenues and were willing to grant (more accurately sell) the liberties townspeople were demanding. By 1100 town folk were obtaining charters of liberties from their territorial lords, either lay or ecclesiastical, that granted them the privileges they wanted. In most cases they obtained their goal simply by an outright purchase (one lump sum money payment) or by regular revenues. The rights obtained usually consisted of four basic liberties in their charters: a testamentary right, the right to bequeath goods and sell property; freedom from military obligation to the lord; written urban law that guaranteed the freedom of townspeople; and the right to become a free person after residing a year and a day in the town. The last provision made it possible for a runaway serf, who could avoid capture, to become a free person in a city. While lords and kings granted such basic liberties, they were very hesitant to allow cities the right of self-government. In most cases, the king or lord continued to actually govern the town through an appointed official called a provost, who collected taxes owed and administered the king's or lord's justice and other laws. Some city charters, however, did grant the right of self government. For example, the city of London received such a privilege from King Henry I in 1130. In their charter, Londoners had the right to choose their own officials to govern them. They also had the right to administer their own courts of law. While taxes were still paid to the king, they were collected by the city's appointees, not the king's.

Frequently, urban communities found that their lords were unwilling to grant them all the liberties they wanted, especially self-government. Bishops in cathedral cities were particularly obstinate in retaining their privileges. In these cities, merchants and serfs lived in the same community; to grant freedom meant the loss of the services of the serfs who tilled the fields outside the city. For a bishop to grant self-government to local officials within his city meant the end of his own authority. Where town folk experienced such tenacity, they often took matters into their own hands by forming an association called a commune and, if necessary, were willing to use force to extract from their lay or ecclesiastical lords their rights. Communes were especially effective in northern Italy, in the regions of Tuscany and Lombardy, where townspeople had the support of local nobles, who were just as keen on wresting power from the clergy as were urbanites. With such support, Italian town residents, in cities such as Pisa, Milan, Arezzo, and Genoa, were successful in the eleventh and twelfth centuries of destroying clerical power and establishing complete self-government, which saw the creation of new municipal offices such as consuls and town councils that governed the city in the name and welfare of its citizens.

Although communes were established in northern Europe, especially in France and Flanders, town folk there did not have the support of rural nobles. Revolts against lay lords were usually brutally suppressed; those against bishops, as in Laon in the twelfth century, were more frequently successful. When they succeeded, communes received the right to chose their own officials, hold their own courts, and administer their own cities. Unlike their Italian counterparts, however, which eventually became completely autonomous, self-governing republican city-states, the towns of northern European did evolve to such status. Instead, in England and France, for example, they remained ultimately subject to royal authority. Medieval cities, then, possessed varying degrees of self-government depending on the amount of control retained over them by the lord or king in whose territory they were located. Nevertheless, all towns, regardless of the degree of outside control, evolved institutions of government for running the community's affairs.

Medieval cities defined citizenship narrowly and granted it only to males who had been born in the city or had lived there for some time. In many cities, citizens elected members of a city council that were responsible for running the city on a daily basis. City councillors not only enacted legislation but also served as judges and city magistrates. Election of councillors was by no means democratic. The electoral process was tightly controlled by the city's mercantile elite—an oligarchy composed of its wealthiest and most powerful families, who came to be called patricians. Councillors were elected from this small cadre of patricians, who kept the reins of government in their hands despite periodic protests from lesser merchants and artisans. In the twelfth and thirteenth centuries, some cities added an executive to the body of councillors, in whose hands was placed the daily governing of the city. Although it varied from town to town, the title of mayor was used to refer to this executive officer. These individuals were either appointed by the king, or lord, or elected from among their ranks by city councillors. In some Italian city-states, the executive known as the podesta, literally a person with power, was brought in from the outside because the city's patricians often feuded bitterly among themselves to decide which of them would assume such control. The podesta was only to rule for one year but occasionally, if he was particularly effective and adept at maneuvering among the city's elite, he was granted a longer tenure, or, if he became especially powerful over the year, he simply established himself permanently by usurping power or taking it by force from the council.

City governments kept close watch over citizens' activities; some historians have used the term "municipal socialism" to describe such scrutiny. To care for the community's welfare and safety, a city government might regulate air and water pollution; provide water barrels and delegate responsibility to people in every section of town to fight fires, which were an ever-present danger; construct warehouses to stockpile grain in the event of food shortages caused by war or bad harvests; and establish and supervise the standards of weights and measures used in the various local goods and industries. Although violence was a way of life in the Middle Ages, urban crime was not a major problem. The community's relatively small size made it difficult for criminals to operate openly. Nevertheless, medieval urban governments did organize town guards to patrol the streets by night and the city walls by day. People caught committing criminal acts were quickly tried for their offenses. Serious infractions, such as murder, were punished by execution, usually by hanging. Lesser crimes were punished by fines, flogging, or branding.

Whatever their condition or degree of independence, medieval cities remained relatively small in comparison to either ancient or modern cities. By the end of the thirteenth century, London was the largest city in England with almost 40,000 people. Otherwise, north of the Alps, only Bruges and Ghent in Flanders had populations close to that figure. Italian cities tended to be larger with Venice, Florence, Genoa, Milan, and Naples numbering almost 100,000. Even the largest European city seemed insignificant alongside Constantinople or the Arab cities of Damascus, Baghdad, and Cairo. For centuries to come, Europe remained predominantly rural. In the long run, the rise of towns and the development of commerce laid the foundations for the eventual transformation of Europe from a rural and agricultural society to an urban and industrial one.

The shrine of Edward the Confessor in Westminster Abbey.

ENGLAND IN THE MIDDLE AGES

In 1066 the death of the childless Anglo-Saxon ruler, Edward the Confessor (so-named because of his reputation for piety), precipitated one of the most important changes in English political history. Edward's mother was a Norman, giving the duke of Normandy a hereditary claim to the English throne. Before his death, Edward, who was a rather weak monarch, acknowledged the Duke's claim and ordered that William's (the Duke of Normandy) ascension to the throne be accepted. In fact, Edward had actually promised William the crown fifteen years earlier. But the Anglo-Saxon assembly, which customarily bestowed the royal power, had in mind a different agenda and vetoed Edward's request. They chose

The most famous account of the Norman Conquest is not a written record but a pictorial one. The Bayeux Tapestry tells the story of Harold of Sessex and William of Normandy through the Battle of Hastings. In the scene at the top, Harold is crowned king of England in Westminster Abbey. In the scene at the right, men cut down trees along the Norman coast to build ships in preparation for the Norman invasion. At the bottom the Normans sack England.

William the Conqueror rides atop his horse during the Battle of Hastings. This was an age when kings were expected not only to lead their armies into battle but also to be mighty warriors, performing extraordinary feats. William of Normandy was certainly such a leader.

instead, Harold Godwinsson, an Anglo-Dane. Harold claimed that on his deathbed Edward had passed the crown to him when he asked Harold to "look after the kingdom." Based on Edward's rather enigmatic request, Harold assumed he was the rightful heir. The Anglo-Saxon lords of England simply did not want to be ruled by a "foreigner." This defiance angered William, who raised an army, crossed the channel and defeated an Anglo-Saxon army, led by Harold, at the decisive Battle of Hastings in 1066. Within weeks of his victory, William was crowned king of England in Westminster Abbey, both by right of heredity and by right of conquest. No sooner was he crowned, than he spent the next twenty years conquering and subjugating the rest of his new country. By the time of his death in 1087, he had made all England his domain.

As a result of his conquests, every landholder, whether large or small, was now his vassal, holding land legally as a fief from the king. William organized his new English nation shrewdly. He established a strong, centralized monarchy whose power was not fragmented by independent territorial princes. He kept in tact the Anglo-Saxon tax system and the practice of court writs (legal warnings) as a flexible form of central control over localities. He was careful not to destroy

Alfred the Great instituted the practice of parleying.

the Anglo-Saxon quasi democratic tradition of frequent "parleying"—the holding of conferences between the king and the great lords who had a vested interest in royal decisions.

The practice of parleying was initially instituted by Alfred the Great (r. 871-899). A strong and willful king who forcibly unified England, Alfred relied heavily on his councilors' advice in making laws. His example was respected and continued under the reign of Canute (r. 1016-1035), the Dane who restored order and brought unity to England after prolonged civil war engulfed the island during the reign of the incompetent Ethlered II (r. 978-106). William, although he thoroughly subjugated the Anglo-Saxon nobility to the crown, nonetheless, maintained the parleying tradition by consulting regularly with them about state affairs. The result was the unique blending of the one and the many, a balance between monarchial and parliamentary interests that has ever since been a feature of English government. Although the English Parliament, as we know it today, did not formally develop as an institution until the late thirteenth century, its tradition began with the reign of William the Conqueror.

For administration and taxation purposes William commissioned a county-by-county survey of his new realm, a detailed accounting known as the *Domesday Book* (1080-1086). The title of the book may reflect the thoroughness and finality of the survey. As none would escape the doomsday judgment of God, so none was overlooked by William's assessors.

The Norman conquest of England brought a dramatic change. In Anglo-Saxon England, the king had held limited lands while great aristocratic families controlled vast estates and acted rather independently of the king. By contrast, the Normans established an aristocratic hierarchy where, depending on their status, the amount of land they held was as a fief from the king. William the Conqueror manipulated the feudal system to create a strong, centralized monarchy. Gradually, a process of fusion between the Normans and Anglo-Saxons created a new England. While the Norman ruling class spoke French, the intermarriage of the Norman-French with the Anglo-Saxon nobility gradually merged Anglo-Saxon and French into a new English language. Political amalgamation also occurred as the Normans adapted existing Anglo-Saxon institutions. The Norman conquest of England had repercussions in France as well. Since the new English king was still the Duke of Normandy, he was both a king (of England) and simultaneously a vassal of the king of France but a vassal who was now far more powerful than his lord. This "French connection" kept England heavily involved in French and continental affairs for several more centuries.

In the twelfth century the power of the English monarchy was significantly expanded by Henry II, the first of the Plantagenet dynasty who reestablished monarchial power after a period of civil war following the death of Henry I, William the Conqueror's son. Henry II was not just the king of England. He also became lord of Ireland, receiving the homage of several Irish princes after permitting some of his leading noblemen to occupy parts of that island. Perhaps more important at that moment than the beginning of English occupation of Ireland was Henry's acquisitions and footholds in France. He was count of Anjou, duke of Normandy, and through marriage to Eleanor of Aquitaine, duke of Aquitaine as well. Henry's union with Eleanor created the Angevin, or English-French empire. Eleanor married Henry while he was still the Count of Anjou and not yet king of England. The marriage occurred only eight weeks after Eleanor's annulment of her fifteen-year marriage to the ascetic French King Louis VII in March 1152. Although the annulment was granted by the Pope on grounds of consanguinity (blood relationship), the true reason for the dissolution was Louis's suspicion of infidelity—Eleanor, it was rumored, had been intimate with a cousin. The annulment cost Louis dearly, who lost Aquitaine and his wife. Eleanor and Henry had eight children, five of them sons, two of whom became the future kings of England, Richard the Lion-Hearted and John. Yet, Henry, despite his vast holdings, was still, by feudal arrangement, a vassal of the king of France! His Angevin empire, as his territory in France was called, made Henry much more powerful than his lord, the king of France. Beginning with Louis VII, French kings saw a serious threat to their own hegemony in France in this English expansion. Consequently, for the next three centuries, the French monarchy pursued a determined policy of containment and expulsion of the English from their nation. Such an effort was not finally successful until the mid-fifteenth century, when English power on the continent collapsed after the Hundred Years' War.

HENRY II

Henry's reign was one of the most important in the early development of the English monarchy. Following his father's death and as a result of the ensuing civil war, royal income declined significantly, and the great nobles, many of whom had resented centralization and the consolidation of monarchial power, used the political chaos to regain their feudal autonomy. Henry, like his grandfather, was not afraid to use brutal force to reassert royal authority. He crushed recalcitrant nobles with ferocity, and once his political hegemony was restored, he successfully implemented administrative reforms and established legal institutions that further strengthened royal government.

First, Henry continued the development of the exchequer or permanent royal treasury that had begun during his father's reign. Royal officials, known as "barons of the exchequer," received taxes collected by the sheriff while seated around a table covered by a checkered cloth (hence, exchequer table), which served as a counting device. The barons gave receipts to the sheriff, while clerks recorded the accounts on parchment that were then rolled up.

Perhaps even more significant than Henry's financial reforms were his efforts to strengthen royal courts and his contributions to the development of English common law. Prior to Henry's legal reformation, justice had been very localized—in primarily county courts and in the courts of the various lords. The king's court had confined itself to affairs relative to the king's rights as a feudal lord. Since William the Conqueror, however, established the king as overlord of the entire kingdom, his successors expanded this jurisdiction to include cases and other legal matters previously handled by the local courts. This expansion or institutionalization of royal legal authority was formalized in 1166 in Henry II's promulgation of the Assizes of Clarendon. The Assizes expanded the number and types of cases to be tried in the king's court. Increased types of criminal acts, as well as property issues, now found their way to the king's court to be heard and tried. Henry's purpose was clear: expanding the jurisdiction of the royal courts extended the king's power and, of course, brought revenues into his coffers. Also, since royal justices were administering law throughout England, a body of common law (laws that prevailed throughout all of England) began to develop to replace the customary law used in county and feudal courts, which often varied from place to place. Henry's systematic approach to legal matters played an important role in developing royal institutions uniform throughout the entire kingdom.

Like his continental counterparts in the twelfth century, Henry became embroiled in the increasing tensions between church and state. Indeed, the most famous (or infamous, depending on which side of the imbroglio one found one's self) church-state controversy in medieval England arose between Henry and Thomas Beckett, Archbishop of Canterbury, the most exalted of all English prelates. The conflict between these two strong-willed individuals centered on two key issues: one, whether the king had the right to punish clerics in royal courts and two, whether legal disputes arising in English courts could be appealed to the papal court for ultimate resolution without royal permission. Since Henry was determined to expand royal power, he viewed such Church prerogatives as an obstacle to his consolidation efforts. Becket, equally determined to sustain Church autonomy by preventing monarchial usurpation of established (and accepted until Henry's reign) Church immunities, asserted that trying clergy for crimes (criminal) in royal courts violated the long-standing right of the Church to try clerics in Church courts. Compounding this church-state power struggle was the fact that Henry and Thomas had been close, personal friends. Becket, prior to becoming archbishop, was one of Henry's closest advisers, and, as such, enjoyed the many "worldly" benefits his position provided. When Henry appointed Becket to be the Archbishop of Canterbury, he expected that Becket, out of loyalty to his friend and king, would do Henry's bidding in all matters. No sooner had Becket put on his archbishop's robes, however, than he

INNOCENT III

underwent a profound spiritual transformation in which he repented for the "sins" he committed while serving as Henry's councilor. To further atone for his past worldliness, Becket decided that he was now religiously obligated to protect the Church's rights. Compromises were attempted between Henry and Beckett, but neither were willing to abandon their respective causes. After Becket excommunicated some bishops who had supported Henry's position, the king, in exasperation, publicly expressed a desire to be "rid" of Becket. Four zealous knights, anxious to please their king, took Henry's utterance literally and on December 29, 1170, assassinated the archbishop at the altar of the cathedral in Canterbury. Becket was martyred by the Church, and three years later canonized as a saint. Henry did public penance for the act and compromised with the Church by allowing the right of appeal from English courts to the papal court. Despite the compromise, Henry had succeeded in strengthening the English monarchy.

Toward the end of his reign, Henry experienced increasing conflict with his nobles over his centralizing policies. Although Henry ultimately crushed the rebels, aristocratic discontent continued into the next century, reaching a climax during the reign of Henry's son, John (1199-1216). Prior to John's ascension to the throne, his brother, Richard the Lion Hearted, ruled England for ten years, most of which time Richard spent in the Holy Land on crusade. Actual power resided with Prince John because of Richard's prolonged absence. Though popular history has vilified John, Richard was just as culpable for policies that aroused aristocratic ire. Burdensome taxation in support of unnecessary foreign crusades and a failing war with France, both of which Richard initiated, turned resistance into outright rebellion during John's regency. Richard had to be ransomed at a high price from the Holy Roman Emperor Henry VI, who had taken him prisoner during his return from the ill-fated Third Crusade. In 1209 Pope Innocent III, in a dispute with King John over the Pope's choice for Archbishop of Canterbury, excommunicated the king and placed England under interdict. To extricate himself and keep his throne, John had to make humiliating concessions, even declaring his country the Pope's fief. The last straw for the English nobility, however, was the defeat of the king's forces by the French at Bouvines in 1214 when John attempted to regain Normandy, which he had lost ten years earlier. With the full support of the clergy and townspeople, English barons revolted against John, forcing him to grudgingly seal the Magna Carta (the Great Charter) of feudal liberties in 1215.

The document limited the monarchial, autocratic power that had been increasing since the Norman conquest, reaching a crescendo with John. It also secured the rights of the many, at least the privileged many, against the monarchy. In the Magna Carta, the privileged preserved their right to be represented at the highest levels of government in important matters like taxation. In short, the Magna Carta was the quintessential feudal document. Feudal custom had always recognized that the relationship between king and vassals was based on mutual rights and obligations. The Magna Carta gave written acknowledgment to that fact and was used in subsequent years to reaffirm the concept that monarchial power should be limited rather than absolute.

THE FRENCH MONARCHY IN THE MIDDLE AGES

The Capetian dynasty of the French monarchy emerged at the end of the tenth century, when in 987, the most powerful noblemen chose one of their own, Hugh Capet, to succeed the last Carolingian ruler of the West Frankish Kingdom (most of present-day France) created in 870 by the Treaty of Mersen. Although they held the title of kings, it was doubtful the Capetians would ever establish their hegemony over all of France. The Capetians controlled as the royal domain only the lands around Paris known as the Ile-de-France. Even that was not entirely under their control; in the eleventh century the Capetians even failed to curtail aristocratic power in their own immediate region. As kings of France, the Capetians were, by feudal arrangement, to be recognized as the overlords of the great lords of France, such as the dukes of Normandy, Brittany, Burgundy, and Aqutaine and the counts of Flanders, Maine, Anjou, Blois, and Toulouse. As has been seen by the exploits of William the Conqueror, Duke of Normandy, the Capetians supposed "vassals" were considerably more powerful than they were. Thus, much of French political history during the Middle Ages is focused on the conflict that often arose between the Capetians and these powerful lords, as the former attempted to expand their power and authority beyond the Ill-de-France.

In their struggle with their vassals, the Capetians possessed some advantages. As kings anointed by God in a sacred ceremony, they had the enduring support of the Catholic Church. The Capetians also benefited from luck. Their royal domain was so small and insignificant that most of the great lords were not very interested in acquiring it by force, especially since it was ruled by the divinely anointed king of France. The Capetians also proved to be a very "prolific" dynasty. Although the Capetian monarchy did not become officially hereditary until 1223, for generations Capetian kings succeeded in producing sons who shared in ruling and then elected kings before their fathers died.

In the twelfth century, Louis VI "the Fat" (1108-1137) and then his son, Louis VII, were successful in solidifying their control over the Ile-de-France. They further strengthened and added prestige to the crown by allying with the papacy and gaining Church support. Their efforts to expand beyond the Ile-de-France, however, were thwarted, and so by the end of the century, the Capetians' territory was still confined to Paris and its immediate environs. But the Louis's kept the monarchial principle alive, and in the thirteenth century, the Capetian dynasty began to realize the fruits of their labors.

It was during the reign of King Philip II Augustus (1180-1223), Louis VII's son, that the power of the French monarch was extended. Philip realized that the key to Capetian expansion and consolidation of power was to drive the English Plantagenets out of France and then annex their territories to the royal domain. Thus in a series of wars against England, culminating in the decisive defeat of King John at the Battle of Bouvines in Flanders in 1214, Philip was successful in wresting from England, Normandy, Maine, Anjou, and Touraine. By the time of his victory at Bouvines, Philip was not only fighting English but their allies as well, the Flemish and Germans under the leadership of the Holy Roman Emperor, Otto IV. As a result of these conquests, Philip not only asserted Capetian hegemony over much of northern and central France but in the process quadrupled, royal income. In short, Philip's victory unified France politically around the monarchy and laid the foundation for French ascendancy in the later Middle Ages.

Like his Plantangenet English counterparts, Philip realized how essential it was to centralize institutions of government to rule his new lands. Philip divided his new territories into bailiwicks, each of which was presided over by a bailiff or seneschal. Bailiffs were appointed to provinces close to the original royal domain, the Ile-de-France region, and seneschals to the more remote provinces. Both of these royal appointees administered justice in the king's name, collected revenues, and served the king's interests in a variety of other matters, ranging from the raising of royal troops to providing escorts for dignitaries and important clerics. Although most bailiffs came from the middle class, seneschals were barons or knights with military experience capable of commanding royal troops when necessary. Bailiffs, seneschals, and their assistants formed the foundation of the French royal bureaucracy in the thirteenth century.

Philip's successors continued the acquisition of territory but, unlike Philip, did not always use force. Through purchase and marriage the same objectives was achieved: the expansion and centralization of Capetian dominion. Much of the thirteenth century was dominated by the man whom many consider to be the greatest of France's medieval monarchs, Louis IX (1226-1270). A deeply spiritual man, he was later canonized as a saint by the Church, an unusual act by the Church regardless of the century. Although possessing a moral character that far exceeded that of his royal and papal contemporaries, Louis was also at times prey to naivete. Not beset by the problems of sheer survival and a reformer at heart, Louis found himself free to concentrate on what medieval people believed to be the business of civilization.

FREDERICK II

Although Louis occasionally chastised popes for their crude political ambitions, he remained neutral during the long struggle between the German Hohenstaufen Emperor Frederick II and the papacy (discussed later in the chapter); and his neutrality proved beneficial to the Pope. Louis also remained neutral when his brother, Charles of Anjou, intervened in Italy and Sicily against the Hohenstaufens, again to the Pope's advantage. Urged on by the Pope and his noble supporters, Charles was crowned king of Sicily in Rome and his subsequent defeat of Frederick II's son and grandson ended the Hohenstaufen dynasty. For such service to the Church, both by action and inaction, thirteenth century Capetian kings became the recipients of many papal favors.

Although Louis ruled through the centralized system set up by Philip, he believed it was his duty to God and to his people to personally guarantee their justice and rights. He sent out royal agents to make sure that his bailiffs and seneschals were not abusing their power at the people's expense. Louis also was responsible for establishing a permanent royal court of justice in Paris, the Parlement of Paris, whose work was carried on by a regular staff of professional jurists. Louis made it increasingly difficult for nobles to wage private wars with each other and eventually outlawed the practice, as well as serfdom within his royal domain, the Ile-de-France. He also gave his subjects the judicial right of appeal from local to higher courts and made the tax system, by medieval standards, more equitable. Louis' countrymen came to associate their king with justice; consequently, national feeling, the glue of nationhood, grew very strong during his reign.

Respected by other European monarchs and possessing far greater moral authority than the Pope, Louis became an arbiter among the European powers. During his reign French society and culture became exemplary, a pattern that would continue into the modern period. Northern France became the showcase of monastic reform, chivalry, and Gothic art and architecture. Louis' reign also coincided with the golden age of Scholasticism, which witnessed the convergence of Europe's greatest minds on Paris, among them Saint Thomas Aquinas and Saint Bonaventure.

Sharing in the religious zeal of his age, he played a major role in two of the later Crusades. (see Chapter 8) Both were failures, and he met his death during an invasion of North Africa. It was especially for his selfless but also useless service on behalf of the Church that Louis later received the rare honor of sainthood. Interestingly, the Church bestowed this honor when it was under pressure from a more powerful and less than "most Christian" French king, the ruthless Philip IV, "the Fair."

In the course of the thirteenth century, the Capetian kings acquired new lands to add to the French royal domain, whether by conquest, purchase, marriage, or inheritance. Although the Capetian monarchs imposed their authority on these accretions, they allowed their new subjects to keep their own laws and institutions. Not until the French Revolution of the eighteenth century would the French move toward a common pattern for all of France. Despite the lack of institutional uniformity, by the end of the thirteenth century, France was the largest, wealthiest, and best-governed monarchial state in Europe.

GERMANY AND THE REVIVAL OF THE HOLY ROMAN EMPIRE

In 918 the Saxon Henry I, the strongest of the German dukes of the defunct Carolingian empire, became the first non-Frankish king of Germany. Over the course of his eighteen-year rule, Henry rebuilt royal power with the use of force and conquest. By the time of his death in 936, Henry had combined Swabia, Bavaria, Saxony, Franconia, and Lotharingia into a consolidated political entity. He secured the borders of his new kingdom by stopping Hungarian and Danish invasions. Although much smaller than Charlemagne's empire, the German kingdom Henry created placed his son and successor Otto I (r. 936-973) in a strong territorial position. Otto was just as adept and clever at statecraft as his father. He maneuvered his own king into positions of power in Bavaria, Swabia, and Franconia. He refused to recognize each duchy as an independent hereditary entity, as the nobility increasingly expected, dealing with each instead as a subordinate member of a unified kingdom. In a truly imperial gesture in 951, he invaded Italy and proclaimed himself its king. In 955 he won his grandest victory when he defeated the Hungarians at Lechfeld. This victory secured German borders against new barbarian attacks, further unified the German duchies, and earned Otto the title, "the Great." In defining Western European boundaries, Otto's victories and conquests were comparable with Charles Martel's earlier triumph over the Saracens at Poitiers in 732.

An integral part of Otto's imperial design was to enlist the support of the Church. Bishops and abbots—individuals possessing a sense of universality and because they could not marry, they could not establish competitive dynasties—were the recipients of much royal largesse. They became the king's royal princes and agents. Because these clergy, as royal bureaucrats, received vast estates and immunity from the mandates of local dukes and counts, they found such vassalage to the king appealing. The medieval Church did not become a great territorial power reluctantly. It appreciated such "gifts" while teaching the blessedness of giving.

In 961 Otto, who coveted the imperial crown, put himself in a position to receive it by responding to a plea from Pope John XII (955-964), who was being bullied by an Italian enemy of the German king, Berengar of Friuli. Pope John thanked Otto for his help by crowning him emperor on February 2, 962. Otto, in return for the Pope's "blessing" and recognition, agreed to accept the existence of the Papal States and proclaimed himself their special protector. The Church was now, more than ever before, under secular control. Its bishops and abbots were Otto's appointees and "placemen," and the Pope reigned only in Rome by the power of the emperor's sword. It did not take John long, however, to realize the royal web of entanglement in which he had placed himself and the Holy See. He joined with Italian opposition to Otto, but the emperor retaliated quickly and decisively to John's "betrayal." An ecclesiastical synod over which Otto presided deposed John and proclaimed that, henceforth, no Pope could take office without first swearing an oath of allegiance to the emperor. Under Otto, popes ruled at the emperor's pleasure or whim.

As reflected in these events, Otto shifted the royal focus from Germany to Italy. His successors, Otto II (r. 973-983) and Otto III (r.983-1002), became so immersed in Italian affairs that their German support base ultimately disintegrated, the result of overly ambitious imperial dreams. Otto the Great's heirs should have looked west for lessons from their Capetian contemporaries, the successor dynasty to the French Carolingians. The Ottonians, by contrast, over-extended themselves when they tried to subdue Italy. As the briefly revived empire began to crumble in the first quarter of the eleventh century, the Church, long unhappy with Carolingian and Ottonian domination, prepared to declare its independence and exact its own vengeance.

THE HOHENSTAUFEN EMPIRE (1152-1272)

During the twelfth and thirteenth centuries, England and France developed centralized,

A likeness of Frederick I from about 1165. Frederick Barbarossa called his realm the Holy Roman Empire, implying a close relationship with the church.

stable governments. In England the Magna Carta balanced the rights of nobility against monarchial authority, and in France the reign of Philip II Augustus secured the king's authority over the competitive claims of the nobility. During the reign of Louis IX, France gained international acclaim as the bastion of enlightened, righteous politics and as the center of medieval culture. The history of the Holy Roman Empire, which encompassed northern Italy, Germany, and Burgundy by the mid-thirteenth century, was quite different. Primarily because of the efforts of Hohenstaufens to extend imperial power into southern Italy, disunity and blood feuding became the order of the day for two centuries. It left Germany fragmented until modern times.

FREDERICK I BARBAROSSA

The investiture controversy had earlier weakened imperial authority. After the Concordat of Worms, the German princes held the dominant lay influence over episcopal appointments and within the rich ecclesiastical territories. Imperial power revived, however, with the accession to the throne of Frederick I Barbarossa (r.1152-1190) (Redbeard to the Italians) of the new Hohenstaufen dynasty, the most powerful line of emperors to succeed the Ottonians. The Hohenstaufens not only reasserted imperial authority but initiated a new phase in the contest between popes and emperors that proved even deadlier than the investiture struggle had been. Never had kings and popes despised and persecuted one another more than during the Hohenstaufen dynasty.

Frederick was originally a powerful lord from the Swabian house of Hohenstaufen when he was chosen king. In need of adequate resources to reestablish his control over the German princes, Frederick decided that the best way to generate such income was to pursue an aggressive Italian policy, which he believed would reward him with the needed income to subdue his German rivals. Frederick's plan was to create a new kind of empire. Previous German kings had focused on building a strong German kingdom, to which Italy might be added as an appendage. To Frederick, Germany was simply a feudal monarchy; his chief revenues would come from the much richer Italian states, which would become the center of a "holy empire," as he called it (hence the term Holy Roman Empire). Consequently, Frederick permitted his cousin, Henry the Lion of Saxony and Bavaria, to rule as "surrogate" emperor in Germany but knowing that Henry held the duchies as fiefs of the king, and that the other German princes recognized Frederick as their overlord. Such an arrangement allowed Frederick to concentrate on Italy. He marched an army into northern Italy where he was immediately victorious. His victory, however, proved short-lived. The papacy naturally was opposed to imperial expansion, for it rightfully feared that the emperor intended to include Rome and the Papal States as part of his empire. Luckily for the papacy, Frederick's threat to papal autonomy was resisted by Pope Alexander III, one of the Vatican's most competent and determined twelfth-century popes. While a cardinal (Roland), Alexander had negotiated an alliance between the papacy and the Norman kingdom of Sicily in a clever effort to strengthen the papacy against imperial influence. Perceiving Cardinal Roland to be a very shrewd foe, Frederick had opposed his election as Pope and even backed a schismatic Pope against him in a futile effort to undo Alexander's election. Frederick now found himself at war with the papacy, Milan, and Sicily. In 1167 these allies drove him back into Germany. The final blow to Frederick's imperial ambitions in Italy came a decade later, in 1176, when an alliance of northern Italian cities, known as the Lombard League, soundly defeated the emperor's forces at the Battle of Legnano. In the final Peace of Constance in 1183, Frederick had little choice but to grant the Lombard cities of northern Italy the full rights of self-rule.

The Normans had a huge impact on English architecture, such as the Durham Cathedral.

Frederick now turned his attention back to Germany where he spent time breaking the power of his cousin Henry the Lion, who violated the emperor's trust by usurping Frederick's authority. Frederick's reign ended with a stalemate in Germany and defeat in Italy. At his death in 1190 he was not, as a ruler, equal in stature to the kings of England and France. After the Peace of Constance in 1183, he seemed himself to have conceded as much, accepting the reality of the empire's indefinite division among the feudal princes of Germany. In the last years of his reign, however, he had an opportunity both to solve his problem with Sicily, still a papal ally, and to form a new territorial base of power for future emperors. The Norman ruler of the kingdom of Sicily, William II (r. 166-1189), sought an alliance with Frederick that would free him to pursue a scheme to conquer Constantinople. In 1186 a most fateful marriage between Frederick's son, the future Henry VI (r. 1190-97), and Constance, heiress to the kingdom of Sicily, sealed the alliance. The alliance proved, however, to be only another well-laid plan that went astray. The Sicilian connection became a fatal attraction for future Hohenstaufen kings. It led them in the end to sacrifice their traditional territorial base in northern Europe to the temptations of imperialism. Equally ominous this union left Rome encircled, thus ensuring papal hostility for decades to come. The marriage alliance with Sicily proved to be the first step in what escalated into a fight to the death between Pope and emperor, resulting ultimately in the complete demise of the Hohenstaufen dynasty.

The period from 1000 to 1300 was a very dynamic one in European history. It witnessed economic, social, and political changes that some historians believe set European civilization on a path that lasted until the eighteenth century when the Industrial Revolution created a new pattern. The revival of trade, the expansion of towns and cities, and the development of a money economy did not mean the end of a predominantly rural European society, but such changes did lay the foundation to new ways to make a living and new opportunities for people to expand and enrich their lives. Eventually they created the basis for the development of a predominantly urban industrial society.

The nobles, whose warlike attitudes were rationalized by labeling them the defenders of Christian society, continued to dominate the medieval world politically, economically, and socially. But quietly within this world of castles and private power, kings gradually began to extend their powers publicly. Although popes sometimes treated lay rulers as if they were their servants, by the thirteenth century, monarchs were developing the machinery of secular government that would enable them to challenge these exalted claims of papal power and become the centers of European political authority. Although they could not know it then, the actions of these medieval monarchs laid the foundation for the European kingdoms that in one form or another have dominated the European political scene ever since.

Suggestions for Further Reading

Marc Bloch, *Feudal Society*, 2 vols. (1961).

Jean Chapelot and Robert Fossier, *The Village and the House in the Middle Ages* (1985).

Karl Leyser, *Rule and Conflict in an Early Medieval Society: Ottonian Saxony* (1979).

H.R. Loyn, *TheGovernance of Anglo-Saxon England* (1984)

J.P. Poly and Bournazel, *The Feudal Transformation, 900-1200* (1991).

Susan Reynolds, *Fiefs and Vassals: The Medieval Evidence Reinterpreted* (1994).

Alfred P. Smyth, *Alfred the Great* (1995).

Chris Wickham, *Early Medieval Italy: Central Power and Local Society, 400-1000* (1981).

David Abulafia, *Frerderick II: a Medieval Emperor* (1988).

Benjamin Arnold, *Princes and Territories in Medieval Germany* (1991).

John Baldwin, *The Government of Philip Augustus* (1986).

Jean Dunbabin, *France in the Making, 843-1180* (2000).

Horst Fuhrmann, *Germany in the High Middle Ages, 1050-1200* (1986).

Chapter 8

THE CHURCH IN THE HIGH MIDDLE AGES, c. 900 to 1216

In 1205 Hubert Walter, the Archbishop of Canterbury, died. His death meant that the most important office of the Roman Catholic Church in the kingdom of England was vacant. Such a Church post was important because it controlled access to a great deal of wealth in the form of Church property in England, as well as revenues of tithes Christians were obliged to give the Church and other fees and gifts that flowed into the Church. Also, with this wealth and property a person serving as Archbishop of Canterbury could be very influential in the political life of England since the kingdom's feudal system of government depended on distributing property as fiefs in exchange for loyalty and service. At the same time, the Archbishop position was important in directing the spiritual affairs of the entire kingdom. Lesser Church posts, implementation of Church policy, issues of morality, and other key religious matters in England were controlled or heavily influenced by the Archbishop of Canterbury.

For all of these reasons, controlling the appointment of the next Archbishop was vitally important to two men in particular in 1205. One was John, King of England. Endlessly restless, given to fits of rage, John was a man that wanted things to go his way. One of the pursuits John cared about was hunting. He had a dozen hunting lodges and traveled with several hundred hunting dogs and their attendants. John was particularly fond of falconry, using trained birds of prey to hunt smaller animals. If one of his falcons failed to return as trained, anyone who found the stray falcon had better return it. John's punishment for anyone attempting to steal a stray falcon points out his capability for cruelty in dealing with someone who dared oppose him: the bird was allowed to eat six ounces of flesh from the guilty man's chest. This imperious nature carried over into his rule of England. John got into a war with the king of France and was notorious for trying, against customary limits of royal power, to rule his kingdom with little or no input from or interference by the barons (the greater English nobles) or anybody else for that matter. Eventually, in 1215, his high-handed approach sparked a revolt of the barons at Runnymeade. Control of the post of Archbishop of Canterbury was something John could use to his advantage in ruling more completely and effectively.

The other man who was interested in the succession at Canterbury was Pope Innocent III, the head of the Roman Catholic Church. Innocent III had his own ideas about who should hold ultimate power in Christian lands such as England. According to him, as the vicar or representative of Christ on earth, the Pope held the highest authority, especially in matters that directly concerned the Church, as did an important Church office like the Archbishopric of Canterbury. Building on earlier developments, Innocent had moved the papacy (the office of the Pope) to its highest level of power and influence.

It is not surprising that these two men came into conflict over the appointment of the next Archbishop of Canterbury. King John very much wanted John de Grey in the post. Grey, although holding a Church post as the bishop of Norwich, was basically a politically involved court favorite who could be counted on to follow King John's lead. John quickly interfered with the Church officials responsible for selecting the next archbishop, getting them to delay election until he had time to secure Grey's nomination. Some of the electors met in secret, however, and chose another man and sent him along to Rome to be confirmed by the Pope. When John learned of this, he rushed to Canterbury and in his enraged state intimidated the Church officials into rejecting the first election and naming John de Grey instead. Grey set off for Rome as well, and Innocent was faced with two men both claiming to be the rightful successor as archbishop. Innocent eventually dealt with the problem by rejecting both claimants and naming his own replacement, the very capable English scholar and church leader Stephen Langton.

What followed was a long, heated struggle between John and Innocent over control of the post. John rejected Langton as unacceptable. The Pope confirmed Langton anyway in 1207. In 1208 Innocent placed England under an interdict, which stopped the performance of key Church duties, and he released all of the king's subjects from their oaths of allegiance to the king. John responded by seizing all the Church property in the kingdom, helping himself to revenues as long as he held the property. In 1209 Innocent excommunicated John, which according to Church teaching condemned John to damnation. Eventually, Innocent convinced King Philip Augustus of France to put together an army in preparation for invading England. By this time, 1213, John's position with his barons was such that he needed to avoid trouble with France and to resolve the dispute with the pope, so he caved in to the pope's wishes. John accepted Langton as Archbishop, gave back all of the seized Church property, promised to repay the money he had appropriated, and gave England to the Pope, receiving his kingdom back as a feudal fief from Innocent and becoming the Pope's vassal in the process.

Chronology

910	Monastery at Cluny founded
1049	Pope Leo IX convenes Easter Synod
1059	Lateran Synod reforms papal selection
1073	Hildebrand becomes Pope Gregory VII
1075	Lay Investiture conflict begins
1095	Pope Urban II calls the First Crusade
1098	St. Robert founds monastery at Citeaux
1122	Concordat of Worms ends Lay Investiture conflict
1173	Peter Waldo begins his ministry
1198	Lothario becomes Pope Innocent III
1201	Fourth Crusade begins
1209	*Regula primitiva* approved for the Franciscan order
1209	Crusade against the Cathari in France begins
1215	Fourth Lateran Council meets in Rome
1216	St. Dominic founds Dominican order
1291	Acre, the last Crusader state on the continent, falls to the Muslims

By the tenth century Christianity was omnipresent in Europe, affecting most every facet of one's life, whether a peasant or a king. The association of the Church with practically every aspect of European society was a distinguishing feature of the Middle Ages, but it was particularly evident during the High Middle Ages. The Church resembled a modern nation-state given that it charged mandatory taxes/tithes, devised and enforced ecclesiastical laws, and was organized under a strict hierarchical structure. However, in the tenth, eleventh and twelfth centuries, the Church struggled to find its place in society. The papacy became more authoritarian, as popes and kings engaged in a power struggle. In addition to the elevated status of the pope, the Church increased its efforts to spread Christianity, and, by doing so, further extended the Church's hegemony. After facing some serious internal difficulties, the Church subsequently reached the height of its wealth, influence, and authority in Europe during the High Middle Ages.

THE ROMAN CATHOLIC CHURCH IN AN UNCERTAIN WORLD

Throughout the ninth and tenth centuries, the formerly grand Carolingian Dynasty deteriorated, and by the late 900's the Carolingians no longer held any significant authority in Europe. As a result, the vast kingdom that was once governed by Charlemagne fragmented into adversarial factions. Feudalism, with its decentralized government, emerged out of the breakdown of the centralized Carolingian government, and strong, commanding men took control over local regions. The aristocracy set up elaborate status-based systems of alliances and loyalty to offer both warfare and protection. The vast structure of feudalism eventually encompassed all aspects of society including the political, military, social and legal realms. Partially due to the lack of central leadership, Europeans endured a period of uncertainty and hardship.

Although the early Germanic invasions had ended, new aggressors arrived starting as early as the eighth century. This time they came from different regions such as Asia, Scandinavia, and North Africa. Respectively, the Magyars, Vikings, and Muslim groups (Saracens/Arabs) stormed the defunct Carolingian empire and left behind a trail of destruction and fear. With this new wave of attacks, it became even more important for locals seek out powerful men for protection; thus, the bonds of feudalism were reinforced.

In spite of the recurrent brutal strikes and widespread insecurity in Western Europe, the Roman Catholic or Latin Church remained a prominent institution with a highly structured bureaucracy. In fact, the church provided the foremost unifying authority in Europe at the time. The Church stepped in to fill the vacuum left by the fragmented governments, and clergymen regularly provided charitable assistance. Also, many secular rulers, even princes and kings, were illiterate while most clerics were taught to read and write in order to study the Bible and compose sermons. This gave the clergy a distinct advantage, and eventually many of the vital tasks of the worldly governments were conducted by learned ecclesiastics.

Land was the most valuable currency and commodity, and the Roman Catholic Church was extraordinarily land-wealthy. The Church owned vast amounts of land, much of it donated by nobles. Many of the gifts of land were given as a reward, as a tithe, or as payment for spiritual services rendered. In the case of donations, the land came with specific feudal obligations. Feudalism was all-encompassing, and through its land holdings, the Church played an active role in the medieval feudal system.

Moreover, since the Church had no military, it was dependent upon the powerful nobility to raise armies to defend the Church's interests. At the same time, in the feudal structure nobles were compelled to demonstrate loyalty and to protect the Church because of the spiritual aid they received. It was a mutually beneficial relationship, but there was frequent dissention. Both sides came to resent the forced allegiance, and in time this resentment led to a disagreement between the secular and religious realms about primacy, particularly between kings and popes.

During the Middle Ages, two impressive domains developed, one in the spiritual realm and the other in the temporal or material realm. The Roman Catholic papacy and the Holy Roman (German) Empire would experience increasing discord from the late eleventh through the thirteenth centuries. At the heart of the conflict was the papal assertion that its spiritual responsibilities took precedence over the concerns of secular rulers. In other words, the pope took the authority to exert his dominion over princes, kings, and emperors. However, not all princes, kings and emperors were going to simply buckle in the face of this proclamation.

Complicating matters was the fact that when German kings wished to expand their jurisdictions, they frequently set their sights on the Italian peninsula. With the headquarters of the pope in Rome, gaining influence over the pope would help German leaders expand into the physical territory they desired in Italy. Just as importantly, controlling the papacy would help further the notion of the Holy Roman Emperor as a religious rival of the pope. These two major powers of the Middle Ages, the Church and the German states, were powerful structures that competed for supremacy. As the Church fell more under the control of German kings, and the competition heated up, one or the other would eventually emerge as the victor.

In the class conscious European Middle Ages, there were three acknowledged social classes: nobility, commoners, and clergy. One was born into either the nobility or the common class, but members of the clergy consciously decided to embrace the clerical life. Within the clergy there was a further distinction between regular clergy and secular clergy. Regular clergy refers to clerics who followed a "rule," generally by taking vows including poverty, chastity, and obedience. Regular clergy lived together in places like monasteries and had limited contact with secular society. On the other hand, secular clergy did not belong to a religious order or take aesthetic vows. Secular clergy were still obligated to vows of celibacy and obedience, but they lived in the world amongst non-clergy or the laity.

The papacy was heavily influenced by lay leaders, and those laymen played a part in choosing popes. The mutual dependence would begin to exasperate both sides involved in this conflict. Eventually secular leaders asserted the divine right of kings, which claims that since a monarch receives his authority from God, no man on earth, including the pope, had the right to interfere with their sovereignty. Conflicts between the secular and religious leaders marked the High Middle Ages.

With virtually everyone in Western Europe participating in some way in the Church (except for Jews, who made up a negligible percentage of the population and were exempt), even the most fearless nobles and rulers obeyed the commands of the papacy. Throughout much of the Middle Ages the papacy boasted such influence over both spiritual and temporal realms that its authority far exceeded that of even the most prodigious Roman Emperors. Why? The pope held immense clout largely based on the anxiety triggered by two sacred weapons in his arsenal. By using excommunication the pope could damn the uncooperative individual to eternal torment. This was no empty threat to medieval Christians who believed strongly in the existence of a literal hell. The pope could also chasten miscreants with the dreaded interdict, which could be used to punish a whole country for the transgressions of an obstinate leader. Interdict, a spiritual penalty, forbade church services and prevented any dispensation of most sacraments such as marriage and confession throughout the country of a disobedient ruler, while allowing only the last rites or death rites to be administered. This was quite effective because a population that feared for its salvation was liable to rise up against a rebellious leader and force him to submit to the Church.

Many clergymen came under moral scrutiny and failed to meet Christian standards set up by the Church. Although ordained clergy took a vow of celibacy and were forbidden to marry, many either wed or had children out of wedlock with mistresses. Even when eleventh century reformer Pope Gregory VII turned his attention to stopping clerical licentiousness, it remained commonplace. This flagrant disregard for the mandatory sexual self-control was given a name by church reformers: *Nicolaism*. This term was also used to describe certain religious divisions that acted as if Church teachings did not apply to their group. The word *Nicolaism* references a passage from the Bible that describes a heretical sect.

The High Middle Ages was filled with conflicts between Church leaders and secular rulers. The role of laymen, non-ordained participants in the Church, in official Church appointments became a serious concern. Men who garnered high-ranking positions in the Church were well aware that certain Church offices could provide

Pope Gregory VII greatly strengthened the Western church. He was among the most powerful and influential popes in the history of the Roman Church.

wealth and authority. As previously mentioned, the Church relied on the nobility to protect its assets from would-be usurpers. Therefore, lay rulers, who were members of the nobility, came to play a significant role in the appointment of hopefuls for coveted Church positions. Lay leaders came to realize that these offices could be bought and sold for a profit. Thus, the history of lay investiture is plagued by corruption.

The papacy claimed exclusive divine jurisdiction, so when lay rulers began exercising the feudal principal of investiture, the Church feared losing control of this domain. The method of investiture entailed conferring (investing) the power and responsibility of a position to the officeholder, generally by giving the individual certain items that represented the office. Originally lay rulers only appointed Church officials, but then they began investing them with spiritual authority by providing physical symbols such as a ring or a staff. This spiritual investiture had traditionally been carried out by higher-ranking Church officials, so when lay rulers began this practice, it created intense debate within the Church.

Lay investiture became unequivocally associated with simony, or the buying and selling of Church offices. The word *simony* is derived from a story in the New Testament Book of Acts. In this account Simon Magus, also called Simon the Magician, tried to buy spiritual gifts and power from St. Peter and was rebuffed. From Acts 8: 18-20:

> 18And when Simon saw that through laying on of the apostles' hands the Holy Ghost was given, he offered them (the apostles) money, 19Saying, Give me also this power, that on whomsoever I lay hands, he may receive the Holy Ghost. 20But Peter said unto him, Thy money perish with thee, because thou hast thought that the gift of God may be purchased with money. (King James Version).

Simony arose when laymen in charge of appointments realized that with many men competing for a small number of lucrative Church jobs, a potential fortune could be made. Consequently, many lay rulers began selling the offices for profit.

As more Church officials acquired their positions from secular rulers, the quality of Church leaders inevitably deteriorated. Many officeholders were attracted to the wealth and prosperity that resulted from the position but were not concerned with upholding the standards of the office. To make matters worse, most of these means-seeking envoys of the Church had no formal training in the tenets and basic beliefs of the institution they claimed to represent.

In the year 918 the first non-Frankish king ascended the throne of the German Empire. Henry I was a Saxon, and he took decisive action in combining many of the smaller duchies of the empire. Henry I was succeeded by his son, Otto I, also known as Otto the Great (936-973). The creation of the German monarchy was largely due to Otto's efforts. Under his leadership the emperor became not only a temporal leader but also a spiritual authority in his land. In 951 and 955 Otto defeated the Italians and Hungarians, which further brought the German duchies under his control.

While Henry I had feared and avoided dealing with high ranking clergy, Otto knew that Church patronage was vital, so he utilized the clergy in his government. His goal was to dominate the Church, then to use its extensive resources to establish the basis of royal power in Germany. He offered German clergy protection from the nobility and took many German clergy as vassals, giving them vast benefices that were then bequeathed to the Church. It was a smart move because since clergymen had taken a vow of celibacy, there was no future possibility of competition for primacy between clergymen's progeny and Otto's descendants.

When Otto defeated the Hungarians, legend says he was carrying Charlemagne's sacred lance. Symbolically, this confirmed Otto as a worthwhile inheritor of Charlemagne's empire. Otto saw an opportunity to ascend to the throne when Pope John XII (r. 955-964) asked for his help in defeating an adversary. Otto provided assistance, and, in return, he was crowned Otto I, Holy Roman Emperor in 962 by the pope. It was a mutually beneficial deal because Otto gave legitimacy and recognition to the Papal States and proclaimed the empire as the special protector of the territory under the *Diploma Ottonianum*. The intimate relationship between the empire and the Church resulted in the Church's loss of power through an increase in royal control over the Church. At the same time, the papacy continued to rely on the protection of the emperor.

After a time Pope John realized that this situation could be detrimental to the Church's sovereignty, so he retreated from the alliance. Pope John then formed a league with the Byzantine Empire, Italians, and Magyars to oppose Otto's administration. The amalgamation of government and church is clearly illustrated in Otto's response to the pope's betrayal. Otto convened a clerical assembly and made a drastic proclamation. In order to assert the supremacy of the emperor over religious leaders, Otto proclaimed that all future popes must swear an allegiance to the emperor before taking office. He proceeded to depose Pope John XII and elected Pope Leo VIII (r. 963–965). Under Otto, the office of the Holy See was subordinate to the office of the Holy Roman Emperor.

By the late ninth and early tenth centuries the Church had lost much of its authority, with the clergy beholden to emperors and kings and the pope being treated as a toy by the Italian nobility. The wealth and military might of the German monarchy were increasing as Holy Roman Emperors progressively took control of the Roman Catholic Church. The Church found itself at a crossroads, and reform was in the air. However, the seeds of change came from an unexpected section of the Church—monasteries.

THE REFORM MOVEMENT

Monastic Reform

The reform movement that spread throughout the Roman Catholic Church can be traced to a transformation effort in western monasticism. Several innovations were underway by the tenth century, particularly at a monastery located at Cluny, Burgundy in France. William the Pious, duke of Aquitaine, founded the Abbey of Cluny in 910 as an austere Benedictine order. The monks held to strict spiritual discipline and maintenance of a high moral standard for clergy. They passionately rejected the subjugation of clerics to earthly monarchs and leaders. In an effort to keep secular leaders from exerting authority over the monks, the cloister was placed under the direct authority of the pope. In this period, with the papacy located in Rome, the Abbey of Cluny was essentially self-governing. The Cluny monks also set out to found "daughter monasteries" or "priories," which formed a network of dependent Cluniac houses dispersed across Europe.

The Cluniac monks were recognized for their piety and devotion to the aesthetic life. They were able to achieve these high standards to a certain extent because of their independence from secular control. Cluniac controlled priories were required to obey specific and stringent guidelines. For one thing, the priories had to live under the strict Benedictine code. All monks were required to take vows of poverty, chastity, and obedience. Also the practice of simony, which had been a problem in other parts of the Church, was forbidden in the election of these monks and abbots. As the Cluniacs' practices and ethics became well-known, they gained respect for their high principles. The laity realized that these monks were actually following the high ideals of the order, and Cluniacs were widely admired and considered an example of how clergy should conduct themselves.

In Germany and England similar movements were launched beginning in the tenth century. But in stark contrast to Cluny, German and British monastic reform was directed by the monarchy. These movements also differed because even though monarchs had the duty to protect these monasteries from secular interference, they also appointed monks and abbots. However, the piety of most of the German and British monasteries did not suffer from monarchial administration, as these kings generally took their obligation very seriously.

Word of the Cluniac accomplishments spread, and soon a call for reform increased among clergy. The effort accelerated when the highest office of the Roman Catholic Church got involved.

The Papal Reform Effort

In the early eleventh century the papacy added its influence to the clerical reform program. German King Henry III (r. 1039-1056) was faced with three men from the nobility who each claimed to be the "true" pope. Henry summarily deposed all three, and appointed Pope Clement II (r. 1046-1047). Clement was a German bishop, and he was the first pope to be placed in office by a German emperor. He took office on Christmas Day 1046, and soon afterwards he officially crowned Henry III as Holy Roman Emperor and conferred the title Defender of the Roman Church. The Defender of the Church was allowed to cast the first vote in a papal election. This prestigious position was not imperative to the outcome of the elections although with a German holding this rank, it decisively reduced Roman nobles' ability to sway papal elections.

Monks lived in poverty and spent their time preaching, performing manual labor, and serving the poor.

When Pope Clement died in 1047, rumors circulated that he had been poisoned, and in the uncertain climate of the Church at the time, it is quite possible. Even though his reign was short, he significantly influenced the coming wave of papal reform by making pronouncements against simony in particular and against other forms of clerical misbehavior in general.

Pope Leo IX (r. 1049-1054) became highly involved in the reform movement, and like Clement II, he stood against simony and promoted celibacy for members of the secular clergy. Leo IX, who was also German, is remembered for his strict enforcement of reform decrees. Until this time the issue of celibacy among the secular clergy had not been a primary concern of reformers. Leo took this issue to heart, and in his travels through Europe to enforce clerical reforms, he found many members of the secular clergy who were married with families. He proceeded to expel many men who violated this regulation. In the spirit of reform, he also placed many Cluniac monks in high ranking positions. During his Pontificate, the hierarchical or tiered structure of the Roman Catholic Church began to evolve into its modern form.

One arduous challenge the Roman Catholic Church faced was a lack of control over the Eastern Orthodox (Greek Orthodox) Church. There were once five patriarchs or bishops who each ruled over an episcopal see, the area over which a bishop exercises authority. This pentarchy included five seats of the patriarchs, which were located in Rome, Constantinople, Alexandria, Antioch, and Jerusalem. The Roman patriarch was considered first among equals, or first in prestige but not in authority. While the Roman patriarch, also called the bishop of

Rome (eventually titled the pope), attempted to gain control of all of Christendom, by the ninth century the Eastern Church in Byzantium had effectively begun to manage the Eastern branch of the Church. The bishop of Rome was the only patriarch in what was once the Western Roman Empire. The bishop of Constantinople and the Byzantine Emperor were located in the physical eastern territory, and Rome was far away. The two branches of Christianity moved further and further apart. When Muslims took Jerusalem, Antioch, and Alexandria, the remaining Christian bishops of Rome and Constantinople each claimed great authority. By the eleventh century the conflict would reach a fever pitch with East-West Schism in 1054.

The roots of the schism or split can be found in disagreements over primacy and the limits of each bishop's jurisdiction. The title of pope had been used since the 200's when Bishop of Alexandria, also called Pope Heracleus, was given this title. In the West, the designation pope could be given to any bishop in the Church. But at that time the title did not carry authority over the entire Christian church or over the other four patriarchs. Eventually the title pope, which means papa or father, was given exclusively by the Roman Catholic Church to the Bishop of Rome, and the powerful office of the papacy truly began to emerge as a force to be reckoned with.

The Roman Catholic Church's assertion of papal control over all Christian churches was challenged by the Eastern Orthodox Church. In the East, the Christian church fell under the governance of the Byzantine Emperor, centered in Constantinople, not under the papacy in Rome. Nevertheless, popes claimed authority over all Christian churches, but the patriarch in Constantinople and the Byzantine Emperor were the *de facto* heads of the Eastern Orthodox Church. In 1054 the estrangement of the Eastern and Western branches of Christianity reached an apex. Cardinal Humbert, a former papal secretary, a cardinal, and a papal legate (official messenger of the pope) under Pope Leo IX. When papal authority was openly challenged by Patriarch Michael Cerularius of the Eastern Church, Humbert was sent to meet with Cerularius, who refused to allow Humbert into his chambers. Much of the dispute had to do with differences in religious rituals, with roots in the Iconoclast Controversy of the eighth century. Humbert and Patriarch Cerularius excommunicated each other in the summer of 1054, and the East-West Schism began. Cerularius closed all Latin affiliated churches in his domain, and the Roman Catholic Church and the Byzantine Empire moved in divergent political directions.

When Leo died in 1054, he was succeeded by men who continued the reform policies. Pope Victor II (1055-1057) and Pope Stephen IX (1057-1059) began to assert themselves more openly against the secular rulers. It is evident that during this period, leaders of the spiritual and temporal realms were at the threshold of a period of conflict. When Pope Stephen died, members of the Roman nobility placed one of their own as pope, Benedict X (1058-1059), who is widely considered an antipope. There were allegations that the election was fixed, so Benedict was forced from his position. Those who supported the reform movement propelled Nicholas II (r.1059-1061) into the Holy See, and Nicholas proceeded to excommunicate Benedict. Also, starting with Nicholas the papacy found a strong alliance with the Normans against emperors, both German and Byzantine.

This upheaval surrounding Benedict and Nicholas brought to light a problem having to do with the election of popes. Specifically, Nicholas believed that secular leaders should have limited influence in the affairs of the Church. Therefore, one of Nicholas' first acts was to address the problem of papal election. In a 1059 Easter synod, Nicholas issued a papal bull, *In nomine Domini*, which assigned the College of Cardinals the sole right to elect a pope. Cardinals, also referred to as cardinal-bishops, are senior prelates in the Roman Catholic Church. While they had been involved in choosing papal successors before, throughout much of Church history there was a requirement of secular approval. This gave nobles and kings a great deal of influence in choosing the pope.

In nomine Domini, sometimes referred to as the Electoral Decree, was significant because it spelled out the exclusivity of the choice made by the cardinals and defined cardinals' power and duty in choosing future popes. But this decree also implied something deeper that emperors and secular leaders would have understood as a threat to their authority in the Church. Nicholas' decree harkened to the Cluniac ideas of free elections as vital to the success of the reform movement. According to historian R.W. Southern, "No doubt the general purpose of this decree was to purify the papacy by cutting it off from the world—especially from the emperor and the local nobility." In reality, this decree had limited success in removing secular rulers' influence over the election of popes; many high ranking nobles still found ways to circumvent the decree and to continue exercising pressure on the cardinals' papal selections.

Politically, Nicholas aligned himself with the Norman princes in Italy, providing a future ally for the papacy against rebellious German and even Byzantine emperors. *In nomine Domini* only provided emperors with a vaguely worded right of approbation; this essentially meant the ruling emperor could give his approval or condemnation of the cardinals' choice for pope, but he had no power of nomination.

Church leaders and secular rulers were entering a period of unprecedented struggle for control over the Roman Catholic Church. After Nicholas' death, Pope Alexander II (1061-1073) became the first pope to be elected solely by the College of Cardinals. Holy Roman Emperor Henry IV (1056-1106) resented the loss of what he believed to be his right to nominate candidates for the papacy, and the liberation of the papacy from the emperor heralded a decline of imperial power. Among the kings of Western Europe, Henry was not alone in this resentment, and the hostility was going to get worse.

The Lay Investiture Controversy

In 1073 Alexander's successor, Pope Gregory VII (r.1073-1085), proceeded to breathe new life into the reform movement. Before his election he was known as Hildebrand, a man who had been actively involved in the papal reform movement for many years. He had served several popes in numerous capacities including papal advisor, legate, and archdeacon. He had also played a vital role in the alliance of Nicholas with the Norman princes. In addition, Hildebrand had been an outspoken supporter of the Electoral Decree of 1059.

In 1075 Gregory issued a document that vigorously asserted the power of the pope within the church and spelled out his rights against emperors and all others who might encroach on papal jurisdiction. This powerful statement, the *Dictatus Papae*, (*Dictates of the Pope*), defined his authority and left little room for argument.

> . . . That the Pope is the only one whose feet are to be kissed by all princes . . . That he may depose emperors . . . That he himself may be judged by no one . . . That the Pope may absolve subjects of unjust men from their fealty.

The papal legates (official messengers of the pope) appointed by Gregory were encouraged to spread his ideas of papal supremacy to other European countries. Gregory did not want there to be any ambiguity; whether peasant or emperor, laymen were always subordinate to the rulings of the pope. According to historian Norman Cantor, "It was . . . the creation of a new world order for Christian society founded on the principle that papal authority alone was universal and plenary." Cantor continues, "It claimed a papal supremacy over monarchy that had never been practiced in European history."

The practice of simony had long been an issue in the Church, with Cluniacs asserting that the practice of lay investiture was the most abhorrent form of simony. Lay investiture involved the appointment of bishops, abbots, and other high ranking church officials by laymen, usually wealthy nobles or kings/emperors. To address this issue, in 1075 Gregory issued a decree that forbade lay investiture in any form. This caused an outcry from powerful secular men who had either meted out these offices to their friends or had sold them for profit. Removal of this privilege would weaken the influence of laymen. For the Church, this was positive because as long as laymen could control appointments of Church leaders, both the authority and the quality of the Church was compromised. Gregory removed this ability with one decree. But the outcry was louder and reached further than Gregory could have imagined.

German emperor Henry IV (r. 1056-1106) would not give up this entitlement without a fight. The assertion by the pope of spiritual authority over worldly leaders combined with the removal of lay investiture threatened to weaken the German emperors to the point of insignificance. Henry knew that if he acquiesced, future monarchs would automatically come under the control of the papacy. Henry defiantly disregarded the new prohibition against lay investiture by appointing a bishop in Milan. Pope Gregory was furious at the challenge and threatened Henry with excommunication. Henry remained undaunted, gathered together the German bishops at Worms, and attempted to depose Gregory. In January 1076, they composed a letter in reply to the lay investiture decree. This letter was harsh and referred to Hildebrand (instead of his papal name) as "not pope but false monk." Henry invoked the ancient idea of the divine right of kings, implying that he, Henry, as emperor had been placed in this position by God.

> And this although our Lord Jesus Christ did call us to the kingdom, did not, however, call thee to the priesthood. For thou has ascended by the following steps. By wiles, namely, which the profession of monk abhors, thou has achieved money; by money, favour; by the sword, the throne of peace.

The letter ended with the words,

> I Henry, king by the grace of God, do say unto thee, together with all our bishops: Descend, descend, to be damned throughout the ages.

In retaliation, Gregory excommunicated Henry and pronounced him unfit to be king. He declared that all German subjects were no longer under any obligation to remain loyal to Henry. The pope also removed all bishops appointed by Henry in February 1076. Unfortunately for Henry, his attempt at asserting his imperial authority proved to be a political disaster.

Henry had inherited the German throne upon his father's death in 1056 when he was only six years old, so for nine years a regent ruled in his stead. When he came into his maturity in 1065, Henry's control over his realm was unstable at best. German nobles and princes had become displeased with the increasingly centralized government, and civil wars wracked the German states. When Pope Gregory deposed and excommunicated Henry, Henry's enemies acted swiftly.

By the fall of 1076 most German bishops had renounced their connection with Henry and prepared to support the nobility in appointing a new monarch. German nobles, led by the Saxons, cheerfully embraced this change in their favor. The pope was scheduled to attend a diet in Augsburg to formally complete the removal of Henry from the throne. Most of Henry's military was afraid to stand with him in defiance of the papal decree, but the bold king refused to repent.

Henry's loyal ecclesiastics convinced him that in order to retain his throne, he must make peace with the pope. But the pope was on his way to Augsburg to complete the formalities in the removal of Henry as emperor. On the journey, Gregory was taken in by Countess Matilda of Tuscany, who had a castle in the small Northern Italian city of Canossa. Some versions of the story say that Gregory had left Rome and headed north toward the Augsburg meeting after learning of Henry's plan to come to Rome to ask for forgiveness. There was speculation that Gregory wanted to complete the process of deposition of Henry before the emperor could ask for absolution. Regardless, Henry caught up with Gregory at Canossa in January 1077. It is likely, given the situation, that Gregory feared a trick. He may have wondered if Henry had rebuilt his military, posing a threat to the pope. However, if Gregory did purposely avoid Henry, he was denying a penitent Catholic (at least on the surface) a chance for forgiveness. Gregory was faced with a dilemma. According to Roman Catholic doctrine, no priest of God can deny a sinner absolution of his sins. Gregory probably remained unconvinced of Henry's sincerity, but to all observers it seemed genuine. The pope eventually backed down, but he did not make it easy for Henry.

At Canossa, Pope Gregory refused to allow the emperor entry into the castle. There are several sources that describe what happened next, but historians remain skeptical regarding how much of the following is factual and how much was fabricated for dramatic effect. According to contemporary documents, Henry waited at the castle gate for entry for three days. Some accounts add that he fasted, wore a hair shirt (an undergarment that was made of coarse animal hair to cause the penitent sinner discomfort), and even that he stood barefoot in the snow during this time.

After several people intervened on behalf of Henry, the pope allowed him entry to the castle. Henry gave every outward appearance of a penitent sinner, kneeling before the pope, kissing his ring, confessing his sins, and humbly asking for absolution and readmission to the Church. When the rebellious German nobles and princes heard of the events through a dispatch from the pope, they remained unwilling to end their insurgence. Even though Gregory did not attend the scheduled meeting at Augsburg, the nobles followed through with the election of a new king, Rudolf von Rheinfelden.

After the show of penitence at Canossa, Henry quickly regressed, going against all the promises he had made the pope. With Henry IV once again securely on the throne, he regained control of his territories, ultimately killing the challenger, Rudolf. He defied the pope's decree yet again and was summarily excommunicated for a second time. But Henry had rebuilt his army with the help of bishops who had decided to support the monarchy in the struggle. The German nobility and the papacy were finding out how difficult it was to make war against a stubborn emperor. Henry declared Gregory deposed (again) and appointed his own, supportive antipope. The antipope, Clement III, crowned Henry IV as Holy Roman Emperor in 1084.

By 1085 Henry's armies forced Pope Gregory out of the papal residence and completely out of the city of Rome. The papacy had enjoyed a continued alliance with the Normans since the time of Nicholas II, so Gregory was saved from Henry's forces. The Normans kept him safe in southern Italy, but the shock and distress suffered by the elderly pope was too much; he died later the same year. But the struggle for supremacy between Church and state was far from over.

Over the next few years each new pope faced the challenge of imperial authority by encouraging rebellions and civil war. Henry IV was succeeded by his son, Henry V (r.1106-1125), who held several titles including Holy Roman Emperor, King of Germany, and King of Italy. Henry V was able to work out a compromise with Pope Calixtus II (r.1119-1124) in 1122 called the Concordant of Worms. The emperor gave up some lay investiture rights in order to settle the conflict. The concordant spelled out the roles of both the Church and secular leaders in appointing clergy. The Church retained the right to elect bishops and grant spiritual authority of the office by presenting a ring and staff. The king had the right to bestow feudal land and become the feudal lord of the bishop. In feudalism, a lord could refuse homage from a vassal; therefore, under feudal law the king was able to reject any candidate for a church office. Kings were no longer able to practice investiture, but they did retain a modicum of unofficial influence over the selection of church officials.

The agreement helped liberate the clergy from many secular constraints, and the gains of the Church heralded the weakening of the imperial authority. The German nobles and princes were able, from this point on, to exert more power in their own regions and to continue their move away from imperial hegemony. Meanwhile, the emperor wanted a return to a more centralized government after the decentralization that had characterized feudalism and the civil wars. The German states were slow to mend their fences, and the region would remain fragmented until the late nineteenth century.

THE CRUSADES

In November 1095 Pope Urban II was at the Council of Clermont, an ecumenical meeting of Roman Catholic prelates and powerful laymen. Earlier in the year Byzantine Emperor Alexius I (r.1081-1118) had asked for help from the West in defeating the Seljuk Turks, who were Asian converts to the Muslim religion of Islam. Palestine, the so-called Holy Land, was being invaded by members of this foreign religion, and Eastern Christians feared losing the territory completely. In the early eleventh century the Turks were moving toward Constantinople, and it was clear they would soon control the city if the advance was not halted.

Since the fourth century, or perhaps even earlier, Christians had regularly made pilgrimages to the Holy Land. They had to pass through the Byzantine Empire before they entered Muslim controlled regions, but even though the trips were dangerous, pilgrims continued making them. However, when the Seljuk Turks and their Muslim allies took control of Jerusalem, they imposed high taxes on the traveling pilgrims.

This discouraged the poor and also angered many Christians who believed Muslims should not be allowed to control the region where Jesus had lived.

In 1071 the Turks defeated Byzantine forces and began a conquest of all of Anatolia or Asia Minor. As they came almost within sight of Constantinople, it was obvious that the Byzantine Empire was in a precarious position. By 1095 when Emperor Alexius asked for reinforcements from Western Christians, it seemed the empire would be lost along with the Holy Land.

Pope Urban had strongly supported and was actively involved in the reform movement that had taken hold of the Church. He had been a monk and prior at Cluny and had served as papal legate under Pope Gregory VII. He believed that it was his duty to defend Christianity any time it was ostensibly under attack. Wanting to bolster the power of the papacy, Urban seized the opportunity to reunite the Christian Church, which had split in a schism in 1054, under his authority—with a resounding battle cry.

But Pope Urban was concerned about the concept of war and the role of Christians on the battlefield, and needed to justify why men of God should kill. The pope, according to historian Jonathan Phillips, "...fused the familiar ideas of pilgrimage, violence, and the need for penance to create a new and enduring concept—the crusade." He promised that if the warriors of France would answer the Byzantine emperor's call for help against the Seljuk Turks, they would receive an incredible reward. Phillips says, ". . . the sins accumulated through a life of violence would be wiped clean and the fires of hell would be avoided." This was an indulgence that allowed these rowdy fighting men to have all their sins forgiven. Only the pope could issue such a plenary indulgence. Apparently Pope Urban had reflected on the role of Christians killing in battle and decided this was a "just" war. This conflict would be so fair and so righteous that it merited a magnificent compensation.

Pope Urban gave a rousing speech at the Council of Clermont on November 26, 1095, and in the process he changed history. The impassioned discourse was masterful in its use of language, obviously meant to stir the emotions of the audience. He described the Muslim Turks as "...an accursed race, a race utterly alienated from God." The descriptions get more graphic and horrific as he describes what these invaders do to Christians. "When they wish to torture people by a base death, they perforate their navels, and dragging forth the extremity of the intestines, bind it to a stake . . . the victim falls prostrate upon the ground."

He continued on, asking the French knights to refrain from fighting amongst themselves and to go on a Church sanctioned mission to seize the Holy Land from Muslim control and return it to Christian governance. Several primary sources from the period say that at the end of the propaganda-laden speech the crowd began to chant "Deus vult," which translates to "God wills it!" and the First Crusade was launched.

The pope then preached the same message in other French and Italian cities, with clergy throughout Western Europe joining in the effort to round up warriors to retake the Holy Land. These forces sewed a cloth cross onto their clothing which symbolized their commitment to fight for the cause. Whether it was to aid Byzantine Christians, to gain wealth and prestige, or simply to earn a plenary indulgence for service, at least 60,000 people set out for the Holy Land.

The First Crusade (1095-1099) marked the beginning of a two-hundred year series of recurrent clashes between Christian and Muslim forces. Historians have tried to make sense of the series of conflicts, and in doing so they created

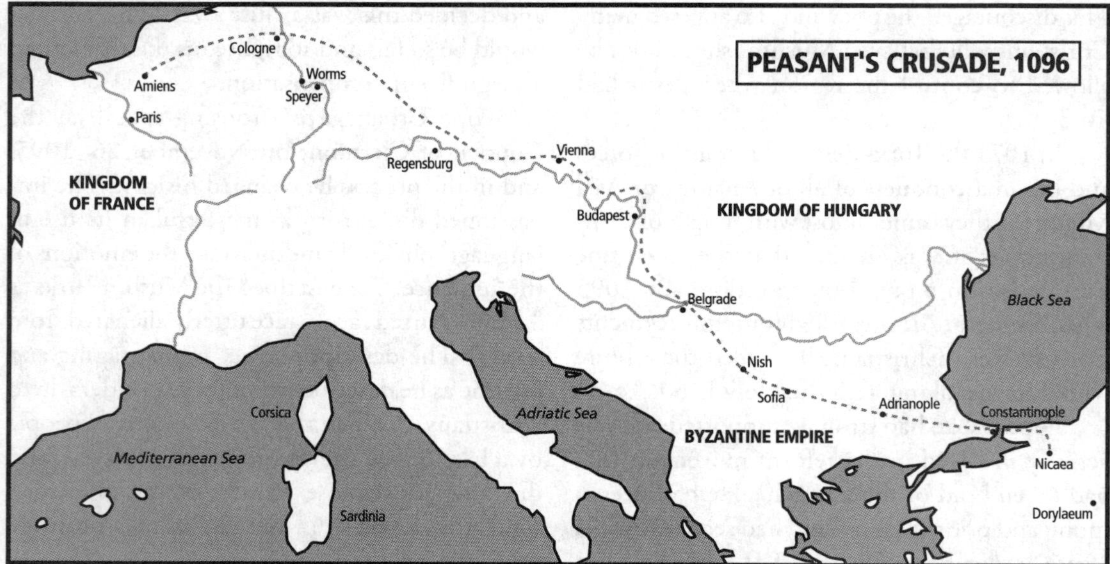

a numbering system for the major campaigns. The eight or nine (depending on the historian) traditionally numbered Crusades span the period from 1095 when Pope Urban made the Clermont speech through 1291 when the last crusader state in the East fell to Muslim forces.

The Peasants' Crusade

Before the noble warriors could get to Byzantium to answer Emperor Alexius' plea for help, a unique band of Crusaders arrived in Constantinople. The nobility had begun planning the armed pilgrimage in 1095 and early 1096, but they required time to organize their forces. In the meantime, a group of impatient commoners decided God was also summoning them to the Holy Land. In the spring of 1096 several large groups of untrained and unprepared people, including women and even some children, set off for Palestine by way of Byzantium.

One of the most colorful leaders was Peter the Hermit, an elderly man who some sources say lived alone in the woods before hearing the call to join the crusade. A chronicler named Ekkehard wrote of Peter: "His feet were bare. He lived on wine and fish and hardly ever, or never, ate bread." Legends apparently arose about Peter because according to Ekkehard, " What he said and did were regarded as little short of divine, so much that the very hairs were plucked from the tail of his mule as relics."

There is speculation that Peter was present at one of Pope Urban's speeches and became inspired to spread the message of crusading. Peter went from place to place beckoning the average person to join him on this journey to serve God. He was enigmatic, a passionate speaker, and his fervor and zeal appealed to many peasants. Perhaps they viewed the proposed journey as an escape from their mundane lives, or maybe they altruistically wanted to play a role in taking back the Holy Land. It is likely each sentiment was represented. Regardless, Peter, along with several other preachers, gathered a force of at least 20,000-30,000 to form what is called the Peasants' Crusade or the People's Crusade. It turned out to be an unmitigated disaster.

Peter the Hermit, Walter the Penniless, and other leaders of these loosely associated groups started for the Holy Land earlier than the official August 15, 1096, date given by Pope Urban. Most had begun to head east by April, and it is likely that the failure of their mission was due, at least in part, to the fact that they arrived in Constantinople and then Palestine before the actual warriors.

This well-intentioned but ill-prepared group of Crusaders did not have enough resources, and they soon ran out of food. As they continued east, hungry and tired, they began to steal food en route. The first group arrived at the border of Hungary in late May, with a second group soon to follow. They were granted passage through Hungary on the condition that they neither pillage nor plunder. However, it was in Bulgaria that the motley band encountered a serious setback. While Bulgaria was technically controlled by the Byzantine Empire, it was by no means friendly to these particular Crusaders. When one of the peasant leaders tried to buy food, he was refused by local magistrates. This left the peasants with few options; unable to procure food by honest means, they seized provisions from locals. Violence ensued, and many Crusaders and area residents were killed.

As the journey continued, many Crusaders starved to death. Many who survived were determined to fulfill the mission, and they continued to Constantinople. When the remnant reached the Byzantine capital, Emperor Alexius ferried them across the Bosphorus to the Asiatic shore where they stayed at Hellenopolis, waiting for more troops from the West. Alexius provided them with necessities, and he warned them to stay out of Turkish territory.

Unfortunately, after a couple of months some Crusaders began stealing from their Greek hosts. After a group of German Crusaders procured a castle, they were surrounded by Turks in a brutal siege. In the battle that followed, many who were not killed were captured and remained slaves for the rest of their lives. Peter the Hermit survived and later became a prior in a monastery. But the noble warriors were on their way, and the First Crusade would have a completely different outcome than the Peasants' Crusade.

The First Crusade (1095-1099)

The first officially sanctioned European warriors arrived in Constantinople in 1097, and Emperor Alexius sent them directly on to Muslim controlled Asia Minor. The Christian soldiers joined the Byzantine military in the fight, and they proved extremely successful. They took Nicaea, and boasted a great victory at the Battle of Dorylaeum. Crusaders took back western Anatolia, the region closest to Europe, and then they marched eastward toward the Holy Land. After

Leaders of the First Crusade included (left to right) Godfrey, Raymond, Bohemund, and Tancred. The forces of these men made up the true military might of the Crusade.

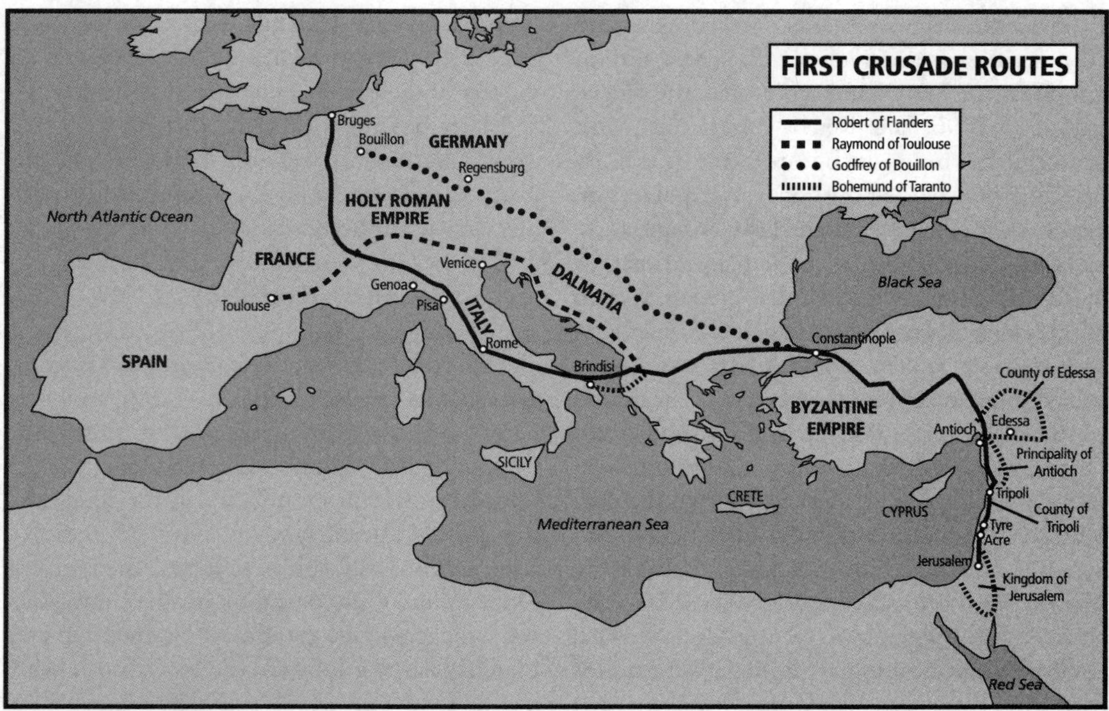

the Crusaders captured Antioch in 1098, they set up a crusader state governed by Bohemond of Tarranto. In Edessa, Godfrey of Bouillon set up a similar state.

The First Crusade to the Holy Land was extremely successful, and the Crusaders believed they had achieved their mission. When Christians captured Jerusalem in 1099, word spread that the worst was over, and the Holy Land was back in the hands of the "faithful." The siege of Jerusalem is a dark chapter in Christian history. A well-known account of this conflict was written by Fulcher of Chartres, a French vicar and participant in the crusade. He relates a horrific scene at the Temple of Solomon where:

> A great fight took place in the court and porch of the temples, where they were unable to escape from our gladiators. Many fled to the roof of the temple of Solomon, and were shot with arrows, so that they fell to the ground dead. In this temple almost ten thousand were killed. Indeed, if you had been there you would have seen our feet colored to our ankles with the blood of the slain. But what more shall I relate? None of them were left alive; neither women nor children were spared.

He describes the spoils of victory taken by Christians:

> Our squires and poorer footmen discovered a trick of the Saracens, for they learned that they could find byzants (gold coins) in the stomachs and intestines of the dead Saracens (Muslims), who had swallowed them. Thus, after several days they burned a great heap of dead bodies, that they might more easily get the precious metal from the ashes.

Crusaders then proceeded to set up a crusader state that included not only Jerusalem but most of the Holy Land as far as the city of Tyre in the north. Godfrey of Bouillon extended his influence and became king of the territory. Consequently, the crusade ended in late 1099 on a high note for Christians. Pope Paschal II (r. 1099-1118), who had ascended the throne of St. Peter upon the death of Pope Urban in August 1099, wrote of the conquest of Jerusalem:

> We owe boundless gratitude to the compassion of Almighty God, since . . . he has designed to wrest the Church . . . from the hands of the Turks and to open to Christian soldiers the very city of the Lord's suffering and death and burial.

The First Crusade was successful since the combined Byzantine and European forces had defeated Muslim warriors and regained control of Palestine. After the First Crusade three crusader states were officially established in the east at Jerusalem, Antioch, Edessa, and then in 1109 a fourth state was established in Tripoli. Crusaders and spokesmen for the Church contended that God was obviously on the side of the Christian warriors, as evidenced by their triumph. In reality, the largely inexperienced, boisterous Christian forces benefitted from disunity and lack of organization among Muslims. The fragmented Muslims were simply unable to band together at first due to internal conflicts, but this was going to change. Westerners would soon realize that their stunning victory was only temporary.

Military Orders of Knighthood

The religiosity of the time produced two well-known military/monastic orders. They were unique because members were warriors who also lived under monastic guidelines, taking vows of poverty, chastity and obedience. The Knights Templar (Knights of the Temple of Solomon) was founded around 1118, but they evolved into much more than originally intended. These men originally banded together to protect Christian pilgrims traveling to Muslim-controlled regions of the Holy Land. They also provided services to pilgrims and Crusaders alike. The Templars learned how to increase their wealth, and they formed a bank with headquarters in Paris. Many significant men, including the pope and several kings, became clients of their early banking system.

Godfrey of Bouillon marches victoriously through Jerusalem, where mutilated corpses litter the streets.

The second order, the Hospitallers, was founded around the same time as the Knights Templar, but it was originally a charitable order, not a military order. The members of the Hospitallers (Knights Hospitallers) worked in and around a hospital in Jerusalem providing care to any sick or injured Christian pilgrims or Crusaders. This changed during the First Crusade after the conquest of Jerusalem in 1099; the Hospitallers set up a charter as a religious and military order much like the Knights Templar.

The Second Crusade (1147-1149)

Pope Eugene III (r. 1145-1153) announced the Second Crusade in 1147 in response to the fall of the crusader state at Edessa to Muslim warriors in 1144. Bernard of Clairvaux was anointed by the pope to preach the Second Crusade, offering the same plenary indulgence to participants as the earlier crusade. This crusade was a failure, as Christian forces attempted to take Damascus in Syria and were overwhelmed by combined Muslim forces. The Muslims continued to advance across Syria and re-conquered Jerusalem in October 1187. Saladin, a Muslim general who controlled Syria and Egypt, gained widespread fame for his leadership at the siege of Jerusalem.

Muslim General Saladin granted Christians access to Jerusalem.

The Third Crusade (1189-1192)

The loss of Jerusalem led to a call for the Third Crusade, yet another attempt to take back lost territory in the Holy Land. Three powerful European leaders responded directly to the appeal: Holy Roman Emperor Frederick Barbarossa (r. 1152-1190), King Richard I of England, also known as Richard the Lionheart (r. 1189-1199), and King Philip II (Philip Augustus) of France (r. 1180-1223). Great victories were anticipated with these strong

Richard the Lionheart led the Third Crusade but never reached Jerusalem.

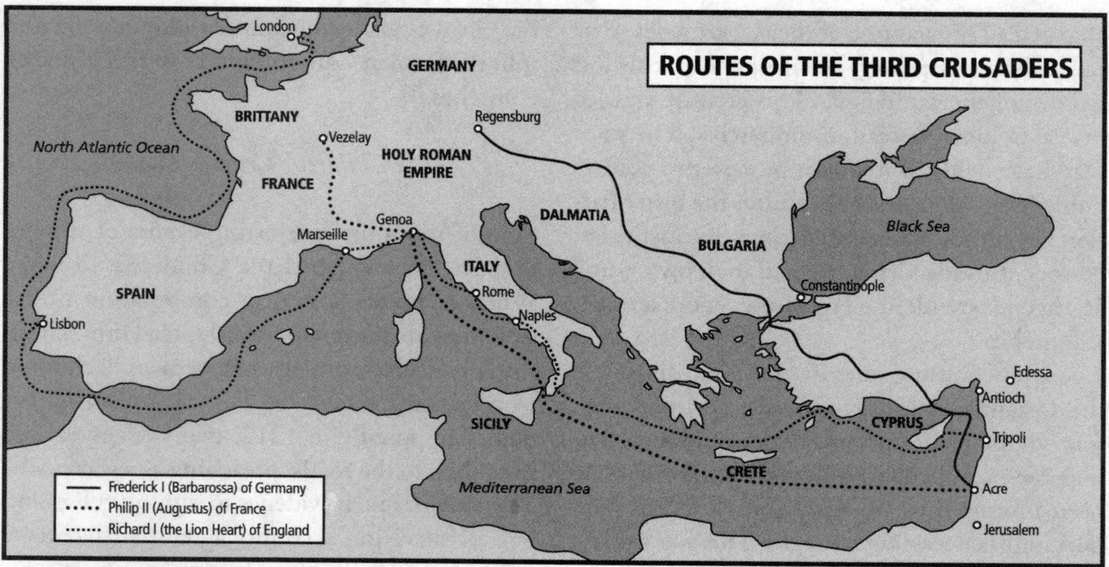

men leading the way, but they were unable to effectively coordinate their efforts, and the Third Crusade fell short of the expectations of most Europeans. Barbarossa was not a young man, but he was determined to lead his troops. They marched through western Anatolia, winning several battles along the way. Unfortunately, the emperor drowned in a river as his forces headed east. Some sources recount that he failed to remove all his armor and was carried away by violent river currents; others say he had a fatal heart attack and died while wading across a river. Regardless of how it happened, the death of the emperor was a blow to the Christian forces. Many of the emperor's German troops deserted the cause and returned home.

The loss of Frederick Barbarossa was exacerbated by the rivalry between the two remaining monarchs, Philip II and Richard I. The kings took control of the European armies in the absence of Barbarossa, but they could not put aside their enmity and unite their armies long enough to gain victory. They had each traveled to the Holy Land separately, and once there, each pursued his own agenda. After taking the city of Acre, Philip called his portion of the crusade a success and went home to France. Richard defeated Saladin in several clashes, but he did not follow through. After signing a treaty that left Jerusalem under Muslim control with a provision that allowed for Christian pilgrimages, he returned to England. After the treaty Saladin gained a reputation for compassion as he allowed Christians to visit Jerusalem without formal papers, and he even commanded his soldiers to watch over Christian pilgrims while they were in the Holy Land.

The Third Crusade achieved very little for Christians, especially since the original objective was to obtain control of Jerusalem. They did establish a crusader state in Cyprus, but Jerusalem remained an unattainable goal.

The Fourth Crusade (1201-1204)

The Fourth Crusade began with the intent of capturing Jerusalem under Pope Innocent III (r. 1198-1216), but the focus soon dramatically changed. This was one of the last crusades to be called for by the papacy, but the pope quickly lost control of the campaign. This crusade was led by the nobility instead of monarchs. The pope may have believed it would be easier to control nobles than kings, especially after the bitter friction and animosity between kings during the last crusade. But the Crusaders had their own vision and agenda, rendering Pope Innocent practically a figurehead.

After choosing sides in a dynastic dispute in the Byzantine Empire, Crusaders turned their forces upon Constantinople, the capital city. The purpose was to collect a sum of money that had been promised to the Crusaders for their support in the succession struggle. This was a direct violation of a papal order that stated that no Christian cities should be attacked by Christians on threat of excommunication. Nevertheless, the Crusaders wanted payment, and Constantinople was sacked in 1204. It was an appalling scene with Crusaders desecrating Eastern Orthodox Churches, damaging the Library of Constantinople, and taking all the wealth they could carry. Much of the stolen fortune was allocated among Venetians, French knights, and any Crusaders who had a hand in the pillage. Pope Innocent was furious, but eventually he took the opportunity to attempt an extension of Roman Catholic authority over the Eastern Orthodox Church.

The Latin Empire of Constantinople was established in 1206 with Baldwin of Flanders as emperor. The Greeks eventually regained Constantinople in 1261, but the relationship between the Latin West and the Byzantine East was irreparably broken. Latin Christians turned against Byzantine Christians, most knights did not even make it to the Holy Land, and many took the opportunity to pillage and plunder, so overall it was a debacle. Some historians cite the Fourth Crusade as the final chapter in the saga of the Great Schism which had begun in 1054 and split the Roman Catholic and Eastern Orthodox Churches.

The Children's Crusade (1212)

One of the more interesting events of the period has been dubbed the Children's Crusade. Whether myth, fact, or a combination of the two, one thing is certain: word spread throughout medieval Europe of a great movement of children who wanted to take the Holy Land for Christians. Supposedly in 1212, two twelve-year old boys took to the roads, preaching a new crusade. There is not much evidence to support this event, but all surviving accounts agree that whatever actually occurred, the ending was tragic.

In France a shepherd boy named Stephen went to King Philip II, saying he had received a message from Jesus to call for a new crusade. Even though the king did not believe the boy's pleas, Stephen started preaching throughout France to anyone who would hear him out. It is said that as he told children about his vision and the need to reconquer the Holy Land, many left their homes and followed him. He told them they would go to Jerusalem with God's blessing and that even the oceans would part for them to cross on dry land. One narrative says that Stephen gathered at least 30,000 children, along with some adult men and women, by summer of 1212. Even though the pope refused to sanction this expedition, they headed east toward the Holy Land.

Stephen's followers began to desert him as they realized the enormity of the task at hand. Most had never been very far from their homes, and the incessant walking day after day was grueling. A number of children died of exhaustion, starvation, and disease. Once the remainder reached the Mediterranean Sea, the waters did not allow them passage. One version says that Stephen's loyal followers then hired several boats to transport them to Anatolia. However, instead of providing transportation, the men who owned the boats sold them all into slavery.

The same year, supposedly, a similar thing happened in Germany led by a boy named Nicholas. He also preached a crusade to children, and he also found many devotees, perhaps as many as 20,000. Nicholas led a large number of the faithful to Rome for an audience with the pope. The pope sent them back home, telling them to return in a few years when they were old enough to take the warrior vows. On the way back to Germany, many of Nicholas' followers died of various causes.

Recent historians believe that there may be an element of truth in the Children's Crusade, but that it is likely that events did not happen in this exact way. It is more probable that chroniclers heard of or encountered large groups of crusaders or those who wanted to be crusaders and embellished the original story. Medieval historian Georges Duby also provides another important fact to consider. Duby notes that the most common Latin word used to describe crusaders was puer, which can be translated as "a young man of low social standing." It is quite possible that later writers mistranslated this word, and the legend was born. One thing is for certain. No one alive knows exactly what happened, but the vision of thousands of children setting out for Jerusalem still captivates the imagination.

Later Crusades

There were four subsequent traditionally numbered Crusades, none of them successful. The Fifth Crusade (1217-1221), the Sixth Crusade (1228-1229), the Seventh Crusade (1248-1254), and the Eighth Crusade (1270) were disappointments to clergy and laymen alike. The high point came during the Sixth Crusade when Jerusalem was briefly controlled by Christians. When the Crusader State of Acre was captured by Muslims in 1291, Europeans lost their last stronghold in the region.

While this chapter has emphasized the specific numbered Crusades, it is important to note that recent medieval historians have included later expeditions throughout the fourteenth, fifteenth and sixteenth centuries in their definition of "crusade." They acknowledge that the conventional crusade numbering system focuses on the two hundred year period of frequent, fierce outbreaks of hostility, and that later the struggles were sporadic.

Impact of the Crusades

While the Crusades are considered a failure for Christians, who remained incapable of regaining significant or permanent control over the Holy Land, the impact of their efforts was far-reaching. One of the most important effects of the Crusades was that it helped speed the breakdown of feudalism. Feudalism, which was based on the economic system of manorialism, depended upon land as a source of wealth. Many warriors who died in the Crusades had no sons, so their land reverted to the king, who in feudalism was theoretically the chief feudal lord. This, of course, allowed kings who had been relatively powerless in feudalism to attempt to end the decentralization of the time. Also, one cannot overlook the obvious; with nobles fighting and dying in large numbers, the kings experienced less resistance from the nobility when imposing new ways to centralize governments around the monarchy. The Crusades also gave many serfs the opportunity to leave the manor and join the throngs of fighters headed for the Holy Land.

Profound devastation marked the relationships between Christians and many other groups. As Crusaders began their quest to the Holy Land, much of their pent-up energy was misdirected toward not just Muslims but also toward any non-Christians. In particular, Jews became targets of violence, especially in France and the German territories. The Jews were in the unenviable position of being caught between two powerful but warring religions, so they were mistreated by both Christians and Muslims. Anti-Semitism was not a new idea; this bigotry had existed long before the Crusades. For centuries some Christians had blamed Jews for the death of Jesus, and the warlike atmosphere of the Crusades seemed to have provided a catalyst for a renewal of anti-Semitic rhetoric. Rumors abounded that they poisoned the drinking wells of Christians, that they murdered Christian women and children, and that they had made a deal with Satan to give them dominance over Christians. Followers of Peter the Hermit during the People's Crusade attacked several Jewish settlements and massacred the inhabitants.

Although the Crusades had an overwhelming detrimental effect, the meeting of Eastern and Western troops led to some positive outcomes. First, both sides had the opportunity to observe and learn from each other. Europeans went into foreign lands and were exposed to different cultures, traditions, and technologies. The Crusades allowed Christians to learn more about the religion of Islam from experience and observation instead of from propaganda. Europeans embraced innovative Arabic ideas such as the numerals 0-9, writing paper manufactured out of cotton, and ship compasses. Trade increased between East and West as Crusaders encountered and brought back new items such as silk, spices, apricots, and sugar that quickly became popular in Europe. Port cities such as Venice and Genoa increased their wealth as they became gateways through which these new exotic items passed. The merchant class began to grow in affluence and importance as the decline of feudalism paired with an increase in trade contributed to the renewal and revival of towns and cities.

INTERNAL CRUSADES

In the aftermath of the Crusades, there was a sudden rise of intolerant attitudes toward those who chose to follow a different form of Christianity. The term "crusade" can be used to describe not only the struggle between Christianity and Islam for the Holy Land but also other efforts by the traditional Roman Catholic Church to expel those who went against orthodox Christian teachings. In other words, the Church had approved certain beliefs as were necessary for a Christian to achieve salvation and eternal life. In Christianity, a heretic was someone who called himself a Christian but at the same time, held some beliefs that were not sanctioned by the Church. For example, in the early days of Christianity followers of Arius believed that Jesus was a created being, and as such he could not be equal to God the Father. People who believed in this purported Arian Heresy were considered heretics. In the Middle Ages several new heresies abounded, and the Church became determined to stamp them out before the heretics lost their salvation and endangered others' eternal souls with false teachings.

Catharism

The Cathari came under fire by the Church for their unconventional beliefs that threatened Roman Catholic theology. The Cathari are also referred to as Albigensians because they were referenced by a medieval chronicler who traced their origins to the town of Albi in France. Some later historians suggest that the sect did not necessarily originate in Albi, but there was undeniably a large following in the area. Regardless, the words Cathari and Albigensians are interchangeable.

While certain beliefs of the Cathari were based in Christianity, there were many tenets considered heretical by Catholics. For example, they embraced the principle of dualism, which teaches there is a virtual split between the evil material and pure/good spiritual worlds. Catharism taught that there is not just one God, but there is a good spirit and an evil one, who are roughly equal in power. Many religions, including the ancient Persian Zoroastrian religion, shared this notion. Albigensians believed that the evil spirit was lord of the material world, and God was lord of the spiritual world. Because the Church, which Catharism alleged was hopelessly secular, existed in the physical realm, it was under the dominion of the evil lord.

This group took the doctrine of dualism to an extreme. They called themselves *perfecti*, and as an outward expression of their conviction that the physical body is evil and the spirit is good, they adopted an uncompromising life of self-discipline and simplicity. Cathari denied themselves any physical pleasure, instilling in their converts the idea that self-denial was the most sincere expression of piety. They asserted that humans are spirits trapped in corporeal bodies. According to Norman Cantor, "The Cathari believed they were the ascetic perfects who achieved a pure spirituality." They thought the Incarnation was fiction because pure spirit—perfection—could not reside in a sinful material body, even for a short time. Critics claimed that the sect also had radical and contradictory sexual beliefs. Stories circulated that they allowed free, uninhibited sex as long as no children were brought into the corrupt physical world. Since the Cathari likewise had a reputation for denial of any sensual or carnal pleasure, that seems illogical, but still, the rumors persisted. Some say it is because the Albigensians believed that sacraments freed the spirit from the sins committed by the body, so that gave them license. To that end, they gained the reputation for infanticide and infant exposure.

Actually, surviving evidence indicates that the Albigensians were sincere, pious, and diligent. Even though they appear to have been compassionate and gentle worshippers, they posed a threat to the mainstream Catholic Church with their radical doctrinal departures. The simple, itinerant, austere lifestyle provided an alternative to the secular and wealthy Latin Church. Many converted because they felt the Cathari were more spiritual and offered a clearer path to salvation. The Albigensians were one of the first so-called heretical groups to gain large numbers of followers and to spread relatively quickly throughout a sizable region. If enough people converted to this sect, of course the established Church would lose members. Catholic clergy claimed the group taught doctrines that endangered converts' immortal souls, and the Church moved against the Albigensians.

As the Cathari gained more members, the mainstream Church first tried to convert Cathari to traditional Roman Catholicism. Saint Dominic began evangelizing in strong Cathar regions, and eventually he created the Dominican order of preaching friars. The Dominicans became one of the most active proselytizers to this group. However, the endeavors were unsuccessful, and Pope Innocent III asked King Philip Augustus of France to start a military campaign against the Cathari. The king was unimpressed at first, but after a papal messenger named Pierre de Castelnau was murdered, perhaps by a member of the Albigensians, Philip allowed the French nobility to participate in a crusade. Beginning in 1209 a formal crusade was launched against these apostates.

During this campaign the French nobility turned against itself, with the nobles in different regions of France warring against each other. Pope Innocent III helped fuel this situation because he offered confiscated land to any warriors who joined the cause to defeat the Cathari.

The end of the Albigensian Crusade is usually marked by the siege and subsequent fall of the Cathar fortress Château of Montsegur in 1244. The stronghold housed at least fifty Cathar monks along with other followers including women, children, and servants. Estimates put the population at five hundred people or so.

In the spring of 1244 after a long siege, those who held to the Albigensian doctrine were given a chance to repudiate their heresy. Most of the monks refused to deny their beliefs, and all who held to their faith were burned at the stake. There were around two hundred who were sacrificed in this manner. The Albigensian Crusade was successful in eradicating the Cathar or Albigensian heresy, but it was yet another example of the prevailing hegemony of the Roman Catholic Church in the High Middle Ages.

The Waldensians

Peter Waldo started a clerical group that the Roman Catholic Church targeted for its heretical teachings. Waldo was a wealthy merchant from Lyons, France who became convinced that men of God should follow Jesus' example of giving up worldly goods and, instead, travel around spreading the gospel. In the 1170's he gave up his affluent lifestyle, took a vow of poverty, and devoted his life to God. He began traveling around France preaching and relying on charity and the patronage of people who believed his message. Waldo was so devout in both word and deed that he inspired many to take up his mantle. His followers became known as the Waldensians or the Poor Men of Lyons. When word of this movement reached high-ranking officials in the Church, the Archbishop of Lyons investigated further. He found discrepancies between Waldensian ideas and the official doctrine of the Roman Catholic Church. One teaching that was contrary to Church creed is *antisacerdotalism*. Advocates of this principle say that the clergy have no special power derived from their position, and that the sacraments one receives from clergy have no intrinsic value. The Waldensians denied several Roman tenets such as papal/priest absolution of sins, clerical celibacy, infant baptism, and intercessory prayers to the saints.

The Archbishop of Lyons made the first attempt to suppress these teachings by accusing the men of preaching without a license. Later when the pope formally backed this decision, Waldo's self-appointed clerics ignored the ruling. In 1181 the Church officially proclaimed them as heretics. The group was excommunicated en masse, but instead of giving up, they continued to travel and preach their interpretation of the Bible. They gained a large following in parts of France and Italy.

Despite the Church's best efforts they were not able to eradicate believers in the Waldensian message. Waldo's theological descendants still exist in modern times, with the current manifestation of the Waldensian Church considering itself part of the Reformed Christian Protestant Church.

CONFIRMATION OF PAPAL LEADERSHIP: The Pontificate of Pope Innocent III

The Crusades illustrate the power of the Church in the High Middle Ages. Even though the campaigns were an overall failure for Christians, the faith that caused warriors to head for the Holy Land helped provide the catalyst for the reform movement that swept the Church. In 1198 Lothario Conti, a member of the College of Cardinals, was elected pope. He chose the papal name Pope Innocent III (1198-1216) and set out to reform the Church in his own way. Innocent deeply believed that the papacy was ordained by God as the head of all of Christendom, but he didn't stop there. He also proposed that in God's perfect order, He had decreed that the pope should have authority over not only the spiritual but also the temporal realm. This was not a unique idea—the problems between Pope Gregory VII and Emperor Henry IV were related to this exact question of supremacy—but Innocent was not an activist reorganizer like Gregory, and he would handle the issue differently. Pope Innocent decided to spread the influence of the Church in two major ways. First he spearheaded an ecclesiastical restructuring movement. He began by centralizing Roman Catholic bureaucracy around the pope. He doubled the size of the Papal States by extending papal control over more of Italy. Second, Pope Innocent was committed to reasserting papal authority in the selection of German emperors.

Innocent is the pope who called for the ill-fated Fourth Crusade (1201-1204) where Christians stormed the Byzantine capital of Constantinople in a fit of destruction. Although he spoke harshly against the atrocities committed by Crusaders, at the same time the pope took the opportunity to exert a measure of control over the Eastern Orthodox Church in Byzantium, which had split from the Latin Church in the 1054 schism. Therefore, from Innocent's perspective, the papacy again presided over a united and universal Christendom. He had no way of knowing this, but ultimately, the violence perpetrated by Crusaders on Eastern Christians in Constantinople widened the chasm between the Byzantine and Latin Christian Churches, and they were never able to reconcile.

Another of Innocent's priorities was to regain leadership over the monarchies of Europe. Holy Roman Emperor Henry VI had died in 1197, and at the time of Innocent's ascension there was no one on the imperial throne. The pope used the resulting disorder to assert papal control over the empire's Italian territory. He restored papal power in Rome and required the Prefect of Rome, the Emperor's representative, to swear allegiance to the pope. In 1202 the pope issued the *Venerabilem*, which gave the pope the right to accept a candidate for emperor or to reject him. At the time of the decree, two candidates were vying for the position, and in the *Venerabilem* Pope Innocent clearly asserted that, in that situation, it was up to the pope to have the last word. After an unfortunate series of events that included papal support of one candidate, changing papal support to the other candidate, and the unexpected murder of one of the hopefuls, Pope Innocent III crowned Otto of Brunswick as Otto IV (r. 1198-1215 or 1218) the official Holy Roman Emperor in 1209. When Otto defied the pope on several issues, including territory he had agreed to cede to the Church, Otto was excommunicated.

French king Philip II (r.1189-1223) was a papal supporter in the conflict with Otto while Emperor Otto found an ally in King John of England (r. 1199-1216). Otto's forces were defeated at the Battle of Bouvines in Belgian territory in the summer of 1214. Otto was left powerless, and he died a broken man in 1218. Upon his death, Frederick II, who had been the rival choice for the throne, was the sole, acknowledged Holy Roman Emperor. During the same period the pope used papal troops to gain control over German provinces in Spoleto, Assisi, and the Sora

King John did little to endear himself to others. He was a disagreeable man whose cruelty and arrogance eventually led to his political defeat.

region.

Similar stories played out in papal relations with England and France. The pope had a nasty dispute with King John of England over a candidate for Archbishop of Canterbury. Stephen Langton was put forth as the nominee by the pope, but King John gave strong opposition to this choice. King John was humbled by Pope Innocent who used feudal law, excommunication, and even placing England under interdict to enforce his will. John was forced to acknowledge the pope as his feudal lord; therefore, the king had to relinquish any control over choosing a candidate for the Archbishopric. The pope had gone over the head of the king, removing king's right as a feudal lord to choose his own vassals. John was sufficiently chastened, so he gave England to the papacy to receive it back as a feudal fief or benefice. This symbolically reinforced the monarchy's subordinate position in Innocent's hierarchical vision.

Although Philip II of France had been a papal supporter, the king was not immune to the pope's efforts to exercise control over secular government. Pope Innocent believed that as Christ's representative on earth he was responsible for upholding morality in Christian territories. A few years after Philip's first wife died, he married Ingeborg, a Danish princess, in 1193. He received not only a large sum of money but also the promise that Denmark would side with France against the English navy. However, shortly after the wedding, Philip wanted to end the marriage. His stated reason for the dissolution was that he realized she was in fact too closely related to him. The pope at the time, Celestine III, refused to dissolve the marriage, but, in defiance, Philip took another wife, Agnes of Merania, in 1196.

When Pope Innocent became pontiff, he declared that the marriage to Agnes was illegal, and he called for Philip to leave his wife. Exercising an overwhelming confidence in the power of the Church, the pope placed France under interdict in late 1199. While Philip continued to refuse, Agnes passed away the following summer. The king was well aware of the political implications if he allowed interdict to remain in France, so he repented. At first, he did not return to Ingeborg, but after a time he acknowledged the marriage and lived with her as husband and wife.

In addition to the political efforts of Pope Innocent III, his reign stands out of the great ecumenical council meeting he convened and directed in 1215. The Fourth Lateran Council is considered by religious historians to be one of the most significant meetings on record. The assembly was attended by hundreds of metropolitans, bishops, abbots, priors, and representatives of the major European monarchies. The meeting reinforced earlier doctrinal statements as dogma and defined many rules for the Church. The Fourth Lateran Council set the number of sacraments at seven and decreed that every member of the Roman Catholic Church must receive the Eucharist a minimum of once yearly. It also reinforced the *Omnis utriusque sexus*, which requires any member who has reached the age of discretion to confess his/her sins at least once yearly to a priest. The Council also defined and reasserted the doctrine of transubstantiation, which is the belief that during the Eucharist (communion) the bread and wine literally transform into the body and blood of Christ as a result of being blessed by a priest. The Council also provided an unambiguous code of behavior for clergy, which banned clerics from, among other things, hunting, performing surgery, and drunkenness. The Fourth Lateran Council provides confirmation of the significance and prominence of the Church during the High Middle Ages. It also furnishes an example of the far-reaching effect of a resolute pope.

The Dominican and Franciscan Orders

As a result of the medieval religious fervor, two new monastic orders were founded in Europe. Members of these groups, the mendicant or begging orders, took vows of poverty and asked for alms and charity in order to survive. The first of these, the Dominican Order, also called the Order of Preachers, was founded in part to combat the Albigensian heresy. Dominic (who later became St. Dominic) wanted to start an order that would value the ascetic standards of the Cathari, but at the same time retain the customary Roman Catholic doctrines. He hoped to convince many of the Albigensian followers to come back to the traditional Church by having well trained men who could easily refute heresies. In 1216 Dominic (1170-1221) began this new order, with papal blessing.

The Dominican Order focused on reaching educated people who would listen to logical Biblical refutations of heretical arguments. The Dominicans, who did not work, devoted themselves to studying the Bible in order to achieve this goal. However, they did not confine their scholarly pursuits to theology. Dominicans became interested in reconciling science and the Bible, and they proudly became intellectual supporters of the Church. One of the most well-known Dominicans was Thomas Aquinas who gave so-called proofs for the existence of God in his work *Summa Theologica.*

The Dominicans were progressive, allowing women to participate in their work. The Order opened its first convent in 1206 in France with a group of former Albigensian women who wanted to continue their service to God. The Dominicans acquired a reputation as frank, intelligent, and open-minded scholars and servants of God. One negative aspect of their service is that they did get involved in the Papal Inquisition. This inquisition began in the early 1230's as a response to the heretical organizations that were springing up throughout Europe. Pope Gregory IX (r.1227-1241) issued a series of papal decrees that, when combined, are referred to as the Papal Inquisition, which was meant to defeat heresy but also to reinforce the teachings of the Church. Gregory wanted trained individuals to carry out this mission, and the Dominicans with their academic approach and deeply held faith were perfect for the job.

The other mendicant order that originated in the High Middle Ages was the Franciscan Order, based on the teachings of St. Francis of Assisi (1181-1226). St. Francis was from a wealthy family, but his life changed when he was taken prisoner during wartime. After that, he heard a sermon that touched him, and he converted to Christianity. His lifestyle became austere, and he went from place to place preaching the gospel and relying on donations, saying he believed totally in God's grace and ability to provide.

While the Dominicans were learned men, St. Francis wanted his followers to be uneducated and to focus on living amongst the commoners. The Franciscans, when juxtaposed with the materialistic Church, provided an unblemished example of Christian piety. The Franciscans were similar to the Waldensians in many ways, but the Franciscan Order believed in submission of all clergy to the pope. These disciples renounced material goods and became itinerant, wandering around proclaiming the gospel in France and Germany. Many men, who were disillusioned with the Church but still wanted to remain Christians, found the Franciscans' honesty appealing. According to St. Francis, his followers were not even allowed to have a permanent residence; rather they were to seek shelter wherever God led them.

The group gained popularity, and as it gained members, it became necessary to impose some sort of structure. Pope Innocent III approved the *regula primitiva* or the simple rule, in 1209, calling them the Order of Friars. Pope Honorius III (r.1216-1227) took this a step further and approved the *regula prima* or the primary rule. They became known as the Little Brothers of St. Francis, an officially recognized part of the Church. St. Francis decided this move was too far from his original intent, and he distanced himself from the group he had founded. He turned over direct leadership of the order to others, but he was always considered their spiritual leader. After St. Francis' death the Franciscan order became more bureaucratic under the governance of the Church, and its members became a positive force in medieval education.

CONCLUSION

The Church in the High Middle Ages experienced an overwhelming drive toward reform that began in the monasteries, spread to the papacy, and finally reached the faithful parishioners and laity. In this period, any breach of rules established by the Church was a severe infraction, no matter the status of the lawbreaker. Those who lived close enough were required to attend mass at least once per week without fail and to dutifully pay their tithes and cheerfully give their offerings. People were expected to keep the fast days as well as the holy days, and it was commonplace for people to report their neighbors for failure to adhere to the rules. A brief example provided by historian William Manchester in *A World Lit Only by Fire*, sums up the atmosphere of the time:

> ...the devout affirmed their Lenten piety by joining a procession led by a priest. Afterwards one marching woman, who had worn a particularly saintly expression during the parade, retired to her kitchen and elatedly broke Lent by heating, and eating mutton and ham. The aroma drifted . . . to passersby . . . (who) brought it before the local bishop, who sentenced her to walk the village streets until Easter, a month away, with the ham slung around her neck and the quarter of mutton, on its spit, over her shoulder . . . . a jeering mob followed her every step.

It was a time of great aspirations to piety, but it was an era when most Christians were illiterate. Knowledge of God's will was imparted through clergy, who sometimes had their own agendas. Consequently, while most people attempted to remain faithful, the medieval world was dominated by an overwhelming fear of and reverence for magic, black cats, broken mirrors, and things that go bump in the night. Religion was vital to people, not on a personal level, but as an intricate part of culture. The Church not only ruled in the areas of politics and social customs, it provided a way to explain the mysterious world, even while religion itself remained enigmatic to most professing European Christians.

Suggestions for Further Reading

Barraclough, G. *The Origins of Modern Germany. (*1946).

Bishop, Morris. *The Middle Ages. (*2001).

Bauer, Susan Wise. *History of the Medieval World from the Conversion of Constantine to the First Crusade.* (2010).

Cantor, Norman F. *Civilization of the Middle Ages. (*1994).

Duby, Georges. *France in the Middle Ages 987-1460: From Hugh Capet to Joan of Arc.* (1993).

Foss, Michael. *People of the First Crusade.* (1997).

Manchester, William. *A World Lit Only by Fire: The Medieval Mind and the Renaissance—Portrait of an Age.* (1993).

Phillips, Jonathan. *The Fourth Crusade and the Sack of Constantinople.* (2004).

Thompson, James Westfall. *Feudal Germany. (1928).*

Chapter 9

Civilization of the Late Middle Ages 1100 – 1300

Westminster Abbey

In 1231, a six-year-old boy named Thomas would stun his teachers at the abbey of Monte Cassino by asking the question, "What is God?" Thomas was born to a noble family in a castle near Naples. Throughout the remainder of his life he continued to ask "what" or "why" when presented with a proposition.

At fifteen, Thomas of Aquino, or Thomas Aquinas, began attending classes at the University of Naples. Under the tutelage of a scholar known as Peter the Irishman, he was introduced to the works of Aristotle.

While still in his teens, Thomas decided to devote his life to God and became a Dominican friar. His family was shocked and disheartened by his decision. On a journey to Bologna, he was kidnapped by his brothers and held in a castle for nearly two years. In an effort to lure him away from the strict discipline of the Dominican Order, his brothers tried to employ carnal lust. A beautiful woman was sent to his chamber to tempt Thomas, but he drove her from his room with a burning log. Unable to corrupt him, his family released him from confinement, and he returned to his life of study and prayer.

Recognizing his brilliance, the Dominicans sent Thomas to the University of Paris, where he studied under the watchful eye of Albertus Magnus. In 1248, master and student moved to Cologne to help the new university in that city. Both men were fascinated by Aristotle's essays and, like so many scholars of their day, chose to ignore warnings issued by Church bureaucrats about the corrupting influence of Greek philosophy.

By 1255, the Dominicans dominated the faculty of Arts at the University of Paris, and they made the works of Aristotle required reading for their students. The following year, Thomas Aquinas was granted the degree of master in theology. As a master, he played an active role in the theological debates that took place at the university. For two years, twice a week, Thomas acted as a challenger in the public debates at the University of Paris. In these debates, he steadfastly maintained that the rational intellect, as a gift from God, could help humanity gain knowledge of God.

In 1265, Thomas was placed in charge of educating young Dominican friars in Rome. There, he began work on the ***Summa Theologica****, a comprehensive attempt to explain all that was known about the relationship between God and humanity. In writing the* ***Summa Theologica****, he returned to answer the question he had raised as a boy at Monte Cassino—"What is God?" By utilizing the logic of Aristotle, Thomas demonstrated that faith and reason were not only compatible, they were complementary.*

Thomas died while on a journey to a general council at Lyons. At the time of his death, his great work had not been completed. He is reported to have said: "All I have written seems to me like so much straw compared with what I have seen and what has been revealed to me."

Chronology

926 Work began on St. Vitus Cathedral in Prague. It was completed more than a thousand years later.

981 The great Islamic scholar Abu Ibn Sina (Avicenna) was born in Bukhara in Central Asia. He attempted to reconcile Greek philosophy with the teachings of the Koran.

1113 Peter Abelard moved to Paris and became a teacher of philosophy.

1144 The consecration of the choir at St. Denis would mark the birth of the Gothic style of architecture in France.

1150 Peter Lombard's ***Four Books of Sentences*** was published. It became the standard theological textbook in the late Middle Ages.

1157 King Henry II of England granted trading privileges in London to the merchants of _Cologne.

1159 Lubeck was founded. It became a major trade center in northern Europe.

1163 Work began on the Cathedral of Notre Dame in Paris.

1167 King Henry II ordered the return of English scholars from Paris. Oxford soon emerged as a center of higher learning.

1172 Islamic scholar Abul Ibn Rushd (Averroes) began to translate and condense Aristotle's ***de Anima*** while serving as a judge in Seville, Spain.

1200 King Philip II of France granted a charter to the masters and students of Paris.

1204 Venetians assisted Fourth Crusade in the conquest of Constantinople.

1241 Lubeck and Hamburg signed a mutual assistance pact that will lead to the creation of the Hanseatic League.

1257 Bonaventure was chosen as Minister General of the Franciscan Order.

1265 Thomas Aquinas was given the responsibility of educating Dominican friars in Rome.

1275 Niccolo Polo presented his son Marco to Kublai Khan.

1278 The Italian painter Cimabue was commissioned to decorate the basilica at Assisi. He was assisted by Duccio and Giotto.

1302 Dante Alighieri was banished from Florence.

1305-06 Giotto painted "the Lamentation" on the wall of the Arena Chapelin Padua.

By the twelfth century, the ingredients of medieval European civilization were all in place. The papal bureaucracy gave spiritual and artistic direction to people throughout western and central Europe. In many regions, kings asserted their supremacy over local warlords. A revival of trade led to a growing prosperity, and prosperity led to greater optimism. Greater stability encouraged innovations in lifestyle, architecture, philosophy, business, and literature. Europeans showed increasing confidence in their ability to control their own destiny and to express themselves in a variety of ways.

TOWNS

The greatest paradox of the Middle Ages is that throughout the entire period, Europe was primarily rural and agricultural. Yet, the beauty of medieval civilization expressed itself most fully in the new and revitalized urban centers during the twelfth and thirteenth centuries.

As noted in Chapter 7, urban growth was closely tied to the revival of trade, which occurred throughout Europe in the eleventh century. Medieval towns usually originated in one of three ways. Some began as centers of lay or church administration. A bishop, abbot, monarch, or great lord would often require the specialized skills of craftsmen to supply his needs. Monarchs and their vassals needed weapons and armor.

Medieval city wall of Donauworth, Germany

Members of the clergy needed ornaments and altar clothes. All people of an elevated station in life desired to set themselves apart from the common people by the clothing they wore. Courts, monasteries, and cathedrals frequently became centers of production.

A second manner of development rested upon the need for security. During the Dark Ages, farmers were plagued by marauding raiders. In response to this danger, they would often flee to a fortification for protection. Some of these local fortifications attracted merchants who viewed local farmers as potential customers. Peasants could exchange a portion of their surplus crop for tools, cloth, or wine. These "farmers' markets" also afforded peasants an opportunity to sell their handicrafts and surplus livestock.

The third explanation for the revitalization of urban centers was put forth by historian Henri Pirenne. Pirenne noted that merchants involved in the new, long-distance trade often united into "companies" or "colonies" for mutual protection as they traveled. Because overland travel was often difficult during periods of inclement weather, merchants tended to congregate at strategically located fortifications along major trade routes. As the trade settlement grew outside of the castle walls, merchants frequently took the initiative in constructing a second, outer wall to protect their homes.

Whether craftsmen, farmers, or merchants were responsible for the rise of an urban center, all medieval towns were centers of production and trade. As such, they brought together the varied classes of medieval society to exchange both goods and ideas. The growth of towns would also lead to the creation of a new and dynamic social class known as the "bourgeoisie" or "middle class." Unlike the peasants and the nobility, they did not derive their wealth from the land. They relied upon skill and intelligence rather than strength and courage. While the incomes of most people in the Middle Ages were fixed by tradition, the wealth of the bourgeoisie was self-generated and unlimited.

The size and appearance of medieval cities varied greatly. The largest urban communities were in northern Italy. Venice, Florence, and Genoa flourished due to their trade connections with the Byzantine Empire and the Levant (the coast of modern Israel and Lebanon). As many as 100,000 people may have lived in Venice by 1200. Centers of production, like London, Bruges, Ghent, and Cologne, could count 20,000 to 40,000 inhabitants. Most medieval towns, however, contained about 5,000 people or less.

Life within metropolitan areas was crude by modern standards. Town dwellers were plagued by fire, disease, unruly livestock, and foul water. Cattle, hogs, rats, and chickens roamed the dirt streets. Human waste was often thrown out in alleyways or dumped into nearby streams. Unsanitary conditions and close quarters made medieval cities fertile breeding grounds for disease. In northern Europe, the popular use of wood and straw as building materials made fire a common hazard.

In spite of the unsavory aspects of urban communities, the lure of wealth, freedom, and entertainment attracted a growing number of Europeans to the cities. In order to succeed, the new middle class needed freedom to run their own affairs. Merchants needed freedom to move about the land in order to trade. Artisans needed the freedom to produce for the market. Moneylenders wanted freedom from church laws against usury. All town dwellers wanted freedom from servile obligations.

The liberties of an urban population were generally defined in the form of a charter granted to them by its local lord. In exchange for the freedoms granted by the charter, the town's people usually agreed to provide the lord with a fixed cash payment. The local lord might also retain certain monopolies, such as the milling of grain. As a result, the middle class demonstrated to the lord that it would be in the best interest of the lord to encourage the growth of the town.

Virtually all charters granted townsmen or "burghers" personal freedom. The standard custom in most of Europe was that if you lived within a town for a year and a day, you would be considered a free person. This rule did not apply to the serfs of the local lord, but it did apply to the escaped serfs of the lord's rivals.

Charters also defined the revenues the lord could derive from the burghers. In addition to an annual revenue, the lord could collect tolls and levy fines. Maximum fines and tolls were stated in the charter.

By the twelfth century, most towns had gained the right of limited self-government. Usually, the burghers could elect local officials, make rules for their inhabitants, and establish courts to try petty offenses. Lords generally reserved judgment on capital crimes and the approval of new taxes. However, the nobles usually preferred to allow the townsmen to administer their own affairs.

Economic activity within a medieval town was controlled by guilds. Both merchant and craft guilds were organized to promote the interest of their members. A town's merchant guild was primarily interested in preserving a monopoly on the local market. The guild assured uniform prices, placed restrictions on outside merchants

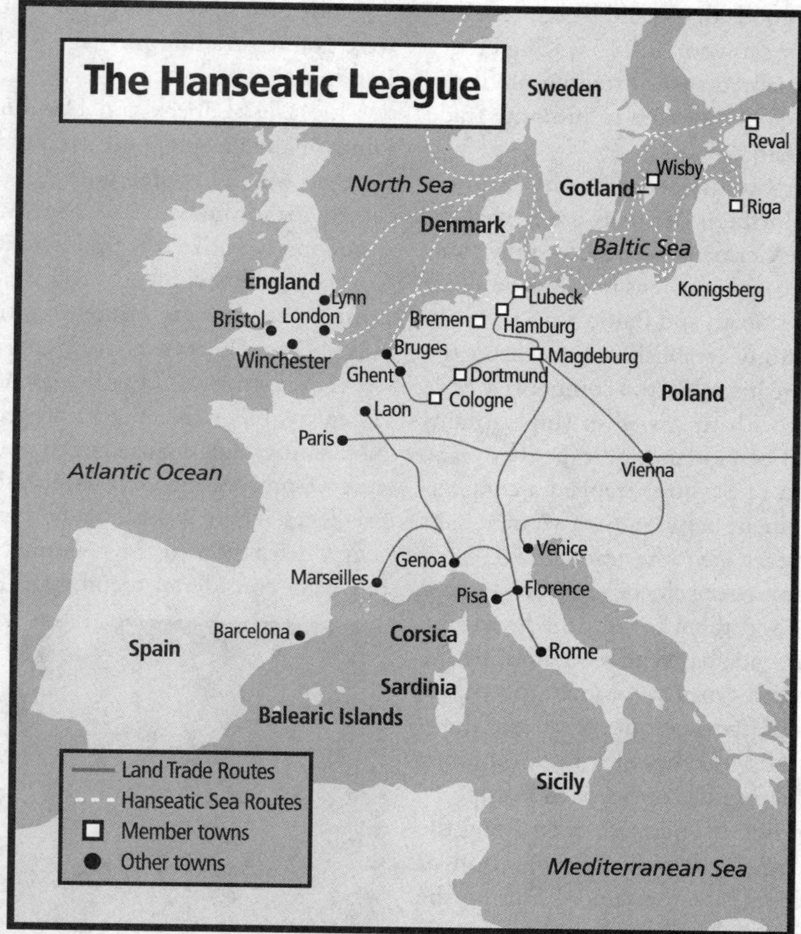

trying to trade within the town, and attempted to prevent any one of its members from dominating the market place.

Craft guilds were designed to regulate the methods and quality of production. The guild determined working conditions, such as limiting working hours. Master craftsmen who supervised the work of journeymen and apprentices dominated the craft guilds. The production of a "master piece" was essential for admission into the ranks of the masters. In addition to these functions, craft guilds provided social services to their members.

THE HANSEATIC LEAGUE

The growth of commerce and urban centers in northern Europe led to the creation of a trade association known as the Hanseatic League. By the early twelfth century, England exported large amounts of wool to the Low Countries. Flemish merchants established trading houses in London to facilitate this trade. By the middle of the century, merchants from various German cities were also active in the wool trade. The burghers of Bremen and Cologne used the rivers into the interior of the Holy Roman Empire to access a wide variety of goods that could be sent to England in exchange for wool. In 1157, King Henry II of England granted special trading privileges to the merchants of Cologne to promote trade with the Germanies.

By the mid-twelfth century, the business community in northern Germany was so well developed that the Germans were successfully competing with the Scandinavians in the trade along the coasts of the North and Baltic Seas. In 1159, the ruler of Saxony established Lubeck on the Baltic Sea to give his subjects a competitive edge in their rivalry with the Swedish ship captains from the island of Gotland. Within two years, Henry the Lion of Saxony arranged a cooperative trade agreement between the two merchant groups. The treaty gave the traders of Lubeck access to the commercial city of Visby on Gotland Island and allowed them to join the Swedes in the Russian fur trade based at Novgorod. By the end of the twelfth century, German merchants were exchanging large quantities of salt and cloth, obtained in western Europe, for furs and forest products originating in northeastern Europe.

The expansion of German trade along the Baltic coast coincided with the migration of Germanic peoples into the region. During the thirteenth century, the Danes and the Teutonic Knights embarked upon crusades against the Slavic-speaking people who inhabited the southern coast of the Baltic Sea. In order to secure their conquests, the German knights encouraged German peasants to immigrate to the region. The interaction of German and Slavic peasants led to improvements in agricultural yields and provided greater incomes for landlords. Many German and Danish lords also sought to enhance their incomes by establishing commercial centers along the Baltic coast. German merchants soon settled permanently in these towns, creating a commercial chain stretching from London to Russia. By the mid-thirteenth century, the Baltic merchants were granted trading privileges in Flanders and London.

In 1241, Lubeck and Hamburg agreed to jointly maintain and police a road that connected the two cities. This vital route also connected the North Sea to the Baltic Sea. Similar agreements were soon negotiated with other cities along the German and Pomeranian coasts. The commercial centers participating in these mutual assistance pacts became known as the Hanseatic League.

The Hanseatic League was never a political entity, but rather it represented a cluster of merchant groups engaged in cooperation for the sake of promoting their international trading privileges. There were actually towns that never sent a delegation to the meetings of the league but were considered members. The merchants

The west front entrance to Westminster Abbey exemplifies several characteristics of English Gothic architecture. The pointed roof and supporting buttresses support a circular, stained-glass window. Statuary adorns the columns and doorway. The archways are severely pointed.

The interior of St. Vitus Cathedral in Prague provides a fine example of the use of ribbed vaults and pointed arches to support the roof. The cathedral was begun in 926 and completed in 1929.

of the Hanseatic League not only dominated the trade in furs with Russia, they helped to move grain from northern Europe to the rest of the continent. The sale of fish and metallic ores from Scandinavia also proved profitable. The power of the league actually increased during the fourteenth century when much of Europe was wracked by famine and disease.

GOTHIC ARCHITECTURE

The growing wealth of the middle class combined with the spirituality of medieval culture expressed itself architecturally in the building of great cathedrals throughout Western Europe. Though merchants and artisans pulled the European economy forward, it was the Church that ultimately gave direction to life in the Middle Ages. The Church, with its growing bureaucracy, could raise money from all levels of society. The upper ranks of the clergy also possessed the ability to organize large projects.

From the middle of the eight century until the mid-twelfth century, the churches and abbeys of Western Europe were characterized by a modification of classical Roman architecture known as "Romanesque." By the late Roman Empire, the Christian churches of the western Mediterranean were primarily rectangular in shape with flat roofs. Known as "basilicas," the interiors of these structures were dominated by rows of columns that supported their roofs. A semi-dome was usually placed over the altar.

Salisbury Cathedral is considered to be one of the best examples of early English Gothic architecture. Steeply pitched roofs and windows with sharply pointed arches are typical of buildings designed during the late twelfth and thirteenth centuries.

Medieval frescoes on the walls of the parish church in Donauworth, Germany.

Most of the early Romanesque churches continued to resemble the basic structure of the Roman basilicas. However, Romanesque architects replaced the flat roofs with round, stone vaults. The weight of the vaulted roofs required massive walls to support them. Windows were small and usually narrow, giving Romanesque churches a dark and fortress-like appearance. Romanesque structures were also characterized by an extensive use of exterior, ornamental sculptures depicting Christ, his apostles, or various symbols relating to Christianity.

By the mid-twelfth century, medieval builders wanted to add light and elevation to churches to inspire those who worshipped in them. The use of ribbed vaults and pointed arches gave rise to Gothic architecture. In addition to the ribbed vaults, flying buttresses were utilized to eliminate the need for massive walls to support the roof. A flying buttress was a heavy pier of stone used to fortify the walls on the exterior of the building. This new method of construction allowed the builder to incorporate large, stained glass windows into the walls of the church. The interior of Gothic cathedrals were filled with color and light as stained glass windows gradually replaced frescoes as the principal means of decorating the interiors of the great churches of Europe.

The new Gothic style first appeared in the Ile-de-France and quickly spread throughout Western Europe. As always, regional variations would be evident. Italian builders refused to abandon the use of massive walls. The Gothic churches of Spain revealed the ornamental influence of the Moors (Moslem invaders from North Africa). Gothic architecture continued to dominate Western Europe for four centuries,

The west front doorway of Westminster Abbey illustrated the skill of medieval craftsmen in sculpting religious statuary.

and it would experience a brief revival during the early nineteenth century.

THE TRANSFORMATION OF ART

The growing popularity of Gothic architecture presented medieval artists with both a challenge and an opportunity. Prior to the twelfth century, the most common form of painting was manuscript illumination. The emphasis on light in the interiors of the new Gothic cathedrals meant that their windows were vast in size. The technique of painting stained glass was perfected during the Romanesque period, but the importance of stained glass in decorating Gothic structures cannot be over emphasized.

The stained glass windows were designed in the great cathedral workshops of Europe. The window itself was not a single pane. Each window was composed of large numbers of small pieces of painted glass held together by lead casings. The artist was literally painting with colored glass as he assembled the window. This process encouraged an abstract style. Figures were often monumental but rarely life like.

As the production of stained glass windows was reaching its height in northern Europe during the first half of the thirteenth century, a second artistic revolution began to take hold in Italy. The Franco-Venetian conquest of Constantinople in 1204 led to a renewed interest in Byzantine art. Throughout the thirteenth century, Italian painters were increasingly influenced by what they referred to as the "Greek manner." At the same time, Italian architects were increasingly influenced by the Gothic style. Italian sculptors were often employed to decorate the exteriors of the new Gothic structures, and they felt the influence of French and German artists. By the late thirteenth century,

The Church of San Giacomo is representative of the Romanesque architectural style so popular during the early Middle Ages.

a group of Italian painters began to synthesize the two styles.

Cenni di Pepo or Cimabue (1240/1250-1302) was among the first to deviate from the neo-Byzantine tradition. In most respects, this Florentine master conformed to the techniques used in Byzantine paintings, but he experimented with both form and style to satisfy the demands of the huge alter panels that he painted. Sometime around 1278, Cimabue was commissioned to work on the basilica at Assisi in honor of St. Francis. He was assisted in his efforts by Duccio di Buoninsegna (1255-1319) and Giotto di Bondone (1267-1337). Continuing along the path blazed by Cimabue, Duccio and Giotto freed Western art from the rigid and frozen style of the neo-Byzantine school.

Duccio's best known work is the main alter of the cathedral in Siena. Known locally as the *Maesta*, Duccio's alter panels reveal a true blending of Gothic and Byzantine techniques with a new attention given to the humanity of the characters being portrayed. The center panel depicts the "Madonna Enthroned" with the Christ child. The painting has a three-dimensional quality absent in earlier medieval paintings. Both Mary and Jesus are depicted in a natural style with pleasant facial expressions.

Most art historians believe that Giotto served an apprenticeship under the supervision of Cimabue, but the student revealed far more talent than his master. Like Cimabue, Giotto excelled when painting on a monumental scale. His most famous murals were painted in the Scrovegni Chapel in Padua during the first decade of the fourteenth century. Like St. Francis of Assisi, Giotto loved the natural world. The realism of his art foreshadowed the works of painters during the Italian Renaissance.

UNIVERSITIES

Christianity permeated the soul of Western Europe in the Middle Ages and the Church regarded itself as the embodiment of Christ on earth. In the Book of Genesis, the earth is described as, "a formless wasteland, and darkness covered the abyss, while a mighty wind swept over the waters." Through the act of creation, God brought order out of chaos. In a sense, the Medieval Church attempted to do the same thing.

The invasions, wars and general chaos of the early Middle Ages impeded the intellectual

growth of Europeans. Throughout the Dark Ages, monasteries and other institutions of the Church preserved and protected Latin manuscripts from the period of the Roman Empire and continued the traditions of a classical education. Clerics also served in the bureaucracies of medieval rulers because few Europeans outside of the Church were literate.

Schools associated with monasteries were generally designed to train young men in the study of the Bible and in the writings of the early founders of the Christian Church, however, by the twelfth century, schools associated with cathedrals were often surrounded by vibrant urban communities. The growing wealth and stability of Europe fostered an interest in a broader education. An expansion of trade introduced new ideas. In Bologna, wealthy merchants created schools to train their children. Merchants in other Italian cities involved in the Mediterranean trade soon

One of the most notable features of the Notre Dame de Paris is the flying buttresses. The cathedral was started in 1163 and the flying buttresses were added between 1230 and 1250 to give support to the structure.

imitated the merchants of Bologna. The earliest universities would emerge from the cathedral schools in northwestern Europe and the more secular schools of Italy.

In a sense, the early universities were associated with the guild system. In the north, master teachers formed educational guilds. In Italy, students controlled the educational guilds.

Due to the Italian focus on trade and municipal government, it is hardly surprising that the scholars of Italy would demonstrate a profound interest in the study of law. The rise of the University of Bologna is associated with the revitalization of the study of Roman law.

Irnerius (1055-1130) is generally given credit for sparking a revival of interest in law. Of obscure origins, Irnerius first gained notoriety as a professor of rhetoric. His renown as a legal scholar is based upon his study of the ***Corpus Juris Civilis.*** During the sixth century, the Emperor Justinian ordered a compilation and distillation of Roman law. This body of Roman law and the legal principles that emerged from it were utilized in the courts of the Byzantine

Oxford University in England grew out of a local school in the town during the twelfth century. The university received its formal charter from King Henry III in 1248.

Empire throughout the Middle Ages. However, the customary law of the Germanic barbarians largely replaced the traditions of Roman law in Western Europe. Irnerius offered his students the first comprehensive commentaries on the ***Corpus Juris Civilus*** of Justinian, as well as contemporary law codes.

To protect themselves from high prices being charged by landlords and store owners, Bologna's students organized two guilds, each headed by a rector. The master teachers (professors) had to agree to the rules set by the guilds and enforced by the rectors. Fines were levied against masters who began their lectures late or who exceeded their time limit. In addition to civil and church law, the young scholars at Bologna could also choose to study rhetoric or medicine.

Greek and Arabs scholars had a great influence on educational developments in southern Italy. Both were intensely interested in finding herbal remedies for diseases. Salerno emerged as the focal point for medical studies in Europe. During the twelfth century, King Roger II of Sicily ordered that those wishing to practice medicine within his kingdom must first be permitted to do so by the masters of Salerno.

The University of Paris was famed for the study of theology and philosophy. By the twelfth century, it had emerged as the greatest center of intellectual life north of the Alps. The strength of the French monarchy offered a stability that helped foster academic pursuits. The prosperity of the town also aided in attracting teachers to the cathedral school of Notre Dame. However, the transformation of the cathedral school into a university was largely due to the quality of its teachers.

In the early twelfth century, Peter Abelard (1079-1142) was generally regarded as the greatest teacher of his day. By all accounts, he was brilliant, egotistical, controversial, and eloquent. As a student, young Abelard had the audacity to challenge his teacher to a public debate. He first gained fame for a series of lectures on the Book of Ezekiel. Following his triumph, he settled in Paris to teach theology. Having little money, Peter boarded in the home of Fulbert, the canon of Notre Dame. He soon fell in love with Fulbert's niece, Heloise, and impregnated her. The couple secretly married, but they tried to hide the union to preserve Abelard's chances for promotion to a high rank within the Church. Feeling that his family had been dishonored, Fulbert hired thugs to castrate Abelard. Following the attack, Abelard entered the monastery at St. Denis, and Heloise became a nun. The castration ended their physical passion, but the two would continue to correspond for the remainder of their lives.

Abelard's reputation was based primarily on his willingness to apply the test of critical reasoning to Scripture and the writings of the fathers of the early Christian Church. He would begin with a proposition. He would then cite quotations written by Christian authorities affirming the proposition. Next, he would cite quotations from the same authors denying the validity of the same proposition. He allowed his students to reach their own conclusions after viewing matters from both sides.

Abelard was no enemy of Christianity. He hoped to use logic to defend the teachings of the Church, but he was frequently misunderstood. His work was condemned on two occasions, and St. Bernard of Clairvaux emerged as a bitter rival within the Church. In spite of his controversial teachings, he never failed to delight his students. When forbidden to lecture on French soil, he spoke from the limb of a tree.

Abelard's notoriety attracted other talented teachers to Paris. By the end of the twelfth century, the chancellor of the school had the authority to license instructors and permit masters to lecture in and around the Cathedral of Notre Dame. Due to limited space near the cathedral, teachers began to set up schools on the left bank of the Seine River. Some time during the latter part of the century, the master teachers organized themselves and began to establish standards for admission into their guild. King Philip II of France officially granted a charter to the masters and students of Paris in 1200.

During the course of the thirteenth century, the masters of arts organized themselves under the leadership of a rector while the professors of theology, canon law and medicine organized themselves under the leadership of deans. After a prolonged struggle, the rector was recognized as the leader of the entire university.

In 1167, King Henry II of England ordered the English scholars at Paris to return home. Oxford soon emerged as the center of higher education in England. By 1209, as many as three thousand students were living in the town.

Students paid low fees for their classes. Their greatest expense came from renting books. Most masters taught by reading from the text of a book, then making extensive comments to explain the passages. Students took notes as best they could in the hopes of later passing oral examinations. Strict rules were established at many universities to prevent physical attacks upon the instructors when they administered their examinations.

Medieval universities always sought to exempt their students from the jurisdiction of local courts. Riots often occurred when local authorities attempted to arrest students for criminal conduct. If a conflict between the students and townspeople continued for an extended period, university officials would usually ask the king to intervene.

SCHOLASTICISM

During the remainder of the twelfth and thirteenth centuries, the scholars of Paris and its sister institutions built upon the philosophical foundation laid by Abelard. Peter Lombard (1100-1160) rigorously applied Abelard's method of logic to his analysis of fundamental theological questions. Lombard's *Book of Sentences* became the theological text at universities throughout Western Europe by 1200.

The reintroduction of the works of Aristotle into Europe during the mid-twelfth century helped to fuel the intellectual rebirth of the period. Ironically, Arab Moslems would introduce the Christian scholars of the West to the writings of the Greek philosopher.

As the Arabs conquered the southern and eastern portions of the Byzantine Empire during the eighth and ninth centuries, they absorbed schools of Greek philosophy. For centuries,

Islamic scholars attempted to reconcile Greek philosophy with the teachings of the Koran. The greatest of these Islamic philosophers were Ibn Sina (Avicenna) and Ibn Rushd (Averroes).

Abu Ali Al-Hussain Ibn Abdallah Ibn Sina (981-1037) was born near Bukhara in central Asia. As a young man, he studied both the Koran and the natural sciences. During his lifetime, he was better known for his abilities as a physician than for his philosophical writings. In his *Canons of Medicine,* he reviewed all medical knowledge available at the time. This encyclopedic work remained the standard text for students of medicine in the Islamic world for six hundred years. Ibn Sina accurately described the function of heart valves in the pumping of blood through the circulatory system. He also recognized the importance of psychology in human health. *Canons of Medicine* was translated into Latin in the twelfth century and became the text book for most medical schools in Europe during the late Middle Ages.

In the *Book of Healing,* Ibn Sina attempted to compile an encyclopedia of philosophical and scientific knowledge. He divided knowledge into two realms—the theoretical and the practical. In the area of theoretical knowledge, he tried to reconcile ideas drawn from the writings of Aristotle and Neoplatonic philosophers with the theology of the Koran.

Like the Neoplatonic writers who influenced early Christian theologians, Ibn Sina taught that all being emanated from a single, creative source. He believed that creative source was God. Using Aristotelian logic, Ibn Sina concluded that since God is a creator by nature and since God is eternal, the process of creation must be eternal.

Abul-Waleed Muhammad Ibn Rushd (1128-1198) was both a physician and a jurist. Born in Cordova, Spain, Ibn Rushd was descended from a family of scholars. At 44, he was appointed a judge in Seville. Inspite of his legal duties, he found time to translate and condense Aristotle's *de Anima.* After two years, he returned to Cordova where he continued to translate and comment on Aristotle's metaphysical works.

Ibn Rushd was clearly Aristotelian in his outlook. He believed that the universe was eternal (without beginning or end), yet, he opposed the concept that an individual soul was immortal. Rather, he believed in the existence of a universal intellect that functioned in individual people. Though the individual perished, the universal intellect continued. Ibn Rushd's philosophical writings seemed to contradict the Koran, and he was vigorously attacked by other Islamic teachers.

To defend himself against his critics, Ibn Rushd advocated the "double truth" theory. Truth is understood clearly in philosophy, but it is expressed allegorically in theology. The teachings of the Koran were true but expressed in such a way that ordinary people could understand them.

In addition to Islamic writers, Jewish scholar Moses ben Maimon or Maimonides (1135-1204) had a major impact on the Christian scholars of late Middle Ages. Maimonides fled his native Spain for North Africa when the puritanical Almoravides conquered the Iberian Peninsula. While serving as a physician to the Sultan of Egypt in Cairo, Maimonides wrote ethical works based on the study of the Torah and the Talmud. His *Mishneh Torah* became a standard guide for Jewish practice.

Maimonides is generally considered to be a religious rationalist. He condemned those who advocated a literal interpretation of the Torah. Rather, he felt that when statements in the Torah clearly contradicted reason, they should be interpreted figuratively.

Maimonides used reason and logic to prove the existence of God using Aristotelian logic.

He viewed God as both first cause and as necessary Being. In spite of Maimonides' successful attempts to reconcile Greek philosophy with Jewish theology, he was condemned by three leading rabbis in France. Having been forcefully denounced by local Jewish leaders, the French Inquisition burned copies of his books circulating in Paris.

The works of Moslem and Jewish scholars began to reach European Christians by way of Sicily and Spain, regions where Christians, Jews, and Moslems lived in close proximity to one another. During the twelfth century, the archbishop of Toledo patronized scholars who translated the scientific works of Aristotle from Arabic into Latin. European intellectuals quickly developed an insatiable appetite for the writings of Aristotle regarding all fields of study.

The early founders of the Christian Church were primarily influenced by the mysticism of Neoplatonic philosophers. The materialism of Aristotle was difficult to reconcile with the spiritualism inherent in Christianity or Islam. Some Church leaders felt that the writings of Aristotle would lead people into heresy. In spite of attempts by religious leaders to ban some of Aristotle's scientific essays, the scholars of Paris continued to read them.

Using the dialectical method developed by Abelard and perfected by Lombard, Thomas Aquinas (1225-1274) reconciled Aristotelian knowledge with the divinely revealed truths of Christianity. He maintained that humans could discover many truths about the natural world through experience and reason. However, supernatural truths are revealed to humanity through the grace of God. On topics where Aristotle seemed to contradict the teachings of Christianity, Aquinas employed Aristotelian logic to refute the scientific conclusions of the Greek master. Aquinas maintained that Aristotle never proved that the universe was eternal because such a proposition was impossible to prove. Regarding other areas of conflict, Aquinas argued that Ibn Rushd had misinterpreted Aristotle or had added his own thoughts.

Thomas Aquinas is generally recognized as the greatest philosopher of his day and his *Summa Theologica* the greatest example of medieval scholasticism. Centuries after his death, the Roman Catholic Church would accept the teachings of Aquinas as its official theology. Yet, in his lifetime, he was attacked for emphasizing reason over faith.

Not all Christian theologians of the thirteenth century were influenced by Aristotle. St. Bonaventure's writings continued to show the influence of St. Augustine of Hippo on Christian thought.

Giovanni Fidanza (1221-1274) was born in Bagnorea in northern Italy. It is believed he became known as Bonaventure because his mother petitioned St. Francis of Assisi to pray for her son during a childhood illness. When the boy recovered, she shouted, "O buona ventura!" which, translated into English means, "Oh good fortune!"

Bonaventure entered the Franciscan Order as a young adult and was sent to study under the famed Franciscan teacher Alexander Hales in Paris. While a student, he met and befriended Thomas Aquinas. In 1257, Bonaventure was chosen Minister General of the Franciscan Order, and he worked hard to end the conflict between Spiritual and Conventual Franciscans. The Spirituals demanded that members of the order maintain a strict rule of poverty. The Conventuals supported Pope Innocent IV's decision to allow the papacy to hold property for the use of the Franciscan friars. Though a Conventual, Bonaventure was respected by the Spirituals for his attempt to curb materialism within the order and for his piety and toleration. Bonaventure gained fame for composing the standard biography of St. Francis of Assisi. Pope Gregory X elevated him to the rank of Cardinal and Bishop of Albano.

Bonaventure believed that reason should be used exclusively to support faith. He denied Aristotle's claim to the eternity of the universe. He also argued that the beauty and goodness of humanity was directly related to the fact that we were created by God. As emanations of God, human beings embody a footprint of the divine nature of our Creator.

VERNACULAR LITERATURE AND DANTE

The Christian Church gave Western Europe a spiritual unity during the Middle Ages and the language of the Church was Latin. Virtually all of the theological and scholarly works of the period were written in Latin. In spite of the universality of Latin, some medieval poets preferred the use of their native languages when producing verse.

During the Dark Ages, the epics and sagas of Germanic peoples were recorded in the vernacular, but few of these early manuscripts survived those turbulent centuries. The heroic deeds of the warrior *Beowulf* were written in an early form of English. The poem provides modern readers with the best example of this type of literature.

By 1100, troubadours were writing, and sometimes singing, love poetry in southern France. Eleanor of Aquitaine (1122-1202) made this form of vernacular poetry fashionable throughout France when she married King Louis VII. During the thirteenth century the love songs of the troubadours would spread to Germany and Italy.

The lyrical poetry of the troubadours was primarily written for the benefit of medieval ladies. Men preferred the *chansons de geste*—narrative poems glorifying political conflict and battle. The greatest of the chansons was the *Song of Roland*. It describes a political rivalry within the court of Charlemagne and later a great battle against the Moslem forces in Spain.

By the late twelfth century, medieval writers and poets were entertaining their audiences with fables, legends, and histories drawn from a great variety of sources. English, French, and German authors wrote of the adventures of the legendary King Arthur and his virtuous knights. Geoffrey de Villehardouin would record his memories of the Fourth Crusade. The legend of the great Christian warrior El Cid was memorialized in Spain.

Dante Alighieri (1265-1321) would emerge as the greatest medieval Italian poet. Dante was born in the thriving city of Florence to a middle-class family. Inspired by the beauty of a young woman named Beatrice, Dante began writing love poetry but lost interest in it when Beatrice died. At the age of thirty, Dante became involved in Florentine politics and was an active member of the "White" faction. In 1302, while Dante was on a diplomatic mission, the rival "Black" faction, with the support of Pope Boniface VIII, gained control of Florence. Dante was banished from the republic. He spent the next twenty years in exile. Dante found employment at the courts of various Italian princes, but he hoped for a unification of Italy under the leadership of Emperor Henry VII. He never returned to Florence and was very bitter about his exile.

Dante's fame rests primarily on his composition of the *Divine Comedy*. Set in 1300, the author is taken on a mythical journey through Hell, Purgatory, and Heaven. The Latin poet Virgil escorts Dante through Hell and Purgatory.

Hell was described as a vast pit where the spirits of the damned are tortured according to the nature and gravity of their sins. Some of these spirits are identified by name. Dante placed Pope Boniface VIII in the eighth ring of Hell even though the Pope was still very much alive in 1300. The bottom of the pit was reserved for Judas Iscariot and Brutus, the leader of the conspiracy to assassinate Julius Caesar.

Purgatory was depicted as a mountain reaching into the sky. Like the pit of Hell, Purgatory consisted of levels or rings. The more petty the sins, the higher the elevation of the sinner. Unlike Hell, the suffering souls of Purgatory retained the hope of release from their torment.

Since Virgil was not a Christian, Dante left him as he entered Heaven. Beatrice, the object of Dante's youthful affection, guided the poet through Paradise. In his assent through Heaven, he saw the apostles of Jesus. Eventually, he was allowed to enter the Empyrean of God, where St. Bernard of Clairvaux acted as his escort and led him to Mary, the Mother of Jesus. His journey culminated with a vision of the Holy Trinity.

Because the *Divine Comedy* was written in Tuscan, rather than Latin, it was accessible to a wider audience. The popularity of the poem helped make Tuscan the literary language of the Italian Peninsula. The ***Divine Comedy*** is also noteworthy as a great synthesis of medieval ideas. Dante presents his reader with an eternal world organized by God. He drew heavily from the philosophy of Thomas Aquinas and the scholars of Paris.

Dante's work indicates that he sympathized with those who wanted to reform the Christian Church of his day. Pope Boniface VIII was placed in Hell for corrupting the Church with his political activities. Controversial figures like Joachim of Floris (1132-1202) were placed in Heaven along side the early founders of the Church. Joachim preached that there were three great epochs of human history. The first was inaugurated by Moses, and it was characterized by the teachings of the Old Testament. Jesus Christ inaugurated the second, and it is spiritually dominated by the teachings of the New Testament. The third epoch would arrive in the future, and the Holy Spirit would direct it. During this final stage of human history, all would live simply and peacefully in a state of Christian anarchy. In the latter part of the thirteenth century, a group known as the Spiritual Franciscans began to preach that St. Francis had inaugurated the coming of the third epoch. The vocal members of the Spiritual Franciscans were persecuted by the Church.

THE ADVENTURES OF MARCO POLO

During the early years of the first millennium A. D. merchants from the Roman world eagerly traded for the spices and herbs of the East Indies and for the raw silk of China. The silk trade survived the fall of Rome and continued to flourish through the early Middle Ages. Greek merchants from the Byzantine Empire gained access to the products of the Far East by establishing trade centers along the coast of the Black Sea and along the coast of Abyssinia (Ethiopia). Wars between the Byzantine Empire and Persia occasionally disrupted the trade but never stopped it. The conquest of North Africa by Arab Moslems put an end to trade between Europe and Ethiopia, but travel along the Silk Roads through Central Asia to China continued throughout the Middle Ages.

The Italian city-state of Venice actively traded with the Greeks of Constantinople (Istanbul) and the Byzantine Empire. The Venetians traded slaves, military equipment, arms, and raw cloth in exchange for the products of the Far East. These same Venetian merchants would transport and assist the warriors of the Fourth Crusade in their conquests of Zara (Zadar) and Constantinople.

The Doge's Palace, Venice, Italy. By the late Middle Ages, Venice had grown wealthy due to her extensive trade connections with Greeks and Arabs in the eastern Mediterranean. Venice was near the height of its power when the Polos began their journey to China.

Once they had conquered the Byzantine capital, the crusading knights established the Latin Empire of Constantinople consisting of Greece, Thrace, and Macedonia. To reward their Venetian allies, the merchants of Venice were granted special trading privileges.

In 1258 Michael Palaeologus (1224-1282) rallied Greek forces in an attempt to drive out the Latin conquerors to recreate the Byzantine Empire. He obtained the aid of Genoese merchants who helped to neutralize the powerful Venetian navy. In 1261, the Byzantine army reconquered Constantinople, and the Genoese were granted commercial concessions within the new empire at the expense of the Venetians.

Just prior to the Greek reconquest of Constantinople, Venetian merchants Maffeo and Niccolo Polo landed in the Crimean Peninsula along the coast of the Black Sea. Traveling eastward into the vast Mongul Empire, the Venetian pilgrims stopped to trade at Surai on the Volga River. They later continued their journey until they arrived at the capital of the Great Khan in 1266. The Polo brothers were greatly impressed by both Kublai Khan (1215-1294) and his splendid city, Khanbalig (Beijing).

The Great Khan was extraordinarily curious about Europe, and he questioned the Polos at length about their religion and culture. The year after their arrival in China, Kublai Khan sent the Venetians back to Italy with a letter to the Pope requesting that he dispatch one hundred scholars to China so that his subjects might become better acquainted with European science and Christianity. The Venetian travelers did not return to their homeland until 1269.

After resting two years in Italy, Niccolo and Maffeo Polo began their return journey to China accompanied by Niccolo's teenage son, Marco, (1254-1324) and two Dominican friars, as well as gifts from Pope Gregory X. The hazards of the journey proved too great for the Dominicans, and they turned back. The Venetians continued their long, overland trek through Armenia, Persia, Afghanistan, and the Gobi Desert. In 1275, Niccolo presented his son, Marco, to the Great Khan at his palace. Marco Polo spent the next seventeen years of his life in the service of Kublai Khan. As a bureaucrat in the imperial service, he visited cities and towns throughout China, Siberia, Burma, and India. He was introduced to the use of paper currency, coal, asbestos fabric, and the imperial mail system. He was greatly impressed by the ability of the Chinese to manufacture large quantities of iron and salt.

The Polos were well rewarded for their services to the Khan, and in 1292 they left China to escort a Mongolian princess to Persia where she was scheduled to marry a prince. Upon delivery of the bride, the Polos made their way to the Black Sea and sailed westward to Constantinople and then on to Venice.

Trade wars between Italian city-states were all too common. In 1298, Marco Polo was captured during a naval battle between Venice and Genoa. While spending a year in captivity, he dictated a recollection of his Eastern adventures to Rustichello of Pisa. Certainly, Rustichello embellished Marco's tales. Published as *The Description of the World*, the book would become extremely popular.

In his own day, many questioned the veracity of Marco Polo's account of his travels. Yet his book provided Europeans with the best description of Central and East Asia for the next two centuries. It fascinated generations of readers and stimulated interest in the wealth of the Far East. Both Prince Henry the Navigator of Portugal and Christopher Columbus are reported to have read Rustichello's lively rendition of Polo's journeys.

CONCLUSION

Historian Joseph R. Strayer expressed the belief that medieval society began to stagnate during the course of the thirteenth century. The accomplishments of Europeans in that century lacked the originality and boldness of the twelfth century. He attributes this in part to an emphasis on legalism and rationalism.

In a sense, his analysis of the period is ironic. The lack of a reliable legal structure plagued the people of Western Europe for six centuries following the end of the Roman Empire. The popularity of rationalism among thirteenth-century

Roger Bacon argued that logic must be supported with experimentation for a theory to be correct.

scholars resulted from the birth of universities in the proceeding century. While Strayer recognizes that the developments of the thirteenth century are a logical outgrowth of trends that first appeared in the twelfth, he fails to see that many innovations appeared in both centuries.

Urban centers continued to show great vigor, and innovation was hardly lacking. In 1241, a mutual assistance pact was signed between the German cities of Lubeck and Hamburg. Smaller cities were later invited to join this association, which came to be known as the Hanseatic League. By 1300, this federation of towns along the Baltic Sea extended from the southern border of Denmark to Novgorod in Russia. The league also maintained "hanses" or factories in London and Bruges to facilitate its business interests in the North Sea region.

The Hanseatic League successfully dominated the trade in North European products like furs, fish, wax, naval stores, and salt for two centuries. At the height of its power in the fourteenth century, more than seventy towns were associated with the league.

Certainly not all scholastic philosophers employed logic exclusively to speculate about theological matters. Franciscan friar Roger Bacon (1214-1292) abandoned the teaching of philosophy to learn mathematics and to conduct scientific experiments. Unlike many philosophers of his time, he refused to rely exclusively on the writings of acknowledged authorities. He preferred to use empirical evidence as the source for knowledge. Although Bacon was often criticized and censured, Pope Clement IV (1265-1268) recognized his ability and defended him. Like Thomas Aquinas, Bacon believed that wisdom and faith were in harmony.

Few European peasants ever heard of the theological debates conducted by the scholars of Paris. Fewer still would have been able to read the *Divine Comedy* or the *Summa Theologica*. Most of those who could appreciate the great writers and teachers of the period lived in the cities and towns. The growing ranks of the new middle class prized literacy and served as a ready audience for new ideas.

Suggestions for Further Reading

Peter Abelard, *The Letters of Abelard and Heloise.* Betty Radice (trans.) (1974).

Thomas Aquinas, *Summa theologiae,* 60 volumes. Thomas Gilby, et al. (trans.) (1964-1973).

John W. Baldwin, *The Scholastic Culture of the Middle Ages, 1000-1300* (1971).

Christopher Brooke, *The Twelfth Century Renaissance* (1969).

Christopher Brooke and Roger Highfield, *Oxford and Cambridge* (1988).

Gabriel Campayre, *Abelard and the Origin and Early History of Universities* (1902).

Alan B. Cobban, *The Medieval Universities: Their Development and Organization* (1975).

Richard C. Dales, *The Intellectual Life in Western Europe in the Middle Ages* (1980).

Elizabeth Hamilton, *Heloise* (1967).

Henry Hersch Hart, *Marco Polo, Venetian Adventurer* (1967).

Charles Homer Haskins, *The Rise of Universities* (1957).

David Knowles, *The Evolution of Medieval Thought* (1962).

David Nicholas, *The Growth of the Medieval City: From Late Antiquity to the Early Fourteenth Century* (1997).

Henri Pirenne, *Medieval Cities: Their Origins and the Revival of Trade* (1956).

Joseph R. Strayer, *Western Europe in the Middle Ages: A Short History,* 3rd edition (1991).

Chapter 10

FROM FEAR TO HOPE, THE 1300'S

Cross from the Ossuary at Sedlec Czech Republic
All the decorations are from skeletons from the Black Death.

ANOTHER SIDE OF THE PICTURE

The history of the fourteenth century is written about men. Men in politics, men in war, men in the Church, and even men in the farm fields fill the pages of books. We have so few references to women that these few ladies tend to stand out as unique. The image of Joan of Arc leading soldiers in an almost holy crusade is one of those moments. Joan, in the early fifteenth century, belongs to the times as she was fighting in the Hundred Years' War that began in the early fourteenth century. As a woman soldier, Joan was not unique, and many women preceded her valiant efforts.

If we look closely, Joan had many predecessors. Isobel, Countess of Buchan, fought for Scottish independence even against her own husband's wishes. Jeanne de Danpierre fought with her husband for the French cause many years before Joan was born. Records about women in this period are sketchy and are mostly about noblewomen, but a few records stand out giving us clues and showing that women did play significant roles.

Phillipa of Hainault was a noblewoman who involved herself in much of the society and culture of the day. She was born in 1311 (possibly as late as 1314; birth records were not well kept, perhaps because so many children died in early infancy). Philippa was the youngest daughter of William, Count of Hainault, Holland and Zealand. An important man in his region, he became associated with Isabella, the wife of Edward II and Queen of England. Abroad to supposedly help her husband's international causes, Isabella was really looking for allies against Edward. In the complex political intrigues of the day, she introduced the idea that her son, the Crown Prince, marry Phillipa in exchange for her father's loyalty to Isabella's cause.

The Crown Prince met Phillipa briefly and agreed, as he was quite impressed with her. The marriage was quickly organized and performed at Valenciennes, Phillipa's home. Edward, however, was represented by a proxy and not even present at the ceremony. Soon the young bride left for England where, on January 24, 1328, another grand rite was held at York. By this time, Edward was king as his mother's plot had been successful and her husband had been forced to resign. After the wedding ceremony, Phillipa should have been crowned Queen, but Isabella refused to give up her own title.

As Edward's attachment and loyalty to his wife grew and his maturity demanded he be the actual king instead of his mother's puppet, Phillipa grew in power and popularity. In 1330, Edward had his mother sent off to a nunnery and her lover Mortimer executed. The new Queen's coronation was splendid, and the couple began a long and productive reign over their English subjects.

Phillipa was, as some historians have called her, a superwoman involving herself in a whole variety of adventures and interests. She introduced England to the weaving of her Flemish homeland as well as techniques for coal mining, which became important to the English economy. She founded Queens College at Oxford, and although no female would attend the university for many many years, her interest in education was important to English society. She enjoyed and supported the writings of

Geoffrey Chaucer and gave grants to the work of the French chronicler Michel Froissart who was living in England during her reign.

In 1346, Edward was away fighting in France, defending his claim to French lands and its crown. Meanwhile an uprising in Scotland threatened English control there and demanded immediate attention. Phillipa called on her English subjects to follow her, and she led them northward to victory. Her campaign was so successful that her troops captured the Scottish king, David Bruce.

The marriage to Edward was on the whole a happy one. Phillipa gave birth to twelve children, nine of whom survived to adulthood—a near record in those days of disease (the plague would hit England several times during her lifetime) and poor medical knowledge. The children, especially the sons, worked together, another near miracle in an age where claims to the throne could destroy even the closest relationships.

In standards we would find hard to endure, Phillipa did suffer through many of her husband's "indiscretions." Edward, as did most noblemen felt was their privilege, had a roving eye and the power to take whatever, or whomever, he wanted. Even in the scandalous time of the accusation that he raped the Countess of Salisbury, the Queen stood firm in her loyalty. Edward's affair with the notorious Alice Perrers (whom he married after Phillipa's death) was the talk of England, yet Phillipa continued to display her royal dignity.

On the August 14, 1369, Phillipa died at Windsor Castle, just a ways outside London. Only two of her sons, her favorite Edward, the Black Prince, and Thomas, were with her as the others were off fighting again for England. She blessed her children and praised the people of England. The writer Froissart wrote this tribute to the Great Lady:

In all her life, she did neither
In thought or deed
Anything whereby to lose her soul
As far as anyone could know.

Phillipa has few modern day admirers because her story is lost in the times of plague, war and political tensions. Her life, however, proves that on the other side of these cherished historical subjects, real people had to struggle and survive and make their days count in the lives of others.

Chronology

1300	Jubilee Year Proclaimed by the Pope
1305-1377	The Papacy resides in Avignon, France: The Babylonian Captivity
1320	First Western written mention of gunpowder
1324	Marco Polo returns to Italy from China
1337-1453	The First Hundred Years War between France and England
1340	Italians construct first paper mill; 7 water wheels drive the "machinery"
1347-1351	The Bubonic Plague
1350	Edward III introduces the foot, yard and acre as measurements
1356	Hanseatic League formed by Northern European merchants
1358	Jacquerie Revolt in France
1369-1405	Tamerlane, a descendant of Genghis Khan, attacks Russia, Persia, Turkey and India, defeats the Ottoman emperor
1378-1414	Popes in France and Rome: The Great Schism
1388	*Canterbury Tales* by Chaucer
1398	Wat Tyler's Rebellion in England
1431	Joan of Arc burned for witchcraft

THE BAD YEARS

In Western Civilization, the number 12 has a fairly good reputation. There were 12 disciples of Jesus; 12 months in a year; 12 inches in a foot; even 12 days of Christmas. In ancient times, there were 12 cities in the leagues of Ionia and Etruria and 12 tribes of Israel; the Romans composed 12 Tables for their laws. Touching on Western Civilization, there are 12 Proofs of Mohammed as a True Prophet. Even today, success can be measured by 12-Step programs. All of this connotes pleasantry, if not happiness, in the balance of 12. In many myths, 12 is the number of completeness.

The number 13, however, is frequently associated with bad times. That the number 13 is unlucky is probably one of the most consistent superstitions of Western Civilization. In the Bible, Revelations Chapter 13 predicts horrible events; the chapter begins ominously and it only gets worse in provoking terrors of the end of the world. Eighty-five percent of the references to 13 in the Bible are connected to something bad and usually horrible. Those looking for connections to the evil even count that the letters in the name Judas Iscariot add up to 13.

Many Christians believe Jesus was crucified on Friday 13, making for many fears as that day periodically arrives. There were, of course, 13 people at the Last Supper (Jesus and his 12 disciples—one of whom betrayed him, making only 12 good people). Across the United States, Europe, and Australia many people refuse to seat 13 guests at their tables, and many hotels and buildings skip 13 when numbering their floors.

In the course of Western Civilization, the century following 1300 was perhaps the most unpredictable and devastating to the population. Each year seemed to bring the world closer to its end. In order to find any hope, the people had to turn to new ideas and new social formulations to survive and make sense of their world.

WEATHER

The economic progress of the 1200s brought an increase in the population and the living standard of Europeans. The textile "explosion" brought new and finer material to clothing and "linens," which proved to be successful in trade all over the Mediterranean. As the new century arrived, there was much hope that growth and prosperity would continue. Success, however, depended on continued good luck as the population was quickly outstripping food and water supplies.

Soon after 1300, tell-tale signs of disaster began appearing. Bitter weather patterns loomed over much of the early part of the century. Some historians refer to the period as "The Little Ice Age." Unexpected drops in the temperature and torrential rains damaged crops of grains and flax, the sources of food and fabric, i.e., prosperity. Wheat, oat, hay, pork and beans were the substance of the European diet, as well as the basis for feeding their stock. With transportation of such crops limited to local circulation, any area hit by bad weather was doomed to poverty and starvation. From 1315 to 1317, almost all of Europe was, at the least, malnourished if not at death's door.

The weakened population suffered another blow when an epidemic of typhoid hit town and country during 1316; cities like Ypres in Belgium, the heart of the flourishing textile industry, lost perhaps 10 percent of their population. Animals, also underfed from the poor harvests, fell prey to disease in 1318, and another poor harvest in 1321 brought more suffering and death. By 1322, poor peasants survived on whatever food they could find, whether it was rancid, bug-ridden, or wormy. Unrest and discontent filled the hearts and minds of the few with any energy; families disintegrated and feudal loyalties were strained. With things going wrong everywhere, surely there was some message that God was sending to His People. By the middle of the century, the bubonic plague made it clear that God's wrath was upon the land.

POPES AND KINGS

During the 1200s, the majority of the popes in Rome held a firm hand on Western Christendom. As keeper of the keys to the kingdom of Heaven, they wielded both religious and secular power. In 1295, a new pope was installed, a strangely unsocial but spiritual man who was surely a sign of God's connection to His world. Before his elevation, Celestine V had lived in the wilds of the Abruzzi forests, hiding out in caves and looking for spiritual guidance. The cardinals elected him to show their dedication to holy ways. Five months after his election, however, the former hermit feared for his soul if he remained the chief priest and in an unprecedented move, resigned from the Holy See.

Benedetto Gaetano, one of the leading advisors to the papacy, was primed to take over in the crisis. His reputation as a great jurist of canon law and as a highly skilled diplomat seemed to make him a perfect candidate, and soon he became Boniface VIII. Some even believed that Gaetano had talked the politically incompetent Celestine to resign in the face of decreasing support for his ascetic ways.

It was definitely a time for a strong leader for many secular controversies were stirring the stability of Europe. Probably the most famous was the long conflict brewing between England and Scotland. The Scots repeatedly declared their independence from the English crown but were dominated by English politics. They appealed to the pope to arbitrate and demanded their freedom from the English, but occupation and control continued. In 1298, William Wallace ("Braveheart") led his troops against the English and, probably betrayed by another jealous Scot, was defeated, sent to England, and executed by drawing and quartering. Boniface warned the English king, Edward I, that Scotland was part of the pope's jurisdiction, but the king continued to rule over the Scots.

Edward seemed unimpressed by papal power. Geographically far from Rome, the king seized every opportunity to increase his own power. In 1294, he had demanded that churches and monasteries pay large sums to gain his protection. Based on an old papal ruling that lords could collect taxes to support holy crusades, Edward demanded that the religious orders pay for his "crusades" against the French.

The Pope had a double problem in dealing with the English. Not only were they defying his edicts, they were constantly tempting the French into war. Such an unstable condition gave increasing powers to the local monarchs at the expense of the Church. In France, Philip the Fair had a similarly disrespectful attitude toward papal positions. He had seized a number of areas previously considered part of the Holy See's possessions. In these wars, Philip had demanded the churches pay large amounts of taxes. France was the most powerful kingdom in all of Europe, and in some ways it was essential that Boniface find some sort of ally. Since working with the kings was impossible, he sought ways to build the power of the papacy above the secular rulers.

The power of the papacy had long been expressed in Papal Bulls, strong statements that carried the punishment of excommunication if disobeyed. (The name has no reference to the animal bull but from the word "bullum," a large lead disk attached to the most important papal documents and then stamped with the holy seal.) Boniface turned to this tool to calm the situation. *Clericis Laicos*, posted in February 1296, declared that secular authorities could not exact any funds or property from the Church unless the Pope gave a special dispensation. Princes who disobeyed the ruling would be excommunicated, meaning that Hell was the final destination of all who broke the rule. While Edward simply ignored the Bull, Philip dealt with it by declaring that no gold, silver, precious stones, weapons or food could be exported from his kingdom, even by the Church. Harassed and pressured by their secular rulers, priests, monks and even cardinals began to petition Boniface to help them. His Holiness responded that he did not mean to forbid voluntary contributions that could aid in the defense of a kingdom. He even added to the compromise by making Philip's grandfather, Louis IX, a saint. The pressure subsided, and for a brief two years the French and English declared a truce.

The year 1300 was a Jubilee year, and Boniface made the most of it. He declared that those who came to Rome to celebrate would be specially blessed. In June, for the Feast of Saints Peter and Paul, 200,000 pilgrims filled the city and rejoiced. Boniface dreamed of reuniting Europe under a papal hegemony. Every country in Europe, and even some from Asia, had answered the call. But, except for the son of the King of Naples, no king or prince could be found in the crowd. Boniface's plan would quickly fall apart.

Misreading the situation and believing that he had a great deal of support, Boniface issued a new Bull to clarify the papal position. In *Ausculta Fili,* Boniface declared that the Vicar of Christ had been placed by God over kings and all temporal rulers. "He is the keeper of the keys, the judge of the living and the dead, and sits on the throne of justice, with power to extirpate all iniquity."

The Bull brought forth all the enemies of the Pope who quickly decided to support the King of France and his struggle against the Church. In fact, some of these churchmen so opposed the power of Boniface they created a false Bull pretending that the Pope had really announced that he had all power in heaven and earth. This "bull" circulated through France and aroused a patriotic cry against the Roman usurper.

The papacy gathered its supporters and called a council to meet in Rome in October 1302. The king declared that all goods belonging to any ecclesiastic who attended the council would be confiscated. The battle continued, although the council finally met with only a few representatives. Two bulls were then promulgated. The first excommunicated anyone who interfered with persons trying to attend the council; the second, the more famous, reasserted papal claims. In *Unam Sanctam*, the basic foundation for the Church position was set down using the famous fathers of the past, especially Thomas Acquinas and St. Bernard. First, there was only one Church and no salvation beyond its organization. Second, only the Roman Pope could dispense the Church's justice. Third, the world was divided into the realms of the spiritual and the temporal. The second was ruled by princes who understood the leadership of the first. Clear and logical, the Bull surely placed the King of France and his allies in error.

Philip quickly had his scholars prepare an answer to the Bull that showed the Pope had overstepped his rightful place. In quick succession, he called his supporters to declare that the Roman bishop was a heretic, made peace with England, and called on that kingdom to join him in his opposition to the treasonous Pope, and supported all the claims of temporal leaders who would join his cause. Boniface was declared a "simonist, robber, and a heretic," and many in Europe looked to Philip to save their souls in this time of crisis.

Boniface retreated to his family estate in Agnagi, declaring that if Philip did not stop his accusations he would be excommunicated. Philip responded by appointing a French prosecutor to charge Boniface with all sorts of ethical, moral and legal crimes. Philip sent troops to capture him. On September 7, 1303, the soldiers arrived and demanded their prey, the Pope. They seized him, but papal troops barred their escape. Finally the French retreated, leaving the aged holy man behind. Humiliated and bruised, Boniface returned to Rome, but on October 11, he died from the shock of the confrontation.

Boniface's successor tried to balance the interests of Church and state and even increased the number of French cardinals. His brief tenure led, in 1305, to the election of a Frenchman who took the name Clement V. With a little pressure from the king, the attractiveness of the beautiful French city, and the prospect of an alliance with the most powerful temporal leaders of Europe, Clement took the papacy out of the divisive Rome. He moved to Avignon in Southern France, just across from the German side of the Rhone River. There popes resided until 1378, living in luxury but under the supervision of the French kings.

Tradition connected the papacy with Rome and the time in Avignon, referred to as the Second Babylonian Captivity in reference to the Jewish captivity by the Babylonians many years before, brought an end to the domination of the Church in Western Europe. Although it would remain the only official Christian Church until the early 1500s, Church policies and leadership came under the critical eye of the secular world.

As the kings and princes of Europe turned their attention from Rome to Avignon, they quickly began to distrust the new set up. They considered (rightly so) the Avignon popes were the puppets of the French kings.

The Avignon papacy tried to establish its supremacy over Christian Europe by beautifying the city. It did so, however, by cutting resources to the parishes, taxing bishoprics, and reducing funds throughout Christendom. It made the selling of church offices (simony) a means of increasing revenue, and the sale of indulgences, documents sold to assure the pardon of sins, became a common practice. Encouraging all priests to raise funds, the popes declared that the practice and "sanctity" of poverty was heretical. The spiritual center of Western Christendom seemed to have more in common with business ventures than with its spiritual traditions of its past.

In the years that popes resided at Avignon, the general populace began to see that spiritualism had been translated into materialism. Few reform efforts were implemented, and the papacy's reputation as the spiritual leader began to suffer. As the crises of the fourteenth century increased, the Church failed to serve its people. Wars devastated land and people and revolved only around greedy land disagreements rather than the spiritual causes of the Holy Crusades. Disease and famine left many dead, and when the plague arrived, many priests were so frightened they refused to perform their duty and administer the sacraments, much less the last rites, which meant that the souls of the dead would be sent to Hell. Once the Church had used the devil and his agents to keep the religious faith of its followers; now it seemed to be turning away from its people and leaving them to be victims of the Evil one. Separated from the traditional means for hope and salvation, the people began to rediscover old pagan rituals and mysticism; the decline of papal power also gave more respect to national leaders and local religious leaders. The luxurious lives of the churchmen did not put emphasis on the road to heaven but rather put the worldly needs and desires at center stage.

ENDLESS WARFARE

Ever since human beings began to record their history, there seems to have been a succession of violence. Whether it was over food, territory, or even women, men lined up to hurt and kill each other. The 1300s were an almost continuous succession of battle, including the vaguely accurate title of the "Hundred Years of War" between the English and the French.

In 1066, William of Normandy had arrived on the Dover shore, and as his troops moved inland, they defeated the armies of Harold the Saxon. The Norman vassal of the King of France believed that he was the rightful heir to the throne of England. The former king of England, Edward the Confessor, had looked to William as his heir until his deathbed revision naming Harold the Saxon as King. After William arrived from Normandy and killed Harold, the English crown passed to his line. From that time on, through intermarriage and conquest, England and France were joined, although not united.

By 1300, France was the undeniable leader of the European political scene. With a population of 21 million, it dwarfed its chief competitor with only a fifth of that number. The concept of "nation" was beginning to take hold. There was a firm belief that peoples from similar ancestors were somehow linked under a social and political organization. Kings had begun to assume a special, almost magical role, an almost semi-divine role that paralleled the positions of cardinals and bishops. As far as Philip was concerned, he was on an equal level with the Pope. When, in 1303, the papacy was transferred to Avignon, the reigning French king made certain that the next six popes paid attention to the needs of the French kingdom.

In England, King Edward was similarly claiming that he had a religious role, and he meant to challenge anyone who lessened the claims of his nation. Maneuvering and bluffing, both kings began a series of threats that would bring their people into some of the worst battles Western Civilization had yet to see.

Philip first turned his vengeance on powerful allies of the Church, the most famous was the Templars. Their power was based on the wealth they had accumulated during the Crusades and their reputation for doing good among the populace; the Templars held a supreme respect from both church and secular circles. Philip began his campaign by forcing the members, particularly the old men, to swear that the Order was a treasonous group threatening the monarchy. If they did not give in easily, they were tortured, sometimes to the point of death, and after confessing, were put to death. In the final days of the Order's strength, the Grand Master was burned at the stake and in his last moments asked God to bring his judgement upon Philip and his Pope. The Templar's Curse seemed very real when Clement died within the month, and seven months later, Philip, hale, hearty and enjoying life, fell dead. Then, his three sons died after reigning only a few years. These sudden tragedies left the throne of France vacant, and a war among its claimants became one of the central events of European history for about 125 years.

In 1328, three contenders sought to become the French king. There was the grandson of Philip, who perhaps had the best claim but was the 16-year-old King of England, Edward III. Edward's mother was Philip's daughter, but she was notorious for her political intrigues, including killing her husband so that her son could rule. The French people feared the return of this evil queen and hoped she would stay in England. The other two claimants were Philip of Valois, son of the brother of Philip the Fair, and Philip Evreaux, son of Philip's half brother. A settlement was made that Philip of Valois would be the new king, and temporarily there was peace.

The Valois line began with splendor but it was soon obvious that the young king had no training for his new vocation and was dominated by his wife, Jeanne de Bourgogne, a woman similar to Edward's mother in style and evil conspiracy. Philip on the other hand was similar to his great grandfather, the now revered St. Louis, and he disregarded the significance of the politics of the day. Philip preferred to pray for guidance and left practical matters to others. In 1337, goaded by his wife and greedy politicians, Philip unwisely confiscated the province of Guienne, considered by the English their territory. The fragile peace that had come with Philip's accession was now destroyed, and Edward declared himself the legitimate king of France as well as England. The complicated alliances from heredity and marriage now divided Europe as each side pressed their connections to gain friends and allies.

Medieval Society

Since the end of the Roman empire, European areas fell into local rule with lords and nobles forming armies to both protect and exploit their peasants and serfs. Three major classes divided the society. The nobility counted on hereditary right to maintain an aura of power and control. The clergy depended on their connection to God to gain respect and authority. Last, the Third Estate was a conglomerate of everyone else. Rich businessmen, lawyers, doctors and other professionals were classed with craftsmen, peasants, landless serfs, beggars and anyone else left at the bottom of the population. This last group made up most of society and was denied most civil and political rights. Of course, the biggest right they were denied was to be part of the warrior class to which the nobility claimed exclusive membership. They were, therefore, dependent on the "protective" services of the nobility. For the peasants and serfs, at least most of them, there was grudging acceptance of the situation. The more wealthy of the Third Estate would slowly make demands to separate from them and eventually would form a middle class.

The concept of chivalry permeated the nobility. Fighting was manhood for the upper class, and every able-bodied noble was trained to defend his and his lord's honor. In the previous centuries, protecting the local people and serving their lords through holy crusades made up much of the obligations of knights, as well as princes and kings. With the journeys to the Holy Land limited, these soldiers turned to other ways of proving they were fit and brave. Tournaments and local squabbles became the order of the day. They were far from glorious, and perhaps the lack of honor and high goals turned the events into vicious personal battles.

Violence was not simply a matter of swords and brute strength. Most soldiers donned about 55 pounds of armor and had to balance themselves on horseback. Even on foot, the weight of the metal made the man awkward during battle, increasing his chances of being wounded or simply falling down. Since the suit of metal covered vital parts, wounds were often to the face, neck or underarms, which were not so easily protected. These wounds were easily infected or led to massive blood loss, causing painful death if the injured was "lucky," or a long, slow and very painful existence if the life of the person were "spared," meaning living with debilitating and crippling injuries.

New weapons added horror to the scene. The longbow, about six feet in length, was invented during the reign of Edward I. It made fighting less personal since it allowed a skilled archer to shoot an arrow at an enemy over 300 yards away, as well as permitting him to "load" quickly and send off many shots in a quick period of time. In 1325, the *pot de fer* was a small handheld cannon that fired an iron ball at the enemy. This device was almost as dangerous to the holder as to its target since it frequently blew up in the face of the person discharging the bullet. Still technology beyond sword fighting and spear throwing began to change the face of war. The nobles rose to the challenge and believed that the only course of action was to kill and win. Their horses had made them the best soldiers, but guns and longbows would eventually change the strategy of fighting. War took on a more impersonal tone as soldiers could kill each other without face to face combat.

Europe at War

At first Edward III demonstrated England's military superiority with a naval victory at the Battle of Sluys. The English did not command the seas with a superior navy but won by using their expertise with the longbow. The French soldiers had little chance against the rain of arrows that flew at them while they hurried to find a way to counterattack. Victory was, however, short lived because Edward did not have a land force to follow his triumph.

In the areas disputed between the two kings, the populace often played one side against the other. In France, however, people tended to lean towards a French king who would be there to protect them rather than a far away overlord who might just collect taxes and confiscate their property. Edward was not seen as a noble rescuer from an evil French king but more often a young greedy royal who wanted to increase his wealth for his own personal motives. By claiming he was the rightful heir to the French throne, he could, however, negotiate with any French noblemen opposed to Philip's rule. The alliances would be tangled and fragile, so the war took on horrendous tones.

In a local battle that has now become infamous, the French and English fought for the dukedom of Brittany. Each side backed a candidate for the French throne, and the French choice was Charles de Blois, the nephew of Philip IV. On the one hand, Charles was an extremely pious man. He prayed everyday and confessed every evening. He put pebbles in his shoes and wore rough clothing to scratch his skin. He slept on straw and tied his body with cords to cut into his flesh so that he constantly knew the sad state of being a sinful human. When it came to warfare, however, Charles had a totally different character. Arriving at Nantes that he claimed as his territory, he impressed the citizens with his seriousness by having his catapults hurl into the city the heads of thirty men he had previously captured.

In Flanders, long under the influence of the English because of their commercial ties for wine and wool, different conditions produced other gruesome scenes. The nobility in Flanders were pro-French while the merchants were supporters of the English. In 1302, the French attacked the town of Courtrai, but the Flemish workers came together to stop the line of invaders. As confusion riddled the French troops, the defenders, armed only with wooden pikes, baited them to cross the canals into the city. The French fell into the pits, and their enemy killed them like ancient warriors had speared animals they trapped in deep holes. According to many accounts, seven hundred gold spurs were taken from the dead and triumphantly hung on the city gates. Twenty-five years later, the Flemish would fall in huge numbers as the French gained a victory at Cassel. Although the French knighthood was to some degree vindicated, the success of the Flemish workers still proved that the average citizen was a useful soldier in times of crisis. The little crack in the nobility's control of the military would eventually grow into the earthquake where citizen armies would terrorize society. (See the French Revolution)

The wars between the French and English not only massacred populations and destroyed large sections of land but damaged the European economy, which had begun to grow beyond its old feudal roots. Both Philip and Edward had to borrow heavily to finance their armies, and when they lost, loans could not be repaid. This was especially true of commercial houses in Italy where the beginnings of commercial banking were starting to challenge the old system of barter. In Florence by the early 1340s, three major banking houses failed thus shutting down the growing economy. Goods sat in warehouses, and salaries went unpaid; people feared that they would starve because they were less dependent on their land-based economy. Perhaps God was unhappy with their faith in materialism; perhaps wars against fellow Christians were great sins; perhaps they ought to return to simple lives as their ancestors had struggled on earth for preparation of the joys of heaven. Perhaps....

THE ARRIVAL OF SATAN'S KINGDOM

If war and economic upheavals were not enough to convince many that God's wrath had come down upon Europe, the year 1347 brought certainty of the fact for it was in that year death

The Black Death decimated populations across Europe, making strong laborers a scarce and valuable commodity. In this medieval illustration, a victim of the plague shows the doctor his large swellings in his armpits and groins.

spread across the continent as eerily as Moses' plague had killed the Egyptians thousands of years before. When it was over, one third to one half of Europe was dead and had died horrible and painful deaths at that.

Although it was not clear to the Europeans, the plague resulted from their quest for luxuries and a higher standard of living. Trade, which had slowly grown during and after the Crusades, brought much more than material goods through the Mediterranean routes. In 1347 in the southern Ukraine—the closest port for bringing goods from China—a mysterious illness began killing the local citizens. At this point the plague had moved slowly, as it had been first seen in China in the 1330s. Panic ensued, and the natives blamed the Italian traders who were in the city at the time. Dead bodies were thrown at the Europeans hoping to get them to take the disease away. The plan was successful in that the plague arrived in Sicily in October 1347. The dying crew was confined to the ship, but no one noticed the exodus of the black rats onto the shore. The rodents, carrying fleas, quickly contaminated the island, boarded other ships heading for the mainland, and brought about one of the most deadly epidemics western civilization has seen. (The United Nations AIDS Program has predicted that the AIDS epidemic will outnumber the deaths due to the plague in 2004; until then the Bubonic Plague has been the deadliest epidemic.)

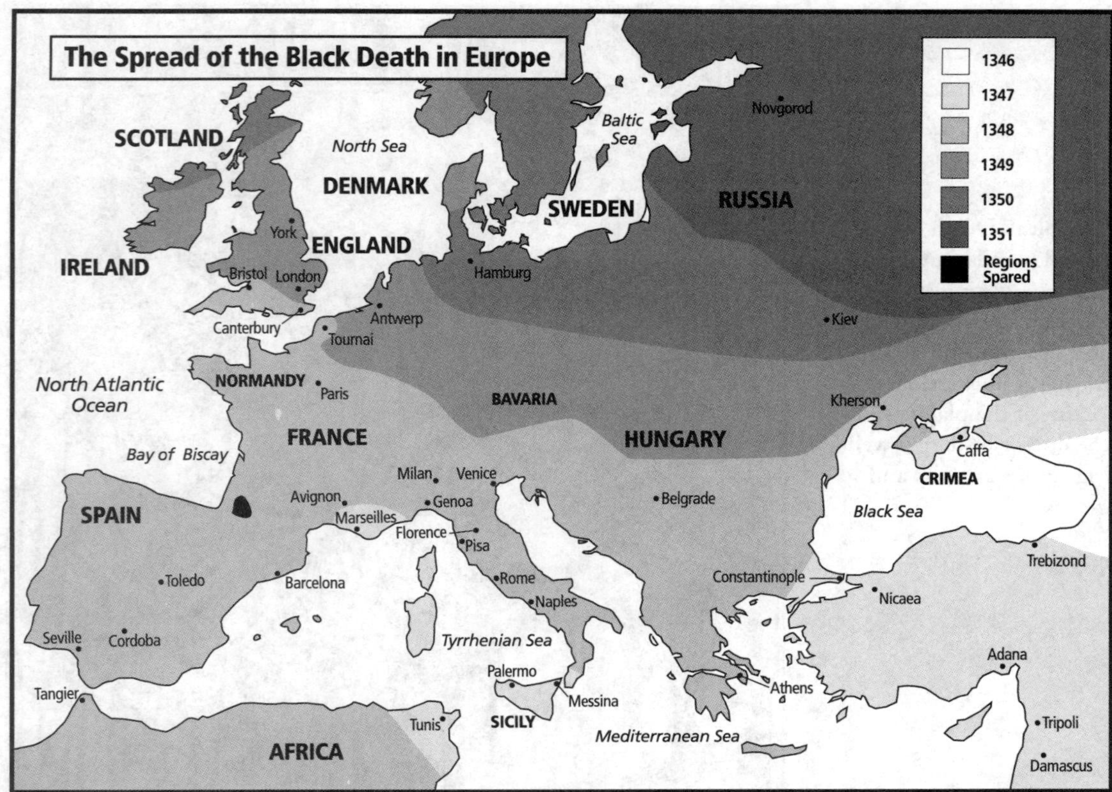

With today's medical knowledge it is hard to understand why the plague was so devastating as many simple sanitary improvements would probably have lessened its effect. Symptoms were, however, so revolting that logical thought may well have been impossible even if scientific knowledge were clearer. The doomed party was bitten by the flea, but fleas were everywhere in society and every class had to deal with the pests—archbishops, merchants, soldiers, peasants, etc. They were so common no one really noticed them; they were simply something to endure. After a bite from a diseased flea, the victim quickly noticed swellings on his body, usually the armpit, groin, or neck. These extremely painful *buboes* could be as large as an apple and gave the disease its name, bubonic plague. As the swelling increased, blood vessels in the patient expanded and burst, leaving black marks on the body. (These did not give the title The Black Death to the epidemic; rather, that came later from a mistranslation of the phrase *altra mors* meaning "dreadful death" but somehow read "black death" around the fifteenth century.)

The dying person gained little consideration from those surrounding him. First of all, the terror caused by the spread of the disease kept family and friends, and even priests, from caring for the sick. Next, everything about the disease was simply disgusting. The body smelled as if it were rotting; breathe, blood, urine, and the oozing sores all created such a stench that it was difficult to approach the person. The wrath of

God was not kind, but then the Judeo-Christian God had promised to send his punishment not only to sinners but to their descendants. It seemed as if all the evil of Western Civilization was now being paid for by the residents of the fourteenth century.

Explanations

Medical knowledge during the 1300s was mostly superstitious. The most famous medical theorist read during this age was the ancient Roman Galen, who had claimed that disease was spread by poisonous vapors that corrupted the air. People were urged to leave marshy areas and come to the cities. There they could hide inside their homes, cover their windows, and try to keep the air cool as heat helped disease spread. The washing of hands and feet was encouraged, but people should be careful washing the rest of their bodies. The dampened skin might attract the vapors and disease might creep into the person. Many people wore flowers on their filthy clothing to ward away the evil air. The childhood rhyme "Ring Around the Rosy" is really a commentary on the period of the Black Death:

> Ring around the Rosy (the pink swellings)...
> Pocket full of Posy: (flowers might drive away the disease)
> Ashes, ashes; (burning of the infected bodies)
> we all fall down! (we shall all die).

This was not a very pleasant picture or interpretation, but surely a realistic view of the despondency of the age.

The plague was uncontrollable. In some places, whole towns were emptied. In some families children died while old people survived. Rich, poor, the plague made no distinction. Some fled the towns and cities for the countryside, bringing the rats and fleas with them, and thus the plague. Some tried lancing the boils and lived; others died of the infections from treatments. There seemed little hope as body after body was placed in the street, and prayers for survival and recovery went unanswered.

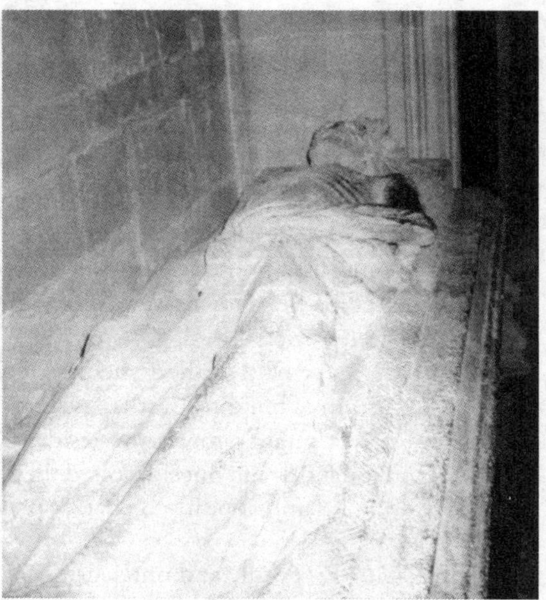

This is a burial image of a person who died from the black plague. (Winchester Cathedral, England)

There were, in fact, two types of the disease. The fleas and rats carried the first form, and then there was a second that was spread by the sneezing and coughing of the infected person. No one in the fourteenth century knew about germs, viruses, bacteria or other microscopic organisms that caused disease. They knew there must be a cause, and although it scurried right in front of them, they could not see it. At one point, many thought cats carried the disease, and they were killed in large numbers, resulting in another increase in the rat population.

The rats and fleas were simply a sign of the times. Medieval life style wallowed in unhealthy filth. Clothes were seldom changed, and baths were probably infrequent since only public bathing houses, few and far between, existed. Many Christians believed that the only personal cleansing they needed to do was to be baptized by the Church. In homes little housecleaning was done, and the streets of medieval towns were filled with garbage and were sewers for all sorts of waste. Bathrooms were not part of the structure of a house. The custom of building overhangs across the narrow streets might protect the residents from rain and too much sun but suffocated them with stale air and damp conditions that helped breed disease.

The plague was deadly and unrelenting. A person might be active and healthy one day, dead the next. Priests and doctors adopted strange costumes, covering their bodies and faces when they chanced the infection by visiting the sick. Within a year, the plague had spread across continental Europe, and in cities it is estimated that 30 to 60 percent of the population died. In 1349 it spread to Scandinavia, Iceland, and Greenland.

Devoted Christians, the population began turning to God with extraordinary prayers. One group, which grew rapidly, revived the ancient custom of flagellation. By marching through towns and beating themselves, they called on God to forgive the sins of all and remove the plague. Frenzied audiences joined in expressing a notion of collective guilt. Everyone needed to appeal to the saints, to the Virgin Mary, to Jesus. St. Roche and St. Sebastian were particularly called upon to relieve the terrors of the plague. The calls, however, went unheeded, and the suffering continued.

A movement known as The Flagellants had a particular affect. Their masochistic practice of beating themselves to unconsciousness became a public entertainment in a grim time. Each member carried a scourge, a wooden stick that had three or four leather strips at the end. The leather strips were equipped with metal spikes so that when they struck the skin, bleeding and much pain occurred. The group would form a circle, strip to the waist (even women), and begin their self-inflicted martyrdom. Many flocked to their appearances to encourage them to whip themselves even harder. Soon these so-called pious representatives were attacking the organized Church and condemning it for not solving the problem. As the insults grew, as well as the horror shows, the Church began to object to the dissidents.

One of the worst side affects of the Flagellant movement was their appointment of the "true cause" of the plague. Since whipping themselves had had little influence on the course of the disease, there must, they claimed, be a source other than Christian sin. That source was obvious to anyone who looked around Christian Europe: Christians could easily blame the Jewish population for its suffering.

The Jews of Europe lived primarily on the outskirts of towns and cities. They had special "quarters," since they were not permitted to own prime land or be an integral part of Christian society. They had, however, served many purposes, especially when it came to Christians finding ways of circumventing Christian law. The rules of the Church had put a great burden on a growing money economy. Christians were forbidden to charge interest on loans; it was simply the duty of a Christian to help others in need, not to make profit from their troubles. Jews, however, did not have to live by such a rule, and some had managed to accumulate enough wealth in the form of money to become large lenders through the "privilege" of earning interest. No one really likes to be in debt, especially to a group that was socially unacceptable. The Church was one of the first to condemn Jewish traders. During the Crusades, soldiers for the holy venture were forgiven any debts to Jewish lenders by a decree from the Church. This was just part of the long tradition of blaming the Jews for the troubles of Christian society.

Many Jewish rituals made them suspicious to Christian society. For one, the Jews were careful in their food preparation as well as in the processes for cooking, lessening sicknesses due to poisons from rotten food. Cleanliness was a practice of their religious devotions whereas Christians needed only to "bathe in their faith." Because of their outcast position in society, Jews often kept to themselves and, worst of all, seemed to be less affected by the sweep of the plague. All this made them an easy scapegoat for explaining why Christians were dying and Jews were not.

Christians noted that Jews would not take water from town wells. The explanation was simple: according to their laws, they had to get "fresh" water from springs. To the Christians, however, the reason was obvious: the Jews had poisoned the wells. In September 1348, eleven Jewish men in a small southern German town were accused of poisoning the town well and after hours of questioning, accompanied by torture, the men confessed. News of their execution spread through Europe, and other communities began to see the cause of the plague—it was not their sin, but the evilness of those who had crucified Christ!

In Zurich, Jews were forbidden to become citizens, one of the least severe "punishments" of the times. In Basel and Brussels, they were herded into wooden buildings and burned alive. In Strasburg, historians estimate that sixteen thousand Jews were killed in 1349 alone. In Frankfort, the Flagellants entered the Jewish quarter and caused such hysteria that the entire population was destroyed. In Mainz and Cologne, they had the same "success." Jews across Europe huddled in their small ghettos waiting for the worst to happen.

Finally in 1349, after the challenge to Church and Papal authority, Pope Clement IV issued a Bull declaring the Flagellant movement heretical and that members would be excommunicated. A few of the leaders were hanged, priests who had encouraged the movement were unfrocked, and all the members were excommunicated. On the secular side, Philip VI of France forbade public self-flagellation and declared that the punishment for such behavior would be death. Several leading Flagellants were beheaded. Anti-semitism was, however, not eradicated. What saved the few Jews remaining, however, was not the outcry against their torture and death, but, in 1350, the sudden and again unexplainable disappearance of the plague.

A TURNING POINT?

Terrible events are the excitement of historical writers since they can speculate on their causes and results. In 1347, the approximate population of Western Europe was 75 million people; in 1352, it was about 50 million. Twenty five million people died within 5 years, a tremendous toll. Entire families were wiped out; whole towns disappeared. Many historians believe that what happened as a result of the Bubonic Plague was the setting up of the foundations for our modern world. A heavy price was paid to bring about our present social, economic and political systems. By the end of the century, only half the number of people that lived in Europe in 1345 populated its territory. Sporadic outbreaks of the plague continued until 1399, when it disappeared until a brief appearance in the seventeenth century.

The first result of the plague was, of course, the drastic reduction of population. Where competition for status, as well as jobs, had been strong before the plague, now workers and even leaders were desperately needed. The plague had not damaged crops, livestock or land plots, so much more material wealth was available to those who had survived. Wages and benefits increased, providing improved life styles. Workers could leave the land their ancestors had tilled with little success and seek better opportunities. Those with traditional power reacted by supporting laws such as the English Stature of Laborers (1351), which stipulated that wages were to remain the same as in pre-plague days, but these could not be enforced because the need for workers was great while the supply was small.

In some areas, such as Florence, Italy, recovery from the economic ruin caused by loans to Edward in the beginnings of the Hundred Years War was assured as the citizens, organized into guilds, began producing high quality products that were demanded across Europe. The need for funds found a few Christian families wealthy and powerful enough to rule the city with the primary interest of business and success determining policy. Roots of the Medici family's control of the city were born out of the plague! Thus, the beginning of the artistic and technological Renaissance came, to at least some degree, from the bite of a tiny flea.

Probably the most significant immediate result of the plague was the negative reaction to the long-term control of society by the Church. For many years, Christianity in Western Europe meant membership in the organization based in Rome. During the plague, the Pope was not in Rome but in Avignon. It was hard not to notice that the city was not protected from the plague. In fact, it suffered as much, if not more, than many other cities.

Also, the Church had preached that living in this world was a time of suffering, a time of preparation for one's journey to Heaven. If life on earth was to be short and miserable, surely God would not mind a few excesses. Even the members of the clergy, especially those at Avignon, indulged in fancy clothes and partying. Years of fear and repression produced a time of celebrating the fact that they had survived the pestilence. Assertiveness replaced compliance; orgies replaced guilt; and European society took on a "this worldly" attitude instead of just seeking the route to Heaven. Many thought it was time to make society a place for the living, not simply a place to prepare for the afterlife.

DIVIDING UP THE WORLD

The French and the English: Claims to the Land

In the complicated realm of allegiances and alliances, European traditions set the stage for a return to war. In some ways, the history of the era can be told through the life of Edward III, King of England from 1327 to 1377. Born in 1312, he was controlled by his mother, the daughter of the French king; she was a vicious woman who fell in love with an equally unscrupulous man, Roger Mortimer. Together these two plotted against Edward's father and taking advantage of his unpopularity, caused a revolt that put young Edward on the throne at the age of 15. Then they had the old king murdered and took control of the kingdom. Their plan failed when Edward, at 18, showed his own strength and had his mother imprisoned and Mortimer executed. His 50-year rule would bring England into the status of world power.

The early parts of the Hundred Years Wars revolved around Edward's claim, through his

French knights charge the enemy during the Battle of Crecy.

mother, to the French crown. The naval battle at Sluys (1340) gave England control of the Channel; and the battles of Crecy ((1346) and Calais (1347) gave the English dominion over much French territory. The catch here was that with these "victories" Edward became the feudal vassal of the King of France and had to pledge his loyalty to him. This meant that even though he was King of England, he was supposed to journey across the Channel, kneel before the Valois dynasty, and promise to protect the French realm from its enemies (some of whom were Edward's allies). Such humiliation was a real problem for Edward, not only ego-wise but in the collection of feudal dues (meaning some of his treasury would have to go to his enemy, the King of France).

By the early 1350s, with the plague subsiding, both sides began pressing their claims against each other, and war was not far off. The French at first declared that Edward must, as tradition demanded, come and make his feudal promises. When he did not come, they moved their troops on to his land and denied him the collection of his feudal rents. Edward retaliated by declaring that he was the rightful king of France, and in 1355, English soldiers began arriving in France to support his claims.

Led by Edward's oldest son, the Black Prince (because he wore black armor), infantry equipped with their longbows swiftly defeated the French cavalry. In the 1356 Battle of Poitiers, the French King, John (Jean) the Good, was captured with his younger son and sent off to England as a great prize. A huge amount of money and land was demanded for his ransom. At first, only a small amount of money was raised, and the English were so frustrated they allowed John to return to France to help raise the money!

Meanwhile, Charles Valois, called the Dauphin (crown prince), tried to combine and organize the French forces. He called a meeting in Paris of the representatives of French society to consider how they would come to his aid and drive out the English. Barely 18 and not ready to rule, Charles had made a strategic mistake. The delegates quickly disintegrated into a squabbling horde that accused Charles' ministers of losing the war. Robert LeCoq, Bishop of Laon, showed that even the Church had little support for Charles and demanded that he release his primary French opponent for the crown, Charles the Bad, King of Navarre (the Dauphin's brother-in-law).

In a series of disastrous events, the weakness of the French situation came to a head. In 1359, the English surrounded Paris and forced the French into the Treaty of Bretigny. The huge ransom for King John was to be paid in three installments, and more land had to be ceded to the English. It looked like the English would dominate French politics.

Within France itself, society was divided about who should rule the country. With varying support, competing groups caused near chaos. In Paris itself, Etienne Marcel, a wealthy merchant, led the Third Estate, demanding they have a voice in the government that had traditionally been run by the nobles and the clergy. Actually Marcel represented only a small part of his "class," as it was composed of a widely separated group. At one end were the wealthy merchants, doctors, lawyers, and other successful non-nobles who did their best to copy the lives of the hereditary nobility. On the other end were the craftsmen, peasants, and landless workers who struggled for survival. Marcel manipulated the lower class and encouraged them to join him against the traditional leaders, the nobility, and the clergy. He even gave those eager to join with him a symbol for their future liberty, red and blue hoods to signify their inclusion in his projects. He was successful enough to drive the fearful Dauphin from the city.

By 1358 another group began to enter the political scene, the peasants of the countryside. Beginning around Beauvais, north of Paris, a group of peasants who were totally frustrated by high taxes and noble privilege broke into a castle and killed the knight and his family. Excited by their success, they moved on to another castle and burned the knight at a stake after raping and killing his wife and daughters. The nickname for French peasants was Jacques, and to assure their anonymity, each member of the group called himself Jacques Bonhomme (John Good Man). The movement has since been called the rise of the Jacquerie. Acts of violence spread rapidly across France. Charles of Navarre took these rebels on as his personal challenge, capturing their leader and beheading him. Soon nobles across France rallied and took revenge by massacring thousands of the insurgents, probably many of them innocent.

Marcel, meanwhile, had problems keeping his coalition together and became desperate for allies. He appealed to Charles of Navarre and the English to help him against the Dauphin Charles. As these forces arrived in Paris, the populace turned against Marcel, and on July 31, 1358, he was beaten and murdered, his naked body thrown into the streets to prove that his movement was as dead as he was.

If this were not enough to tear France to near anarchy, a third group began to have its own effect on the scene. As armies came and went on official missions led by royal officers, there were periods of "non-fighting." They could hardly be called peace because throughout the land, marauders or Free Companies attacked whomever and wherever they pleased, taking what they wanted, not only in goods but livestock and women. They left the French countryside as vulnerable as in the days of the Barbarian raiders. It took over thirty years for the French to stabilize the situation.

Both England and France suffered from the years of war. Although a brief peace was made in 1360, war resumed by 1369. A new French commander began to make inroads into English success, including a brief invasion into the English territories. Now it was England's turn to be distracted by troubles at home.

New Ways of Government: The Case of England

The English have long prided themselves with their organized "representative" government and many of the hallmarks of Western Civilization have English precedents. The Magna Carta of 1215 formed the precedent of no taxation without representation; the courts of Henry II and III instituted the notion of a jury of peers for trials. During the passage of these ideas into procedures, the real benefactors were the upper classes, and they were not in any way "democratic" or inclusive when they were first presented.

In 1295, Edward I had reached out to broaden his base of support against the nobles who had forced previous rulers to give up some of their power. Needing money for campaigns and court expenses, he called Parliament but invited two knights from every shire to attend. In an attempt to strengthen royal power, Edward solidified a tradition that would lead eventually to establishment of the House of Commons.

Edward III was similarly a practical man who, especially after the unpopularity and demise of his father, wanted the support of his people. His wars against France demanded that he look favorably on petitions and demands of his subjects. Throughout his reign, Parliament grew stronger and met to consider the needs of the "nation." This did not mean the monarchy felt any desire to represent the common people, but a sort of notion about sharing power began to develop.

The exclusion of the majority of English "citizens" from the government and their exploitation was clearly demonstrated in 1381 with a massive protest that demanded that the rulers consider the needs of the majority. In the early fourteenth century, the Court of Common Pleas, the civil court of England, decided that it did not have time for the legal problems of peasants. This basically denied the lower class access to the protection of the law. It also indicated that there was so much business for the courts that little could get done. For the peasants, local lords equaled justice, and the idea of the King's law was compromised.

During the Bubonic Plague, perhaps as many as half of the English people died. It was particularly devastating to the poor who were the workers of the once-growing English economy. Now the nobles demanded that the peasants work even harder to keep their lowly positions on the manors. If they even tried to understand the law, they were limited because it was written in an almost foreign language, "law French" handed down from the days when William of Normandy became the conqueror of the island.

"Wat Tyler's Rebellion"

The Peasants' Rebellion centered around a specific event against a specific person, but the event and the person symbolized the plight of all the peasants. In 1381, a tax collector arrived at the hovel of a peasant named Wat Tyler. He demanded that Tyler's daughter, aged 15, was of taxable age and grabbed her, stripped her naked, and assaulted her. Tyler, who was working near by, heard the screams of his wife and daughter and came running. Hammer in hand, he smashed the tax collector's head to pieces. His neighbors cheered him and agreed to follow him to London to protest their treatment.

As they traveled across England, they were joined by two other groups led by John Ball and Jack Straw, itinerant priests who had called upon the peasants to invade London. By now there were 100,000 followers. They broke into the city, tore open the gates of prisons, and beheaded every judge and lawyer they could find. The leaders demanded that this was a cause for justice not looting and forbid their followers to take any goods as they moved through the area. Now they surrounded the building where Richard II, England's 18-year-old king, huddled among his advisors. As a few nobles tried to escape, they were caught and killed. Richard pleaded with the

John Ball recruited peasants to revolt against their lords. He was later executed

mob; he asked what they wanted and they cried out, "We will be free forever, our heirs and our lands." Richard, realizing he had little to oppose them, agreed and blessed them.

With the promises of the king, many of the peasants left to go home and take care of their fields and families. A few days later, Wat Tyler stood at the front of the remaining peasant "army." On horseback, Wat slowly rode toward his king and the Mayor of London. Trusting that all was well, the two men met and exchanged greetings. Suddenly the Mayor of London, who later claimed he thought Tyler had insulted the king, knocked the rebel leader to the ground and slit his throat. Richard charged into the enemy claiming that only he was their rightful lord, and his momentary bravery saved the day. The crowd dispersed. Tyler's head was placed on a pike outside the city; Ball and Straw were soon captured and beheaded.

Richard had promised to forget the violence of the rebels, but when the leaders were dead, he arranged trials for the rebels. Altogether, 1500 peasants were hanged all over England. The trials were presided over by the king's judge who told the jurors that any votes against the crown were treason, and they would be hanged if they did not convict the criminals. Freedom and justice for the lower class would have to wait until another century.

DEFINING CRACKS IN THE SYSTEM

The Rise of Secular Literature

From the beginning of the century, hints of social change slipped between the major political events. Literature in the vernacular encouraged a return to literacy, and legends about the power of the individual began to creep into the expectations of Europeans.

As the fourteenth century developed, more and more writers picked up the theme of the nobility of the individual against the traditional institutions of society. Dante's (see the previous chapter) commentary became very popular, and a new generation of writers began to question the foundations of medieval society.

Born in 1270, Marsillius of Padua was a physician and theologian. In the controversies that arose between popes and secular leaders, the Holy Roman Emperor, Louis IV of Bavaria, was excommunicated and denounced by the Pope. Louis called upon Marsillius to search for sources to justify his rule. The result was the *Defensor Pacis* (Defender of the Peace), a long discourse published in 1324. The basic points were (1) all power is derived from the people; (2) the ruler is the people's delegate; (3) there is no law but popular will; (4) the Church should be under the ruler; (5) it should only deal with worship and it should be governed by councils, not by just one man. Louis was probably as upset by these clearly revolutionary statements as the Church, and the ideas were not, at first, widely circulated. They were, however, another new precedent, and the interest in the role of "the people" began to grow.

In Italy, the poet Francesco Petrarca (known as Petrarch) was similar to Dante. Born in 1304, he also fell in love, as a young boy, with "Laura" who inspired him to give up his access to a rich, materialistic life to write poetry. Here he praises the individual whose thoughts and feelings were in conflict with the ideals of medieval asceticism. He rediscovered the writings of Plato and other Greek intellectuals and admired their work. In some ways this set the stage for the next century's "renaissance" of the classics of the ancient world. Petrarch stressed the individual's expressions of love, a sort of spiritual notion. He also condemned the materialism of the Church and pleaded with the popes to return to Rome and a simpler style of life than they were practicing in Avignon.

For present day English and American audiences, the most famous of the fourteenth-century "English writers was Geoffrey Chaucer, the poet and chronicler whose *Canterbury Tales* have become a classic. Chaucer was born sometime around 1340 to 1345 to a family that was connected closely with nobles who recommended them for government service. Over his life time he was chosen as a local official and served as a diplomat well into his senior years. In 1359 to 1360 he served with John of Gaunt (one of Edward's III sons) in France and was captured. He was ransomed for a small amount (16 pounds). Not scarred by the episode, he served again in France in 1369 and 1370. These adventures plus his rich imagination made for a fertile source of many stories.

Petrarch studied and preserved many of the forgotten works of the ancient Romans and Greeks.

The *Canterbury Tales* again focus on individuals and their trials and tribulations through

***The Canterbury Tales* written by Geoffrey Chaucer is famous for its poetic tales of life during a pilgrimage.**

life. Many tell sad stories of their grief and pain, their humiliation at the hands of others. The tales rapidly became popular, and besides his official positions and military service, Chaucer became well known through the kingdom. He was popular enough that in 1374, the king granted him a gallon of wine every day for the rest of his life. This was improved in 1398 to a ton of wine a year. In 1399, the new King Henry IV granted him all sorts of royal honors for his service to the crown and the people of England. As with the uncertainty of the date of his birth, questions remain about the exact time of his death, but it is usually considered to be in October 1400.

New Ways of Getting to Heaven

With the papacy in Avignon, controlled by the French king, and the Church itself struggling to clarify its doctrinal positions, critics of its message, as well as its organization, began to appear. Muddled within the political and social issues of the day, religious dogma was slowly changing. The universities of Europe were torn by religious feuds. The faculties were primarily made up of clerics with different emphases. French and Italian universities tended to be seats of Church law due to their connection with the papacy. Other Christian intellectuals were less dedicated to orthodox opinions.

John Wyclif

Perhaps related to the political stress between England and France, voices against traditional interpretations of the Church began to be heard and listened to in England. Most noteworthy was that of John Wyclif, professor at Oxford. He received support and interest from such powerful men as John of Gaunt, Edward's III son and Richard's II uncle.

Born in 1330, Wyclif studied at Oxford and in 1374 became the Rector of Lutterworth. Here he began writing down his thoughts on Church policy. In his pamphlet, *On Civil Lordship,* he strongly opposed the great accumulation of wealth that the Church had made a major part of its activities. He wrote that the Church should not own property or be involved in any matters other than spiritual issues. He even suggested that a Pope who was involved in worldly power was nothing more than an agent of the devil, and even called such a person the Anti-Christ. In other doctrinal ideas, he declared that priests had no special powers, including the supposed power to turn the bread and wine used in the Holy Eucharist into the Body and Blood of Christ (the Roman Catholic doctrine of transubstantiation). The Scriptures, he claimed, were the only law for the Church and that any conflicting Church policy or doctrine, even Papal Bulls, were irrelevant. Wyclif said that each Christian needed only a personal relationship with God to understand His role on Earth. Because he was so convinced of the need for every person to learn about God's ways, he translated the Latin Bible into English and encouraged its circulation.

Wyclif attracted a large following beyond the circles of the university. His belief in educating the ordinary Christian led him beyond writing, and he sent preachers out to the parishes to speak to their congregations in the vernacular rather than in Latin. Soon his followers became so numerous that they were grouped under the name "Lollards." The name came from a Latin term meaning to sing softly and is loosely meant as "mumblers." Sometimes connected with Wat Tyler's rebellion, the Lollards were concerned about the treatment of the lower class but beyond that they were inspired by Wyclif's theological challenges to the traditional Church. In 1382, Wyclif's association with the revolt cost him support in the nobility, and his books were banned. He died at home on December 31, 1384.

The Lollard movement continued and, in 1395, the followers presented their twelve "Conclusions" to Parliament. Much of this was a criticism of the role of the Church and the clergy in English society. They demanded some relief from taxation by the Church and questioned the doctrines of transubstantiation (changing the bread and wine) as well as the "feigned" divinity of Church leaders. In 1398, opposition to the group was so strong that Wyclif's body was dug up, burned at the stake, and his ashes cast into a nearby river. As more religious and political struggles continued, the Lollards played their role as a persecuted group. Many were hanged or burned for their beliefs, but the ideology continued to threaten the orthodox positions.

The Great Schism

The Church went through further challenges and humiliations. In 1377, Gregory XI went to Rome to see if some compromises could be worked out. He realized that he did not have the support of the Italian cardinals so he decided to return to Avignon. He died before he could leave, and the College of Cardinals took this as a divine sign (or at least a political opportunity) and, in 1378, elected Urban VI to lead them as the Holy Father. Soon after, the French cardinals declared Urban's election null and void and elected their candidate, Clement VII, to take charge in Avignon. Now Western Christendom was ruled by two popes, both who excommunicated the other. Europe became split between advocates for each side. Both popes demanded church taxes be sent to them; both declared that any obedience to his opponent would cost the person his soul and heaven. It was a very confusing situation.

This Great Schism caused the rise of the Conciliar Movement, which supported the notion that the Church should be ruled by a group of advisors not just one man. Most of the dogma of the fourteenth century declared, like "Unam Sanctam," that only one person could head the Church but in fact there were now two popes and great arguments about who the "real" pope could be. In 1409, the Council of Pisa met to consider the crisis. They decided that a council could combine the best sense of the Church. The 500 members called upon Gregory VII of Rome and Benedict XIII of Avignon to help bring the schism to an end but neither pope would come and both declared the meeting invalid. The council, however, moved to solve the problem, deposing both popes and declaring a new election. Alexander V was chosen, and the result was that there were now three popes in Western Christendom as well as the Patriarch who ruled the Eastern Church based in Constantinople. (The split of the Roman Empire into Eastern and Western parts was not only political, it was spiritual; Roman Popes claimed supremacy across Christendom, but the Patriarch of Constantinople in the East claimed he was Christendom's spiritual leader. See material in previous chapters.)

In 1414 the Council of Constance met and finally resolved the situation. They deposed the Pisan Pope in 1415; the Roman Pope resigned; and the Avignoese Pope was deposed in the summer of 1417. Now, with no official Pope sitting anywhere, the council met in November 1417 and elected Martin V to return to the Vatican. The turmoil all this confusion had caused greatly lessened the power and the prestige of the papacy.

John Hus

Attacks on Church policy and traditions even began to be heard in the middle of the continent. John Hus (1371 – 1415) had read some of the writings of John Wyclif. The books of the English theologian had arrived in Bohemia (part of modern day Czechoslovakia) as its princess, Anne, married Richard II. Here religious doctrine was bound to the political situation. German and Slavic conflict over control of central Europe gave the Bohemians a strong nationalistic feeling. Many of the Holy Roman Emperors were appointed by a council of electors that was usually controlled by the papacy; their secular power was to rule the area where Germans and the Bohemians resented this "outside" authority. When Hus proclaimed that the Church should only be a spiritual body and that Christ, not the Pope, was the head of the Church, he began a crusade that called Bohemians to formulate their own church doctrines. He preached against the selling of church offices, indulgences, and the abuses of the clergy and the papacy.

At first King Wenceslas IV supported and protected Hus from Church prosecutors. Hus grew bolder and condemned the Church's call for an indulgence to fund a crusade against the King of Naples. Here the Church was asking its people to give money for a war against a fellow Christian. Collection of the indulgence in Bohemia was small, and the Church began to move against Hus. Although the politics of the time would have supported him, Hus refused to cooperate. He preached sermons on the perfection of humans and told his parishioners that only "he who dies, wins." For Hus, there was little to value in this world's existence.

Soon Hus cut himself off from the political forces that were trying to protect him. Summoned to the Counsel of Constance, he was promised safe passage by the Holy Roman Emperor, who at this point was Sigismund the King of Bohemia. Once there, however, he was tried for heresy, convicted, and on July 6, 1415, burned at the stake. Later, Martin Luther and Johannes Eck would argue about Hus' fate. Luther concluded that both popes and councils, being human, could make mistakes.

The Hussites did not disappear when their leader died, and he was pronounced a martyr by his supporters. In fact, they began to become more vocal on the political and religious scenes. Two groups formed around his doctrines. One was the Ultraquists (or Calixtines), a conservative group of nobles and wealthy townsmen that denounced only practices specifically forbidden by the Bible. The other was the Taborites, composed mainly of peasants, who accepted only those practices found in the Bible. The second was closer to Hus' views.

Both suffered as Rome sent, between 1420 and 1434, five "crusades" against them. Jan

Zizka led the Hussites against Rome, and in 1420 the "Four Articles of Prague" stating their position was published. War against Rome produced greater friction between the two Hussite groups, and in 1434 the Ultraquists defeated the Taborites. The conservatives then entered into negotiations with the Church and made several compromises. The Taborites continued to resist and became the Bohemian Brethren. Some of this party laid the basis for the present Moravian Church while others would join the Lutherans in their objections to the Roman Church.

Besides the religious significance of the Hussite defiance of the Church was their introduction of an infant technology into their defense. Since the beginning of the 1300s western Europe was toying with gunpowder and its use in military situations. Upon his coronation, Edward III had received a manuscript showing a *pot de fer*, an explosive device that shot a missile into the air. In varying attempts, the device was used to drive a projectile towards the enemy. By 1338, the French were using the techniques to fling iron arrows toward the English, and all noted that with some reliability, this could be the weapon of the future. When the Hussites went to war against the Church, they used handguns and cannon to weaken their enemy and then ran their cavalry into the opposing army. The technique was successful, and a new form of warfare was born. And so in their search for religious and political freedom, reformers changed the way men could efficiently kill each other!

On the other hand, proponents for different religious emphases were not so involved in violence. Both Wyclif and Hus claimed the only authority for Christianity was the Bible. They emphasized the spiritual side of the Church's message. Roman Catholicism was not without its champions for spreading their faith through visions and mysticism. Building on the traditions of, for one, St. Francis of the thirteenth century, Catherine of Sienna (1347-1380) became one of the most notable heroines of the fourteenth century. Born 23rd of 25 children, Catherine was the daughter of a successful dyer and the granddaughter of a poet. At age 6 she began having visions of Christ, and although her family pushed her to have a "normal" life, she gave herself to spiritual missions. When the family sought to set up an engagement to marry, she cut off her hair and stayed prayerfully in her room. Finally they consented, and she became a lay worker for the Dominican order. As Catherine's mission became her life, she called upon the popes to return to Rome from Avignon and give up their extravagant life styles. She wrote beautiful stories and poems focusing on an individual's search for peace with God. These remain Italian classics. Today, Sienna is an attraction to those who wish to perform a modern pilgrimage.

In the fourteenth and early fifteenth centuries, the Church continued to dominate politics and attempt to rule in the secular world. In central Europe, its biggest challenge was the constant pressure from Turkish, meaning Moslem, attacks and inroads. Here the expansion of the "infidels" threatened the survival of Christianity. Local lords, such as Vlad (great grandfather to the famous Vlad Dracul) in Wachovia, traded their religious loyalties for political protection. If the Christian support were stronger, the areas faced Rome, if the Moslems offered more safety, then the choice was to bargain with them.

In the West, Church influence was closely related to the fortunes of the English and French as they continued their wars against each other. The agonies of the rising infant form of nationalism were intimately related to the structure of the Church. Rulers, as well as individuals, began to choose what they thought supported their secular positions, justifying their power. The stage was set for a reformation of the Church.

BACK TO THE WAR

English Dynastic Problems

In 1377, Richard II began his reign at the age of 10, following his grandfather Edward III. The old king, as well as Richard's father, the Black Prince, had been popular heroes, and Richard had a great deal to live up to. His early reign was dominated by John of Gaunt, his uncle. Richard did prove his strength during the Peasants' Rebellion, but soon political battles with the nobility would prove to weaken his powers as king.

Medieval superstition could probably have predicted the outcome of Richard's reign. He married well, first to the daughter of the Holy Roman Emperor and then to Isabella, daughter of the King of France. He had, however, no children from either marriage, and so no heir to the throne.

Richard's choice of advisors was also a sign that all was not well. During the late 1380s, five members of his "loyal opposition" appointed themselves Lords Appellant and found five of Richard's closest advisors guilty of treason. They were executed. In 1397, not realizing the political situation, Richard forced Parliament to find the Lords also guilty of treason. Three were executed, and two were banished. Among those exiled abroad was Henry Bolingbroke, John of Gaunt's son, and Richard's cousin. Soon after this, John of Gaunt died, and Richard foolishly confiscated his land breaking any alliance he had with the powerful Bolingbroke.

With troubles multiplying and an uprising in Ireland, Richard left for the Green Isle to settle things there. Taking advantage of the king's unpopularity and that he was "out of town," Bolingbroke returned and convinced Parliament that he should be king. They elected him and deposed Richard. Henry, with excellent military skills, sent his soldiers off, and they soon captured Richard. It was 1399 and Richard was sent off to prison, where, a year later, he was mysteriously murdered.

Henry's usurpation of throne caused him many problems both politically and personally. Richard's supporters revolted and kept the new king engrossed in suppressing rebels. In a misconceived action against the Church, Henry had the Archbishop executed, antagonizing many across his divided land. In his personal life, he married Joan of Navarre who had many strange habits and, actually, was convicted of witchcraft in 1419. When he developed (probably) leprosy, and then epilepsy, the popular opinion was that God was punishing him for his misdeeds and sins.

The last two years of Henry V's reign were controlled by his son, Henry VI. Born in 1387, this Henry seemed to have been a natural born soldier. At 14 he fought the Welsh in behalf of his father, and at 16 he was again triumphant at the battle of Shrewsbury. Soon, he put down revolts by the Lollards and an assassination plot by nobles still loyal to Richard II.

Henry's foreign battles slowly distracted his opposition away from other claimants to the throne although he was never secure. He made demands against the French king and in the Treaty of Troyes in 1420, he was "awarded" Catherine, the king's daughter. He then demanded his feudal rights to the duchies of Normandy and Anjou. When Charles ignored him, England went to war with France. At the famous battle of Agincourt, Henry's 5000 exhausted soldiers were pitted against five times as many French soldiers. The conflict between the various French generals, however, gave Henry the day. Shakespeare immortalized Henry with his supposed St. Crispin's day speech, encouraging his troops to follow him to glory. Charles, King of France, was so impressed that he passed over his own son and named Henry as his heir. If Henry had lived only a little longer, he would have worn the crowns of both England and France. A life of warring and partying caught up to Henry, and in 1422 he died, never seeing the son his wife in England had just born him.

With a baby on the throne of England who had a strong claim to the crown of France, English and French politics became more and more intertwined. The struggle for power is never nice, and the claims to rule rise above civility. The War of the Roses soon ensued, and cousin versus cousin played the English scene in intrigue as well as murder. Now the stage was set for wars between the great grandsons and supporters of Edward III. The War of the Roses would muddle English politics until the victory of the Tudors at Bosworth Field in 1485.

Meanwhile in France

If the English political scene were filled with treachery, the French political scene was filled with insanity. Charles VI was born in 1368 and was crowned at the age of 12. A pleasure loving young man, he left most of the governing to his uncles. In 1382, however, the tax burden on the population caused a series of revolts and Charles, with the help of his brother, Louis of Orleans, took over and began their own style of ruling. They brought back a number of their father's advisors who were of humble origin and could be influenced by the brothers. In 1385, he married Isabeau of Bavaria. She was 14, and he was 16. They filled the court with fun and partying. All this seems pretty much the rule for royal courts.

In 1392, however, Charles suffered an unknown illness. He had high fevers, and his hair and nails fell out. After that, he was subject to strange moods and behaviors. A few years later, he rode with some knights when suddenly he picked up a sword and killed four of them. At a masquerade ball that he and the queen gave, he and some others wore light, flowing costumes. Charles and his revelers caught fire, and only by chance was he saved while the others burned to death. By 1398, the general opinion was that the king was possessed, and even the Church tried to exorcise him. He began to tell people he was made of glass and they must not touch him. He had special clothes made with metal rods to protect him from breaking. In 1405 he decided that he should not even change his clothes and after months of his wandering in filth, his advisors paid some men to paint their faces black, hide in the King's closet, and jump out at him in the middle of the night. This shock treatment did cause a brief return to the king's attention to cleanliness.

During the time Charles was moving back and forth between sanity and insanity, the queen, Isabeau, found it increasingly difficult to behave well. After producing a number of children with the mad king, she began a close relationship with his brother. The queen was never known for her propriety, and she and Louis traveled together and partied as much as she had with the young king. Louis was deeply involved in war with John the Fearless, Duke of Burgundy. When John had Louis killed, the unfaithful Isabeau became John's close friend.

To make matters even worse, the succession to the throne was in doubt. In 1419, the supposed crown prince was discredited by his own mother who claimed he was illegitimate. The prince's reputation was further defeated when, after meeting John the Fearless, the Duke was hacked to death. As turmoil filled the royal palace, the demented king was left to strangers who simply tried to keep him out of trouble. If he wished to be dirty, they agreed; if he had a few sane moments, they humored him back into fantasy. In 1422, the poor disheveled king died, only a few months after his son-in-law and supposed heir, Henry V.

Most of Charles' sons died young and his successor, Charles VII, feared bridges (where he had seen John the Fearless murdered), and had all sorts of food psychoses. Many historians believe that Charles VI had porphyria, which created his mental problems. They point to many relatives who had similar, if less dramatic, symptoms. And as Charles' daughter Catherine married Henry V of England and their oldest son went mad, perhaps this is a connection to the "Madness" of King George III, ruler of the British Isles during the American Revolution.

THE LAST OF THE WAR

The last years of the Hundred Years War are frequently glossed over by historians, suggesting it as not terribly important to European politics. In the Treaty of Troyes, the French princess was given to the English king, and then the French king made Henry his heir instead of his own son. French patriotism began to stir, and a new ending to the war was written. Although the tale of the next few years was written in mysticism and miracles, what probably turned the tide was the introduction of technology.

The romantic symbol of the new patriotism was a saintly young woman, Joan of Arc. The daughter of a small landed peasant, Joan was born in Domremy in the province of Champagne. She began hearing voices as a teenager and soon defined them as Saints sent from God to give her holy messages. Whereas the voices of Catherine of Sienna had led the Italian woman to serve the poor, Joan's voices asked her to save France. Dressing in men's clothing, she traveled to find the Dauphin and aid his cause. Domremy was devoted to the crown prince, even though the Burgundians and their allies, the English, controlled the area.

At first the prince's advisors refused to let her see him, but after several tests, including recognizing the Dauphin even though he was disguised, the idea that Joan held a holy mission began to be considered. At this point, the French had suffered so many defeats that almost any hope would have sounded encouraging to the desperate French. Joan also validated her claim by asking the men to go to a church and look behind the altar for an ancient sword. When they found it, they were sure Joan had a special calling.

Now Joan, dressed in men's clothing that was strictly forbidden in medieval days, led the Dauphin's troops to Orleans, which had long been controlled by the English. They were victorious in capturing it. It was May 1429 and within the next month, the French had another victory at Patay. On the July 17, Charles VII was crowned at Reims, and Joan felt triumphant.

The crowning of the new king did not unite the French forces, which continued to court English support when it pleased them. In May 1430, Joan was captured and turned over to Bishop Pierre Cauchon for L10,000. Cauchon was an agent of the English, and they greedily accepted the young woman who had defeated their troops and called for the English king to abandon his claims to France.

At first Joan was simply imprisoned; the conditions were dirty, dark, and quite foreboding. She was forced to sign a statement that she

Joan of Arc is cheered by townspeople after successfully leading French troops to victory against the English in the north of France.

would never again wear men's clothing. She tried not to hear the voices and to weather the inquisition but she heard the saints tell her that she did not have long to live, and returned to wearing her soldier costume. In 1431, she was tried as a heretic and in late May, only two years after her victory at Orleans, she was condemned. Joan, calling on her saints to lead her to heaven, was burned alive on Rouen's old market square. Her martyrdom was an inspiration to her followers, but she remained unrecognized as a saint until the Church determined that a great mistake had been done; Joan became a saint of the Church in 1920.

Things were rapidly changing on the war front. The alliances between England and various French nobles were falling apart. After the Peace of Arras in 1435, the Burgundians, long tied to the English, abandoned their allies and began to cooperate with the French forces. In 1436, Charles VII retook Paris, and the slow but steady consolidation of France began to have an effect on the war's progress.

In 1450, the French finally found an answer to the English longbow. For many years they had been working on improving the *pot de fer*, the gun, and now had established an improved gun powder that made the weapon more reliable. In the "tradition" of the Hussites, and even the

Joan of Arc was found guilty of sorcery and heresy and burned at the stake. Later, Joan was canonized as a saint.

Flemish peasants, the Battle of Formigny saw French gunners decimate the English troops and the French cavalry ride over their mangled bodies. Soon after, the French took back Normandy. The end was in sight.

1453—A REAL TURNING POINT

The events of history are not neat and organized. Historians, however, create orderly time lines. Thus a chronology often confuses the student and places artificial boundaries on the connections of the past. In many ways, the "calamitous" fourteenth century did not end until 1453 when the basis for a new age and new opportunities began to appear.

Two major events framed the year of 1453. On the Western shores of Europe, the guns and cannon of Formigny and Normandy were moved to Castillon where the French destroyed the last English land army. When the fighting was over, the armies just faded away. No formal truce or conditions of peace were signed. Perhaps the long years of war had convinced the rulers, negotiators, and even the people that fighting would surely begin again. But, for awhile the French and English turned to their own matters.

In England, Henry VI became so insane that a Protector, Richard of York, was assigned by Parliament to run the country. Soon the houses of York and Lancaster plotted against each other and the War of the Roses tore England apart. Peace would not be restored until the Battle of Bosworth Field, at the end of the fifteenth century, was won by a new player, Henry Tudor.

For the French, victory allowed them time to concentrate on their own internal confusions. Charles VII died in 1461, and his son Louis XI claimed the crown. The Dauphin had spent much of his earlier years in revolt against his father and had even been exiled for attempts to gain the throne before his father's death. Finally as king, Louis dismissed many of his father's advisors and began to coordinate his power by enticing other nobles to his court. Shifting coalitions gave Louis some general control over the country, and he worked hard to make the crown supreme in France.

In central Europe, the Papacy and the Holy Roman Emperors would continue the struggle for a balance of power. Here was the new battleground for Christianity as the Turks, who now controlled the Muslim empire, increasingly crept towards the prize of Constantinople.

The Eastern capital of Christendom was, by this time, totally surrounded by Moslem lands. On May 29, 1453, Sultan Mohammed II used "giant bombards" to crash the five walls protecting the city. Once the walls were breached, the city passed into his control, and Christianity became a persecuted religion. The Hagia Sophia, probably Christianity's most spectacular church, was converted to a mosque, and all of Christendom mourned its loss. (Soon, in Rome, the Pope would call for the rebuilding of St. Peter's to take the place of the Hagia Sophia and glorify Christianity.)

Many defeats for the progress of Western Civilization were represented in 1453, but many new opportunities were on the horizon. The mid-fifteenth century would see the birth of people who would change the world and bring Western Civilization into the leading power of world politics and culture, as well as social, political, and religious reform.

In Genoa, Christoforo Columbo was born in 1451. Not too far away, in a little town just outside Vinci, Leonardo arrived; although illegitimate, he would be "adopted" by his father's family and find his way to Florence and great fame. 1456 saw the birth of Henry Tudor who would one day reign over England as Henry VII and produce a line of kings and queens who would change the course of English history. In the same year, Johannes Gutenberg first used moveable type and began a revolution of dispensing information not unlike the explosion which has occurred through the use of the computer. Vasco da Gama, who discovered a route around Africa to India and the Spice Islands, was born in 1467; Copernicus in 1473; and Michelangelo in 1475. Lastly (although this is far from a complete list), 1483 saw the birth of a young German monk and scholar whose soul, tortured by medieval concepts of a judging God and the horrors of Hell, gave Europe new avenues to Heaven. Building on the ideas of Wyclif, Hus and others, Martin Luther declared that each man's soul was his joy and obligation and that faith, not works or even membership in the Roman Church, was the "truth which sets us free."

The traditional institutions of the old world view were giving way, and the importance of each individual, whether they could hold a gun or discover an idea to protect themselves, was becoming part of a new way of looking at this world. The heroes of this new age would be those who took risks and affected the communities around them. The modern world was being born.

Suggestions for Further Reading

Peter F. Ainsworth, *Jean Froissart and the Fabric of History: truth, myth, and fiction in the Chroniques* (1990).

Giovanni Boccaccio, *The Decameron*

Edward P. Chaney, *The Dawn of a New Era, 1250-1453* (1962).

Geoffrey Chaucer, *The Canterbury Tales*

G.G. Coulton, *The Black Death* (1929).

Kenneth A. Fowler, *The Age of Plantagenet and Valois: The Struggle for Supremacy, 1328-1498* (1967).

David Herlihy, *The Black Death and the Transformation of the West* (1997).

Johan Huizinga, *The Waning of the Middle Ages* (1968).

Richard Kieckhefer, *European Witch Trials: Their Foundations in Popular and Learned Culture, 1300-1500* (1976).

Francesco Petrarch, *Letter to Posterity, Canzoniere*

Christine Pizan, *The Book of the City Ladies*

Edward Porroy, *The Hundred Years War* (1965).

Shahar, Shulamith, *The Fourth Estate: A History of Women in the Middle Ages* (1986).

Barbara Tuchman, *A Distant Mirror: The Calamitous 14th Century* (1978).

Chapter 11

THE RENAISSANCE 1350 TO 1650

QUEEN ELIZABETH I

Artemisia Gentileschi, a young eighteen-year-old aspiring painter, sat beside her father, Orazio, in a courtroom in Rome. The time was January 1612. On trial was Agostino Tassi, Artemisia's former teacher and an artist friend of her father. Eight months earlier, in May 1611, Agostino had raped Artemisia. Orazio, seeking justice for his daughter, sued Tassi. The trial, which lasted seven months, was like the rape itself, an ordeal Artemisia hoped never to have to endure again. It seemed as if the Italian legal system favored the rapist rather than his victim. During the seven-month trial the judge had Artemisia tortured with thumbscrews in an effort to painfully force her to recant her story about the rape. Fortunately, the heroic young girl endured the pain and testified that Tassi, while teaching her how to paint, tried to seduce her. He became angry when she rejected his sexual advances and forced himself on her. Artemisia fought back, physically resisting the assault. Finding a knife lying nearby, she picked it up, wounding her attacker. Unfortunately, the knife inflicted little permanent damage on Tassi. Infuriated, he began to beat his student, and his strength and brutality were too much for a seventeen-year-old girl to fight off. Tassi completed the rape and then promised to marry his victim. Artemisia then testified that she later consented to have sexual relations with her rapist because she feared he would rape her again and because she hoped sex would make him keep his promise to marry her, which would restore the honor the assault had taken away.

Of course, Tassi never married Artemisia and at the trial denied that he had raped the young woman. His background, however, suggested otherwise. Previously, he had faced trial for murdering his wife but was acquitted for lack of evidence. He had also served a prison sentence for incest after siring several children by his brother's wife. Tassi believed he could beat the rape charge just as he had beaten the earlier murder rap by hiring people to commit perjury during the trial. His strategy backfired when Pietro Stiattesi, a witness Tassi hired to attack Artemisia's character, decided to tell the truth. Stiattesi testified that Artemisia was telling the truth and that Tassi had paid him to lie. Consequently, Tassi was convicted. Artemisia believed for a few minutes that justice had finally prevailed. Her euphoria was short lived, however, when the judge sentenced the rapist to serve only eight months in prison. The judge explained that women were not equal to men, and thus rape was not a serious enough crime to warrant a more severe punishment.

Artemisia, devastated by the rape, the ordeal of the trial, and the lax sentence, felt that she could no longer live in Rome. She married Stiattisi, the man who had testified on her behalf, and moved to Florence where Artemisia became one of the best artists the Italian Renaissance produced. Art historians believe that her victimization by a rapist and an unjust legal system is reflected in her paintings. Strong female figures dominate much of her work. Perhaps, as a rape victim, Artemisia was attempting through her artwork to right the wrongs done to women by the Renaissance legal system and create a more just society.

Chronology

Around 1350	Renaissance Begins
1375	Francesco Petrarch Dies
Around 1385	Jan Van Eyck Born
1397	Manuel Chrysoloras Comes to Florence
1400s	Gunpowder Invented
1422-1461	Charles VII Rules France
1434-1464	Cosimo de' Medici Rules Florence
1452	Leonardo da Vinci Born
1434-1494	Sforza Family Rules Milan
1450	Treaty of Lodi
1453	Mehmed II Captures Constantinople
1455-1471	War of the Roses
1455	Printing Press Invented
1469	Laura Cereta Born
1480	Spanish Inquisition Begins
1484	Charles VIII Invades Italy
1492	Columbus Sails to America
1494	Pietro Medici Forced into Exile
1500-1527	High Renaissance Period
1500	Baldassare Castiglione Writes *The Courtier*
1508	France Invades Italy, forms Cambrian League
1516	Sir Thomas More Writes *Utopia* Erasmus' Greek New Testament Published Concordat of Bologna
1519	Charles V named Holy Roman Emperor
1522	Habsburg-Valois Wars Begin
1527	Charles V Sacks Rome Niccolo Machiavelli Dies
1547	Miguel de Cervantes Born
1594	Shakespeare forms the King's Men
1616	Artemisia Gentileschi joins Florence Academy Of Art
Around 1650	Renaissance Ends

THE ITALIAN RENAISSANCE

A medieval visitor who could transcend time and visit Florence, Italy from the fourteenth to seventeenth centuries might have difficulty believing he or she was in a society and culture much different from the Florence of Dante's time. People still lived in an Aristotelian and Ptolemaic universe and continued to accept the medieval Christian worldview. Both the universe and society were still perceived as hierarchical. The Gothic style of art was still present, especially in northern Europe. In education, scholasticism flourished even though it was under attack by a new liberal arts curriculum, which used literature as its base. Among common people, the pietistic movements that swept Europe during the 1300s continued unabated.

Despite the similarities to medieval Florence, the visitor would have sensed something new in the air. A new tone, a new atmosphere, new attitudes about life, and an important shift in thought had occurred. These changes were the result of secularism, individualism, and humanism. European people had rediscovered classical antiquity and began to appreciate the legacy of Greek and Roman scholars in a new way. While medieval authors, scholars, and poets such as St. Thomas Aquinas and Dante had read, admired, and used ancient writers like Cicero, Aristotle, Plato, and Virgil, their writings emphasized service for God and the Christian faith. Renaissance scholars broke with this tradition, viewing instead the classical world as a culture with its own integrity that was worthy of study for its own sake. In addition to ancient writings, Renaissance people also rediscovered classical art and architecture. The study of antiquity created within the Renaissance person an admiration for the wisdom and achievements of the ancient Greeks, Romans, Egyptians, and Hebrews. This regard for the ancient world was so great that Renaissance scholars began to imitate the elegant literary style, art, architecture, moral realism, politics, and government found within the ancient world. Life within the Greek polis and Roman commonwealth provided standards of civic and personal life that Renaissance scholars found worth imitating.

European nations underwent vast changes that affected virtually all aspects of life on the continent from the fourteenth to the seventeenth century. This interest in and flowering of intellectual and cultural life is called the Renaissance. Italy was the first European kingdom to experience the Renaissance in the late 1300s. After about a century, the Renaissance moved from the Italian Peninsula across the Alps into northern Europe, changing society as it went.

Several factors produced the Renaissance. First, it was the result of urbanization. By the late fourteenth century Italian cities were flourishing economically. Their populations had swelled, their wealth had increased, and their physical size had expanded. Second, was an emphasis on literacy. The trade and commercial relations that developed in the 1300s made literacy necessary for an individual to gain material wealth and prosperity. Merchants had to fluently speak several languages and understand how to use mathematics to be successful. The need for language and math skills gave rise to the need for formal education, which heightened the intellectual development of middle and upper class people. Third, creation of a middle class was necessary for the Renaissance to occur. Prior to the thirteenth century, the wealth of Italy was in the hands of the upper class and the Roman Catholic Church. In the thirteenth and fourteenth centuries the urban middle class was created when trade with Asia and the Middle East increased. The wealth the middle class earned from this trade enabled them to lead a life of comparative luxury and leisure. They now had time and money to enjoy art, literature, and culture. Without the urban middle class sponsorship of artists and writers there likely would not have been a Renaissance. Fourth, feudalism began to wane. The invention of gunpowder in the 1400s enabled kings to defeat feudal knights with standing armies comprised of common men. This caused nobles to lose their monopoly over military defense, which eventually caused them to lose social status. Furthermore, as trade and commerce among the middle class increased, the nobility often had to turn to bankers and merchants for financing, creating huge debts that caused nobles to lose their economic status at the apex of European societies.

Before the Renaissance could occur in any part of Europe, an economic foundation had to be laid. From 1000 to 1300 numerous commercial and financial changes occurred, including an increase in the political power of self-governing cities, an increase in Europe's population, and the opening of new trade routes to Asia and the Middle East that spawned commercial growth. Without such developments, artistic, literary, political, educational, and religious changes associated with the Renaissance could not have occurred.

Northern Italian cities led the way. During the eleventh century a revival of trade and com-

Venice, Italy, bordered by the sea and crisscrossed by canals, was forced to build upward instead of outward. It was one of the richest cities in Europe. Renaissance merchants gained both wealth and political power.

merce had begun. Venice, Genoa, Milan, and other cities profited handsomely from trade with the Middle East and northern Europe, growing rich as a result. Geography was important in Italian cities monopolizing trade between Europe and Asia. Their location along the Mediterranean coast of southern Europe perfectly situated them to act as middlemen in the trade between East and West. Wealth garnered from this intercontinental trade provided resources that permitted the Renaissance to happen.

Florence was the first Italian city to experience artistic and literary activities that signaled the beginning of the Renaissance. Although Florence was an inland city, not as well suited to profit from foreign trade as were other Italian cities, it nevertheless possessed great wealth derived from control of papal finances. Florentine merchant and banking families served as tax collectors for the Roman Catholic Church, a position they used to provide banking services in North African and European cities, including London, Paris, Barcelona, Marseilles, Morocco, Tunis, and Algiers. These banking families, like the Medici, profited from their activities and used the money to develop commerce and industry in their native Florence, creating a city that was the most prosperous in Europe for a time. The wool industry was the most important industrial development in Florence. Florence traders acquired fine wool from northern European countries, especially England, Scotland, and Spain, and turned it into high quality cloth. Florence's textile industry employed thousands of workers. Traders then carried this cloth throughout the known world (Europe, Africa, and Asia) where it brought tremendous profits that were plowed back into Florentine industry.

Important also to the Renaissance was the political independence of northern Italian city-states. Milan, Florence, Genoa, Pisa, Siena, and other cities were comprised of independent merchants and craftsmen who did not owe feudal allegiance to Italian nobles. To maintain their independence, northern Italian merchants formed Communes, organizations devoted to keeping merchants and cities free from control of feudal nobles. Communes often had to construct walls around cities, enact ordinances to regulate and control commerce, and maintain law and order to prevent nobles from taking control of Italian city-states. Communes financed these activities by imposing taxes on the city's inhabitants. Most of the cities in northern Italy gained their freedom in the twelfth century when nobles who previously controlled them recognized the economic opportunities independent cities presented them. Nobles also could profit from the riches of cities. They could, for example, form business partnerships with urban merchants engaged in foreign trade, investing heavily in commercial enterprises in return for a share of the profits. Over time these business ventures between noblemen and merchants produced a new social class, an urban aristocracy. Marriages between wealthy merchant families and hereditary noble classes were not uncommon and strengthened the ability of northern Italian cities to maintain their independence.

The urban aristocracy tightly controlled Italian cities. Most residents were not given citizenship, which required that a person own a substantial amount of property, have high social status, and have resided in the city for a lengthy period. Most urban dwellers did not meet these requirements and consequently had no voice in their government. In general, *signori*, an urban king, or *oligarchies*, a small number of urban aristocrats, from 1300 to 1500, ruled Italian city-states. Cosimo de' Medici, for example, ruled Florence from 1434 to 1464 and Lorenzo de' Medici ruled the city from 1469 to 1482 as *signori*. Likewise the Sforza family controlled Milan from 1434 to 1494. Most *signori*, like the Medici and Sforza, were despots who followed no law but their own. They made and enforced ordinances that enabled them and the merchant aristocracy to maintain power, wealth, and influence. *Oligarchies* generally had constitutions, but they were structured to ensure that political power remained in the hands of the urban nobility. Wealthy merchants and other members of the urban aristocracy made the laws, controlled the courts that enforced and administered these laws, and interpreted the constitutions to suit their needs. Venice, for example, had a population that exceeded ninety thousand during the first quarter of the fifteenth century, but less than three hundred of its residents controlled the government. Practically every other Italian city-state not controlled by a *signori* existed under similar conditions. Only a few wealthy men held all the political influence. All challenges to the *signori* or *oligarchies* were crushed. Whenever residents protested their exclusion from power and the heavy tax burden that they bore, the ruling classes in Italian city-states ruthlessly used the military and police power to regain control and "put the lower classes in their place."

ITALIAN STATECRAFT, WAR, AND FOREIGN POLICY

Five Italian city-states—Venice, Florence, Milan, Naples, and the Papal States (Rome and territory governed by the Pope)—controlled Italy during the Renaissance. Of these five "city kingdoms," Venice was perhaps the most important. It was an international power during the fifteenth century. The oligarchy of merchants and bankers that controlled the city dominated its trade around the world and even established colonies outside Italy. While the other four cities were not as powerful as Venice, they exerted much influence over their neighbors. Milan and its ruling Sforza family controlled smaller towns and cities in northern Italy. The Papal States, along with Florence, controlled central Italy, while Naples was dominant in the south. These major city-states influenced politics in and controlled smaller cities in their vicinity while jockeying for influence and fighting for territory among themselves. They made treaties, engaged in spying, arranged marriages between families in other cities, and used any

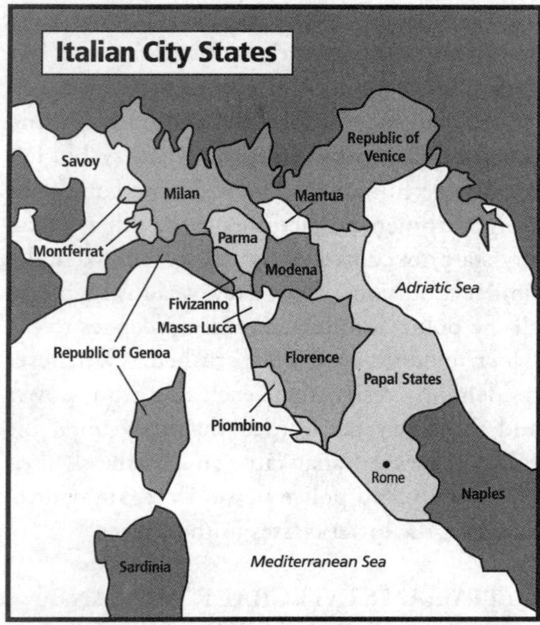

available advantage to enhance their wealth, increase trade, and obtain territory.

Italian cities also took action to prevent one state from becoming dominant. If the military power of one state increased until it was stronger than the other kingdoms, various cities combined against their stronger neighbor. This "balance of power" system, established in 1450 by the Treaty of Lodi, was a prelude to that which countries in northern and western Europe later devised to maintain peace. When Francesco Sforza, the Venetian leader, usurped the position of Duke of Milan in 1450, for example, war broke out between Venice and Milan. Florence and Naples combined their armies with those of Milan to oppose Venice and the Papal States. Cosimo de' Medici, the Florentine prince, aided Milan because he feared that Venice might become too powerful. Previously, he had made an alliance with Venice but switched sides to prevent Venice from dominating the Italian Peninsula. Naples, likewise, joined the war for similar reasons.

Wars fought by Italian city-states during the Renaissance caused what might be termed "modern diplomacy" to arise. The Italian cities were the first states to build permanent embassies in foreign capitols and staff them with full time ambassadors. This development occurred largely because Italian city-states constantly needed to keep watch on economic and political happenings abroad to protect their own military and economic interests.

The tremendous wealth of Italian city-states attracted attention from foreign powers, which led to numerous invasions of the peninsula. Venice, Florence, Milan, the Papal States, and Naples were unable to stop these invasions because of their inability to unite against a common foe and because they sometimes sought outside help against each other. When Florence and Naples signed a treaty to jointly take territory from Milan in 1493, for example, Milan invited France to defend the duchy. Charles VIII, the French monarch from 1483 until 1498, thus invaded Italy in 1484. French armies were so powerful that they easily defeated the Italian kingdoms, seizing Florence, Rome, and Naples, exiling the Medici from Florence and reestablishing a republic. The French invasion marked the beginning of a period of wars and controversy in Italy that lasted several generations.

France, in an attempt to further its political, economic, and territorial ambitions in Italy, invaded the peninsula a second time in 1508. Louis XII entered into an agreement with the Papal States and Maximilian, the Hapsburg Emperor, to form the Cambrian League. The purpose of this alliance was to take colonial territory from Venice. When France betrayed Rome and the Papal States, Pope Leo X formed a new alliance with Spain and Germany to drive France from Italy. In return, Charles V of the House of Hapsburg was named Holy Roman Emperor in 1519. His success, however, was short lived. French armies again invaded Italy in 1522, beginning a series of conflicts known as the Hapsburg-Valois Wars. Almost continual warfare on the Italian Peninsula took a costly toll on people, livestock, the government, and the economy. Rome, the imperial city, was captured and sacked by Charles V in 1527. For the most part, Italy was controlled by foreign powers until it achieved unification in the nineteenth century. Had Italian kingdoms been able to look beyond parochial interests in the fifteenth and sixteenth centuries and unite as a nation, the history of the western world likely would have been altered. Certainly, Italy could have repelled the foreign invasions and, perhaps, with its wealth and industry assumed a position of dominance in Europe.

One good thing did, however, come out of the wars in Italy. Invading armies exported cultural and intellectual developments achieved by the Italian Renaissance to northern and western Europe. Had these conflicts not occurred, the Renaissance might not have spread outside Italy.

THE ARTISTIC RENAISSANCE IN ITALY

Art is perhaps the feature most associated with the Renaissance. The reappearance of classical styles and an emphasis on harmony and balance were important features of Renaissance art. Many forms of art flourished during the fifteenth and sixteenth centuries, including painting, sculpture, and architecture. From 1500 to 1527, a period historians call the High Renaissance, Italy's most famous artists—Leonardo da Vinci, Raphael, and Michelangelo—labored in Rome, producing masterpieces like the statue of David, the Mona Lisa painting, the ceiling of the Sistine Chapel, and other equally impressive works. Rome, Florence, Venice, and other Italian cities were centers for artistic achievement.

A distinctive and vitally important feature of Renaissance art was the discovery of perspective and the change it produced in humankind's mental vision of the world. This change is evident in paintings by the masters Botticelli, Masaccio, Ghirlandaio, da Vinci, and other Renaissance artists. The qualities that perspective gives to art—illusion of depth, the capturing of a moment in an event, the sense of movement, careful attention to detail, and an accurate representation of nature—are evident in Renaissance work.

Artists in Renaissance Italy generally did not produce art for art's sake. Rather, they produced art for profit, working on commission for a wealthy merchant or ruler. Production of art for the masses meant the artist had little status as a professional. An individual's reputation as an artist was directly related to the amount of money he or she earned from powerful patrons like the Medici family, who spent vast sums on artistic commissions. Important artists like Leonardo da Vinci and Michelangelo became wealthy on commissions from these art patrons. Da Vinci earned in excess of 2,000 ducats a year at a time when common laborers lived on less than 250 ducats annually. Michelangelo earned 3,000 ducats for painting the ceiling of the Sistine Chapel. This enabled him to turn down a commission for work on St. Peter's Basilica because he was wealthy enough to live comfortably for the rest of his life.

Not only did artists become wealthy, they also achieved high social status within Renaissance society. The Holy Roman Emperor Charles V picked up a paintbrush the artist Titian had dropped, a reflection of the status of artists. Contemporaries sometimes perceived Renaissance artists as geniuses. This marked a break with the Middle Ages. Then, it was generally thought that God expressed himself by giving artists the ability to create. Thus, according to medieval philosophy, God created all artwork by using individual artists. Renaissance people, in contrast, believed that the artist created art. Unlike medieval thought, which did not recognize individual originality, the Renaissance celebrated it. Renaissance people thought that art was not only the creation of the artists but reflected his or her own individuality, personality, and style.

Not only did art enrich the artists but it enhanced the lifestyles of wealthy individuals in Italian city-states. During the Middle Ages homes and castles of princes and wealthy merchants were generally sparsely furnished. As wealth increased in the Renaissance, elaborate and artistic decorations found their way into houses and castles. Rooms were filled with paintings, portraits, statues, elaborately carved furniture, woven tapestries, and other artifacts. Churches and private chapels, likewise, were decorated.

Lorenzo de' Medici was a patron of the arts.

Italian Renaissance society viewed art as power. Individuals in the Italian city-states commissioned artists to complete works to display their wealth and power or to celebrate their family name. Kings, oligarchs, wealthy merchants, and guilds hired artists and commissioned works to make the lower and middle classes aware of their influence and prestige. Such individuals and groups spent enormous sums on paintings, ornate buildings, portraits, and decorative burial chambers to display their wealth. Lorenzo de' Medici, for example, claimed that the Medici had spent over 650,000 gold florins commissioning works of art and architecture from 1435 to 1470.

Themes Renaissance artists depicted were different than those medieval artists conveyed. Instead of dealing with spiritual themes, as artists in the Middle Ages tended to do, Renaissance art was more secular. Individuals who were the subject of portraits, for example, were often painted in a romantic setting. Giotto, a Florentine painter who lived from 1276 until 1337, was one of the first artists to express realism in portraits. His use of facial expressions and various body poses represented a break from the stiff poses and artificial looks that characterized medieval portraits. Likewise, the Florentine painter Masaccio, often called the father of modern painting by art historians, pioneered the use of light and shade to make his work more accurately reflect the real world.

Sculpture also reflected realism. Donatello, an artist working in Florence during the first half of the fifteenth century, created statues depicting differences in human nature. His work drew from ancient artists in Greece and Rome. He moved away from the medieval display of the naked human body in a spiritual context, creating nude human forms in which individual self-awareness was evident. Other artists, including the famous Michelangelo, also glorified the human body. *David*, Michelangelo's depiction of the Hebrew king in his triumph over the Philistine giant Goliath, shows a male that is youthful, strong, self-confident, and certain of victory over his larger opponent. Female figures were treated in a similar manner. Rather than being depicted as stiff and formal, they were shown as full figured, voluptuous, sensual, and sexual. Artistic treatment of the human body is a reflection of the secularism of the Renaissance. Religion was beginning to lose its grip on the artist as well as the literary scholar.

INTELLECTUAL ACHIEVEMENTS

Renaissance men and women living in fourteenth and fifteenth century Italian towns and cities were conscious that they inhabited a new world vastly different than that of the Middle Ages. The first man to publicize the dawning of a new age was the poet Francesco Petrarch. His poetry and writings indicate that he believed a new age of light had replaced several centuries of darkness that began with the downfall of the Roman Empire. For Petrarch, the first four hundred years of the millennium after the birth of Christ marked the apex of western civilization. When Germanic tribes invaded Western Europe beginning in the fourth century, a "Dark Age" was inaugurated. These Dark or Middle Ages lasted a thousand years, from 400 A.D. to 1400 A.D. During this dark millennium knowledge was stagnant, scholarship almost nonexistent, and people lived a brutal, barbaric lifestyle largely devoid of art, literature, and the finer things in life that had characterized Greco-Roman civilization. Petrarch, however, believed Greco-Roman civilization was reborn in Italy during the fourteenth century. This rebirth, or Renaissance, as the French called it, witnessed a remarkable record of human intellectual accomplishment. Three intellectual changes marked the Renaissance: secularism, individualism, and humanism. Each of these developments represented a change from medieval European attitudes and is the foundation upon which Western society is built today.

Secularism

Secularism is a fascination with the temporal rather than the spiritual world. Medieval thinkers were more concerned with God and religion than with secular life. Their writings usually focused on heaven and eternal salvation rather than on human life on earth. St. Augustine, for example, maintained that there were two kingdoms, the spiritual one of God and the earthly one of humans. God's kingdom, according to St. Augustine, should be sought while the human kingdom should be shunned. Renaissance scholars, however, tended to be less concerned with the world of God and more concerned with the human condition in the earthly world. Renaissance thinkers did not reject spiritual matters but focused more on the temporal world. Unlike medieval monks and scholars who often abhorred material possessions, Renaissance people often pursued material wealth.

These changing attitudes about materialism had their roots in the economic changes Italy experienced in the thirteenth and fourteenth centuries. As merchants became richer, their attitudes toward wealth changed. The richer they became, the more material comforts and pleasures they could afford. Money gave bankers and merchants in Florence, Rome, Genoa, Venice, Milan, and other Renaissance cities the wherewithal to commission art and the leisure time to enjoy it. Consequently, they began to view life from a different perspective. Instead of seeing the purpose of life as a difficult struggle to obtain heaven, Renaissance men and women viewed existence as an opportunity to enjoy life. What the revival of classical thought in the Renaissance enabled the upper crust of society to do was redirect their attention from preparation for paradise to a concern for living here and now. Renaissance people were unwilling to accept the self-denying, world-rejecting monastic view of life that had dominated medieval culture, and they were dissatisfied with a worldview where human beings were merely pawns in a larger game plan of God. Instead, Renaissance people cultivated family life, endorsed the wise use of wealth, and actively involved themselves in worldly affairs. The temporal world was seen not as a Babylon, or as merely a rest stop on the long pilgrimage to heaven, but as a place where people, using critically and intelligently the wisdom of the ancient past, could realize their potential.

Writings left behind by Renaissance men of letters reflect the temporal world that dominated thought. Lorenzo Valla, an Italian humanist, in *On the False Donation of Constantine* (See Chapter 6) challenges the Catholic Church's claim to have authority over human life. He concluded that an eight-century deed known as the Donation of Constantine, giving the Roman Church and its Pope vast lands in Western Europe, was fake. The Emperor Constantine had not, in fact, given the Church jurisdiction over this land. Valla's evidence that the Donation of Constantine was a forgery questioned Church claims that it had control of earthly life. How could an institution that purported to be concerned with spiritual matters use a forged document to gain control of a large land area? Valla also discovered serious errors in St. Jerome's translation of the Greek Testament into the Italian language. Valla's work called into question the Church's credibility. He showed that reason and scholarship could be used to challenge previously accepted facts of the medieval world. In another work, *On Pleasure*, he challenged the medieval view that the spiritual world was the highest good, maintaining that earthly pleasures, including food, drink, wealth, art, and sex, were equally as good.

Other writers also concentrated on the sensual. Giovanni Boccaccio in *Decameron* created characters, including husbands, fathers, priests, businessmen, who enjoyed life and pursued temporal and material objects rather than spirituality. Unlike medieval literature, which viewed sensual pursuits with contempt, Boccacio and other Renaissance authors made sensuality and materialism respectable goals to be sought. They supported their views by drawing upon the works of ancient Greek and Roman authors.

Secularism also pervaded the Roman Catholic Church. For the most part, high ranking Church officials—popes, cardinals, and bishops—were scions of wealthy Italian merchants and banking families. They were reared in households who pursued material wealth, patronized art, and sought sensual pleasures. As Church officers, they continued to do these things and seldom did much to discourage the new secular spirit that pervaded upper levels of Italian society. The Church itself spent enormous sums commissioning artists and architects to create works and design buildings that enhanced the power and beauty of Rome. The Papal Chancellery, constructed from 1483 to 1511, is considered an architectural masterpiece of the Renaissance. St. Peters Basilica was demolished in 1506 and replaced with a new structure; Michelangelo was hired to create the building's dome, which is perhaps his greatest work. Thus, the Church partook of and encouraged secularism rather than condemning and attacking it. The Church's attitude did not mean that it had forsaken spiritual matters altogether. Rather, Church officials tried to strike a balance between the

***Decameron*, by Boccaccio, was the first major prose piece of the Renaissance written in the vernacular tongue.**

spiritual and temporal worlds, recognizing that both were important to human existence. Most people living in Renaissance society remained Christian, continuing to follow basic teachings of Christ and the apostles. Even learned men who questioned medieval religious doctrine remained loyal to the Church and Christianity. They were neither atheist nor agnostic but simply viewed religion from a more worldly perspective. Religious themes were still present in Renaissance art, literature, essays, and architecture but so were temporal and material themes, which had been largely absent from medieval works.

Individualism

A second intellectual development that characterized the Renaissance was individualism. While medieval Europe produced renowned personalities like St. Augustine, their achievements were not celebrated as personal accomplishments but as spiritual accomplishments. St. Augustine, as the Bishop of Hippo, wrote his greatest work, *City of God,* to glorify God. Christian beliefs discouraged medieval men from seeking personal glory. This mode of thought and behavior changed with the Renaissance. Individual personality and achievements became important. Artists, architects, and men of letters openly competed with each other and boasted whenever they bested an opponent. Renaissance men sought fame, glory, and attention. Each one tried to accomplish as much as possible while alive so that society would notice. Individual genius was celebrated by Renaissance Europe, and individuals were urged to reach their full potential as human beings. Renaissance men did not follow the "herd mentality." They were not afraid to be different from their neighbors. Consequently, the Renaissance produced individuals who relished their own individuality and who were not afraid to celebrate it. Michelangelo, Gentile Bellini, Leonardo da Vinci, Raphael, Valla, Boccaccio, Benvenuto Cellini, Leon Battista Alberti, Niccole Machiavelli, and other Renaissance figures are remembered for remarkable individual achievements. They and others developed a large body of art and literary work as a result of individualism. Had these men been part of medieval society, the modern world might not have remembered them because most likely they could not have accomplished what they did in a medieval society. They distanced themselves from other people and provided a sense of historical distance from medieval Europe.

Humanism

A third characteristic of the Renaissance was humanism. The Florentine writer Giovanni Pico della Mirandola was its leading advocate. His work, *Oration on the Dignity of Man*, rejected the medieval notion that the distinctive thing about humankind was its place on the Great Chain of Being; instead, he stressed that the individual had an intrinsic worth and that the highest form of religion was to respect human dignity. People can best worship God, Pico held, by respecting themselves and fellow human beings while cultivating individuality to the highest possible level. Intellectual development and the pursuit of knowledge should be goals sought by each individual. Although Pico and other humanists held Christian beliefs and values, their fundamental outlook on life was somewhat different. Whereas medieval Christianity emphasized the sinfulness of humans, the lack of control people had over their destiny, and the unlimited ability of God to forgive, humanists stressed the grandeur of man and viewed God as being relatively uninvolved in the world after creation. While God ultimately judged each human life and decided whether the individual suffered heaven or hell, the deity did not intervene directly in life. Human beings were directly responsible for their life because they had freedom to choose. An important component of humanism was skepticism. Renaissance humanists did not accept Christian, pagan, and classical authors and documents at face value. Rather, they questioned their authority, conscious that time and historical context separated the two ages and knowledgeable that ancient texts often disagreed with and contradicted each other.

The origins of humanism, like most aspects of the Renaissance, lie in antiquity. Italian cities rediscovered ancient texts produced by Greek, Roman, and Egyptian authors. Pope Nicholas V, for example, collected over nine thousand ancient manuscripts, which were eventually housed in the Vatican library that Pope Sixtus IV had constructed. The term "humanism" is derived from ideas of *humanitas* found in ancient texts written by Cicero. In the Ciceronian sense, *humanitas* refers to the educational and literary knowledge needed by civilized beings. Leonardo Bruni, a Florentine historian and lecturer who lived from 1370 to 1444, was the first scholar to use the term humanism to describe the study of ancient texts to understand human nature. These ancient texts focused on individuals, their accomplishments, and their intellectual abilities. Their study led Renaissance scholars to reject the medieval idea that people were merely helpless sinners with no control over life. Instead, humanists emphasized the innate dignity, intellectual abilities, creative talent, free will, and ability to determine the course of life present in all people.

In fact, one can argue that the catalyst for the Italian Renaissance was the rediscovery of ancient texts. Although classical texts were present in monastic libraries, the urban middle classes did not read them during the Middle Ages. At the beginning of the Renaissance, however, the messages ancient texts contained about individualism and secularism were particularly relevant to the new commercial society arising in Italian cities. Furthermore, Renaissance scholars realized that the meaning of ancient texts was often lost or altered by poor translators and thus studied ancient forms of Latin and Greek so that they could read classical texts in their original form. Knowledge of ancient Greek was greatly enhanced when the Byzantine scholar, Manuel Chrysoloras, came to Florence in 1397. This need by Renaissance scholars to find texts closest to the original as possible led to the development of modern philology, textual criticism, and literary and historical scholarship. The study of ancient texts caused Renaissance scholars to admire classical Latin. Because many of the ancient texts they were fascinated with were written in classical Latin,

Renaissance intellectuals viewed it as superior to the language used by Latin writers of the Middle Ages. Consequently, men of letters during the Renaissance imitated ancient authors, writing highly stylized manuscripts in classical Latin. They even went so far as to try to recreate Plato's Academy from the fourth century A. D., using the Socratic method of questioning and dialogue to uncover knowledge.

Humanism gave rise to the concept of the Universal or Renaissance person. This was an individual who was well-rounded enough to do many things. The idea of the Universal person first surfaced in *The Courtier* written by Baldassare Castiglione around 1500. According to Castiglione, the Universal person should speak several languages fluently and be knowledgeable about art, literature, and philosophy. If wealthy, the Universal person should patronize artists and authors while always conducting himself in private and public with the grace and dignity that only knowledge could provide. A good example of a Renaissance man was Leonardo da Vinci. During his lifetime (1452-1519) he was a painter, engineer, anatomist, botanist, optician, and inventor. He theorized about the Law of Gravity two full centuries before Sir Isaac Newton, designed an airplane that influenced other designers, including the Wright brothers, drew the first complete anatomical charts of the human body, studied the principle of optics, and theorized about energy conservation. In addition, his paintings the *Last Supper* and *the Mona Lisa* are among the greatest art works in history.

LITERATURE, WRITING, AND PAINTING

Literature was an important component of the Italian Renaissance. Florence was the dominant city in literary prose, producing great writers, while Ferrara dominated poetry. Francesco Petrarch (1313-1375), the first individual to recognize that a new age had dawned, greatly influenced Renaissance literature. A student of classical literature, he perfected the sonnet as a literary form. His writing style was copied by other Renaissance literary figures. Likewise, Giovanni Boccaccio (1313-1375) helped shape Italian prose and *Decameron*, a collection of stories, influenced novelists into the fifteenth and sixteenth centuries.

Italian Renaissance poetry was centered in Ferrara, a duchy ruled by the Este family located north of Florence and the Papal States. One of the most important Ferraran poets was Matteo Maria Boiardo. He wrote scores of poems during his life from 1434 to 1494. His most famous, *Orlando Innamorato*, was modeled after the medieval *Song of Roland*. He tried to recapture the vitality of the ancient knights long after their time had passed. Ludovico Ariosto (1474-1533) wrote Italy's greatest epic, *Orlando Furisos*, while Torquato Tasso (1544-1595) focused on the First Crusade to the Holy Land in *Jerusalem Delivered*. Other poets too numerous to mention were also part of the Renaissance.

The Renaissance produced writing in genera other than prose and poetry. Niccolo Machiavelli wrote about politics, government, and statecraft. His most famous work, *The Prince*, rejects metaphysics, theology, and idealism in favor of political realism. Machiavelli distinguished between what ought to be and what is, between the ideal form of government and the pragmatic conditions under which government actually operates. *The Prince* told would-be rulers how to gain and maintain power in the real world. Contrary to the popular view, Machiavelli was not some ogre or Anti-Christ who created a new immorality. He was a diplomat who served the Republic of Florence, the government that

The invention of the printing press eliminated the laborious process of copying books by hand and thus accelerated the spread of literature.

came into existence when Pietro Medici, son of Lorenzo, was forced into exile in 1494. For the next eighteen years, Machiavelli lived under and loved the Florentine Republic. At the age of twenty-nine he joined the government headed by Piero Soderini, who was elected *Gofalonier* (President for Life) in 1502. Machiavelli saw service in the diplomatic corps, where he distinguished himself, until war destroyed the republic in 1512 and again brought the Medici to power. Florence had insisted on allying itself with France against the Papal States and Spain. When France withdrew its protection from Florence in 1512, the city was at the mercy of a hostile pope and his Spanish allies. Machiavelli formed a citizens' army (city militia) to defend Florence but saw it crushed by a stronger Spanish force. Machiavelli was captured and tortured by the Medici before being allowed to retire to the countryside where he wrote numerous books, including *The Prince, A History of Florence, Discourses, The Art of War*, and *Mandragola*. Although he hoped to return to governmental service, the opportunity never presented itself. Machiavelli died in 1527, awaiting a call from a new government that had come to power in Italy. Charles V defeated Papal armies in 1527 and sacked Rome, allowing republican forces in Florence to oust the Medici and restore democratic government for a short period. Machiavelli hurried back to Florence, eager to regain a diplomatic post. Unfortunately, leaders of the new government, like most people, had read and misunderstood *The Prince*, which caused them to fear and distrust Machiavelli. The hopeful Machiavelli became ill and died before learning that the Florentine governing council had voted against employing him as a diplomat. Yet, even after death, Machiavelli survives through the pages of *The Prince*. He was the first politician to truly understand the art of power politics that has shaped the modern world.

THE PRINTING PRESS

The invention of the printed word made literature available to the upper and middle classes. A form of printing that developed in China reached Italy as a result of trade along the Silk Road. The Chinese began to reproduce printed characters carved into blocks of wood that were inked and then pressed onto paper. Using wooden blocks to print characters and words as the Chinese did was expensive and time consuming. Europeans found a more efficient way to print. Johannes Gutenberg of Mainz, Germany is credited with inventing moveable metal type in 1455. There is evidence, however, that Johann Frist and Peter Schoffer also had a hand in creating moveable type and thus modern printing. These men created a system whereby individual letters could be put together to form words and sentences on paper. Since each letter was interchangeable with all other letters, words and sentences could be arranged in any format to print any text in existence.

Paper also was important to Renaissance printing. Medieval European scribes had written on animal hides. Because sheepskin, calfskin, and other animal hide parchments were expensive, few copies of ancient or medieval texts were produced. Arab traders had brought paper, which was relatively inexpensive when compared to animal skins, to Europe during the twelfth century. The Chinese had invented a process to manufacture paper, and Arab traders began to sell the product in European markets. Europeans quickly learned how to make their own paper, which printers could easily acquire.

The invention of the printing press had a tremendous effect on Europe. For the first time, large numbers of people had access to literature. The availability of books increased because their production cost decreased, which enabled middle and upper class merchants to collect their own private libraries. Simultaneously, the printing press facilitated communications among scholars and the general dissemination of knowledge. In 1456 Gutenberg printed his first Bible; within a half-century scores of presses had been established. By 1500 there were over 70 printing presses in Italy, 50 in Germany, 40 in France, and lesser numbers in England, Switzerland, and the Netherlands. The largest and most important press was located in Venice. It was operated by Aldus Manutius and named the Aldine Press. Classic works of ancient Greek and Latin literature, as well as the best works of Renaissance authors, were published. It employed approximately six hundred workers and produced about 15 percent of all books printed in Europe.

Printing affected many aspects of European life. It enabled governments and businesses to effectively use propaganda. Governments could easily disseminate their viewpoints to the masses, while merchants and shopkeepers could engage in a subtle use of propaganda called advertising. Propaganda gave rise to political parties that competed with each other on ideological grounds. Localism and provincialism were eventually replaced by nationalism. People who lived in diverse geographical locations could be united by the printed word and form a common or national identity.

Printing also had an effect on the lives of ordinary people throughout Europe. Because life was tedious, most people sought relief from boredom through reading. Although many books dealt with religion in the early years of printing, printers eventually produced books on practically every imaginable subject.

RENAISSANCE SOCIETY

Although the Renaissance was one of the most important events in Western Civilization, it did not mark the beginning of the modern age. Renaissance society and Renaissance people were, in many respects, closer to medieval men and women than modern people. Yet, the Renaissance concern with secular and religious life laid the intellectual foundations for the modern world. Despite this emphasis on humankind rather than God, most people living during the Renaissance retained their Christian faith. With the exception of a few scholars, most Renaissance people did not question the authority of the Church or the basic tenets of Christianity. Even Italian humanists were not atheist, agnostics, or skeptics. The scores of religious art works and written manuscripts produced by Renaissance scholars that contain religious themes provide evidence that religion remained important during the Renaissance.

A small mercantile elite dominated Renaissance society. It was generally not democratic, and most lower classes of people did not fully participate in it. Renaissance culture and society were created by a small number of highly educated, intellectual writers and artists for an elite population. These elites did not understand, or much care, about the common man and woman. In fact, the Renaissance created and perpetuated a gap between highly educated members of society and the undereducated that persists even today.

Education was a central concern of Renaissance humanists. Numerous essays, letters, and books were written on the subject. The most influential was Castiglione's *The Courtier*. Castiglione maintained that men (not women) should undergo both academic and physical development. The ideal man should have a broad understanding of all academic disciplines, be able to dance, be able to understand music and art, and be proficient at fighting. Education should be structured to teach these things to all young men, especially those from rich merchant or banking families.

Peter Paul Vergerio, another Renaissance scholar, devised a program of education similar to Castiglione's and linked it to the interests of the state. In a letter written to Ubertinus, the ruler of Carraia, Vergerio maintained that the state had an interest in using education to create modern citizens. His program outlined in this letter advised that students study history because it teaches virtue from past examples, ethics so that virtue itself can be learned, and public speaking or rhetoric to develop eloquent oratorical skills. Vergerio also maintained that teachers should be individuals with high moral standards who would provide good examples for students to imitate and who would "repress the first sign of evil." He called his education program "liberal arts" because it was designed to allow the individual to obtain wisdom and practice virtue.

Women

Education, scholarship, and artistic endeavors, like most public activities during the Renaissance, were considered male activities. With a few exceptions, women were not allowed to attend universities and could not practice law or medicine, go into banking, or become teachers. Legally, women were considered to be the property of their fathers until marriage when they became the property of their husbands. (This ideal is still reflected in modern marriage ceremonies when the father traditionally gives the bride away.) Females who attempted to enter male-dominated professions faced much ridicule, suspicion, and opposition. Educational opportunities for women were so limited that less than two hundred women in all Europe owned books, an indication that literacy rates were low.

The status of women during the Renaissance actually declined when compared to the Middle Ages. Access to property and political power for upper class women was less than during medieval Europe, and the ability of women to shape society was almost non-existent during the Renaissance. Ordinary women still performed the same economic functions in Renaissance Europe as their mothers and grandmothers in previous epochs. Farm wives and daughters helped husbands and fathers complete agricultural tasks while urban women performed domestic duties and other feminine tasks. Countless women across Europe functioned as midwives, cooks, seamstresses, maids, laundresses, and house servants. A few women worked in industry. The Italian textile industry, for example, employed women as weavers and silk winders. Shipyards in other European countries often used women to make canvas sails. Widows who possessed the required skills sometimes ran their deceased husband's businesses and were occasionally admitted to membership in guilds.

Occasionally, Renaissance women overcame barriers placed in their way by achieving an education. A few remarkable women from upper class families managed to obtain educations equal to their male counterparts. Such women were taught how to read, write, and do mathematical calculations. They then could learn the ancient languages, which enabled them to read classical literary texts. Such educational advances enabled a few women to produce scholarly works of their own. After the printing press was invented, at least twenty-five Italian women wrote books that were published. Other Renaissance women exchanged letters with male and female colleagues on academic topics, engaged in heated debate with scholars, and produced great works of art.

Isotta Nogarola was one of the most remarkable women the Renaissance produced. She was born in Verona, Italy, in 1418 to a noble family that took pride in educational achievement. Nogarola's aunt, Angela, had been highly educated and when her father died, urged Nogarola's mother to provide her daughter with a classical education, which was atypical for women at that time. Martino Rizzoni, a prominent educator, was hired to tutor Nogarola and her sister, Ginevra. The sisters learned quickly and soon became well known among Italian humanists. Ginevra married in 1438 and, as was customary, completely abandoned her academic pursuits. Isotta moved to Venice, a more cosmopolitan city, where she lived until 1441 when she returned to Verona. Determined never to wed, she spent the majority of her life pursuing academic matters. About 1450 she began to correspond with Ludovico Foscarini, a humanist politician. Their letters provided material that Nogarola drew on to produce several books, including her two most famous, *Dialogue on Adam and Eve* and *Oration on the Life of St. Jerome.*

Another remarkable woman that overcame sexist prejudice was Laura Cereta. Her life from 1469 to 1499 illustrates both the successes and failures of Renaissance women. Like Nogarola, Cereta was a scholar who had difficulty overcoming social prejudices against talented women. Until she was nine years old, she lived in a convent where her education began. She left the convent with her father, a Brescian nobleman and Lombardy government official. He taught Cereta to speak several languages and instructed her in mathematics, philosophy, history, theology, government, and classical literature. Education provided Cereta with self-esteem and a desire to become a scholar like Petrarch, her hero. Marriage to a merchant at the age of fifteen interrupted her studies. Like most Renaissance and some modern women, Cereta was forced to choose between marriage and a career. She could take a husband, bear children, participate fully in social life, and assume domestic duties or live life similar to a hermit, withdrawn from the larger world. After choosing marriage, Cereta fully expected to abandon scholarly pursuits until the unexpected death of her spouse from Bubonic Plague eighteen month after the wedding, which opened new opportunities. The young widow found an outlet for her grief in the pursuit of knowledge. Prior to her death in 1499, Cereta wrote numerous letters to contemporary scholars defending her ideas about a liberal education for women.

Although women labored in studios throughout Italy, credit for the artwork they produced usually went to their husbands and fathers who owned the studios. An exception was Sofonisba Anguissola. Born into an aristocratic Cremonan family about 1532, she, along with her five sisters, were taught music and painting in accordance with ideas on female education her parents gleaned from Castiglione's *The Courtier*. Sofonisba showed artistic talent as a result of this training and was allowed to study formally with Bernardino Campi, a local painter. Her family encouraged Sofonisba's painting. In 1557, her father persuaded the great Michelangelo to send Sofonisba several drawings that she could paint and return for him to evaluate. Sofenisba's work so impressed Michelangelo that he invited her to serve a two-year apprenticeship under him in Rome. During the apprenticeship she painted a portrait of the Duke of Alba that pleased him so much that he secured her a position at the court of King Philip II of Spain, a job she held for twenty years. The Spanish royal family valued her work so highly that King Philip gave her away when she married a Sicilian nobleman, Fabrizio de Moncada, in 1569. The royal couple, Philip and Queen Isabella, patronized her work. Sofonisba's most famous work is *Portrait of a Couple*, a painting that depicts a husband holding his wife with a tender touch while the couple stare at the viewer, a trait found in most of her work.

Sofonisba inspired other female artists throughout Europe. One of them was Artemisia Gentileschi. Her father, Orazio, himself an artist, taught Artemisia how to paint after her mother died. Orazio also arranged for Artemisia to study under the master painter Caravaggio where she developed a style in which light and dark contrasts were used to convey emotions. Artemisia, at the age of seventeen, completed her first critically acclaimed work, *Susanna and the Elders*, a painting depicting a vulnerable young girl in a world filled with dangerous men. Even after marriage, Artemisia continued working as a painter, one of only a few women to do so. Her signature masterpiece, *Judith Slaying Holofernes*, was painted after she left Rome for Florence where several members of the Medici family, the scientist Galileo, and descendants of Michelangelo patronized her. In the masterpiece, Judith is depicted as a strong, heroic woman who beheads Holofernes, the Assyrian oppressor of the Hebrews. The painting reveals not only Artemisia's technical talents but her use of bold colors conveys a strong sense of emotion to the viewer. Other works that Artemisia painted also depicted strong female figures, including *Madonna and Child, Self-portrait as the Allegory of Painting*, and portraits of Cleopatra, Lucretia, Minerva, and Mary Magdalene. In 1616 she was the first female artist granted membership in the Florence Academy of Art, the most prestigious artistic society of the seventeenth century.

Despite some success in the literary and artistic world, careers for most Renaissance women were non-existent. Medieval women were relatively equal to men in regards to love and sex, but

Renaissance humanists created a double standard for men and women. Castiglione and others proclaimed that woman's proper place was in the home. They maintained that men and men alone participated in public life and separated sex from love. For women, sex was permitted only in the marriage bed, while men, even married ones, pursued sex outside matrimony. Women were required to remain virginal until marriage and then were generally relegated to social roles as wives and mothers. Any talent or career aspirations a wife might harbor were put aside to promote those of her husband and male children. Laura Cereta, Sofonisba Anguissola, Artemisia Gentilischi, Isotta Nogarola, and other Renaissance women who overcame social barriers to achieve scholarly and artistic prominence were the exceptions. Most women had little hope of developing their talents and abilities to their utmost potential.

Females living during the Renaissance were often victimized by rape. Legal evidence from Italian city-states indicates that rape was treated in a casual manner. It was not even classified as a felony. Noblemen committed many rapes. Punishment for a nobleman convicted of raping a noblewoman ranged from a small fine to about six months in prison. Punishment for a nobleman who raped a woman not born to the noble class was non-existent. These light sentences were handed down during a time when shoplifting was punished by bodily mutilation, when heresy was punished by burning at the stake, and when forgery resulted in beheading. The only time rapists were severely punished occurred when a child under the age of twelve was raped or when a common man raped a high-ranking noble woman. Assaults by working class men on noble women were punished more severely because such assaults often had social and political consequences, especially if they resulted in pregnancy. In general, Renaissance society believed that rape did little harm to its victims.

Renaissance women who tried to overcome gender barriers usually faced ridicule and scorn from both lay people and scholars. Females could choose marriage and full participation as women in society or scholarship and social isolation. Marriage prevented most women from fulfilling their scholarly ambitions. With marriage came children and domestic responsibilities that prevented study. Also, males felt threatened by educated females. Most Renaissance men believed that learning was contrary to a woman's basic nature. Education, they believed, would make a woman cease to be a woman. Intelligent women, such as Laura Cereta, who were accomplished scholars faced severe attacks from male counterparts because they threatened to break the male dominance in the intellectual world. Most girls during the Renaissance from upper and middle class families received at most a minimum education in painting, music, and dance. The purpose of this education was to enable them to attract husbands. Girls were educated in various social graces so that after marriage they could grace the husband's household and attract scholars and artists to the manor. Women were not educated to participate in politics or business.

Minorities and Slavery

Women were not the only minorities that suffered from discrimination in Renaissance Europe. Ethnic minorities faced not only discrimination and prejudice but persecution as well. Italy and other Renaissance nations contained a small number of ethnic and religious minorities during the Middle Ages and into the Renaissance. Even though the overwhelming majority of Europe's population was Roman Catholic, a minority of the population in eastern areas of the continent were Eastern Orthodox Christians. In worship services they used either the Greek or Slovonic rites rather than those of the Roman Church. Christians in western nations, however, viewed practitioners of Orthodoxy with suspicion, as Renaissance people did not tolerate religious diversity

Another religious minority in Renaissance Europe were Muslims. Islam reached Europe by two routes—from the Middle East and North Africa. The Moors, Islamic people from northern Africa, invaded Spain and France and controlled parts of both nations from the Middle Ages into the Renaissance. In 1492 Spanish armies controlled by Isabella of Castile, the warrior queen, captured the last Moorish stronghold at Granada. Following a brief period of religious toleration, Isabella demanded that the thousands of Muslims living in Spain convert to Roman Catholicism. Those who refused were expelled from the Iberian Peninsula. Faced with eviction, thousands became Christian, but thousands more gave up their property and material possessions, fleeing Spain for Africa, Asia, or other European countries. Many lost their lives after leaving Spain due to religious intolerance elsewhere.

Although Islam was virtually destroyed on the Iberian Peninsula, it existed in Eastern Europe as a result of warfare with the Middle East. The Ottoman ruler, Sultan Mehmed II (1451-1481), captured Constantinople, the Turkish city that straddled the boundary between Europe and Asia in 1453. After taking Turkey, Mehmed launched a military campaign in Southern and Eastern Europe. His armies took Athens in 1456 and eventually conquered all of Greece. Later, he captured territories in the Balkans, including Serbia, Bosnia, Herzegovina, and Albania. Mehmed allowed the populations he had conquered to convert to Islam. As a result, Islam became firmly established in Eastern Europe.

Renaissance Europe also had a small population of Jews who managed to survive despite various waves of persecutions. No minority religious or ethnic group was treated as poorly in Europe as were Jews. They often underwent forced expulsions from European countries or were forced to convert to Christianity to escape execution. Occasionally, Jewish populations in Italy and other Renaissance countries were protected by princes or ruling families. However, in most countries Jews were prohibited from owning land, which meant that agriculture was closed to them. Consequently, European Jews became an urban people, working as butchers, peddlers, bankers, pawnbrokers, notaries, writers, servants, and various other occupations not legally closed.

Hatred and prejudice against Jews was so bad that Jewish communities during the fourteenth century were often blamed for any disaster that befell a community. One such example was the Bubonic Plague. Christians throughout Europe accused Jewish neighbors of poisoning wells or placing evil spells on victims of the Black Death. Of course, such accusations were untrue. Bubonic Plague was actually spread by germs that lived in fleas carried by rats that infested Renaissance houses. Many communities afflicted by the plague believed that God was punishing them for allowing unchristian Jews to live within the city. The only way they believed they could rid themselves of the plague was to expel or exterminate their Jewish population. As a result, Jews in hundreds of localities experienced waves of terror that cost them their homes, wealth, and often their lives.

Africans were another minority that lived in parts of Europe during the Renaissance. They came from numerous tribes and religious groups on their native continent. Most were used as domestic slaves in wealthy homes at the height of the Renaissance. African slavery is traceable to the Roman Empire. Africans, along with white slaves, had come into Europe after being captured in war. After the Roman Empire fell, slave traders continued to sell people to rich families. When the Bubonic Plague reduced Europe's population in the fourteenth century, the resulting reduction in the labor force caused the demand for slaves to increase. Thousands of slaves from Africa were brought to Europe. These individuals were captured and sold into slavery by Portuguese and Spanish traders in markets at Barcelona, Marseilles, Seville, Genoa, Pisa, Naples, and other localities. So many Africans were imported into Europe during the Renaissance that they comprised between 3 and 10 percent of the urban population

Europeans often viewed Africans as evil. Prior to the age of discovery, the European world-view was limited. Most Europeans had no contact with Africa. What they knew of it was based on Biblical stories. Europeans generally saw Africa as a far away place inhabited by dark people who were either pagan or heretical Muslims. Contact with an "advanced" European civilization, most believed, would improve the African race. Europeans also suffered from racial prejudice and bias against Africans caused by the scant Biblical knowledge about the continent they valued so highly. European religious scholars maintained that Christ, who was good, was of light skin pigmentation. Black, which represented Satan, was evil. Therefore, theologians speculated that black skinned Africans were created by the devil in his image and were evil while whites, created by a light skinned God in his image, were good. Lucifer, or Satan, was usually depicted as a black man in Renaissance art. Unfortunately, Renaissance scholars ignored historical and archaeological evidence that indicated Christ was most likely dark skinned.

Europeans also regarded Africans as objects of curiosity. Black servants, because of their skin pigmentation, were valued because they were different. Some noble households even kept black servants as "court jesters." In 1491, Isabella, the Duchess of Mantura, gave orders to purchase an African girl with as dark a skin as possible to use for entertainment. Isabella wanted to train the girl to be the "best buffoon in the world." Most Africans, however, were not used for entertainment. They usually performed numerous tasks from farm laborers to prostitutes.

Other minorities, including whites, also served as slaves in Renaissance Europe. Tartars and Turks, for example, were occasionally sold at slave auctions in Ancona, Genoa, Pisa, Venice, and other cities. Like their African counterparts, these slaves performed multiple tasks from serving on ships, working as domestics and in factories to herdsmen, grape pickers, and craftsmen. It appears that race, in contrast to American slavery in later centuries, played little role in Renaissance slavery. Individuals were enslaved not because they were black but because their people sold them into slavery or because they were captured in war. Modern scholarship indicates that race did not become an important factor in slavery until the seventeenth century. Renaissance people kept slaves because, like women and art, they were indications of wealth.

THE NORTHERN RENAISSANCE

Italy was not the only European country to experience the Renaissance. Nations in the northern portion of the continent also underwent a revival of art, learning, and culture, but it occurred somewhat later than in Italy. During the last half of the fifteenth century Italian ideas and culture began to move into European territories across the Alps. At that time, students from Belgium,

Holland, France, Germany, England, and Spain ventured to Italy to partake of the new "classical learning." When they returned home, they brought Italian ideas about government, nature, society, people, religion, and the economy with them. Northern Europeans, however, interpreted Italian views on ancient Greece and Rome, individualism, humanism, art, literature, music, religion, and education in light of their own cultural traditions. In general, the northern Renaissance was more Christian and less secular than in Italy. This is not to say that Italian Renaissance scholars and artists were not Christian, for they certainly were; however, Italians focused more attention on worldly themes than did scholars north of the Alps who often emphasized Biblical thought.

The Renaissance was slower to move into Northern Europe because the region did not contain many large cities and lacked the large number of middle class merchants who supported art and literature in Italy. Also, the cultural traditions and languages of people in the North did not have as direct a connection to the Greece and Rome of antiquity as did those in Italy. The court and the knight, rather than the city and merchant, dominated northern European culture until near the close of the fifteenth century.

Humanism as reflected in northern European nations is more aptly labeled "Christian Humanism." Its practitioners were interested chiefly in development of an ethical lifestyle that could best be achieved by fusing together the best parts of Greek, Roman, and Christian cultures. Once Christian and classical values were combined, northern humanists believed an ethical individual and an ethical society would result.

An important component of northern European humanism was its emphasis on logic and reason. Northern scholars adopted Socrates' view that each individual possessed knowledge within that could be extracted through logical reasoning. To arrive at the correct answer, a person had to question preconceived notions. Reason, rather than dogma, was the key to developing an ethical person and society. Humans could, through use of reason, institute reform within society and its institutions. Christian humanists rejected the medieval view that human beings were by nature evil. Instead, they stressed that even though people often committed sins, human nature was basically good. In other words, Christian humanists believed that if given a choice, more often than not, human beings would opt to do good. The key to improving human existence was education, which taught the individual to exercise reason to solve all dilemmas. Only by being educated to use their rational faculties could humans become pious individuals who fashioned just and ethical societies and lived Christian lives in them.

One of the most important Christian humanists was Sir Thomas More, an English lawyer and diplomat. Born in 1478, he lived his teenage and young adult years in London Charterhouse, a Catholic monastery operated by the Carthusian order. He left the monastery, married, and was sent by Henry VIII as ambassador to Flanders. His signature work, which he wrote while in Flanders, was *Utopia*. This work, penned in 1516, represents the first time that a European had written about a socialistic society. In *Utopia,* More creates an island community located somewhere in the Western Hemisphere inhabited by scholars. In this utopian society the government provides each child with a free education. After reaching adulthood, individuals continue learning by dividing their day between work and study, working six hours and studying six hours. Also, in *Utopia* there was absolute equality in society, as property was held in common. All profits from business activities were divided among the population. Greed was not a problem on this island paradise. Precious metals, like gold and silver, were valued so little that they were often used to make chamber toilets. Rather than fighting over money, Utopians used gold and silver to prevent wars. They simply paid enemies not to attack. Utopia's inhabitants lived a carefree, ideal life that was not beset by the problems England faced during More's lifetime. The utopian legal system placed mercy above justice, punishment, and retribution. All people lived in nice houses that contained glass windows (Glass was a symbol of prosperity in sixteenth-century England.), fireproof roofs, and gardens. Water flowed fresh and clean while goods in stores and markets were free. Each individual took only what he or she needed to live. All people dressed alike except for priests. However, women were somewhat subordinate to men but did receive military training. Wars of conquest were prohibited. Religion was flexible and not bound by dogma. Utopia was a perfect society because its people lived by reason, making their government, social institutions, and economy perfect.

More's career was cut short by his execution in 1535. After his death, his ideas survived. *Utopia* rivals the plays of Shakespeare as the most read sixteenth-century English work. His view that greed and the acquisition of material objects promoted civil disorder and crime were revolutionary in the sixteenth-century world. He clearly rejected earlier Christian notions that crime existed because individuals were sinful. Because legal systems in England and elsewhere protected private property and encouraged the acquisition of material things, society was responsible for war, crime, violence, poverty, and a host of other social ills that plagued humankind. Improvement in the human condition was achievable only by reforming social institutions that were corrupt.

A close friend of Sir Thomas More was the Dutch scholar, Desiderius Erasmus. The illegitimate son of a priest and a physician's daughter, he was born in Rotterdam around 1466. (His exact date of birth is unknown.) When both parents died in his youth, poverty forced Erasmus to enter a monastery. Although he hated the monastic lifestyle, he received an excellent education at the famous Brethren of the Common Life School at Deventer, developing while there an excellent knowledge of the Latin language and profound appreciation for classical literature. The school also instilled into Erasmus its pious *devotio moderna*, a new type of lay spirituality that emphasized free thought and open religious discussion that greatly influenced northern humanism. Later, Erasmus was ordained as a priest and became a monk at the Steyn, an Augustinian monastery. His stay at the Steyn from 1486 until 1493 was brief. His dislike of other monks, poor health, and love of the classics caused Pope Leo X to grant him a dispensation, allowing Erasmus to permanently leave the monastery. In 1494, he became secretary to the bishop of Cambrai in France, which allowed him to enroll at the College de Montaigue at the University of Paris. He spent several years there but claimed to hate its "stale eggs and stale theology." In particular, Erasmus disliked the scholastic theology and systematic philosophy that dominated theological studies at the university. He was drawn to a new discipline, classical philology, and would place the field in the service of religion. In 1499, Erasmus found employment as a tutor in England where he met humanists John Colet and Sir Thomas More. He became fast friends with both men. Colet especially influenced Erasmus; his ideas enabled the young Dutchman to apply humanistic principles to Biblical scholarship.

Erasmus was a prolific writer. His first known publication was *Adages*, a collection of eight hundred wise sayings from ancient Latin texts. This

Eramus was one of the most celebrated humanists in Europe.

work became popular because it made the wit and wisdom of classical texts and authors available to the masses of people who could not read Latin. *Adages* popularized such modern sayings as "to leave no stone unturned," and "where there is smoke, there is fire." After *Adages* established him as an author, Erasmus published *Handbook of the Christian Soldier* in 1503, which stressed the importance of Christian faith in everyday life. In 1504 and 1505 he published an edition of Cicero's and St. Jerome's letters along with Valla's *Annotations on the New Testament*. Erasmus's most important works were *Praise of Folly* (1509) and *The Greek New Testament* (1516). *Praise of Folly* was a work that criticized abuses in both the Catholic Church and European society. Erasmus hoped that his criticism would promote a purer, simpler form of Christianity. Thus, he condemned "the cheats of pardons and indulgences" the Catholic Church dispensed so readily as well as worship of the Virgin Mary before Christ. Even the Pope was not spared criticism. Erasmus wrote: "Now as to the popes of Rome, who pretend themselves Christ's vicar, if they would but imitate his exemplary life...." *Praise of Folly* was popular reading even though the Catholic Church banned it. After moving to Basel, Switzerland to be closer to his publisher, Johann Froben, as his nine-volume edition of the writings of St. Jerome was being printed, Erasmus published his second most important work, *Novum Instrumentum*, a translation of the Greek New Testament. This work marked progress in higher textual criticism. Erasmus used his knowledge of classical languages to produce an improved version of the Bible translated from the best Greek manuscripts available. He believed, as he explained in the introduction, "that the sacred scriptures should be read by the unlearned translated into their vulgar tongue..." and that "Christ wished his mysteries to be published as openly as possible." The Catholic Church was displeased with Erasmus's improved Bible. Church officials preferred that the official Latin Vulgate be read. Consequently, in the mid-sixteenth century the Greek New Testament, along with all of Erasmus's works, was placed on the Church's *Index of Forbidden Books*.

The phrase, *philosophi Christi,* best describes the fundamental theme found in Erasmus's work. He believed in a simple, ethical piety that imitated Christ. His views contradicted the dogmatic, ceremonial, and factious religious worship present within the Catholic Church. Erasmus criticized anybody or any institution that let doctrine interfere with Christian humility. He taught that Christianity was found within the individual rather than in an institution called church. Christianity is Christ; it is not a building, a priest, a Bible, or a ceremony. To Erasmus, what Christ did and said was more important than anything theologians wrote or anything the Pope decreed. Erasmus, like most humanists, believed the classics from ancient Greece and Rome would prepare the individual's mind to receive God's truth. Furthermore, he believed the classics were worth studying for their own intrinsic value. All people who read from them were bound to improve their outlook on life and likely to become ethical people.

Even though Erasmus is remembered as a critic of the Catholic Church, he was not an early reformer. In fact, he criticized Martin Luther for breaking with the Catholic faith. When accused of being a "heretic Lutheran," Erasmus said that he did not write *Julius Excluded from Heaven*, a satire published in 1517 that describes a swaggering warrior-pope who is denied admission to heaven. Later, a copy of the work was found in Erasmus's handwriting! In the 1520s Erasmus and Luther engaged in a heated debate over free will and predestination. Erasmus published *The Freedom of the Will* in 1524, which argued that Luther's conception of predestination was incorrect. Because he had disagreed with Luther, Erasmus, fearing for his life, fled Basel in 1529 after the Protestant Reformation came to that city. He settled in Freiburg where he lived for six years before returning to Basel where he died in 1535.

Erasmus was a pacifist who hoped reason would eventually prevent wars. He rejected the idea of St. Augustine that a "just war" was possible. In *Complaint of Peace* (1517) Erasmus argued that "war incessantly sows war, vengeance seethingly draws vengeance, kindness generously engenders kindness." Erasmus was particularly opposed to the Crusades and holy wars of the Middle Ages. He strongly opposed the Catholic Church's involvement in such wars. He thought the Church and all Christians should preach peace and set an example of nonviolence for others to imitate rather than engaging in military alliances, wars, and violence.

Erasmus was one of the first humanists in northern Europe to support classical study for women. Although Erasmus sometimes ridiculed women and believed they were inferior to men, he did not think that they were incapable of learning. He advocated that daughters of the rich, at least, should be educated in the classics. His views were shaped, in part, by having been impressed with the work of Margaret Roper (1504-1544), the daughter of Sir Thomas More, in translating his work on the Lord's Supper into English. This prompted him to write an essay entitled "Dialogue Between an Abbot and a Learned Lady" in which Erasmus has an educated housewife tell an unlearned abbot that "if man can't play their parts, they should get off the stage and let women assume their roles." Erasmus also maintained that study for women was a weapon against an idle mind and would produce a virtuous woman.

Although Erasmus and Sir Thomas More brought recognition for humanistic thought to England and the Netherlands, every country in northern Europe produced a brand of humanism unique to it. In the Germanic kingdoms humanism celebrated nationalism. This nationalistic slant is particularly evident in the work of Conrad Celtis (1459-1508), one of the most important German humanists. Born into a peasant family at Wurzburg, Celtis attended a number of colleges and universities before Holy Roman Emperor Frederick III named him Germany's first poet laureate in 1487. While a student, Celtis became disturbed by Italy's claim to have a superior culture to the "barbarians" in Germany, Poland, Russia, France, and England. This disgust with Italian claims of superiority caused Celtis to urge fellow Germans to challenge Italy culturally much as they had earlier challenged Roman legions militarily. Other than lyric poetry, for which he is well known, Celtis translated *Germania*, the writings of the Roman historian Tacitus, introduced the writings of Hrosvit of Gandersheim, a tenth century author who wrote poetry, history, and drama, and wrote his own history of Germany entitled *Germany Illustrated*. All the translations from antiquity, as well as Celtis' own personal writings, were produced because he wanted to show the world, as well as his countrymen, that German culture was equal to that of Italy or any other nation.

The most celebrated humanist Germany produced was Johann Reuchlin. Born in Pforzheim in 1455, his early education was at the Brethern of the Common Life School. Later, he attended universities at Basel, Freiburg, Orleans, Paris, and Tubingen. He traveled widely and during visits to Italy met the famed humanist Pico whom he came to admire. Trained as a lawyer, Reuchlin served as an aide to the Duke of Wurttemberg and represented the Swambian League from 1502 to 1512. He left the legal profession a few years before his death in 1522 and taught Greek and Hebrew at the universities of Ingolstadt and Tubingen. Reuchlin is most noted for his study of Hebrew. He maintained that it was impossible to understand the Old Testament without reading it in Hebrew, its original language. In 1506, he published a Hebrew grammar book, *The Rudiments of Hebrew*, to guide other scholars interested in the Old Testament and other ancient Hebrew manuscripts. This book represents the first Hebrew grammar book written by a Christian author. Later, in 1517 he wrote *On the Cabalistic Art*, which showed the relationship between ancient Greek, Hebrew, and Christian beliefs.

Reuchlin's work with Hebrew texts provoked much debate within Germany. Johann Pfefferkorn, a scholastic scholar who had converted from Judaism to Christianity, like many religious converts, wanted to advance his new faith at the expense of the old one. Consequently, he attacked Reuchlin and scholars inspired by Reuchlin to study ancient Hebrew texts from a humanistic perspective. In *A Mirror for Jews* Pfefferkorn stated that the government should ban, confiscate, and burn all Hebrew books. Several Catholic monastic orders, including the Dominicans of Cologne, supported Pfefferkorn's ideas, fearing that humanistic Hebrew scholarship threatened traditional scholastic Christian ideas. In 1519 Emperor Maximilian I implemented Pfefferkorn's ideas, ordering all Hebrew books to be burned. This began a controversy known as the Reuchlin Affair. Reuchlin responded that rather than destroying Hebrew books, Christians would become closer to God if they studied these books intensely. Pfefferkorn published a pamphlet directly attacking Reuchlin, stating that he was ignorant. Reuchlin, forced to defend his scholarly reputation, wrote the *Letters of Famous Men*, a collection of statements by noted humanist scholars supporting his idea that the study of Hebrew would enhance Christianity. The Reuchlin Affair continued until 1520 when Pope Leo X issued an edict ordering Reuchlin to stop expressing his views. Even though friends urged him to join Luther in condemning the Catholic Church, Reuchlin refused and obeyed Pope Leo X's order. He died two years later still in the Catholic fold.

Lesser-known German scholars included Ulrich von Hutten (1488-1523), the Humanist Knight, who defended Reuchlin against Pfefferkorn. His most famous work, written with Crotus Rubianus, was the *Letters of Obscure Men*, a work deliberately written using poor Latin grammar to poke fun at those who attacked Reuchlin. Unfortunately, Huten and Rubianus tainted *Letters of Obscure Men* with anti-Semitism, which lessened its value. When the Pope banned *Letters of Obscure Men,* its sales increased, bringing more attention to it authors.

Caritas (1466-1532) and Willibald (1470-1530) Prickheimer, a brother and sister duo, were also part of the German Humanistic Renaissance. Friends of Celtis, the Prickheimers produced numerous works. The most important was Caritas' *Memoirs*, which documented the early history of the Reformation in Nuremberg, the Prikheimers' hometown, and Willibald's translation of major classical Greek and Latin authors, including Xenophon, Plutarch, Ptolemy, Thucydides, Galen, Aristophanes, Aristotle, and Gregory of Nazianzus.

Jacob Wimpfeling (1450-1528) was the most important Rhenish humanist Germany produced. His most famous work, published in 1500, was *Germania*, a history of the German states. Wimpfeling devoted most of his energy to education, proposing to create a humanist school in Strasbourg. Unfortunately, Strasbourg's leaders rejected his idea.

Humanism also made its way into France and Spain during the European Renaissance. Unlike German humanists, who largely rejected Italian influence, French humanists openly embraced Italian scholarship. One of the most important French humanists was Francois Rabelais. (He lived from about 1490 to 1553; his exact date of birth is unknown.) Like the Italian humanistic work that he used as a model, Rabelais' work was distinctly secular. His most important works, produced between 1532 and 1552, were the literary comedies *Gargantua and Pantagruel*. Modern scholars place them among the world's greatest comic literature. These works are written so that they can be read on several levels: as the funny adventures of the giant Gargantua and his son, Pantagruel, as a romantic comedy starring Gargantua and Pantagruel, as a critique of French society, as a demand for humanistic education, and as a spoof of Christianity. Gargantua and Pantagruel travel throughout the world, meeting numerous people with whom they have comedic chats that provide readers with important information on government, politics, religion, economics, philosophy, and education.

Another important French humanist was Guillaume Bude (1467-1540). As head of the royal national library at Fontainebleau, he was perhaps the chief French authority on classical works. His formal training was as a lawyer, but he rarely practiced. Instead, he studied ancient texts. Because Greek and Latin scholarship was almost non-existent in France, Bude had to teach himself. The work that solidified his place as France's and one of Europe's leading classical authorities was *Commentaries on the Greek Language*, published in 1529.

Lefevre d' Etaples (1450-1536), a contemporary and rival of Bude, also developed a reputation within France and Europe as a humanist scholar. In 1492 he visited Italy where he met and was greatly influenced by Pico. After returning to France, he developed the Aristotelian Renaissance, an educational method that used knowledge of ancient history to study classical texts. Toward the end of his life, Lefevre grew interested in Christian mysticism. His most important publication was *Commentary on the Epistle of St. Paul.* In this work, Lefevre focused on Paul's idea that heaven is attainable only by the grace of God and that the life an individual lived on earth had little to do with salvation.

Cardinal Jimenez de Cisneros (1436-1517) was largely responsible for the flowering of Spanish humanism. Born into poverty, he studied law and theology at the University of Salamanca prior to working for the Catholic Church in Rome. Eventually he returned to

Spain as a Franciscan friar and Church officer. When Spanish forces subdued the Moors in 1492, Queen Isabella appointed him as her private chaplain. Cisneros used his influence to promote humanism throughout Spain. His most significant achievement was founding the University of Alcala in 1509. Creation of this university was part of a reform of the Catholic Church throughout Spain that Cisneros oversaw. The Church reforms were intended to force Catholic priests and other Church officials to live morally upstanding lives. Cisneros believed that priests needed a university devoted to Biblical scholarship. Consequently, the University of Alcala was made into one of Europe's centers for the study of ancient Greek, Hebrew, and Latin texts. Alcalan scholars published the first multilanguage Bible. Greek, Latin, and Hebrew texts were written in parallel columns, much as modern Gospel Parallels will provide texts from different English Biblical translations side by side. Cisneros believed that the study of classical Biblical texts would produce priests who were more moral, who understood more about the Bible, and who, thus, would set a better example for their parishioners.

Another important Spanish humanist was Juan Luis Vives (1492-1540). However, Vives did not spend most of his career in Spain. After completing the early part of his formal schooling in Valencia, his place of birth, he left Spain at the age of seventeen to attend the University of Paris. After graduation, he became a professor at the University of Louvain. While there, he produced one of his most famous early works, *The Fable of Man*, in 1518. Shortly thereafter, the English monarch, Henry VIII, hired Vives as Princess Mary's private tutor. In England, Vives also taught at Oxford. His English sojourn resulted in over fifty books detailing his humanistic ideas. In particular, Vives believed that education should produce a moral citizen, which he held could most easily be achieved by studying ancient classical and Christian texts. Vives, like Erasmus, stressed that women should receive formal education (different than that men received) to create a woman full of wisdom, morality, and goodness. His most famous work on female education is *On the Education of a Christian Woman*, written for Princess Mary in 1523. Vives' success in England did not endure for his entire life. After criticizing Henry VIII for divorcing Catherine of Argon, Vives fled England to avoid execution, settling in Bruges (a town in the Low Countries) where he lived out his life.

Northern Renaissance Art

Art, like literary works, produced as part of the Renaissance in northern Europe also generally contained distinctive literary themes. The center of Renaissance art in northern Europe was the Low Countries ruled by the Duke of Burgundy. Within the Low Countries, Flanders produced some of the greatest artists.

Jan Van Eyck was one of the greatest artists from Flanders. Born about 1385, he is most famous for a type of three-dimensional oil painting. He achieved this effect by using a base of tempera on canvas over which were applied multiple coats of oil-based paints. Van Eyck's use of oil and tempera allowed him to paint with meticulous detail and realism that came to characterize all Flemish art. The Virgin Mary was one of his favorite subjects. Van Eych's technique allowed viewers to approach the Holy Virgin from the familiar perspective of family relations. His most famous painting is *The Virgin Mary and Child*. Viewers of this painting are drawn to the subject's robe and crown jewels. The realism with which Van Eyck depicts them adds an aura to the painting that transfixes the viewer to such an extent that it feels almost as if the subject and viewer are in the same room. Van Eyck was also famous for using a technique in which contemporary subjects were placed in a Biblical setting. Wealthy patrons hired Van Eyck to paint them in the company of the Virgin Mary, Baby Jesus, or other Biblical characters until his death in 1440.

Hieronymus Jerome Bosch (1450-1516), a Flemish contemporary of Van Eyck, also used religious themes in his paintings. Bosch, however, approached art differently than Van Eyck. Rather than producing work with realism, Bosch used fantasy, folk legends, and color to depict his religious message. His *Death and the Miser*, for example, depicts a miser in the throes of death agonizing over his ill-gotten gold that is controlled by rats and toads while an angel offers him the crucifix. In other words, he can choose earthly wealth and eternal damnation or heavenly bliss.

Many art historians regard Peter Paul Rubens as the greatest Flemish school painter of the Baroque period. He studied art in Italy before opening a large studio in Antwerp, Belgium. The Antwerp school attracted students from most European countries. Rubens used his students and instructors to paint sections of massive paintings he designed and became famous for. His work was in great demand at courts across Europe. He was commissioned to paint portraits of royal figures, such as King Philip IV of Spain. Like most Renaissance painters, his work depicted Biblical scenes. One such painting was *Descent from the Cross*.

Germany, like the Low Countries, also produced remarkable artists during the Northern Renaissance. German art stems from the tradition of quality its craftspeople developed. Renaissance artists extended the techniques and styles of German craftspeople to the fine arts. Simultaneously, the German nobility increased its patronage of the arts, which enabled artists to earn a living.

Albrecht Duer of Nuremberg is the best-known German Renaissance artist. His work reflects his craft background. As a youth, Duer served an apprenticeship under his father who was a goldsmith. His work as a goldsmith later enabled Duer to master numerous styles and techniques. In 1486 he found employment with a painter and woodcut designer, Michael Wolgemut. Duer worked for Wolgemut for four years, traveling throughout Germany and the Holy Roman Empire, but realized that if he wanted to become a master artist he must study Italian works. In 1494 and again in 1505 he journeyed to Italy. After each trip he earned important commissions from Holy Roman Emperor Maximilian I. After Maximilian's death in 1519, Duer visited the Netherlands where he studied the Flemish art of Van Eyck and others. Duer also befriended Martin Luther, believing the Protestant reformer had brought Christianity back to its first-century roots. Duer's art work made him wealthy. He lived in a large home near the Nuremberg Castle. Over the course of his life, he produced about 75 paintings, over 100 engravings, over 1,000 drawings, 250 woodcuts, and books on geometry, fortification, and the human body. One of his most famous paintings is the *Self Portrait*, which shows the artist looking like Christ but wearing a fur coat to show his prosperity. The *Self Portrait* was actually one of a series the artist produced. Duer most likely suffered from psychological illness. Throughout life he was prone to bouts of depression that sometimes lasted for weeks.

Two German contemporaries of Duer also became important Renaissance artists. Lucas Cranach (1472-1553) and Hans Holbein (1497-1543) did not master all the techniques and styles that Duer used but, nevertheless, both earned handsome commissions from wealthy patrons. Cranach, like Duer, came from a craft background. As a youngster, the Franconian learned engraving from his father. From 1500 to 1503 he served as court painter for Duke Frederick the Wise in Vienna. He often incorporated Biblical themes in his artwork. His paintings of early leaders of the Protestant Reformation in Saxony, including Martin Luther and Philip Melanchthon, are important to historians studying Reformation art.

Holbein, from Augsburg, was one of the few German artists who did not have a craft background. His father, Hans Holbein the Elder, was a well-known artist in his own right. He sent his son to Italy to study with Italian masters. Following his Italian sojourn, Holbein the Younger traveled throughout Europe creating commissioned art. In Basel, Switzerland he earned excellent fees providing illustrations for books published by Johann Froben, Erasmus's publisher. In addition to book illustrations, he also received commissions for portraits of Swiss nobles. Holbein also spent time in England where he painted portraits of famous people, including Thomas Cromwell, Sir Thomas More, Erasmus, and Anne of Cleves, a German princess who became one of Henry VIII's many wives.

Another famed German artist was the sculptor Tilman Riemenschneider (1460-1531). Although Riemenschneider is not in the category of Michelangelo or Donatello, he was a good artist. He is most remembered for the wooden alters he produced. Born in Heiligenstadt in the Erchsfeld, Thuringia, he moved to Wurzburg where he was admitted to the guild of painters, sculptors, and glaziers. Toward the end of his life, Riemenschneider was tried and tortured because he publicly sympathized with German peasants during the Peasant Revolts from 1524 to 1526. Like Duer, Riemenschneider was most likely afflicted with some sort of psychological disorder as he often experienced long bouts of depression.

The Iberian Peninsula produced El Greco. This famed artist used a style called Mannerism, popularized by Michelangelo. Mannerism was a reaction against the simplicity and symmetry of High Renaissance art. It allowed the artist to incorporate strange, abnormal things into his work. This style allowed artists to reflect individual perceptions and feelings, to paint in a "mannered" or "affected" way.

Literature

Literature, especially that written in the vernacular languages such as English, French, Spanish, and German, flourished in northern and western Europe during the Renaissance. English writers were the most important literary figures during the Renaissance.

Of all English writers, literary scholars regard William Shakespeare (1564-1616) as the most talented. The Bard of Avon, as Shakespeare is sometimes called, came from a wealthy family in Stratford-upon-Avon. His father was a glove maker and government official while his mother's family owned a substantial amount of land. He began writing in his early twenties and continued until his death. By 1592 he had moved to London where he was an actor and playwright. In 1594 he, along with other London actors and playwrights, formed a theatrical company, the King's Men, with whom he remained until he retired to his birthplace in 1611. During the course of his writing career, Shakespeare produced in excess of thirty-five plays, as well as numerous poems. He was an excellent playwright in two different genera—tragedy and comedy. He produced unrivaled masterpieces in both. Tragedies he wrote included *Hamlet*, *King Lear*, and *Macbeth*. His most beloved comedies included *Much*

Ado About Nothing, and *A Midsummer Night's Dream*. Shakespeare's plays convey a sense of history, politics, and world affairs, as well as English and foreign culture. Several of his plays, including *Julius Caesar* and *Antony and Cleopatra,* deal with ancient historical events while others, such as *Richard III* and *Henry VIII,* offer critiques on events closer to Shakespeare's own historical time period. The Bard of Avon did not hesitate to set plays such as *Othello*, *The Merchant of Venice*, and *Two Gentlemen of Verona* in other countries, including Italy.

Shakespeare was an excellent psychologist. He completely understood many aspects of human behavior, which is evident in his plays. Characters he created bring to life every conceivable mood human beings are capable of experiencing—searing grief, airy romance, rousing nationalism, deadly hatred, betrayal, and humor. His work shows a familiarity with a wide variety of subjects—astronomy, politics, statecraft, alchemy, warfare, seamanship, intrigue, love, hate, life, and death.

Shakespeare was part of what English historians term the Elizabethan Renaissance, sparked by the reign of Elizabeth I (1558-1603). This period produced other remarkable literary figures like Christopher Marlow (1564-1593*),* Edmund Spenser (1552-1599), Sir Philip Sidney (1554-1586), and his sister, Mary Sidney (1561-1621). Marlow came from a working class background but earned degrees from Cambridge as a result of having received a scholarship to the prestigious university. He wrote seven plays and several volumes of poetry. His most important plays were *Edward II*, *Dr. Faustus*, *The Jew of Malta*,

Some of Shakespeare's most famous works include: ***Hamlet*****,** ***King Lear*****,** ***Romeo and Juliet*****, and** ***Macbeth*****.**

and *Tamburlain.* Marlow probably would have produced many more plays had he lived longer. Unfortunately, he died in a barroom brawl at the age of twenty-nine. Spencer was the most important English poet of the Renaissance. His greatest work, *Faerie Queene,* glorifies Elizabeth I. Like most poets and literary figures, Spencer believed Elizabeth I was the greatest monarch Europe had produced. The Sidneys were friends of Spencer, as well as being important literary figures in their own right. Philip produced several volumes of poetry. His major work was a prose romance entitled *Arcadia* and a scholarly work, *Defense of Poetry.* Mary is noted for writing religious poems, translating Petrarch into English, producing beautiful elegies, and dramatic dialogues. Her most important work was a metrical version of *Psalms.*

Miguel de Cervantes (1547-1616) was Spain's greatest Renaissance literary figure. Cervantes spent most of his life impoverished. Born at Alcala de Henares, he wandered from place to place, holding a variety of low paying jobs. Forced to leave Spain after fighting a duel, he fled to Rome where he worked for a Catholic cardinal until 1570 when he enlisted in the Spanish army to fight against the Ottoman Turks. A few years later he fought in North Africa, where a ship he was on was captured by Moorish pirates who sold Cervantes into slavery in 1575. The Spanish government freed him in 1580 by paying the pirates a ransom. He returned to Spain where he chronicled his mishaps and wartime exploits in *Pictures of Algiers.* Cervantes then married, worked for the Spanish government, and was jailed for financial mismanagement. Despite the hardships, Cervantes wrote his masterpiece, *Don Quixote de la Mancha*, a scathing social satire. In the novel, Cervantes ridicules the Spanish nobility with a knight who was ready to tilt at windmills and who was a born loser. The novel also gives the reader a glimpse of Spanish and European society, especially its intolerances, injustice, and disregard for human beings.

France produced numerous novelists and poets during its Renaissance, including Francois Villon, called the thief, Louise Labe, the ropemaker's wife, Clemont Marot, and Queen Marquerita of Navarre. None of these writers were as important as Christine de Pisan (1363-1434). The daughter of an astrology professor employed by the French monarchy, Thomas de Pisan, Christine was the first woman to write professionally and the first published feminist. As a result of her father's presence at the French court, Pisan attained a superior education, which included instruction in Greek, Latin, French, and Italian literature, despite objections from her mother that learning would hinder Pisan's marital chances. Despite her mother's fears, Pisan mar-

Miguel de Cervantes became a popular Renaissance author when he wrote *Don Quixote.*

ried Etienne de Castel, a nobleman from Picardy who served as secretary to Charles V until the monarch died in 1380. Thereafter, her fortunes suffered. Thomas de Pisan lost his position with the new king, Charles VI, and died in 1385. In the fall of 1390 Pisan's husband also died from illness while traveling with Charles VI to Beauvais. Pisan, at the age of twenty-five, was left with three children, a niece, and mother to support. In addition, she was the defendant in several lawsuits over her late husband's debts. Even though few opportunities for women to support themselves outside marriage existed, Pisan was determined to emulate Petrarch, her idol, and earn a living with the pen. She supported her family by writing poetry, copying books, and working as a notary. About 1393, she began to have success with poetry and literature. Her most important book was *The Book of the City of Ladies* in 1405. This work put forth the revolutionary idea that women were equal to men. She refuted all arguments that supported female inferiority, including those from the Bible. Previously, Pisan had touched off a debate that lasted throughout the Renaissance called the *Querelle de Femmes* (quarrel over women). This debate began when Pisan wrote *The Letter to the God of Love*, criticizing Jean de Meun's work, *Romance of the Rose,* for its misogyny. A heated exchange occurred between Pisan and Meun that attracted attention from other scholars. Pisan published a sequel to *The Book of the City of Ladies* entitled *The Treasure of the City of Ladies,* a handbook on etiquette for all women, including queens, servants, housewives, barmaids, and prostitutes. In this work Pisan urged all women to support each other because they could never be secure in marriage or work. Other works Pisan wrote included *The Body of Policy*, an advice handbook for kings, *The Book of Feates of Arms and Chivalry*, a work Henry VII liked so well he had it translated into English, *Book of Peace*, a text about the need for education, and *Hymn to Joan of Arc*, who Pisan viewed as an heroic woman and example of feminism.

Although German literature developed later than that in other northern European countries, Germany produced important literary figures during the Renaissance. Sebastian Brant (1457-1521) and Hans Sachs (1494-1576) were the most significant figures writing in vernacular German. Brant, a poet and lawyer, was known for poetic satire. His most famous work was *The Ship of Fools* published in 1494. Sachs, like Brant, was a master satirist, who was a prolific author, writing over 4000 songs, 1,700 folk tales, numerous poems, and about 200 plays.

MONARCHS

The literature, art, and other achievements of the Northern Renaissance could not have occurred without the support of strong monarchs. Like the merchant class in Italian city-states, monarchs north of the Alps patronized art, literature, and their creators while simultaneously creating strong nation states. These monarchs, who included Louis XI of France, Henry VII of England, Ferdinand and Isabella of Spain, and others are often called the "new monarchs" because they ruled with a strong hand and pursued nationalistic goals. Even though they had not read Machiavelli's works, they utilized principles he identified to maintain power. The new monarchs believed they were sovereign and tolerated no dissent. All opposition was immediately suppressed. The nobility, which during the Middle Ages had exerted sovereignty over territory within nations, were forcefully subdued. The new monarchs demanded absolute loyalty. Loyalty was achieved by reliance upon civil officials to collect taxes in towns independent of the local nobility. Middle class townspeople, especially merchants and artisans, were willing to pay taxes to a central government in return for protection from armies and knights employed by feudal landowners. This tax revenue was then used to crush local nobles and force their allegiance to the monarch. The ultimate result of this was the creation of the modern nation-state, which was perhaps the greatest political achievement of the Renaissance.

France

The modern nation-state developed differently in France, England, and Spain. France had been seriously weakened by the Hundred Years' War. The monarchy was weak, the population had declined, business was in disarray, and farm production was low when Charles VII ascended to the throne in 1422. Under his rule, which lasted until 1461, France became one of the strongest nations in Europe. He made peace between the Burgundians and Armagnacs who had fought a civil war in France for more than thirty years and drove English armies from all French provinces except Calais by 1453. In addition, he imposed taxes on various items, including salt and land, to provide the royal treasury with a steady and reliable source of income. Much of the revenue Charles VII received was used to strengthen the French army. He created the first permanent army for the monarchy, organizing it into calvary and archery units. These changes eventually gave France the most formidable army in Europe. Charles VII also curtailed the power of the Roman Catholic Church. In 1438 he proclaimed in the Pragmatic Sanction of Bourges that a general council was superior to the Pope, giving the French monarch authority to appoint Church officials and collect Church revenue. In effect, Charles had taken control of the French Church from the Roman Pope and greatly strengthened the monarchy.

When Charles VII died in 1461, his son, Louis XI, became the French monarch. Nicknamed the Spider King because of his ruthless nature, Louis further strengthened the monarchy. He promoted industry and commerce, using tax revenue generated to enlarge the army. Under Louis XI commercial treaties with England, Portugal, Spain, and the Hanseatic League, allowing foreign craftsmen and products into France and French products into foreign markets, were negotiated. The Spider King also used his strong military to subdue rebellious nobles, take control over independent towns, and annex territory, including Burgundy, Anjou, Bar, Maine, and Provence.

French expansion continued after the Spider King died in 1483. The marriage of Louis XI (1498-1515) to Anne of Brittany added the Duchy of Brittany to France. In 1516 Francis I and Pope Leo X signed the Concordat of Bologna, which repaired the relationship between the papacy and the French monarchy. This agreement overturned the Pragmatic Sanction of Bourges and gave the Pope authority to take the first year's income from French Church officials. In return, the Church gave the French monarchy the right to choose bishops, abbots, and other top Church officials. Since French kings could appoint Church officials, they controlled Church policies and practices. The monarchy had created a national Church.

England

England also experienced nationalism and had strong monarchs during the Renaissance. Several strong monarchs increased the power of the national government. Edward IV (1461-1483) began the process of healing England from the ravages of the War of the Roses. From 1455 to 1471 two noble factions, the Yorks and Lancasters, fought a civil war. This War of the Roses, so called because the Lancaster symbol was a red rose and the York symbol was a white rose, devastated England, hurting commerce, industry, agriculture, and people. Edward IV, a member of the York faction, defeated the Lancasters in 1471 and rebuilt the English monarchy that had lost much of its authority during the war. He, along with his successors, brother Richard III (1483-1485) and Henry VII (1485-1509), the first Tutor king, destroyed the power of the nobility and established law and order throughout England. Methods used by all three rulers were brutal, lethal, ruthless, efficient, and conducted largely in secrecy.

One device these English kings employed to strengthen the monarchy was to bypass Parliament. Before Edward IV became king, the monarch was dependent on Parliament for revenue, a condition made necessary by the high cost of the Hundred Years' War. Since the nobility dominated Parliament, they controlled the monarch by holding the purse strings. It was impossible for the English kings to fight wars without Parliamentary approval and financing. Rather than seek the approval of the nobles who controlled Parliament, Edward IV, Richard III, and Henry VII used diplomacy to conduct foreign policy rather than war. The use of diplomacy meant that the English monarchy was no longer dependent upon Parliament for financing, which curtailed the influence of the nobility within the government.

Another device English monarchs used to increase their power was the Royal Council. This institution consisted of about fifteen middle class men with backgrounds in law or business. Generally, aristocrats were excluded from the Royal Council, which conducted its business at the pleasure of the monarch and dealt with all matters the king requested. Its scope included legislative, executive, and judicial authority. The Royal Council used terror and secrecy to dispose of threats to its authority. The Star Chamber Court was the most notorious device the Royal Council employed, which derived its name from stars painted on the courtroom's ceiling. People tried within this infamous institution were not permitted access to evidence prosecutors had compiled against them. Court sessions were held in absolute secrecy, judges ordered victims tortured to attain bogus confessions, and jury trials were forbidden. Although such practices violated English common law, Henry VII and other English monarchs effectively used the Court of the Star Chamber to control the nobility.

English monarchs also broke the power of the nobility by formulating and pursuing governmental policies that benefited the upper middle class. Influential people engaged in commercial farming or business pursuits disliked violence, chaos, and crime. Consequently, the English national government enacted laws promoting peace and order to secure support from the upper middle class. In return, the upper middle class generally did not object to institutions such as the Star Chamber Court, especially if it was used to punish criminals and prevent future crime.

English kings bypassed nobles in regards to law enforcement. Because England did not have a permanent army or a permanent governmental bureaucracy, Henry VII, Richard III, and Edward IV empowered local judicial officials to act on behalf of the central government. These Justices of the Peace, usually large landowners elected by local voters, enforced laws, punished criminals, collected taxes, controlled wages, set prices, inspected scales, and regulated personal moral behavior in the name of the king. During the Middle Ages, English noblemen had carried out these functions.

Henry VII was the most ruthless English Renaissance monarch. Serious, secretive, economically conservative, and utterly brutal, he made Great Britain one of the leading nations in Europe. He accomplished this by encouraging industrial development, especially in the wool and textile industries, and strengthening the navy and merchant marine so that Albion's products could be sold worldwide. Henry also turned back an Irish invasion and made peace with Scotland by marrying his daughter Margaret to the Scottish king. When Henry VII died in 1509, the England he left was a wealthy, peaceful, prosperous nation on the verge of becoming a world power.

Spain

Spain did not experience the same kind of nationalism during the Renaissance that England and France experienced. Until the eighteenth century Spain existed as a loose confederation of states with each one having its own legislature, courts, system of taxation, and separate monetary system. Two monarchs, Ferdinand and Isabella, did, however, strengthen royal authority in Spain at the expense of Spanish nobles. This was accomplished by investing with royal authority an old medieval institution, the *hermandades*, or brotherhoods. Ferdinand and Isabella gave the *hermandades* power to apprehend, try, and punish criminals. Leaders of the brotherhoods took orders from royal officials and often acted on behalf of the monarchy.

Like their counterparts in England, the Spanish monarchs curtailed the power of the Spanish nobles by using a Royal Council. They prohibited aristocrats from serving on this governmental agency, which greatly reduced the influence of Spain's largest landholders. Ferdinand and Isabella gave themselves the right to appoint council members. They appointed only middle class artisans and businessmen to the Royal Council. Most council members had training in Roman law and owed allegiance to the monarchy. Ferdinand and Isabella invested the Royal Council with tremendous power, making it the central feature of Spanish government during their reign from 1474 to 1516. This institution had complete authority to make, enforce, and interpret Spanish laws.

Ferdinand and Isabella used the Catholic Church to exert control in Spain. Like Charles VII in France, the Spanish monarchs got authority to appoint Church officials. An agreement was negotiated with the Spanish-born Pope, Alexander VI, under which Ferdinand and Isabella was given the authority to appoint bishops throughout Spain and its holdings in Latin America. This authority enabled the Spanish monarchs, whom the Pope gave the title "Catholic Kings of Spain," de facto authority to create and control a national Church. Revenue the monarchy received from the Church enabled the monarchs to create a strong army, which was used to drive the Moors from Granada in 1492 and complete the *reconquista*, a struggle to recapture Spanish lands that Muslim Arabs had held for eight centuries.

Ferdinand and Isabella, like other European Renaissance monarchs, utilized terror to exert control over their subjects. The device they used most frequently was the *Inquisition*. In 1478, Pope Sixtus IV issued a decree allowing governments to establish tribunals to root out religious heretics in Catholic countries. On September 28, 1480, Ferdinand and Isabella ordered tribunals established in Spain. The Spanish Inquisition, as these tribunals were called, was used primarily to curry favor with the Spanish population, which was suspicious of the large minority of Muslim and Jewish converts to Catholicism residing on the Iberian Peninsula. Ferdinand and Isabella realized that most Spanish Catholics hated the Arab and Jewish Christians who had been forced to convert during the fifteenth century. If the royal government protected the *conversos,* it likely would lose support from the population, but if they were not protected, rioting was likely to occur in towns when Spanish Catholics attacked the conversos. Ferdinand and Isabella decided to win popular approval and prevent rioting by establishing the Inquisition.

Although Isabella allowed the Inquisition to come to Castile, she demanded that Pope Sixtus relinquish control over the inquisitors and the confiscated wealth to the government.

Compounding the problem was that the conversos, who numbered about 250,000 in the Spanish population of more than 7,000,000, held prominent positions in business and government, which enabled them to exert influence disproportionate to their population. Conversos, for example, held about 30 percent of the positions on the Royal Council, controlled the Spanish treasury, served as archbishops, bishops, and abbots in the Spanish Church, intermarried with the nobility, held prominent positions in medicine and law, created successful businesses, and served as tax collectors. The fact that conversos held prominent positions within Spain produced jealousy and racism within the Catholic population. Traditional Spanish Catholics insisted that the conversos had abandoned Christianity and reverted to their Jewish or Muslim roots. Catholics invoked racism to use against conversos, maintaining that ethnically an individual was what his or her ancestors were before conversion. Thus, a person whose ancestors were Jewish or Muslim remained a Jew or Muslim even after conversion to Christianity. This racial theory, which violated Biblical doctrine, evolved to hold that all conversos were evil and controlled by Satan. Spanish Catholics maintained that the immoral and malicious conversos were by their ethnic nature criminals and thus could not be converted to Christianity. Furthermore, Spanish anti-Semitism alleged that Jews were plotting to control all governmental and religious offices in Spain unless they were stopped. This, anti-Semites believed, posed a threat to Spanish national unity. The Inquisition was thus created and used to rid Spain of these perceived threats and the heretical conversos. The Inquisition, although primarily a Catholic device to uphold Catholic faith, was not controlled by the Church in Spain. Rather, Ferdinand and Isabella controlled and used it to politically unify Spain. The tribunals commonly employed torture to force confessions from Jewish and Muslim converts to Catholicism, as well as from Protestants. After the Inquisition had been created, Ferdinand and Isabella expelled by royal edict all Jews from Spain in 1492. The royal couple demanded that Spain develop as a nation unified by Catholic orthodoxy, free from Muslim and Jewish influences.

Nationalism that developed in the Renaissance produced a wave of overseas exploration that eventually led to the establishment of colonies. Northern European countries led the way across the ocean.

EXPLORATION AND EXPANSION

Toward the end of the Renaissance, the strong monarchies and nationalism they generated caused northern and western European nations to begin a period of overseas exploration and expansion. This "Age of Expansion," as the period from 1415 until 1650 is often called, resulted in the migration of Europeans to other continents and European political, economic, and social control of North and South America, coastal regions of Africa, India, China, Japan, and many Pacific islands.

Before significant oceanic exploration could occur, improvements in navigation and technology had to take place. Before the Renaissance brought its technological revolution to Europe, navigational methods were primitive. Viking sailors, the best medieval Europe produced, calculated their position on the ocean by viewing the sun with the naked eye. They could only guess at the speed their ships traveled and the distance covered. However, all this had changed by the middle part of the fifteenth century.

By that time European sailors were using various mechanical devices to help with navigation on the open ocean. The most important navigational device was the compass. Invented by the Chinese, the compass was a simple tool that consisted of a magnetic needle fastened to a piece of wood marked with directions. Since the magnetized needle always pointed toward the earth's magnetic North Pole, navigators could always determine the direction their ship was traveling. In addition to being able to mechanically determine direction of travel, ship captains could also fix their precise location on the ocean's surface by using the astrolabe, quadrant, and sextant. All three instruments enabled navigators to measure the altitude and position of stars in relation to the earth's surface and thus precisely locate a ship on the ocean. Used in conjunction with the compass, ship captains could correctly and accurately record direction, distance, location, speed, and use maps to plot courses through waters of the known world.

Not only were improvements in navigation made, but Europeans also benefited from better ships. The medieval European ship was a relative small vessel with one sail, high sides, and wide bodies, with a steering rudder on its side. The sail was useful only if the wind blew from behind the ship because it could not be rotated. For locomotion these ships often relied upon slaves to man oars. Over time, modifications in ship design occurred. Important changes included more, larger, and adjustable sails. By using a sailing tactic called "tacking" and a new type of rigging developed by Arabs called the lanteen sail, ships could position various sails to travel into the wind. No longer did ships have to travel in the direction the wind blew, now they could move against it. European ships in the fifteenth and sixteenth centuries also became longer, sleeker, faster, and more stable and improved rudder designs made them more maneuverable. Such improvements were first manifest in Portuguese caravels and carracks during the 1400s and in Portuguese, Spanish, French, Dutch, and English galleons in the 1600s.

Another important technological innovation that made possible European exploration was the use of gunpowder. Although its origins are not clear, most likely the Arabs invented gunpowder around 1,000 A.D. The Chinese, who had traded with Arabic peoples, were using gunpowder when Marco Polo visited Carthay (the European name for China). Europeans were quick to find a military use for this invention. During the early years of the fourteenth century gunpowder was used to shoot objects from cannons and eventually small arms were invented. Without gunpowder, cannon, and personal firearms, it is doubtful that Europeans could have prevailed in war against Native Americans because of the small number of European soldiers that could be sustained in the New World.

The modern age of exploration began with Portugal during the fifteenth century. Portugal's exploration began largely as a result of Prince Henry the Navigator's quest to make contact with the nation of Prester John. According to legend, Prester John was a Catholic priest who governed a Christian state somewhere in Africa or Asia. Prince Henry, being a devout Catholic and thus anti-Muslim, wanted to contact Prester John in hopes of forming a Christian alliance that would encircle Muslim nations. To achieve this objective, Prince Henry undertook a major exploration along Africa's western coast. Although Prince Henry personally did not sail on any of these voyages, his financial assets were critical to their success. Portuguese explorers, who may or may not have believed in the existence of Prester John, realized there were vast profits to be made in Africa. Portuguese ships left Cape St. Vincent, the westernmost point on the European continent, under the authority of Prince Henry. Their captains, who were paid handsomely by Prince Henry, pushed farther south and west. In 1445, Dinis Dias sailed around Cape Verde and passed beyond the Sahara Desert. On a voyage in 1455, Alivse da Cadamosto sailed up the mouth of the Senegal and Gambia Rivers and discovered the Cape Verde Islands. At the same time, the Portuguese had found and colonized the Madeira

The triangular sails of the caravel were augmented by square sails to help catch the wind from many directions.

and the Azores Islands in the Atlantic Ocean west of Portugal. After Prince Henry died in 1460, his exploration program was continued under various Portuguese monarchs. However, Portugal was no longer concerned with contacting Prester John. The goal was to find the southern tip of Africa, sail around it, and reach India, China, and Japan. If Portugal could discover a water route to Asia, it could control the spice trade, which had been dominated by Italian and Arab traders for centuries.

In 1488 Portugal achieved its goal of sailing around Africa. Bartolomeu Dias rounded the Cape of Good Hope at the southern tip of Africa and saw the Indian Ocean for the first time. Dias had to turn back before reaching Asia because his sailors were afraid to go farther. Ten years later, Portugal finally found its ocean route to Asia. Vasco da Gama set sail in 1497 intending to go beyond the Cape of Good Hope. The next year da Gama reached India. Later expeditions reached China. Portugal had achieved its goal of dominating the spice trade. After reaching India, Portugal began to build a commercial empire in Africa and Asia. This was accomplished by establishing numerous trading posts at places such as Sao Tome and the Cape Verde Islands, Ceylon, and Malabar, India. Portuguese control was completed in 1509 when a Muslim fleet was destroyed in a naval battle at Diu in the Indian Ocean. This victory ensured that Portugal would be the dominant power in Asia. By 1550 Portugal had a world monopoly on the spice trade. Its empire stretched from the Persian Gulf to the Pacific.

Portugal, after discovering an oceanic route to Asia, mostly lost interest in further explorations westward across the Atlantic. However, a storm blew the ships of Pedro Alvares Cabral off course in 1500, and he reached the coast of Brazil, which eventually became a Portuguese colony. With the exception of Brazil, Portugal established few colonies in the Western Hemisphere. Exploration and colonization of North and South America was largely left to other European countries, including Spain, England, France, and the Netherlands.

Jealous of Portugal's success and fearful of its power, Spain wanted to challenge Portugal's mastery of the seas. Like Portugal, Spain sought an ocean route to the riches of Asia. An Italian sea captain, Christopher Columbus, persuaded Ferdinand and Isabella in 1492 that a third trade route to Asia could be discovered by sailing westward across the Atlantic. Spain's fear of Portugal's increasing power, coupled

Vasco da Gama

King Ferdinand and Queen Isabella are pictured here with Christopher Columbus.

with Columbus' promises of gold, glory, and colonies, caused Ferdinand and Isabella to take a chance on this Italian sailor. Spain provided Columbus with three small ships: the *Nina, Pinta*, and *Santa Maria*. Columbus set sail for China in August 1492. After stopping for repairs and supplies in the Canary Islands, it took Columbus just over a month to cross the Atlantic. He landed on a small, flat island in the Bahamas, probably Samana Cay. Columbus erroneously believed he had landed on an island near the Asian mainland and thus called the native people he encountered *Indios* (Spanish for Indian). Columbus then explored parts of Cuba and an island he called Hispaniola (today Haiti and the Dominican Republic). After capturing several Native Americans as proof that he had reached Asia, Columbus returned triumphantly to Spain. There, he was knighted and given the title Admiral of the Ocean. Isabella and Ferdinand believed Spain had found a short route to the wealth of Asia. Columbus made several more voyages to the Americas between 1493 and 1504. He explored numerous islands in the Caribbean and on his third voyage reached Venezuela in South America. On his fourth voyage in 1504, he visited the southern tip of North America, briefly exploring Honduras, Nicaragua, Costa Rica, and Panama.

Eventually, some Europeans realized that Columbus had not reached Asia but a new continent. One was the adventurer Amerigo Vespucci. An Italian like Columbus, Vespucci was part of a Portuguese expedition that explored the coast of South America in 1499. In 1500, he published a series of vivid and largely fictional descriptions of the lands he visited. Vespucci was the first European to describe the lands Columbus reached as *mundus novus*, or New World. In 1507, a geographer, Martin Waldseemuller, published a map depicting lands west of Europe as a separate continent, which he labeled America in honor of Vespucci.

The harbor at Genoa from where Columbus began his journey.

Columbus returned to the court of Ferdinand and Isabella with gifts and natives from the New World. The explorer's tales of vast gold deposits persuaded the king and queen to finance further expeditions.

Largely as a result of Columbus' exploration, Spain replaced Portugal as Europe's most dominant nation. In 1573, the Spanish explorer Vasco Nunez de Balboa crossed the Isthmus of Panama, seeing the Pacific Ocean for the first time. In 1520, a Portuguese navigator sailing for Spain accomplished what Columbus failed to do—find an ocean route to Asia. Ferdinand Magellan sailed around a passage at the tip of South America into the Pacific Ocean that was named the Straits of Magellan in his honor. Magellan eventually reached the Philippine Islands where he died after a fight with the native people. Finally, one of his ships reached Spain by sailing around the tip of Africa, marking the first time a European ship had circumnavigated the Earth. Other Spanish explorers, including Ponce de Leon in 1513, Cortez in 1519, and Pizarro in 1531 continued Spanish explorations throughout the Western Hemisphere. As a result of Columbus' explorations, in the Treaty of Tordesilles Spain claimed all of the Americas with exception of Brazil, which was awarded to Portugal. In 1580 Spain gained control of Portugal and for a time controlled all of the New World where they forced into submission Native American people and largely destroyed their cultures through warfare and disease.

Five years after Columbus' voyage, England sent Giovanni Caboto (John Cabot), a Venetian sea captain, on an exploratory expedition to North America. Cabot, in 1497 and 1498, explored along the Atlantic coast from the Chesapeake Bay to Newfoundland. Like Columbus, Cabot sought an oceanic route to Asia westward across the Atlantic or, as he referred to it, a Northwest Passage. Cabot's voyage in 1497 represents the first recorded Trans-Atlantic voyage by an English ship although some evidence indicates that English fishermen might have accidentally landed in Nova Scotia and Newfoundland in the 1480s. Regardless, English historians give Cabot credit for discovering North America. The English based their territorial claims in the New World upon Cabot's voyages. Perhaps Cabot would have undertaken further explorations had he not died on his second voyage to America in 1498. John's son, Sebastian, continued England's explorations. In 1508 and 1509 he sailed across the Atlantic attempting to find a Northwest Passage to China, but success eluded him. He did, however, explore in the Hudson Bay region of North America, which England claimed.

Ferdinand Magellan

After Sebastian Cabot failed to find the Northwest Passage, England lost interest in the New World for about seventy-five years. When Elizabeth I took the throne, English interest in overseas exploration revived. The driving force behind exploration under Elizabeth I was Sir Humphrey Gilbert. Originally, Gilbert wanted to do what the Cabots had not done, find the Northwest Passage. Earlier, Gilbert published a book on the subject, speculating about where such a passage might be located. He also promised readers, who might be potential investors in an expedition to find a northern route to Asia, that wealth awaited those smart enough to find a new trade route. In 1576, Gilbert convinced Elizabeth I that it was in England's national interest to find the Northwest Passage

In 1576, at the behest of Gilbert, the Queen sent Martin Frobisher to find the Northwest Passage. Frobisher sailed into Labrador where he captured an Eskimo, taking him and the kayak he was paddling from the Atlantic. Frobisher returned to England with the Eskimo and a small sample of gold ore. After assayers determined that the ore contained gold, Elizabeth in 1577 organized a joint stock company to construct a fort and mining operations in Labrador. This company financed two expeditions by Frobisher in 1577 and 1578. During these trips to Labrador Frobisher captured three more Eskimos and brought back two thousand tons of gold ore. The Eskimos, like the first one in 1576, died soon after arriving in England, and the gold ore was not real after all. Frobisher had brought back "fools gold" (iron pyrite). This mistake ruined his reputation.

Gilbert, distrusting Frobisher, had refused to invest in the 1577 and 1578 expeditions. When Frobisher returned with fools gold, Gilbert took advantage of the explorer's misfortune. He persuaded Elizabeth to grant him a charter to

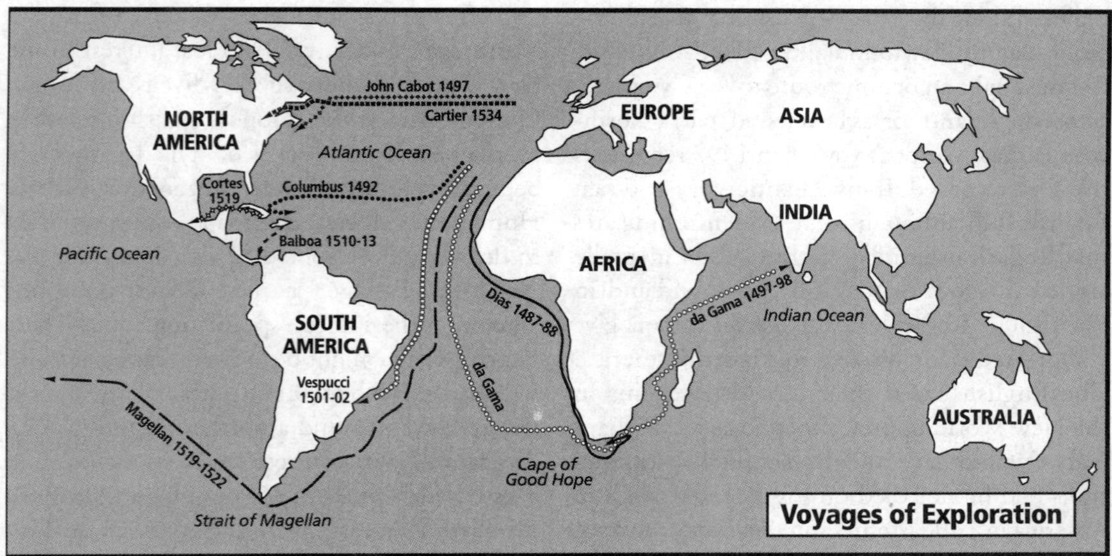

explore, settle, and govern all territory in North America not occupied by Christian people. The English charter completely disregarded all claims Native Americans had upon land in the New World. Gilbert, for some time, had tried to convince the Queen that England should be more interested in land than gold.

Gilbert set sail in 1583. He reached Nova Scotia where the voyage was aborted due to bad weather. On the return voyage to England Gilbert's ship sank during a storm. His death prompted his stepbrother, Sir Walter Raleigh, to attempt to colonize the New World for England. Raleigh received permission from Elizabeth I to explore and establish a colony in North America. The result was the ill-fated adventure at Roanoke Island. In 1584, Raleigh dispatched an exploring party, which surveyed Roanoke Island off the coast of present-day North Carolina. The next year Raleigh dispatched six hundred men to the colony. These men, many of whom were soldiers, raided Spanish ships in the Caribbean before leaving about 108 of their number on Roanoke Island. This attempt at settlement failed due to poor relations with nearby tribes of Native Americans. After one year, the colony was abandoned, and the Englishmen returned home. In 1587, Raleigh tried again to settle Roanoke Island. Like the earlier one, this second attempt to plant an English colony in North America was doomed for failure. John White headed the Roanoke Island settlement, which included women and children. Within a year, the Roanoke settlement vanished. Its disappearance is one of the biggest mysteries in history.

England's next attempt at colonization in North America was successful. In 1606 the English government granted a charter to investors for the Virginia Company. Initially, investors in the Virginia Company dreamed of finding gold and silver but soon realized these minerals were not available along the Atlantic seaboard. They then attempted to make money by trading with Native Americans and establishing an agricultural colony in North America. In December 1606, the Virginia Company sent Captain Christopher Newport and 144 men on three ships, the "Susan Constant," "Godspeed," and "Discovery," to

Sir Walter Raleigh

establish a colony near Roanoke Island. Thirty-nine of the men died on the Atlantic crossing, but, in May 1607, the survivors landed at a site they named Jamestown in honor of King James I. This settlement, in territory Raleigh had earlier named Virginia after Elizabeth I, the so-called Virgin Queen, became the first permanent English colony in North America.

The English and Spanish had rivals for control of North America. France and the Netherlands explored and colonized areas in the New World. French claims in North America were based on explorations by Giovanni da Verrazzano in 1524 and Jacques Cartier in 1534. Verrazzano, an Italian mariner, sailed westward across the Atlantic under the authority of Frances I. He explored along the East Coast from South Carolina to New England, claiming all this territory for France. Cartier, following in Verrazzano's wake, led three expeditions between 1534 and 1542 through the St. Lawrence River Valley, reaching sites where the modern cities of Montreal and Quebec are located. Because the French were interested in trading with Native Americans, Cartier established the first French colony in 1541, but the effort failed due to political upheaval in France. It was not until 1608 that the French successfully established a settlement in Canada. Samuel de Champlain

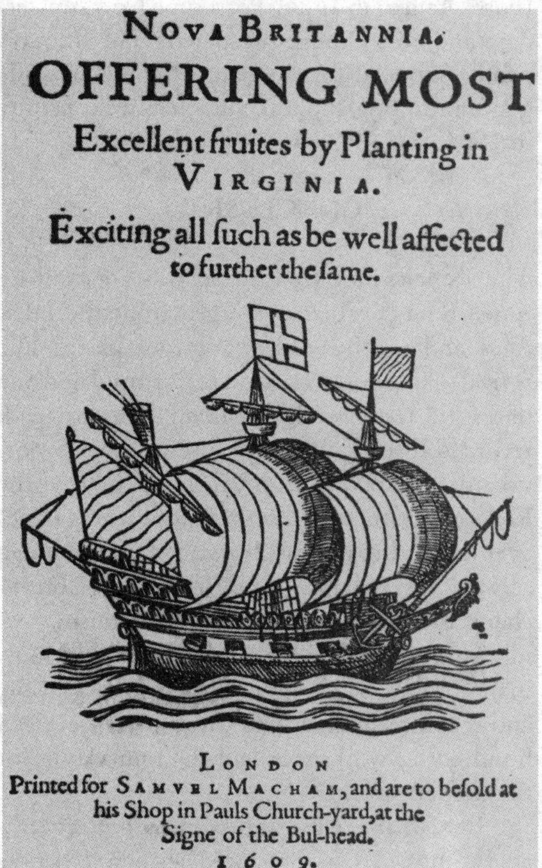
NOVA BRITANNIA.

OFFERING MOST

Excellent fruites by Planting in

VIRGINIA.

Exciting all ſuch as be well affected to further the ſame.

LONDON

Printed for SAMVEL MACHAM, and are to be ſold at his Shop in Pauls Church-yard, at the Signe of the Bul-head.

1609.

built a fort at Quebec on the St. Lawrence River and sent out explorers who claimed the Ohio and Mississippi River Valleys and all territory surrounding the Great Lakes for France.

Dutch claims to North American territory were based on the explorations of Henry Hudson, an English sea captain. In 1609, Hudson, in the employ of the Netherlands, was sent to search for the Northwest Passage. He explored Delaware Bay, New York, the Hudson River, and Hudson Bay. Like the French, Hudson was interested in establishing a fur-trading network with Native Americans. To achieve this objective, the Dutch established forts on Manhattan Island, which they called New Amsterdam and at Albany (Fort Orange) in 1624. For a time New Amsterdam and Fort Orange prospered. The Iroquois people supplied furs in return for Dutch trade goods until England forcefully seized the colony in 1664.

CONCLUSION

The Renaissance in Europe was an exciting time. The continent emerged from the Dark Ages, and a revival of learning took place. The revival of interest in classical texts stimulated one of the greatest periods of human creativity in all recorded history. Italy, because it was the most urbanized part of Europe, first experienced the Renaissance, but northern European countries eventually became as thirsty for knowledge as were the Italians. The Renaissance forever changed western civilization. Humanism, secularism, and individualism became the dominant modes of thought throughout Europe, and scholars imbued with these ideas produced hundreds of works that laid the foundation for the modern world.

Remarkable men and women did remarkable things. Artists produced numerous works influenced by the ancient civilizations. Artists became celebrated figures in Renaissance countries. Wealthy patrons viewed art as power and commissioned artists to produce works to impress others with their status and wealth. Literature and other forms of scholarly writing were also important. Aiding the literary works produced in the Renaissance was the printing press. For the first time in history, it was possible to reproduce the printed word many times over.
Nationalism was also an important component of the Renaissance. Strong monarchs in various countries, taking advantage of nationalistic feelings, unified their countries and sent out voyages of exploration to other parts of the world, beginning a process that, over time, saw European influence permeate the entire world. Statecraft became an important component of government, especially in Italy where so many independent city-states existed.

Despite these achievements, the Renaissance was marked by inequality for women, stigmatized by slavery and traumatized by war. However, a few women overcame social barriers and participated in the Renaissance, producing scholarly writings and artwork. Despite the achievements of a few, most women did not fully participate in Renaissance society. They were, at best, second-class citizens who were subject to many inequalities and an unjust legal system.

Even though inequality and injustice were part of society, scholars often date the beginning of the modern world to the Renaissance. This amazing period of artistic, scholarly, political, and literary achievement influenced many events to come. The Protestant Reformation was one such event. The Renaissance emphasis on humanism, individualism, and secularism would, in the sixteenth century, give rise to the Reformation, perhaps the greatest religious upheaval Europe would witness.

Suggestions for Further Reading

Hans Baron, *The Crisis of the Early Italian Renaissance: Civic Humanism and Republican Liberty in the Age of Classicism and Tyranny* (1966).

James Beck, *Italian Painting of the Renaissance* (1981).

Marvin B. Becker, *Civility and Society in Western Europe, 1300-1600* (1988).

Thomas G. Bergin, *Boccacio* (1981).

J. M. Clark, *The Great German Mystics: Eckhart, Tauler and Suso* (1961).

Alistair C. Crombie, *Medieval and Early Modern Science* (1961).

Amos Funkerstein, *Theology and the Scientific Imagination from the Middle Ages to the Seventeenth Century* (1986).

Richard A. Goldthwaite, *The Building of Renaissance Florence: An Economic and Social History* (1980).

J. R. Hale, *Machiavelli and Renaissance Italy* (1966).

J. R. Hale, *Renaissance Europe: The Individual and Society, 1480-1520* (1978).

George Holmes, *Florence, Rome and the Origins of the Renaissance* (1986).

George Holmes, *The Oxford History of Italy* (1997).

George Holmes, ed., *Art and Politics in Renaissance Italy* (1993).

J. Huizinga, *Erasmus of Rotterdam* (1952).

Christiane Klapisch-Zuber *Women, Family and Ritual in Renaissance Italy* (1985).

Christiane Klapisch-Zuber, *A History of Women* (1994).

Paul O. Kristeller, *Renaissance Thought and Its Sources* (1979).

Lauro Martines, *The Social World of the Florentine Humanists* (1963).

M. M. Phillips, *Erasmus and the Northern Renaissance* (1956).

Chapter 12

THE REFORMATION

Martin Luther, the second son of a German copper miner who had become a mine owner, was alone and frightened while crossing a field during a severe thunderstorm. Without warning, a loud clap of thunder and a bolt of lightening knocked Luther, a man in his early twenties, to the ground. The experienced terrified him. He began to see his short life passing in front of his eyes. Thinking that he was dying, Luther cried out to St. Anne, the mother of the Virgin Mary and the patron of travelers in distress, that he would enter a monastery if God allowed him to live. Miraculously, or so he thought, the storm abated. Luther arose, thanked God and St. Anne, and continued on his way. The thunderstorm experience changed Luther's life and the history of Western Christianity. Because Luther had promised St. Anne that he would enter a monastery and devote his life to God if he were spared, the young German faced a dilemma. His father, Hans, an omnipotent figure who dominated the Luther household, was determined that his second son would become a lawyer, a profession that would enable Luther to earn a handsome living and offer many opportunities for the family's upward social mobility. Hans had spent considerable money and endured personal deprivation to see that his son received a good education. Eventually, Luther earned a Masters' degree with distinction in 1505. At his parents' behest, Luther enrolled in law school but never studied law. Without consulting Hans, Luther entered the Order of the Hermits of St. Augustine on July 17, 1505, keeping his vow to St. Anne. Hans was furious. He ranted and raged, thinking that the money and personal sacrifice he had expended to make his son a lawyer had been wasted. Little did he know that Luther would begin a revolution twelve years later that would completely change western civilization.

Luther's decision to enter a monastery was actually an attempt to resolve a long-standing spiritual conflict within his mind. The young German was obsessed with his own sinfulness and tormented by guilt. He joined a monastery hoping that life as a hermit would enable him to be forgiven of his earthly sins and absolve him of guilt. Luther was a conscientious friar, pursuing every possible way of penitence, including lengthy fasts, prayers, self-denial, frequent confessions, and self-flagellation. None of these acts relieved the sense of guilt he felt at being a sinner until another extraordinary experience in a castle tower (restrooms were located in castle towers) at Wittenberg, where he served as a university lecturer on theology, alleviated his guilt. While in the tower, Luther received what he believed to be a visionary insight from God that brought peace to his troubled mind. Prior to the tower experience, he could not understand how a sinner could receive anything from God other than being cast in hell's fiery pits. In the tower vision, however, Luther understood that God was merciful and just. This insight enabled him to develop the principle of "justification by faith" upon which the Protestant Reformation was based. Luther now understood that God forgave sinners and made them righteous through the gift of grace, which was achieved by faith. Luther then began to question activities within the Catholic Church, such as the sale of indulgences, that violated this "truth" God had revealed in the Wittenberg castle tower. In 1517 Luther nailed his Ninety-five Theses to the church door in Wittenberg, beginning the Protestant Reformation that shattered the unity of Western Christendom. Had the young German become a lawyer, as his father wanted, the Protestant Reformation might not have occurred, and Luther most likely would not have had an influence upon the world a half millennium after his life ended.

Chronology

1483	Martin Luther born.
1484	Ulrich Zwingli born.
1509	John Calvin born.
1517	Ninety-Five Theses composed.
1519	Leipzig Debate with John Eck.
1520	Luther branded as a heretic by a Papal Bull.
1521	Luther's ideas published in three pamphlets.
1521	Diet of Worms.
1521-1555	Habsburg-Valois Wars
1524-25	The Peasant's War
1525	Luther marries a former nun.
1527	Henry VIII requests an annulment of his marriage to Catherine of Argon.
1529	Term Protestant first used after Diet of Speyer.
1529	Zwingli meets with Luther at Marburg
1533	Calvin converts to Protestantism.
1534	Calvin flees from France and goes to Geneva.
1534 lish	Acts of Supremacy passed by Eng- Parliament.
1535	Melchiorites gain control of Munster
1535	Order of Ursuline Nuns founded
1536	Calvin publishes *The Institutes of the Christian Religion.*
1541	Calvin establishes a theocracy in Geneva.
1545	Council of Trent convened.
1549	Book of Common Prayer Written.
1553-1558	Bloody Mary reigns in England.
1558	Elizabeth I becomes English Queen.
1560	John Knox creates Calvinist church in Scotland.
1563	Thirty-Nine Articles composed.
1564	Book of Common Order Published.
1572	St. Bartholomew's Day Massacre.
1585	War of the Three Henrys begins.
1588	Spanish Armada defeated.
1598	Edict of Nantes
1618	Thirty Years War begins.

BACKGROUND TO THE REFORMATION

For sixteenth-century Europeans, the most momentous event in their lives was not overseas exploration, nationalism, or the Renaissance but the Protestant Reformation, an event that shattered the unity of Western Europe under the Roman Catholic Church. Two sides within Christianity—the protestors, or Protestants, and Catholics—arose, and each believed that its views and doctrines were righteous while those of the other were heretical. This confrontation between Catholics and Protestants throughout Europe lasted for more than a century, produced countless wars, and killed thousands of people, leading one wit to comment, "more people have been killed in the name of God than for any other reason."

The Protestant Reformation occurred among such a wide complex of change that scholars often regard the sixteenth century as the transition from medieval Europe to the modern age. By 1500, the Renaissance, after a century and a half in Italy, blossomed on both sides of the Alps. In intellectual circles classical antiquity furnished the inspiration for arts and learning, and the courtier had replaced the monk as the "ideal" person. Commercial expansion and overseas exploration had broadened the horizons of Western Europe while secularism and humanism had created a strong interest in temporal things. The emphasis of the medieval manorial and guild economy on community welfare was being replaced by individualistic capitalism that emphasized profit making. Middle class people were challenging nobles and high-ranking church officials for power, privileges, and prestige. Peasants and artisans were becoming impatient with medieval obligations and restrictions. The increasing power of national monarchies, which upheld the principle of state sovereignty, reduced the power of the Catholic Church, its Pope, and the Holy Roman Empire, institutions that during the Middle Ages had largely controlled the Christian Commonwealth (*Corpus Christianum*). Amid all this change, the Protestant Reformation fragmented the ecclesiastical unity of Western Europe.

Despite the secular tendencies the Renaissance stimulated, the sixteenth century was still a religious age, and the Reformation was primarily a religious movement that involved most people in European societies. From one perspective, the Reformation was a religious revival whose main concern was salvation. Individuals took religion seriously, and it was a way of life. Sixteenth-century Europeans looked to both the church and state to foster religious life. Religious issues were closely tied to economic, political, and social issues. Demands for social justice usually were couched in religious language taken from the Bible. It is difficult to understand why people vexed by social, economic, and political changes they did not understand would also support religious reform.

The need for reform in the Church was a theme found within Christianity almost from the time of its inception. Early Christian monasticism, the Benedictine Rule, the Cluniac, Cistercian, and Franciscan movements were all motivated by a desire to bring Christian life into conformity with the highest Christian ideals. The medieval conflict between church and state began as an attempt to free the church from political control, which had subordinated Christian values to political expediency. Medieval reform, however, was not permanent. After a few years the Church, like the ancient Israelites, strayed from the "will of God" and needed to be taken back to its original commitment. In the century and a half before Luther began his reformation, most serious efforts within the Church had failed. The Englishman, John Wyclif, for example, had been declared a heretic. Jan Hus and Girolamo Savonarola had been burned at the stake. Desiderius Erasmus had been ordered to keep quite, and the Roman Church banned his books. Church councils, which had been called from time to time, accomplished little. Popes, bishops, abbots, and priests often behaved immorally. Monks were perceived as being fat and lazy. Not all Church officials fit these perceptions but enough did to give the Church a bad reputation. The behavior of Church officials, coupled with the corruption, was enough to undermine respect lay people had for the institution. When various individuals began criticizing the Catholic Church, common people, aware of problems within the Church, began to take allegations of the detractors seriously.

PROBLEMS IN THE CHURCH AND ORIGINS OF THE REFORMATION

Dissatisfaction within the Roman Catholic Church was apparent by the first decade of the sixteenth century. The authority of the Pope had been declining for over two centuries. Three events—conflict with German Emperor Frederick II in the thirteenth century, the Babylonian Captivity from 1309 to 1376 when Philip the Fair forced the Pope to live in Avignon, France so that he could control the Church, and the Great Schism from 1378 to 1418 when three individuals claimed to be the true Pope—weakened the Church. Even though the Council of Constance had ended the Great Schism by 1418, it encouraged the Concilian Movement, an attempt to give papal authority to Church councils and make the papacy a constitutional monarchy. The Concilian Movement failed largely because Wyclif and Hus convinced secular rulers to oppose it. Their action, which probably delayed the Reformation for a century, was an indication that Western Christendom faced serious trouble.

Further weakening the authority of the Church was secularization produced by the Renaissance. Popes, like many people in Europe, became increasingly concerned with worldly things. They behaved like kings, employing diplomacy and war to gain territory, surrounding themselves with an elaborate court, and patronizing artists and writers. From the perspective of many observers, the papal concern with temporal matters seemed more important than the Pope's religious duties. Various popes, including Alexander VI and Julius II, used their spiritual authority to raise money for non-religious activities, such as building palaces, funding private armies, etc. Although funds available to the Church increased as a result of these practices, corruption within the Church became widespread. Wealthy individuals and families could purchase high ecclesiastical offices. Usually nobles who bought Church offices did so not to further religion but because such offices could be used to attain wealth and power.

Abuses were also apparent at lower levels within the Catholic Church where the religious life of most Europeans took place. Priests at parishes in local villages, like most of the European population, were peasants who lived in abject poverty. To raise funds for themselves and the Church, parish priests sometimes granted forgiveness for sins in return for money. Some lay people viewed such practices as an attempt to sell divine grace. Parish priests also vulgarized religion, sometimes combining religious and pagan symbols into daily life.

By the beginning of the sixteenth century, critics of the Catholic Church attacked it on three fronts: immorality within the Church, the lack of knowledge of parish priests, and clerical pluralism. These things made it seem that the Church was not fulfilling its religious mandate and meeting the spiritual needs of parishioners. These attacks occurred largely because over the centuries the Church had become more institutionalized, more formal, and its doctrines were supported by a detailed system of canon law, theology, pomp, and ritual. Increasingly, Church officials promoted as important the sacraments and the role of priests in performing them. Moreover, the doctrine that good works, fasting, self-denial, and charity must accompany faith was becoming more dominant within the Church.

Immorality was a big problem. It particularly manifested itself in the requirement that priests and Church officials remain celibate. This practice, which dates to the fourth century, was often violated. Parish priests, as well as higher-ranking Church officials, including Pope Alexander VI, commonly had sexual relations with females in

Public burnings ensured that the crowds would witness the execution and hear the agonizing screams of the dying.

their congregations. Sometimes these priests even lived with concubines, sired children, and raised families. Immorality was not confined solely to sexual transgressions. Clergy often appeared in public wearing fancy clothes, gambled, and drank alcoholic beverages to excess. Such conduct, which contradicted Church doctrine and teaching, caused lay people to view Church officials as hypocrites.

Clerical ignorance was another problem. Even though Church law required priests to be educated, bishops rarely enforced this regulation because it was difficult to find educated people who wanted to become priests. Consequently, priests were often poorly educated. Many could barely read and write. They understood the Bible little better than the parishioners they ministered to. Church record books were usually not well maintained. Records of deaths, births, and marriages were sometimes inaccurately recorded, if they were recorded at all. Financial records were usually in disarray. Because of these problems, which could be solved by having an educated clergy, Christian humanists and other Renaissance intellectuals who valued learning criticized the poorly educated priests, mocking them as they recited Latin words in Mass that neither priest nor parishioner could understand.

Clerical pluralism also provided ammunition critics used to attack the Church. Many Church officials held several *benefices* or Church offices simultaneously. This meant that absenteeism was a problem. It was impossible for one official to regularly visit different offices they held in various countries and carry out the spiritual duty each office required. However, these officials collected revenue from all offices held. Priests were usually hired by absentee office holders to perform the spiritual duties each office entailed. These priests were paid a small fraction of the revenue the office holder collected. Thomas Wolsey, an advisor to England's Henry VIII, for example, held the position as Archbishop of York for a decade and a half before he visited the diocese he controlled. Antoine du Prat, the French diplomat under Louis XII, served as Archbishop of Sens without ever visiting a church in his diocese. The only time he was ever in a church in the diocese he controlled was for his own funeral. It was common for Italian church officials to hold high offices in foreign countries that they seldom, if ever, visited. Yet, these absentee foreign officials collected revenue from benefices in England, France, Spain, Germany, and other countries. Clerical pluralism and absenteeism created resentment within congregations and others at the local level, leading to harsh condemnation of the Catholic Church. Critics complained about the way money changed hands every time a new bishop was appointed.

A fundamental problem with the Roman Catholic Church by the sixteenth century was that it simply did not provide for the spiritual needs of local parishioners in an acceptable manner. Most laypersons wanted a more personal relationship with God than the elaborate pomp and ritual present in the Church enabled them to have. They found little comfort in formalized institutional rituals because such practices had little meaning unless the believer could find within them the presence of God. Part of the difficulty was due to the fact that the Catholic Mass was conducted in Latin, which most people did not understand.

Some individuals who wanted a closer personal relationship with God turned toward mysticism because its practitioners stressed religious freedom and individualized worship. Mystics rejected Scholastic theology that dominated the Catholic Church, denounced its authority, and turned to the ancient scriptures and writings of early figures within the Christian Church for guidance. St. Augustine's writings particularly influenced Mysticism. Mystic religious groups had arisen in European cities by the sixteenth century. Such groups were particularly numerous in Germany. By allowing individuals to engage in private devotions, they met the spiritual needs of Christians in ways the Catholic Church could not. One of the largest Mystic organizations in Germany was the Brotherhood of the Eleven Thousand Virgins. Its members met regularly to sing hymns and read psalms. By 1450 over one hundred Mystic societies existed in Hamburg, a city that contained only about eleven thousand people. Other cities in Germany, Italy, and other countries contained similar groups.

Officials within the Roman Catholic Church tried to suppress Mysticism and ordered Mystic societies to disband. These efforts at suppression met with little success. Itinerant preachers traveled throughout Europe spreading Mystic doctrines and beliefs. At every place they preached Mystic evangelists exhorted listeners to communicate directly with God. Mystic ministers told the large crowds they drew to rid themselves of corrupt priests, free themselves from the institutionalized doctrine and ritual of the Catholic Church, and seek a deeply personal relationship with God.

One of the most famous and popular Mystic preachers was Girolamo Savonarola, a Dominican friar who wanted to outlaw materialism and secularism present throughout the Catholic Church. Everywhere this Italian friar preached hundreds, and perhaps thousands, of lay Christians flocked to receive his message. In 1496, for example, he preached in Florence, Italy and presided over a tremendous bonfire fueled by the burning of secular items that included "heathen literature," art, cosmetics, gambling devices, and other worldly items. The tremendous following Savonarola attracted, along with his condemnation of secularism within the Church, drew the attention of Catholic officials. Eventually the Pope issued a warrant for his arrest and had Savonarola executed for heresy.

Another Mystic group was the Brethren of the Common Life. This group was active in Holland. The lay people that organized it tried to imitate Christ in their daily lives. They lived simple lives and performed daily acts of charity, such as feeding the hungry, providing shelter for the homeless, and aid to the sick. The Brethren did these things because they believed Christ taught all Christians to do them. In addition, members of this Mystic society also taught in local schools. Through their teaching, the Brethren of the Common Life urged students, many of whom were training to be Catholic priests, to develop an inner, personal relationship with God and to provide opportunities for future parishioners to develop the same kind of relationship with their God. Thomas Kempis, a member of the Brethren of the Common Life, even wrote *The Imitation of Christ* that was widely read in Holland. In this book he exhorted Christians to view Christ as their role model and lead a simple, unadorned life similar to that the Savior had led. By the mid-fifteenth century the Brethren of the Common Life had spread beyond Holland into Germany. There they would influence many people, including Martin Luther.

LUTHER AND THE BIRTH OF PROTESTANTISM

The problems in the Catholic Church prior to and during the first two decades of the sixteenth century caused Martin Luther (1483-1546), a German Augustinian monk, to officially break with the Church and launch the Protestant Reformation. Even though he did not intend to break away from the Church, Luther was appalled at conditions within the institution. He believed the institution had strayed from practices, beliefs, and teachings of Christ, the Apostles, and first-century Christians.

Luther was particularly troubled by the Catholic practice of selling indulgences. An indulgence allowed sinners to be forgiven of their sins and repair the relationship with God the sin had broken. According to Catholic teaching, individuals who sin become estranged from God. Reconciliation can only occur if the sinner confesses the sin before a priest and is given penance to perform. Penance usually amounted to requiring sinners to reject the wrong and then reciting certain prayers or performing some kind of community service or good deed as atonement for the evil. However, the Pope insisted that because the Church was the embodiment of Christ upon earth it had the authority to grant sinners forgiveness for any sin they might have committed. The doctrine of indulgences was originally developed in the twelfth century so that the Pope and bishops could reward crusader knights for fighting to free the Holy Land from Muslim infidels. Individuals who received an indulgence from the Church, it was believed, would not face punishment for their sins while alive on earth or after entering purgatory. These individuals, at the moment of death, would be granted immediate entry into heaven. Luther was especially upset that people who bought indulgences believed they could commit any sin afterwards without having to confess the sin and do penance.

The event that disturbed Luther most was Pope Leo X's selling of indulgences to raise funds

Martin Luther, German scholar, was one of the fathers of the Protestant movement.

to construct St. Peter's Basilica. In 1517 Albert of Magdeburg, the Archbishop of Mainz, Halberstadt and Magdeburg (an example of clerical pluralism), had received a special papal dispensation to simultaneously hold all three offices. He had borrowed money from the Fuggers, a wealthy Jewish banking family in Augsburg, to pay Leo X for the dispensation allowing him to hold all three offices. As part of the agreement, Leo X had authorized Albert to sell indulgences to raise money to repay the Fuggers and fund construction of St. Peter's Basilica. Albert hired John Tetzel, a Dominican friar, to sell the indulgences near Wittenberg where Luther was teaching in 1517. Tetzel was one of the first people to engage in modern advertising. To sell indulgences, he constructed a chart with different prices for different sins and composed a "cute" but disturbing slogan "As soon as coin in coffer rings, from purgatory the soul springs." Individuals could purchase indulgences not only for themselves but also for dead relatives.

Frederick of Saxony, one of the seven electors within the Holy Roman Empire, and the ruler of the German principality where Wittenberg was located, forbade Tetzel to sell indulgences in the Duchy of Saxony. Tetzel simply moved across the border to Jutenborg, Thuringia where he continued to preach and sell indulgences. Many Saxony residents, including some of Luther's students at the University of Wittenberg, crossed the border and purchased forgiveness for their sins. Luther, a Biblical scholar, had found no scriptural authority allowing the Church to grant indulgences. Furthermore, he believed that Tetzel was cheating German citizens out of their hard-earned money. He found it objectionable that the Catholic Church was making worthless promises to people that their sins would be forgiven when the Church did not have the authority to grant forgiveness. Luther's studies told him only Christ could forgive sin. Since the Church had no official doctrine on the sale of indulgences, Luther believed the matter was open for academic discussion.

Luther wrote a letter to Archbishop Albert stating his objections to the sale of indulgences. This letter contained a document written in Latin called the "Ninety-five Theses on the Power of

Indulgences." After Luther's death, Philip Melanchthon, one of his disciples, claimed that on All Hallow's Eve in 1517 Luther posted the Ninety-five Theses on the door of Wittenberg Castle Church. Whether Luther nailed this document to the church door is controversial. Some historians have concluded that the event never occurred. Nevertheless, Luther's argument in the Ninety-five Theses was that the sale of indulgences trivialized the penance sacrament, contradicted Biblical teaching, and caused Christians to forgo charitable penance. By the end of 1517 the Ninety-five Theses had been translated into German and were being read and discussed throughout the German principalities.

Luther's Ninety-five Theses was not intended to signal a break with Catholicism. The document stated what Luther believed to be the Biblical position on indulgences. Luther maintained that there was no Biblical basis for indulgences and rejected the notion that salvation could be purchased through an indulgence or achieved by performing good deeds. Instead, Luther maintained that salvation came only by the grace of God. There was nothing that an individual could do in the earthly life to obtain salvation. God granted salvation to individuals for reasons known only to the deity. Luther also maintained that the Pope could only remit temporal punishment imposed by the Church, that every Christian was saved so long as they accepted grace even if they did not purchase an indulgence and criticized papal wealth.

As word of Luther's attack on indulgences spread across Germany, the money Tetzel collected from their sale declined. This caused the Dominican Order to launch an attack on Luther, whom they perceived to be a presumptuous Augustinian. The Dominican attack was based in part on a longstanding rivalry with the Augustinian order. Augustinian beliefs were more liberal (more likely to question church practices) than those held by the Dominicans, who were defenders of Church orthodoxy and who would later play a prominent role in the Catholic Inquisition. In fact, Luther and other Augustinians often mockingly split the Dominican name into its two Latin parts *Domini canes*, which means dogs of the Lord. Initially, church officials, including Pope Leo X, took little interest in the controversy, regarding it as simply a dispute between friars. Eventually the controversy became so widespread that the Church could not ignore it. In 1519 Luther, in a public debate with John Eck, a prominent scholar, at Leipzig that attracted a large audience, challenged the authority of both the Pope and the Council of Constance, maintaining that both had been wrong when John Hus was convicted of heresy and burned at the stake.

In 1520 Luther wrote three brief essays outlining his views. The first, entitled *An Address to the Christian Nobility of the German Nation*, was an appeal to German nationalism. In this essay Luther urged his countrymen to reject the authority of a foreign pope. All Christians, said Luther, constitute the body of Christ (the Church) and have a responsibility to heal a defective institution and rid it of abuses such as indulgences. The second essay, *The Babylonian Captivity*, criticized the seven sacraments from which the Catholic Church derived much of its power. Luther argued that the Bible authorized only three sacraments—penance, baptism, and the Lords Supper (the Eucharist). The third letter, *Liberties of the Christian Man*, outlined Luther's position on salvation, faith, good works, and grace.

Pope Leo X responded by condemning Luther's theology, ordering that his books be burned, and excommunicating him unless he publicly recanted within two months. Luther responded by burning Leo X's letter and calling the pontiff an Antichrist. Charles V, the Holy Roman Emperor, ordered Luther to defend his views before a diet (assembly) at Worms, a city on the Rhine, in 1521. When directed to disavow what he had previously said and written, Luther refused, stating that he could not go against his conscience or Biblical scripture. His refusal to recant prompted Charles to brand Luther an outlaw and issue an order for his arrest. Even though it was illegal to do so, Duke Frederick III of Saxony offered Luther protection against German and Church authorities, officials he viewed as foreign usurpers. Frederick had Luther taken to Wartburg Castle where the monk lived for a year. Ironically, Frederick never broke with the Catholic Church. His actions, however, enabled the Protestant Reformation to continue. Without his protection Charles V would probably have had Luther burned at the stake.

Luther's break with the Catholic Church was complete. From 1520 to 1530 he developed a theology different from Catholic orthodoxy. The theological principles Luther devised became the basic tenants all Protestant sects who were part of the Reformation followed. Lutheran theology was firmly rooted in Biblical scholarship.

Luther devised five primary doctrines that became the foundation for all Protestant theology. First was the principle of salvation. Traditional Catholic doctrine held that salvation resulted from faith and good works. Luther rejected the notion that good deeds played any role in salvation. Instead, he taught that the Bible clearly indicated salvation results solely from faith. There is nothing, Luther said, that humankind does to achieve salvation. Individuals are saved because God arbitrarily decides, for reasons known only to the deity, to grant certain people grace. Taking the sacraments, giving to charity, or doing good in everyday life would not save someone unless God granted that person grace. God, not people, Luther believed, initiated salvation.

Second, Luther rejected the Catholic notion that religious authority resides in two places—the Bible and traditional Church teachings. Rather, Luther stated that religious authority resides only in the Bible, which he believed was the word of God revealed to humans. Each person was free to interpret the Bible as his or her conscience dictated. For Luther, it was important that each individual read and study the Bible and then reflect on its teachings amid the presence of other Christians in a communal or church setting.

Third, Luther maintained that the church was the body of Christ and that all Christians, not just clergymen, were part of the institution. Catholics had previously taught that only priests were part of the Church, and, therefore, only priests were allowed to partake of wine during the Eucharist. Luther allowed the congregation to drink the wine, which lessened the authority of priests. Furthermore, Luther abolished much of the Catholic pomp in religious services, which simplified the liturgy and further decreased the power of priests.

Fourth, Luther developed the concept known as the *priesthood of the believer*. This is the idea that individuals can understand God's will as revealed in the Bible through prayer without the aid of priests. Nor, do people need a priest or church to attain salvation. God will grant grace outside church without the presence of a priest endowed with special powers. In other words, each believer can serve as his or her own priest and together all Christians share responsibilities Catholics reserved for priests. This idea was completely alien to Catholics whose theology made a clear distinction between clergy and laity. Since the doctrine of the priesthood of the believer meant that it must be possible for every person to read the Bible, Luther translated the Latin Bible into German, finishing the task in 1534.

Fifth was the doctrine of *consubstantiation*, which differed from the Catholic idea of *transubstantiation*. Catholics believed that during the Eucharist words uttered by the priest consecrated the wafer and wine, miraculously transforming them into the actual body and blood of Christ. Luther rejected this idea. His doctrine of consubstantiation held that after consecration the bread and wine changed spiritually so that the presence of Christ was found, but the wafer and wine were not really transformed into the body and blood.

Luther's basic principles were first codified in the Augsburg Confession of 1530. After his German Bible was published in 1534, Luther's new Christianity was doctrinally complete. Although Luther lived until 1546, he did little after 1534 to further spread his beliefs. Yet, the revolution he launched over the sale of indulgences would spread throughout Europe and around the world, producing wars and social change in its wake.

RELIGIOUS VIOLENCE AND THE PEASANT REBELLION

Luther's condemnation of the Catholic Church and its religious authority encouraged oppressed people across Germany to revolt. The first violence related to Luther's new theology occurred in the summer of 1522 between German princes and knights. Imperial knights, who usually owned only one castle and owed their allegiance to the Holy Roman Emperor, felt oppressed by the growing power of independent towns and the local princes who controlled vast territories in Germany. Since German princes usually held ecclesiastical offices, the imperial knights, who believed they represented the emperor, used Lutheranism to justify launching an attack on the Archbishop of Trier. This war, which lasted about a year before the knights were defeated, caused Luther's opponents to criticize Protestantism for inciting violence and undermining law, order, peace, and stability.

Lutheranism also was used to justify the peasant revolts that swept across sixteenth-century Germany. German peasants were particularly attracted to Luther's doctrines because he came from a peasant background. Peasants generally looked upon Luther as a hero because he had defied the authority of the Catholic Church, which was viewed by peasants as perhaps their greatest economic oppressor. German peasants took Luther literally when he proclaimed in *On Christian Liberty* in 1520 that Christianity makes humans "the most free lord of all and subject to none." Uneducated peasants who followed Luther's teachings understood the words to mean that Christ would liberate them from their earthly oppressors—the Church and government.

The peasant revolt began in Swabia in 1524 and within a few months spread throughout southern and central Germany. Citing Luther's beliefs, peasant representatives gathered at Memmingen in 1525 to compose a list of twelve grievances. The articles of grievance condemned ecclesiastical and temporal lords for practices that made peasant life difficult. Among the grievances, peasants wanted common land that nobles had seized returned to villages, freedom for serfs, an end to religious taxes or tithes, prohibitions on hunting and fishing lifted, excessive rents and fees for religious services lowered, unlawful punishments abolished, an end to death duties (the practice of peasant families being forced to give the church and nobles their best horses or cows when a death occurred in a peasant family), and the right to choose their own pastors. They also insisted that their revolt be judged by Biblical scripture rather than temporal law.

At first, Luther personally sympathized with the peasants' cause because he admired their unceasing toil and as a peasant child himself had experienced the drudgery of everyday life peasants endured. In 1525 Luther published *An Admonition to Peace,* which criticized German nobles and blamed them for causing the revolt: "We have no one…to thank for this…rebellion, except… lords and princes, especially…blind bishops, mad priests, and monks…. You do nothing but flay and rob your subjects…until the poor common folk can bear it no longer." However, when Luther realized that peasants were rebelling against all authority using his theology, he turned against the peasant rebellion, ignored the oppressive life they endured, and wrote *Against the Rapacious and Murdering Peasants*, a pamphlet that authorized German nobles to destroy rebellious peasants unmercifully until peace was restored. A few months later the Peasant Rebellion was crushed; its participants believed Luther had turned his back on a just cause, ignoring Biblical teachings that supported revolt. However, Luther did not see it this way. When he used the word "freedom," Luther meant freedom to obey the word of God without interference from the Roman Church. Freedom did not mean opposition to legally instituted governments. In fact, as Luther refined his theology, he increasingly demanded that Christians support the state, that the church be subordinate to government, and condemned rebellion. Luther wrote "that nothing can be more poisonous, hurtful, or devilish than a rebel." Luther's critics maintained that he opposed the Peasant Revolt and supported the state because he realized that he and his faith needed the protection of German princes to oppose Roman Catholicism. Had Luther supported the Peasant Revolt, Germany's secular rulers likely would have denied him protection from Catholic authorities, condemning him and his movement to an early death. Regardless of why Luther opposed the Peasant Rebellion, historians estimate that German princes killed over seventy-five thousand peasants before crushing the revolt in 1525.

THE SPREAD OF PROTESTANTISM

Despite violence, such as the Peasant Rebellion that was associated with Lutheranism, the new faith spread across Germany and throughout Europe. Important to its spread was the printing press, which enabled publishers to rapidly reproduce Luther's writings and disseminate his ideas everywhere. Equally important was Luther's ability to turn a phrase. He was a gifted writer and speaker who expressed himself extremely well. Some scholars have maintained that only Shakespeare equals his use of language. Nevertheless, language was the sword that Luther, the peasant's son, used to seriously wound the Catholic Church.

Many people were attracted to Luther's ideas. Peasants, Renaissance humanists, nobles, merchants, and princes found desirable Luther's call for a simple religion based on personal faith and scripture and the abolition of elaborate ceremonies. Humanists across Renaissance Europe had advocated many of the same reforms. Ulrich von Hutten (1488-1523), for example, was a celebrated German humanist who joined Luther in advancing the Reformation. The conservatism within Lutheranism made it possible for anyone who accepted the idea of justification by faith and the authority of scripture to join the church. Converts could, with some modification, keep much from the Catholic faith they had grown up with, including the liturgy, music, and church organization.

One of the most important things that attracted rulers and nobles to Lutheranism was materialism. Since Lutheran theology did not permit the church to hold vast amounts of land or acquire substantial wealth, any prince who accepted the Protestant faith could confiscate the land and wealth controlled by Catholic monasteries, churches, and high officials in their kingdom. Although this strategy was risky because Emperor Charles V was a staunch supporter of the Catholic faith and could take away the title of prince from any German nobleman, if successful it could enrich the prince. Eventually, enough German princes risked alienating the Emperor by becoming Protestant that they developed enough strength to resist Charles. Protestant rulers convened at the Diet of Speyer in 1529 and produced a document protesting the Emperor's order that no new religious idea would be allowed in Germany. In fact, this is the origin of the word "Protestant." After Speyer, all non-Catholic Christians would be called Protestants. In 1530 the Lutheran princes further upset Charles V by voting to support the Confession of Augsburg, a document containing the basic principles of the Lutheran faith. Faced with this opposition, Charles threatened to use military force to crush Protestant princes. They responded by forming a military alliance against the Holy Roman Emperor at Schmalkalden, Saxony in 1531.

War did not occur between German Protestant princes and Charles V until 1546. From 1531 until 1546 German Protestants consolidated their power, enticed other princes to join their ranks, and negotiated with the Pope about returning to the Catholic fold. When the Roman Church was not willing to accept Protestant demands that Lutheran theology be made part of the Catholic faith, it became clear that war could not be averted. In 1546 German princes and Charles V fought a brief conflict. Charles easily defeated the weaker German princes, but his victory did not destroy Protestantism. Luther's theology had advanced too far by the time Charles acted. About half of the German population had become Protestant by 1546. There were so many Protestants in Germany, particularly in the northern and eastern principalities, that it was impossible for the Holy Roman Emperor to destroy Lutheranism. There were also pockets of Protestantism in southern cities like Nuremberg, which was the German center of Renaissance Humanism.

Catholic princes in Germany also made it difficult for Charles to destroy Protestantism. They feared the power the Holy Roman Emperor had amassed and were reluctant to help him assert control across Germany, refusing to provide German troops. Thus, Charles had to use Spanish troops to fight Protestant princes, which caused the German populace to resent this foreign intrusion. Historians believe that the use of Spanish troops caused even more Germans to become Protestant.

From 1546 to 1555 sporadic fighting occurred in Germany. Although Charles V was a staunch defender of the Catholic faith, his actions were partly responsible for the spread of Lutheranism. The Holy Roman Emperor did not understand or try to solve political, religious, social, and economic problems Germany faced in the sixteenth century. Rather than devoting attention to Germany, he was more concerned about Flemish, Spanish, and Italian territories he controlled. He also faced a threat from Turkish Muslims who besieged Vienna, ruled by Charles' brother, Ferdinand, in 1529 and went to war with the Valois kings of France five times between 1521 and 1555. Consequently, Catholic rulers of France supported German Protestant princes when they challenged Charles V's power. France wanted to keep Germany divided to weaken

Charles. This struggle between Catholic France and Charles V, called the Habsburg-Valois Wars, fought over Habsburg lands due to the marriage of Maximilian and Mary of Burgundy, ironically promoted the spread of Protestantism.

As Protestant numbers increased, they became more formidable, and in 1555 a diet at Augsburg was held. This meeting produced a settlement between Catholics and Protestants in Germany. According to the agreement, known as the Peace of Augsburg, each German prince could determine what religion his kingdom would follow without interference from the Roman Pope or the Holy Roman Emperor. The Peace of Augsburg signaled that the unity of Western Christendom had ended and that Lutheranism would be safely entrenched in Germany. Other reformers, imitating Luther's example, also broke with the Catholic Church and carried Protestantism throughout Europe.

REFORMERS AND RADICALS

One of the most important reformers was the Swiss humanist Ulrich Zwingli (1484-1531). He introduced the Reformation into Switzerland. On January 1, 1519, less than two years after Luther composed his Ninety-five theses, Zwingli, a Catholic priest and disciple of Erasmus, informed his congregation that he would no longer preach sermons taken from official Catholic sources. Using the New Testament Erasmus had translated, he stated that he would cover the entire book from Matthew to Revelation. Like Luther, Zwingli believed a personal study of scripture was necessary to lead a Christian life. From 1519 to 1522 he developed a theology similar to Luther's. Zwingli's doctrine rejected priests serving as intermediaries between God and humankind, allowed ministers to marry, and disavowed the notion of purgatory.

Despite similarities, Zwingli's theology was vastly different from Luther's. Unlike Luther, Zwingli believed individuals were basically good and only needed discipline imposed by the church to lead Christian lives. To accomplish this, he created a magisterial tribunal comprised of ministers and lay people to enforce religious law. Whereas Luther made a distinction between religious and secular authority, Zwingli saw the two as being one and the same. Zwinglian tribunals were thus given authority to enforce all laws, secular and religious, excommunicate wayward Christians, rule on moral questions, require church attendance, and spy on parishioners using a network of informers. In short, Zwingli created a Protestant faith more dependent on the individual and less reliant on grace than Luther could accept. When Luther and Zwingli met in 1529 to work out differences in their theology, a disagreement over the importance of the sacraments prevented them from reaching an accord. Zwingli saw the sacraments as symbols of grace God previously bestowed on the individual whereas Luther believed God was actually present in the ceremony to bestow grace when the sacraments were administered. Under Zwingli's system, baptism and communion, for example, were not necessary; Luther saw them as central to the Christian faith.

The most important reformer other than Luther was John Calvin (1509-1564). Born in Noyon, France, Calvin studied law at the

University of Paris before beginning a crusade to make the world Protestant. As a young man, Calvin underwent an experience that changed his life. He called this event his "sudden conversion" but refused to elaborate about it. Whatever the experience was, after its occurrence in 1533, Calvin converted to Protestantism, becoming its foremost sixteenth-century spokesperson. The theology he developed had a greater impact on subsequent generations than any other reformer, including Luther. Calvinistic doctrine greatly influenced the government, economy, society, attitudes, and character of Europeans and their settlers in various American colonies.

After his sudden conversion French authorities charged Calvin with heresy. Thereafter, he hid from authorities for more than a year until he moved to Basel, Switzerland. While living at Basel, Calvin wrote *Institutes of the Christian Religion* (1536) that discussed his religious doctrine. This essay contained the five principles central to Calvin's theology. First is the idea that humankind is totally depraved. Calvin theorized that humans, by nature, are evil and will almost always do wrong. Second is the concept of unmerited grace. Calvin maintained that all people who became sinners when Eve consumed the forbidden fruit in the Garden of Eden were damned to hell. However, for reasons known only to God, some sinners were given salvation. Yet, this grace was not earned. People who were saved could do nothing to earn or merit heaven. God arbitrarily chose the saints and condemned all others to spend eternity in hell. In other words, according to Calvin, God, not human beings, was sovereign. It did not matter how morally upright a life people lived on earth. They still could go to hell. Third is the notion of limited atonement. Calvin stressed that although God granted salvation to undeserving human sinners, the number of people who receive atonement for their sins was limited. God chose only a few people to enjoy heavenly bliss in the afterlife. Calvinists referred to the chosen ones as the Saints or the elect. The vast majority of people were condemned to eternal hell. Fourth was the idea of predestination. Calvin concluded that God had decided who was damned and who was saved before people were born. This decision, which was made before a child was even in his or her mother's womb, was completely independent of the earthly life an individual might lead. Fifth is the idea of irresistible grace. Calvin declared that God's will would be done regardless of what any human might do. Individuals granted grace had no choice but to accept salvation just as those sentenced to hell could not change their fate. God's grace was irresistible, and the deity's power was absolute. People were, Calvin said, "as meaningless to God as grains of sand upon the seashore."

Shortly after defining his basic theology in the *Institutes of the Christian Religion*, Calvin moved to Geneva, where he remained until his death. In 1541 he accepted an invitation from Geneva's citizens to establish the Protestant faith in the Swiss city after it deposed its prince who was also a Catholic bishop. Calvin established a theocracy to govern both Geneva and his church. A group of deacons and church elders controlled the theocracy. A body of lay elders, called the consistory, made decisions about both church and state in Geneva, enforced laws, excommunicated wayward Christians, and punished sinners. Strict discipline and a high degree of organization characterized Geneva and other communities controlled by Calvinists.

The Reformation produced individuals and religious sects even more radical than Luther, Zwingli, and Calvin, who primarily represented moderate to conservative Protestantism. Left wing Protestant sects that embraced the Reformation were called Anabaptists. Controversy between mainstream and liberal Protestants erupted over the sacrament of baptism. Calvin, Luther, and most mainline reformers, wanting to preserve church authority, held that the individual became part of the body of Christ (the church) at the moment of baptism. This meant that infants who were baptized became Christians at the moment of immersion. Anabaptists, however, rejected infant baptism. They believed that only mature adults should undergo baptism. Radicals insisted that only mature adults, capable of exercising free will, could consciously accept grace and become Christian. Thus, Anabaptists insisted that all adults who had undergone infant baptism be re-baptized. (The term Anabaptist means to baptize again.) They maintained that there was no scriptural basis for infant baptism because immature children could not understand the concept of grace.

Generally, Anabaptist sects, each one unique, are characterized by several commonalities. All accepted the idea of religious diversity. They did not reorganize the church in an institutional form, did not allow priests, believed that personal communication between God and the individual was paramount, and valued religious tolerance. Anabaptists sought to recreate the Christian community they believed had existed during the first century after Christ's execution, a voluntary group of believers who had attained salvation. Anabaptist sects rarely numbered more than one hundred individuals. Many sects wanted to completely isolate themselves from the world, live a Christian life as they saw it, and set an example for worldly sinners to follow. Anabaptist sects were also generally eschatological, that is, they believed in the imminent coming of Christ. Some even went so far as to create "communistic" societies in which members held everything in common, including material possessions and husbands and wives. Mystical Anabaptist sects lived isolated, hermit-like lives completely apart from the world. They often experienced some sort of psychological trance, which they believed indicated direct contact with God. Each Anabaptist church and sect was completely independent of all other groups, chose its own ministers and officials, made its own laws, and devised its own theology. Some Anabaptist sects were the first Christian churches to accept women ministers while others allowed only males to preach. Most Anabaptists refused to hold civil offices and some were pacifists, refusing to serve in national militaries or fight for any reason.

Anabaptists also held that only a few "true believers" really achieved salvation and that church and state should be separated. Anabaptists believed that no government should promote any religious view. Nor did Anabaptists think individuals should proselytize, meaning Anabaptist sects did not force their religious views on others. Instead, Anabaptists allowed people to make up their own minds about religion.

Radical views meant that Anabaptists were destined to remain in the religious minority. Mostly, such sects attracted the poor, the dispossessed, the uneducated, and the downtrodden from Europe's urban areas. Also, because Anabaptist ideas threatened the church/state relationship during an age that made no distinction between the two institutions, these minority sects often faced persecution, religious hatred, and violence. Political and religious leaders in Protestant countries, including Luther, Calvin, and Zwingli, believed that separation of church and state would inevitably led to the creation of a completely secular society, which they opposed. Since Anabaptist ideas threatened existing governments, churches, and societies, members of radical sects often experienced brutality sanctioned by mainstream religious leaders. Some

European towns drove Anabaptists out of the community while others maimed, tortured, and killed members of these radical groups. Many Anabaptists were burned at the stake for heresy, while others were brutally beaten to death, drowned, hanged, or drawn and quartered.

The assault on Anabaptist sects began in the mid-1520s in Germany and quickly spread throughout Europe. An imperial diet in 1529 condemned to death all Anabaptists. Consequently, most of their leaders were violently executed. One of the best examples of violence against an Anabaptist sect was suppression of the Melchiorites at Munster, Germany. The Melchiorites attracted a large number of industrial workers and craftspeople. In 1534 this Anabaptist sect gained political control of Munster and established a Christian community according to Melchiorite ideas. They instituted a legal code that, among other things, established the death penalty for wives who did not obey their husbands and forced women to marry or face banishment from the community. Women who refused to marry or leave the city were executed. Melchiorites rule also introduced into Munster polygamy, burned all books except the Bible, and preached an eschatological religion.

Religious and secular leaders perceived what the Melchiorites had done at Munster as threatening society. Catholic and Protestant rulers united, sent an army to attack Munster and rid the city of Melchiorite ideas. This assault was successful. Many Melchiorites were killed; a few escaped to Poland, England, and the Netherlands.

THE ENGLISH REFORMATION

Across the English Channel the Reformation took a different turn, having economic and political causes in addition to religious ones. The official split with the Catholic Church occurred when King Henry VIII, wanting a male heir in 1527, requested that Pope Clement VII grant an annulment to his marriage to Catherine of Argon. Previously, Pope Julius II had given Henry a special dispensation, which allowed him to wed Catherine who had been married to Henry's brother, Arthur. In asking for the annulment Henry stated that if Princess Mary, the child produced by his union with Catherine, inherited the English throne, anarchy would result. He also maintained a legal marriage to Catherine had never existed because of her prior marriage. Clement VII was a weak pontiff whose focus at the time was on Luther's Reformation in Germany and on the Habsburg-Valois War in Italy. Clement refused Henry's request for an annulment because he did not want to provide more ammunition to Protestant reformers who criticized the Church by saying that popes replaced God's law as revealed in scripture with their own rules. Henry's divorce petition claimed that Julius II erred because his special dispensation violated God's rule that a man could not marry his brother's widow. Had Clement recognized Henry's argument and granted the annulment, Lutherans would have used this to convince more people to join the Reformation. Compounding the situation was the sack of Rome in 1527 by Charles V, Catherine's nephew. Since Charles was in complete control of Rome, Pope Clement delayed action on Henry's request; he was afraid to annul the marriage of Charles V's aunt while the Holy Roman Emperor controlled Rome.

After Clement refused to grant the annulment, Henry joined the Reformation. He removed the English church from papal control and made himself head of the institution. In 1533, at Henry's request, Parliament passed the Act in Restraint of Appeals, which legalized the English Reformation by forbidding church officials to submit legal appeals to the Roman Pope. Instead, English churchmen were required to submit all religious disputes to the English monarch. Thus, Henry VIII became the highest religious authority in England. Later, Parliamentary laws more firmly codified the Reformation in Britain. The Act for the Submission of Clergy in 1534 required priests and all other church officials to obey the king's rules and forbade Christians from publishing theological principles without consent of the monarch. The Supremacy Act, also passed in 1534, made the English monarch the official head of the Anglican Church. Henry's opposition was unexpected because he had previously written an essay attacking Luther and the Reformation, for which the Pope had named him "Defender of the Faith" in England.

While these acts made the break with Rome official, they caused controversy within England. A few Parliamentary representatives and other officials opposed passage of England's Reformation laws. Sir Thomas More, for example, resigned his chancellorship because he could not support leaving the Catholic fold and making the English monarch head of the Anglican Church. John Fisher, the Bishop of Rochester, also objected to the English Reformation, accusing the English clergy of cowardice when most did not protest when Henry removed the church from Rome's control. More, Fisher, and others who opposed the English Reformation were beheaded.

From 1535 to 1539 the English Reformation continued. Henry and Thomas Cromwell, his most influential advisor, abolished the monastery as an institution and confiscated its wealth. Monks, nuns, and abbots were driven from their homes. All monastic lands were taken; much of it was later sold to the upper and middle classes because the government needed money to finance various wars. The redistribution of lands also strengthened the rich and made them dependent upon the English king.

Because the English Reformation occurred more for secular than religious reasons, initially the Anglican Church kept many Catholic beliefs, doctrine, and practices, such as transubstantiation, celibacy for priests, and confession. After Henry VIII's death, however, the English church became more Protestant. During the seven-year reign of Edward VI (1547-1553), Henry's son, Catholic practices and theology were replaced with Protestant ideas. Archbishop Thomas Cranmer ordered a simplification of the Anglican liturgy. The *Book of Common Prayer* was written

Edward VI wanted the country to be Protestant.

Anne Boleyn, mistress of Henry VIII, demanded that he annul his marriage to Catherine, causing an international controversy.

in 1549. Protestant ministers began to roam the English countryside, spreading Calvinistic, Lutheran, and other religious doctrines.

After Edward's death, his half-sister, Mary Tudor, the daughter of Catherine of Argon, tried to undo the English Reformation. During her brief reign from 1553 to 1558 England faced religious instability. She rescinded most laws Henry VIII and Edward VI had enacted to further the Reformation. In their place, Mary passed legislation that completely returned England to the Catholic fold. Mary's religious changes, along with her marriage to the Spanish prince Phillip, son of Holy Roman Emperor Charles V, were not received well by her English subjects. When Mary began a campaign to persecute Protestants, many fled England, settling in countries where the Reformation was more firmly established. Under Queen Mary's rule, hundreds of Protestants, especially ministers and other leaders, were executed, earning her the name "Bloody Mary."

Mary's death brought her sister, Elizabeth I, to the throne. Under Elizabeth's reign from 1558 to 1603, religious stability slowly came to England. Because Elizabeth was raised Protestant, she rescinded Mary's laws that had returned England to Catholicism. However, Elizabeth was not overly zealous initiating religious reforms. When she became queen, she faced pressure from Catholics who wanted England to remain part of the Roman Church and a group of Protestants called Puritans who wanted the Anglican Church to become Calvinistic. Puritans were especially vocal and political. They wanted Elizabeth to rid the English church of all vestiges of Catholicism. Elizabeth, who was perhaps the best monarch in English history, steered a middle course between Catholic and Protestant extremists. She gave England more religious freedom and toleration than it had ever had. Even though all English people were legally required to be Anglican, Elizabeth generally allowed her subjects to practice whatever religion they wanted so long as they did not try to force their beliefs on others. Nor was the Queen a strict doctrinalist. She demanded that peace and order be maintained throughout her realm and in religious services but did not precisely define how English services were to be conducted. Laws enacted by Parliament during her reign, called the Elizabethan Settlement, were not unreasonable. They required that every English man and woman attend Anglican services; those that refused faced fines rather than execution or imprisonment. English bishops in 1563 drew up and approved the *Thirty-nine Articles* that briefly outlined Anglican beliefs. All Anglican services were required to be conducted in a uniform manner. The English language was used in services, Anglican priests were allowed to marry, and monasteries were prohibited from reopening. Still, these reforms were modest when considered in light of what Catholic and Protestant extremists wanted.

The Reformation in Scotland and Ireland was more radical than in England. John Knox, a staunch Calvinist, was the most important Reformation figure in Scotland. In 1560 he persuaded the Scottish legislature to pass legislation creating a Calvinistic Church. The Catholic Mass was forbidden. Any Scottish citizen who attended mass could be executed. Everyone was required to attend the Presbyterian Church, which was controlled by ministers called presbyters instead of bishops, which Knox founded. Calvinistic theology was introduced into Scotland. Knox, who previously had studied with Calvin in Geneva, attempted to create a theocracy in Scotland. The Presbyterian Church utilized a simple worship service dominated by hell fire and brimstone preachers. The *Book of Common Order* that Knox published in 1564 was adopted as the official liturgical tool in the Presbyterian Church.

Both James V and his daughter, Mary, Queen of Scots, opposed the Scottish Reformation. The Scottish monarchs were staunch Catholics who allied themselves with other Catholic monarchs in Europe. Because the Scottish monarchy was weak, James and Mary were powerless to stop the spread of Calvinism throughout their realm. Numerous Scottish nobles, who dominated Parliament, supported the Reformation. They saw religious change as a means whereby they could wrest more power from an already weak monarchy.

Ireland did not undergo a complete Reformation as Scotland did. In 1536 the English government ordered the Irish Parliament to pass legislation instituting the Reformation. These laws abolished the Catholic Church, made the English monarch head of the Irish church, outlawed monasteries, and created an Irish church similar to the English Church. The ruling class, which was primarily comprised of English nobles, quickly converted to Protestantism. However, the largest majority of the Irish population remained Catholic because they did not accept the political legitimacy of their English rulers and Parliament. Maintaining their Catholic faith was a way for the masses to defy their oppressive English rulers. The Catholic Church had to function as an underground institution. Its property was confiscated and sold. Profits went to England. Monasteries were destroyed. Despite these hardships, Catholicism survived in Ireland. Catholic priests and bishops became national leaders in the Irish resistance to English rule.

THE CATHOLIC REFORMATION (Counter Reformation)

After Luther began the Reformation in 1517 it quickly spread across Europe. By 1547 all England and Scandinavia had become Protestant. Most of Germany and Scotland, as well as parts of France and Switzerland, were following the doctrines of Luther, Calvin, Zwingli, Knox, or some other reformer. The spread of Protestantism meant that the Catholic Church had lost its control over millions of Christians and had witnessed the confiscation of thousands of acres of real estate property and had lost millions of dollars in annual income. Faced with these problems, Catholics began to put the Church's affairs in order. Reforms within the Church were instituted as a result of the Protestant Reformation. Catholics refer to these reforms at the Catholic Revival while Protestants call it the Counter Reformation. Whatever its name, lasting changes in the Catholic Church resulted, and after 1540, with the exception of the Netherlands, no substantial number of people in a European geographic area would become Protestant.

Certainly, reform within the Catholic Church was needed. Protestantism had spread across Europe, taking several countries out of the Catholic fold. Even in countries that remained loyal to the faith, the Church had lost much of its influence. There also was no unified Catholic doctrine on justification, salvation, or the sacraments. This situation began to change in 1534 when Paul III was elected Pontiff. When his reign ended in 1549, the Catholic Revival was firmly established. Pope Paul III began to root out abuses within the Church. He tolerated little corruption from lay priests, high ranking bishops, or abbots and created the Roman Inquisition, which used violence to stifle dissent.

Paul's primary strategy to reform the Church was convening an ecumenical council that met at Trent, Italy in 1545. The Council of Trent, as it was known, met off and on for eighteen years until the work was finished in 1563. Delegates to the Council of Trent were instructed to reform the Catholic Church and induce reconciliation with wayward Protestants. Lutherans, Calvinists, and other Protestants were initially asked to participate. Those who attended insisted that the Bible was the sole authority of God, which made reconciliation difficult to achieve.

Throughout the Council's existence, national politics intruded on its religious mission. Representatives from Western European countries demanded that Rome share power while delegates from Italian states wanted the Church's power centralized under the Pope. Charles V refused to allow discussion on any topic he believed would upset Lutherans in his realm. If Lutherans were upset too much, Charles was likely to lose more land to Protestant German princes. Likewise, French representatives opposed reconciliation with Protestants because they wanted to keep Germany weak. So long as Lutheranism divided the German states, the less authority Charles V had. A religiously divided Germany meant that France, unified under Catholicism, would be stronger.

Despite the intrusion of national politics and the stubbornness of Protestants regarding the importance of Scripture, achievements of the Council of Trent were remarkable. Numerous decrees were issued at the meeting. The most important one rejected Protestant positions on Scripture, sacraments, and free will. The Bible was not, according to this decree, the sole authority on religious matters. Tradition, as well as rulings by the Pope and church officials, was also important. Moreover, the Council of Trent decided that all seven sacraments are valid representations of God's grace. Priests were the only people authorized to administer the sacraments. Delegates also reaffirmed the Catholic position that humans possess free will and that good works in conjunction with faith are necessary for salvation. The elaborate rites and ceremonies that had become part of Catholic worship remained part of the faith.

Numerous decisions of less importance were also handed down from Trent. Many abuses within the Church were corrected. Ecclesiastical discipline was strengthened; bishops were now required to live within the diocese they governed. The sale of indulgences was abolished, priests who lived with women were ordered to embrace celibacy, bishops were required to visit every church within their diocese at least once every two years, and every diocese was ordered to create a seminary to educate priests. St. Jerome's Latin translation of the Bible was made a holy book, and priests were required to preside over marriage ceremonies. The Council also established the Inquisition and the *Index of Forbidden Books* to root out dissent and inform Catholics about books the Church considered heretical.

Although the Council of Trent did not affect reconciliation with Protestants, it did create a renewed spirituality within the Church. Criticism of the Catholic Church abated after most abuses were abolished. Decisions made at Trent remained important to Catholics for centuries afterward.

The Catholic Reformation involved more than simply the Council of Trent. New Religious orders also came into existence. They developed primarily for two reasons—to improve morality within the Church and provide education for clergy and lay people. The two foremost orders were the Society of Jesus (Jesuits) and the Ursuline Nuns. Ignatius Loyola (1491-1556) founded the Jesuit Order in 1540. He believed the Protestant Reformation had occurred because of low spiritual moral within lay people. The antidote for the Reformation, he believed, was found in ministering to the spiritual needs of individual Catholics. Loyola molded the Jesuits into a highly centralized group whose members were willing to go to the far corners of the world in service to the Church. Individuals who wanted to become Jesuits had to undergo a novitiate (probationary period) of two years rather than the standard one-year period required of other religious orders. The Jesuits became known for the schools they established. Jesuit monks educated children from both common and noble families. Over time, Jesuits exerted tremendous political influence, especially on the nobles and kings who had been educated in the order's schools.

The Ursuline Order of Nuns, founded by Angela Merici (1474-1540), focused on educating women. Originally established in 1535 to battle Protestant heresy by educating girls according to Catholic doctrine, the order eventually spread outside Italy, becoming known worldwide for its mission. The Ursuline goal was to make society more moral by teaching women who would become wives and mothers about Christian love. It was then hoped these Christian women could influence husbands and sons to exercise greater morality both inside and outside the home.

New religious orders were not the only institutions established as part of the Catholic Reformation. In 1542 Pope Paul III created the Inquisition to fight the spread of Protestantism within Catholic countries. The Roman Inquisition consisted of six cardinals who were given authority to act as a court to try individuals accused of heresy. This institution was given the power to issue warrants, arrest, try, imprison, and execute heretics. Trials run by the Inquisition were not fair to the accused. Judges accepted hearsay evidence. Accused heretics were not always informed of what they were charged with and torture was often applied to extract confessions. In countries controlled by Catholic monarchs Protestant heretics were effectively destroyed; in non-Catholic countries the Inquisition was not effective.

RELIGIOUS WARS

Wars plagued Europe for almost a century. From the 1560s to the 1650s countries fought over many issues, but religion was a common denominator in all the conflicts. Religion caused Catholics and Protestants to oppose each other. Both faiths saw the other as heretics and were convinced that God wanted all heretics destroyed. Catholics and Protestants developed a hatred for each other that bordered on fanaticism. This hatred caused members of both Christian sects to treat each other cruelly. Catholics executed Protestants by burning them at the stake;

Protestants executed Catholics by drawing and quartering (ripping the body apart by hitching horses to all four limbs). Even corpses were not spared. Dead bodies were often mutilated as a warning to other heretics.

One of the most fervent anti-Protestant rulers was Philip II of Spain (1556-1598), the most powerful monarch in the world at the time. He ruled Spain, most of Italy, the Netherlands, most of South America, and parts of North America. Despite his vast possessions and wealth, Philip was not satisfied. He intensely disliked the Protestant Reformation and also hated Muslims who controlled parts of Africa and the Middle East. Philip believed that Islam and Protestantism were enemies of the Catholic Church; consequently, he wanted to destroy both. Philip waged a successful campaign in the Mediterranean against the Muslims. A naval victory at the Battle of Lepanto against Muslim forces curtailed Islamic power in the Mediterranean and made Philip a hero in the Catholic world. However, his successes against Islam did not translate into victory against Protestant forces.

One of the most serious setbacks for Philip was in the Netherlands, which he had inherited when his father Charles V abdicated in 1556, dividing his territories between Ferdinand (Charles's brother) and Philip. Problems arose because the Dutch considered Philip to be Spanish whereas Charles was one of their own, having been born in Ghent and raised in the Netherlands. Unlike Charles, who was Flemish in language and lifestyle, Philip spoke Spanish and the Dutch perceived him as a foreign ruler. In 1559 Philip named Margaret, his half sister, as ruler of the Netherlands and ordered her to destroy Protestantism in the kingdom. She quickly established the Inquisition to root out Protestantism. The problem in the Netherlands was not Lutheranism but Calvinism. Calvin's teachings had attracted a following among the Dutch middle and working classes. By the 1560s, Calvinist enclaves existed in most Dutch towns and the religion was well financed by bankers and merchants throughout the seventeen provinces that comprised the Netherlands. Margaret's immediate problem was raising capital to finance efforts to destroy Protestantism. Despite protests from the Dutch legislature that taxes were already too high, Margaret raised them. Her actions caused Dutch merchants, businessmen, and bankers who opposed the tax increase to unite with Calvinist leaders being persecuted by the Queen.

In 1566 working class Calvinists, faced with high food costs coupled with high taxes, revolted. Incited by Calvinist preachers, fanatical mobs attacked Catholic churches and their parishioners. The Catholic cathedral of Notre Dame at Antwerp, along with thirty other churches, was destroyed. Alters were smashed, windows broken, tombs opened, books were burned, and priests were killed. From Antwerp the violence spread across the Netherlands and throughout the Low Countries.

Philip II dispatched a Spanish army commanded by the Duke of Alva to crush the Dutch rebellion. In addition to using the Inquisition against Protestants, Alva established an institution called the Council of Blood. To finance the Spanish campaign, he increased taxes even more. On March 3, 1568, Alva's troops executed over fifteen hundred Protestant heretics. Protestants were publicly hanged, and rebel bands were ruthlessly slaughtered by Spanish forces as the troops sought to suppress treason and heresy. Often innocent people were killed. Two Dutch noblemen, for example, were executed because they demanded that Philip alter his repressive policy. The executions and tax increases, which produced economic hardship, caused Dutch

Protestants to completely turn against their Spanish oppressors. Over the next ten years a civil war was fought between Protestants and Catholics in the Netherlands. Generally, Protestant forces won the war. In 1572 a group of Dutch sailors, whom the Spanish called "sea beggars," captured Brill, a North Sea fishing village. Their success prompted revolts in other Dutch towns. Spanish troops were dispatched to recapture Brill and other towns that had fallen to rebel forces but were defeated in 1574 when the dikes were opened, flooding Spanish troops who were only twenty-five miles from Amsterdam. In 1576 Protestants in all seventeen Dutch provinces united under the leadership of William of Orange.

Philip II sent his nephew, Alexander Farnese, the Duke of Parma, to crush the revolt. Farnese captured numerous towns in the southern provinces, including Ghent, Bruges, Maastricht, Tournai, and Antwerp. The fall of Antwerp was the last significant Spanish victory in the Netherlands. Farnese's success also meant that the Netherlands would be divided religiously. In the ten southern provinces Farnese conquered, Calvinism was stamped out. Protestants residing within them were either forced to become Catholic or migrate to a Protestant province. These ten provinces, called the Spanish Netherlands, remained under control of the Habsburg dynasty, eventually becoming the country of Belgium. The seven northern provinces William of Orange controlled remained Protestant. In 1581, led by Holland, they signed the Treaty of Utrecht, declared their independence from Spain, and created the country of Holland.

Philip and Farnese refused to accept the political division of the Netherlands. They tried to subdue the northern provinces after 1581. Protestant Holland repeatedly asked Elizabeth I, the English monarch, for military assistance. England faced a serious dilemma. If Elizabeth helped the Dutch she would anger Philip II and likely produce war with Spain. But, if Spain conquered all the Netherlands provinces Philip would likely attack England to restore the Catholic religion in Albion. Compounding the problem, the Dutch revolt had harmed the English wool industry. The Netherlands was the largest market for English wool cloth. When it collapsed, Elizabeth's government lost tax revenue. The execution of William of Orange in July 1584 and the Spanish victory at Antwerp frightened Elizabeth. She believed that if Spain crushed the Dutch resistance Farnese would turn his army against England. Thus, Elizabeth I sent money and soldiers to help Dutch Protestants confront the Catholic armies of Spain in 1585.

Farnese insisted that before Spain could defeat the Dutch it must also defeat England and halt Elizabeth's support of the Protestant Netherlands. Philip agreed with Farnese because he had spent a fortune fighting the Dutch but had little to show for it. Upsetting Philip even more was the execution of Mary, Queen of Scots, Elizabeth I's cousin and heir to the English throne, on February 18, 1587. Mary, a staunch Catholic, had hatched a plot to assassinate Elizabeth and take the English throne for herself. Philip II, wanting to restore England to the Catholic fold, had provided Mary financial support. Had Mary's plot worked, English support of the Dutch rebellion would have ended and Spain could have completed its Dutch conquest. After the plot failed, Elizabeth had Mary beheaded. Pope Sixtus V (1585-1590), after learning of Mary's death, was so upset that he offered Philip one million Italian gold ducats if Spain invaded England. Philip, after consultation with his military advisors, decided to assemble a large fleet to attack England.

The powerful Spanish Armada set sail to attack England. Bad weather and superior English naval tactics, however, forced the crippled fleet to withdraw in defeat.

On May 9, 1588, the Spanish Armada left Lisbon. This fleet, which consisted of about 130 ships, was one of the largest ever dispatched against an enemy. Unfortunately for Spain, England could assemble a larger fleet. About 150 English ships fought the Spanish Armada in the English Channel. The English ships, which were generally smaller, faster, more maneuverable, and had greater firepower than their Spanish counterparts, carried the day. Particularly damaging to Spain was England's use of fire ships that ignited and burned Spanish vessels. England destroyed about a third of the Spanish fleet. On the return voyage to Spain several more ships sank in a storm off the Irish coast. Less than seventy Spanish ships survived to return home.

The defeat of the Spanish Armada did not immediately end the Netherlands war. Fighting continued between Protestants backed by England and Spain until 1609 when Philip III (1598-1621) signed a treaty in which Spain recognized the independence of the seven northern Dutch provinces. The English victory over the Spanish Armada meant that Philip II had failed to restore Catholicism to most parts of Europe. It also marked the ascension of England as the world's foremost naval power. Spain never again seriously threatened England.

France, like England, experienced war as a result of religious differences. Luther's writings had reached France by 1518 but attracted few converts. When Calvin's *Institutes of the Christian Religion* was published in 1536, large numbers of French Catholics adopted the Protestant faith. These converts were called Huguenots. Calvinism appealed to them in part because Calvin was French and wrote in the French language. Most French Huguenots lived in cities such as Paris, Lyons, Meaux, and Grenoble. Despite widespread persecution, which included burning at the stake, the numbers of French Calvinists grew, reaching about 9 percent of the population by 1560.

The Spanish galleon was a mainstay of the powerful Spanish Armada.

Civil war, rooted in religion, engulfed France in 1559 and lasted for thirty-six years. The weak French monarchs, all sons of Henry II, the last strong king France produced for a generation, were unable to maintain order. Francis II, who became king in 1159 after Henry II's death, died after ruling for only seventeen months. His successor, Charles II, who ruled from 1560 to 1574, was controlled by his Mother, Catherine de' Medici. Henry III, who succeeded to the throne in 1574 and ruled to 1589 experienced psychological problems due to guilt he experienced because he was homosexual in a society that did not tolerate gay people. It was not until Henry IV (ruled 1589-1610) became king that peace and stability came to France.

French nobles took advantage of royal weakness. Various nobles adopted Calvinism in an attempt to intimidate Lutheran princes in Germany and use religion to declare their independence from the king. In southern France Huguenot leaders, for a time, created a semi-autonomous state. Estimates indicate that perhaps half of all French nobles adopted Calvin-

The English ship was narrower, with gun ports along her side, which made her clearly superior to the Spanish galleon.

ism at some time. Clashes between Protestant and Catholic nobles were inevitable given the weakness of the monarchy. Among the nobility the real issue was power while among the working classes it was religion. Calvinists and Catholics viewed each other as heathens. Violence erupted throughout France. Not only did Catholic and Protestant armies led by various nobles clash, but violence often occurred at daily events, such as weddings, funerals, baptisms, and worship services. Catholics attacked Protestants and Protestants attacked Catholics. Huguenot ministers often exhorted their flocks to raid Catholic churches and destroy statues and art objects that Protestants viewed as idols. Likewise, Catholic priests urged parishioners to kill the Huguenot heretics.

The most notorious act of violence in France occurred on August 24, 1572. Called the Saint Bartholomew's Day Massacre, the event occurred when Huguenot nobles gathered for a wedding uniting Margaret of Valois, sister to the Catholic King Charles IX, to Henry of Navarre, the foremost Protestant leader. The marriage was intended to bring reconciliation to the warring Catholic and Protestant factions in France. Catherine de' Medici, who several times in the French civil war switched sides, felt that her Huguenot allies were becoming too strong and apparently ordered attacks on Protestant leaders gathered for the wedding. On the eve of the wedding Henry of Guise had Admiral Gaspard de Coligny, a Protestant leader who had replaced Catherine de Medici as primary advisor to King

Queen Elizabeth went to St. Paul's Cathedral for a service to celebrate the defeat of the Armada dressed in elaborate garb.

Charles, attacked. This event touched off rioting and violence in Paris that killed most of the Calvinist leadership. Only Henry of Navarre escaped. Within a short time, religious violence spread from Paris to the countryside. All French Provinces were engulfed in war. From the Saint Bartholomew's Day Massacre until early October Catholics slaughtered over ten thousand Huguenots throughout France.

This bloodshed produced the War of the Three Henry's. The conflict was a civil war between factions led by Henry of Guise, a Catholic nobleman, Protestant nobleman Henry of Navarre, and King Henry III who succeeded Charles IX in 1574. For fifteen years France experienced civil conflict. Even though Henry III was Catholic, he fought against Henry of Guise because the Catholic Guise faction had formed an alliance of Catholic nobles called the Holy League whose goals were to eradicate the Huguenots as well as overthrow the monarchy.

Several events brought the War of the Three Henry's to an end. One was the defeat of the Spanish Armada. When England defeated the Armada, Henry of Guise lost his principal backer, Philip II of Spain. Henry III then had Henry of Guise assassinated. A few months later Henry III was also assassinated. The deaths of two of the three Henry's meant Henry of Navarre, the lone survivor, could take the French throne. He ruled as King Henry IV from 1589 to 1610. Even though he was Protestant, Henry IV realized that the majority of the French people were Catholic; therefore, he converted to Roman Catholicism in 1593 so that most French citizens would accept him as king. However, he issued the Edict of Nantes in 1598, which allowed Huguenots to legally hold worship services and exist as a religious minority throughout France.

THE THIRTY YEARS WAR

The Holy Roman Empire in Germany and central Europe were not immune from religious war. Conflict between Protestants and Catholics rocked the region, killing millions from 1618 until 1648. Known as the Thirty Years War, this conflict was the bloodiest of all wars that resulted from the Reformation. Central Europe was ravaged by this conflict, and every principal monarch in Europe eventually became involved.

Problems leading to the Thirty Years' War date to the Augsburg settlement in which each German prince acquired the right to determine whether his lands would be Catholic or Protestant. Catholics became alarmed when Protestants violated the Augsburg peace by expanding into German Catholic bishoprics. Catholics were particularly concerned about the aggressive spread of Calvinism. Since the Augsburg agreement was between Lutherans and Catholics, Calvinists ignored it, converting German princes at an alarming rate. Lutherans, like Catholics, also feared the spread of Calvinism into Germany. They believed that the Augsburg peace was in danger of collapse if the advances of both Calvinists and Catholics were not halted. Compounding the problem was that Jesuit missionaries had convinced several Lutheran princes to become Catholic. Lutheran principalities responded by forming the Lutheran League in 1608; Catholics in turn created the Catholic League in 1609. The primary goal of both alliances was to stop the other from enlarging its territory.

The war began after Ferdinand of Styria, a staunch Catholic, was elected king of Bohemia in 1617. He angered Bohemian Protestants in 1618 when he abolished laws enacted by the previous ruler, Emperor Rudolf II, that in 1609 had allowed Protestants to worship freely within Bohemia. Bohemians rebelled. Since the Bohemian king was elected, the electors declared that Ferdinand had been deposed. In his place they chose Fredrick II of Palatinate, the leader of Bohemian Calvinists. Violence erupted with the occurrence of the Defenestration of Prague. Protestants, upset with Ferdinand, threw two government officers from the window of a Prague castle on May 23, 1618. Both men miraculously survived after falling approximately seventy feet to the ground. Catholics maintained that angels caught the men, gently lowering them to the earth while Protestants claimed that a deep pile of horse manure softened the fall. Regardless of what happened, the Defenestration of Prague marked the onset of the Thirty Years' War.

The conflict escalated over time. From 1618 to 1625 it was primarily fought in Bohemia. This conflict was essentially a religious civil war between Ferdinand and his Catholic allies trying to reclaim the throne from Fredrick and his Calvinists allies. In 1620 Catholics won a major victory when they defeated Fredrick's army at the Battle of White Mountain. Ferdinand, who had also been named Holy Roman Emperor, took back the Bohemian crown. He unleashed persecution on Bohemian Protestants, forcing most to become Catholic and executing those who refused. By 1630 Protestantism no longer openly existed in Bohemia.

In 1625 the war escalated. King Christian IV of Denmark (ruled 1588-1648) intervened on the Protestant side. Largely ineffective as a military commander, Christian was unable to stop advances by Ferdinand's forces. Albert von Wallenstein, the commander of Catholic forces, won numerous victories over Protestant armies. By 1627 his army had began to attack

Protestant strongholds in the northern regions of the Holy Roman Empire. Catholic forces took control of Silesia, Pomerania, Jutland, and Schlesuwig. Protestants had lost so much territory in Germany by 1629 that Ferdinand issued the Restitution Edict, which ordered all property taken from Catholics since 1552 returned. The Restoration Edict alarmed Lutheran princes throughout Germany. They feared that Ferdinand and the House of Habsburg he represented would eventually subdue all of Germany. Consequently, they united against Ferdinand, forcing the Holy Roman Emperor to fire Wallenstein at an electoral diet in 1630.

Protestant fortunes began to improve in 1630 when Swedish king Gustavus Adolphus (ruled 1594-1632) brought an army to support oppressed Lutherans. The French king, Louis XIII, wanting to weaken the Habsburgs in central Europe, provided financial support for Sweden. In 1631 Adolphus decisively defeated a Habsburg army at Breitenfeld. After Adolphus was killed in a victory over Catholic forces at Lutzen in 1632 and after a Swedish army was defeated at the Battle of Nordlingen in 1634, France entered the war. Even though France was a Catholic nation, its forces supported Protestants because the French monarch wanted to stymie the advance of Habsburg power. The French intervention marked the beginning of the international phase of the Thirty Years' War. Over the next fourteen years French and Swedish armies ravaged Germany. More than a third of Germany's population was killed, agriculture was virtually destroyed, and economic devastation occurred when several German princes debased their currency. The war caused an economic depression that engulfed the entire European continent, causing deflation and falling commodity prices for the first time in over a century.

The Thirty Years' War lasted so long because no ruler had the ability and resources to win a complete victory. Fortunately, the primary conflict ended in October 1648 when the Peace of Westphalia was signed. Peace was achieved when two agreements, the Treaties of Munster and Osnabruck, were signed. France and the Habsburgs agreed that German princes would be sovereign and independent. Each prince could rule his territory as he saw fit, make any law he wanted, and determine what religion his subjects would follow. The Holy Roman Empire was effectively destroyed. Germany was now controlled by over three hundred princes, which meant that centralized authority represented by the Holy Roman Empire had ended. The position of France and Sweden in the European power structure improved. France received two new territories, the provinces of Alsace and Lorraine. Sweden received territory in Pomerania, Bremen, and Verden. In addition, the independence of Protestant Holland was recognized, and France got the right to intervene in German affairs. The issue between Catholics and Protestants was settled when the Westphalia Peace expanded the Augsburg agreement of 1555 to include Calvinists as well as Lutherans and Catholics. All three religions could legally exist in central Europe. This did not mean that religious toleration was accepted. German citizens usually followed the religion of their prince. In practice, principalities in northern Germany were Protestant while those in southern Germany remained Catholic.

WOMEN AND WITCHCRAFT

The Reformation introduced new ideas regarding women, marriage, and sexuality. Whereas Catholics saw marriage as a holy sacrament that could not be dissolved once the union was completed, Protestants viewed marriage as a legal contract between two individuals. Each partner under this contractual arrangement was legally required to fulfill various marital responsibilities. Wives were expected to maintain and manage the home, engage in charitable work, help husbands with farm or business work as the need arose, bear, rear, and tend children, and provide sex for husbands on demand. Women were generally discouraged from working outside the home because outside employment would interfere with homemaking duties. A husband's responsibilities, in contrast, included providing food, shelter, and clothing for his wife and children. Men generally worked on the farm or ran the business from which he earned the family's livelihood.

Although Protestant thought, as evidenced in literature about marriage, stressed that husbands, as head of the household, should rule their families fairly and justly, many husbands behaved like tyrants. Protestant writers justified the verbal and physical abuse women suffered as punishment for sins committed by the Biblical Eve. Men, they said, were also punished because God required them to work on a daily basis, earning their family's living "by the sweat of his brow."

Like Catholics, Protestants stressed sexual fidelity within marriage. Because marriage was perceived as a contract, Protestants permitted divorce for various reasons, including adultery. Protestants also allowed ministers to marry, which lessened the problem created by priests taking female lovers. Women who had been priests's concubines could legally become their lovers' wives.

Although civil governments in both Catholic and Protestant nations licensed prostitution houses, the world's most ancient profession was frowned upon. Legally licensed prostitution establishments catered only to single males. Some Protestant countries paid government employees to live in the houses to ensure that married men did not partake of their sensual pleasures. Even though prostitution was legal throughout Europe, it reflected a double standard in sexual morality for men and women. Single males were free to satisfy their sexual cravings while women, with the exception of prostitutes, were expected to refrain from sexual intercourse outside marriage.

Even though Protestant women were expected to remain virginal until marriage, Luther, Calvin, Zwingli, and other Reformation leaders believed that celibacy was not necessary to lead a religious life. Luther maintained that God delighted in sexual activity so long as it occurred as part of marriage. Words Luther wrote a friend in a letter provide evidence of his views regarding sex: "Dear lad, be not ashamed that you desire a girl, nor you my maid, the boy. Just let it lead you into matrimony and not into promiscuity, and it is no more cause for shame than eating or drinking." Nuns in former Catholic countries were encouraged to marry after their convents were abolished. Marriage, Protestant reformers believed, provided women with economic, emotional, and cultural benefits while alleviating repression of sexual desires. Still, the emphasis was upon sex within marriage. Women who expressed their sensuality too openly or who behaved differently from the norm might be accused of practicing witchcraft.

The century of the Reformation witnessed the persecution of numerous women for practicing witchcraft. A belief in witchcraft was widespread throughout Europe. Educated and non-educated people alike believed that witches were real. Most people believed the earth was the battlefield between God and the Devil. Illness, injury, bankruptcy, deaths, or any misfortune were often blamed on witchcraft. Witches were generally thought to be older women who consorted with Satan and as a result possessed mysterious powers. Occasionally, younger women and children might be accused of witchcraft. Tradition held that witches rode broomsticks to *sabbats* (meetings with the Devil and other witches). At these sabbats witches supposedly engaged in wild sexual orgies with Satan and male witches called warlocks. These sexual escapades, which people believed included lesbian sex with other witches, supposedly lasted all night. Between bouts of sex, witches were believed to dine on the flesh of human babies.

Europeans generally believed that witches were married or widowed women who desired more sex than they were having. Women older than fifty were especially prone to accusations of witchcraft largely because they possessed some of the characteristics Europeans attributed to witches—aged, wrinkled skin, limbs crippled with arthritis or other diseases, deafness, poor eyesight, malnutrition, thinning hair, and various psychological disorders. Moreover, these women might practice midwifery and folk medicine, healing sick people with roots, herbs, and other folk cures. Moreover, most women accused of witchcraft did not follow the mild, meek roles assigned women in European society. Instead, they behaved aggressively, spoke their mind, and refused to be subservient to men.

The Protestant Reformation contributed to the witch hysteria that swept across the European continent from 1560 to 1660. Protestants, especially Calvinists, feared Satan's power and the religious wars wrecked havoc across Europe, creating much insecurity. Because reformers believed witches worshipped Satan, witchcraft was considered heresy. As a result, governments and religious reformers denounced witchcraft. Anyone suspected of witchcraft was subject to horrible prosecution. Thousands of women accused of witchcraft were executed across the European continent. Authorities in several southern German principalities burned over three thousand witches. Switzerland killed even more. Although the exact number of women tried for witchcraft will likely never be known, one estimate is that over nine million throughout the world stood accused over several centuries. Between 1450 and 1700 at least nine thousand people were tried for witchcraft on the European continent. Over half were found guilty and condemned to death. England, for example, executed about one thousand witches from 1560 to 1740.

Scholars differ about the cause of the European witch hysteria after the Reformation occurred. Most likely the fear of witches and the executions resulted from a variety of factors. First, most people believed in witchcraft. They tended to blame witches for life's misfortunes and feared the power of witches. Anything that could not be readily explained was usually blamed on witchcraft. Second, Protestant ministers preached strong sermons warning congregations about the Devil's power. These sermons created fear in the minds of ordinary people. Some began to look for signs of witchcraft in neighbors. Third, Christianity stressed a repression of sexual desire. All the sexual activities attributed to witches, some scholars believe, represented the repressed urges of sexually frustrated Christians. Fourth, witchcraft provided an easy means for tight knit, local communities that stressed social and cultural conformity to rid themselves of nonconformists. Anyone who did not behave like others in the community was likely to be accused of witchcraft. Fifth, the Christian belief that women were more susceptible to the Devil's intrigues likely played a role in the witch hysteria. European Christians believed that women inherited a tradition from Eve of being deceived by Satan. In light of this belief it is no wonder that women were accused of practicing witchcraft far more often than men. Whatever the reason for the witch persecutions, they took a tremendous toll on European women. Thousands were executed as witches at various times in European history.

CONCLUSION

When Luther nailed his Ninety-five Theses to the church door in Wittenberg, Western Christianity was forever changed. All of Western Europe would never again practice the same faith. Religious unity under the Catholic Church was forever broken. Other reformers, following Luther's example, disavowed Catholic doctrines and formed numerous Protestant denominations. John Calvin was the most strident of these reformers, creating a theocracy in Geneva. Calvinist ministers fanned out across Europe preaching the gospel as they saw it. Anabaptists, the most radical of Protestant groups, gained a foothold in parts of Europe. Henry VIII created a state controlled church in England as part of the Reformation.

Suggestions for Further Reading

Roland H. Bainton, *Here I Stand: A Life of Martin Luther* (1955).

William Bangert, *A History of the Society of Jesus* (1772).

William J. Bouwsma, *John Calvin: A Sixteenth Century Portrait* (1988).

John Calvin, *On God and Political Duty.* John T. McNeil, ed. (1950).

Owen Chadwick, *The Reformation* (1964).

Patrick Collinson, *The Religion of Protestants* (1982).

Jean Delumeau, *Catholicism Between Luther and Voltaire: A New View of the Counter-Reformation* (1977).

H. J. Hillerbrand, *The Reformation in its Own Words* (1964).

Anthony Kenny, *Thomas More* (1983).

James M. Kittelson, *Luther the Reformer: The Story of the Man and His Career* (1986).

Bernd Moeller, *Imperial Cities and the Reformation* (1972).

E. A. Payne, *The Free Church Tradition in the Life of England* (1952).

Bob Scribner and Benecke, Gerhard (eds.), *The German Peasant War of 1525: New Viewpoints* (1979).

W. A. Shaw, *A History of the English Church 1640-1660.*

Max Weber, *The Protestant Ethic and the Spirit of Capitalism* (1958).

Index

A

B

C

G

H

N